THE THEATRE AT WAR

RELAXATION

The Theatre at War

by
Basil Dean

*With thirty-one plates in half-tone
and seven illustrations in the text*

George G. Harrap & Co. Ltd
London Toronto Wellington Sydney

First published in Great Britain 1956
by GEORGE G. HARRAP & CO. LTD
182 High Holborn, London, W.C.1

OC0265155

Composed in Bembo type and printed by
Western Printing Services Ltd, Bristol
Made in Great Britain

1000176395

*Dedicated to all the ENSA artistes
who went overseas to entertain the troops,
especially the parties that, without fuss or bother,
cheerfully gave of their best
in circumstances that were sometimes dangerous
and always difficult*

ACKNOWLEDGMENTS

I am indebted to many friends and associates of the war years for some accounts of local incident not disclosed in the official reports and for many personal stories. In furnishing me with this cement of human interest they have enabled me to present a more complete edifice than would otherwise have been possible. Invaluable advice and criticism during the course of the work came from Clemence Dane, Desmond Young, Collie Knox and others. To all of them my warm thanks are due, as also to John Drummond of Megginch, without whose persistent propulsion I should never have reached the end of the road. And I remain grateful for the wise sympathy of my sister-in-law, the late Violet Dean, in the first days.

Some of the photographs are from the archives of the Imperial War Museum; others came from our own photographic department at Drury Lane or from private contributors; a few are the result of my own efforts as a cameraman. I wish to thank all those who have granted permission for their use, and the Still Department of Ealing Studios for preparing so many of them for reproduction.

I have to thank the proprietors of *Punch* for permission to reprint certain cartoons.

I am indebted to Richard Blake for making the preliminary selection of illustrations and for preparing the Index. Finally, I have to thank Berta Nicoll for her unflagging interest, despite the typing and retyping, the checking and rechecking of all-too familiar chapters.

CONTENTS

The First Phase
THE END IN THE BEGINNING

The Second Phase
THE SWELLING SCENE

The Third Phase

CLIMAX AND ANTICLIMAX

ILLUSTRATIONS

PLATES

PAGE

IN THE TEXT

INTRODUCTORY

IN company with the butcher, the baker and the candlestick-maker, actors, singers and musicians went forth to the Second World War. Some wore His Majesty's uniform; others marched under the banner of the Entertainments National Service Association (ENSA) to the cheers of the onlookers, with an occasional sneer by way of overtone. The entertainment army grew from the smallest beginnings until all non-combatant members of the theatrical, variety and musical professions became involved in its affairs in one way or another. And the demands for equipment were so great that the manufacturers of theatre and cinema equipment, the scenery and lighting contractors, costume and property makers and the like found themselves compelled to set on one side an ever-increasing proportion of their annual output to meet the requisitions of the Department of National Service Entertainment, the official title for the administrative machine built up round the ENSA idea.

Such a mobilization of entertainment had never before been seen, and never will be again; just as well that it should be so, for the demand grew beyond manageable proportions, so that mistakes were made, and quality sometimes fell short of expectation. In the nightmarish wars of the future the struggle for mass preservation will dominate the national effort, even though rationed entertainment—sound and vision—should be piped to the new troglodytes in their atom-proof shelters. Therefore, in the historical sense, ENSA's record will remain unique.

The entertainment world is different from all others in that its hours of work and leisure are basically the reverse of those of its audiences. It is a world apart, with a freemasonry peculiar to its members; it does not take kindly to interference, either from within or without its ranks. Behind the glitter there lies a jungle where rampant individualism is the life-blood of success and only the fittest can survive.

Music-hall comedians, and others who aspired to that title, used ENSA as a sort of Aunt Sally, especially those who found it inconvenient to devote more than a minimum of their spare time to the work, covering their moral retreat behind a smoke-screen of abuse. When the national emergency demanded the sacrifice of competitive salaries in favour of standard rates of pay, the temptation of the commercial engagement was thereby increased for those whose sense of duty was weak. On the other hand, the managers naturally preferred the tops of the bottles to the dregs, and were actively concerned to see that ENSA did not get at the milkman first. Changing the analogy to express other and wider differences, the paths of professional and official conduct did not run in parallel; they crossed and recrossed one another and sometimes ran in quite opposite directions, and, doing so, became inextricably mixed up with the human side of the story. The publicity aroused by this domestic warfare concealed from the public the scope and value of the work. Nevertheless, vast numbers of young men and women savoured the delights of music and the living drama for the first time through ENSA. In audience-making alone, as distinct from its work for national morale, it was in some part both the cause and the effect of changes that are still going on.

I make no apology for the inclusion of personal matters, because this is also my own story during the war years. Furthermore, if I am to remain true to my purpose of providing a faithful account of the seven years of ENSA's existence I must set all down in as near to chronological sequence as I can manage, hoping that in the end both those with a taste for theatrical history and those who prefer the lighter side will be able to follow the main outlines of a complex pattern. Anyhow, I want to present the whole picture before parts of it fade from memory and before the accumulation of papers and documents that clutter up my office are sent to the knacker's yard or blown sky-high in the ultimate bombardment.

To the thousands of artistes and technicians who have waited so long for this record of their struggles and achievements I express my regrets, as also to all those inadvertently left unmentioned. There has been a mountain of facts to sift, and my pen no more adequate to the task than a child's spade.

London,
  1951–55

THE FIRST PHASE

The End in the Beginning

*Cover design for
the first Garrison Theatre (1916)
by George W. Harris*

CHAPTER ONE

REVEILLE

HAVE you ever watched children throwing stones into a pond and wanted to join in, hunting for larger and larger stones to fling, until the widening ripples cover the whole surface and melt away against the further bank? ENSA began rather like that when four theatre men sat down one Sunday morning in the summer of 1938 in a charming little Regency house in St John's Wood, home of Leslie Henson, to ask themselves the question, "What shall the Theatre do if there is a second world war?" The other three were Owen Nares, Godfrey Tearle, and myself. A desperate fellow named Hitler was throwing stones into the ocean of world politics. We wanted to throw stones, too, so as to stir the theatre world into preparation for what was to come.

As we strolled up the path to that first meeting—Owen Nares had popped in on his way to golf; it was as casual as that—Leslie made a characteristic entrance to the view, hailing us from his dressing-room window, an enormous shaving brush in one hand and his face half-covered with soap, and demanding cheerfully when the first concert party was to be formed, as he had thought out a good gag about Hitler. Godfrey Tearle was very impressive, I remember, with a grave, judicial air that seemed to give weight and substance to the proceedings. Years later he confessed that he had been mainly thinking—Poor B.D.! He's got a bee in his bonnet; but we must humour him and do our best to help. Owen Nares, detached but conscientious, naïvely suggested that he should be the transport officer, as he liked driving. And it was agreed that I should write a pamphlet setting out our ideas. This pamphlet was later circulated to Members of the House of Commons and to public departments; it is reprinted without alteration as an appendix to this story. No prophet, I must confess to some twinges of pride in the degree of accuracy with which the war-time uses of entertainment were forecast in it. The meeting that began so portentously ended with hilarity as Leslie told stories of his 'Gaieties' housed in the huge theatre in Lille during the First World War. In the light of what finally came out of those early talks, this first approach

may sound rather juvenile. Nevertheless, the world-wide organization of
ENSA began just so.

2

The story really begins much earlier than that—in the early months of
the First World War to be exact, when thousands of young men brought
up in the ways of peace found themselves trudging through the countryside, dummy rifles and wooden cartridges made in Japan in their hands,
and the certainty of victory in their hearts.

The Colonel of my training battalion was an elderly dyed-in-the-wool
volunteer, brought up in the days of dark green uniforms and shiny black
leather accoutrements and accustomed to shouts of "Saturday night
soldier!" from impertinent small boys as he marched his self-conscious
troops through the streets of Victoria's England. Now, in the frosty
autumn days of 1914, he found himself leading eager recruits up and down
the green hills of North Wales and through the beech-brown lanes of
Cheshire, his conception of the warfare that lay ahead made up of romantic notions of what went on in the Crimean War, coupled with an
enthusiastic study of the tactics of the Boer Commandos, with Mr
Kipling somewhere in the background of his mind for inspiration.
Nevertheless, he understood the need for maintaining the morale of young
men brought up in homes where bloodshed was only read about, never
imagined as a personal experience. There was no radio in those days, just
a few inadequate cinemas showing out-of-date silent films in near-by villages. To make matters worse our battalion was still under canvas, the
tents surrounded by deep trenches full of muddy water, and winter rapidly
approaching. As he stumbled and lurched his way forward at the head of
the line of march the Colonel's mind was full of schemes for keeping us
out of mischief. I like to think of him as the first Welfare Officer of the
British Army, but of course Florence Nightingale was that. All the same,
he was a gallant old man.

One day, during a more than usually tedious exercise when all the songs
had died in the men's throats and depression had settled like a cloud upon
the marching column, the Colonel called me to his side. He knew I had
been an actor and a producer of plays, for he lived near Liverpool in
peace-time and had modestly supported our efforts to found the Liverpool
Repertory Theatre.

"How about some shows for the men?" he demanded, abruptly.

"Shows, sir?" I replied, pretending not to understand.

"Yes. You're an actor chap, aren't you? Can't you get up some concerts or plays? Tell you what! We'll have a competition. Each company

shall get up a show; then you and I'll pick the best team for a battalion concert party and play 'em against other units!"

This was certainly a sportsman's way of tackling the problem.

Shortly after this conversation our battalion was moved into winter quarters at Aberystwyth: several rows of lodging-houses on the outskirts of the town, those allotted to the officers being right on the sea front. They had been stripped of every item of furniture. When the north-westerly gales blew in from the Atlantic the window frames rattled like castanets, and newspapers lying on the floor went scurrying into corners, chased by the icy blasts coming up through the floor-boards.

There, in the evenings, I set about the task the Colonel had laid upon me, determined that my own B Company should come out on top in the eliminating round of concerts, held in a little café in the High Street. In the spring we were moved inland to a vast new hutted camp at Oswestry, recently completed save for the roads, of course; these were an afterthought. Here our Colonel renewed his activities as a theatrical manager, and soon a battalion entertainment unit was formed. The concerts were such a success that the regimental canteen could not hold all the visitors, and the beer-swillers began to grumble at the interruption of their pleasures.

Success brought the Colonel credit at divisional headquarters; also, it went to his head. Perhaps he already saw himself as a famous impresario after the war. At all events he decided to "go professional," as he termed it, and ordered me to London, "to get some actresses, and wigs and costumes." Scenery was provided by the pioneer sergeant, who made large wooden frames and covered them with latrine canvas, which George Harris, the distinguished artist from the Liverpool Repertory Theatre, by now renamed the Playhouse, who was later to be the designer of most of my post-war productions, quickly converted into scenery. I remember a gay terraced garden, complete with nymphs and fountains, that he created one day between breakfast and retreat, to the great astonishment of the fatigue men, who stood watching him through a pall of smoke from the barrack-room stoves, and maintaining a running fire of comment, most of it unprintable, that was highly amusing to George, who gave as good as he received.

Very soon both the divisional generals stationed at the camp demanded organized entertainment for all units in training. This created a major problem of accommodation, for there were no camp halls or central institutes then; and the duck-boards that were deputizing for the missing roads sat upon billows of mud which made entry into the canteens a high adventure.

3

One night in the Mess I overheard the Senior Major discussing with the Commanding Officer ways of spending the rapidly accumulating P.R.I. funds. These funds, made up of rebates on sales in the canteens, were paid by the catering contractors to each occupying battalion to be expended upon various comforts and amenities for the men. The senior officer responsible for the disposal of the money was the President of the Regimental Institute, hence the name. In the teeming camps of those days the regimental officers often found themselves in control of more money than they knew what to do with. To hand the excess funds back to the Command Paymaster was unthinkable. No army in war-time has a particularly strong sense of responsibility towards public funds; those who are doing the fighting not unnaturally feel that the civilians should be left to pay the bill, with unfortunate after-effects upon the national economy. All this was before the advent of the Army Canteen Committee, first version of the present NAAFI. Whoever thought of the basically simple idea of a central authority to control all these matters in the soldier's own interest not only has saved the country large sums of money, but has secured a steadily improving service of amenities for the troops.

It occurred to me that here was the solution of the problem. Each battalion should make a contribution from its P.R.I. funds towards the cost of building a theatre for the whole camp. Luckily, the place was still in the hands of the civilian contractors, so the War Office need not be consulted. At a meeting presided over by the Camp Commandant[1] the money was quickly forthcoming. Armed with a special pass, I hurried off to interview Harry B. Measures, the Director of Barrack Construction, taking with me some sketch-plans that I had worked out with George Harris for the proposed theatre. The main features of these plans provided the basis for all camp theatre design in both World Wars, as may be seen by a glance at the photographs reproduced in this book.

Measures, a cheerful, energetic man and the most rapid chain smoker I ever met, was just then enduring the full blast of public criticism for delay in completing the new camps, a delay which, as a civilian, he naturally said was entirely due to War Office muddle. Delighted at the prospect of carrying out an unorthodox proposal behind the backs of the military big-wigs, he redrew our sketch-plans, made a special journey to the camp to select the site and to instruct the contractor, and then stood by the

---

[1] Lieutenant-Colonel H. Worsley-Gough, C.M.G.

project until it was completed. Afterwards he told me he regarded it as a good joke at the expense of the brass hats.

As our theatre, with its high stage roof, drew near to completion it became the most conspicuous building in the camp. We had helped ourselves to all sorts of bits and pieces whilst building the place, so we shook in our shoes at the news of a forthcoming general inspection by the G.O.C.-in-C. Western Command (Lieutenant-General Sir William Pitcairn Campbell). However, by a skilful use of the port decanter after lunch, our General secured his promise to open the theatre officially in a month's time.

There was the usual rush to get the building ready, and we had to comb the nominal rolls to find men with technical experience as stage hands and electricians to run the place for us. Eventually, I put Sergeant Bryant, an N.C.O. from my own regiment, in charge of the stage, and very well he ran it, too. He must have remained in the business ever since, for only the other day I found him presiding over the stage-door at the London Palladium. The magnificent air with which he passed me through the waiting crowds on my way to see Gracie Fields was an unconscious tribute to our happy association so long ago.

There was tremendous enthusiasm on the opening night. If the performance, a mixture of amateur and professional items, was not particularly good, the Mess dinner beforehand was first-class. From the moment when General Campbell at the end of a thumping speech announced that he wanted more camp theatres in his Command and as soon as possible, success was assured.

Twice-nightly performances were given seven days a week, plays of all kinds alternating with film shows, with two and sometimes three special concerts on Sundays. The demand for seats was so great that tickets had to be rationed among the various units. On one occasion the principal singers of the Beecham Opera Company came down and gave excerpts in costume from several operas; among their number were Edna Thornton, Frank Mullings, Robert Radford and Foster Richardson.

Shortly before these events, thanks to a good memory and the habit of clear exposition learned in the theatre, I had managed to gain a 'distinguished' at the Command Musketry School. As a result of this I was made brigade musketry officer, and spent long hours on the boggy ranges of Prees Heath, lost in a mist of dreams of what I could do for troop entertainment if I were given the chance. This must have caused considerable embarrassment to the musketry instructors of the Regular Army whose work I was supposed to supervise.

"Outer, three o'clock. Don't snatch, Private Williams. How many more times! George Robey: I wonder if he'd come? Squeeze the trigger. Forefinger and thumb."

"Ever seen Leslie Henson, sergeant?"

"Sir?" Obviously he thinks me an imbecile.

Leslie had written to say that he would bring down the full Gaiety Company on the following Sunday, including himself, David Burnaby, and the Gaiety Chorus, in a specially written revue entitled *How's Yer Father?* or *Any Complaints?*; but he did not tell me that the company proposed to write it among themselves on the train travelling between Paddington and Shrewsbury. The performance was certainly hilarious, with Melville Gideon at the piano (for orchestra), the comedians at the top of their form, and an attractive chorus of little girls, many of whom were later to have successful careers in the theatre, including Joyce Barbour, Avice Kelham, and Mercia Swinburne.

Musketry instruction and theatrical management made up a peculiar combination of duties. There was the further distraction of waiting daily for the appearance of my name on the draft list for France. Early one morning the summons came. As I watched my batman collecting my things for embarkation leave, feeling decidedly blue and refusing to think any more about the theatre, I was summoned to the orderly room, where I was abruptly told that my embarkation leave was cancelled: I was to report immediately at Command Headquarters in Chester. No reason was given: had they found out about the spare timber and that roll or two of roofing felt? I was in a state of mild panic when I arrived. A staff colonel of the period (and in those days some of the senior officers were certainly period pieces) told me I was transferred to Western Command with instructions to organize a camp theatre at Kinmel Park, near Rhyl, on the same lines as Oswestry.

It was in this little theatre that J. B. Priestley spent much of his spare time during the months of training. Years later, when I came to produce some of his plays, he told me the theatre at Kinmel Park was the one bright spot in a prospect dominated by mud and whitewash. So our scheme helped to foster the genius of one of Britain's leading dramatists. The third and last theatre Harry Measures built was at Ripon, in Northern Command, where General Sir John Maxwell was Commander-in-Chief. I was allowed to organize this by arrangement between the two commands; so the theatre was larger than the other two; it had canteens for N.C.O.'s and men, as well as an officers' lounge-bar.

The rapid growth of the scheme, for which there was no War Office authority, began to alarm the Command staff. So far it had been financed by contributions from the P.R.I. funds in each camp; but the impending

H.R.H. THE DUKE OF KENT WITH A CONCERT PARTY FOR THE R.A.F.

T.M. KING GEORGE VI AND QUEEN ELIZABETH TALKING TO VIOLET LORAINE AND BINNIE HALE ON THE STAGE OF THE THEATRE ROYAL, DRURY LANE, BEFORE THE DISPATCH OF THE FIRST PARTIES TO FRANCE, NOVEMBER 1939

In the background: Leslie Henson and W. Macqueen-Pope.

GARRISON THEATRES NEAR AND FAR (1)

INTERIOR OF THE FIRST
GARRISON THEATRE IN
WORLD WAR I:
PARK HALL CAMP,
OSWESTRY, 1916

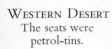

WORLD WAR II: ONE
OF THE CONVERTED
RIDING-SCHOOLS

WESTERN DESERT
The seats were
petrol-tins.

R.A.F. THEATRE,
SHILLONG, ASSAM

departure for the Front of some of the contributing battalions now raised an awkward problem. They were likely to lose touch with their invest-ment; and what regiment was to make up the losses, if any were incurred?[1] Unless the scheme were to be officially adopted by the War Office, it must sooner or later come to an end. I had already drawn up a memoran-dum setting out the progress to date and giving my ideas for the future. This I sent to Edward ('Eddie') Marsh, then Private Secretary to Win-ston Churchill at the Admiralty, with a naïve request for Army Council approval. Eddie replied that the procedure was not so simple as that, and it might be months before I heard anything.

Early in 1917 I was called to the War Office. The yeast must have been at work beneath the surface. The Western Command staff thankfully said good-bye to their responsibility for a scheme which nevertheless they had come to look upon as their own, and I mounted the steps of the War Office for the first time, feeling rather cocky. My pride was lowered a few days later when I received a request from an illiterate corporal left in charge of the stage at Kinmel Park, asking for special leave. He wished to marry the girl of his choice, and the matter appeared to be pressing. The letter was addressed to "Captain Vassilene, the War Office."

4

At first I worked under Colonel Gordon Leith, who was in charge of a branch of the Quartermaster-General's Department known as QMG 11, which acted as liaison between the Army Council and the newly formed Army Canteen Committee. Later I was transferred and placed in charge of the Entertainment Branch of the renamed Navy and Army Canteen Board (N.A.C.B.).

Now began an experience of Army administration and of large-scale planning that was to stand me in good stead in the years to come. We built many fine theatres, the last and most elaborate being at Catterick, in Yorkshire, opened by H.R.H. the Duke of Connaught in March 1918.

The Branch ran its own companies, each with a repertoire of plays and a cast of actors selected to suit the particular type of entertainment. There were drama companies, musical-comedy companies, revues, farce com-panies and so on. The redoubtable Fred Melville of the Lyceum Theatre supplied and produced all the melodramas; I say "redoubtable" because

---

[1] This problem solved itself, for when the Navy and Army Canteen Board took over the theatres each battalion was repaid the amount of its original contribution, plus a share of the profits, which in the case of Oswestry amounted to 6s. 6d. for each £1 invested.

he consistently refused to be intimidated by the official atmosphere in which he found himself. Upon one occasion he was asked to inspect and report upon a large circuit of privately owned camp cinemas on Salisbury Plain. In response to public agitation the War Office had proposed that they should be compulsorily purchased. Fred's report, formally addressed to "The Secretary, War Office," was commendably brief:

DEAR SIR,
re Albany Ward Circuit
My advice is "don't."
FRED MELVILLE

Robert Evett, of Daly's Theatre, looked after the musical comedies, Sir Frank Benson appeared in Shakespeare, while the facetious, always urbane Douglas Furber wrote and acted in our camp revues, unveiling before my astonished eyes as he did so all the mysteries of the professional gag-book. Jack Hylton was the conductor of the principal musical-comedy company. He was an elusive, shy young man in pince-nez glasses, whose thoughts seemed always to be somewhere round the corner while he was talking to you. One felt he knew all the time the road he intended to take, even though one might be propelling him gently in the opposite direction. Thorpe Bates organized the Sunday concerts, spending his time between our headquarters and Daly's Theatre, where he played the romantic hero in *The Maid of the Mountains* eight or nine times a week. His deep-breathing and chest-expansion exercises much amused our typists at lunch-time; he was taken more seriously at night. George Harris came down from Liverpool to design stages, scenery, costumes, programme covers, posters; all with a fund of invention, a furious speed and a technical expertise that I have only once seen equalled, and that was by Rex Whistler.

The companies included many people who won fame for themselves later on. Among the girls was Dodie Smith, for a short while an unruly member of the Farce Company. Complaints of slackness and insubordination in this company had been received for some time. So, during a hurried visit to Bulford Camp I called a rehearsal of one of the plays; it was a mothy farce called *Niobe: All Tears*. Unfortunately, the General kept me talking and I arrived late for the rehearsal, only to find that Dodie, tired of waiting, had commandeered the bus and gone back with other malcontents to the hostel some miles outside the camp for lunch. In the afternoon I gave her a severe lecture on the importance of discipline. She was quite unmoved and retorted that, if she had waited any longer, the lunch would have been cold. I became heated while she remained cool, her conversation exasperatingly irrelevant: she didn't think the play very funny, she didn't like her part; and the hostel lunch *was* cold anyway. Miss

Dodie Smith ceased to be a member of our Farce Company. We did not meet again until some ten years later, when she marched into my office in John Street, Adelphi, with a copy of her first play, *Autumn Crocus*, tucked under her arm. I had asked the author of this sentimental comedy, written with much delicacy and feminine insight, to call and discuss it with me; I looked forward with interest to meeting the shy young authoress. There entered a spirited, bird-like creature, dressed to kill in high-button boots and a white hat with something pink at the top, looking rather like a French can-can dancer from the Casino de Paris. I quite failed to recognize the rebellious 'Niobe' of the camps. She listened to my smooth compliments, then heaped coals of fire upon my head by quietly reminding me that the last time we had met I had given her the sack.

In the spring of 1918 Douglas Furber and I wrote a camp revue together, with some lyrics by Ronald Jeans, which we called *Merry-Go-Round*. The music was contributed by all the best-known light composers of the day, including Archibald Joyce, Howard Carr, Harold Samuel, Emmett Adams, Herman Darewski and, finally, Ivor Novello. When I went to see Ivor at his flat—it was our first meeting—I remember being struck by the aura of happiness that surrounded him. Bright, gay little tunes seemed to come dancing out of his head as he sat down at the piano to play the music he had composed for us. The revue was a sensational success, and there was talk about bringing it into Daly's Theatre; but then the Armistice was signed and the actors hurried back to their normal professional work. Twelve months later I too was demobilized, and began immediately the exciting adventure of running the ReandeaN Company with Alec Rea.

A regular entertainment service, including the provision of circuits of properly equipped theatres and cinemas, became a commonplace of World War II, but it was quite a new idea then, as new as the citizen army that Britain had mobilized for the first time in many centuries. And it was this original conception of the Garrison Theatre at Oswestry, built and paid for out of the soldiers' own funds in the First World War, that made possible the birth of ENSA in the Second.

CHAPTER TWO

THE USUAL CHANNELS

SKIP now the intervening years—they add nothing to this particular story—and turn again to the time of Munich. In 1938 the Theatre was passing through one of its periodic phases of decline. Plays of outstanding merit were even fewer than usual and acting had grown stale and accustomed. Moreover, the Nazi menace was making people restless, and disinclined to spend money on entertainment. While the theatrical managers continued their search for box-office success the minds of their audiences drifted farther and farther away from the business of daily living to concentrate upon the greater drama taking place across the Channel. It was a schizophrenic condition for everybody. Yet I found no cause for complaint, producing in close succession spectacular melodrama at Drury Lane, *The Story of an African Farm* at the New Theatre and a series of plays in partnership with J. B. Priestley, mostly at the St Martin's Theatre, which, ever since the happy ReandeaN days, has always been like home to me, and culminating in the production of *Johnson over Jordan*,[1] again at the New Theatre, in the spring of 1939. In all of them there were fascinating opportunities for pursuing my experiments with new staging and lighting techniques.

The most successful production was Priestley's own Yorkshire comedy, *When we are married*. This merry play is Priestley at his best, with his particular gifts of humour and observation of English idiosyncrasy well displayed. The final rehearsals were interrupted by my engagement to speak at the annual convention of the Institute of Journalists at Keswick, where Hugh Walpole, proposing my health, praised me for pursuing what he called a middle policy in the theatre, a compliment of uncertain value. I returned to my London flat in time to take in the early-morning milk and newspapers announcing the Prime Minister's departure for Germany.

The opening performances in Manchester took on a disembodied air as empty seats in the theatre contrasted with the full, anxious hearts in the streets outside. The scanty audiences hardly noticed what was passing on

---

[1] It was in the part of Johnson that Ralph Richardson took such a notable step forward in his career.

the stage, holding their ears cocked for news of the whereabouts of Mr Chamberlain and his umbrella. (That article later became a joke not only of the English music hall, but in foreign countries too. "Voici mon Chamberlain," exclaims a famous French actress to whom I am introduced in Paris, waving her umbrella in my face, presumably as a sign of international goodwill.) By the time the play reached Blackpool the Prime Minister had taken himself off for the second time. The tension was finally broken on the Saturday morning by his return with a promise of "peace in our time." George Black came to the performance that afternoon and prophesied success for us in London; but when I talked to him about my plans for mobilizing the Theatre for the approaching conflict he laughed in my face, so eagerly had public opinion turned to thoughts of peace everlasting.

As the glare of Munich faded away, its place taken by the rose-dawn promise of peace—a shepherd's warning—our little committee faded away too, although during the following winter I used occasionally to persuade Leslie Henson into my flat to talk things over. A sense of urgency about our scheme nagged at me continuously. I was convinced that war would bite deeper into the social structure than ever before, and that we of the Theatre would have a great opportunity to prove our worth in the national emergency. It was important to seize that opportunity at the right time. We were unlikely to have 'greatness thrust upon us.'

Early in 1939 our committee was resuscitated and enlarged. Sir Seymour Hicks agreed to become controller and so give the profession a lead. Thanks to his energy and bonhomie, more and more people became interested in our ideas. While he hurried to theatrical meetings and in and out of the clubs, stifling the ridicule and jealousy, 'glad-handing' everybody, making them think that perhaps there might be something in the idea after all, I strove to widen and deepen the foundations of the scheme. Enthusiastic support for my pamphlet from numerous back-benchers in the House of Commons had not taken us very far. Who would give us the necessary authority and finance when the opening thunderclaps sent every one scurrying for shelter?

2

The problem had three sides: civil, military and professional. Which should we tackle first? To provide for the civilians in the war factories we should have to persuade a Government Department to include the necessary funds in its vote. Troop entertainments presumably meant the War Office. Within the profession the theatrical organizations would have to be persuaded to make sacrifices and to co-operate with each other. For several weeks Seymour and I sat uneasily on the horns of this trilemma. In the end we tackled all three together.

On April 6, 1939, the Lord Privy Seal (Sir John Anderson[1]), who was then in charge of Home Security, received us both at the Home Office. Mr Robert Wood[2] was with him. Seymour tried to enliven the atmosphere with a blithe description of our ideas, throwing in a few Garrick Club quips which wrung a wry smile from the dour Scot watching him across the table. Sir John asked some searching questions, and Mr Wood wanted further copies of the pamphlet; we then withdrew with the promise of an official reply in due course. As we retreated down the gloomy corridor, escorted by one of those silent, battered-looking messengers that I always find more intimidating than the ministerial presence itself, Seymour plucked my sleeve and whispered, "He'll forget all about it before he's finished his tea." This was not so, for on May 6 we received a letter from Robert Wood giving us the Minister's official blessing. This we thought to be great progress at the time. The stone which we cast into the pond at that interview set up the strongest ripples in the following year, but unfortunately they did not travel in our direction.

In the course of my search for contacts within the Services I got into touch with Arthur Tedder,[3] whom I had not met since we were at school together. He dined with me at the Garrick Club. Very little changed through the years, he had the same charm and imperturbable good humour, lightened by a boyish smile. He reminded me of the time when we appeared together in the annual play for the school charities, I playing the leading part of Dick Bultitude in *Vice Versa*, and he one of the other boys. The following year he took my place as 'leading man' before going on to Cambridge. Now, beyond cordial approval of the scheme, he could do little to help me, as he was not in a branch of the Air Ministry that concerned itself with such matters. But this renewal of contact was to bear fruit later on.

To raise a matter of this kind 'through the usual channels' is always slow and difficult, particularly at a time when the authorities are preoccupied with more serious matters, but there was nothing else for it. Our early efforts at the War Office were not encouraging. Patronizing smiles appeared behind clipped moustaches at the interviews. Clearly we were just a little mad. "Whoever heard of mobilizing actors for national service? If war does come it will be serious. Let 'em join the army!"

Seymour soon tired of tramping down corridors in search of elusive

---

[1] Now Lord Waverley.
[2] Later Sir Robert Wood, Secretary to the Ministry of Education.
[3] Now Marshal of the R.A.F. Lord Tedder.

encouragement. Later on, after the war had begun, he used to delight in telling a malicious story of his attempted interview with a certain general whom he called 'Sprike.' He had been told this general could facilitate the transport of artistes to France. So he presented himself at 10 A.M. at a certain room in the 'War House,' on the door of which were various numbers and letters of the alphabet, described by Seymour in his rapid manner as follows:

"You know the sort of thing, old boy. XYZ, small 2 in a bracket. Colonel Snooker-Poole, Dep:Director, small a, two brackets."

"General Sprike in?" says Seymour.

"Well, actually—er—no, sir. This isn't his office any longer. Actually, if it's about transport for actors I should try Q Movements, General Sprightly. He's the proper person to see."

Arrived at this department, Seymour demands to see General Sprightly, only to be told he is away on inspection.

"Oh," says Seymour, "well, could I have an appointment when he gets back?"

"Actually an appointment *could* be arranged, but it wouldn't be any use, as the matter doesn't concern him. I think General Sprike's your man, sir."

"But—I've just—been sent—here! Never mind. Where is he?"

"Down the corridor, second staircase on the right, one floor down. Sergeant, show Sir Seymour."

Arrived there, Seymour is told the General's office has again been moved. After knocking on a number of doors where similar explanations of the General's non-appearance are given, the party, now grown to the size of a deputation, finally arrives at a door with General Sprike's name on it in large letters, the time, according to Seymour, now being about noon. The room is occupied only by a staff-sergeant.

"Can I see General Sprike, please?"

"Very sorry, sir," replies the staff-sergeant. "General's not here any more. He died last week."

Summer time came in, but no one could alter the clock of events in Europe. The hours of peace were growing shorter, not longer. Making no headway with the War Office, we began to think more and more of my association with the Navy and Army Canteen Board of the First War. This was now called the Navy, Army and Air Force Institutes (NAAFI), the fuller title symbolizing the extension of its responsibilities to include the Air Force. I submitted a memorandum to the Corporation on April 18, outlining our plans for entertainment in the event of another war and suggesting that NAAFI should undertake financial responsibility

C

for the military side of our provision. The memorandum was accepted in principle on April 27. In fact, the Corporation had continued to provide small concert parties and music-hall turns in special circumstances, such as the summer canvas camps, ever since the First War. So their acceptance involved no new principle, merely an extension of existing practice. On May 1 I agreed to act as an honorary liaison officer between the NAAFI Corporation and the theatrical world, while the various entertainment interests were being cajoled into line by Seymour. On May 2 the Corporation issued a statement to the Press, and on May 5, in reply to a private Member's question in the House of Commons, Sir Victor Warrender,[1] Financial Secretary to the War Office, supplied Government confirmation of the preliminary arrangements: a prompt and businesslike proceeding throughout, and a refreshing change from our experiences elsewhere. . . . This briefly explains how NAAFI, an organization existing primarily to provide drinks and edibles for the troops, came to be concerned with professional entertainment. The arrangement puzzled many of ENSA's friends, but it was one for which I was initially responsible.

The third side to our problem, the co-operation of the entertainment organizations, made no progress at all. The first impact of a great war on the Theatre is catastrophic; it is later on that the box-office boom starts. The new war was to prove no exception to the rule. Meanwhile, with livelihoods in jeopardy, both managers and actors refused to contemplate the problems which another world war would bring to the profession.

3

Tired of knocking my head against a brick wall, I went to America, ostensibly to confer with Richard Aldington about the dramatization of his novel, *Seven against Reeves*,[2] on which we had agreed to collaborate, but actually to get away from the London atmosphere of 'alarm and despondency.'

The easy hospitality of America could not lighten the dark background of anxiety about events at home. I spent much of my time like an itinerant preacher, distributing copies of my pamphlet to incredulous theatrical friends, and going daily to the World's Fair, staring at the raucous crowds in the amusement park, and marvelling at the immense resurgence of power implicit in the Russian pavilion.

By July I was in Paris, making a nuisance of myself there too. This time it was Frank Vernon, distinguished producer of the play *Milestones*, and his wife Virginia who had to endure my missionary zeal. They tried to

---

[1] Now Lord Bruntisfield.   [2] The war killed this project.

distract me with nightly visits to the theatre and the opera. No one could resist their cultured and amusing companionship, nor the hospitality of the many French artistes whom we visited after the performances. On our last evening we sat at a favourite café on the Boulevard Saint-Germain, watching the homing crowds under the whispering plane trees in the summer night. I began to imagine British khaki among the variegated colours: of course, there would be another Expeditionary Force, and that meant entertainment. The others were talking about the opera we had seen that night, but I brought the conversation back to my preoccupation: "The contribution of the Theatre to national morale will be immense; but we must organize beforehand." I was throwing stones again. Turning to Virginia, I asked her casually if she would help us to arrange hotel accommodation and billets for the artistes, and perhaps contact French theatre people, if we needed their help. She said she would if Frank had no objection.

"Oh, Basil," said my wife anxiously, "do be quiet. How can there be another war when nobody wants it?"

"Garçon!" called Frank. "Four beers! . . . There *will* be another war. You've a tremendous idea, Basil. Virginia must help if you want her."

There was silence between us as our unspoken thoughts went running on. Soon it was past closing-time. The waiter, who had been gloomily picking his teeth at the side of the awning, snatched his tip and hurried away.

Frank died at Dieppe in the spring of the following year. It was only then that I realized what a personal sacrifice it had been for him to give up the devoted companionship of his wife when he was in such poor health. His approval of my suggestion was in reality a last gift to his country in time of need.

4

Back in London the prevailing mood was one of apprehension. The personal problems which the coming of war would present were the principal topic of conversation. I spent the early part of August at Little-stone, in Kent, in the company of Anthony Kimmins and his wife, discussing the revision of a play he had written, and pondering the purchase of Gun House, a charming Queen Anne property on the outskirts of New Romney, which I thought, in the event of war, would be more accessible than my home in Essex. Although I bought the place, we never lived there; it was requisitioned, and suffered greater damage from the British coastal troops who occupied it than from the bombs and machine-guns of the enemy. Our relaxations were fishing for shrimps, which the children dignified by the name of prawns, and contemplating the shipping in the Channel through Tony's big telescope, mounted in the bay-window. That sailor's look in anticipation of foreign travel, of dangers to be courted and overcome, came into Tony's eyes as he waited for his call to rejoin the Navy.

The pages of my office diary for the second half of the month are filled with entries of meetings. First came general meetings to which all branches of the profession were invited. These were quarrelsome affairs. One of them broke up in disorder because an agent demanded that his association should control the booking of the variety artistes, to which the V.A.F.[1] representative replied that this was national service and not to be controlled by anyone! The Incorporated Society of Musicians claimed to represent a higher order of being than the Amalgamated Musicians' Union; this too made collaboration difficult. At another meeting the name of our association was finally chosen. We had begun by calling ourselves the Actors' National Service Association (ANSA), but this was objected to as being too narrow a flag for all to march under. I submitted as alternative the Entertainments National Service Association (ENSA); this was finally agreed after Leslie Henson had characteristically remarked that if we kept to ANSA we should be accused of knowing all the answers.

Sub-committees were formed to deal with this and that; but the major question as to the best constitution for our Association to adopt, one that would give it a separate existence and at the same time enable it to set up the contemplated business arrangements with NAAFI and with Government Departments, remained intractable because of managerial suspicion. This had been growing ever since the managers realized that my plan was going to come to something after all. Here was a new impulse stirring in the Theatre, one that already had a measure of official encouragement. Whither would it lead them? Perhaps ENSA would take over all the theatres before long? The note of personal sacrifice had been sounded too suddenly in unaccustomed ears. Thanks, however, to Walter Payne and Bronson Albery,[2] of the Society of West End Managers, and to P. M. Selby, President of the Theatrical Managers' Association, both these bodies did eventually give their formal support.

On August 31 I gave a talk on the Empire wavelength about our plans. While I was at Broadcasting House the news of Hitler's invasion of Poland came through. It was exciting to listen to the comments of the monitoring staff as they picked up little bits of news from the various foreign stations. Later the producer escorted me down into the main hall, where I was surprised to observe a large number of young men dashing into the build-

---

[1] Variety Artists' Federation.   [2] Now Sir Bronson Albery.

ing and disappearing at speed down corridors. They presented a surprising similarity of appearance; raincoats, no hats, long hair and carrying attaché cases. It was the opening long shot in an American super-film of World War II. "Where are all those people off to?" I asked.

"Hush," said my escort, placing a finger down one side of his nose. Then, bending over me—he was a tall, willowy person—he whispered, "War stations!"

Outside I shivered in the early-morning mist. So it had come at last! Had I bitten off more than I could chew? Would it ever be possible to keep such a team of wild horses within the shafts? Well, I'd started the scheme. It was up to me to go through with it. I got into the car. "Quite good, sir," said my driver.

"Good?" I exclaimed. "Why, this means war! Oh, you mean my broadcast."

5

It was now only a question of days before war was declared, so I decided to spend what remained of peace with my family in Essex. I telephoned to NAAFI Headquarters and told them where I was going, adding half jocularly, to conceal the nervous tension I felt, "Give me a ring when you want us to mobilize!" On Sunday morning my family and some friends were gathered in the Long Room at Easton Manor, listening to the quiet voice of Mr Chamberlain telling us we were at war, just after the bells of the ancient village church on the opposite side of my yard had ceased to ring. We had had barely time to take in the news when we heard the siren from the neighbouring town of Dunmow. I shepherded the party into the cellarage, although the protection afforded by the floor above was of the flimsiest description. Half an hour later we were out in the sunlight, waiting to receive our first batch of London evacuees. The next morning, as I was on my way down to the lake for a swim with my daughter, the telephone rang. Against the background of giggling evacuee children I heard a quiet voice say, "How soon can you get back?" It was the General Manager of NAAFI.

"Why? D'you want us to start right away?"

"Yes."

"Oh, very well. To-morrow."

That was all. My stomach gave a funny little twitch, and I went indoors to pack.

In quiet homes all over England similar scenes must have been taking place that Monday morning; hardly worthy of note, perhaps, except in their similarity: no drama, no excitement, just packing up. For my family there was heartache too, because we were not going to live at Little Easton any more.

I drove straight to NAAFI H.Q. at Imperial Court, Kennington. London had a different feel about it from the previous week. The people in the streets and tubes and buses wore an air of relief and certainty about them. Even the buildings had a sense of purpose, standing there in the September sun, as though their stones wanted to share our decision; just a trick of personal consciousness, of course, but a strange effect while it lasted. . . . My secretary was waiting for me in the small office allotted to us. Two desks, chairs, a typewriter and a small pile of stationery, but no telephone. However, either Post Office engineers or R.E.'s—I forget which—were busily engaged in laying emergency lines; and we managed to get two extensions the next morning.

6

A pandemonium of ringing telephones, interviews with over-enthusiastic volunteers in corridors and on the street, arguments with managers —one thought dominated my mind throughout those first days: speed, speed, speed! How soon would the troops demand their shows? How soon could we persuade the entertainment world to adopt a constitution for ENSA?

At a special joint meeting of the Society of West End Managers and of British Actors' Equity I made an urgent appeal for immediate action. The Managers wanted to consult other bodies with whom Hicks and I were already in contact, to discuss and discuss, and yet again to discuss. I knew that both the War Office and NAAFI were anxious to know whether we could deliver the goods. Already splinter groups were forming. A manager in Scotland had launched a scheme of his own; Harold Holt had offered to give free concerts in the new camp halls; it was easy to foresee the waste and confusion that would result unless a central organization were formed. The stalwarts of the last war were sound enough. Both Jack Hylton and 'Tommy' Bates were among the first to offer their services. Indeed, it was gratifying how promptly all the survivors of the old Entertainment Branch rallied to ENSA's call when war came again, slipping quickly into their places without fuss or uncertainty, seeming to know exactly what was expected of them. Their cheery voices down the telephone were a great comfort: "Ready when you are. Where are the Headquarters?"

This was another problem. Although the theatres had been closed, we had neither funds nor authority to take one of them over for our use.

During the week W. A. Abingdon, whom I had installed as stage director of the Theatre Royal, Drury Lane, in 1924, and who was another recruit from the old Entertainment Branch, rang up and suggested that we should take over Drury Lane, where attendances at Ivor Novello's *Dancing Years* had become very thin, so much so that at the closing performance the previous Saturday Ivor had invited the audience in the upper parts of the house to fill up the stalls, whereupon the evening had developed into an impromptu concert with Ivor as the star turn. (Yet this was the production that ran for several years at the Adelphi Theatre when the management later brought it back to London, making Novello a rich man!) The installation of ENSA at the famous theatre was later described as a piece of brilliant imaginative planning. If that be so, the first of the credit must go to Abingdon. When he rang up that morning it took me a minute or two to recover my breath and to realize the significance of the proposal; then I undertook to persuade NAAFI to agree.

Meanwhile Seymour Hicks made a further attempt to reconcile the warring interests. He took the chair at another representative meeting on September 8. The proceedings were unruly from the start. Every one seemed to be resentful of something or other. Many were inclined to blame ENSA for the closure of their theatres; others said it would take their business away from them. Agents wanted to know if they were going to get their commissions, actors their exemption from military service. Many of the disputants had obviously given no thought at all to what lay ahead. In vain Seymour pleaded, pointing out that the conditions of the new war would be quite unlike those of the last; there would be general black-out, air raids and so forth. Through all this I kept as quiet as possible. I had flung so many stones into the pond by now, aroused so much jealousy, that silence seemed the wisest course. The fog of disputation and tobacco smoke was at its densest when a very important manager 'made an entrance'—there is no better way to describe it—into the tiny room and, under the influence of an excellent lunch, launched a vicious attack on me. Why had he not been invited? (His office had, of course, received an invitation.) The whole thing was out of order. Under whose authority were we acting, etc., etc.? All the questions people ask when they are flushed and angry and not in good debating humour. Encouraged by the warmth of his own eloquence, he moved that the whole project be abandoned.

The meeting was kept from open disorder by Seymour's adroitness. But we had reached an impasse. Angry groups broke off into separate argument; the buzz of talk was deafening. Then I was summoned to the telephone in another room by Macqueen-Pope, who had taken office, as it were, as the ENSA Public Relations Officer. It was a message from NAAFI. I returned to the meeting and whispered the news into Seymour's ear; we were taking over Drury Lane as our headquarters from the following Monday. "That settles it then," said Seymour. There was a quality in the silence that followed his announcement which convinced me that sabotage of ENSA was not finally quashed. The meeting was adjourned until the following Thursday (September 14) at Drury Lane.

By this time I was extremely worried lest we found ourselves bogged down in a morass of talk while the troops were demanding entertainment, a situation from which the profession could only emerge looking very foolish. There seemed no reason to anticipate anything untoward as a result of the postponement of my plan that ENSA should have a corporate existence of its own and be financed by the various public bodies for whom it provided entertainment. There would be time later on to draft a constitution that would be acceptable to the profession and make possible the granting of official status. Nevertheless, I viewed with much disquiet the possibility of having to hand ourselves over to NAAFI as part of the 'give-aways' that went with the groceries ranged on the shelves of their canteens. In fairness to the Corporation it must be stated here that it was quite willing to accept my plan for a separate ENSA; and I did, in fact, hold several conferences to that end with the deputy general manager. That the idea did not go forward was not the fault of the Corporation.

On the day before the meeting was to be resumed at Drury Lane, I took the decisive step and told Seymour we should waste no more time in talk. The only way to get things started quickly was to have an Entertainment Branch of NAAFI to do the managerial side of the job, and to regard ENSA as a sort of recruiting agency attached to that Branch. Seymour loyally accepted my view. The meeting was cancelled, and an official statement issued to the Press, the opening and closing sentences of which read as follows:

> The organization for the provision of entertainments for His Majesty's Forces both at home and abroad is now completed. The Navy, Army and Air Force Institutes will be responsible for the organization, control and finance of the entertainments. The Entertainments National Service Association (ENSA) will provide the entertainment asked for through various committees. . . . The entertainments are scheduled to begin on Monday week, September 25.

And they did. We were off!

CHAPTER THREE

HORSES FOR COURSES

ONCE more I found myself in charge of the Theatre Royal, Drury Lane. As I went in by the stage door on that Monday morning and surveyed the vast stage, stripped to the waist for its new task, and the darkened scene-dock, with its racks piled high with dusty backcloths, I felt the spur of the new responsibility for the first time. The sight of abandoned scenery usually makes me sad; it is like wreckage on the seashore, witness to lost hopes and frustrated endeavour. But this time it had the reverse effect. My mind slid back fifteen years to my single-handed and presumptuous effort to convert this shrine of English theatrical tradition into a National Theatre. All the incident and high adventure of that Christmas production of *A Midsummer Night's Dream*, carried out in the face of angry opposition from the Drury Lane Board (although Sir Alfred Butt had himself made the first tentative suggestion, never thinking I would take it seriously), flickered like a silent 'movie' across my mind. Then I remembered the overwhelming success on Boxing Night; and I felt better. I hurried through the auditorium and up to the front office to take over my charge formally from the house manager.

Abingdon was with him, waiting to receive instructions on his new job. He was to take charge of the staff, recruit the secretaries and typists and look after the internal running of our headquarters, a responsibility that eventually covered the work of hundreds of men and women of many trades and crafts. Soon we were joined by Stanley Bell, another old friend, whom I had first met in 1913 when he was stage director for Sir Herbert Tree. He had a distinguished record in the First World War, joining the Royal Naval Air Service and spending much of his time with the Grand Fleet. After that war he had established a further reputation as the best mind of his generation on the technical side of stage production. Many an ingenious stage effect, the credit for which has gone elsewhere, owes its origin to Bell's inventive skill and imagination. For example, he was the first man to make an ice spectacle possible on the stage, adapting a ship's refrigeration machinery for the purpose. This was used in Sir Oswald Stoll's production of *St Moritz* at the London Coliseum.

These two men were prominent in the small circle of enthusiasts to whose loyal support through the whole of the war I was to owe so much, a Prætorian Guard that never allowed itself to lose sight of the ideal of national service for which ENSA stood. Many other 'Prætorians' will come to mind in the course of this story, filling key positions in their various artistic, technical and administrative capacities with a confidence that seemed always to keep abreast of mounting responsibility.

Contrary to what might be supposed, we did not begin to discuss important plans in loud and confident voices, nor did I give any orders on that first morning. We sat rather mum, wondering what to do next, and trying to shelter from the rain of telephone requests already pouring in to the inadequate Drury Lane switchboard. After the first shock of inundation the senior telephonist, Mrs Easthope, rose to the occasion and tackled the situation with quiet efficiency.

While Abingdon and Bell went off to allot dressing-rooms as offices I retired to the little room I had occupied before and which was again to be my office for the next seven years. I remember walking up and down the square of purple carpet, wondering which of the many problems to tackle first: the shows, their organization, their finance or their distribution. In effect we were embarking upon a new Supply Service for the troops, and everything had to be worked out from scratch. My head started to buzz.

At the end of the day I was sitting at my desk, still feeling overcome by events, when there was a bang at the door.

"Come in!" I cried. "What is it? Time to go home?"

"No," said Stanley Bell, pointing to a hand-painted sign which Abingdon was nailing into position. "We've just painted a label for your cell."

I congratulated him on his artistic skill, adding involuntarily, "Of course, later on we must get these things done properly."

As he left the room, somewhat crestfallen, I could have kicked myself for being so tactless. A few minutes later I recrossed the big stage on my way home alone. A large black cat sprang towards me, rubbing himself against my legs. He was miaowing loudly as though protesting against the broken rhythm of his life backstage. With the silly superstition of most stage folk I wondered if this were a lucky sign or not, got into my car and drove away into the black-out.

2

During that first week Seymour Hicks came bustling in, anticipating an early invitation to take a glittering company of stars to entertain the

Guards. Instead I installed him as Controller in the big Board Room at the far end of the main foyer, famous in the annals of Old Drury as the room in which Sheridan wrote *The School for Scandal*. It was later re-named the Conference Room, and was in such demand that a Conference Secretary had to be appointed to regulate the queue of councils and com-mittees waiting to use it.

"What do I do now, Basil?" asked Seymour. "Go out to lunch?"

"Wait for the flood," I replied grimly, and left him.

He was soon dealing with a steady stream of callers. Leading actors and actresses from the London theatres, now unemployed, had come to offer their services, along with crowds of lesser-known artistes. Also, elderly officers with a gleam in the eye and an unwonted air of exhilaration, their well-worn uniforms smelling faintly of mothballs, came seeking enter-tainment for their reserve units. They were requested to join the queue waiting outside the door. Usually loud laughter punctuated the interview going on inside. After a week or so the resourceful Seymour had evolved his own method of dealing with the congestion. One day, noticing a remarkable speed-up in the rate of his interviewing, I asked him how he managed to get rid of people so quickly. "Watch me," he chuckled. Then, flopping into the chair at his desk, he began talking to an imaginary prima donna anxious to offer her services. The telephone rang. "Damn," he said, and picked up the receiver. Apparently the Under-Secretary of State for War wanted to see him at once. Seymour apologized to the imaginary opera star and rose to show her out. "So sorry, but you see how busy I am. Delighted to have your help. Will you write? Good-bye." A deep bow and the little piece of make-believe was over.

"Very amusing, Seymour, but how is it worked?"

He invited me round to his side of the desk and pointed to a push button screwed to its under-side. This was connected to a telephone box on the wall. A gentle pressure from his knee, and lo! the telephone call cut short any interview that threatened to become tedious.

We began to suffer the usual embarrassments of an untried organization flung suddenly into gear and expected to travel at top speed without doing harm to its bearings. The over-eager and inexperienced secretaries detailed to acknowledge the flood of correspondence made mistakes which, amusing enough to look back upon, were very irritating at the time. For example, Sidney Bernstein, the well-known cinema impresario, received a postcard in reply to his offer of help on the film side, stating that "we shall be happy to call upon you to entertain His Majesty's Forces at the earliest possible moment"—presumably with parlour tricks! And Mrs Percy Pitt, widow of the man who had been artistic director of Covent

Garden for many years, was requested, also on a postcard, "to attend on Tuesday next with practice dress for an audition." Why such important offers were not brought to me I do not know, except that behind the tremendous façade of Drury Lane there was as yet little or no machinery to run the administration.

As we began to build up the different types of entertainment we used to hold informal meetings to decide who could be roped in to help. On such occasions Seymour would assume a tragic air, belied by the mischievous twinkle in his eyes, and say:

"Oh, you can't ask him. He's engaged already."

Committee Member: "Engaged?"

Hicks: "Haven't you heard? In Hollywood. Joined the cast of *Gone with the Wind UP!*"[1]

3

The first ENSA concert was given at Old Dene Camp, Camberley, on Sunday, September 10, 1939; it was organized by Thorpe Bates, in charge of the newly formed Concert Section. The party included Frances Day and Arthur Riscoe. Leaving London by a circuitous route in motor-cars, the artistes were transferred into bren-gun carriers a mile or so from the camp in order to preserve the highly secret information as to its whereabouts. Unfortunately, this was fully revealed in the National Press the following morning, complete with photographs. However, as Frances pointed out, it was doubtless a useful exercise for the Security officers.

The following Sunday a party, including Beatrice Lillie, Helen Hill, Annette Mills and Jack Warner, went to the Hurlingham Club for the R.A.S.C.; Harold Holt organized light classical concerts with some of his best artistes, and Jack Hylton went into action with his Bands Division at important military centres. Jack Buchanan, concealing as usual his shrewd business sense behind an insouciant carelessness, began quietly preparing a musical show on individual lines with which he started a series of visits to units stationed in or near London. Later the show achieved high popularity in France. These were but testing samples, so to speak, whilst we made ready for a regular service of entertainment to cover the whole country.

Greatrex ('Rex') Newman, producer of the Fol-de-Rols and other concert parties, and for years a brilliant contributor to many of London's lighter entertainments, including the Co-Optimists, had been one of the first to put his name down on the inaugural committee. He now reported

[1] Elsewhere this quip has been attributed to Wardour Street, but it is a typical sample of Seymour's wit, and I was present when he made it.

at Drury Lane for 'active service.' This was a great accession of strength, because Newman is a recognized authority on a type of entertainment always popular with the troops and comparatively easy to handle. It was largely his influence that has raised concert-party entertainment above the level of the sand-buskers that were the admiration of my childhood. In an astonishingly short space of time he sorted out the best of the seaside parties, all of which had been closed down on the outbreak of war, and made them ready to tour the camps, in which work he was ably seconded by Thorpe Bates.

It was on a Saturday morning exactly three weeks after the declaration of war that the first fifteen concert parties, consisting of over one hundred artistes, were assembled on the stage, complete with wardrobe, travelling stages, transport and so forth. The din was tremendous as they said good-bye to their friends, lost and found again their 'props,' exchanged notes with their managers or bombarded Rex with questions. Armfuls of last-minute costumes were being brought down from the sewing-rooms, while portable stages and equipment were shouldered into the waiting lorries at the stage door. Reporters with notebooks were everywhere arranging picture groups for their cameramen. Presently Seymour stood on a theatre basket and asked for silence. "Hold it a minute. Look this way, Sir Seymour, please. Smile, girls." (Flash.) "Thank you." Then, in his best style, Seymour exhorted them all to do their best for the honour of ENSA, their own profession in general and the British Army in particular. Hurrah!

A Christmas Fol-de-Rol . . .

The bitter weather that lasted throughout the first Christmas of the war will not be forgotten by those first ENSA parties, as they slithered along the icy roads in the black-out towards remote corners of the country, least of all by the Fol-de-Rols. Rex Newman had persuaded his famous concert party to give a much-needed Christmas Night show to a lonely unit somewhere in Berkshire, after which they were due to open a commercial engagement at Tunbridge Wells on Boxing afternoon. This meant an early-morning start and the cancellation of their private plans. After a series of mishaps the artistes arrived, hungry and cold, to find the troops had not been notified and were already far advanced in their own preparations for a festive evening. The proferred entertainment was accepted with reluctance after the door of the canteen had been slammed in the manager's face by an orderly who thought it a practical joke. The troops had eaten all the Christmas fare, so the artistes went supperless to bed on the floor of an unheated Y.M.C.A. hut, hastily partitioned with blankets. The next morning cold shaving-water for the men, outside latrines for the women and well-stewed NAAFI tea for both sexes completed the catalogue of amenities. The company arrived back at Tunbridge Wells ten minutes after the advertised time for the Boxing Day matinée, teeth chattering with cold, the women bordering on hysteria, to find Newman impatiently awaiting their return, and wondering if he should return the money taken at the doors. The dialogue that followed is unprintable. Now, whenever he asks his artistes to give a performance for charity he is greeted with shouts of: "Another ENSA show at Christmas?"

"LOOK, DEAR, A CONTRACT FROM ENSA!"
By permission of the proprietors of "Punch"

CHAPTER FOUR

WARDOUR STREET REVISITED

THE most popular form of entertainment for the troops is the cinema, not so easy to handle as the radio but less difficult than live entertainment. Nevertheless, it is worthy of note that, as the war progressed, the demand for living personalities to relieve the tedium of military training and the strain of watch and ward grew in something like geometrical progression. Men and women divorced for long months from their normal lives sought unconsciously for the renewal of their humanity by contact across the footlights with the singers and dancers, the pretty faces and bright costumes, even the too-crude jokes of the comedians. Purpose was renewed, enthusiasm rekindled and the lift to morale noticeably greater by these means than in the case of mechanized entertainment. But none of this was apparent in the beginning, and the demand for film shows arose overnight.

On August 25 I had both spoken and written to Dave Griffiths,[1] the President of the Kinematograph Renters' Society (K.R.S.) that year, inviting the support of his society in general terms for our plans, and had received a sympathetic response. A few days later I wrote again, informing him of the measures already taken and calling for a practical demonstration of support. The reply was evasive. Evidently something was going on behind the scenes. . . .

Here I must interrupt the story to explain the business structure of the Film Industry which is not easy of comprehension to the layman, although its broad outlines may be better known now than at any previous time because of the wide publicity given since the war years to the efforts of British film magnates to obtain a reasonable share of that El Dorado of their dreams, the American market: a mirage, the pursuit of which has broken the hearts and emptied the pockets of more than one pioneer.

The Industry is roughly divided into three interdependent parts: the producers who make the films, the distributors (or renters, as they are called in Britain) who distribute them—*i.e.*, let them out on rental—and the exhibitors who show the films to the public in their cinemas. This

[1] Now Sir David Griffiths.

division is not entirely arbitrary. In many cases the financial interests of members of the different groups are closely interlocked, sometimes entirely controlled the one by the other. Each section has its own trade association with its established commercial practices and negotiating machinery for governing its relations with the others and with Government departments, such as the Treasury and the Board of Trade. In this tripartite structure one partner is always the dominating factor; and in Britain at this time it was usually the distributor, for he receives the money paid by the exhibitor for showing the films to the public, and it is to him that the producer must look for the return of his capital investment. Since the majority of films shown in Britain are American-owned, it follows that the American members of the renters' trade association (the K.R.S.) hold the dominating influence. This technical explanation is admittedly over-simplified, but it will serve for the purpose of this story.

The standard-size-film (35-mm.) programme to which the troops were accustomed in civil life could only be shown in permanent buildings with properly equipped projection rooms (or by mobile projectors with expensive generating plant, mounted on heavy lorries). The military camps in existence before the war were already being catered for in this wise by contractors who had either leased the garrison cinemas built by the Entertainment Branch of the N.A.C.B. during the First World War, or had built new ones of their own on sites, known as encroachments, granted them by the War Department. The films shown in them were for the most part out-of-date, the more recent pictures not being available because of the proximity of cinemas in the neighbouring towns which were invariably protected from this form of competition by barring clauses. Also, the small numbers of men in camp in peace-time had not warranted the higher prices demanded by the renters for more recent releases.

General mobilization changed this condition overnight; but the agreements under which the contractors operated their cinemas could not be so quickly changed. Moreover, ENSA's arrival upon the scene threatened to rob them of a rich harvest. Understandably, the renters were reluctant to throw over their peace-time clients. On the further question of newer and better films for the now teeming camps, they were certainly not prepared to enter into any arrangements, even with the existing contractors, that would prejudice the business of commercial cinemas in the neighbouring towns, which the men would presumably visit when on leave.

The entertainment halls now being built in Hore-Belisha's new militia camps would also require a regular service of full-size films. With this in view, a Film Council had been proposed during the year of rearmament to advise on the running of these places, consisting of an equal number of

GARRISON THEATRES NEAR AND FAR (2)

Burma

Second Front Circuit: Opera House, Düsseldorf

Rome

Calcutta

48

ENTERTAINMENT ON WHEELS

(1) VANS FOR THE FACTORY SCHEME. (2) RECORDING TRUCK PRESENTED
BY GERTRUDE LAWRENCE. (3) FIRST CONSIGNMENT OF PORTABLE STAGES
BEING ASSEMBLED AT DRURY LANE

members of the Cinematograph Exhibitors' Association (C.E.A.) and of the K.R.S., together with the Director of Public Relations at the War Office (Major-General Beith[1]) and other War Office representatives. When war broke out the council was still in process of formation. After NAAFI had pointed out that its continued existence might conflict with the new entertainment mandate the plan was abandoned.

The position regarding sub-standard (16-mm.) film was different. Hitherto, distributors had not taken the sub-standard market very seriously; they had usually disposed of these rights in their films to film libraries for small lump sums after the other rights had been fully exploited, which meant that the films were several years out of date before they were shown in miniature. The sub-standard has certain physical advantages which made it the ideal solution to a large part of our problem. It is printed on non-inflammable stock, and can be shown over small projectors mounted in light vans and using the local electric supply. Thus entertainment could be taken to men in the most lonely places, such as gun sites and small canvas camps, where the need was often greatest, without the necessity for heavy transport, motor generators and special fire precautions. But it was not worth while planning so if only old films were to be made available. Moreover, a large number of small projectors would be required. Those made in America were considered to be the best, but few of them were available in Britain. Import licences would be needed to build up stocks, and arrangements made to encourage the manufacture of the best British models; all of which depended upon the willingness of the Industry to set on one side the normal trade practice with regard to the delayed distribution of its films on 16-mm. stock. This could not be taken as a matter of course, for at the outset of a major war executives are anxious about the future of their businesses and unwilling to grant concessions before their implications are known. . . . Such was the general position regarding film entertainment at the beginning of the war.

2

An experienced man was needed to take charge of our Cinema Division. The general manager of the company I had formed to distribute the pictures made at Ealing Studios seemed the most likely. His attitude had been the reverse of friendly at the time of my leaving that organization; but personal feelings had to be set on one side and the best volunteers secured for the various jobs if we were to succeed. Mistakes could always be rectified later on. This was unquestionably the right policy—indeed,

[1] Better known to the general public as Ian Hay.

D

the only one—but when later in the war I discovered in myself a constitu-
tional dislike of getting rid of misfits, even though I might suspect them of
disloyalty, I ran into difficulties. Too often I left matters alone until serious
mischief had been wrought.

There was no such anxiety in this case. Ben Henry proved an excellent
leader of the division, efficient, energetic and, although somewhat brusque
in manner, possessed of genuine enthusiasm. He understood thoroughly
the ramifications of Wardour Street and was a pertinacious negotiator,
although he found the political manœuvring of the Service Departments
very trying to the temper. Many a time he would come bursting into my
office with the light of battle in his eyes because of some recently discovered War Office futility, or, alternatively, with a gleam of triumph
softening his aggressive stare because he had won the common sense of
an argument. The scent of his big cigar wafting round my little office provided welcome relief from almost unbearable tension; it created an atmosphere of confidence and good living that was balm to the daily frustration. I sometimes wonder why it is that film executives have such a fond-
ness for over-size cigars. Perhaps it serves to hide an inferiority complex, a
pricking of the conscience for the large salaries they gather in for themselves. . . . Ben Henry worked loyally and hard throughout the war for a
nominal salary, according to the light that was in him; and he thoroughly
deserved the modest recognition that eventually came his way.

The first step was to overcome the hesitancy of the K.R.S. In the course
of the inconclusive interviews and guarded correspondence that now
ensued it became clear that the Society wanted direct contact with the
War Office. Apparently brass hats and official notepaper had not lost
their glamour, and the dictatorship of the printed form had not yet begun.
"It might be best if we ran the whole thing ourselves. Anyway, we prefer
to wait and see what happens": such was the general tone of speech and
letter. But we could not afford to wait if we were to fulfil our mandate.
Already there were other Richmonds in the field, and local *ad hoc*
arrangements were springing up all over the place. At this point Michael
Balcon, who had taken my place in charge of production at the Ealing
Studios, wrote to the War Office and offered his services. The offer was
referred to me and I was grateful for 'Mick's' contribution towards the
solution of our immediate problem. He obtained a number of mobile
cinema vans, equipped with 16-mm. projectors, from various organizations that were accustomed to hire them out for electioneering purposes.
Meanwhile, with the co-operation of Major R. P. Baker, the managing
director of Ealing Studios, Ben Henry got together a supply of films,
including all those made at Ealing, and worked out a system for running

the new service. The example of Ealing was followed by the other British members of the K.R.S., while the American members wrote to their New York offices, urging that their more recent pictures should be reduced to sub-standard size especially for our purposes.

It was a great thrill when Ben Henry came bounding into the office one morning to announce the unqualified success of the first showings of 16-mm. programmes in canvas recreation tents on Salisbury Plain.

"It's terrific. It's marvellous! Absolutely clear pictures. No trouble at all. The boys went mad. Have a cigar?"

The service began on October 2, 1939, and quickly spread all over Britain and Northern Ireland, subsequently following the troops into every theatre of war.

3

The emotional stirrings that accompany the outbreak of a major war breed numerous Sir Galahads, armed *cap-à-pie* in a golden armour of distorted fact, ready to ride forth and fight to the death on that greensward which is the floor of the House of Commons, or in the correspondence columns of the public press, in defence of the soldier's rights. The amount of genuine grievance set right by these means is questionable, but their nuisance value is enormous. The Andrew Aguecheeks of the Civil Service may be able to cut a caper, but it is the patriotic Sir Tobys who can "cut the mutton to't."

In this instance the champion of the soldier's weal was Sir Adrian Baillie, a wealthy M.P. who had had some contact of a dilettante nature with film-making in India before the war. He sounded the battle-cry of better films for the troops while the many complexities I have described were still unresolved, and entered the lists at the head of yet another Army Film Council that, phœnix-like, rose from the ashes of its forerunner. But the flamboyant interviews in which he trumpeted his style and title to be the Army's film champion alarmed the renters, who sensed in his statements the possibility of even greater interference with their freedom of action than was probable in dealing with professional people like ourselves. The renters' disapproval grew stronger after one or two meetings with Sir Galahad and his posse of advisers. Eventually the champion was persuaded to retire from the lists, having achieved nothing more than a welcome hastening of the renters' decision to support us.

My suggestion that an independent Film Entertainments National Service Association (FENSA) should be formed to work in liaison with ENSA, with Ben Henry as an *ex officio* member from Drury Lane, was now unanimously approved.

The co-operation of the Industry being assured, the American members vied with the British in their willingness to lower trade barriers and to secure the early release to the troops of the latest pictures, printed both in standard and sub-standard size. The legitimate interests of exhibitors were safeguarded by our giving a general undertaking not to give films within a two-mile radius of a commercial cinema. As a further safeguard, E. J. Hinge, the President of the Exhibitor's Association for that year, was appointed Honorary Cinema Adviser to NAAFI. In that capacity he dealt with border-line cases (*i.e.*, situations just without or within the two-mile limit), and quashed the objections of local exhibitors whenever he felt that these were unreasonable and likely to cause deprivation to the troops concerned.

The FENSA committee remained in being for the whole period of the war; it controlled the release of all the films required for H.M. Forces, both for static and mobile cinemas, and it settled the standard rentals to be paid to the members of the Society for the different classes of films. Thus the arrangements, hammered out with much strenuous argument and counter-argument, proved to be so finely tempered as to withstand the stresses and strains of departmental politics. It is as well to add for the benefit of the general reader that a very large sum of money was saved to the public purse as a result of the concessions obtained from the Film Industry through FENSA.

◇◇◇

Moving Pictures . . .

Our mobile cinemas were soon reaching out to the remotest corners of Britain. In 1941 one of them visited a gun site outside a tiny hamlet in Wales. The performance was given in the chapel, the only building that possessed electric light. In exchange for its use the villagers sat at the back in their Sunday best. Many of them had never seen a film in their lives. The picture was *Convoy*, and when the dive-bombing sequences began half a dozen of the older village women took fright and ran out screaming in Welsh. Nothing would induce them to go again. "If that iss the fillums, ENSA can keep them, look you!"

At Barra, in the Outer Hebrides, a similar first encounter with the new terror got no farther than the title of the Gaumont Newsreel. As the figure of the old-time watchman began to ring his bell the islanders stampeded, bowled over the operator, trod on his projector and vowed never again to enter the haunted hut.

CHAPTER FIVE

MORTAR WITHOUT BRICKS

NO sooner had we made a start with concert parties and mobile cinemas than the cry was raised that the legitimate theatre was being neglected. Why were no plays being given to the troops? Well, we had been told that no garrison theatres were available.[1] I knew that several of them had been burnt down by Dominion troops impatiently awaiting demobilization after the First War; and the parent of them all, my own theatre at Park Hall Camp, Oswestry, had been similarly destroyed by fire a year or so later. But what had become of those on Salisbury Plain and at other places where there were permanent military installations? I set forth on a voyage of discovery.

The search was not rewarding. The best buildings had been handed over to contractors to run as camp cinemas. My mouth watered as I thought how quickly they could have been made ready and fit for their original purpose. But their occupants saw no reason to abandon the fat years now in prospect merely for my asking. And the rentals they demanded as compensation for loss of trade were exorbitant.

At Catterick I was so envious of the former Garrison Theatre, with its fine stage designed by George Harris, now being run as a cinema but looking very dilapidated, that I used to go out of my way to avoid passing it whenever I visited the camp. Eventually we were forced to convert a small cinema that had originally been an Army gymnasium into the Garrison Theatre—an arrangement that remained totally inadequate for that vast camp, even though the building was extended and re-equipped and, later, had a gallery added to it.

It was the same at Bulford, where George had fashioned a modern theatre, complete with stage grid, out of an old institute building. How angry he would have been to see his model theatre put to such use! There I met an old acquaintance in the person of the Area Commander, Major-

---

[1] The only permanent building immediately available to us was the Royal Artillery Theatre, Woolwich. This was placed at our disposal by the Littler family and reopened under ENSA management on Sunday, October 22, 1939, with a concert given by Jack Hylton and his Orchestra. Subsequently George Black arranged a number of variety programmes for us there.

General Freyberg, V.C.,[1] the famous New Zealander. He marched me all over the camp, waving his little leather-covered swagger stick at buildings he thought might suit our purpose, to which I made the inevitable reply: "No use, General." Finally, he exploded in wrath and said he intended to take over the old Garrison Theatre, "whether the War House likes it or not." This was just good-hearted talk, not a threat he could carry out. At Tidworth near by we took over the permanent building we had used before. Here our stage manager from the First War was in charge and still carrying on the good work.

In Aldershot a large building known as the Albuhera Hall, used before the war as the Command Boxing Centre, was handed over to us for conversion into a garrison theatre, on condition that it could be reconverted into a boxing ring at twenty-four hours' notice. Fortunately Ernest Joseph, the NAAFI architect, had co-operated with me in former days and understood thoroughly the requirements. With his help this hall and a number of disused riding-schools in the Aldershot and Salisbury Commands, fine, lofty buildings, built of brick, were taken over and skilfully adapted as theatres. Their facilities were much praised by the star companies that later visited them.

Albuhera Hall was full of the most baffling echoes; they seemed to vary in intensity and direction with each row of seats. Stanley Bell solved the difficulty by hanging three swathes of hessian canvas between the open steel trusses of the roof to the full length of the hall, a simple remedy that he used later to correct similar faults in converted buildings up and down the country. After Bell had finished tinkering with these places, their acoustic problems, often severe because of low concrete ceilings, were almost invariably solved.

A Showman's Tale . . .

The Garrison Theatre, Aldershot, soon became enormously popular. Success was due as much to the energy and lovable character of its manager as to the merit of the shows. T. C. ('Tommy') Wray, for many years general manager for George Dance, had come out of semi-retirement to do this as his war service; he carried out the assignment with enormous energy and aplomb, no detail being too small to escape his attention. For some time he lived on the premises, and was known to turn to and scrub

Now Lieutenant-General Lord Freyberg, V.C., G.C.M.G., K.C.B., K.B.E., D.S.O.

the place out if the daily fatigue party failed to arrive. He was known to all the troops as 'Poppa.'

No performance was complete without a speech from Poppa at the final curtain. It was always the same speech. Although the men soon knew it by heart, they refused to leave the theatre until Tommy had made it. After announcing the programme for the ensuing week he concluded by reminding the men that nowhere else in the world could they see such wonderful and varied entertainment as at—the last words to be shouted in unison, lento—"your *very own personal*—GarrISON THEA—TERR—[extra loud shout]—ALDERSHOT!!" (Perhaps it was here that some of the present-day audiences of the Players' Theatre learned their habit of boisterous collaboration.)

Accustomed to lavish pre-war poster advertising, he complained bitterly when the paper restrictions compelled us to replace the weekly 6-sheet bills by permanent announcements painted on oilcloth. Determined not to be done out of his advertising, he volunteered to tour a loudspeaker van around the district if NAAFI would provide the van. This was sent to him. On the first morning, eager to exploit its possibilities to the full, he drove the van along the parade grounds, announcing in stentorian tones the latest ENSA attraction. Very soon, from every doorway of every canteen, institute or sleeping quarter, men came tumbling, putting on their steel helmets, adjusting their equipment and carrying rifles and gasmasks. Military police drove up in jeeps; officers appeared at orderly-room doors strapping revolvers to their Sam Browne belts; M.T. drivers started revving up their transport.

Tommy was delighted that his van was such a sensational success. He was unaware that the troops had been told the first warning of invasion would be by loudspeaker from the parade ground! He was highly indignant when the provost marshal, stifling his laughter, threatened him with close arrest for a breach of Security.

2

The conversion of riding-schools amounted only to a few drops in the empty bucket of our requirements. Then it occurred to me to find out what was being done about entertainment halls in the new Belisha camps. The more one poked one's nose into things without waiting to be asked the better, in the prevailing hurly-burly. A branch of the Quartermaster-General's Department (Q.M.G./7) turned out to be responsible. So I rang up and invited myself round to see the plans.

Colonel Sinauer's office staff seemed quite glad to see me and produced a set of standard designs for the new camp halls. These bore a strong family resemblance to the garrison theatres of the First War so far as the auditorium lay-out was concerned; but at the stage end the available space had been divided into three portions, with the centre one, framing the cinema screen, shaped like a slice of cake. The outer portions were intended for a chair store and boiler-room respectively. A grand piano in front of the screen would fill the entire stage, so that ingenious methods of extrication would have to be used if the prima donna were inclined to stoutness! Such requirements as side entrances or space in which to hang scenery and curtains had been disregarded. When I pointed out the deficiencies to the draughtsmen they were quite surprised.

Fortunately only two of the halls had been completed. There was still time to set matters right. I persuaded Colonel Sinauer to telegraph and suspend all further work on entertainment halls throughout the country. Then I borrowed the set of plans, hurried back to Drury Lane and turned Stanley Bell on to the job of making them practical, telling him to remove all encumbrances from the stage and to put the dressing-rooms in an additional corridor across the back of the building. The revised plans were approved, the small additional cost being swallowed up in the feverish outpouring of the national millions that was now taking place.

As the War Office authorities had no idea how to set about equipping the halls, I persuaded them to let us do the job at Drury Lane and, later, induced NAAFI to pay for it as part of their mandatory duty. Eventually our technicians designed and fitted all the stage and cinema lighting, besides equipping each hall with tableaux curtains, stage draperies and tip-up seating, all set out in good theatre style.

The practical value of Drury Lane as our headquarters now began to show itself. The old theatre possesses workshops and technical facilities unlike those of any other theatre in the Kingdom. Not only did we make, or assemble, the components for all the stage and electrical equipment required for the static theatres and cinemas at home, but also those for similar installations in countries as far apart as Iceland, the Middle East and India. As the years rolled on, bulky equipment such as travelling stages and portable switchboards poured out of those shops in ever increasing quantity, thereby saving enormous sums of public money, since sub-contractors' profits were eliminated, and standardization by theatrical experts became the rule.

By these means a circuit of more than fifty permanent garrison theatres-cum-cinemas was quickly made available for the use of the Army at comparatively slight expense to the Corporation, and with standard equipment of our own design. I regarded this as an excellent stroke of business on my part, although much of the credit was due to NAAFI and various departments of the War Office for their sensible and quick reactions to the proposals.

3

Unlike the War Office, the Air Ministry had no previous experience in designing buildings for entertainment. Their general-purpose institutes were not suitable, neither were the hangars, which were too large and lofty, although both were often ingeniously adapted by the highly skilled air-craftsmen on the spot. Also, the R.A.F. expansion programme was further advanced, so that the architects were less willing to retrace their steps. By the time the technical staff at Drury Lane came into the picture it was too late to do more than give general advice and provide theatrical equipment when it was asked for. In the end we found ourselves servicing several hundreds of these adapted theatres. Although they were not to be com-pared with the Army theatres as buildings they enabled ENSA to do some of its best work.

The memory of those performances at R.A.F. stations during the Battle of Britain and the subsequent Blitz is deeply cherished by all ENSA artistes. To be allowed a small share in those festivals of the human spirit, for such in effect they were, was an unforgettable experience. The huge, dimly lighted hangar with a stage about the size of a pocket-handkerchief at one end, that seemed only to accentuate the curves of the steel roof; row upon row of officers and aircraftmen, joined later in the war by girls with shining faces in clean WAAF uniforms, with usually a basket chair or two dragged out of the mess and set in front for the station com-mander; the gusty enjoyment of the performers as they feel the pulse of their audience—all set in an atmosphere of strain and alertness, high courage persistently understated, tension relieved by riotous blasphemy that is, in fact, not blasphemy at all. . . . In a sudden silence in the programme the loudspeaker summons pilots and crews away to duty. The show goes on: it must always go on; it is the rule of life. But the jokes of the comedians acquire an added zest, as the audience drowns its thoughts in louder laughter. . . . The aircraft slip away in the night sky, their crews echoing the choruses over the inter-com:

"Wizard show, what!"

"R-O-L-L OUT THE B-A-R-R-E-L."

"That comic put up a black all right. Did you see the old man wince?"

"Let's have a BAR-R-E-L OF FUN."

"How about a prang with the blonde?"

"R-O-L-L OUT THE B-A-R-R-E-L."

"WE'VE GOT THE BLUES ON THE RUN."
(*Boom! Whine! Crash!*)
"Look out, chaps! This is it!"
How quickly the war-time slang has passed out of currency! . . .

In the Black-out . . .

Flanagan and Allen were giving an ENSA concert at one of the bigger
R.A.F. stations. Bud Flanagan was standing at the stage entrance to the
converted hangar in his Home Guard uniform waiting for the show to
begin when the Station Commander passed by. It was a dark, moonless
sky.
"Nice night for the Jerries—eh, what!" said Bud with a grin.
"Stand to attention, sir, when you talk to me!" bellowed the Commander.
"Certainly, sir, by all means," said Bud, suiting the action to the word,
whilst the Commander hurried away to the softly whistled tune of
"Underneath the arches!"

CHAPTER SIX

POLICIES AND POLITICS

THE entertainment service I had in mind was radically different from anything known in Britain before; and it had no counterpart elsewhere. Indeed, other nations were to copy us in time. Air warfare had forced dispersal of the troops as a matter of common safety. Therefore entertainment would have to be taken to them rather than they to it. Unfortunately neither the Army nor the R.A.F. had any organization for receiving and dealing with mobile entertainment on this scale; and the blessed word Co-ordination had scarcely been thought of. There were no direct channels of information between us and the various commands and formations; yet the War Office, obsessed by the word 'Security,' was reluctant to give us any information as to where the troops were encamped. In consequence, the distribution of shows began under a system of personal contacts that was in fact no system at all. Seymour would meet some one in the Garrick Club whose nephew was second-in-command of a unit somewhere in the New Forest, and "could he have a show, please?" Whereupon Seymour, with the utmost zeal, over a glass of port would reply:

"Certainly, my dear fellow. Any time you like."

Such promises left us to find out where the units were stationed, and this required the diligence of a Scotland Yard detective. The telegrams which were delivered at Drury Lane in handfuls often included cancellations of shows that had already been sent out; occasionally cancellation preceded the original request. Enterprising officers discovered that a visit to Drury Lane "to get something out of ENSA" meant forty-eight hours away from camp amongst "the bright lights." (In fact, there were no lights but only a romantic darkness.) In consequence, their units had more frequent entertainment than others. Concert parties arrived at camps only to find the victims flown; sometimes an amateur party was discovered in occupation of the pitch. In one instance the professional manager 'tossed for it' with his opposite number, and, having lost, graciously gave place to the amateurs, then led his party to 'the local,' where they all spent a jolly evening, for which escapade he was duly sacked, although he protested he was merely the unfortunate victim of circumstances.

It became a matter of urgent priority to bring order out of the prevailing chaos. The War Office was too busy with mobilization to bother about us, and equally so the NAAFI, delivering its cakes and ale. We must fend for ourselves. I hurried round the country, visiting each Command Headquarters in turn, armed with a copy of the W.O. Letter of Authority to NAAFI. I asked for the appointment of a staff officer at each Command Headquarters to undertake the work of collecting and co-ordinating the requests for entertainment and forwarding them to Drury Lane each month, and for similar appointments in the military areas into which the Commands were subdivided and, ultimately, with each division. As there was no War Office authority, the work would have to be undertaken voluntarily.

2

Returning to London, I found everybody bewildered by the avalanche of requests for entertainment. To say that we were inundated is a precise description. The NAAFI Corporation began to wonder what it had let itself in for. Since the formation of the first Entertainment Branch it had always regarded entertainment as one of the amenities for which it was responsible, in a mild sort of way; but this was a very different thing. In my early talks with the Corporation I had often spoken of mobilizing the entire Entertainment Industry, but this was dismissed as a typical piece of theatrical extravagance. Now it looked like coming about, unless stopped in time. Nevertheless, the mandate had been accepted; and the dispersal of a large proportion of the NAAFI profits by way of ENSA must now be envisaged. The question was what proportion? Since the idea of a corporate existence for ENSA had been dropped, surely NAAFI was entitled to restrict development to the requirements of its own policy?

A brief digression on the subject of NAAFI itself may help to make the position more clear. NAAFI is not a Government body; it is a trading corporation that belongs in effect to the three Services, for whom it provides a variety of articles of food and drink over and above the basic rations, as well as certain amenities. It is, in fact, the Serviceman's 'Co-op.' Official representatives of the Service Ministries sit on the Board to approve and co-ordinate its general policy. Treasury sanction is necessary in matters involving financial policy or large-scale increases in its commitments.

Its trading profits are considerable, astronomical during a great war, but so, too, is the scale of its operations. The public has always been inquisitive about these profits, the usual criticism being that they are either too large or improperly distributed. This is untrue, for both the control and the distribution of the profits are closely supervised. The profits are shared between the Navy, the Army and the Air Force in proportion to the amount of trade each Service does with the Corporation, after deduction of proportionate shares of the running costs, in accordance with normal commercial practice. In addition, each unit receives a monthly rebate on its canteen earnings, a sort of interim dividend to be expended for the unit's sole benefit. Under the Draper Report, issued after the official inquiry into the Corporation's affairs at the end of the First World War, this rebate was to be reduced on the outbreak of the war to a standard 6 per cent. as a safety measure to cover increases in the operating costs in supplying the troops in the field, and also as an insurance against the heavy losses of material to be expected from active warfare—a wise provision, as the losses sustained by the Corporation at the time of Dunkirk clearly showed.

Each Service has its own internal arrangements for the distribution of its share of what might be called the bulk profit; and many important Service charities, run for the benefit of the men or their wives and children, are largely dependent on payments from this source. In considering the financing of ENSA those responsible for distributing the bulk profits were concerned to see that the prior claims of their charities were fully met and not pushed on one side for the sake of war-time entertainment. Also, since the amount of profit varied with each Service it seemed only logical to argue that the amount of entertainment should vary in like proportion; but such a mathematical argument could not be sustained. There were psychological and operational factors to be considered. For example, the strain imposed upon the bomber and fighter crews of the R.A.F. entitled them to prior consideration. They were already in the front line before the Army had even begun its war. Again, men stationed on a lonely gun site with only limited canteen facilities should be given priority above the claims of men stationed near large towns. I was convinced that ENSA could only fulfil its mission if it were planned and operated with such broad considerations in mind and without regard to the fluctuations in NAAFI profits. So it was to that end I turned all my thoughts, being convinced that the authorities would come to the same view sooner or later.

The Corporation's concern over the extent of its commitment was due to fear of adverse criticism from its customers, who were also owners of the business and often thought they knew how to run it better than the present managers. This intrinsic subservience also explains the contrast between the reluctant attitude of the Corporations towards ENSA's urgent desire to expand and its ready co-operation in routine matters. Further, the older 'canteeneers,' whose traditional alternation of arrogance with servility (according to the military rank of those with whom they were dealing) did not make for popularity, regarded profit-making as their primary duty. Consequently they were disposed to resent the intrusion of younger men, drafted from the business world outside as the war progressed, bringing with them ideas that seemed designed to spend money rather than to make it. ENSA and its staff were regarded in this light. "We work hard to make money; all ENSA does is to spend it," was a criticism often heard among them.

3

The R.A.F. was receiving its ration of entertainment through Army channels; this was difficult to arrange because the R.A.F. administrative areas did not correspond geographically with those of the Army. It was not long before the airmen began to complain that they were getting the dirty end of the stick. Anxious lest the system of allocation should break down almost before it had started, I asked Stanley Bell to become R.A.F. Liaison Officer, in order to secure as close co-operation as possible with the Air Ministry. At the Ministry, in charge of R.A.F. amenities, he discovered an old shipmate from his days with the Grand Fleet in the person of Group-Captain Halahan.[1] It was largely due to the foundations of confidence laid by these two good friends that ENSA's efforts were better appreciated at the Air Ministry than at the War Office. The situation took a perverse turn when the Army began to complain that the R.A.F. were receiving better treatment than they were. But similar co-operation at the War Office would pay similar dividends, a fact of which Graham John, whom I appointed to be Army Liaison Officer at about the same time, never ceased to remind the staff officers with whom he came into contact.

The Navy's proportion of the NAAFI profits was the smallest of the three, and already fully earmarked before we came upon the scene. So there was considerable heart-searching among the responsible Admiralty officials and much delay before the Navy took part in the general scheme. Meanwhile I had strict orders from NAAFI to give the Navy no shows for the present, an order to which we applied the Nelson touch whenever we could,[2] slipping in occasional concerts at Naval ports such as Portsmouth, Greenock and Rosyth.

[1] A distinguished Air Vice-Marshal who had retired before the war and had now volunteered to resume active service in a lower rank.

[2] In May 1940 I had a letter from Major Mavor, R.A.M.C., who was James Bridie, the dramatist, serving in *Atlantis*, the largest British hospital ship. The ship was without entertainment of any kind and needed a film projector and some films. Hospital ships were 'No man's land' so far as we were concerned. However, by 'borrowing'

It was not until some time in 1941 that a regular ENSA service to the Royal Navy was started. To mark the occasion Beatrice Lillie and Evelyn Laye and an ENSA party gave a special concert at the opening of a new canteen at Rosyth by the Commander-in-Chief, Home Fleet. Prior to that the position at Scapa Flow had been relieved by a number of highly successful concerts which Evelyn Laye organized independently of us, the out-of-pocket expenses being met out of the funds of the Home Fleet. Later, when the financial argument was over, Evelyn joined ENSA, and her manager, T. Fitzgibbon, became the R.N. Liaison Officer at our Headquarters. Meanwhile R.N. ships were fully provided with film entertainment through the Royal Naval Film Corporation, founded, before the war, by Lord Louis Mountbatten,[1] and run under the direction of Arthur Jarrett.

4

To begin with, all entertainments were given free, a policy with which the theatrical profession and all of us at Drury Lane were in cordial agreement, but later circumstances compelled us to consider the arguments in favour of charges for admission. They were very strong. First of all, the money received from admission charges would go to swell the sum the Corporation was prepared to spend, thus enabling more entertainment to be given. Secondly, the general consensus of opinion was that the men would appreciate the entertainment more if they had to pay a few pence for it. In this view we were supported by the experience of the last war, when not only the entertainment at home, but also many of the Army's own divisional concert parties in France, notably Leslie Henson's 'Gaieties,' charged for admission as a matter of course. Thirdly, the free system was inequitable since the men who did not go to the entertainments, for whatever reason, were in effect paying for those who did. Finally, there seemed no reason why the principle of payment should be accepted in the case of private contractors working cinema concessions in the permanent camps and not in the case of ENSA, when the effect of free admission would be to reduce the amount of entertainment the men received. These arguments were submitted by the War Office and the Air Ministry to their Commands throughout the country before any decision was taken.

To enable admission charges to be made it was necessary to divide the entertainments into different categories so as to take into account the vary-

a spare projector from our stores and assuring NAAFI that we should get the films without paying film hire, we were able to 'wangle' things. It made me happy to do this service for an old friend.

[1] Now Admiral of the Fleet Earl Mountbatten of Burma.

ing conditions of performance and the numbers of men to be entertained. A stage play or a costumed concert party could not be sent to a handful of men on a lonely gun site. Such locations needed very simple shows, which in their turn were unsuitable for the larger camps. It was not so much value for money that dictated the ultimate decision to make the smaller entertainments free as business common sense, for the cost of collecting admission money from a very small audience would exceed the revenue. After full consultation at Drury Lane I worked out a system of categories and a range of prices[1] that were eventually authorized.

There is a fascinating tale to be told of those 'sing-song' parties—four-handed, two-handed, down to the solitary exponent of the soldiers' beloved 'squeeze-box,' troubadours of the modern style, equipped with Spanish and Hawaiian guitars, progressing along the byways in motor-cycle combinations where the use of a van or small car was not justfied: a story compounded of cheerfulness and courage, of meagre talent and boundless confidence that disdained criticism and maintained an obstinate belief in the value of its contribution to national morale. And if discerning eyes and ears sometimes decided otherwise—well! were the troubadours of old always in tune?

Some of these units remained in being for five years and more, winter and summer, totting up remarkable scores in their tireless peregrinations, reckoning their performances by the thousand and their travelled miles by the tens of thousand, journeying a hundred miles and more (in one case 194 miles), just to give one brief performance, dodging the Blitz and the flying bombs on the gun sites, buried in snow-drifts in the winter, or waiting for summer weather to find their way to the distant Faroe Islands, their audiences varying from three to three times three thousand—disastrous temerity!—but it made no odds to them.

Mr Churchill, writing of his return to the Admiralty, has referred to the emotion aroused in him by the sight of his old war maps in their

---

[1] *Category A.* For permanent Garrison Theatres and Cinemas:
Plays, musical and dramatic, Concert Parties and other full-scale entertainments, including standard-size film programmes:
1s. (seats reserved prior to performance 1s. 6d.), 6d. and 3d.
Category B. For institutes, converted gymnasia and other buildings used temporarily for entertainment purposes:
Programmes similar to those in Category A but given by smaller mobile companies carrying their own portable stages:
1s., 6d. and 3d.
Category C. Mobile Cinemas (16-mm. sub-standard):
Free.
Category D. Sing-songs:
Free.

FIRST FILMS FOR FRANCE
THEATRE LORRY 'CHALKS IT UP'
SOUVENIR OF LAST CONCERT IN
H.M.S. "HOOD"
EVACUATED STAFF PARADE AT
DRURY LANE

Will Fyffe performing at the Same Concert

Ernest Bevin inaugurating the Ministry of Labour Scheme of Lunch-time 'Ensatainments' for Munition Workers: Woolwich Arsenal, 1940

accustomed case in his room. In my humbler sphere I found myself repeating the actions and reactions of the First War. It was so when I visited the camps and strove to win back the garrison theatres. And now I found myself drafting a letter to H.M. Customs and Excise for remission of Entertainment Tax in precisely similar terms to those set out in 1917. Under the terms of the remission wives and girl friends were admitted to the entertainments provided they were accompanied by men in uniform. Civilians working in the camps who were in possession of passes certifying the fact were also admitted.

It was originally intended to begin charging for admission on November 11—a significant date—but some bright mind at the War Office, to prove his solicitude for the soldiers' welfare, altered the official memorandum after it had been approved, and made two prices for the cheap seats, namely 3d. and 2d. The additional expense of collection involved in this flight of fancy had not occurred to him. The memorandum had to be revised; and it was not until December 4 that the system of charging for admission to certain categories of entertainment came into operation.

Despite the sounding of opinion beforehand, there was quite a hullubaloo. Some commanding officers demanded that entertainments given in their regimental institutes be given free, because the institute was the soldier's club, and entertainment interfered with other amenities for which the soldier did not pay—a legitimate argument that evaded the other issues involved. NAAFI area managers raised objection to the use of the institutes because it interrupted the counter sales and took men away from the bars. Private soldiers wrote to their M.P.'s, accusing NAAFI of more profiteering. Members duly rose in the House to repeat the charge. Actors joined in defending the soldiers' right to receive free entertainment. The logic of this point of view, advanced by professional actors, was a little confused.

It is impossible to make formal ending to these preliminary chapters in which I have tried to describe some of the turmoil and scramble of improvisation that followed the beginning of ENSA. Our ship had been launched and now began to bump its way down the rapids. From now on the tale of its progress has a nightmarish quality, as the stream of urgencies carried it faster and faster past the rocks of official obstruction. It was a Flying Dutchman, growing in size as it sped through the night—yes, even while the bombs were falling—but never sailing fast enough to outstrip the flow of new ideas that kept crowding in upon the crew.

E

CHAPTER SEVEN

FAIR STOOD THE WIND FOR FRANCE

THE Expeditionary Force went off to fight in France before the general shape of our organization had declared itself and long before such matters as charges for admission had reached the stage of public controversy. That is the main difficulty in writing this story; the pattern of events is never wholly clear. One can only follow an individual thread for a short way in the general design before it becomes lost in a multiplicity of others.

As soon as I heard that the departure of the Army had taken place I began to cast longing glances across the water to where lay our real job. My first request for permission to go to France to see things for myself brought no result. Then one afternoon, as I was crossing the rotunda at Drury Lane, I noticed the Cinema Officer in close conversation with a chaplain of the R.A.F., the Rev. H. A. M. Paget-Wilkes, who had just flown over from France, where he was stationed in a highly secret locality. The chaplain wanted to know if we could let him have some films and a projector or two, as the men urgently needed entertainment. There had been rumours for some days that the R.A.F. was actually in contact with the enemy; now here was confirmation of it. When I demanded the whereabouts of the force the chaplain made mysterious reference to a place called Panther. This was an obvious code word; it was not till some time afterwards that I found it stood for Rheims and that our Advanced Air Striking Force (A.A.S.F.) was spread out in a number of villages in front of that city. Henry hurriedly procured a couple of projectors and some films with which the chaplain flew back to France the following day. A week or so later he turned up again for more supplies. Meanwhile we had arranged with the Paramount Company in Paris to take over their large cinema in Rheims twice a week for special showings of English-speaking films to which the R.A.F. were to be admitted at special rates. Supplying the equipment and those first films had a curious aura of romance about it. Perhaps it was the secrecy; perhaps it was the sense that here we were coming to grips with the actual problem. Yes, I think it must have been that; we had begun to serve the troops in the field.

I decided to renew my attempt to break through the barrier of pre-occupation at NAAFI Headquarters and to obtain the necessary authority to go overseas. Following my first application a letter had been sent to Lieutenant-Colonel Peters, the Officer Commanding the Expeditionary Force Institutes (E.F.I.) (which was the name of NAAFI overseas), requesting him to find out whether the authorities would like entertainment for the men, and, if so, of what kind, and where it was to be sent.

On October 16 I again wrote to NAAFI, urging that my visit be expedited. I attached to my minute an extract from that day's *Daily Mail*, pointing out that it was the third day in succession that war correspondents had referred to the lack of entertainment, and that we should be severely criticized for lack of initiative if action were not taken soon. I also took the precaution of backing up my application to NAAFI with a surreptitious call upon Sir Victor Warrender at the War Office. Red tape was not strong enough to withstand the combined onslaught; the next morning an early telephone call to my flat informed me that permission was granted for the visit.

Arriving at Boulogne on October 19, I was met at the quayside by Peters, who drove me to his headquarters at Arras—for Security reasons referred to officially as 'Brassard.' As we drove along Peters strove to 'put me in the picture.' He was still spending a lot of time trying to find out where people were. The various branches of G.H.Q. were dispersed amongst a number of villages on the outskirts of Arras—sorry!—'Brassard.' This was a necessary air-raid precaution, but it made communication very difficult. The military telephone system was only to be used for urgent priority messages; the civil lines were hopeless. The troops were even more dispersed than the staff, so he failed to see how entertainment was possible without a great deal of transport, and he had none to spare. As for the audiences he was quite sure G.H.Q. would never agree to the use of Army transport to bring them to places of entertainment after dark. However, we could see what they had to say: 'So-and-so' was easy; General X was notoriously difficult, and as for 'old Y'—he always said 'no' to everything.

I did not pay much attention to his gossip. My mind was full of a sense of mission, so that the familiar sights and sounds of France took on a mysterious and romantic quality, due once again to a super-charged consciousness. It was a typical October day with a pale blue sky and mist, and frost, evidently not the first of the season. The leaves of the tall poplar trees bordering the roads were falling in brown and yellow cascades. Berries were red on the bushes at the edges of the woods; overhead, starlings and rooks were wheeling and chattering, and everywhere the smell that is France. All the warnings of a hard winter were plain to see, but my mind was not on the weather, nor on the delights of *tourisme*. The real war had come at last, and I was actually in France in a staff car on my way to British Headquarters in the service of ENSA.

The next morning Peters took me to the various branches of G.H.Q. Our first call was upon the Quartermaster-General, Major-General Lindsell, who had set up his headquarters in a small château on the outskirts of the village of Saint-Pol. His office was a tiny *cabinet* on the first floor, approached by a winding stair. The room retained its attractive French character, although stripped of all its furnishings, save a small buhl writing table crowded with War Office files and correspondence in wire trays and a heavy military field telephone, together with the General's cap and swagger stick. A British 'barrack issue' coal scuttle was beside the fireplace, stacked with small birch logs in the French way, a practical symbol of Anglo-French co-operation.

As we were shown in the General was struggling to make himself heard over the telephone. Throughout the war the vagaries of this uncertain instrument were a constant source of irritation to its victims. I was to see officers suffer every degree of rage, hate and frustration in their encounters with the evil genie that dwelt within that heavy metal box; handles wrenched off the instrument in the last degree of blind fury and, upon one occasion, the instrument itself hurled to the ground, where it broke its silence with a long complaining gurgle.

"Is that the War Office?" (Buzz.) "*Is—that—the—War—Office?*" (A buzz loud enough to burst the ear-drums.) "Le Havre! But I don't want Le Havre." (Pip! Pip!) "No, this isn't R.E.M.E. This is the Q.M.G., General Lindsell." (Sundry whirrings and wheezings.) "Oh, ring off!" (A crackling sound and a mild electric shock for the General as he vigorously grinds the handle.) "Sergeant! I told you I wanted the War Office. Never mind Table A. Get me the War Office. And be sharp about it!"

The General turned to greet us, slightly flushed by his encounter with the genie. The slight air of self-importance—pomposity is too strong a word—that hung about all senior officers in those first days, caused by their sense of mission perhaps, since after all the opportunity to which they had dedicated their lives was now upon them, soon gave place to a naturally genial manner. He briskly examined my proposals, pointing out the transport difficulties involved in sending artistes to France and conveying them about the military areas, particularly as the French Army zones were intermingled with our own, so that the British military pass would not be valid everywhere. However, these were matters to be discussed with the Adjutant-General. In so far as the 'Q' staff were concerned, we should have every support. Throughout that campaign in France he kept his word. We remained responsible to 'Q,' so there were no manufactured difficulties, only genial understanding, co-operation and, now and again, a little chaff.

The Adjutant-General had established his headquarters in a farmhouse on the outskirts of another near-by village, to which a large military policeman now directed the car, but Peters already knew the way. Another still larger policeman escorted us across the muddy farmyard, scattering the ducks and hens, whose loud clucking mingled incongruously with the tapping of typewriters. We were shown into a small waiting-room where a staff-sergeant, seated at the usual trestle table, was entering correspondence in a register. Across the passage in the kitchen of the farmhouse an important conference was in progress. A deep, booming voice, which I took to be that of the Adjutant-General, appeared to dominate the discussion. The sergeant grinned pleasantly at me, and asked when the Army was going to get some entertainment. Presently he wrote our names on a slip of paper and disappeared into the next room. The booming voice went on and on.

I began to feel nervous about the forthcoming interview. The title of Adjutant-General was an awesome one to a mere civilian. My visit might interrupt the daily preoccupation with campaigning in a foreign country: dispatch riders bearing urgent messages, secret telephone calls to the War Office and the like. Yet there was so little evidence of the romantic bustle I had anticipated that it seemed impossible to believe that France was at war and that troops of a friendly power were in occupation of these peaceful villages; just an occasional British uniform, an Army lorry or two, and that was all. No wonder the Americans had already nicknamed it 'the phoney war.' It was as though the nations, suddenly confronted with a war all had talked about and none had wanted, were shocked at their own wickedness and uncertain how to begin it. We know now that the rape of Europe was in preparation, but at the time the ordinary man could only sense without understanding the lack of reality.

Presently a brigadier of the General Staff came in. He had a pair of thin, steel spectacles perched on the end of his nose, and waved a long cigarette-holder in a rather charming dilettante manner. He assured me that the A.G. would not be long, and then turned his attention to a pile of papers in a wire basket on the desk. With a pout and a muttered excuse he left the room without finding what he was looking for. A moment later another staff officer came in. This one had a large pair of spectacles on the top of a bald head. Obviously the defect in his vision was of a different character. He too turned over the papers in the tray; he too failed to find what he was looking for, and, without so much as a glance in our direction, scurried from the room. The booming voice sounded louder and sharper. Yet a third staff officer appeared. He wore a pair of half-spectacles which gave him a learned quizzical look. He was no more successful in his search than the others, although the booming voice was now rapping out commands to "find the damn thing and be quick about it." This officer apologized most charmingly for keeping us waiting. He need not have done so, for I was having a fine time. After the search had apparently been abandoned the staff-sergeant returned, lifted a book out of another wire tray and uncovered the precious document. Taking this with him, and with a knowing grin at us, he said, "The A.G. will see you now, gentlemen. This way, please." As I rose to follow him I could not help thinking what a funny scene in a revue the paper-chase would make: Leslie Henson could play all the parts.

2

Lieutenant-General Brownrigg was seated at a trestle table in the middle of the kitchen. At his back there was the usual open French hearth, and on the blank wall facing him a very large map of Northern France, dotted all over with little flags mounted on pins. All signs of the farmer's occupancy had been removed.

He acknowledged our "Good mornings" abruptly and told us to be seated, launching without hesitation into a disquisition upon the importance of entertainment in war. As he warmed to his subject he began to stride up and down the room and to illustrate his remarks by banging on the map with his leather-covered stick. Whenever he did so some of the little flags fell upon the floor, from which the elderly brigadier dutifully rescued them. It was a most useful geography lesson, if somewhat peripatetic. I decided to wait until it was over before putting to the General the list of precise questions I had brought with me. When he began to falter, as if his subject were exhausted, and to express doubt as to the possibility of 'laying on' entertainment for a long time to come, because the Army was on wheels and widely dispersed, I judged the time had come for concrete proposals, and made the obvious reply that entertainment could be put on wheels, too. I explained the success we had had with 16-mm. films on Salisbury Plain and pointed out the advantages of using sub-standard film units in forward areas in place of the more cumbersome and dangerous full-sized projectors. This satisfied the Adjutant-General, who made a ruling there and then that all mobile cinemas in the forward areas were to be of the sub-standard type. And he gave added point to it by demanding double the number of units allowed for in my preliminary plan.

As to 'live' entertainment, continued the General, well, that was more difficult. Preparation for it on the lines of communication and at the base ports might begin now, but it would depend on the course of military operations when it would be allowed in the forward areas. In any event female artistes would never be permitted. Entertainments should be allocated among the various units by entertainment officers sent overseas for the purpose. (Another instance of the casual way in which an essential link in the ENSA organization chain was first forged.) Yes, in the forward areas admission would be free and at the bases there would be a scale of nominal charges, similar to that being discussed at home.[1]

The General gobbled the various items of my plan as they were put before him, regurgitating them in short, rapid sentences that carried the maximum of authority. Then he embodied his agreement in an official letter, dictated before we left the farmhouse. I was delighted to have such co-operation. The General came with us to the door, reminding me once more that under no circumstances were female entertainers, as he called them, to be sent to France. . . . The hens were still clucking in the farmyard as we drove away to our next interview.

The rest of that day was spent in visiting other branches of the headquarters staff, some of them so hidden away that it was like an adult game of hide-and-seek, with motor-cars, code words and mystifying initials as instruments of the fun.

First, then, to the Provost Marshal to ask him to send instructions to the Passport Office in London regarding the issue of the necessary travelling permits; thence to the Director of Military Intelligence (D.M.I.) to find out what steps he proposed to take to screen the artistes, some of whom were of foreign origin and acting under professional names. Screening was a procedure very little known to the public at that time, but it would certainly be embarrassing if Miss X, the celebrated cabaret artiste, were to be turned back at Boulogne by a young subaltern wearing the green flash of Intelligence because her grandmother had been of German origin. A set of regulations would have to be laid down to cover the difficulty. Next, to a mysterious department known as 'Q Movements' to follow up a suggestion made by the Adjutant-General that artistes returning home might be accommodated on the leave boats that would shortly ply between Le Havre and Southampton. In later stages of the war I learned how to keep in the good graces of the Movement Officers, for

[1] These charges were finally fixed at 10 francs for officers, and 5 francs and 2 francs for other ranks.

without their co-operation and that of the R.A.F. it was impossible to make journeys at short notice in any of the theatres of war. One soon learned the way of it, but to begin with I had only the vaguest notion of their duties and importance. . . . To end the day, a conference with the war correspondents in the hope that they would mention our plans in their dispatches home, so that parents, wives and sweethearts, to whom the separation of foreign service was a new and trying experience, would know that the entertainment of their menfolk was not being neglected.

Early next morning, in a borrowed staff car, I set out to contact the Air Commodore in command of the A.A.S.F. at Rheims, to see how Paget-Wilkes' film shows were getting on.

And thence to Paris, where the obese night porter at the Hôtel Plaza Athénée shocked me by his complete indifference to the war and everything to do with it: a whiff of that defeatism that later burst over Europe like a huge bubble of poison gas. Virginia Vernon telephoned to me at daybreak to tell me she was standing by for orders, and had already contacted the President of the French Syndicate of Theatrical Managers who told her an official organization for the entertainment of French troops, to be known as Le Théâtre aux Armées, had been authorized. I jumped at this opportunity of collaboration with our allies; it bore fruit a few months later in two joint entertainments, one given at the Paris Opéra and the other at Drury Lane; the course of the war prevented any wider application.

Next, an early call upon our Military Attaché, where I was received with that cocoon-like courtesy that effectively hides from the visitor whether the impression he is seeking to make has been achieved or not. I was passed on to a branch of French Intelligence, known under the initials B.C.M.C. There I was interviewed by a certain Capitaine Desouch, who with much charm elaborated the difficulties and then explained the enormous efforts he proposed to make to dispel them.

Billeting of the artistes was going to be difficult. Virginia would be called upon to play a more exacting role than had seemed likely when she had so light-heartedly offered her services in the summer. As no date had been fixed for the dispatch of 'live' entertainment, we had to content ourselves, she and I, with an intelligent anticipation of requirements, briefing each other as best we could and leaving it at that.

The next day, elated and confident, I caught an early plane to London and went straight to Drury Lane, where a Press conference was awaiting me. The Board Room was packed with reporters, evidence of the public interest in what was going on in France. The shower of questions, some spiteful and others designed to stir up the argument still raging in Wardour

Street as to whether we were to provide the film entertainment in France or to leave it to some rival body, drove away the elation and left my confidence swimming in the air. I had come home!

"I take it the selection of films will not be all 'B.B.C.'?"

"If ENSA supplies the films, will they be out-of-date?"

"What about new American films? Will the boys see them?"

"Have you got a uniform, Mr Dean?"

"*Not in this war, no.*"

"Would you like one?" To which my only reply was an uncomprehending stare.

"Are the artistes going to wear uniform?"

"*Not so far as I know, but cinema operators will be enlisted into the R.A.S.C. (E.F.I.).*"

Although some newspapers expressed disappointment that women would not be allowed to go to France, there was no cause for complaint in the way our plans for the B.E.F. were put before the public.

3

In the spring of 1939 I had interviewed Gracie Fields at her house in St John's Wood and persuaded her to join with Sir Thomas Beecham, Sir John Martin Harvey and other leaders in building up our Central Committee. We had not met since the Ealing days, but to have known and worked happily with Gracie is to find oneself treated as one of the family for all time. Heartening, too, to receive her ready promise of support, and all the more disappointing a week or so later to receive a letter from her agent, saying that Gracie would rather "go about it in her own way should, unfortunately, anything of this nature be necessary," and concluding with the cheery prophecy that there was not going to be a war for a long time to come.

Shortly after the war broke out Gracie underwent a major operation. Rumours began to spread that she might never appear in public again. Then one morning I received a message from the nursing home to say she was better and wanted "to go and sing to the boys in France" as soon as she was well enough; she wanted to return thanks for her recovery. Despite the A.G.'s prohibition of "female entertainers" this was not an offer to be disregarded. I telephoned to the Q.M.G. in France and told him Gracie had been ordered to Capri for convalescence, but would like to give two or three concerts on her way through. To our great joy permission was granted. As there had not yet been time to create an overseas organization I decided to go to France myself to settle the details with the Army authorities, leaving the Drury Lane staff to cope with arrangements in London.

Seymour, as the Controller of ENSA, had planned to lead the first party in France, but when he heard about Gracie's offer he generously offered to act as her compère. As it was obvious that Gracie, weakened by her operation, would not be able to sustain the entire programme herself, a number of other prominent artistes volunteered to go too.

There were to be two concerts, one at Douai in the afternoon for the First Corps and another in the evening at Arras for the Second Corps. Virginia Vernon had already contacted the theatres and made all the preliminary arrangements for billeting the artistes. The authorities proposed to organize a strict ballot for the seats to ensure that every unit within reach was represented in the audiences.

When it became known that Gracie was on her way to sing to the men in France her journey there became a triumphal progress. Outside the hotel in Folkestone, where she spent the night before sailing, the usual crowd of autograph hunters mingled with women relatives of the soldiers overseas. They brought flowers and little gifts. She cracked the usual jokes, facetiously inviting "old man" Hitler to come and enjoy himself; quite unimportant, except to illustrate the gay spirit in which she left her sickbed, pursuing health, but putting duty first.

She was accompanied by Monty Banks and the faithful Mary Barrett, her secretary-companion and nurse. They journeyed by road to Paris, where Virginia had arranged she should rest for twenty-four hours before undergoing the emotional ordeal that lay ahead. On the way the car became entangled in a convoy of army lorries. As they drew abreast a Cockney voice shouted, "Why, it's Gracie Fields!" Immediately the whole convoy was in an uproar, drivers stopping their vehicles and crowding round the car to demand a song. One request led to another. Then an infuriated transport officer arrived on a motor-cycle to ask "What the blank blank was going on?" When he saw Gracie clinging to the door of the car for support and singing at full pitch the abuse died away in his throat, and he remained in the middle of the road, straddling his motorcycle, with his eyes popping and mouth wide open. She gave a full-sized concert by any ordinary reckoning before the convoy got under way again. The most amusing part of the incident for Gracie was when a boy from Accrington complained bitterly that he had not recognized Gracie first; that honour had fallen to a pal who was only a Cockney.

4

The great day, November 15, was misty and dull, but the little square in front of the theatre at Douai had quite a festive air, displaying a huge banner across it with "Welcome to Gracie" painted in large letters, and many flags of the Allies festooning a boar's head in the little restaurant opposite. The inhabitants of the ancient town had decided to make their own welcome for *la grande vedette anglaise*. Their eagerness to help in the preparations showed itself in many touching ways. Expensive carpets were borrowed from a château near by and spread on the stage, and in Gracie's dressing-room baskets of flowers surrounded a comfortable couch for her rest. Seymour needed a bouquet of red carnations for his contribution to the programme. An old lady with two sons in the Maginot Line stripped her little greenhouse for the purpose. To cap all, the proprietor of the restaurant prepared a sumptuous *déjeuner* which Gracie was too nervous to eat.

Daylight was already failing as the first concert began; but the men were there, some of them, two hours before. They filled the little market square, marching in, squad by squad, under their N.C.O.'s; others were packed in lorries and Bren carriers, so many men from each unit or formation. Here and there little groups stood apart, wearing a look of disappointment on their faces because they had not been lucky in the draw.

The old-fashioned theatre, with its little tiered boxes and narrow, steeply raked galleries, supported on slender iron pillars, was packed. The committee that organized the ballot had been scrupulously fair. A large stage box was crowded with men from a Scottish regiment who had evidently decided to double its capacity, for they were sitting on each other's knees. In the next box members of a headquarters staff sat beside their orderlies. In another corner a general stood behind a corporal, and refused the offer of his place. Excitement flew in gusts round the waiting audience and betrayed itself in sudden laughs, shouts and wisecracks with meanings clear only to the initiated. The artistes waiting on the stage were no less excited; some of them were trembling, all had a sense of a great occasion. In her dressing-room Gracie, dressed for the performance, lay on the couch, Monty watching her anxiously on one side and I on the other, and Mary Barrett at the foot, vainly offering her champagne. She was trembling like a frightened child.

At last the show was to begin. Seymour Hicks went on to the stage as compère and struck just the right note: This was to be Gracie's evening. The regular ENSA concerts would start in a few weeks' time, when many of the artistes they would see that afternoon would 'call again.' Other stars, such as Jack Buchanan, Leslie Henson, the Crazy Gang and so forth, would follow. This announcement set a match to the enthusiasm, and the burst of applause nearly blew the roof off.

All the artistes, caught up in the wonder and thrill of the occasion, gave better than their best; a cliché, but a true description. Dennis Noble began the programme by singing the Prologue to *Pagliacci*. I have never heard Dennis sing better. Then followed Claire Luce, Tom Webster (the *Daily Mail* cartoonist) and some adorable little dancing girls, known as the Four Ascots. Item after item was received with such rapturous applause that one wondered whether the audience would have any enthusiasm left for the star they had really come to see, now standing in the wings, leaning heavily upon me for support and still in a violent tremble. I put my arms round her to prevent her collapsing altogether.

"Feel all right?" I whispered.

"Yes, luve, thank you, only mah knees wobble a bit. Hope I won't disappoint you."

Gracie walked on to the stage through a barrage of sound that drowned midway Seymour's opening sentence of introduction. My throat went dry, and I caught myself gulping back some tears. Looking round at the others, I saw that they were in the grip of the same emotion. Gracie made a supreme effort to steady herself. Putting her fingers in her mouth and whistling shrilly, she shouted: "Now then, lads, no muckin' about!" With this touch of Lancashire vernacular the emotional atmosphere dissolved into laughter.

She began by singing *Sally*, the theme-song of the first film she had made with me so long ago. Anxious for the men to join in the choruses of the various songs, she whistled up Tom Webster, who was standing in the wings, and made him go to the easel on the stage and write out the words on his large sheets of sketching paper. Sometimes she would be too fast for him and, lightning artist though he might be, Tom's calligraphy would fall behind her singing. This led to vigorous cross-talk between them, as Gracie stopped her singing to watch his pencil scampering after her notes. On one occasion he outstripped her and made her sing the last line over again to make sure he was right. All of which made the fun uproarious and homely and intimate and completely suited to the occasion. The applause seemed unending. Staff officers and those in charge of transport began to glance anxiously at their wrist-watches, wondering how they were going to get her through the black-out in time for the next concert.

At Arras it was the same thing all over again, only more so: the crowded, exuberant audience, the nerves and tension. Here there were Lancashire boys in the audience and a Lancashire orchestra in the pit, which pleased Gracie very much. Some bandsmen of the regiment, borrowing a number of instruments from a friendly French unit, had conducted a series of vigorous rehearsals of her better-known songs. Admittedly the tempi were somewhat erratic, but that added to the fun, for Gracie was soon beating time for the self-appointed conductor, with a running fire of amusing criticism worthy of Beecham in his best vein.

A small box had been reserved for the Mayor of Arras. This gentleman arrived in good time, accompanied by his *chef de pompier* and other officials, only to find the box packed with stalwart Scots. The altercation that ensued in voluble French and good broad 'Hielan' was only terminated by the strain of *La Marseillaise*, which compelled all to stand to attention. The Mayor decided to watch from the wings. Unfortunately they too were crowded; so much so that the artistes had great difficulty in getting on or off the stage, reminding me of an eighteenth-century print of a performance at Drury Lane I once had in my possession. The Mayor was undeterred. He called for some wooden boxes and seated himself in the middle of the stage behind the back-cloth, where his *chef* obligingly cut eyeholes in the canvas for them both. As the municipality owned the theatre I presumed "M. le Maire" could do what he liked with his own, and did not feel called upon to protest at the mutilation of his scenery.

5

It had occurred both to Macqueen-Pope in London and myself in France that if the B.B.C. were to broadcast a portion of one of the concerts it would be like a direct message from the troops at the Front to their families at home. But their officials were unprepared for such a revolutionary proposition. Admittedly, it was put to them only a week before the concert was due to take place—short notice in peace-time, but under war conditions all they were entitled to expect. Pope kept in daily contact with me by telephone through the War Office, telling me of his efforts to overcome the various objections that were raised. His pertinacity was eventually rewarded. At noon on the day of the concert I received a teleprint signal to the effect that there would be a fifteen-minute broadcast in the Home Service that night, immediately after the nine o'clock news. The London evening papers issued contents bills: "Gracie broadcasting from France to-night"; these were the last contents bills that were issued for the duration of the war.

Many will remember that first broadcast, how moving it was. The sound of those soldiers yelling the choruses made every mother in the British Isles imagine her son's voice to be amongst them. The B.B.C. had reason to be grateful to Macqueen-Pope for his persistence, for without it they would have missed one of the outstanding broadcasts of the first winter of the war. Even so, there was much public criticism, led by Seymour on his return home, of the action of the Corporation in taking only fifteen minutes of the concert. Gracie's voice over the ether was like a Verey light piercing the fog of official censorship. It brought the human side of the war home to every listener and afforded one more striking example of the triumph of personality over red tape.

CHAPTER EIGHT

GRAND CHAIN

NOW that Gracie had 'jumped the gun,' preparations for a regular overseas service had to be speeded up. Although the Government order to close the theatres had been rescinded, new productions to fill the gaps were not ready in all cases, so that many of the most popular stars were available to us. Naturally they preferred the glamour of foreign service across the Channel to performing in draughty women's institutes, huts, marquees and other inadequate buildings in the outlandish places to which the troops at home had been dispersed. We were not disposed to criticize them. It was right that the men overseas should have the best of what was going. Moreover, the war held an element of romantic adventure in it for most people, despite the black-out. The bombing of civilians had not yet begun, and Drury Lane was crowded with volunteers. Here our Controller was at his best, acting with energy and determination in sorting out the wheat from the chaff and terminating many an unfruitful interview by his secret telephone technique with the greatest possible charm. He was assisted by an able overseas executive that included the heads of the various ENSA sections, Lena Ashwell, who did such notable work for the troops in France during the First World War, and Harold Holt.[1] Prominent also in this first group of planners were Leslie Henson, Jack Buchanan, Thorpe Bates, Greatrex Newman and Jack Hylton. It was not long before I was able to send a memorandum to NAAFI setting out our plans in detail.

As this early memorandum became the blue print from which all succeeding arrangements for overseas theatres of war were developed, it might be as well to set down its main points here. Dealing with the entertainment first, the maximum number in each party was to be fifteen, including the manager. Each visit was to last for four weeks. (Later the contracts contained an option giving us the right to extend engagements for a further month.) Maximum salary, exclusive of billeting and rationing, was to be £10 a week, with a minimum of £4 per week for the

[1] When Harold Holt resigned in the spring of 1940 Eric Evenett, a member of his staff, took over the Concert Section, sharing the work with Thorpe Bates.

chorus, which was higher than the Actors' Equity rate at that time. Billeting and rationing would be the responsibility of the Corporation. Each party would be provided with its own bus or coach for the artistes and a five-ton lorry carrying a portable stage, motor generator and lighting equipment. Parties would also carry their own pianos.

On the administrative side there would be Service Committees, similar to those now coming into operation at home, to whom the ENSA staff would make known the amount available. Our overseas staff would become members of the R.A.S.C. (E.F.I.), and be subject to military discipline. Officers would be commissioned in the ordinary way; enlisted men would be promoted to be warrant officers and N.C.O.'s as merit and circumstances dictated. The staff would take instructions on all professional and technical matters from the civilian organization at Drury Lane, while in respect of military matters, they would be responsible to the senior E.F.I. officer in the Command or Area concerned.

As the same broad principle of taking the entertainment to the men was to be followed overseas as at home, I proposed to divide the British Army Zone into four areas and to set up four 'entertainment posts' for administrative purposes, one for each Area. No. 1 Post, which was also to be our Main H.Q., would be at Arras, within easy reach of General Headquarters, with other posts at Rheims (No. 2), Le Havre (No. 3), Rennes (No. 4). Each post would have an establishment of officers, N.C.O.'s and men, with a senior officer in charge of the whole at No. 1 Post. The Service Committees would meet each week at our posts to settle the allocation for a fortnight hence. Drury Lane would send notification of the forthcoming bookings to our H.Q. in France one month ahead of the dates. Our overseas staff would be responsible for booking the local halls—or *salles des fêtes*, as the French call them—and for hiring the larger theatres and cinemas.

Finally, each entertainment post would be allotted its own transport for delivering parties to the locations and bringing them back at night. To avoid a pile-up of vehicles within an area, transport would not come back empty, but return with new parties for the areas. Thursday would be 'removal day,' when a sort of general post would take place.

Q.M.G./France gave cordial approval to the whole of these arrangements, and officially confirmed them in a general instruction issued towards the end of November.

GRACIE FIELDS AND MAURICE CHEVALIER
A SPECIAL SHOW FOR ACK-ACK TROOPS,
DRURY LANE, APRIL 1940

GRACIE'S AUDIENCE AT A FACTORY

"LET 'EM ALL COME"

"WE'RE ON THE AIR!"

BROADCASTING AN ENSA HALF-HOUR: ELSIE AND DORIS WATERS AND GORDON HARKER

RECORDING FOR TROOPS OVERSEAS: JACK BUCHANAN WITH GERALDO'S ORCHESTRA

CHILDREN'S MESSAGES FOR THEIR FATHERS IN WEST AFRICA BEING REHEARSED BY VICTORIA HOPPER, CHRISTMAS 1940

2

Their Majesties King George VI of his line and his Queen visited the Theatre Royal, Drury Lane, to inspect the ENSA work on the afternoon of Friday, November 24. We were told they would spend a maximum of three-quarters of an hour there. In the end they stayed for two hours and a half and were reluctant to leave. As it was war-time we had only about two days in which to make our preparations. These had to be kept very secret. The visit had been arranged by Macqueen-Pope, our publicity officer, who, amidst all the bustle and preparation for overseas, had developed a habit of mysterious hint-dropping and then, 'nanny-like,' refusing to tell me. Of the many services that 'Popie'—the nickname by which he is affectionately known in Fleet Street—rendered ENSA in those early days this was the most important.

We planned to give the King and Queen as complete a picture as possible of all that was going on. The vast stage at Drury Lane and its immediate environs was divided into stamping grounds for the various stars and for other activities, while at the back of the stage Abingdon placed rows of sewing-machines so that the Queen might see the wardrobe women at work without having to climb the stairs, and in the big workshops behind were gangs of stage hands waiting to erect mobile stages in record time.

The Call Sheet, summoning the artistes for the occasion, an historic document that has regrettably been lost, read something like this:

THEATRE ROYAL, DRURY LANE
VISIT OF T.M. THE KING AND QUEEN
ENSA Call Sheet

ROTUNDA	Orchestra Rehearsal	(Jack Hylton)
BOARD ROOM	Central Committee	(Sir Seymour Hicks)
BALLET ROOM	Gang Show	(Ralph Reader)
BAND ROOM	Ensa Music Hall	(Will Hay)
GREEN ROOM	Ensa Drama Company (Eight Bells)	(James Mason and Co. Directed by Henry Oscar)
MAIN STAGE FRONT	The Gaieties	(Leslie Henson and Co. Violet Loraine, Binnie Hale)
REAR	Revue	(Jack Buchanan, Fred Emney, Elsie Randolph and Co.)
STAGE RIGHT	Radio Rehearsal	(Godfrey Tearle)

All shops, workrooms and offices to be in full operation.

W. ABINGDON
Staff Control

F

A scout was placed in the passage leading from the stalls to the stage to give warning of the approach of the Royal visitors. Everything was to begin when this scout gave the signal, but he was so keyed up with nerves that he gave it too soon, shouting (in a stentorian voice intended for a stage aside), "They're here!" Immediately the most appalling din burst forth, as every one strove their utmost for attention; Jack and Elsie's tap dance competing with Leslie and Vi Loraine and Binnie Hale in full song in the foreground; James Mason fighting hard in an *Eight Bells* scuffle to drown Godfrey on the opposite side of the stage; and, over all, the clatter of sewing-machines and the thunder of dozens of hammers vigorously striking at nothing in particular. Once all these pent-up energies had been let loose Abingdon and his assistants had the greatest difficulty in stopping the riot of sound. When the actual arrival was signalled everything began again, only rather sheepishly and one at a time, which was just as well.

Their Majesties were met at the main entrance by Sir Murrough Wilson, the Chairman, and other senior officials of NAAFI, and by Sir Kenneth Barnes, Alec Rea and myself, representing ENSA. The party proceeded up the main staircase to the rotunda, where Jack Hylton was giving an impressive orchestral rehearsal, although the music in question was only *Run, Rabbit, Run*. In the Board Room the Main Committee was in session under the Chairmanship of Sir Seymour Hicks. Those present included Sybil Thorndike, Lilian Braithwaite, Lena Ashwell, Martin Harvey, Harold Holt and many more. Seymour's idea was to show the Committee at work, allocating the entertainments, and not just talking. For this purpose he had provided himself with a large map, into which he was busily sticking little flags when Their Majesties entered. In a speech that was perhaps more romantic than precise, he described the system and the wonderful results already achieved. He was momentarily nonplussed when the Queen, with a charming smile, asked him why some of his flags were blue and some red. The King, with a twinkle, covered Seymour's hesitation by saying, "Oh, they use red when they run out of blue!"

Their Majesties went everywhere, saw everything and encouraged every one. Up and down the winding staircases, on to the stage, and in and out of those historic rooms where David Garrick dressed and where Richard Brinsley Sheridan wrote *The School for Scandal*, down into the underground ballet room within the walls of the original theatre built by Sir Christopher Wren, into the famous scene-painting rooms where the giants of the past exercised their art—nothing was left out. In the property shop the King and Queen watched the almost extinct craft of stage-property-making, with the giant heads and trick effects of the pantomimes of long ago grinning at them from the dusty shelves behind their backs. In the big runway that divides the stage from the workshops a lorry was being loaded with equipment for France, and a small sing-song company, ready to leave immediately for the country, watched its equipment being loaded into the small van that was to be the sole means of transport for months to come. Their Majesties watched the dress rehearsal of Leslie Henson's 'Gaieties' from the stalls for a while, joining in the old choruses and asking if there were no new ones. Afterwards they went up on the stage, crossing the gangway over the footlights to chat with the company.

So little was known about ENSA that the King had not been briefed, as is customary on such occasions, and kept plying me with questions. He was obviously amazed at the growth of the organization within so short a time. At one point he turned to me and asked:

"Who pays for all this?"

"NAAFI, sir," I replied.

"Good," said His Majesty, "stick to it, they've plenty of money." Then he looked with a merry twinkle at Sir Murrough Wilson, who grinned— perhaps I should write 'like a Cheshire cat,' except that I am not quite sure what that expression means.

One likes to think that the enthusiasm seething about Drury Lane that afternoon and the pleasant informality of the occasion were some relief to the King from current anxieties. So far as ENSA was concerned the visit had a wonderful tonic effect upon our morale. This reached concert pitch when on the following Sunday the first of the ENSA companies set out for France.

3

Seymour opened our regular service across the water, although his visit was for two weeks only, because his duties as Controller necessitated an early return to Drury Lane. The party included Dorothy Ward, Claire Luce, Tom Webster, Bertha Wilmott, Billy Russell, Lance Fairfax and the Four Ascots. Leslie Henson's 'Gaieties' went over at the same time. His party included Violet Loraine (singing *If you were the only Girl in the World* to the troops as she had done to their fathers before them), Binnie Hale and Gavin Gordon, and the Debroy Somers quintette. There followed in quick succession Jack Buchanan's Musical Show, with Elsie Randolph, Fred Emney, Syd Millward and his Nitwits (an orchestral combination very popular with the troops), Ralph Reader's Gang Show, an all-male party designed for the forward areas (I hesitate to write "front line" in view of the inactivity of the 'phoney war') and the first[1] of the Variety Companies which Will Hay organized under the general name of 'ENSA Music Hall.'

In December a special party got together by Lady Louis Mountbatten,[2] at the instigation of Frances Day, began a series of performances at Arras. With Frances went Edythe Baker, Paddy Brown, Sutherland Felce, Harry Jacobson, Norman Hackforth and Lyle Evans. This party was originally planned as an independent effort, but when ENSA began overseas the sponsor immediately got into touch with me and placed the party at our disposal. Lady Louis went with the party just to see things for herself. I believe it was due entirely to that first contact that we owed her invaluable help and support throughout the war.

During the week before Christmas Lupino Lane closed the Victoria Palace in London and took over the *Me and My Girl* company. On Christmas Day Gracie Fields, not yet fully recovered in strength but greatly benefited by her brief visit to Capri, opened a short series of performances at Rheims for the R.A.F. Over the holiday period, too, there was Will Fyffe with a company that included Jasper Maskelyne (of Maskelyne and Devant), Albert Whelan and John Sharman, who managed the company. At the beginning of the year Harold Holt took out Jeanne de Casalis, Marian Davis and Jane Carr, Lilian Keys, and, later, Gwen Farrar. The first of the special parties organized by Lena Ashwell and Thorpe Bates included (besides Thorpe Bates himself) Parry Jones, Gladys Ripley and Victoria Hopper. George Formby was another star who went over in the spring. For good measure, which was indeed pressed down and running over so far as accommodation both for shows and artistes was concerned, there were many of the best-known dance bands under their popular leaders. These included Jack Hylton (Arthur Askey joined him for his short tour), Jack Payne, Joe Loss (with whom was Charlie Chester, later to become a radio star), Billy Cotton, Ambrose and Carroll Gibbons.

The best of the established concert parties now left the home front to begin a life of globe-trotting that ended only with the last hostilities; they followed the British troops into every theatre of war from Iceland to the Far East. They were popular because their well-balanced entertainments, if not of high artistic merit, were always good value for money. They were the mainstay of our overseas service.

[1] This party arrived at Cherbourg on December 11 and left Le Havre for home on January 21, after giving performances to British and French troops occupying the Maginot Line over Christmas. Among the members of the company were Beryl Beresford and Leslie Hinton, Harry and Marjorie Ristori, Keith Wilbur and the Griffiths Brothers in their well-known pantomime comedy act of the horse.

[2] Now Countess Mountbatten of Burma.

Working hard, too, on the morale front were a number of sing-song units and, of course, the 16-mm. mobile cinema vans, giving two and three performances a day in barns and sheds. The schedule was further extended by the formation of a Lectures Section under the chairmanship of Lena Ashwell. Its members included Dr J. J. Mallon, Harold Nicolson,[1] M.P., and Gerald Christy of the well-known Lecture Agency.

Q.M.G./France was scared of this development at first, but appreciated the entertainment as well as the educational value of the lectures when the list of subjects was shown to him. Among those who gave popular lectures were Escott North, James Hogan (on football) and Sir Paul Dukes (Secret Service in Finland and Russia). In the New Year our production planning staff began mapping out programmes that were bolder and wider in scope than those that had gone before. One of these was to be a visit of the Vic-Wells Ballet, about which there were a number of official telegrams in which the company figured as "the Welsh ballet," despite my attempts at correction. Originally it was proposed that the company should go first to the troops and then pass into Belgium and Holland, where a tour had been arranged by the British Council. But the Intelligence Staff insisted that the order of the visit be reversed for Security reasons. This meant a delay of four weeks, so that the visit to the B.E.F. could not take place before May. As it happened, the delay lasted four years and not four weeks, for the Ballet did not reach France until the spring of 1945, by which time our forces there had been renamed the British Army of Liberation.

Of the individual stars John Gielgud was preparing to go out in Shakespeare; Harry Lauder wanted to go but his doctors would not permit it, so he went to Orkney and the Shetlands instead! A number of play companies were being formed, manned by first-class actors and actresses. On the film side, twenty mobile vans, carrying 16-mm. double projectors, were now at work in the forward areas, and permanent cinemas had been opened in Arras, Lille and Le Havre. Contact had been established with the Canadian Forces in readiness for the supply of entertainment parties specially suited to their tastes. At a later stage of the war these were known as the 'ENSA Maple Leaf Companies' and were very popular.

As the result of three-sided correspondence between G.H.Q., the War Office and ENSA, it had been agreed that the principal Army Bands should tour the British zones in company with ENSA artistes. We had already tried out this plan with the R.A.F. Central Band under Wing-Commander O'Donnell. At first he had been chary of this co-operation, but his objections had been overridden by Halahan at the Air Ministry.

[1] Now Sir Harold Nicolson, K.C.V.O., C.M.G.

From now on the R.A.F. Central Band gave us enthusiastic support for the whole period of the war: a practical example of how senior officers can set the tone of mutual help between organizations. In the contemplation of these plans I was blissfully free from any nagging thoughts as to who was to pay for it all.

The main bulk of this entertainment was delivered overseas within a period of six months. A task of such magnitude, complicated by war-time restrictions in a foreign country, was entirely without precedent. If there had been time for reflection, the staff at Drury Lane might have anticipated nothing but praise for what they had accomplished. They would have been disillusioned. Such was the inactivity, and consequent boredom, of the troops that there were many complaints of inadequacy, and the cry was always for more, more! mingled with vociferous criticism whenever the shows fell below standard or the lecturers soared into the realm of education. I am not going to say that the troops were spoilt in the matter of entertainment during the 'phoney war'; but it was something very like that.

The Magic Slide . . .

Tschiffely, famous traveller and author of *Tschiffely's Ride*, was among the lecturers who visited the B.E.F. during that winter. Upon one occasion he arrived at a *salle de fête* in a small French village to give his lecture to a unit quartered there, and found quite a number of men already seated watching the operator making ready the magic lantern. As he wore a black overcoat and a large black hat, he looked like a Nonconformist parson in the dim light. When they saw him the men began to slip out one by one. Looking up from his notes, Tschiffely whispered to the operator to put on a slide of semi-nude native women from South America. This caught the eye of the last man to leave, just as he was about to go through the door; and lo, silently, unaccountably, within a matter of minutes, the place was full again.

4

Among the multiplicity of events with which we were concerned during that first time in France one stands out in recollection, gay and successful, against the background of approaching fury. The French counterpart of ENSA, Le Théâtre aux Armées, had made little headway, although it enjoyed the official support of the French Government and, in particular, of the Minister of Education (M. Albert Sarraut). Whenever possible, French troops in the vicinity of our men were invited to the

ENSA shows, but nothing could alter the fact that the British were now receiving a regular service of entertainment and the French troops were not. This did not escape the notice of the German propagandists. So I was glad when Lord Ivor Spencer Churchill approached me on behalf of an organization in which he was interested, known as Art et Tourisme, whose avowed object was to promote *la solidarité Franco-Britannique*. He proposed that a combined Franco-British entertainment should be given on April 16 at the Paris Opéra in aid of Le Théâtre aux Armées. I set high hopes on this initial collaboration with the French theatre managers but had some difficulty in persuading NAAFI to allow us to carry it through. The project was eventually agreed to when Maurice Chevalier, one of the stars to appear in the programme, volunteered to fly to England later and give a return performance at Drury Lane Theatre for our troops.[1]

Half the items were to be provided by the French, and the other half by ENSA. Besides Maurice Chevalier, the French contribution included a military band, a portion of the Opéra Ballet and a fine choir of volunteers from the Czechoslovak Air Force. We sent Jack Hylton and his orchestra, Gracie Fields, Jack Warner and 'Stinker' Murdoch. Maurice Chevalier agreed to introduce Gracie Fields over the air immediately following his own contribution, and I was asked to announce the programme, partly in French and partly in English, to which I agreed with some trepidation. Part of the performance was to be broadcast by the B.B.C. and by Radio Paris.

All these arrangements having been mutually agreed and the attendance of the President of the French Republic promised, the performance was set down for Tuesday, April 16, 1940. Jack Hylton's Orchestra and the English stars arrived from London the night before, in readiness for a full rehearsal on the stage of the Opéra at eleven o'clock the next morning.

The main French item was described on the programme as a "*ballet surprise.*" This I had been told would be fully rehearsed beforehand, so as to free the stage for Hylton's orchestral rehearsal; but the usual optimism had betrayed those responsible for the time-table. When our people went to the theatre they found the whole place in confusion, not unusual on

[1] This return concert took place at Drury Lane on April 30, 1940. Once again Gracie Fields appeared with Maurice Chevalier; they sang a duet together. Others in the star programme were Seymour Hicks, Jack Hylton and his Band, Leslie Henson and Binnie Hale, Sydney Howard and Arthur Riscoe, and Louis Levy and his cinema orchestra. The audience consisted of representatives of all three Services and some small detachments of French troops in England. The performance took place in the presence of the Duke and Duchess of Kent, to whom the stars were afterwards presented. The portion of the concert which included Maurice Chevalier and Gracie Fields was broadcast, the broadcast fee being used to defray the cost of Maurice Chevalier's special plane from France (arranged by the Air Ministry).

the morning of a gala performance. In the foreground rehearsals of the ballet were being held, some of the dancers in practice dresses, others in the special costumes designed for the occasion by the famous French artist *le Caporal* Vertès. At the back of the huge stage gangs of men were bringing in scenery or nailing up rostrums, whilst others, perched on high ladders, were touching up scenery under the direction of an artist in painter's overalls and bow tie, a Caporal cigarette drooping from his lips in conventional style. Violent argument between the choreographer and the *metteur-en-scène* alternated with directions to the dancers and the clatter and banging of carpenters and electricians.

Jack Warner and Murdoch and the others strode up and down, waiting impatiently to take the vocal measure of the vast auditorium, while Gracie Fields sat quietly in the stalls munching sandwiches. Hylton's musicians lounged in the wings, watching the proceedings with cynical amusement. When the spectacle ceased to amuse they engaged in wordy battles with the French stage staff as to the whereabouts of their instrument cases. Later the trumpeters and saxophonists, tired of waiting, began to play impertinent little trills behind the scenery, embarrassing the French orchestra rehearsing a soft fiddle passage with the ballet. Presently, patience exhausted, they began to converge slowly upon the harassed dancers. Then the choreographer, stepping back, trod on the corns of a trumpet-player. A British oath, formal French bows of apology, and on again! It was now two o'clock in the afternoon, and still no lessening of the racket. Finally Jack Hylton, who had been itching to intervene for the last hour, sidled up to me and whispered in his native Lancashire, so great was his agitation:

"Eeh, Basil, ye'll 'ave to do something. This is just a b—g—r's muddle!"

Together we strode to the centre of the stage, interrupting an altercation between the *maître de ballet* and the chief electrician, and announced our intention to rehearse the English programme. Round about five o'clock the French staff took polite revenge on us by turning all the lights out and going home before our rehearsal was half done.

Thus far the proceedings had not exemplified the *solidarité Franco-Britannique* advertised on the programme, and I was in much anxiety as to the final outcome. However, in due time the great tableaux curtains of the Opéra parted, disclosing stage and auditorium to each other. Here was calm, dignity and poise where a short time before had been rage, tumult and frustration.

The opera house was *en fête*. Standing in the *coulisse*, one could feast one's eyes upon the glittering spectacle. In the foreground sat many leaders of French life and letters, escorting the dowagers in black silk with lace col-

larettes stiffened with whalebone, strings of pearls and diamond ornaments
in their hair. I can see them yet, those women, looking so aristocratic and
grey and tired as they sat stiffly in their seats, applauding gently the expensive entertainment they had been dragged out to witness. Paris had certainly turned up in force. In addition to the President of the Republic
(Albert Lebrun), the Prime Minister (Paul Reynaud), the Minister of
War (Édouard Daladier) and the British Ambassador (Sir Ronald Campbell) were there. It proved to be the last performance given in the famous
building before the occupation of Paris by the Germans.

To fit the more important items into the broadcast the order of the
programme had been changed. Jack Warner now immediately preceded
Maurice Chevalier. To my astonishment and Maurice Chevalier's disgust,
Jack opened his turn by singing Louise in the best Chevalier manner, straw
hat and all: an excellent idea for the Chelsea Palace, but hardly suitable for
the Paris Opéra with Chevalier in the programme. I cannot possibly reproduce Maurice's remarks as he stood by me in the wings; most of it was in
the Parisian argot which I do not understand, but there was one word
which I did understand, and that is unprintable. Warner came off to
generous, if somewhat shocked, applause, and I anticipated physical combat in the wings between the two famous stars—quite like an eighteenth-
century affair, I thought—but Maurice was silenced by Jack's bland
suggestion that he should imitate him in return.

The first two songs sung by Gracie were received politely, but with no
appreciable loosening of the stiff necks in front. The third item was a
comedy number, and Gracie evidently decided to take things into her own
hands. As Harry Parr Davies played the opening bars she suddenly took off
a lovely little fur cape she was wearing and flung it into the orchestra,
shouting in broad Lancashire, "Eeh, this is a bit dull. Let's 'ave some fun!"
An unusual technique for the Opéra audience, but Gracie's instinct won
the day, so that when the end came the stiff necks were on their feet,
clapping and laughing by turns: one of the most unexpected conquests
that I have ever seen Gracie make.

At the reception afterwards the ENSA artistes were presented to the
French President by the British Ambassador, whilst Reynaud and
Daladier talked animatedly of l'esprit de l'orchestre de M. Hylton.

5

Apart from the ten days or so of each month spent in France, my time
was divided between Drury Lane, where the showers of paper that daily
descended on my desk competed for attention with the practical work of

building up the internal structure of the organization, and hurried visits to the camps, where the equipping of the new entertainment halls and the conversion of the disused riding-schools was now proceeding.

Building up the structure was interesting enough, but there were times when I longed to take a hand in the practical work of production, particularly in the Drama Division; but there was never enough time. Even the two or three special performances for the Ack-Ack troops of General Pile, which we gave at Drury Lane, had to be left to others. The long reports and the estimates of future expenditure required by NAAFI were usually written late at night, when nothing came between me and the silence of my own thoughts but an overworked secretary and a persistent night telephone. . . . It was a merry-go-round without the merriment; but I had climbed on to it of my own free will, and until some one stopped the infernal thing there could be no thought of dismounting.

It was a relief from the endless pressure to join the audiences on special occasions, such as when Commanders-in-Chief or members of the Government were present, and to know the thrill of having had a share in bringing the people so much enjoyment.

One of the earliest of these visits remains sadly in my memory. It was a few days after the return of Gracie Fields from her Christmas visit to the B.E.F. (on Sunday, January 7, to be precise), when she gave two concerts for the Royal Navy at Greenock, officers and men coming ashore in detachments from the warships in dock and at anchor, and filling the large hall to overflowing. This was another of our 'Nelson touch' naval occasions, which Gracie had asked for because she did not want the sailors to feel she was neglecting them for the men in France. When NAAFI heard about it I came in for a severe wigging, but I protested that the broadcast fee had enabled us to cover all the expenses (well, nearly all), so our dastardly attack upon the soldiers' funds for the benefit of the sailors was forgiven.

After the concert the artistes had supper in the *Hood* with Admiral Whitworth, his personal staff and the ship's officers. At the end of a delightful evening each of us was presented with a photograph of the ship, signed by the Admiral. The loss of the ship with its gallant company so soon afterwards gave mournful significance to these carelessly tendered mementoes.

CHAPTER NINE

MARCHING AS TO WAR

M OST of the officers and N.C.O.'s required to run our organization were in France before Christmas, although it is only fair to say that at no period of the war had we sufficient staff overseas. This short-handedness added to the initial difficulties that arose as the new officers felt their way. The work called for tact and firmness at all times, and the exercise of a high degree of self-discipline, often in circumstances that encouraged the opposite. Entertainment was always in short supply, and demands from senior officers made impartiality difficult to maintain. Extravagant praise when the shows were good alternated with a certain amount of bullying when they were the reverse, which made it difficult for our officers to retain their sense of proportion. Moreover, the hours of duty were different from those of the troops they served, and responsibility to a civilian body at home too frequently came into conflict with military pressure overseas.

Some of the artistes regarded service in France as a kind of Cook's tour, during which such matters as the care of personal luggage, passports and military permits, and compliance with French currency regulations would be looked after on their behalf by kindly Olympians in uniform who had nothing else to do; but they suffered disillusionment when they found out that personal inconvenience was inseparable from the service. They could not understand when allocations were changed or cancelled because of troop movements, general 'stand-to,' or other military reasons, and put all down to our inefficiency. Some of the stars, when they reached a comfortable well-appointed theatre where they were playing to good audiences, objected to being moved out after two days, or even one day, when it was quite plain that only a fraction of the troops in that neighbourhood had been able to see them. But there were others who realized that to carry on without grumbling brought its reward in less wear and tear on the individual and more appreciation from the troops.

Seymour caught the exhilaration of working for the B.E.F. like the rest of us. But the impact of his exuberant personality upon our still rickety organization was disastrous. His tour was conducted in a blaze of glory which left our inexperienced officers blinking their eyes at the passing of a theatrical comet, whose trail of brilliant suggestion completely destroyed the first green shoots of discipline and left nothing in their place but flowery promises that soon withered in the sunlight of reality.

One of his suggestions was that our ENSA Headquarters should be transferred to Paris, but it did not require the gift of prophecy to foresee the result of allowing Paris to become the lodestone for British artistes sent to France to entertain the troops. Another idea was that stars should be flown over by the R.A.F. to give special concerts at the request of senior officers with whom Seymour had personal contact, an arrangement that would please the stars who liked to bask in the glamorous light that surrounds distinguished commanders in the field and doubtless flatter the vanity of those able to obtain their exclusive services: everybody would be happy, except the less fortunate troops whose officers could not boast of direct contact with the stage. The unequal distribution of entertainment that would follow upon such a plan was obvious. Our senior officer then in France was swept off his feet by Seymour's magic, and came back to London with him to finalize the plan without troubling to inform anyone at Drury Lane that he had left the organization in France without its chief.

All of us at that time were hag-ridden by our enthusiasms. The artistes were excited by the totally new experiences they were undergoing, the officers uncertain of their authority; for my part, I was obsessed with the desire to make ENSA a model organization in all respects. It is a mistake to surrender oneself to the domination of a single idea; it may give one strength and persistence, but it also inhibits one's ability to manœuvre round obstacles. Perhaps it is for that reason that Lady Louis Mountbatten once said jokingly that I behaved like a tank when a principle was at stake. This I took as a compliment at the time, but now I am not so sure.

By the Way . . .

There was a brisk little correspondence in January between the Provost Marshal at Arras and ENSA H.Q. there, regarding the arrest by the civil police at Douai of a small party of girls on their way to the theatre. Because they were dressed in slacks and could not speak French they were regarded as spies—not a very obvious way of concealing one's identity!— and taken to the police station, whence they were rescued by a gallant captain of the R.A.S.C., ably seconded by an officer of our French allies. The correspondence concluded with a stiff note from a pompous D.A.A.G., threatening the girls "with a worse fate if they persist in walking about French towns in fancy dress."

2

Throughout those first days in France, Virginia Vernon worked with a sort of desperate efficiency, booking hotel accommodation, meeting trains and aircraft, soothing the ruffled feelings of French hôteliers when parties failed to arrive on time. Our military staff began by treating her, and welfare matters generally, with pleasant condescension, an attitude that was exemplified by the behaviour of one senior officer who used to pat her on the back and call her "dear lady," conduct which enraged Virginia and showed a considerable ignorance of feminine psychology. It would have been laughable if it had not sown the seeds of mutual dislike so that ultimately there grew up between them an impenetrable hedge, effectively preventing either from seeing any good in the other.

Virginia was born into the world of the theatre. Consequently she knew how to cope with the many little personal difficulties that arise in life behind the scenes. Here she had an advantage over our inexperienced staff, whose treatment of the actors oscillated between two extremes, some behaving as though they were soldiers and subject to military discipline, others indulging in back-slapping and wearing a 'to Hell with this military stuff' air: both attitudes were resented.

The bands were always the most difficult to handle, not only because of their numbers and the amount of heavy baggage they carried, but also because there was less discipline among them. After the successful wooing of some difficult hôtelier it exasperated Virginia to find her efforts brought to naught by the misbehaviour of one of these parties. Many were the wordy battles which she waged with recalcitrant musicians. But no one was ever in doubt as to who was left in command of the field; it was always Virginia, eyes flashing, nostrils quivering, while the baffled drummers and saxophonists retreated clattering down the tessellated hallways of the little French hotels. It was not their misbehaviour that mattered to her; it was the resulting loss of a first-class billet. Yet it must not be thought she was compact solely of regimentation. For example, it was due to her insistence that NAAFI was eventually persuaded to make a refreshment allowance of so many francs per meal for each artiste. Apart from helping the performers, this alleviated some of the financial strain on the officers' messes, especially their younger members, who felt themselves constrained to entertain artistes in return for the entertainment given to the men.

Since Virginia speaks French as instinctively as she does her native tongue, the habit grew of addressing her as *Madame*, after the manner of the French people with whom she was in such constant and voluble argument. It followed her to England after Dunkirk. And it was as Madame Vernon that she became generally known, being so addressed by officials, factory superintendents, high-ranking officers and ENSA artistes everywhere.

3

The weather was exceptionally severe that winter. Severe frosts alternated with brief thaws in which drizzles of rain froze as they touched the ground. Soon the roads were covered with ice to the depth of several inches, which made them well-nigh impassable, while the ports were fogbound for days at a time, so that the ships in which the artistes were to cross the Channel could not sail.[1]

Most of the travelling was done by road, using Army lorries, hastily converted for passenger-carrying. The seats had few springs; the flapping canvas sides were no protection against the bitter cold, and the mica windows effectively obscured any view of the countryside during the short hours of daylight. Efforts were made to mitigate the hardships by a liberal use of Army blankets and petrol tins converted into hot-water bottles, but when I gave orders for the hire of French motor-coaches wherever available the Corporation sent me a minute stating that the hire of luxurious coaches was to be avoided as it would lay NAAFI open to the charge of extravagance. On the disorganized French railways, occasionally used for the longer journeys, parties frequently lost their way, even though some of their number could speak French. When to this general picture of ferocious weather and inadequate transport there were added such stringent conditions of black-out that the striking of a single cigarette lighter was enough to cause an appreciable reflection in the snow, it was not surprising that parties arrived at their destinations one or two hours late; it was more surprising that they arrived at all. In some cases there was no surprise because, in fact, they never did arrive!

Under these conditions it was only to be expected that our first casualties were caused by transport and not by bullets. Violet Loraine and Binnie Hale hired a taxi one afternoon to visit the War Memorial at Vimy Ridge, and were hurrying through the dusk to rejoin the Henson party for the evening show when the taxi came into collision with a military lorry emerging from behind a farm cart, heavily laden with sugar beet. The lorry came off best. Both artistes were injured, Vi Loraine so seriously that

[1] ENSA was permitted to use both military sea routes in transporting the artistes: Southampton–Le Havre for the larger parties; Folkestone–Calais for the small units.

her husband, Captain Edward Joicey, was flown out in a specially chartered plane to be at her bedside.

We had made a rule that all artistes must travel in the transport provided and under the care of the ENSA staff. This was the only possible way in which supervision of their movements could be made effective. But the accident, coming as the climax to a number of incidents in the first three or four weeks, pointed to a degree of slackness on the part of our staff that might end in disaster.

4

Thoroughly alarmed, I hurried back to France in the middle of December. The Cinema Officer came with me. The prospect of having to dispense with certain officers made me feel very uncomfortable. Nevertheless, I reflected, it would mean promotion for officers able to take the places of those who had found the task beyond them. After obtaining official approval of the changes I proposed to make I set out from Rennes at first light for Arras, accompanied by Ben Henry and taking with me our senior officer in the L. of C. area, who was to take over command of our main headquarters. The previous day there had been a silver thaw. Now there was fog and ice and again bitter cold. During the night, so I was informed, over one hundred heavy lorries had been piled up in that military area alone. As we slid cautiously by, there they were, lining the roads in various drunken attitudes: literally dozens of Army vehicles of every sort and description.

Apart from the hazards of the way, that journey is also memorable for the Strange Affair of the Missing Overcoat. We had stopped for lunch at the principal hotel in a pleasant market town: an excellent meal, somewhat long-drawn-out, as is the French habit. While conversation at our table revolved round the evident delight of our military companion at renewing his First War contacts—I found it impossible to be stirred by the news that only yesterday he had bumped into "old Brigadier So-and-so, who used to be No. 2 to the D. of S. and T. on the Rhine," or that Captain A was now a full Colonel and had married the Town Major's daughter after all—I transferred my attention to a couple lunching in the opposite corner: a large, prosperous, bearded Frenchman of the Midi and an attractive young woman, decidedly too smart for her surroundings. They finished their meal and rose to go. Taking his overcoat from the stand, the Frenchman followed his companion into the main part of the hotel. During a pause in the flow of military jargon at our table I wandered into the market-place, preparatory to leaving. Ben Henry took his coat off the stand and followed me. The pale sun had momentarily driven away the fog and was warming the earth again. We got into the car and had been driven slitheringly a few miles in pleasant somnolence when Ben woke up with a start and said:

"I've got the wrong overcoat!"

"How the Hell do you know?" I asked, peevish at being woken up.

"There's a list of cinema locations in the inside pocket. Besides, though it's the same colour as mine, this one is too big."

Instantly my mind was full of thoughts of spies and the Fifth Column; those cinema locations could be useful to the enemy. We drove back to the hotel, while our military companion set forth in pompous tones the swift action he proposed to take. I told the proprietor we had seen another customer take a coat of similar style and colour off the peg.

"Ah, oui," he exclaimed, "c'est Monsieur le Baron X."

Although I did not catch all the proprietor's voluble French, his customer was evidently a very important man indeed.

"Pardon. Un moment." And he disappeared down the corridor. Presently he returned to make a number of embarrassed excuses.

"M. le Baron is engaged. M. le Baron is entertaining a friend," etc., etc.

"To hell with that!" exclaimed Ben Henry, in a tone of sharp alarm. "I want my coat."

"Mais, M. le Baron is with M'selle; he—he is, vous comprenez?" The explanation ended in a despairing shrug.

Comprehension spread over Ben's astonished face like a pink sunset after rain.

"You've had it, Ben," I interposed. "We'll just have to wait."

And wait we did, drinking coffee and cognac by the big window in the thin sunlight whilst the customer concluded his amour. Later the head waiter handed Ben Henry the overcoat with a grave air and many apologies. The contretemps delayed us for over an hour, and it was after midnight when I guided the car into Arras, sliding and lurching like a drunken sailor through the icy fog, with an electric torch for the last two or three miles.

Two days later, Ben Henry having finished his tasks and gone home, I set out for Rheims to see that all was ready for the concert which Gracie Fields was to give on Christmas Night, half an hour of which was to be broadcast in the B.B.C. Home Service. Layers of ice several inches thick now covered all the main roads of Northern France. I began to wonder how much of the long journey we could cover before darkness compelled us to halt, but my driver evidently had his own ideas, which did not include any regard for my personal safety. As we slithered along the main street of one village great trees loomed up out of the fog, forming vast arch-

GRACIE AMONG
MY 'PRÆTORIANS'
(See Appendix Five
for key.)

DEPARTURE
PLATFORM

THE ROUTING
ROOM: "WHERE
ARE THEY NOW?"

ENSA's Coming-of-age Luncheon Party at the Savoy Hotel is presided over by
H.R.H. the Duke of Kent, May 27, 1941

ways through which the shop-fronts glinted like the windows of some
ghostly cathedral. Then the trees began to stagger like giant drunkards
as the contents of one shop larger than the rest (an *épicerie*, as I remember)
leered at me first through one window of the car and then through the
other. We had turned completely round and were speeding down the
road the way we had come. "That was a bit of orl rite," said my cheerful
Cockney. We arrived at Rheims in the late afternoon, nervous and shaken;
at least, I was, and more confirmed than ever in my dislike of all forms of
winter sport.

5

That Christmas Night concert was a tremendous success, repeating the
scenes and excitement of the previous month at Arras. But the whole plan
was very nearly wrecked by transport difficulties. At the last minute Jack
Hylton's orchestra was unable to go; so Jack Payne volunteered in his
stead. His band was fulfilling a broadcasting engagement during the week
before Christmas at Bristol, and it was found impossible to cancel its
engagement for the Saturday night. To enable the party to get to Rheims
on the Sunday, which was Christmas Eve, NAAFI allowed us to charter
a special plane, but the flight had to be cancelled because of fog. With the
help of 'Q' Movements, War Office, we secured last-minute reservations
on the Folkestone–Calais route. Once more General Weather deployed
his forces, immobilizing the boat and smothering our disgruntled musicians in a genuine 'pea-souper.'

Meanwhile we waited at Rheims for news of the wanderers, living
through a forty-eight-hour bombardment of telephone calls and messages
from here, there and everywhere, with excited telephone operators growing more incoherent as Christmas Day advanced and teleprint signals
even more misleading because more positive in their misstatements. At
one time we were assured the party would positively arrive within the
hour, and half an hour later that they were already in Rheims.

During the discussions the previous night as to what was to be done if
Jack Payne's band failed to arrive in time Gracie had produced a tattered
sketch from her basket of theatrical properties, and a cast had been settled
which consisted of Gracie, Monty Banks, Mary Barrett and Harry Parr
Davies, the composer, who was again acting as Gracie's accompanist.
After a good deal of chaff he had agreed to play the part of Gracie's lover,
provided at least half of it was cut out. . . . It now being noon on Christmas Day, we went into vigorous rehearsal. Most of the time was spent in
spirited backchat between Gracie and Monty, each complaining that the
other was stealing the best 'business.' At the performance Monty's start-

G

ling improvisations, verbal and gymnastic, delighted the troops, but reduced Gracie to such helpless laughter that she forgot to 'feed' him with the correct lines, and the so-called dramatic sketch ended in Marx Brothers confusion, Harry Parr Davies remaining mute for the entire performance, despite all my efforts in the prompt corner: as sharp an attack of stage-fright as ever I saw. After the concert was over I received the last teleprint of the day from Virginia. She was hoping to dispatch Jack Payne and his Orchestra the next morning.

Boxing Day: two concerts that evening in the packed cinema in Rheims, this time complete with the band and Jack Payne. The next day the whole party set out for Arras to give two concerts, at the first of which the improvised sketch once more made its appearance, the band being late again because of failure to comply with transport instructions; thence to Rennes and finally to Cherbourg, whence Gracie left for England, having, in her two visits to the B.E.F., given concerts to token audiences of all the units in France.

Hogmanay

Another outstandingly successful visit to the B.E.F. over this period was made by Will Fyffe. His concert for Scottish troops on New Year's Eve was broadcast in the Home Service. In the afternoon he was invited to appear at a concert for French charities in the town where he was staying. He knew only a few words of French, and felt very nervous as he strode on to the stage. But, espying a gold-braided French officer in a box and wishing to pay him a compliment, he bowed low and, pointing to himself, said, "Regardez, Écossais," which started things going with a round of applause. His turn was greeted with storms of laughter, especially the pathetic bits. At the end Will stood in the centre of the stage, overcome with the warmth of his reception. Then he looked across at John Sharman watching from the wings and muttered in broad Scots, "Eh, mon, they didna' understand a wurrd."

6

In the New Year I made visits each month to France, usually by A.D.L.S.[1] plane; and Richard Llewellyn came with me as my personal assistant. He had joined us at Drury Lane within a week of the outbreak of war, adding a vivid splash of colour to the human scene there in more senses than one. Using his quick intelligence and Celtic gift of fantasy where the facts of a situation required embellishment, he devoted himself with aplomb to

[1] Air Daily Letter Service.

whatever task came his way, irrespective of whether he knew much about it or not.

He began by taking charge of our transport section, but after a time the more stolid imagination of the NAAFI officials refused to follow the higher flights of his fancy in justification of his requisitions, so he gave that up. Later he took charge of the Passports and Permits Section and spent long hours at the French Consulate, charming visas out of the Consul-General at immediate notice. Whether that official really believed all the stories of urgency and august authority that were told him, or merely surrendered his Gallic logicality to Richard's fascination, will never be known.

Richard's love of colour was expressed not only in his personality and mode of life, but in other ways. In the flush of first success as a novelist (*How Green was my Valley*) he purchased the most surprising wardrobe for a young man of exceptional fashion in war-time. One 'creation' was of a startling shade of green, with shirt and collar of paler hue, suede shoes and a violet tie, all of the first quality. When he appeared in this outfit at an important committee meeting it caused a minor sensation; as Richard fully intended it should. But the temptation was too much for Rex Newman's wit; he leaned across the table to me and whispered, "How keen was my valet!"

I was too engrossed with daily problems to bother about the discomfort which air travel caused him—it made him unbearably sick—until one day a chance remark overheard at Drury Lane uncovered a whole range of amiable devices that he employed to persuade me to use other means of transport. One bitterly cold morning in March he came into the office at Arras where I was giving some last-minute instructions before going home.

"Met. report, sir."

"What the heck do I want with the Met. report?"

"There's a fog. The A.D.L.S. won't get away to-day."

"Nonsense, of course it will."

"I thought perhaps you'd prefer to go by boat, as——"

"Anyway, ring up Glissé and find out."

He left the room disconsolately, and I had a queer sensation of having said something like that before.

There were some amusing 'cards' among our overseas staff, men who were more used to giving orders than to receiving them. But their new commanding officer was rightly concerned to instil the rudiments of military discipline into his Falstaffian army. Hence such minutiæ as standing to attention when addressed by an officer were sometimes insisted upon to the point of exasperation. But ours was a theatrical organization, despite the uniform, and attempts to quash the normal freemasonry of the entertainment world were not regarded favourably. The boys who ran the sing-song vans, accustomed to the witticisms of the Charing Cross Road and the brisk exchanges of Blackpool and Brighton in the holiday season, had abundant exercise for their sense of comic situation.

The commanding officer had arrived in Arras with a fine new pair of riding-boots of which he was very proud. Some of the more mischievous spirits decided to provide him with a Rosinante. They borrowed an ancient steed, subsequently described as having a back like a washbasin, provided it with a jockey's saddlecloth cut from an Army blanket, saddle and bridle, and tied it to the railings outside headquarters. The ringleader, one Sergeant X (well known in his particular branch of show business), then mounted the stairs, entered the Major's office and saluted smartly, saying, "Your horse is at the door, sir." "What the hell do you mean, X?" said the Major, momentarily taken aback. "Sent over from No. 1 Remount, sir." He saluted and left the room without further word. The Major, overtaken by curiosity, went downstairs to find out what was going on. When he saw the animal tethered to the railings he exploded with violent anger, unaware that the Sir Tobys and Sir Andrews of the unit were observing him from behind a near-by hedge.

7

A little back-room tussle requires mention here because of its later repercussions.

In the late spring the strength of the B.E.F. was increased by a third Corps under the command of Sir Ronald Adam. One of its divisions— the 44th, to be exact—was fortunate in that the late Sir John Jarvis, Bart., M.P., had induced several well-known business firms to present them with full-size projection equipment (35 mm.), promising that the names of the donors would be advertised by means of slides thrown on the screen.

It became my duty to point out to the energetic and slightly cantankerous Sir John how his proposals would affect the general plan. First of all, it would be unfair for his cinema units to be used solely for the benefit of one division, particularly if they were to be supplied with films and serviced by our staff. The old cry of inequality of distribution once more. Secondly, to advertise on the screen the names of the firms presenting the equipment was not only contrary to Army Council policy, but would not be permitted by the K.R.S., who controlled the supply of films. Thirdly, if 35-mm. projectors were used by the 44th Division other units in the forward areas would also want full-scale films.

Unfortunately Sir John seemed incapable of altering his ideas on the subject. On several occasions I lunched with him at Claridge's. At the first of these feasts he held out every inducement to me to let him have his way, going so far as to say that he felt he could help me in other ways, whatever that might mean. On the next occasion he produced a draft deed for the cinema projectors and invited me to become one of the trustees. It contained the usual legal phrases about good care and mainte-nance, but when I asked him what would happen if the projectors were destroyed by enemy action he replied that in that event the trust deeds would become null and void, which seemed a logical answer.

As he continued to insist, even after the 44th Division had embarked, that the projectors were for their sole use and should be allowed to go forward with them, I decided to stand back and let the generals fight it out among themselves. Eventually the Corps Commander brought A.G./ and Q.M.G./France round to Sir John's view. Between them they decided to allow the big projectors to go forward after all. A profitless story, to which their destruction by the advancing Germans before they could be used provided the epilogue.

8

What a strange war it was! No battles and seemingly few preparations for one; some tank-traps and pill-boxes and barbed wire in the forward positions along the Belgian frontier, and that was all. Would such puny obstacles really keep out the Germans when the time came? And that visit to Lord Gort's headquarters in the big château, hidden from the road by tall trees—every one so courteous and helpful, and the General anxious for entertainment to be given at the château for the clerks and orderlies. Would the enemy wage war with similar poise and dignity? As a non-military person I lacked the knowledge that would give me the answer, but I wondered just the same.

Occasional high-flying German reconnaissance planes set off the air-raid warnings in the French towns, but the troops soon grew accustomed to the daily visitations and took little notice. Apart from the difference in the siren's note, there was nothing to distinguish such occurrences from those taking place in any garrison town in England. So regular were the visita-tions that Seymour brought home a story of how he was stopped in a street in Lille by a French gendarme who warned him that it was eleven o'clock and that every morning German machines came over at that hour. Then he looked at his watch and up at the sky, and added, "*Hélas, monsieur*, to-day he is six minutes late."

Arras, the heart of the British military zone, had a holiday air as the troops, a little self-conscious in their new Hore-Belisha battle-dress, whiled away their time in the immemorial fashion of troops waiting behind the lines for a battle to begin, lounging in the cafés, window-shopping or crowding into the kiosks to buy coloured postcards to send to girl friends at home.

There was a restaurant on the corner of the square facing the main railway station, which was nightly crowded with young officers enjoying the rich onion soup for which the place was famous, as well as the attrac-tions of the equally famous young lady at the cash-desk. She was dark, petite, with beautiful teeth and bright, twinkling eyes. I was never quite sure whether it was the onion soup or the mademoiselle that caused Richard to find so many excuses for taking me there. When I was pre-vented he would go there himself. His manner after these solo visits was designed to create an impression of personal triumph in the face of the keenest competition. Later a rumour went round the B.E.F. that the young woman was a German spy, but when I discussed it with Richard he merely nodded his head knowingly, as though to say, "This counter-counter espionage. Very dangerous. Very difficult." The little restaurant was a cheerful, friendly place; and it was sad to see it again towards the end of the war, silent and forlorn, its glass windows broken and boarded, and to know for a certainty that the young lady at the cash-desk had been taken away and shot.

It was in this restaurant that Richard Dimbleby came to me one even-ing and said, "You've just been on the air." "What!" I said. "Oh, well, not you actually; but Lord Haw Haw. He doesn't like ENSA and says the troops have to be paid to go and see your shows!" The German propagandists had begun to recognize the value of our work.

The two houses in the Boulevard Faid'herbe that we occupied as headquarters were part of a row of old houses patched up during the reconstruction of Arras after the First World War. They stood back a little from one of the main military routes to the South behind narrow strips of neglected garden, divided from each other by high brick walls. One afternoon I was standing at the front window of the main office, waiting for a telephone call and idly watching a procession of British tanks from one of the base ports go rumbling by when, to my astonish-ment, the wall on my left began to sway along its whole length; then it leaned gracefully over and collapsed on to the front path in a pile of rubble and a cloud of dust. "Jericho," murmured the sergeant standing behind me. And I wondered vaguely if this were a premonitory sign of things to come.

CHAPTER TEN

IN THE NEWS

CRITICISM is good for the soul, we are told. On that reckoning alone ENSA must have been redeemed many times over. The trite comfort, usually offered to sufferers under the lash by those who are not, contained a good deal of truth in our case, for the successive waves of misrepresentation drew the original band of volunteers closer together in defence of what they were doing, so that there was no fury like that of an ENSA official scorned.

Opening my newspaper one morning, I was confronted by a row of portraits of the chairmen of the various ENSA committees, all famous names. As a caption to each portrait there was a brief statement of the subject's whereabouts the previous day: those encountered at Drury Lane had not been standing on their heads, so they were obviously idling away their time; others doing normal professional work at film studios or elsewhere were treated as remanded persons who had jumped their bail. The intention behind the article was to encourage the public mind to lick its chops over the approach of a scandal of considerable dimensions. The onslaught gave me a shock; it was the complete opposite of what volunteers for national service were entitled to expect.

The distinguished names on our committees seemed to heighten the general impression in Fleet Street that ENSA was nothing but an extravagant lark. Large sums were quoted at random in the Press as our spending money, the general implication being that a large part of it would be wasted on inflated salaries for useless managers. One prominent reporter who came to interview me said he had been reliably informed that my salary was £15,000 a year. He refused to believe that the leading officials at Drury Lane had made personal sacrifices of any kind.

Such animosity was difficult to understand. Admittedly, a voluntary banding together of all branches of the Entertainment Industry, not for personal advantage, but for a single national purpose, was difficult to believe in—"There must be a nigger in it," thought the cynics. Macqueen-Pope put it more tactfully when he said, "It was something quite new and therefore suspect."

The recurrent arguments about the unsuitability of our shows (either too high-brow or too low-brow), and what was vulgar and what was not, call for separate consideration later on, when the reasons for all that occurred will fall into perspective, for this after all is a story of things done rather than of those left undone or as they might have been better done. But enough may be here set down to show the heavy responsibility borne by Macqueen-Pope as our public relations officer, for we were certainly in the news!

2

In France it was the static warfare, confined, as far as the land forces were concerned, to minor bickerings on the Saar front, that brought about the bonfire of ENSA publicity by which the frustrated war correspondents strove to keep public interest in the 'phoney war' alive. All the same, I longed for the more mischievous of them to leave the regimental messes and the warmth of their comfortable hotel billets to see what really went on at the ENSA concerts, especially in the forward areas. I was convinced they were missing many human stories that their editors would have welcomed, and the public been delighted to read. By way of contrast one or two of the younger correspondents became too enterprising, finding their way past the stage doors under the pretext of interviewing the artistes. When I protested on one occasion that the chorus girls' dressing-room seemed an unsuitable *venue* for this purpose I was blandly told that war correspondents had the right to interview anyone from the Commander-in-Chief downwards. . . . Although our misadventures in France provided the critics with a plentiful supply of ammunition, it was of such mixed calibre that the charges rarely fitted the weapons of invective employed, and so there was a high proportion of misfires.

Some of the stories made good holiday reading for girls and boys during the Christmas holidays. There was that one about the failure of Billy Cotton and his band to appear at a special R.A.F. concert due to take place some seventy miles forward of where the band was billeted. Some distance along the main road the military police directed the coach conveying the band on to a side road, whither it had been preceded by a military lorry carrying the instruments and theatrical equipment. Proceeding along this road a short distance, the coach was stopped at a bridge by some French engineers who jumped down from the parapet and told them that it was not safe. While Billy Cotton was arguing with them the bridge collapsed, leaving the band separated from its trumpets and trombones by a river in flood. This fantastic occurrence won headlines as a flagrant example of ENSA waste and muddle.

Then there was LOVE ON THE WESTERN FRONT: headlines to a too romantic story of how a party of ENSA artistes had been left stranded on a railway platform for a whole day in the bitter cold, of how they had been rescued by the lucky arrival of a gallant figure in R.A.F. uniform, who turned out to be a long-lost friend of one of the young actresses, and how from this chance reunion young love was born. The truth was more matter-of-fact, for the young lady in question was already comfortably engaged to this officer before his arrival at the station, half an hour late, to escort the party to comfortable billets.

The complaints of dissatisfied artistes on their return home added to the general din, whereupon Madame Vernon, indignant at the implied reflection upon her own efficiency, entered the lists. Her reports, which poured into Drury Lane in a steady stream, showed a progressive decline from circumspection into frankness. Of a certain variety artiste she wrote: "Mr X was inclined to refresh himself too well, and this interfered with the carrying out of his duties." When the complaints of a famous band were publicized she reported as follows:

> This band played whoopee at the Hotel C at B on New Year's Eve, where they left a big bill which Mr Monty Banks had to pay, including the cost of an enormous mirror which members of the band removed from the wall and used as a dance floor, so that it broke to pieces. May this be regarded as war damage, please?

When the first ENSA Music Hall returned from France three of its leading members—Will Hay, Albert Whelan and Billy Russell, all prominent in the Water Rats (the well-known benevolent society of the music hall)—were so impressed with their experiences that they wanted the public to know about them. A deputation was arranged for the following day to which the Press were invited. In the morning an important newspaper published under banner headlines the surprising news that the Water Rats were joining the War Office in an attack upon ENSA! Representatives from all the papers, except the one which published this story, came to Drury Lane, where they listened with astonishment to the eulogistic terms in which Will Hay and the others spoke of our organization in France, and to their caustic comments on recent reporting.

One newspaper began its account of an interview with Jack Payne with a flaring headline: SACK THE LOT! As this was a solution of the matter with which I did not agree, I challenged the bandleader to open debate in a forum to be provided by the Gallery First Nighters' Club. It was in buoyant mood that I went to the Criterion Restaurant the following month to debate our iniquities. Jack was prevented by a concert engagement from being present. However, there were plenty of critics 'in the body of the hall.' Hannen Swaffer was in the chair. Over an acquaintance of many years my relations with this Dickensian personality have alternated between cordiality and a polite indifference. To win his support when I was convinced I was in the right of a matter became an important achievement, whatever previous controversy lay between us. On this occasion he gave me strong support and used his sarcastic wit to good effect. The proceedings were faithfully reported in the Press, and ENSA won a resounding victory.

MONTAGE:

A fevered condition such as this has to reach its crisis before it can be cured. In our case it came quite unexpectedly with the threatened publication of a canard that might have had serious consequences. One Friday evening, towards the end of January, the deputy general manager of NAAFI telephoned saying that he had heard that all ENSA live entertainment in France was cancelled as from the following Sunday. Why had he not been informed, and what was the explanation? I said it was news to me, but I would telephone to G.H.Q. and find out. I did so, and received the terse reply: "No truth in it. We've had the 'War House' on the wire twice asking if it means that enemy action is imminent. Can't you keep your people quiet?" I retorted that the story had been circulated from his end and we were just as upset as G.H.Q. The Brigadier replied gruffly that he would look into it and rang off. Pope then told me that one of the biggest dailies intended to publish the story, although he had warned Fleet Street the rumour was incorrect. Realizing what a bad impression this would make and sensing its larger implications, I rang up the night editor (it was then about 10 P.M.) and gave him the gist of my conversation with G.H.Q. With some reluctance he consented to withhold publication, realizing, I suppose, that the risk of annoying the War Office was greater than the opportunity to have another slap at ENSA.

There were distinguished correspondents in France who took no part in this racket, men like Philip Gibbs and Douglas Williams of the *Daily Telegraph*, who always gave the true reasons for our various mishaps. Their fair reporting did much to steady the position.

3

Macqueen-Pope was installed in the principal dressing-room on the prompt side of the stage, where the most famous actresses of past and present generations have dressed for their parts. This had been converted into a publicity office. The walls of the room were covered with posters and charts, the most prominent being a newspaper contents bill of 1919, autographed by Lloyd George, displaying in large letters the words: PEACE SIGNED. Here 'Popie,' assisted by Harold Conway, was to be found from early morning until late in the evening, surrounded by typewriters, telephones and mountains of Press cuttings: here he played the part of 'Sir Valiant' with the utmost effect, striking down misrepresentation and calumny wherever he found it. When he was not interviewing reporters he was emitting pressurized jets of propaganda to wash away the mud that was continually being flung at ENSA by all sorts and conditions of people, apart from the Press: by those with a zeal for uplift in soldiers' entertainment and those who held the view that soldiers only wanted to laugh and that to object to vulgarity in wartime was absurd and puritanical, by dissatisfied artistes in search of publicity, and, of course, by the inevitable soldier's widow whose only son had written to tell her he had never seen an ENSA show and did not believe ENSA existed, except to pay huge salaries to out-of-work actors.

Pope brings the priceless gift of enthusiasm to all his work for the theatre, and a love for it so deep and romantic that he seems able to summon the ghosts of the great stage figures of the past to throw aside their cerements and to make a series of personal appearances entirely for his benefit. And who is to say him nay? It is enough for this master of collated incident to make some innocent and romantic (in a theatre sense) adornment to a story he is telling and to repeat it two or three times for it to become unalterably fixed in his mind as a verifiable fact.

The value of his services to ENSA at the beginning can scarcely be overestimated. The organization was growing so rapidly, and the areas of possible misunderstanding were becoming so large, that the facts had to be clearly and forcibly stated day by day, if public confidence were not to be irretrievably lost. His wide knowledge of the theatre, as well as of the darker ways of Fleet Street, his popularity in both circles and his dogmatic ebullience enabled him to emerge the confident victor from every controversy in which we were involved. There were times when he must have slept with the telephone glued to his ear, for my calls for help were assured of a response, no matter at what hour they were made.

4

Although the adverse publicity showed that we were able to stand fire it took up a great deal of time, since each Press story had to be carefully checked and its grosser extravagances refuted. Enthusiasm was running high among our own people, but in the face of this constant disparagement, and with the inevitable frustrations of the war, morale would fall rapidly unless means were found of stimulating it. Moreover, some of the stars thought it was beneath their dignity to work for ENSA,[1] and that it might result in their becoming mere cogs in a vast entertainment machine.

Skilful and sustained publicity would be needed not only to maintain the morale of our own staff, but also to overcome these prejudices. One morning I was passing by the Y.M.C.A. building in Tottenham Court Road, fretting about the failure of a certain star to come up to scratch, when I looked up and saw the Red Triangle. How many of our soldiers on foreign service must welcome that symbol of friendliness and good cheer! Now here was an idea! A sign! A badge of service, too; something to build up the corporate idea of ENSA. I hurried back to Drury Lane and asked Seymour to suggest some one who would design a badge for us, one that could be cheaply and quickly reproduced in different materials, something quite simple, I said, like London Transport or the Y.M.C.A. Seymour suggested the President of the Royal Academy, Sir Edwin Lutyens—he usually went to the Garrick Club for lunch; we would tackle him at once. We found Lutyens at the Club. He made a preliminary sketch on the back of the menu card there and then: 'just the job,' as the wartime slang went. Sir Edwin took the rough sketch back to his office and

[1] As early as December 14, 1939, the following reference had appeared in the *Continental Daily Mail* to the work in France: "When I was in Paris I spoke to Noël Coward about it. I cannot quote his comments, but at least I can repeat his remarks: 'Please tell every one that I have nothing to do with entertaining the troops.'"

the following day sent me the completed design, drawn to scale, and coloured red, white and blue, just as he had promised.

The first use of the design was as a badge for men's buttonholes, and as enamelled brooches for the women. These badges and brooches were proudly worn at first, but whenever we came under fire from the Press I noticed they had a tendency to disappear. Whereupon I issued a directive to all the staff, urging them to wear their badges on every possible occasion, particularly in difficult times; to do otherwise was like taking off one's uniform in the face of the enemy. Artistes going overseas were told to wear it always. Ben Henry presented me with one in solid gold, a gift which I treasure to this day. In fact, I forced the use of the sign at every opportunity. Reproductions of it were made in the form of shields which all the concert parties were instructed to carry with them and to display on either side of the stage or outside the doors of the hall where they were giving performances. Failure to do so drew an instant rebuke on to the heads of the party managers.

Coloured posters are an established advertising medium in the entertainment world. ENSA used them freely. The senior designer, Denis Wreford, was a brilliant draughtsman, keenly receptive of new ideas which he transferred to the drawing-board with amazing speed. Some of his posters became well known throughout the theatres of war; there was one I particularly liked, entitled 'World Theatre,' a name subsequently given to a series of broadcast plays by the B.B.C. One of the earliest designs arose out of my desire to express the buoyant, aggressive mood of our entertainments. The design showed the white cliffs of Dover and the Union Jack flying defiantly in the breeze. Underneath was a quotation from Shakespeare's *King John*:

> Come the three corners of the world in arms,
> And we shall shock them!

Unfortunately its issue coincided with an outburst of vulgarity among the ENSA comedians. So my poster had to be hurriedly withdrawn.

5

The NAAFI Corporation was in two minds about our publicity. This did not worry me unduly; it could be in as many minds as it liked, for aught I cared. But the conflicting instructions issued from time to time were an embarrassment. It was not so much that these gave expression to a policy opposite to our own as that they showed a jealous misunderstanding of the requirements of theatrical publicity. They also showed how the desire to bask in the ENSA limelight conflicted with the NAAFI view of itself as an august Government agency.

Very early on I received a minute from the Corporation insisting that wherever the name of ENSA appeared there, too, must NAAFI appear. This was easy to control in our advertisements and printed programmes, but in other directions quite impossible. The Press was accustomed to giving theatrical people liberal publicity, and they were accustomed to receiving it; no pompous minutes from NAAFI were going to stop that. After the film squabble was over I received another minute from the Corporation (on November 21, 1939, to be precise) requesting me to reduce publicity to its absolute minimum; statements that were essential should be impersonal and should receive the prior approval of the Secretary of the Corporation. Further, the desirability of retaining the services of Mr Pope and his assistant was questioned.

After consultation with my closest associates I showed the minute to Pope. He said nothing but went straight back to his office and typed out his resignation, which I found lying on my desk when I returned from lunch—a dramatic procedure quite in keeping with his character. I refused his resignation, and sat down to reply to the minute while the mood of indignation was still upon me. Among other things I pointed out that distinguished artistes giving their services either voluntarily or at salaries below their market value were entitled to the fullest publicity; if it were not accorded to them through the proper channels, they would either obtain it for themselves or gradually drift away from the work.

We won that first tussle with NAAFI, as we were to win others subsequently, but the upset lasted for several weeks and left us all badly shaken. The effort was not wasted, for out of it we gained the strength and the wisdom to deal with the more serious attacks and ambushes that lay ahead. If the Corporation's attack upon our independent way of going about things may be regarded as distant musketry fire, and the Press attacks as the exploding of blank ammunition, at least we learned from them how to keep our heads down when the heavy artillery and tanks of the War Office opened up against us, to say nothing of the commando raids of private M.P.'s in search of notoriety.

An incident that occurred several months later reminded us that the cold war over publicity was still going on. Coaches and cars were liable to be held up for identification purposes at the gates of camps and aerodromes during the winter black-out; so ENSA labels were affixed to the windscreens of all our transport vehicles. No sooner did this come to the ears of the Corporation than I was instructed to have the NAAFI equivalents pasted alongside them. Thus, a simple means of identification was made confusing for no good reason. Was it beer or actors the driver had brought through the night? The welcome would have been cordial in either case, although one well-known producer was in doubt about the matter, for when in the black-out a guard presented a drawn bayonet at his chest and shouted, "Who goes there?" he replied in terrified surprise, "William Armstrong."

NAAFI's own publicity was admirable towards the end of the war. The early suffusion in the ENSA limelight had shown the way to a good deal of it. At a time when cooks and counter-hands were in short supply an advertisement appeared in the national papers announcing that the ENSA audiences at home now totalled twenty-five millions, and reminding the public that an efficient canteen service alone made this possible. The advertisement was headed "The Greatest Show on Earth." Whether it helped the recruiting of cooks for the canteens is uncertain, but one can imagine the skeleton of P. T. Barnum rattling its bones fiercely at the heading.

6

It must not be thought that the many difficulties that are here set down robbed us of zest to carry on the work. Quite the contrary. They were but salt to the dish. Without doubt many mistakes were made at the beginning; and the reasons for some of them were not made clear at the time. In France the early confusion could have been avoided if more time and thought had been given to the work of preparation, but we should have kept the men waiting some six or eight weeks longer while the staff work was being completed. I take reponsibility for the course followed. As it was, the men got the entertainment, and, well! we got the criticism.

Throughout that first winter my personal relations with the War Office and with Q.M.G./France were excellent. When the Press agitation was at its height I asked him to obtain candid opinions from all the formations in France and to report the result to the War Office. Great care was taken in the preparation of this report, which summarized the opinion of the whole B.E.F. The small mobile cinemas came in for high praise, as did also the sing-song units. Regarding the larger parties there was a reflection of the grumbles that had appeared in the Press in the statement that:

Artistes must be prepared to travel in charabancs and to put up with poor accommodation.

Another quotation threw light upon the Press controversy:

The attack in the Press against ENSA entertainments has been in the main untrue and unjustified; it has done harm, rather than good.

Attached to the copy of the report which General Lindsell sent me was a cheery personal letter, which ended: "Stick to it, ENSA. You are doing good work to help win the war."

It was now late spring. The weather had improved, and still the war remained static. More and more artistes and managers crowded to Drury Lane, anxious to share in the fun of entertaining the troops. More and more committees; more and more temporary offices at Drury Lane; more and more demands for shows; several Army theatres at home now made ready; requisitions for stages for the R.A.F. by the dozen—there seemed to be no slackening of growth, no end to it all. Could this be war?

Faster and faster whirls the merry-go-round. No hope of stepping off now; the machine is moving so fast that it takes complete control of one's being, one's thoughts, one's physical existence. And then with a violent jolt and a rasping of nerves the gay whirl is over; over before we have time to relish our new-found efficiency. . . . The Germans have turned us out of France.

CHAPTER ELEVEN

EVACUATION

BRRRH! *Brrrh!* Hateful thing a dentist's drill! Was I in the dentist's chair? How did I get there? *Brrrh! Brrrh!* Absurd. Must be dreaming. I'm in my flat in London. . . . Gradually the persistent buzzing of the telephone at my bedside, muffled to avoid waking the household in the night hours, forced me out of dream consciousness. I glanced at my watch. It was six o'clock in the morning.

"This is the teleprint room, War Office."

"Oh, yes," I said sleepily.

"You remember you asked me to let you know when the balloon went up?"

"Yes, yes," I said, instantly awake.

"Well, it's happened. The Germans invaded Holland and Belgium at four o'clock this morning."

"Hold on a minute," I said, as he was about to ring off. "Will you send a signal for me?"

"Where to?"

"Brassard. O.C. E.F.I. Entertainments."

"Be quick, then. We're flooded out with signals. What is it?"

"Just one word. 'Hamlet.'"

"That all?" He was too busy to express more surprise, and rang off.

The date was Friday, May 10, 1940.

For a while I lay stretched out on the bed, abandoning myself to the rush of an overpowering excitement, my mind empty of all but odds and ends of thought that chased each other round and round, nothing concrete. . . .

During my March visit to France, sitting in the office at Arras going over things with our senior officer, I had suddenly said to him:

"I think we ought to have an evacuation plan."

"Evacuation?" he said, his eyes goggling with surprise.

"Yes, one never knows. I've an uneasy feeling about all these arrangements of ours."

"Why?"

H

"They're too static. We seem to be running an entertainment business, not taking part in a war. Supposing the Germans advance suddenly?"

"They're miles away the other side of Belgium."

"They went through pretty quickly last time. And even if the Army goes forward our people will be in the way at first. I suggest we plan it like a military operation; put all the entertainment parties into columns in charge of the military staff at each entertainment post and then, at a given signal, withdraw them along second- or third-class roads clear of the advancing troops. The entertainment can then be regrouped ready to be called forward whenever G.H.Q. gives the word. In any case we reduce the risk of casualties."

The major caught on to the idea eagerly, and we spent the rest of the morning discussing the plan in rough outline. It was agreed that he should work out the details on paper, allotting the military staff and the transport for each column and plotting the routes to be followed, obtain the approval of G.H.Q. and send the blueprint to me in London. The names of the ENSA parties making up each column would depend upon their whereabouts at the time the signal to move was given.

"We shall need a code word," said the major. "What's it to be?"

"Something theatrical, so that the signal doesn't get mixed up with anything of a military nature. I suggest 'Hamlet.'"

I was not conscious of any premeditation in respect of our conversation that morning. It would be tactless to use the word 'intuition,' because in matters relating to the war Hitler had acquired a sinister monopoly of its use, but I distinctly remember the inner surprise I felt as I put forward the idea. In proof that our conversation was not entirely defeatist, we agreed upon a number of other code words to indicate the towns where the ENSA Headquarters might be when the general advance took place. They were all well forward of the positions we occupied during the 'phoney war.' I still possess the piece of squared paper, torn from a field service notebook, on which we made out the list: 'Othello' for Brussels, 'Lear' for Ghent, 'Shrew' for Mons, 'Midsummer' for Antwerp, 'Andronicus' for Ostend, and so on. It was years before we went into those places, by which time such juvenile expedients were unnecessary.

I had a standing invitation to lunch at the Q Staff Mess. As I entered the dining-room that day General Lindsell looked up with a friendly smile that mitigated the patronizing tone of his voice.

"Well, and what have you been up to this morning?" he said.

"Well, actually, sir," I said nervously, as I sat down beside him, mentally kicking myself for the verbal cliché, "actually, I've been getting ready a little evacuation plan."

"Evacuation?" He sat bolt upright with surprise, and the heads of the other senior officers seated round the table jolted upwards in unison.

"Good God! We're going forward; we're not going back." And the red-tabbed pairs of shoulders heaved with merriment.

"No doubt, sir," I said, "but when you do, my people are much better out of the way for the time being, so I'm getting ready a plan to pull them out and down to the back. You can always call us forward when you want us."

"Well, well," said General Lindsell, "you may be right there." He looked at me with quizzical interest, as though surprised a mere civilian should think of such a thing.

It was fortunate for the speedy operation of the plan that the General had placed me on the short list of those permitted to use the military tele-phone lines to France, and had also cleared the way for us with Army Signals, so that messages about arriving artistes could be delivered promptly in all areas. Similarly, incoming teleprints were delivered at Drury Lane by War Office messengers with commendable speed. At Christmas-time I had added some personal lubrication of my own to the smooth-running lines of communication, beseeching the head of the teleprint room at the War Office to give me early information of any major occurrence likely to affect us. The innocuous bribery drew its reward in the lottery of events here described. Certainly, we had nothing to complain of about War Office co-operation in those early days.

My 'Hamlet' signal was received at our H.Q. in Arras at 9 A.M. on May 10, and by noon of the same day all our troupes of 'motley' in the forward areas had been assembled at the concentration points where they were given hot meals and issued with seventy-two hours' dry rations for emergency use. "Utensils for brewing tea will be provided for each M.T. vehicle" had been thoughtfully added to the draft instructions by Madame Vernon.

By 2 P.M. some twelve companies were en route to the back and by nightfall safely stowed in billets out of the way. The ENSA evacuation (Operation 'Z' we called it) was a complete success, despite some delay in concentrating the Music Hall unit playing at Lille because of Will Hay's frenzied anger at the bombing which was going on; he persisted in rush-ing up and down the street, shaking his fist at the aircraft overhead and shouting violent oaths as he pocketed pieces of spent shell for souvenirs.

2

Meanwhile at home we waited anxiously through the forenoon for news. We knew that both Arras and Lille had been bombed; beyond that nothing. There was no means of finding out whether my signal had got through. It was impossible to use the telephone, and all other means of communication were blocked. As the power and swiftness of the German stroke became more apparent my anxiety grew deeper. So, early in the afternoon, I decided to go to France myself and to take Richard Llewellyn with me. My usual route to Glissé airport, just outside Amiens, was impossible that day because all the R.A.F. planes were ferrying back to France senior staff officers whose hopes of a 'spot of leave' over Whitsuntide had been so rudely interrupted. However, we managed to scramble on to an overloaded mail-plane leaving Hendon for Paris. Richard made the journey sprawling uncomfortably on a heap of mailbags that reached nearly to the roof of the fuselage. Judging by his flashing eyes and merry grin, present thrills were drowning the prospect of a bumpy crossing which otherwise would have obsessed him. As the plane flew low over the airport buildings before setting course for France we could see the machine-gunners squatting on the roofs behind their tripods and sandbags, like guns behind the butts waiting for the driven grouse. Fortunately for the occupants of the surrounding houses no birds came their way that afternoon.

Amidst the crowding anxieties about our own 'family' I was worried by an added responsibility, flung into my lap just as the plane was about to leave, a large and youthful one at that, as the following letter will testify:

> THE BRITISH COUNCIL,
> 3, HANOVER STREET,
> LONDON, W.1.
> 10th May 1940
>
> DEAR MR BASIL DEAN,
> Will you please take this letter as your authority from the British Council to receive the members of the Sadler's Wells Ballet on evacuation from Holland and Belgium, and to arrange for their safe conduct to England.
> Yours sincerely,
> A. J. S. WHITE
> *Secretary General*

Arras had the air of a country town at the end of the annual race-meeting, its sleepy life no longer stirred by the thousands of strangers in its midst, the shops no longer in cheerful conspiracy to circulate the additional money that had come their way. Now the troops were gone, and the shopkeepers had resumed their somnolence; even the civilians had left the streets. Might they be indoors packing their bags?

I lodged at the Hotel Univers, a charming inn of the eighteenth century or, maybe, earlier, built round the sides of an ancient courtyard paved with cobbles in the French way, with a large plane tree at one side of it. The interior, with its high, narrow passages, thin panelled doors and casement windows, was sufficiently old and dilapidated to gratify the taste of the most romantic American tourist.

I awoke on Whitsun morning to the sound of all the bells of the city ringing out in bright dissonance. Distant gunfire provided the contra-bass, and the high whine of the air-raid siren added to the clamour. By the time I was fully awake the warlike sounds had gone, leaving the peaceful Whitsun bells in possession of the sound-track. I got up and began to shave, using a little stainless steel mirror that I carried with me everywhere during the war years. This I tied with a shoelace to the knob of the shutters, where it swayed to and fro in the draught ever so gently and ever so annoyingly. There were cheerful British voices below me. I peered into the courtyard, bright in the spring sunshine. Two or three staff cars were drawn up to one side, the drivers lounging against the bonnets or sitting in the driving-seats, smoking cigarettes inside their cupped hands, waiting for their officers to finish breakfast. While I was looking out of the window more aircraft came over, but this time much nearer. The drivers began talking excitedly to one another and pointing up into the sky. I could not see what they were pointing at because of the overhanging eaves of the roof. Then I heard a loud Cockney voice shouting, "Blimey, there they are. Look out for the shrapnel, boys." One of the drivers disregarded the warning, so his Cockney friend shouted again, "Bill, don't be so bleeding silly, mate. It's shrap-nell!" I thought I could detect a pattering sound on some near-by roofs, as though very large hailstones were falling. I had been observing the scene with a certain detachment, for, like most civilians at that time, I had yet to learn that discretion was the better part of curiosity and that it is the bomb you do not hear that kills. But the disappearance of the drivers and the pattering on the rooftops reminded me there was no sense at all in standing in front of double windows during an air-raid. I hurried downstairs in search of coffee, one side of my face unshaven and a cut on my chin, vaguely conscious of an anticlimax in this first experience of an air-raid in the Second World War.

It was a relief to spend the morning at our headquarters, congratulating the commanding officer and his staff on the efficient working of the evacuation plan. Discussion on various matters of detail was interrupted every quarter of an hour or so by the droning of air-raid sirens and the popping of anti-aircraft guns. Presumably these were only German 'recce' planes keeping a watch on the movements of British transport going forward into Belgium.

"When are YOU proposing to move out?" I said to the commanding officer after one of these bursts of activity.

"I belong to G.H.Q.," he replied pompously. "Can't move without their authority. You mustn't give me orders," he added warningly. "We're not civilians like the artistes."

"Quite so," I said. "Suppose we go across to G.H.Q. and ask permission for you to move back? There's no sense in your being stuck up here now the artistes are hundreds of kilometres behind you. Besides, things seem to be warming up."

As in the streets of Arras, so at G.H.Q., the same atmosphere of activity abruptly suspended, only here upon a more intimate scale, as though a household had turned out to witness some unusual event just down the road. Gone were the busy staff officers and the aura of high-level decision that surrounded them. A lonely brigadier, some clerical sergeants packing up or destroying papers, an orderly or two disconsolately sweeping out the fire-grates were all that remained. The brigadier regarded me balefully, observing that entertainers were in the way at a time like this; they ought to be sent home or down to the L. of C., and he proposed to issue an order to that effect. He showed no surprise when told they had already gone, and agreed nonchalantly to the withdrawal of the military staff; it was one responsibility the less for him.

Any feeling of importance we may have had was effectively dispelled by this lack of official interest in our doings. In its place I felt a sickening sense of responsibility, which the written authority to withdraw, received by dispatch rider that afternoon, two days after the artistes had gone, did nothing to dispel. We began to plan the withdrawal of the entertainment posts: Nos. 1 and 2 to Boulogne, which for a hectic week or so became our Rear H.Q. The Post at Rheims, now No. 4, which had some small units of entertainment right in the Maginot Line, as well as some with the Saar Force, to be gradually withdrawn with its military personnel to join No. 5 in the south; No. 3 Post (which included the Administrative H.Q., Technical stores, Film Exchange and Accounts) to remain at Le Havre for the present.

In normal times these rearrangements would have been easily and quickly made. But now the gremlin of the military telephone reared its head and supervised our activities from a mysterious exchange in

Paris known as 'Table A.' (Its French pronunciation made it sound more mysterious.) This I assumed to be a portion of the French trunk system given over to operation by British Army Signals. If so, it was an example of miscegenation at its worst, the casualness of the French operators making triumphant union with British obtuseness, and the presiding gremlin encouraging the nuptials.

A civilian like myself was very liable to make Security mistakes while speaking on the military telephone. The only indication of such a transgression would be to find oneself cut off by the telephone censor—in midsentence more often than not. The abrupt termination, through one's own mistake, of a connexion it had possibly taken two hours to obtain was peculiarly exasperating. In any case the movements being planned that day were the responsibility of the O.C. So I followed his hour-long struggles with the gremlin with a mordant interest, even to the length of going with him at ten o'clock at night to the Arras central exchange (where the instrument panels were too heavy to throw across the room) in an endeavour to grip the attention of the mysterious 'Table A,' and to discharge my commission for the British Council by directing the Sadler's Wells Ballet to come through the British lines to Arras, whence I would undertake to get them home. I soon gave up that task as hopeless, and was relieved when I returned home to hear that the ballet had managed to get out of Holland at the last moment, although minus its scenery and baggage. Thus ended my brief responsibility for the safety of the famous company. The following morning I made a hurried dash to Rouen, already bursting at every concierge's lodge with weary and excited refugees. Here Madame Vernon had somehow managed to secure accommodation for the considerable concentration of artistes as well as two rooms in one of the hotels for our provisional headquarters, a delicate negotiation only concluded after her stream of voluble and forceful French had induced the protesting manager to submit. He held his return fire until my arrival, when I was received with similar volleys. My verbal artillery not being capable of equally rapid answer, I retired elsewhere.

3

The removal of the artistes from the area of immediate operations being safely accomplished, my thoughts turned back to Drury Lane, where the burden of responsibility was daily growing heavier. It was a shuttlecock existence: in France I worried about Drury Lane; at home I longed to be 'out there' sharing in the experiences.

The next day Richard and I drove very early in the morning to Glissé, hoping to pick up a plane for home. The airfield looked forlorn and deserted in the cold morning light; not a plane to be seen on its grass-covered runway; not a vehicle of any sort in the deep ruts of dried mud that surrounded the group of Nissen huts. Yet somewhere beyond the horizon war was raging viciously. As we stood there looking about us, the whispering in the long grass seemed to be full of rumour. A young officer who presently came out of one of the huts could tell us nothing. He had been left in charge of the field when the station commander was called forward. The A.D.L.S. was suspended; that he did know. Our chance to return home that way was gone. As to whether there would be an aircraft going to England later, "he really couldn't say; but even if there were he had no authority to put us on it." While we argued uncertainly a plane came in from England, loaded with young R.A.F. pilots returning from leave or sent over to replace casualties. They came tumbling out of the aircraft down the little tubular-iron ladder, carrying haversacks and over-night bags and wearing a pretence of boredom belied by the strained look in their eyes. They made straight for the operations hut and the telephone in search of further orders. Information was a scarce commodity everywhere in France in those first days of the real war. After waiting another hour or so in indecisive mood we motored to Amiens in the hope of catching a train to Calais.

Here Richard's peculiar combination of charm and assurance stood us in most admirable stead. He secured permits to board the last train from Paris to Calais that night. The coaches were crowded to suffocation with a distinguished company of officials and others scurrying for home: many passengers were standing in the carriages as well as the corridors. How Richard managed this I do not know, nor how he induced the Hôtel du Nord at Calais to reserve rooms for us, seeing that it had already officially closed its doors. When we arrived there it was after midnight. The night porter told us the only other guest was an Ambassador; it was for him and not for us the management had reluctantly consented to stay open, although the staff had been dismissed and the electric light cut off. Richard was soon engaged in a spirited bilingual conversation with the porter, whose resistance to Celtic charm melted like ice-cream in the sun. The Ambassador had gone early to bed, as he proposed to board the packet at an early hour. Richard, joking and laughing and flashing his white teeth, proceeded to arrange matters for our comfort, mesmerizing the night porter into finding us drinks, biscuits and cheese. Extracting a promise of an early call in the morning, we retired to undress by the light of our torches and to pass a comfortable night in two of the best rooms in the hotel. The other passengers from the train went on board the boat waiting in the harbour;

she was due to sail at 8 A.M. It was to be the last sailing, after which the cross-Channel service was closing down.

Unfortunately the porter forgot his commission to waken us, and it was half-past seven when I sat up and looked at my watch. As a person subject to train fever I viewed the prospect with grimness. I shouted to Richard next door. He remained irritatingly calm and collected, although he seemed literally to jump into his clothes.

"We'll catch the old tub, don't worry," he said, as he sauntered down the passage in search of his 'ancient' to give him a good wigging for the non-appearance of the coffee he had ordered. Ten minutes later Richard led the way to the quay, followed by the porter and a small boy carrying our luggage. It was 8.20 A.M. Yet the packet was still waiting, her rails lined with tired, anxious passengers, whose disdainful looks proclaimed their disgust that wealth and position had not protected them from an uncomfortable night. I observed with relief that the main gangway was still down waiting to receive—might it be us since every one else had embarked? Hundreds of pairs of eyes followed our progress along the deserted quay, up the gangway into the ship. As we drew near, sailors hurried forward to take the luggage, and Richard drew back deferentially to let me pass. No sooner had our feet touched the deck than the ship sprang to life: gangways were lifted, ropes cast off, and a whistle was blown. Soon we were hasting out of the harbour, the captain obviously nervous lest German aircraft should take it into their heads to pay Calais a breakfast visit.

The whole proceeding left me quite mystified. Noticing the deferential glances cast in our direction, I began to ask questions. Richard's replies were cryptic.

"How did you get them to wait for us?"

"I didn't."

"But . . ."

"The captain sent across to tell the Ambassador he was waiting, but that gentleman had already popped on board, so I said we wouldn't be long."

"My God, Richard, you've got a nerve."

"Well, well," said Richard with a grin. "Pity we missed that coffee."

4

As the situation worsened the artistes' relatives grew more and more anxious. The officials at Drury Lane were inundated with inquiries. Their replies varied according to temperament and the name of the depart-

ment to which inquiries were addressed. While the Drama Division became evasive and portentous, duly reflecting the high drama of events,
Transport Branch would reply laconically: "No boats in to-day." A one-
time music-hall soubrette was unlikely to have her fears assuaged if her
question as to the whereabouts of her tap-dancing daughter were met by
a cheery: "Search me, duckie," from the Variety Division. My own
answer to such questions was that of course everybody was safe and sound
in the care of our officers but, much as I should like to do so, I could not
say where for Security reasons. No one knew what a desperate prevarication that was.

A private responsibility was adding to my anxieties. My wife had begun
a series of broadcast concerts with the R.A.F. Central Band under Wing-
Commander O'Donnell from Arras on May 3, which was interrupted by
a brief attack of tonsillitis. On recovery she had insisted on returning to
Le Havre to join another ENSA party, and was still there. About a week
after my return I woke up suddenly one night, thinking I heard her calling
to me in a loud voice, as though she were in danger. I glanced at my
watch; it was 1 A.M. The message was so unmistakable that automatically
and without reflection I rang up the teleprint room and asked them to send
a signal through to Le Havre, instructing our H.Q. to return all artistes in
the area immediately. It was only as I set the receiver down that I realized
I had involuntarily given way to private anxiety. Was I morally justified?
Yes, for sure. At the present rate of German advance Le Havre would soon
be vulnerable; it was already a forward position, and we had been told to
move out of such places. By good fortune the message got through; it
resolved the doubts of the officer in charge, who was already contemplating the removal of the Stores and Film Exchange as well as the artistes.
The ENSA party that included my wife left Le Havre by the last boat out
of the port: and on the following day Frascati's Hotel, where they had been
staying, was partially demolished by a direct hit. On her return my wife
confessed that on the night in question she had suddenly lost her nerve,
found herself longing for me to call her home.

5

In company with every one else during those last days, I could do
nothing but wait, my mind agape at Giant Catastrophe in its mad rush for
the Channel Ports. Then, as the miracle of salvation began to disclose itself
on the Dunkirk beaches, I realized ENSA was missing an opportunity
for service. Although the Press references were very guarded it was
clear that the flood of rescued men pouring into the southern camps

raised serious problems of welfare. Here was where we could help. It was useless to bother the harassed War Office; we must act for ourselves.

At dawn on the morning of May 31 Stanley Bell and I set out by car for a quick tour of the camps in the Aldershot and Southern Commands. We visited first the R.A.F. Station at Halton and thence worked our way south and west. At Salisbury we separated, Stanley going one way, I the other. I had already told Drury Lane to telephone to all cinema managers in the south and west to open their cinemas at once, if they had not already done so of their own accord, and to keep them open from 10 A.M. to 10 P.M., giving non-stop film shows free until further notice. As each camp was visited the manager was told to set up *ad hoc* arrangements with his nearest neighbour for the exchange of film programmes. In many cases those who had projection experience took turn and turn about with the regular projectionists. Meanwhile, Stanley had told the Variety and Concert Party Sections to dispatch as many extra units of live entertainment as they could muster within the next twenty-four hours to the West Country by car, with orders to concentrate at Bristol. As the torrent of humanity increased (they could no longer be called troops, for they were without arms or unit formation of any kind; Frenchmen, Belgians and British in seemingly inextricable confusion, as they jostled one another in long lines in the dining-halls and canteens), the camp commandants gave orders for our theatres and cinemas to remain open at night for use as temporary sleeping accommodation. It was deeply moving to watch the serried rows of men, too exhausted either to laugh or applaud, dropping into deep sleep whilst George Formby and other favourites performed their antics on the screen.

Stanley and I met again that first evening in Bridport. The town was crammed to suffocation. In a small pub to which we had been directed for accommodation by a brother Mason of Stanley's we exchanged impressions and made further plans, listening to the seething soldiery (yes, that is the only adjective to use) expressing blasphemous resentment at what had happened to them. There was a typical 'Sergeant Troy' in the bar whose loud-mouthed criticism of the junior officers of his Ack-Ack unit in seizing the only available transport and making for the French coast, leaving their N.C.O.'s and men to fend for themselves, was gaining angry corroboration among his listeners. These dismayed men, savagely wounded in their pride, were seeking relief in bitter criticism of those set over them. We promised each other that whilst the war lasted we would never speak of what we had seen and heard that night, and we never did. Throughout those visits to the camps, and colouring all my thoughts, was a feeling of joy that in tiny measure we had been permitted to serve the troops in the aftermath of their escape.

6

During my hurried dash to Rouen I had held a staff conference, at which I suggested that the entertainment should be reorganized in mobile columns, able to keep close behind the troops as they moved about the country and ready for use when called upon; each column to consist of both 'live' and cinema units, and to have its own military personnel, including at least one commissioned officer in charge. Although our men had neither the transport nor the technical equipment nor the necessary staff experience, a start was made with the new system by splitting up into small groups two large parties that remained in France after the bulk of the live entertainment had gone home (namely, Will Hay's Empire Music Hall and the Strolling Players), and using them like the sing-song units, which also had stayed behind. In company with the mobile cinemas they were attached for periods of a few days at a time to the regrouped formations and to the fresh troops from Britain, including the 51st Highland Division and the Canadians.

The mobile cinemas were a great boon as they provided an up-to-the-minute service of relaxation. The operators, inspired by the welcome they received, enjoyed driving their vans into villages in the most forward positions, unrolling the screens, switching on the generators and giving a show within a matter of minutes. One or two of them had some narrow escapes. In one case, at a village called Vitry-le-François, our operator was rolling up his screen at one end of the village as German tanks were entering at the other.

I was anxious to see how our plan for mobile columns was working out in practice, but the Authorities flatly refused my application to return. On June 10, G.H.Q. requested all female artistes to retire from the country— the last of the A.T.S. would be leaving that day—but the male artistes should stay as entertainment was still badly needed. Before they could be regrouped the authorities at home intervened, and ordered all 'live' entertainment to return immediately.

7

The original intention in planning our retirement had been to keep out of the way of the advancing British troops; it proved fortunate that the scheme also had the effect of turning the thoughts of our staff away from

the Channel Ports—where they would inevitably have been caught up in
the military retreat, with severe casualties as an added probability. Nevertheless we did suffer one casualty, Lieutenant Hobson, a young accounts
officer. He had been sent up to Arras from the head accounts office at Le
Havre to deal with the increased volume of accountancy in the forward
areas.

Hobson was a pleasant, fair-haired young man to whom everything
happened with such tragic suddenness that, looking back, it seems as if
Fate had determined to rush him headlong to his destiny. He had just
qualified as an accountant when he was specially commissioned and sent
out by NAAFI to augment our inadequate Accounts Branch. Assured of
his commission, he had married before going out to France. When No. 1
Post was closed down, still goaded by Fate, he had volunteered to remain
behind with his clerk to settle the artistes' bills at the various hotels and
any other outstanding accounts in the town. This work was not finished
until Tuesday midnight: too late to rejoin the main body at Rouen,
according to instructions. As he had given up his billet, Hobson decided
to spend the night at the Hôtel Univers and go to Rouen the next day.
In that decision Fate played the ace of spades, for towards morning the
hotel was bombed, and the wing in which Hobson and, as it so happened,
a King's Messenger were sleeping suffered a direct hit. Both were killed
outright. The only means of identification of Hobson were his fair hair
and a pocket-book containing a photograph of his young wife. . . .
The commanding officer concluded his brief report on the matter as
follows: "In the same action the O.C. lost all his personal kit."

8

The majority of our uniformed staff had neither the military training
nor the ingrained discipline essential to the safety of a fighting soldier in
retreat. The reports show that they came through the ordeal magnificently. As I scan them and reflect upon the swiftness of the catastrophe it
seems remarkable that this heterogeneous collection of cinema technicians
and theatrical managers dressed up in uniform did not scatter like chaff
before the rampaging enemy. Instead, they kept their heads and clung to
their cherished equipment, their cinema vans and films and mobile stages,
as the disciplined Guardsman clings to his rifle. This may have been due
partly to the instinctive loyalty of all show people towards 'the show,' but
it also reflects the highest credit upon the commanding officer and the
handful of men with previous military experience who worked with
him.

The pillar-to-post retreat involved the evacuation by sea of over 200 artistes and the packing, unpacking, repacking and transport of many tons of valuable film and technical machinery and equipment. Yet entertainment did not cease entirely, and by the end of the first week in June 240 ENSA shows were once more being scheduled each week, two-thirds being film programmes.

The staff had a rough time during their trek to the south, frequently sleeping in cinema vans or on the portable stages, because the towns and villages where they stopped en route were crowded with refugees, and any spare time that might have been given to a search for accommodation was used in giving impromptu shows to troops on the move. During the course of one of these jostlings the personnel of one Entertainment Post handed in their spare underclothing to the official laundry over-night. The corporal sent to retrieve them the following morning found that the laundry had been evacuated and the underclothing with it. There followed a plaintive request to Drury Lane to be allowed to spend up to 100 francs per man on new underclothing, "as the O.C. is anxious that the men should not become verminous." This seemed a creditable ambition.

Although the conditions were tough, the projectionists, the 'song paraders' from Blackpool and the managers from all those places where the more vociferous forms of show business are concocted, revelled in the opportunities for the display of their raffish humour. Nevertheless, the commanding officer, determined that his little army should not be regarded in a Falstaffian light by the Authorities, decided that his men must be capable of self-defence, so their spare time was filled in with vigorous rifle and bayonet drill. It is difficult to believe these warlike preparations would have been of much avail, in view of what we now know of the speed and efficiency of the German war machine, but at least they showed that the spirit was willing.

Any attempt to direct the staff overseas from London was out of the question. Nevertheless, I tried by a series of teleprints and telephone messages to keep myself in touch with what was going on. Occasional messages from the commanding officer, written on pages torn from his field service notebook and brought back by concert party managers, were a help, and so, too, were the odd scraps of news picked up here and there. But suspense grew unbearable as the 51st Division surrendered and the *Lancastria* was sunk. The last report to reach me from the O.C. had been too cheerful: "The mails are straightening out [*sic*]; reports will be dispatched daily in future: the last of the artistes are gone, but could they be sent out again soon? And more mobile cinemas, please!" . . . All this confident assertion, and then—silence.

The gaps in the story were not closed until all were safely home and the commanding officer had made his final report:

> I received instructions to evacuate the country that night. The port given was No. 463, St. Malo. . . . Upon arrival at St. Malo I was informed that personnel could be accepted but the equipment would have to be dumped. In view of the fact that this unit had up to that moment not lost any equipment and thereby earned a reputation, I was reluctant to accept this instruction. . . . I was informed that if I cared to risk the journey with my personnel and vehicles to Brest, 190 miles away, I would be able to get everything back to England. This was put to the officers and men, and every one volunteered to make for Brest. . . . Upon arrival at Brest I was informed that there were only two passenger boats in the harbour and there was little likelihood of any cargo boats arriving to take off vehicles and equipment. . . . After some discussion with the Captain and ship's officers I managed to get the personnel on board, and it is worthy of note that this was only done through [their] being pulled through a hole in the ship's side. Officers were the last to go on board and the Adjutant climbed up the ship's side. The party eventually arrived at Plymouth on the morning of June 17, when I telephoned to you. . . .

The work of the projectionists continued even during the Channel crossing because by some ingenious means or other our 'indomitables' managed to smuggle two of their mobiles into one of the ships, where they gave non-stop film shows—demanding as admission money a share of the rifled NAAFI stores with which the troops on board had thoughtfully provided themselves. Packets of cigarettes were high in the scale of currency, but bully beef, cheese and chocolate were higher still, for our staff had had nothing to eat since they left Rennes twenty-four hours before.

Our contingent in that overcrowded ship comprised eighty officers, N.C.O.'s and O.R.'s, and 'one civilian, female,' Madame Vernon. She arrived in England in the clothes she stood up in, and with no other belongings at all, except what she had been able to stuff into a haversack. After twenty-four hours' rest the military personnel assembled on the stage of Drury Lane Theatre, where it was my privilege to thank them for the inspiring manner in which they had upheld the name of ENSA. Madame Vernon was not there; she was out with my wife, buying herself some new clothes, a necessary preoccupation that prevented her sharing in the general satisfaction at an honourable anticlimax.

CHAPTER TWELVE

MR BEVIN JOINS THE QUEUE

WHEN Ernest Bevin joined the Government as Minister of Labour and National Service and, in company with the other Labour leaders, called for an all-out effort from factory and workshop and farm, he let it be known that his plans to stimulate output included music in the factories. Here was a chance of carrying out some of the promises made in that first pamphlet of ours. On May 27, 1940, the *Daily Telegraph* published a letter over the joint signatures of Seymour Hicks and myself, announcing ENSA's intention to inaugurate a service of lunch-time concerts for munition workers, wherever approved by the authorities. The concerts would last for half an hour each and be given inside the factory areas, so as not to compete with commercial enterprise, thus honouring the undertaking we had given at the beginning of the war to the professional associations.

We did not consult NAAFI before writing the letter. We wanted to get the idea over first and argue about it afterwards. The day before publication I mentioned the matter to the General Manager. His reply was non-committal. But on the following morning I was handed an official communication that was distinctly minatory in tone. Amongst other things it pointed out that the Corporation could not permit any interference with my duties as its Director of Entertainments. In reply I stated that I had not accepted the position of a whole-time employee of NAAFI, that ENSA had been formed for certain national purposes and that, whilst I would see that all the Corporation's rules and regulations were obeyed, particularly with regard to the expenditure of funds, I should resist any interference with ENSA's liberty of action in the professional field.

At the time that our letter was published we had no preconceived ideas as to how the factory concerts should be organized. The first step was to write and ask Bevin if he would support our proposal in general terms. This drew an immediate request for a talk from Godfrey Ince,[1] the civil servant closest to Bevin at the time, who, without any prevarication or

[1] Later Sir Godfrey Ince, G.C.B., Permanent Secretary to the Ministry of Labour and National Service.

conversational manœuvre, told me the Minister was interested and would like further details: what kind of entertainments were proposed and how often? Had the Minister of Supply, Herbert Morrison, been approached about the Royal Ordnance Factories? There were strings of questions to be considered and answered before a complete scheme could be drawn up; but it was evident from our conversation that this might become an important part of ENSA's work.

The broad outlines of the scheme began to take shape in my mind even while we talked, but on my way back to Drury Lane I was assailed with the usual doubts. Unlike the military side, all concerned with the factory scheme would be starting from scratch: audiences, factory managements, the Ministry and ourselves. A great deal of information would be needed —about the factories, their size, location, distance from town centres, means of transport, existing or prospective facilities in the canteens or recreation halls (*i.e.*, whether they had stages or space in which to erect them), the times of the meal-breaks and so on—before a general plan of organization could be worked out. Above all, we should want to know whether the factory managements would welcome the entertainments.

The first question was, who was to pay? Obviously NAAFI funds could not be used. Beyond realizing that fact, I had given the problem little thought, preferring to wait and see how far the Minister was prepared to go towards taking us under his wing.

My precipitancy in allowing ENSA to start work without a separate legal and financial existence was now coming home to roost. We discovered to our chagrin that NAAFI objected to an organization created under its wing being used at all to entertain civilians. Since it regarded ENSA as an integral part of itself, the Corporation had no authority to approve a development that lay outside its terms of reference. Furthermore, it did not understand why we wanted to bother our heads in the matter; there was enough to be done already. And the possibility that ENSA might grow into a fully fledged department free of NAAFI leading-strings, its publicity value lost to the Corporation, was distasteful to certain senior officials. However, since we had in no wise abandoned our original ideas, it was essential to combat this attempt at restriction. Future development would be impossible once NAAFI acquired psychological as well as material dominion over our affairs. The former we never conceded, and we hoped to escape from the latter eventually.

The Minister shied at the major financial operation that virtual separation from NAAFI would involve at this crisis of the war. I therefore suggested he should adopt the principle of 'paying for what he had,' plus a percentage for overhead expenses: a simple arrangement that would

I

have the effect of reducing NAAFI's administrative costs. As the matter was urgent, the Treasury agreed to this unorthodox procedure, but insisted that NAAFI should continue to act as bankers. The arrangement saved a great deal of time and money. In effect, it meant that henceforward Civil Departments authorized to provide entertainment for war-workers could indent upon NAAFI for ENSA entertainment. Once again we had to turn aside from our search for independence in order to shoulder the immediate burden. *THE MINISTER WANTED ENTERTAINMENT NOW!*

2

Welfare supervision in the munition factories was just then coming into being, for which purpose the Ministry of Labour had opened twenty divisional centres. It was decided to make a start at these and at the Royal Ordnance Factories. This would heap enough on to the ENSA plate for the time being. Our staff were to contact the Ministry of Labour officials at these centres, who would give them lists of the factories to be visited. I drew up a form of questionnaire to be completed in respect of each factory. There was opposition from some of them, mostly those known to be backward in their labour relations, a condition that often accompanied the most arduous work. Such factories produced a heavy crop of negatives to my first question: "Do you desire to receive lunch-time concerts from ENSA?"

As the flood of completed forms poured into the secretariat the magnitude of the new task took on the proportions of a nightmare. I particularly remember one lovely summer week-end spent in my stuffy office with two loyal secretaries, sorting and collating the information, while downstairs Stanley Bell worked hard upon one of his beloved charts that was to set out in diagrammatized form the organization as we conceived it. I hardened my heart against the longing glances of the girls at the bright sunshine filtering through the dusty window while they bent perspiringly over their typewriters. Above their heads the old-fashioned office clock was ticking away the hours of lost leisure. It was no use; the work had to be done.

I had decided to base the plan of organization upon existing military commands and areas, the only difference being that for our purposes the areas would not be known by their military names but be numbered consecutively from John o' Groats to Land's End. Each area was given a combination of letters which I worked out by combining the first and last letters of the alphabet and working through it in that way. As there were twenty-six military areas this fitted quite well. Each factory in each of these coded areas was given a number. Thus, a factory might have a code number of BY 12. This was to meet the requirements of Security, which did not wish the names of factories and their locations to be mentioned in correspondence. As each area came into the scheme an organizer would be installed in a small office with a clerk, a typewriter and a telephone. There he would direct the day-to-day work of the artistes and maintain contact with the Labour Welfare officials and the factories. Wherever possible organizers would be given offices in the existing Labour Exchanges to save expense.

3

The entertainments were divided into three classes. Scheme 'A,' by far the largest, consisted of half-hour entertainments given in the lunch- and supper-breaks, so as to cover both day and night shifts. To begin with, each factory on the Ministry's approved list was visited by one party each week. In many cases a party worked two factories on the one day, so the work was not light. When the industrial output was at its highest, in the years '43 and '44, the ration was stepped up to two parties each week in the case of factories doing the most strenuous work. This entailed the use of nearly 200 parties on Scheme 'A' alone. Scheme 'B' consisted of con- certs corresponding to the Category 'B' entertainments for the troops, given to workers in lonely districts who had no other facilities for enter- tainment. The same admission charges were made as in the case of the Services, entertainments being given in the Miners' Welfare Institutes, wherever miners were included in the scheme, and in recreation halls run by the Hostels Corporation, many of which were fitted with admirable stages.[1] The third Scheme, designated 'A/B,' comprised similar entertain- ments to those falling under Scheme 'A,' but given to war-workers whose conditions of work did not make it possible for them to assemble in a canteen. Such were the steel men in South Wales and the ironstone workers in the Cleveland district of Yorkshire. Later on a considerable service of mobile cinemas, showing not only entertainment films but propaganda subjects made for the Ministry of Information, was added for more remote factories, for lonely building-sites, and for the Women's Land Army.

The half-hour parties were similar in size and composition to the sing- song units devised for the Army, but somehow that title did not seem suit- able for crowded factory audiences, hurriedly swallowing their meals while they listened. Besides, the Minister might not think he was getting

[1] Our Equipment Division laid out the stage lighting plans for these hostels and provided much of the material.

his money's worth! One day some one came into my office with a grouse. He'd too many of these "bloody ensatainments" to get together. Couldn't he do something bigger? He glared at me, expecting a return broadside. But I told him he had invented an excellent name, and we would adopt it forthwith. He was so astonished that he forgot to grouse any more. So all the small parties became known by that name, with the words Military and Labour suffixed for purposes of classification.

Transport was undertaken by the factories, an assembly-point for the artistes being agreed with the ENSA Area Office. As the service grew more extensive the factories found their transport obligations increasingly difficult to fulfil. So NAAFI bought vans and coaches on the account of the Ministry, and the organizers were given driver-assistants to run them and to help in the offices. The vans had a distinctive appearance, with the word 'Ensatainments'—copied from my handwriting after the transport manager had playfully asked me to write the word out for him on a piece of paper, pretending he could not spell it—painted on the sides, together with an admirably designed poster by Denis Wreford, announcing 'Ministry of Labour Concerts' against a background of guns and aeroplanes.

4

Bevin was no man for delay, once his mind was made up. Before I submitted the plan of organization he had already pushed on one side NAAFI's objections and obtained Cabinet approval. Also, he had spoken to Morrison, whom I was to see immediately to obtain his formal consent to the inclusion of the Royal Ordnance Factories.

I had not met Herbert Morrison for several years, not since a chance encounter at the Labour Party Summer School at Easton Lodge. Now I found him occupying a small, unimposing room in a new block of offices in John Street, Adelphi, that had replaced the row of lovely Adam houses, where, during the middle twenties, I had my offices on the first floor of Number 5. (Archibald Batty, the actor, and his wife and an extremely noisy baby occupied the flat above.) The front room with a beautiful Adam ceiling, its centre medallion carefully restored and painted in palest green flecked with gold, and the walls and deep window embrasures pine-panelled, gave me surroundings in accord with that happy period of my career. Now in its place there was a concrete box with typewriters, telephones and filing cabinets; a film setting for American Big Business perhaps, but it did not suit Morrison at all. He appeared to be much overworked, as he clutched his forehead in perplexity. "Now, what do *you* want?" he said, without pausing to acknowledge my greeting. Relief spread over his face when he learned that all I wanted was approval of a scheme for which he would have no responsibility.

There were the usual alarums and excursions in the profession, when it became known that we were going to run an officially sponsored entertainment service for the factories. On July 9 Walter Payne, on behalf of the Entertainments Protection Association, a loose combination of all the managerial bodies, sent a telegram to the Minister, protesting that such entertainments, wherever given, "will seriously jeopardize employment in and stability of this industry." Seymour and I pointed out that all the theatrical trade unions and managerial associations were represented on the ENSA Central Committee, which, at a meeting on the previous day, had agreed unanimously that ENSA should undertake the scheme. We need not have worried. The Minister rejected the managerial representations out of hand; and the work began.

5

The first concert was given in one of the canteens at Woolwich Arsenal on July 22. The Minister had promised to be present, but he could not leave Whitehall before noon, and it took half an hour to get to Woolwich. The concert was due to go on the air at 12.30, so this was cutting things rather fine. To find out the short cuts Stanley Bell 'went over the course' beforehand with my driver, and on the morning of the concert rode in a pilot car just ahead of us. During the drive I talked rapidly to Bevin about our plans, and all that we hoped to do. He made no comment; just sat there, thinking of other things. All the new Labour Ministers wore a rather pompous air of responsibility in those days. While this fittingly proclaimed their honesty of purpose, a dash of 'Melbournism' might have helped them occasionally to throw off their cares. As we drove through the gates of the Arsenal, Bevin suddenly asked me what he should say. Pressure of work was so great upon him that he could not give his mind to any fresh task until it was immediately in front of him. I was flustered by this unexpected question at the last minute. Already little knots of workers were hurrying towards the canteen. Then a phrase jumped out at me like an advertising slide on the screen. "Tell them it's to maintain the rhythm of the job." The look of weary abstraction on Ernie's face disappeared as he clambered out of the car. "That's it," he murmured. "The rhythm of the job."

Seymour was supporting me loyally in this new essay, although, organization not being one of his strong points, he had decided to confine himself to the collection of suitable artistes, of whom large numbers would be needed. For this opening occasion he had arranged a special programme with Joan Cross, Will Fyffe, Arthur Salisbury's quintette, and himself to act as compère. When Bevin saw the rows of excited faces and heard the tuning up of the little orchestra in readiness for the broadcast and the glad cries of "Hallo, Ernie!" almost drowned by the loud clatter of plates and dishes being hurriedly taken away for washing up, a glint came into his eyes; and the instinct of showmanship, never entirely absent from the politician's make-up, began to assert itself. I felt he wanted to compère the show himself. Fortunately I was able to reassure him that his speech at the end would be included in the broadcast. (He was to have his fun later on when he compèred some programmes for the B.B.C. from his native district of Bristol, not without raised eyebrows from Ministerial colleagues.) The broadcast gave the scheme a fine send-off with the public, in spite of the fact that the two iron tables on which Bevin stood to make his speech went 'pong-pong' every time he shifted his weight, so that over the air it sounded as though he were being most rudely interrupted.

6

When Seymour and I first made our proposals to the Ministry of Labour, C.E.M.A. had already given some concerts of classical music under private arrangements with certain factories. These had been sufficiently successful to surprise those who had remained sceptical of any genuine love of serious music among the masses. CEMA had neither the staff nor the administrative experience to undertake the far-flung national programme which Bevin contemplated. This was something of a relief to me because, although CEMA had got in first and I was not prepared to indulge in 'body-snatching,' our own intentions in this matter had been disclosed long ago in my pamphlet.

Throughout the war years I used to meet Bevin fairly regularly on Saturday afternoons in the hot room of the Turkish bath, a place where it was difficult to observe formality. He soon put me on Christian-name terms with himself. At these vaporized meetings I used to report progress, and received much wise advice in exchange. It was during one of the first of these encounters that Ernie confided to me that he thought CEMA's early efforts were "too 'ighbrow!"

Let me admit at once that the average CEMA party was of a higher standard than our average. But our parties came to be numbered by the dozen, whereas CEMA provided but few. When the area organizers sent the CEMA parties to the rougher works the cacophony of kitchen sounds proved too great a handicap after the silence and attention of

Queen's Hall, and the artistes suffered from a disastrous lack of appreciation. This our area organizers liked to exaggerate, which encouraged George Smith in his pursuit of mediocrity. In time these avoidable mistakes became fewer, but they left their mark upon the relations between the two organizations. Eventually, in response to Miss Glasgow's request, CEMA was allowed to select its own factory dates, notifying our organizers beforehand so that room could be made for them on the official allocation lists.

Out of that first contact there grew up a general impression that, whereas ENSA might be a large, perhaps over-large, purveyor to the lowest common denominator of taste, CEMA was synonymous only with the highest artistic integrity. Maynard Keynes, the Chairman of CEMA, did little to counteract the misapprehension. In fact, it suited his policy to encourage it, as subsequent events proved. The rivalry was a useful mental spur to our efforts, and the sections responsible for our factory parties were under constant fire from 'upstairs' whenever cheap and nasty material made its appearance in their programmes. Nevertheless, it was irksome to find ourselves regarded as the chain-store of the concert world while CEMA dealt only with the custom-built trade. We had our exclusive counters, too, for the display of the finest musical wares, but we did not waste time preening ourselves so much; we went out into the market-place, amidst the rough and tumble of common living, in search of converts to good spirits and the common weal.

7

The two men responsible for the day-to-day running of the scheme were both members of the multitudinous family of Smith, George of that name representing ENSA, and F. W. H. Smith, C.I.E., a senior official of the Ministry of Labour. They established a basis of mutual confidence, so that the service was developed with great speed and an almost complete absence of official obstruction. George came to us from the hard-bitten world of Wardour Street, where he had made a considerable reputation by producing those deplorable quota 'quickies' so economically that the standard price of £1 per foot of film shown on the screen, which was all the American distributors could be induced to pay for them, returned him a comfortable profit.

He had promoted the old adage, "Take care of the pence and the pounds will take care of themselves," into a whole philosophy of life, in the pursuit of which his æsthetic standards may have suffered damage but his commercial practice had been exact, not to say parsimonious, an estimable trait when it comes to the expenditure of public money. He spent his week-ends at his home in the country, indulging his passion for turning things to good account. On Monday mornings his office at Drury Lane resembled a miniature Covent Garden: flowers, fruit, vegetables, chickens, an occasional duck, and, above all, eggs, were all to be had there—at a price!—to the profit both of the producer and his customer. I remember one autumn morning, encountering George in one of the corridors of the theatre, carrying a basket stacked to the brim with some remarkably fine bunches of grapes. When I asked him how he managed to grow such fine fruit he replied in a singularly humourless voice that he supposed it was because he always relieved himself against his vines.

George Smith did a loyal job for ENSA, working incredibly long hours every week for all the years of the war, a remarkable feat of endurance, seeing that he reached his seventieth birthday while he was with us. He established the closest contact with the area organization throughout the country, and insisted upon the most meticulous reporting of every incident, toward and untoward. Ultimately he became so devoted to these Ensatainments that all his geese became swans. His passionate defence of indifferent parties because they cost a few pounds less than their fellows was an understandable loyalty towards his own philosophy, but a betrayal of ENSA standards that had some harmful repercussions.

8

The type of entertainment calculated to give the maximum relaxation within the allotted half-hour and to overcome the competition of heavily shod feet stumping over bare concrete had to be discovered by a process of trial and error. In general we found that comic stories and patter were as much out of place as the ultra-refinement of some of the CEMA artistes. Even when a successful formula for the lunch-time concert had been evolved it was difficult to prevent it from becoming stereotyped or dull by constant reproduction, a problem that must dog the footsteps of many a B.B.C. producer.

The standards of the parties varied. In certain cases artistes were slack, which threw more work upon the conscientious ones. It must have been during the autumn of 1940 that I visited an engineering works in the Leeds Area which was turning out heavy shell-cases in great numbers. A director of the works invited me to walk through the engineering shops while we were waiting for the lunch-hour. He first introduced me to the manageress of the canteen, who asked with a certain air of mystery whether I had ever tasted real Yorkshire pudding, to which I replied with a tactful negative. Before there was time to appreciate the significance of her question I was led away to the shops. . . . At the machines women had replaced the men. Watching them at work, their faces drawn with fatigue, their oily hands guiding and controlling the ruthless power, I thought— these women are the real heroes. Just then there was a muttered impreca- tion and a hoarse cry of "Mind tha'sel" as a tiny slip of a woman nearly knocked me flat with a trolley-load of shell-cases. This was no place for romantic reflections! Besides, it was time to go and inspect our own war effort.

The canteen was packed: rows of faces, shining, work-tired faces on all sides, united in a simple expression of anticipation. Then in between the narrow dining-tables, dodging the canteen waitresses, sniffing the food-scented air, came the artistes, five minutes late, the women in untidy slacks (women of a certain shape and age should take a backward glance at themselves in the mirror before adopting male dress) and the men in mufflers and caps. They made their way to the piano on the little plat- form with a self-conscious air of indifference to the hearty applause they were given.

They were not an attractive party, the raucous comedian perfunctorily snapping up his 'feed' lines from the vamping pianist while his nostrils dilated at the smell of food from the adjacent kitchen; the faded soprano with over-large dentures whose efforts to look pleasing only met with uncomprehending stares; the baritone with an air of Blackpool about him. Their lack of talent could be forgiven, but their casual regard for the eager audience was surely the crowning sin! To say that I 'saw red' is merely to beggar description with a cliché. I left the works, feeling so humiliated that I forgot to thank the cook for the lightest and tastiest Yorkshire pudding I had ever eaten.

After this occurrence I issued circular instructions that may have given offence in some quarters but were definitely needed in others: in all cases afternoon frocks or stage costumes must be worn by the women, and costume or evening clothes by the men. The company must remain seated at the back of the platform, and not come on one by one after tiresome intervals which meant the loss of the audience's attention. Since the enter- tainments were part of a national plan to boost the war effort it was un- necessary for compères to tell the audience of the sacrifices they were making to entertain them. Finally, I did my utmost to curb the detestable practice of saying "thank you" after each song or item in a programme, and the even more infuriating trick of reacting to weak applause by saying, "Thanks—both of you."[1]

[1] Comment: At a concert given to 1500 workpeople in the Manchester district a workman jumped on the stage at the end, and, waving his cap, yelled, "Three cheers for the audience," amid the delighted shouts of his pals.

Not all the concerts were given by Ensatainment parties. Very early in the scheme the Minister obtained permission from the War Office for the use of well-known military bands. We paid for the transport and made a nominal contribution to the band funds for each performance; the factories provided the men with a hot meal. There was the usual protest from the Musicians' Union, most troublesome of all the theatrical trades unions, who claimed that the soldier-musicians should be hired at ordinary professional rates. The claim was refused, and many famous military bands provided a useful change in our weekly bill of fare. Stars could not often be spared to take part in the scheme because it would have been an uneconomical use of their time; but their appearances were more frequent when we arranged factory broadcasts in collaboration with the B.B.C. Sometimes radio favourites like Bebe Daniels and Ben Lyon, when they were broadcasting from Bristol, would lend a hand; and George Formby spent a memorable week at the beginning of September 1940 at the huge Ordnance Factory at Chorley, in Lancashire, giving concerts at midday and midnight in each of the various canteens in turn, always before different audiences, which gives an idea of the size of the place.

Although the entertainments were not all of a high quality, the regular break with routine, the chorus singing and general air of jollification, the looking forward and the looking back, brought succour to the tired human spirit. There was unanimous testimony from every type of factory and every class of war-worker, from the vast ordnance factories to the humblest party of Land Army Girls, that this was so. One factory, doing particularly tiresome and monotonous work, had a superintendent with a statistical turn of mind: he claimed a definite improvement of five per cent. in output after each ENSA concert. And Dr Jacques wrote from Chorley to say that both factory output and food consumption at the canteens went up after each series of concerts, providing "an index of the effects of the concerts on the minds and bodies of the workers."

If ENSA had not given a single entertainment for H.M. Forces, its existence would have been fully justified by its work for the Ministry of Labour and National Service, to say nothing of the Ministries of Agriculture and of Fuel and Power, who later joined the queue.

9

One day I was asked to go and see Mr Bevin immediately; he had a new job for us, urgent and secret. As I hurried down to the Ministry I could not resist a feeling of pride at receiving this personal summons. The more

ENSA was treated as a public service the better. When I arrived the Minister was too busy to see me. In his stead Godfrey Ince told me that serious difficulties had arisen in Orkney over the defence works now being constructed around Scapa Flow. The civilian contractors were behind schedule. The Admiralty said it was because they could not get enough labour to work there. Most of it came from Eire, and the men so disliked the lonely conditions—there was a total lack of entertainment, for one thing —that few of them could be induced to stay beyond their initial contract of service. So there was a constant ebb and flow of casual labour, which was causing dangerous delays in the work of safeguarding the anchorage. The Minister wanted to know what ENSA could do to help.

The works were scattered about the various islands in highly secret locations, so the problem of administration would not be easy. It would be further complicated by the storms that were sometimes severe enough to immobilize all road and sea transport for days together. Also, there was an embarrassing absence of accommodation for female artistes in the islands. This had severely hampered Evelyn Laye's special concerts for the Navy. Nevertheless, I told Godfrey Ince ENSA would undertake the job— provided hostel accommodation was built for the artistes, and suitable buildings made available in which to give the performances.

Taking Stanley Bell with me, I went off to see things for myself. Stanley knew the conditions of Scapa well from his service with the Grand Fleet during the First World War. We left Hendon on August 28 in a special aircraft of the Fleet Air Arm, and flew up the East Coast at a height of about 500 feet so as to keep out of the way of marauding enemy planes. It was a fine morning in early autumn with high white clouds floating lazily in the pale blue sky and a soft haze over the sun. Soon we were skimming along the Yorkshire dales, sometimes flying so low between the folds in the hills that the sheep cropping the clover grass looked up with surprise at our intrusion, and, doing so, let us see the lustre of their eyes before they ran away, bleating with alarm. The wide sky seemed empty and tenantless, when suddenly round a bend in the hills came another low-flying aircraft, heading straight for us. Our pilot jerked his aircraft 90° to starboard, and I was flung violently out of my seat. Really, hedge-hopping is a most unpleasant mode of flight, I thought, but there! flying instructions must be obeyed.

We landed at the Fleet Air Arm station at Kirkwall at four o'clock. In the mess we were surrounded by officers and civilians who pelted us with questions, mobbed us in fact, for were we not the harbingers of the long-awaited entertainment? Glamorous girls! Pretty dresses! Lights! Women and song, in fact; the Navy to provide the rum.

That afternoon there was time only for a hurried glance at the Temperance Hall, Kirkwall, then being fitted up as a cinema for the Navy, before hurrying on to Hoy, where the Admiral Commanding Orkney and Shetlands[1] (known as ACOS for short) was awaiting us. He gave us a Naval welcome which included an excellent dinner. After the port and the usual loyal toast the Admiral invited me to explain my mission in detail, as he had only received the briefest Admiralty signal. I had scarcely time to open my mouth before his 'flags,' an officer of the R.N.V.R., remarked that ENSA was not required at Scapa: the Services were quite capable of organizing entertainments for themselves. This momentarily winded me, but before I had time to reply the Admiral went pink in the face and ordered 'flags' off to bed in his best quarterdeck manner. The young man's departure, although momentarily embarrassing, enabled the conversation to range more freely. ACOS ended the evening in a state of enthusiasm, and made a signal summoning senior representatives of all the Services and of the civilian authorities to collaboration.

Two days were spent in battling through mud and rain and oh! such wind (anyone who has crossed Hooton Bay in a barge in a rough sea knows well what I mean) to visit all the locations where entertainment was badly needed. It was apparent that each Service was struggling to act independently of the other. Co-ordination of the entertainment for the general good had not occurred to anyone, or, at least, none felt it his duty to propose it.

I put forward my plan to a full-dress conference of all concerned, summoned by ACOS, before I left Scapa. This was simply to provide a co-ordinated service of live and film entertainment which all could share. The Navy and the Army were to convert or make available buildings within their control for use as theatres and cinemas. With the aid of the civilian contractors the Admiralty was to build and equip two hostels which NAAFI would run. The Corporation would also be responsible for finance and accountancy, but the ultimate cost would be borne by the Ministry of Labour and National Service. Finally, it was to be known as the Orkney Entertainment Scheme, and run by one of our experienced officers in collaboration with a local entertainment committee.

There was a certain amount of reluctance on the Navy's part about sharing with the others; but Admiral Binney let it be known that officers who opposed the scheme would incur his displeasure. The civilians were entirely dependent upon invitations to Service entertainments; so I knew we could depend upon them to build the hostel accommodation with speed. The promises of the Army representatives to requisition premises

[1] Admiral Sir T. H. Binney, K.C.B., K.C.M.G., D.S.O.

and help with transport were less certain of fulfilment, but at least there was unanimity in the general enthusiasm.

Both the Admiralty and the Ministry of Labour accepted the proposals. The hostels were built and equipped in record time, and Major J. H. Haygarth, our senior officer from France took over the initial organization.

Through Mr Bevin's intervention we now had the opportunity, which I had long desired, of working under a Cabinet Minister to whom we would be directly responsible for results, and who was not concerned to restrict our outlook. If the Orkney Scheme could be made to work satisfactorily, might it not become the prototype for a co-ordinated system of national-service entertainment to cover the whole of Britain? This would result in the saving of millions of pounds of public money, to say nothing of manpower and commodities of which the country might shortly be in need. At last the way seemed clear for those larger plans of which I had dreamed. Much depended upon the success of the prototype.

Tail Feathers . . .

One of the first stars to visit Orkney under the Scheme was Leslie Henson. On his way to the cinema to arrange the opening performance he met a padre going in the same direction. "First house or second?" he asked cheerily. "Both," replied the padre gloomily. "It's my duty."

During the course of his month's stay Leslie took some of his party to a remote location where the men were said to be desperate for relaxation. It was a long and circuitous journey. They arrived to find the troops had been moved out that afternoon, except for one old soldier and three young recruits left to maintain the site. Somewhat dashed in spirits, Leslie decided to give the show. A girl with an accordion opened the proceedings. At the end of her turn the old 'sweat' who had been sulkily reading his newspaper in a corner of the hut was asked how he liked it. "It used to be quiet round here!" he said, resuming his paper.

CHAPTER THIRTEEN

LILIES OF THE FIELD

AFTER Dunkirk the national war effort burgeoned forth in all directions. It was like the second half of a tornado of which the evacuation from the beaches was the suspenseful centre. In conformity with that false calm ENSA found itself for a short while officially *in vacuo*. However, we went engrossedly about our business, shortening sail and battening down the hatches against the threat of German invasion. We introduced a series of measures designed to keep parties in circulation as long as possible. The number of artistes in each of the larger parties was not to exceed twelve. The use of framed scenery was forbidden; in future, it was to be painted in dyes and made to be rolled up and put into baskets. (This regulation paid us good dividends in the later campaigns, when our designers were able to provide most ingenious and effective settings for remote and primitive theatres in the Middle and Far East.) Artistes' baggage was limited to one package per person, apart from hand luggage; stage furniture and properties were severely curtailed.

If invasion came we would not be allowed to distribute entertainment under our existing system. That much was clear. I decided to treat the existing military Commands as entertainment zones. Upon receipt of a stand-still order all parties would remain in the zones in which they happened to be at the time, where they would be controlled by our Regional Committees, assisted by senior executives from Drury Lane, sent out to act as directors with full authority within the zones for the period of the emergency: 'rural deans,' as Rex Newman dubbed them.

These preparations had little reality for me. Neither the gangs of workmen with concrete-mixers building road-blocks and drilling the roads for mines, nor the forests of barbed wire and tubular scaffolding on the seashore, nor the painting out of the names of railway stations and the removal of signposts, so that, as one drove about the country, one was compelled to use maps, as in a remote foreign country, could convince me there was really going to be an invasion. After all, it was a thousand years since we had suffered foreign conquest. One could not be expected to get used to the idea again within the span of a thousand hours or so.

❖❖❖

Sack Race . . .

It was in connexion with the invasion emergency that I visited a Divisional Headquarters at Tunbridge Wells, where I met Henry Sherek, larger and more urbane than ever, but somewhat shaken by 'Monty's' invasion order (just issued) that all staff officers wishing to retain their jobs must undergo physical training, including running before breakfast. This was a little hard on Henry, whose first attempt at this race to avoid the 'sack' left him severely shaken.

2

Apart from the minor difficulties with NAAFI, due mainly to our makeshift constitution, our relations with the official world had been cordial without exception. It is important to stress this happy childhood in contrast to the bullying we were about to receive in the school of experience. This freedom from interference largely existed because the professional soldiers at the War Office were too busy to bother about a business they did not understand; but now the mobilization day of the amateur, anxious to ginger up the professionals and show everybody how to do things, had arrived.

Before Armageddon II the word 'welfare' had not its present wide application. In the public mind it was usually associated with the activities of religious and philanthropic bodies, or with the Factory Acts and the more enlightened management of some of our basic industries. Anyway, the word lacked popular appeal, smacking too much of the poor-house with its atmosphere of patronage, of good deeds for the luckless, and even more unwelcome to the romantic journalists who lauded the spirit of British independence, unaware how soon the characteristic would be evaporated in the crucible of war, as the giant compressors of the Government machine closed in upon the national life.

Welfare came late to the Army, so it had to make its own niche. As the war progressed the niche became a platform, crowded with officers of every sort and degree, standing up boldly for all the world to watch them directing the humble efforts of the philanthropic bodies beneath them. If this attitude involved a measure of interference with the work, and if some of the volunteers now found themselves pushed off the platform—well! that was just too bad.

ENSA, first of the new voluntary organizations to achieve national prominence, obviously merited early attention. A chance remark at a War Office conference in April 1940 which I attended disclosed the fact that a committee under the chairmanship of Lieutenant-General R. H. Hain-ing, appointed by the War Minister to inquire into the organization of Welfare for the Army, was proposing to include entertainment in its field of inquiry. On my suggestion that it might be as well to consult pro-fessional opinion on the subject, the General and one member of his com-mittee called at Drury Lane on May 1 to hear what ENSA had to say. Before our statement was made the General in a burst of frankness explained that another member of his committee was not present because he was busy writing the report. Evidently their minds were already made up. An air of perplexity, not to say suspicion, pervaded the meeting. It was as though I had shot down a *rara avis*, and now stood respectfully by while the committee examined the plumage and asked each other what sort of a bird it might be.

It was decided that entertainment should be the perquisite of a new Directorate of Army Welfare, under the Adjutant-General. This meant that, in spite of NAAFI's close connexion with the Quartermaster-General, ENSA would henceforth be regarded as an 'A' matter by the War Office. I did not appreciate the significance of the change at the time.

The circumstances of the war tended to make each new directorate extremely jealous of its rights; anything that trespassed upon its work-preserve was automatically to be condemned. So, as the Haining decision brought NAAFI (and its problem child, ENSA) into closer contact with Army Welfare, a chain-reactor of friction was gradually set up. The hard-working NAAFI officers overseas, who found so many of their best ideas filched from them, regarded Welfare Officers as 'the lilies of the field,' and sometimes referred to them as such. But this did not prevent them from being jealous of our entertainment officers also, who, in their turn, were guilty of a kind of snobbish superiority in their dealings with NAAFI and of quite a degree of mulish obstruction when Welfare Officers were obviously trying to do a good job of work. At this remove one can be philosophical and laugh about all this; but during the year of anxiety, when the nation was arming itself with broom-handles and sporting rifles, there were few subjects of laughter between the civil population and the Service Ministries. Against such a background it is easy to trace the rapid deterioration in the former pleasant relations between ENSA and the War Office.

"CATHEDRAL STEPS": BEFORE ST PAUL'S CATHEDRAL, SEPTEMBER 25, 1942

144

THE CROWNÉD FIGURES IN
PRAYER BEFORE THE WEST
DOOR: EDITH EVANS AND
HENRY AINLEY

"CATHEDRAL STEPS"

LESLIE HOWARD AS NELSON
(HIS LAST PUBLIC APPEAR-
ANCE), MARY CLARE (ANY-
WOMAN), FRANK CELLIER
(ANY-MAN)

3

And so the Directorate of Army Welfare came into being; at its head marched Lieutenant-General Sir John Brown, one of the few Territorials to achieve high rank in the Army, following a distinguished record in the First World War. I took the opportunity of studying his personality at close range, when he asked to be shown over Drury Lane. He seemed to be a pleasant, amiable fellow, mildly interested in the theatre. At our first full-dress meeting, held on August 7, 1940, he began by stating that he had no desire to "take over ENSA," thereby proclaiming that possibility. It was apparent that behind his cheerful inquisitiveness, culminating in the suggestion that his 'Number One'—at that time an expert in the marketing of petrol, I believe—should visit each office at Drury Lane in turn to find out how things were done and to suggest possible improvements, the General held strong views as to the importance of his Directorate in the future scheme of things.

The relative positions of staff officer and theatrical manager were now strangely reversed, Sir John eagerly putting forward his suggestions, only to find they had been considered and either adopted or rejected long since.

DIALOGUE EXTRACT: *not quite verbatim, but nearly so*

Sir J: The Army should organize its own entertainments.

Myself: Professionally, do you mean, General?

Sir J: No, no. Form our own units and train them ourselves.

Myself: We already have a number of well-known producer-stage managers[1] working with the Army and the R.A.F.

Sir J: How do you mean?

Myself: They are attached to units for a certain time, organize and produce the shows, and then move on somewhere else. We are proposing to send many more out.

Sir J: I must inquire into that. Meanwhile you'd better not send any more for the time being.

[1] Amongst the well-known artistes and producers who gave service to the troops in that department of ENSA's activities were: David Burnaby (mainly musical shows and revues for the R.A.F.), Leon M. Lion (who staged a number of dramas), Martin Lewis (plays and concert parties), Jack Miller (in general charge of this work in the Isle of Man; now stage director at the Theatre Royal, Drury Lane), Frank Marshall (now general manager of Drury Lane), Frederick Lloyd (now general manager of the Gilbert and Sullivan Opera Company), Frederick Tomlin (who staged a remarkable production of *The Wandering Jew* by R.A.F. amateurs, who made their own scenery and properties; this production was subsequently broadcast), John Deverell (very popular with his farce productions), Claude Beerbohm (handicapped by the loss of his teeth, so that he found it difficult to speak for himself), Reginald Palmer (musical shows), Cecil King (one-time stage director for Herbert Tree).

K

Myself: Very well.

The General changes the subject.

Sir J: Now about this ENSA vulgarity——

Myself (hotly): We haven't a monopoly of dirt, General! Some of the Service shows I've seen——

Sir J: That's only just letting off steam. It's different with professionals.

(*A hit there, I thought.*)

There was another snippet of conversation about this time that I recall:

Sir J: Amateurs are the second line of entertainment.

Myself: But I've already said that!

Sir J: Oh! Where?

Myself: In my last memorandum.

Sir J: Nothing seems to have been done.

Myself: Excuse me, General. ENSA has done quite a lot.

Sir J: I'm glad to know that.

I went on to explain how a number of amateur companies in each Command, in the selection of which we were being greatly helped by Geoffrey Whitworth, of the British Drama League, were to be placed on approved lists and given help in the way of transport, etc. In the South-west, Cyril Maude, our chairman, using the authority of his great name, was insisting upon his prior approval before any amateur groups came under this assisted scheme.

Sir J: Cyril Maude? Is that the actor?

Myself: Yes, the actor.

Sir J: Excellent! But we must do more than that!

And he did.

4

Welfare Officers set about encouraging the amateurs with a will. Various associations and groups with high-sounding titles distinguishing them from ENSA were formed, and in Northern Command, where General Sir Ronald Adam, Commander of the 3rd Corps in France, was now Commander-in-Chief, a Director of Amateur Entertainments was appointed. Such appointments called into question the competence of our own Regional Committees, the majority of whose Chairmen were prominent men of the theatre, such as Emile Littler (in charge of the Southern Region) and T. D. Clarke, of the famous Argyle Theatre, Birkenhead (who looked after our affairs in the North-west). Our Scottish Committee, whose President was Sir Harry Lauder, was run with great energy and efficiency by Horace Collins, a successful theatre owner and manager north of the Tweed. He had already secured the co-operation of all the leading Scottish artistes, many of whom had already toured the camps and been to France.

Soon the amateurs were swarming like bees round the more accessible camps, and in the scramble some simple truths about entertainment, such as that quantity cannot make up for lack of quality, were lost sight of. On one occasion two coaches conveying fifty-three would-be Thespians arrived at a camp to give a performance timed to last for one hour and a half. The organizer, on being asked why he had brought so many people, said it was "to make up for the good party who were unable to come owing to illness." Frequently our Sunday bookings of films at the big garrison theatres had to be cancelled at short notice to allow the amateurs to perform their plays. The B.E.F. men in particular were not to be fobbed off with amateur entertainment. They made effective protest by walking out in the middle of the show, or by slowly 'counting out' the bad comedians.

All this activity was costing the amateurs money. Advertisements were inserted in provincial newspapers calling for funds to enable the local 'Hamlets' and 'Charley's Aunts' to do their duty. In certain towns recourse was had to the Lord Mayor's Comforts Funds, and in other places the appeals were supplemented by special performances, for which the assistance of professionals available in the district was sought. This did not help us with the theatrical trades unions, many thousands of whose members were unemployed at this time. Then Commerce began to rear its ugly head as amateur organizers announced the scales of fees they proposed to charge units or Command Funds to cover expenses; this led them inevitably along the primrose path towards admission charges, whereupon the political atmosphere among the trades unions became highly charged indeed. It must not be thought we were hostile to the amateurs. No, our opposition was aroused by the disorganization that followed upon the deliberate attempt of Welfare Officers to set the amateurs up in rivalry against us.

5

The outstanding achievement of the amateurs was in Northern Ireland. On the outbreak of war a meeting was held, presided over by the Lord Mayor of Belfast, at which it was decided to form the counterpart of ENSA in the Province, and to seek affiliation with us in London. This body became known as the Northern Ireland ENSA (N.I.E.N.S.A.). For the first twelve months of its existence it had to rely entirely upon amateur effort to entertain the troops. All we could do in the way of practical help was to send over two mobile cinemas, and meet the general expenses of the organization by monthly payments from NAAFI funds.

The early success was due largely to the energy and sound business sense of its Chairman, Alexander Dalzell, J.P., a prominent Belfast citizen who had formed the original committee and then hurried over to London to study our organization and ways of doing things. But, as the months went by and more and more troops were poured into the Province, the burden became too heavy for amateurs to sustain, especially as the more talented and able-bodied amongst them were gradually absorbed into military service. Standards fell rapidly, and when child prodigies became the chief stand-by it was time to call a halt. I went to Northern Ireland to discuss the position with the G.O.C. (Lieutenant-General Franklyn). It was clear that the monthly payment of 'danegeld' would no longer satisfy requirements, as NAAFI had hoped. But it was not until a year or so later that we were able to set up a full-scale professional service, under the direct control of Drury Lane. This was known as the Northern Ireland Entertainment Scheme.[1] NIENSA took over the functions of a regional committee, and through its Chairman loyally co-operated with the officials we sent over to run the scheme.

Such was the familiar pattern of amateur entertainment throughout Britain: first enthusiasm and early success followed by a period of declining standards and then dissolution. It was not to be wondered at, for in the hard circumstances that were forced upon the nation there was little energy for amateur or diversionary effort.

6

Doubtless you are acquainted, dear reader, with the process known as 'empire-building'? It is a kind of mathematical pyramid: the loftier the rank of the man at the top the more extensive the staff required to support him in that elevated position. The number of junior N.C.O.'s required to sustain a staff sergeant, or subalterns a captain, or majors a brass hat, and so on, can be worked out in precise terms, known by the august title of 'establishment.' The ingredient that is essential to the support of your pyramid is Function—real, fancied or acquired. The wider the range of Function the taller the pyramid and the higher the rank of the officer at its head, which is the same proposition stated in reverse. It is, too, a kind of game, fascinating in the rewards it brings to the successful participants. And the opponent to be most aware of is the expert, for he knows all about Function, or should do.

---

[1] A note amongst the ENSA papers gives February 13, 1941, as the opening date of the Scheme, when a party that included Frances Day, Mai Bacon, Lyle Evans, Arthur Anton, Norman Hackforth, Hugh French and Cyril Smith began its tour with special performances for the troops in Belfast.

In the course of their participation in the game Army Welfare took unto itself a new Director-General: Major-General Willans, another Territorial officer who had won distinction in the First World War. Willans had none of that anxious look of the office general, dreaming nostalgically, behind the semi-retirement of his desk, of the whitewashed posts of the Aldershot parade grounds. He wore the air of a professional Staff Officer with confidence. And he had similar confidence in the ability of his newly acquired directorate to achieve Function in all branches of Entertainment.

Shortly after his appointment, hoping to establish friendly relations between us, I invited him to lunch at the Savoy Restaurant. I had scarcely finished ordering the meal before he fired his first question at me:

"Tell me, what do *you* do in the theatre?"

Not a bad opening gambit for a newly appointed Staff Officer determined to stand no nonsense. Clearly he had made up his mind that I was a difficult person to deal with; and, as the meal progressed, it also became clear that he was not going to bother himself overmuch about the theatrical point of view; it was we who must stand to attention while the tables of military law, order and authority were read out to us. Entertainment was a commodity to be dispensed and administered in appropriate doses by the staff of Army Welfare. Such a lack of comprehension was to lead him into egregious error, as, for example, when he interrogated Herbert Griffiths, the Area Organizer for the Aldershot Command, regarding the quality of our Sunday concerts.

Griffiths, formerly musical director of the London Coliseum, was a conscientious and experienced musician and an enthusiastic worker. His Sunday evening concerts at the Garrison Theatre, given by famous staff bands stationed in the Command, such as Kneller Hall, with the help of artistes sent down each week-end by the Concert Division, were an established success. He had supplemented these arrangements by organizing talent from within the Forces under the title of 'Stars in Battledress,' a scheme that, with its title, was later annexed and run by Army Welfare. Griffiths was also a hot-tempered fellow who possessed a type of loyalty that is not uncommon in the theatre: the production with which you are immediately concerned is always the best production and the management that employs you is always the best management.

"Tell me about these Sunday concerts," said the General haughtily. "Are you sure they're quite suitable?"

"They're very good shows indeed," said Griffiths. "Last Sunday we had Moiseiwitsch down here."

"Moiseiwitsch? Moiseiwitsch? Ah! Let me see! He's a juggler, isn't he?"

"No, sir," replied the outraged musician, "he's a jockey!"

There was also a new Adjutant-General at the War Office in the person of Sir Ronald Adam from Northern Command. The fracas over Sir John Jarvis' cinemas had stirred up clouds of suspicion in this general's mind about ENSA and about myself that were never wholly dispersed. Despite his unfailing courtesy, conversation between us remained oddly formal, even upon social occasions, as when we found ourselves staying at the same headquarters abroad. Maybe this stiffness was because I was not subject to orders in the same way as a member of the Army Staff. Indeed, the General once complained to the Chairman of NAAFI that he never knew what to say to me because I was a civilian and could do as I liked. He did not realize that my obsession was a harder taskmaster than ever he would have been.

7

It was well that our organization now possessed safe moorings in public opinion through its Regional Committees,[1] located in each military Command, and drawn to an apex of influence through the eye of a Central Committee in London under the Chairmanship of Lord Tyrrell of Avon, of which each Regional Chairman was a member. Without such moorings to which it could attach itself for moral support ENSA would undoubtedly have been carried away in the storms of contending influences that from now on continued to burst over it.

The first hint of the wrath to come was contained in an Army Council Instruction (A.C.I.) that NAAFI entertainment was to be reduced by 50 per cent. Two days before its issue NAAFI sent for me, gave me the news and told me to halve the cost of the service immediately. When I protested that one could not turn entertainment on and off like a tap—there were such things as artistes' contracts—I was cut short by the reminder that it was—AN ORDER!

Before Dunkirk the ration of professional entertainment had been roughly at the rate of one show a fortnight. With the return of the B.E.F., the arrival of Dominion troops and the additional call-up, the ration had now fallen to about one entertainment in every six or seven weeks. A further reduction of 50 per cent. would call into question the value of the whole service.

A few days later, fortified to the point of resolution by the War Office order, the Corporation followed up its instructions to reduce cost by suggesting that we should abandon Drury Lane as the ENSA headquarters and sack Sir Seymour Hicks. The last measure was quite ridiculous, for

[1] See Appendix Four.

his departure would rob us of the only senior producer available to undertake general supervision of the shows; at the most it would save some £20 or £30 a week. As for our removal from Drury Lane, that meant disregarding all the arguments previously advanced as to the enormous savings being effected through the use of its workshops. When the accountants eventually worked out for us the amount of financial saving that the cuts would effect, and this was found to be at the rate of some £160,000 per annum only, we determined to fight the reduction by every means in our power.

By way of parenthesis, the Air Ministry took the strongest exception to the unilateral action of the War Office. It could only result in the R.A.F. receiving a negligible allocation, whereas, in view of the Battle of Britain and what followed, their needs should be regarded as paramount. The inter-departmental breeze was only stilled by our agreeing to provide additional shows exclusively for certain of the larger R.A.F. stations; but the Air Ministry regarded this as a temporary solution only.

Our Central Committee met on Monday, July 8, to consider a Memorandum of protest which I had drafted. Lord Tyrrell took the Chair, and there was a full attendance. As I sat listening to the flood of complaints about inadequacy, reported by each Regional Chairman in turn, I could not resist a little thrill of pride that the framework of organization that we had constructed was not only holding, even though all its rivets were not yet in place, but had so proved its worth that the prominent men and women sitting round the table were prepared to fight for its continuance.

The Memorandum posed a general question to which an early answer was requested:

Is the work which ENSA is doing to entertain the troops of value in maintaining national morale at this time or not? If the answer is "Yes" then the saving of £160,000 per annum, secured by cutting the supply of entertainment in half and thereby depriving large numbers of men of professional entertainment altogether, is obviously the wrong policy. If the answer is "No" then the work should cease.

A resolution, proposed from the Chair, was added, condemning the reduction and requesting that the order be rescinded without delay. Lord Tyrrell undertook to bring both papers to the notice of members of the War Cabinet and the Army Council, while Sir Kenneth Barnes was to forward them to NAAFI.

Perhaps the Memorandum was worded with needless acerbity. After it had gone I felt it might have been better to tone it down a little. And yet, in the jostling crowd of ideas and ambitions that flooded the offices of

Whitehall at that time, if one did not strike out with one's elbows now and again one might easily find oneself jammed between the door and the wall, one's cherished plans swept into the official wastepaper basket, to be conveyed quietly and painlessly to the incinerator and thence to oblivion.

Our President was well aware that the matter at issue was the future existence of ENSA. He knew that a scheme was gestating at the War Office that would duplicate our organization in every respect, but so far his letter-writing had brought no result. One day he insisted upon my accompanying him to an interview with Lord Croft, then Under-Secretary of State for War. He seemed very frail as he tottered up the steps of the main entrance to the 'War House.' Poor old man! Why should he bother? I'm sure he'd much rather stay at home, somnolent over *The Times*. We began slowly climbing the marble staircase on our way to Lord Croft's room. Here he seemed to hesitate and, turning to me, with a hushed voice said:

"I think after all I'd better go in alone. They get so cross whenever your name is mentioned."

I felt like a private soldier being 'crimed' before his company officer at Office Hours. At any moment I expected the harsh command of the sergeant of the guard: "Cap off, right turn, quick march. Private Dean, sir. NAAFI. Charge: Talking to Cabinet Ministers without permission."

I was left waiting in the corridor for about ten minutes, and then a messenger came along and said Lord Croft wished to see me. As I entered the room the two old gentlemen were laughing and exchanging reminiscences. The Minister looked up at me with a suspicious glance from under his eyebrows:

"Of course, I really have no business to be talking to you at all."

"Why not, sir?" I asked.

"Fraternizing with the enemy," he said, chuckling.

8

Our opponents had the advantage of War Office authority behind them, in addition to its long experience in the conduct of office battles. While the result of the opening skirmishes over live entertainment remained uncertain Army Welfare decided to extend their front by opening an attack on the cinema position on the opposite flank, thereby displaying a nice appreciation of tactical principles. The announcement of their intention to purchase and run 300 mobile cinemas in competition with those we were already running was received with incredulity in Wardour Street.

"Well, they just can't do it—that's all," declared our Cinema Officer, in between outraged puffs at his cigar. "There isn't that much equipment in the country." But when this was followed by a request to the K.R.S. for a scale of reduced charges for film hire both exhibitors and renters became alarmed: the exhibitors because they realized that the employment of that number of mobile cinemas giving free entertainment to so many men and women of the Armed Forces (shortly to number four million) would be extremely hurtful to their business: the renters because they realized that, if they agreed to the request, the War Office would be acquiring a large part of their annual output of films at rentals considerably below those paid by the commercial renters. This would deplete the revenues and disturb the good trade relations between exhibitor and renter, a situation to be avoided like the plague.

ENSA's own relations with Wardour Street had now been established on a basis of complete confidence, as between the FENSA Committee representing the renters and our Cinema Officer representing the Cinema Division at Drury Lane. Consequently, while the Trade were too scared to say "No" outright to the War Office, they met the overtures with coolness, inquiring why it was desired to disturb the existing arrangements. In doing so they were not concerned with our finer feelings, but with their own legitimate interests. But the 'empire-builders' at the War Office were not to be repulsed as easily as that. Assuming eventual consent, they went ahead with their plans.

Early in October I received an invitation to a luncheon to be given by the Army Council at the Dorchester Hotel to leading members of the C.E.A. and the K.R.S. H.R.H. The Duke of Gloucester, K.G., was to be in the Chair. The object of the gathering was to thank the representatives of the Film Trade for their generous assistance over the new War Office plans. It was not clear why I had been invited to this feast of reason, unless it were as a witness of my own discomfiture. From the feelings openly expressed up and down Wardour Street the War Office was plainly heading for disaster. Therefore I tried to warn the Authorities, tactfully, to hold their horses.

The luncheon duly took place on Tuesday, October 22, 1940. All the members of the Army Council were there, including, I remember, the new C.I.G.S. (General Sir John Dill) and the two Under-Secretaries of State. When His Royal Highness rose to speak the atmosphere 'below the salt' became highly charged with embarrassment. The Wardour Street tycoons are men of notoriously independent mind, and at the time the film trade was extremely prosperous; they were not to be bulldozed in that fashion. The Presidents of the two Societies rose in turn to reply, and regretfully announced their Societies could not agree to what was proposed. It seemed as though the ensuing silence would never end. Each man tried to avoid his neighbour's eye; expensive cigars were allowed to go out, or fell from nerveless fingers into the coffee cups; the magnates looked like condemned men awaiting the electrical discharge that would blast their recalcitrancy into eternity. . . . We rose respectfully in our places as His Royal Highness passed slowly by the long table and out of the room, followed by the generals, whose empurpled necks bore witness to their anger.

On the following morning the General Manager of NAAFI accused me over the telephone of engineering a most flagrant insult to the Duke of Gloucester, and threatening me with the full pains and penalties of Cabinet exposure. What that might mean for me I could not imagine. The affair was duly reported to the Cabinet, and Sir John Anderson, as Lord President of the Council, held a private inquiry. I heard no more of the ridiculous charge of my complicity in the matter. I make reference to this incident not out of a desire to resuscitate a forgotten scandal, but because it is essential to my story of our struggle for survival.

9

Hostilities now broke out along the entire ENSA front. The Press resumed its attacks upon us for inadequacy, even *The Times* joining in critical comment. (A sympathetic talk with Geoffrey Dawson and an invited perusal of our documents soon put a stop to that. Thereafter, at intervals throughout the war the news editor, Alan Pitt Robbins, a friend since the first days of the ReandeaN management, would send correspondents into the Home Commands to write descriptive articles on our work in camp and factory that were of inestimable value in letting the public know the truth.) The theatrical trades unions were summoned to the pursuit with a 'view-halloo' from Mr Tom O'Brien,[1] of the stage-hands' union, who got up at the Trades Union Congress to propose that ENSA should be dissolved and its place taken by a new and larger organization to be run by the Trades Unions—with managerial assistance, of course. The Musicians' Union held a meeting at Victory House, in Leicester Square, at which one bright spirit appealed for a 'combination' with Russia; this would solve the entertainment problem and find everybody work, which ENSA had failed to do!

---

[1] Now Sir Tom O'Brien. When Macqueen-Pope brought him to see me afterwards, and I told him the facts, he generously admitted his mistake; and thereafter gave ENSA his support.

Army Welfare entered a new champion into the lists in the person of George Black, then at the height of his success as the rejuvenator of British variety. His appointment as Honorary Entertainments Adviser to the War Office shook NAAFI so much that the General Manager of the Corporation requested the Air Ministry to give me a similar appointment, which proposal the Under-Secretary of State (Lord Sherwood) readily accepted.

In the late autumn of 1939, during a lunch with Seymour Hicks and myself at the Garrick Club, George Black had volunteered to close the Palladium for a week and to send the whole show over to France, adding jokingly that it would be amusing if the public arrived at the theatre one fine day to find the usual contents bills replaced by a curt notice: "Gone to France." But somehow or other I always felt that we had failed to catch his enthusiasm and that he remained critical, not to say suspicious, of my personal intentions. In fairness it must be recorded that after the politico-theatrical arguments were over George Black did occasionally use his influence to secure us additional entertainment.

By this time Seymour had gone to South Africa to give some lectures for the British Council, taking Lady Hicks with him. When he first proposed the trip I could not do otherwise but agree, although I knew we should greatly miss his good humour and high spirits, and his ingenious way of brushing official obstacles to one side, either by ridicule or plain disregard. However, we were not entirely without friends. Harold Nicolson helped us a good deal at the Ministry of Information; he had been a member of our Lectures Section, disbanded after Dunkirk, and knew a good deal about us. And J. B. Priestley came along to Drury Lane with his pipe and was photographed in friendly attitudes in various odd corners of the building, preparatory to writing a sympathetic article for *Picture Post.* . . . Nevertheless, the need for reinforcement of our position was urgent.

I remembered my interview in the spring of 1940 with Lord Lloyd (proconsul of Egypt and founder of the British Council—that red flag to Lord Beaverbrook's taurus) about taking the Vic-Wells Opera and Ballet to France and thence to Holland: "We should have met long ago. If you are ever in any difficulty don't hesitate. Come and see me." Why had I not thought of him before? His wise advice would help to clear my mind.

I went to see him one Saturday morning in late September. That part of Whitehall had been hit the night before, and, as I drove into the great courtyard of the Foreign Office and round to the left to Lord Lloyd's office, repair gangs were at work, shoring up damaged cornices, removing the broken glass and nailing up doorways. He listened to what I had to say, told me to send him a memorandum (which he promised to put before the Prime Minister) setting out all the facts and then rang up Brendan Bracken at No. 10 Downing Street to ask for the co-operation of the M.O.I. When Bracken refused to see me Lord Lloyd looked at me with a shrug of the shoulders, as much as to say, "It's only what I expected." The sirens sounded another raid warning. He took no notice; just went on quietly talking, but after a little while, when the barrage began, he said, "I think you'd better clear out, but send me that paper and I'll see what I can do." For some reason I neglected to do so immediately, and by the time the paper was ready George Lloyd was dead.

10

The smoke of the conflict now reached the rarefied atmosphere of the House of Lords. Colonel Lord Nathan, Welfare Officer at Eastern Command (so alive to the political value of welfare work for the troops that by one means or another he had extorted from us more than double the number of mobile cinemas allotted to other Commands and, not unfairly, was taking considerable credit to himself for the exploit), rose in his place on November 6, 1940, and in the course of a highly tendentious speech[1] suggested that if the Army could not get enough entertainment from ENSA it should create its own organization.

I began to see more and more clearly that the only way out of our difficulties lay in securing official status under the Government. Only thus should we possess the requisite authority to co-ordinate the requirements of troops and civilians. Now that the fog and the bombs had begun to descend upon the land, blotting out the countryside and whole streets of the cities with riotous impartiality, co-ordination was essential both financially and practically and also, so far as we were concerned, politically. Surely our work for the factories had clinched the argument for regarding ENSA as a national service and not merely as a canteen amenity? But it was futile to look to NAAFI to bring it about. We must stand to our own guns and work hard for the success of the Orkney Scheme. Later there would have to be an Entertainments Board, responsible to a Cabinet Minister, and with authority to override conflicting interests and to arrange through the Treasury for the necessary finance.

All this was going to take time. But after a week or two I could no longer control my impatience. I decided to mention the matter to Bevin at one of our unorthodox meetings. He approved the idea, asked me to prepare a short memorandum[2] and promised to discuss the matter with

[1] Hansard, Vol. 117, Cols. 633–639. Lords Session 1939–40.   [2] See Appendix Two.

the other Ministers concerned. Not long afterwards, as he sat wiggling his toes in the steam room, Ernie confided to me that a departmental committee was to be formed to make recommendations for the future organization and control of all national-service entertainment.

The immediate battle was won, it seemed; and when later I received a letter from Lord Croft, saying that he "wanted entertainment in full blast and hoping we would do our utmost to provide it," I knew it was so. What I did not realize was that this success put the possibility of whole-hearted co-operation between Army Welfare and ourselves farther away than ever. From now on its relations were to be set in a pattern of critical rivalry towards us, to which all its subsequent directors would find themselves obliged to conform. And it made no difference when, after Sir John Brown's retirement from the Army, we invited him to inspect and report upon the shows offered to us by the commercial theatre for service overseas. In fact, it made matters worse. Antagonism had been so deeply etched that there was a sharp protest from the War Office at our daring to offer an appointment to its ex-Director-General of Welfare.

CHAPTER FOURTEEN

ENSA COMES OF AGE

AN Inter-departmental Committee of Inquiry was called into being by Mr Bevin in the autumn of 1940; Lord May was its Chairman. I suggested his appointment as a way of getting round any objections that NAAFI might raise to the creation of an entertainments board. He was then acting as Treasury Adviser to the Corporation. As the Chairman of the Economy Committee of 1931, which produced the political dynamite of the famous May Report, and of the subsequent Import Duties Advisory Committee, he obviously wielded considerable influence at the Treasury.

George May's brilliant career with the Prudential Assurance Company, of which he eventually became the Secretary, had given him a unique experience of life as it is negotiated in the City. This experience had not been wasted. Indeed, he was a man upon whom it might confidently be stated no experience was ever wasted. He was an astute negotiator and understood fully the value of inducing the other participants at a conference to play their cards first. One could imagine him as a superb poker player. He walked with an upright carriage, retaining to the end of his life a slender, imposing figure, although rapidly failing sight caused him to throw his head slightly forward. His speech was slow and hesitant, and his use of short, clear terms evidence of long commercial training. The embroidery with Whitehall turns of speech that he occasionally permitted himself was a luxury, designed to show off with delicate inadvertence his familiarity with high matters.

In committee he would sit at the table—silent, impassive, with the benevolent look of a bird of prey after a good meal. At the same time something warned you there was always the risk of a sudden scratch if you went too near. When his turn came to speak he would slowly polish his eyeglass with a white silk handkerchief and screw it into his eye, while all present waited for 'wise saws and modern instances.' More often than not, however, he would begin with a carefully selected item from his repertoire of *risqué* stories. Some of these were good, but some were only of schoolboy standard; in any case after a few months one knew them all.

It was amusing to glance round the table and watch the look of bored resignation that came over people's faces when Lord May began to split open another chestnut. After a while it dawned upon me that there was method in this madness. Here was an example of the military 'softening-up' tactic as practised by a civilian. The Chairman was successfully boring his audience while sorting things out in his own mind before coming in for the clinch.

The three Directors of Welfare—for by this time the other Services had adopted similar nomenclature to the Army—were nominated members. The Naval representative, Captain Blacklock, R.N., D.S.O., a distinguished officer of the submarine service in World War I, was previously unknown to me. His monosyllabic utterances in committee certainly entitled him to represent the 'Silent Service.' Asked to give his opinion on a proposal, he would reply somewhat after this fashion:

"Well, if we try that—er—thing there it should be all right. . . . I mean —er—if not, we might try some—er other thing. At least—er—well— there we are!"

This peculiar mode of speech concealed an absolute integrity of purpose so far as the Navy was concerned and a genuine concern for the welfare of the ratings.

General Willans preferred not to serve, but sent a staff officer in his place. Group-Captain Halahan remained our staunch supporter throughout the whole time that he was at the Air Ministry. Among the civilian members Godfrey Ince, on behalf of the Ministry of Labour, was a tower of strength in the first days. He knew Mr Bevin's mind on the matter and was invaluable in establishing the necessity for an impartial inquiry; but, owing to rapidly increasing responsibilities, he had to give place before the committee's report was published to F. W. H. Smith, who continued to represent his Ministry until towards the close of the war. Mr R. S. Wood,[1] of the Board of Education (as that Ministry was then named), exercised a watching brief on behalf of CEMA; he was not immediately concerned with the discussions between the Services, although he had been a member of the Haining Committee.

As Chairman of the Inquiry Lord May had no intention whatever of involving himself in details: for that purpose he obtained the services of a civil servant, Mr P. Goldberg, who had been his personal aide on previous Treasury Committees, and for whom he had a high regard, so much so that he refused to begin the work until his temporary transfer had been arranged.

Mr Goldberg was possessed of an inquiring mind and a determination

[1] Now Sir Robert Wood, K.B.E.

to convince himself that there were no mysteries in back-stage matters that could not be solved by clear thinking and the superior competence of the civil servant. Upon one occasion he declared that running ENSA was "as easy as running a string of sausage shops": a choice of analogy that baffled me. Anyhow, Mr Goldberg was clearly a formidable person, and, as my sole contact with the Inquiry was to be through him, it was evident I should have to wrestle mightily to save his soul from heresy and to make him see the true light—that which shone upon ENSA!

It was important that at the outset the Inquiry should be in possession of the full story from ENSA's point of view. But time was short. So I departed with my senior secretary for the NAAFI hostel at Hindhead, where we laboured night and day without interruption for a week, surrounded by piles of documents, preparing a complete and detailed report, to which I added an outline of my proposed co-ordination plan.

In preparing the report I spared neither man nor matter, but stated the facts, attaching copies of all the minutes and correspondence that had passed, irrespective of whether it were discreet to do so or not. I had not allowed for the assiduity of the Civil Service, and was both amazed and a little scared when I found out that mimeographed copies of this voluminous report had been circulated to the committee members, some of whom had sought to obstruct or destroy ENSA and now found themselves incontrovertibly exposed.

2

Although the administrative machine, as I am now about to describe it, did not take final shape until the end of 1941, there was enough of it there by this time to hope for the hallmark of Government approval. And it was to remain substantially the same for the remaining years, even though additional cogs, balances and governors, all designed to assist speed and smoothness in working, were put into position after the issue of the Report.

The ENSA side of the work was divided among a number of Divisions and Sections, a Section being regarded as junior to a Division, and promoted to the higher denomination when an increase in the volume of work demanded it. Alternatively, Divisions sometimes comprised two Sections, where the types of related work made this desirable. The NAAFI side (which dealt with purely administrative matters, such as Accountancy, Contracts, etc.) was divided into Branches. This separate nomenclature was more than a personal whim; it tended to keep the channels of entertainment-making free from routine.

The day-to-day work of the ENSA Divisions and the NAAFI Branches

SIR HENRY WOOD AND MYSELF ON THE ROSTRUM WAITING FOR
THE PERFORMANCE TO BEGIN

"CATHEDRAL STEPS" WAS GIVEN A SECOND TIME ON THE
FOLLOWING SUNDAY AMID THE RUINS OF COVENTRY CATHEDRAL

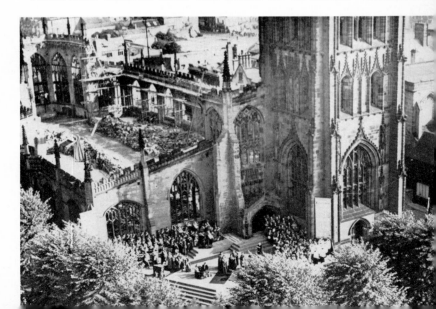

Music by the Hallé Orchestra (Conductor Albert Coates) in the Palace Gardens in Front of Salisbury Cathedral

Salute to the Red Army: Royal Albert Hall, Sunday, February 21, 1 The Grand Climax

was linked together by internal committees, or 'Executives,' as I called them, whose main function was to prevent the various offices from turning themselves into watertight compartments. In the hectic conditions under which we were living this was a matter of the first importance, otherwise the right hand of the organization would not have known what its left was doing. The members of the 'Executives' were senior officials from both sides of the organization. They were nominated by myself and were obligated to meet once a week and to furnish me with single-page minutes of their proceedings. The Senior Committee was the Co-ordination Executive, which was given overriding authority in respect of such matters as the co-ordination of our activities generally and the planning of additional services at home and abroad.

Below the Executives and working to their specific instructions came the personnel of the various Branches, Divisions and Sections. Here there had been a number of adjustments since the first days. At the beginning many of the front-line managers and organizers of entertainment were too busy with their own affairs to undertake the whole-time service that we required. Consequently, men less prominent in the profession found themselves in positions of control where they lacked authority to deal with those whom they wished to engage. As rumours of our impending recognition by the Government began to be bruited abroad, some of the more prominent managers, whose businesses had dwindled to nothing in the Blitz, became critical, considering they should now be asked to assume directive authority. But it seemed grossly unfair to throw over those who had come forward first for the sake of later help, especially in view of the strong probability that the senior men would drift away again as soon as business began to improve. The situation put us at a disadvantage, bearing in mind that the theatre is an intensely snobbish profession within its own ranks, despite its easy manners and outward appearance of unconventionality.

The liaison officers for each of the three Service Departments and for the Ministry of Labour and National Service (known by their various initials as R.N.L.O., A.L.O., R.A.F.L.O., and E. (Ensatainments) M.O.L.L.O.) had their own offices and separate staffs. They were of course key-members of the various Executives.

The Regional Committees were now complete. The chairmen and some of the more active members were also members of the ENSA Central Committee. Upon more than one occasion this top committee was called upon to make known the national as opposed to the professional point of view on major issues, and thus to influence Government Departments before final decisions were taken.

L

On the professional side a number of advisory councils were formed whose members were men and women of high distinction in the particular field in which they were called upon to advise, or were representatives of the professional Trades Unions. The lists[1] of members of the various councils and committees show how wide the net had been flung. I drew up terms of reference for each council and conferred regularly with the chairmen upon matters of general policy, but, unless requested to do so, I did not attend council meetings. When I did it was usually because some problem had arisen that affected either general policy or the work of other councils. The ENSA official in charge of the Division with which each council was directly concerned acted as its secretary, working closely with his chairman and discussing with him the agenda for each monthly meeting. By these means Policy and Practice were induced to walk hand in hand; or, should I say they ran?

All the councils and committees gave continuous and valuable service; they were far from being mere window-dressing. And the system of delegated responsibility under which they and the Executives at Drury Lane worked made nonsense of the charge of dictatorship that was flung at my head towards the end of the war, when routine control was still being exercised by the same Prætorians that had first rallied to the ENSA flag.

3

Public expenditure upon entertainment always arouses criticism. The replacement of the private patron by public subsidy is still quite a new thing and was newer still in the war years—so it behoved us to see that our financial arrangements were above reproach.

At the outset I asked NAAFI to control all expenditure directly through their own Accounts Branch at Drury Lane. The accounts were audited by an independent firm of auditors. Later on Treasury supervision was added. The freedom from personal anxiety over the day-to-day expenditure was an immense boon, as it left me free to range over future aspects of the work. Before long we were compelled to create a separate branch to deal with finance and financial estimates, as distinct from the routine work of accountancy. To this new branch I gave the name of Finance Control; and NAAFI appointed O. J. T. Llewellyn to take charge of it, in which position he had ever to be on the alert to explain and justify the constant twisting and turning of the entertainment kaleidoscope, as the demand from overseas grew or changed direction, and home requirements continued to increase instead of falling in sympathy. It says much for

[1] See Appendix Four.

Llewellyn's efficiency and tact that he succeeded in retaining the confidence both of the Treasury and the Corporation throughout the financial turbulence in which he worked.

The method of financial allocation had grown up since the days of hand-to-mouth feeding by NAAFI. When the factory concerts began and public money became directly involved I suggested to Sir Alan Barlow, the senior Treasury official responsible for the matter, that a ring fence should be put round expenditure by agreeing beforehand the annual amount within which monthly estimates would be submitted. In an endeavour to make the money go as far as possible I divided the financial year into two six-month periods: the first from April to September inclusive, to be regarded as the summer period when entertainment would be on a lower scale, and the second beginning in October, when money saved in the first period would be used to swell the sum available for winter entertainment. Later on, when the service became virtually world-wide, these nice adjustments had to be abandoned in favour of a straightforward division of the financial year into thirteen four-weekly periods, and global estimates prepared accordingly.

After the cut and thrust of private enterprise I had expected to find working with the Treasury somewhat difficult. Nothing of the sort. The civil servant's approach to every new problem is guided by established precedent or previously accepted principles. Learn to appreciate this and the way to whole-hearted co-operation is open to you. I found I had little difficulty in obtaining agreement to the expenditure of comparatively large sums of money, always provided that, as I say, the proposition 'came under the umbrella'; but quite senior officials would argue like the devil over the expenditure of a few pounds, simply because the requisite principle had not previously been established.

4

And now here is the appropriate place to mention two senior Prætorians, who would have received earlier notice but for my desire to choose the most significant moment in our story to draw attention to the value of their work. It was mainly their influence, increasingly so after Seymour left, that made possible the smooth running of the vast machine now beginning to revolve with increasing power and momentum at Drury Lane.

Alec Rea, the first of these, had been my close friend and associate since the founding of the Liverpool Repertory Theatre in 1911; he was the first half of the name ReandeaN, under which title we achieved success together after the First World War. As my deputy Alec presided over the Co-ordination Executive and a number of *ad hoc* committees where his business training enabled him to present the problems in clear and simple terms. He did not hesitate to expose with devastating clarity the occasional follies to which all were subject, myself included.

Sir Kenneth Barnes, Administrator of the Royal Academy of Dramatic Art, acted as General Secretary of ENSA for the duration of the war, in which capacity he sat like St Matthew at the receipt of custom, gently imparting innocuous information to distinguished but inquisitive visitors and less gently reminding some of the rougher elements who found themselves occupying beds in the NAAFI hostels of the rudiments of house-training. The benedictory manner, adopted out of past habit towards departing students of R.A.D.A. as he bade them go forth and prosper, was invaluable in turning the edge of complaint and leaving the aggrieved with the comfortable certainty that justice would be done. When, quite unaccountably, Lord Esher (whose unconventionality at council meetings always outraged Alec's sense of business propriety, reminding him, so he said, of Harry Tate) lost his temper with the routine procedure laid down for the regional committee of which he was chairman, a matter quite outside my power to alter, it was to Kenneth that I turned instinctively for the soft answer that turneth away the wrath unreasoning.

Kenneth was also chairman of the Advisory Labour Council, which was made up entirely of Trades Union officials. Its formation had followed upon a suggestion made by Godfrey Ince when the factory concerts were started. This council was extremely inquisitive about all that went on. As I read its minutes I admired the skill with which Kenneth habitually steered the flow of disputation into the calm waters of acquiescence.

There were occasions when he did cause me the gravest anxiety, such as when he took me to lunch at the Garrick Club in his car. This fearsome vehicle, worthy of Harry Tate's at its most decrepit, was literally tied together with string in certain of its secret parts. Our journeys across Covent Garden amid the departing lorries were navigational exercises of rare peril, Kenneth taking the helm with sublime courage and ruthless indifference. When, sometimes, his passenger list included Alec Rea and perhaps two other senior men, it did seem as though the future of ENSA depended upon a shoelace.

◇◇◇

Stranger than Fiction . . .

A certain Mr B, a man of independent means, sought employment with ENSA. It was a strange new world, in which his neat gloves and bowler hat seemed out of place. He was given the job of circulating confidential cables round the various offices. One day, as he was leaving the stage door for lunch, attired as usual, he was given a priority cable for Sir Kenneth Barnes, who had been dealing that morning with actors brought back from America by the British Government for service with us.

"Cable from New York, sir," said Mr B, as he walked into Kenneth's room.

"How are you?" promptly replied Sir Kenneth. "Have you seen Mr Rea?"

"No," replied the astonished messenger.

"Come along, you must see him at once."

Followed by Mr B, Kenneth 'gate-crashed' a production conference over which Alec was presiding.

"Oh, Alec, this is Mr Cable from New York."

Rea was about to introduce Mr B to the meeting when some one recognized him and asked him "what the hell he wanted?"

"Only a signature for a cable from New York," replied Mr B, producing the missive from his pocket. Whereupon he bowed and left the conference room, wondering what all the fuss had been about.

5

It was fortunate that the main lines of our organization had already been drawn before the period of intensive probing into our affairs began, for no sooner had I submitted my Memorandum with its supporting documents than Lord May sent his newly appointed assistant round to Drury Lane to ask questions. There followed a testing time for all our senior people, as one by one they were 'hauled before the beak,' who sat in my little office and pelted them with wordy interrogations.

Sometimes discussion and argument went back and forth between Goldberg and myself until nine or ten o'clock at night, long after the witnesses had been sent home, and we, judge and prisoner, had been left to wrangle on alone. Then, weary and exhausted, we would find ourselves staggering along the silent passages towards the stage-door by the light of my torch. There my driver, Guenigault (pronounced 'Guineagold' by the staff, not as a measure of his worth, although he certainly carried that many carats, but as a workaday habit), would be chatting with the fire-guards in the stage-doorkeeper's office while he waited for me. Soon we would be hasting through the streets—I sitting in front beside him, peering into the black-out and hoping to reach the dubious shelter of my flat before the opening of the barrage. Upon such occasions I was grateful as much for this Channel-Islander's taciturnity, that yet managed to convey a sense of companionship, as for his superb driving.

Mr Goldberg took several weeks to prepare the committee's Report, during which time I grew heartily sick of his constant questioning. But as the long discussions drew to a close it seemed as though we were winning every point. There were some last-minute hagglings, due to my insistence upon the inclusion of my complete exoneration from complicity in the sad affair of the film lunch, before a copy of the final draft was sent to me.

Then one day I received a pressing invitation to lunch with Lord May and Colonel Benson at an inn somewhere in the Thames Valley where I was assured the steak was particularly good. I was embarrassed by the praise showered upon me by those who hitherto had been so critical and exceptive, and by their very broad hints at the recognition I should receive "*after* I'd agreed to the draft Report." I remember so well how sharply I rejected the notion that I sought anything but the triumphant vindication of ENSA. I remember, too, saying that I knew Mr Bevin was willing to act as our Ministerial sponsor in the House of Commons, to which amiable aspiration Lord May returned no answer.

It was always Mr Bevin's intention that the Entertainments Board, which he hoped would be formed as a result of the inquiry, should be placed under the Ministry of Labour. Naturally this was also the summit of our hopes. But further study revealed how neatly and expertly my plans had been filleted of the bones and sinews of that independence for which I had been fighting, much as a sole is prepared at the side table by the *maître d'hôtel*—an operation that you watch with intermittent interest while talking to fellow-guests.

Responsibility for national-service entertainment was not after all to be placed in Ministerial hands. Financial control would be strict; but of political control there would be none. We shall see the effects of this omission in subsequent happenings. I had scarcely time to appreciate its significance before Lord May, accompanied by his faithful henchman, Goldberg, came into my room, and demanded my acquiescence in the Report, which was to be submitted to the Cabinet immediately. . . . And then one day at lunch, not long afterwards, Lord May told me with a sly chuckle how he had been round to see Bevin and persuaded him to abandon his proposed responsibility to Parliament. He would never tell me what he had said to induce the Minister to change his mind, only hinting darkly at some service that he had rendered Ernie when first he came into the public eye at the time of the great dock strike.

6

The Report, the only one on the control of theatrical entertainment ever to be circulated as a Government paper, appeared in March 1941. I have a copy of it before me as I write. It bears striking testimony not only to the brilliance and efficiency of Goldberg's drafting, as he delicately castigates the War Office for their folly and me for tactlessness in attempting to impose good works upon unwilling recipients, but also to Lord May's skill in piloting the Report to unanimous adoption.

Official authority for our existence was implicit in the third of its findings:

> The ENSA organization under the general supervision of NAAFI and of the National Service Entertainments Board should henceforth be recognized as the sole source of supply of professional entertainments for any section of the community for whom entertainments (other than concerts promoted by the Council for the Encouragement of Music and the Arts) are provided out of public or semi-public funds.

The Inter-Departmental Committee was to be reconstituted as a National Service Entertainments Board with a Finance and Organization Committee to deal with day-to-day administration. As public funds were to become increasingly involved, a Treasury Finance Officer was to be appointed to this Committee with overriding authority, so as to secure ultimate Treasury control over expenditure, while leaving NAAFI as the banker and supervisor of accounts. Thus the system whereby the volume of entertainment provided for each Service was made dependent upon the proportion of its NAAFI profits which that Service was prepared to see spent on ENSA was ended. Henceforth, the allocation of entertainment was to depend upon the relative numerical strength of the three Services and the degree of urgency that lay behind the claims presented from time to time to the Board.

The Report came down heavily on the side of Co-ordination and called upon the War Office to encourage active co-operation with the ENSA Regional Committees. ENSA Area Organizers were to be appointed to distribute the entertainments, and I was to be known as Director of National Service Entertainment. A well-deserved tribute was paid to the flexibility of NAAFI control that had enabled such rapid expansion to take place. There was also a recommendation[1] that certain whole-time ENSA

---

[1] This recommendation was never properly implemented.

personnel should receive special consideration for deferment from military service.

Objection Overruled . . .

Following precedent whenever a fresh ENSA development took place, the London Theatre Council induced its Chairman, Lord Esher, to propose that the various managerial bodies and Trades Unions should be represented on the Board with the object of improving ENSA's efficiency. At that time Lord Esher himself and representatives both of the managers and of the actors were already serving on various ENSA councils and committees, so the proposal seemed to call into question the efficacy of the help they were already giving. The suggestion was turned down.

7

Government acceptance of the Report having been signified by the Lord President of the Council (Sir John Anderson), the decisions embodied in it were published as official orders by each of the Service Ministries and circulated as printed instructions to all Ministry of Labour offices throughout the country.

Co-ordination of entertainment now being part of official policy, it became my duty to work out the details and to put them into practice. This was relatively simple, being the logical development of that early makeshift when I had visited the Home Commands and asked for the unofficial appointment of entertainment officers. The ENSA Regional Chairmen took up official positions as Chairmen of National Service Entertainment Committees set up at Command level. (We did not use the word 'Command' for fear of confusing them with military appointments.) They were assisted by whole-time Regional Supervisors. Area Committees were formed in each of the twenty-six military areas. Officers from the Services and from the Ministry of Labour were appointed to all these committees. Where the factory scheme was not being operated Ministry of Labour representatives were not appointed; the same applied to the Navy in certain cases.

I had asked for co-ordination of supply as well as of administration, so it was agreed that the Entertainments Board should meet once a month and decide in general terms the amount to be allocated to each Service and to Civil Departments; its Finance Committee would sanction the estimate of costs prepared for me by Finance Control at Drury Lane. Notification of each month's supply would be sent to the Regional Committees, and by them apportioned among the various areas; the Area Committees would meet later in each month, to share out the entertainment among the units and formations. The Regional Supervisors and Area Organizers would then get on with the professional job of administration. Finally—as Army Welfare was now to run its own mobile cinemas while we continued to run those required for the R.A.F. and for the Ministry of Labour building sites, etc.—we asked the War Office to appoint their own representatives to the F.E.N.S.A. Committee, so that there would no longer be any competition in respect of renters' terms nor of situations where films were to be shown.

For a few weeks after the issue of the Report we were busy appointing Regional Supervisors and additional Area Organizers and in obtaining premises for them. When all was ready Stanley Bell drew up one of his famous charts, setting out the Military Commands and Areas, together with the names and office addresses of all the co-ordination personnel. As I was seeking unanimity for my plan, how better to achieve it than in an atmosphere of refreshment and momentary good living? I invited the three Directors of Welfare and F. W. H. Smith, of the Ministry of Labour, to be my guests at a luncheon at the Garrick Club on May 20. To my great relief, all accepted. There, in a small private room after an excellent lunch, I produced my chart and obtained the unanimous approval I sought.

It was about this time that changes were made in the higher direction of NAAFI. Benson, the General Manager, retired with a knighthood but retained his seat on the Board, and a whole-time Chairman entered the arena in the person of Lancelot Royle,[1] who brought with him from the world of commerce many new ideas and some old ones, including the simple concept that arrogance towards the customer did not pay, even though he might be in the wrong. One was bound to admire a certain tensility of character that enabled him to maintain a tactful front at all times, even though there were occasions when one might sense a determination to order things quite otherwise. The new Chairman took no part in our negotiations beyond expressing the view that any goodwill that ENSA might acquire properly belonged to NAAFI. But he welcomed the Report and did his utmost to assist in the carrying out of its provisions.

The Co-ordination scheme proved of benefit to all, and saved vast sums in staff, office expenses, transport and everything else. There was nothing very surprising or original about it, except its imposition at a time when co-ordination among the various agencies fighting the war was not popular.

[1] Now Sir Lancelot Royle, K.B.E.

8

There was great rejoicing in the ENSA tents when the results of all this political striving were made known. I had not the heart to spoil the jubilant atmosphere by voicing my misgivings, nor to object when some of our valiant Prætorians proposed that we should invite ourselves to lunch, and ask the Service Chiefs, the heads of NAAFI, and some members of the Government to be our guests.

The lunch took place on May 27, 1941, at the Savoy Hotel. It was exactly twenty-one months since the work had begun; so this was a coming-of-age party and the proper occasion for inviting the family circle and professional friends to join us, although, our parentage being so doubtful, we realized we must pay for the party ourselves.

All the friends and relations turned up in force to celebrate our arrival at the years of indiscretion. The Treasury, in the person of the Chancellor of the Exchequer,[1] was there as family trustee, having reluctantly paid out the child's allowances, grumbling the while that they were more than the estate could bear. Lord Croft, representing the Army, was like a querulous elder sister who always thinks more should be done for her side of the family. As for the R.A.F., a sympathetic aunt, too worried about her own annuity to take sides in the argument, it was represented by Lord Sherwood, Under-Secretary of State for Air. Mr A. V. Alexander, First Lord of the Admiralty, was the jolly, much-travelled uncle, who always makes it his business to keep out of family rows. Then there were the Ministry of Labour representatives, those appreciative neighbours from 'down the street,' happy to champion the cause of the boy who had now grown up.

General Willans was the only official *invité* who was absent. The list of distinguished guests was a long one and included many leaders of the musical, theatrical and variety professions, and of the cinema industry, who, even though they might not be closely connected with our work, felt instinctively that the occasion was momentous. It was indeed so, for it marked a turning-point in the muddled history of the relations between the State and the professional worlds of Music and Drama.

Thanks to the influence of Lady Louis Mountbatten, the late Duke of Kent, who was taking an active interest in our affairs at this time, having visited Drury Lane on February 27 and been particularly delighted to see how well the R.A.F. was treated, had consented to take the Chair.

[1] The Right Hon. Sir Kingsley Wood, P.C., M.P.

I felt definitely 'pixilated' as I went into the anteroom where His Royal Highness was shaking hands with the notabilities introduced to him by Lady Louis. In spite of my extreme nervousness I had that inner sense of elation that every theatrical manager experiences at one or other of his first nights, a feeling difficult to describe but tangible and irrefutable: his play is a good one, well produced and well acted, and the time is psychologically ripe for its production; above all, his patrons are in good humour and ready to meet his efforts half-way. Yes, I felt the function would be a success. In view of the presence of Royalty we had to observe a strict time-table. It was only a few minutes after one o'clock, then, that His Royal Highness led the long procession of guests into the banqueting-room.

There must be few people whose digestions thrive on the obligation to speak at a public banquet. For my part such occasions seem interminable; but all too soon the voice of the toastmaster boomed out in tones that have no counterpart in the vocal world, save perhaps among ring-masters: "My lords, ladies and gentlemen, see that your glasses are charged, and pray silence for His Royal Highness, the Duke of Kent, your Chairman."

After praising the work we were doing, and telling his listeners that ENSA was now giving some 1700 separate shows of all kinds each week, the Duke went on:

"This lunch has been arranged to commemorate what is really a unique departure in the history of the English stage—Government recognition of the work of ENSA. I don't propose to go into any details over the very controversial subject of Government support, recognition or control of art. The subsidizing of Music and a National Theatre are questions which have been and are still debated by all who are interested in those professions; and they apply almost exclusively to peace-time. Government recognition of ENSA has, however, come about because the Entertainment Industry has been faced with a special problem due entirely to war conditions. It has come about, too, at a time when the Industry is brought together as never before to try to do all it can to help this country. So there is now a great opportunity to try and get a lasting result to help the Industry after the war and enable it to produce even finer results than before."

This passage set my mind wandering off into the paths of frustration it had so lately trod. Only the necessity of remembering what I had to say in reply pulled me back in time. Anxious not to sound stiff or pompous, the usual effect of nerves on my outward seeming, I took the opportunity of tilting with the Chancellor of the Exchequer; it was a chance that was unlikely to recur. In an amusing reply he promised to give due consideration to my plea for more money: a pleasant lunch-table promise that broke no hearts!

And now the nerves in my head began to tingle with excitement as the voice of the toastmaster rang out again:

"Your Royal Highness, my lords, ladies and gentlemen, pray silence for the Right Honourable A. V. Alexander, Member of Parliament, First Lord of the Admiralty; Mr Alexander."

An historic announcement was about to be made; one that would set everybody alight in a positive bonfire of excitement. But first of all I must explain that, as I was about to take my allotted place at table, one of the Admiralty representatives had whispered some news into my ear that made me want to whoop for joy. When I suggested to the First Lord that he should mention it in his speech he was astonished. "Don't these people know already?" asked 'A.V.' "I think not, sir; most of them were already here before it was broadcast."

The First Lord was on his feet:

"I feel that I am speaking on a rather important naval occasion; I think that is the term." A momentary hush, as a little chuckle of excitement ripples along the top table amongst those in the know. "Members of ENSA have entertained in the last few months officers and gallant men in the *Hood*." (Memory catapulted me back to a certain night in January 1940 on that ship at Greenock, the officers plying us with pink gin, and Gracie Fields, all smiles, signing photographs and kissing the Admiral 'good night.' . . .) "You will feel as I feel about their last great gallant sacrifice." Pause, and then, raising his voice as though to drown his own emotion: "But the British Navy has in all its decades of history taken good care to avenge things of that kind. That is why this morning at eleven o'clock the *Bismarck* was sunk." (Uproar!) "I always felt most irritated before I went to the Admiralty and our great Prime Minister was First Lord when a very traitorous and unscrupulous German propagandist used to say, 'Where is the *Ark Royal*?'" (Excited laughter.) "Well, last night the *Ark Royal* put two torpedoes into the *Bismarck*." (Renewed uproar.) "And this morning further torpedo bombers from that ship joined with other gallant officers and men of the Royal Navy in finishing the ship—their latest and best—for good!"

The B.B.C. had refused to record any part of the proceedings, although its Director-General (Dr F. W. Ogilvie) was among our guests. Therefore we had taken the precaution of making our own recordings of the speeches. Realizing the opportunity they had missed, the B.B.C. now asked permission to use our recording of the First Lord's speech in their evening news bulletins. This made Macqueen-Pope dance with joy, as he politely insisted upon full credit being given to an ENSA occasion.

The gathering broke up in an atmosphere of success and achievement; much handshaking, little jokes and excited laughter. But I was conscious of a sinking feeling at the pit of my stomach. Why do novelists write of a sinking heart, for I find that in such situations it is always the stomach that is affected?

The Duke had touched off the true significance of what was happening to the theatre world. His words were buzzing in my head, all mixed up in uneasy diapason with my own reply. True, we had won a partial victory, but it carried within it the seeds of defeat. The plan to make ENSA a separate entity, with a Minister authorized to speak for it in Parliament, had failed—failed largely because of the false move I had made in the beginning. And yet, I reminded myself, without NAAFI's prompt support ENSA could not have provided the troops with a far-flung service of entertainment within a few weeks of the outbreak of war.

TALLY ONE

(as at the time of the issue of the Government Report: MARCH 1941)

The general service of entertainment to troops in Home Commands
began on . . . . . . September 25, 1939
That for the British Expeditionary Force began on . November 22, 1939
Ministry of Labour 'Symphony Concerts for War Workers'
began on . . . . July 22, 1940

HOME FORCES:
Number of companies performing each week 250
Number of shows, live and cinema, each week . . . 1250

WAR FACTORIES:
Number of companies performing each week 100
Number of shows each week 850

B.E.F.:

	Live:	Cinema:
Total number of performances:		
(from November 1939 to June 1940) . .	2381	3157

Total Certified Attendances from September 1939 *to March* 1941:
HOME FORCES 14,949,173
B.E.F. . . . . . . 1,166,199[1]

WAR FACTORIES: No record was kept of attendances at Ministry of
Labour concerts, but the number was estimated to be in excess of the
total for all Service Departments combined.

Thirty-four garrison theatres and 185 garrison cinemas had been built, converted and/or equipped for the Army and the R.A.F., and were now open
seven days a week.

[1] Excludes the figures after the German invasion of Holland and Belgium, the
returns for which were lost.

THE SECOND PHASE

The Swelling Scene

HEADNOTE

This phase of the story covers the years of waiting, years in which the national frustration sought relief in various ways, among them an inordinate demand for entertainment. Efforts to supply that demand led to a vigorous scramble for a place next the rails for every hobby-horse capable of carrying its rider into prominence. This had delayed the start of the race and later halted the operation of sound principles. ENSA's view of the course was continually blocked by the boring tactics of rival entrants, so that the redemption of our repeated promises to follow the fighting troops everywhere seemed just round the corner—our Tattenham Corner—when, in fact, it was much farther away.

To omit reference to these matters would be to leave the account incomplete and, in respect of some later episodes, almost incomprehensible. Nevertheless, the general reader may prefer to lower his field-glasses when he comes to Chapters 19 and 20, and direct them towards other incidents along the course that may interest him. For example, there is the story of what was accomplished in the realm of Music and, to a lesser extent, in Broadcasting. The influence of ENSA in these matters was developed greatly in the later stages of the war, and continued through the years of reconstruction even until the present day.

CHAPTER FIFTEEN

THE MERRY-GO-ROUND

1

Smoke and Smother

THE Blitz arrived at the Theatre Royal, Drury Lane, at five minutes before midnight on October 15, 1940, when a 500-lb. bomb hit the roof, passed through each of the galleries in turn and exploded in the pit. The war-head became detached from the main part of the bomb and crashed through the pit floor on to the fire-watchers sheltering in the bar underneath, but for which accident none of the party would have survived. Incendiaries followed the bomb down half an hour later and burnt

M

out the orchestra stalls; but, thanks to the theatre's fire appliances and the energy of the night-staff, the blaze was confined to that area.

There was a brooding silence as I drove up to the portico the next morning. The entrance lobby, or rather the suite of temporary offices that now occupied that space, was empty. I hurried towards the stalls, where I was met by Macqueen-Pope, armed *cap-à-pie* in boiler suit and the white helmet of the A.R.P.—he was our Chief Warden—and holding in his right hand a gleaming axe, with which he appeared about to decapitate me. In terse, dramatic accents he told me what had happened.

"Any casualties?" I demanded.

"Denis Wreford's got a bit of a scratch. Of course," he added inconsequently and with a rueful air of lost opportunity, "this would happen on my night off! They ought to have sent for me." (Impossible, for the telephone system had been wrecked. It was a month before communications were fully restored.) The auditorium was in a shocking mess; broken chandeliers and rows of charred and sodden seats, the air still heavy with plaster dust, and the safety curtain blown several feet up the stage, where it hung precariously like a giant, crumpled handkerchief. The stage staff were busy shovelling up the debris and lowering the remaining chandeliers to safety inside the stage boxes. No one else was to be seen.

"But where is everybody?" I demand irritably.

"Seymour has just been in and ordered every one out of the place until we find out whether it's safe."

"How about the offices?"

"Not been touched," said Pope.

"Very well, then. Get everybody back. Work must go on."

The various little cafés and coffee stalls in the immediate neighbourhood, crowded with our clerks and typists, chattering excitedly like young rooks blown from their nests by the first explosion of the squire's shooting party, were soon empty again.

Although the theatre escaped further direct hits, this solitary bomb put a stop to its use for public performances for the remainder of the war. The gallery, the two circles and the pit were all out of action. We managed to patch up the front stalls as far as the cross gangway and use them for the various audition and production committees which sat there in more or less continuous session for the next five years.

The theatre remained vulnerable because of the huge area of its flat roof. Many incendiaries were hurled into the street below by our fire-watchers; and, as the surrounding buildings came under fire, there was frequent straddling, which invariably blew out the windows. Upon one occasion they had to be replaced twice within twenty-four hours, which drew lewd comments on Hitler, Goering and Co. from our undismayed Cockney staff.

Another time I had gone across to the Aldwych Tube Station to attend the first ENSA concert to be broadcast from an underground shelter.[1] From a little stage mounted in the middle of the track, just large enough to take a piano and himself, George Formby was making the shelterers forget their anxieties, as they sat on the tiered beds along the platform, or on the track itself, laughing and joining in the choruses. After the concert I made my way back to the street level with a member of the staff, through lanes of tired men and women who crowded the passages and stairways, calling out their thanks to us as we went by. A heavy raid was in progress. I was fortunate that night. While we had been underground the whole of the window to my office with its frame had been blown across the room, landing on the large settee which stood against the opposite wall. Everything above a height of a few inches upon the desk had been swept away.

One never knew who would arrive at the theatre homeless after the previous night's raid. One day it was a manager in the Variety Division, an ex-acrobat named Bob Ricardo. He had been removing a kettle of hot water from the gas-stove when his flat received a direct hit. Blown out of the window, he had landed on top of a heap of rubble in the yard with the kettle still in his hand. Arriving at Drury Lane at the usual time the next morning, he explained his escape by saying it was because he knew how to fall properly.

Upon another occasion it was Seymour Hicks who had been marked down by Fate; his flat in Chelsea was hit. Convinced that the mishap was a warning, Seymour decided to take out an insurance policy for the benefit of his family.

"How long for?" I asked.

"Just a year," he said. "If nothing happens by that time I shall be all right."

A few days later he told me the insurance agent had been to see him. "A funny little man with twittering eyes and an emaciated smile," said Seymour. "Kept on filling up forms for me to sign and asking me all sorts of questions. Asked me my age next birthday, and when I said seventy he nearly fainted. Then he twittered at me through his glasses and said, 'Oh, but, Sir Seymour, actuarially, you are already dead!'"

One of the senior secretaries had the most extraordinary ill-fortune; she

[1] The series of shelter concerts was made possible through funds provided by Dr J. J. Mallon, of Toynbee Hall. The series did not long continue, because after the money gave out no other private or public agency could be found to provide more. The inaugural concert was introduced by Admiral Sir Edward Evans ('Evans of the Broke'), now Lord Mountevans.

was bombed out three times in succession. With invincible good humour she decided she was wasting her time trying to find a place to live; she would make her home in one of the new air-raid shelters underneath the stage, and if the theatre had a direct hit, well, she would go up with it, and that would be that. Her principal worked in one of the larger dressing-rooms, and her own office was the anteroom to it, complete with washing accommodation and built-in wardrobe for her clothes. So she would not fare too badly. One night she was invited to an engagement party by one of the other girls. The evening was a merry one, and it was late when she returned. Unable to find the right switches in the black-out, she undressed in the dark and did not put her clothes away. Hurrying back to the office in the morning to tidy up before the arrival of her boss, she was distressed to find that an important article of clothing—to wit, a pair of knickers—was missing. Her principal arrived in the middle of the search, and gave her leave to go out and do some essential shopping. Later in the day she came giggling into his room with the missing garment tucked under her arm. "It's all right. I've found them," she said. "And where d'you think? They were filed under K."

2

"Put that Light out!"

Pope undertook his duties as our Chief Warden with the same enthusiasm with which he fought our battles in the Press. He was fond of giving lectures to his squad on various aspects of A.R.P. work. Upon one occasion he gave a practical demonstration of the rescue of a man suffocated by smoke. Tying a handkerchief round his nostrils, he called for a volunteer to represent the body. Egged on by the others, the heaviest man in the class stepped forward and lay prone on the floor. Popie tried to edge the 'body' forward with his hands between his knees, but with no effect at all, until the model lifted himself on his heels and the palms of his hands, when he shot forward with apparent ease.

"You see," said Popie triumphantly, "it's just a knack!"

Whenever a warning was sounded he rightly insisted upon everybody leaving their offices and going into the shelters underneath the stage. I must have added to his anxieties considerably. My lack of discipline in this regard was not due to foolhardiness, nor was it courage, as I found out when driving home through the air-raids after factory inspections or visits to the camps. It was simply that my sense of mission had by this time become an obsession, and the comparative quiet and freedom from telephone calls saved valuable time.

At home it was different; one was no longer absorbed in urgent tasks, and the necessity to appear cool and indifferent imposed a strain which I found difficult to hide. During the first evening raid on London, when the absence of a barrage made us all feel lonely and defenceless, my family passed the night in the temporary air-raid shelters in the basement of our block of flats, listening to the chatter of the foreign refugees: the women silent for the most part, with frightened eyes, the men voluble and inquisitive, arguing fiercely among themselves as to how far away the bombs were when they fell. Squatting on top of the bulkhead that supported one of the huge boilers were the driver and the conductor of a bus abandoned in the street above when the siren sounded, the driver in his long white coat, smoking cigarettes and airing his knowledge of Russia to a silent but receptive companion.

"In Russia it's the economic factor that counts, mate." (*Crrrash!*) "Coo! That was a near one. Now, if you remember, Karl Marx said——" (*Crrrash!!*) "Nearer still! Ever read 'Das Kapitull'?"

"Well, not the 'ole of it."

"You oughter. It's smashin'." . . .

As we did not like the thought of being buried alive we soon decided that sheltering underground was not for us. We preferred to judge the progress of the battle from upstairs, counting the blazes in the night sky and in the morning refreshing our jaded spirits by listening to the greetings of the milkmen as they dumped their milk-bottles in the doorways along the street.

"Bit lively last night, eh? They got six of 'em, though."

"Oh, where?"

"Search me. One pint or two?"

One Saturday evening my wife and I were the guests of Geraldo at a party in a famous restaurant after an ENSA broadcast to America. The raid was particularly heavy, so we all got up to dance; it was the best thing to do. As we did so the whole floor rose and fell as though we were at sea, and the glass lustres tinkled like tiny pagoda bells. A moment later, or so it seemed, the manager rushed up to tell us the Café de Paris had been hit and dozens of people killed, including Poulsen and 'Snake-Hips' Johnson, the band leader. We told him not to be an ass, frightening his guests with rumours, and went on dancing. Again, it was the best thing to do.

Our staff was expanding so rapidly that people's names were pasted on the outside of the doors to assist identification. "And who d'you think you're talking to?" demanded a senior secretary of an impertinent junior. "Dunno, I'm sure," replied the girl, glancing up at the outside of the door

"Label's fallen off." Tempers were evidently growing short under the strain. I came to dread the look of brave anxiety on the girls' faces.

Then one day I was so late back from a camp inspection that I passed the night at the Waldorf Hotel. One had become accustomed to swaying walls as the bombs fell, but that night a big one landed on Covent Garden tube station. The floor of the bedroom seemed to rise up to meet the ceiling; the unaccustomed motion made me feel quite sick. Perhaps this was the last straw in the load of responsibility. At all events my resolution wavered, and I began to make plans for the evacuation of ENSA from London, much to every one's relief. Copies of all important documents were sent down to one of the hostels at Hindhead, and a section of the Accounts Branch began to function from there, in readiness for any emergency. The two Sections of the Cinema Division (distribution and technical) had earlier been moved to our Southern Regional H.Q. at Salisbury, a common-sense precaution in view of the large stock of films and projection equipment we had now accumulated. But after a while we all seemed to catch our second wind, so I ordered all administrative staff back to London, feeling secretly rather ashamed of myself.

The life of challenge and uncertainty that we led in the passages and dressing-rooms of Drury Lane had its counterpart out in the country among the artistes and managers. Leslie Henson told me of a girl in a four-handed party who had one of her fingers nearly severed by a small shell splinter. She was sent to hospital, but on the next day insisted on getting up to rejoin the party, explaining that there was no need to bother about her finger: "she didn't have to play the piano; she was only a singer." At Weymouth the warning was sounded during a concert at the Whitehead torpedo works. As there were over two hundred people in the canteen the party decided to carry on. One of the performers was a variety artist with a one-string fiddle. He had scarcely begun his turn when a bomb fell near by. A portion of the glass roof of the canteen collapsed, the audience disappeared under the canteen tables, and the pianist crouched under the minipiano, but Fred and his fiddle played on. The bomb was followed by machine-gun fire, and a bullet plopped through the stage six inches from the fiddler's foot; whereupon he joined the pianist under the piano. When the Area Organizer drove over the following day the little fiddler was a trifle apologetic. "I'm sorry I stopped when the bullet came through the stage—I hope you don't mind—but, honestly, nobody much was listening."

Our offices in some of the seaports had a particularly bad time. At Southampton we were given two rooms in the Labour Exchange to begin with. The Exchange received a direct hit early in August 1940. The steel filing cabinets belonging to the Exchange were blown up, but the ENSA papers stored under the table in a wooden tea chest were undisturbed. We were moved to another building, which was bombed out in its turn. Next we occupied a back room on the first floor of Lily Langtry's old home. The front of that house was wrecked. The following morning an inspector from the Ministry of Works ordered ENSA out; but the Area Organizer declined to go, saying he was sick of these constant moves. "Why," he said, as he leant with his shoulder against the wall in practical demonstration, "the place is as safe as a house." An unfortunate comparison, for the ceiling fell in, as he followed the window-frame out into the yard. The artistes' hostels were not immune. 'Billy' Armstrong, visiting one of them with his Liverpool Playhouse Company, protested when the matron marshalled the actors in the kitchen, insisting that they should place saucepan lids on their heads in case of shrapnel. He declared the protection inadequate.

The phrase that grew to common use, "You're all right until your number's on it," reinforced for us the unwritten law of the theatre that the show must go on. Concerts were continued despite the Blitz, and, if perchance a factory was so badly hit that no concert was possible, the party moved on elsewhere. After the Coventry raid the artistes were back on the job again within a week, giving performances amongst the still smoking ruins, with the hose-pipes lining the ruined streets to provide water for drinking as well as for extinguishing the fires.

3

The Inspector calls

It was good fun showing Lefebure,[1] the newly appointed Treasury Finance Officer, round Drury Lane to initiate him into the mystical absurdities of 'show business.' I was so anxious to impress him with our worthiness that it is only in retrospect that I realize what a strange new world it must have appeared into which he had suddenly been dropped.

We fenced with each other a good deal to begin with as I fought down my suspicions of official interference and as he constantly applied the Treasury yardstick to our plans, only to discover that it was invariably a few inches too long or too short by our reckoning. Our unorthodox ways of doing things caused him much amusement; it was fortunate that the saving grace of humour prevented him from falling into the pit of contempt, whence his views of our proceedings would obviously have been somewhat restricted. Eventually his shrewdness reached a working understanding with my intransigence.

[1] C. H. Lefebure, o.b.e.

To follow Lefebure's initiation into our Dionysiac revels will afford the reader a good opportunity of viewing as it were through his eyes the teeming life now going on at Drury Lane. As we tour the offices in his company it will be necessary to make some chronological jumps, because, of course, the process of learning all about us occupied our Treasury man for many months, and even in that time things were constantly changing, developing and moving forward.

To begin with, we shall have quite a struggle to get into the stage-door. ENSA's war-time occupation of Russell Street, in which the stage-door is situated, was almost complete by this time. We had taken over the greater part of Drury House opposite, and also the Fortune Theatre; so that on most days the short, narrow street was a seething mass of NAAFI lorries unloading scenery and equipment, recording vans, taxis disgorging actors late for rehearsal and ENSA coaches loading artistes and their baggage for home and foreign parts. Here and there, dodging fearsomely among the horses, backing lorries and gesticulating porters, musicians might be seen; judging by the risks they ran, ready to sacrifice their personal safety for the sake of the precious saxophones and cellos they hugged to their panting chests. Every now and then lorries and carts from Covent Garden Market would reassert their peace-time privilege of early-morning parking in the street and refuse to move when the Thespian rush began, despite the efforts of the police and of Bill Abingdon,[1] dictator of the famous stage-door. This is evidently one of those days: we had better try the main entrance.

Half-way up the grand staircase at Drury Lane there hangs a large oil painting by Romney, although some detractors prefer to regard it as 'of the school of' only. Macqueen-Pope has, of course, the appropriate story attached to it. It was discovered in an attic, covered with dirt and grease, at the time of the last rebuilding of the theatre in Alfred Butt's day, and had presumably been given to one of 'The Lane's' managers, either as a

---

[1] Abingdon, who was now known as Staff Control, carried out his complex duties with a stolid devotion to written instructions, from which an amiable lack of imagination never once permitted any deviation: a disposition of inestimable value in the atmosphere of recurrent crisis in which he laboured. Amidst all the comings and goings at Drury Lane, that incessant spewing forth of men and women through the stage-door into all the theatres of war, each with his burden of personal worries and anxieties and all of them possessed of 'artistic temperament' in some shape or form, amidst American importunity and British red tape, doodle-bugs and NAAFI regulations, I never once saw Bill Abingdon lose his head, nor fail to close his office door punctually at 6 P.M., after which he remained deaf to all entreaties until 10 A.M. the following day. No, that is not quite true, for I do remember one occasion when Bill 'blew up,' as the saying goes: that was when he studied the first requisition for theatrical equipment for the U.S. Army in Europe. The list included several hundred portable stages and £5,000 worth of grease paint!

gift or in payment of a debt, and then forgotten. As I take Lefebure up the staircase this first morning he pauses before it, staring at a quotation from Churchill's "so many and so few" speech, which had been printed in bold letters on paper and pasted over the glass in front.

"What's the picture?"

"It's supposed to be a Romney."

"Insured?"

"Not the faintest idea."

"Better see about it," says Lefebure importantly. "We can't have the Treasury responsible."

We pass among the dust-sheets covering the bomb-damaged orchestra stalls as a sad, mousy little lady emits a piercing shriek from the stage.

"What on earth's that?" says the startled Lefebure.

"Just another audition; it goes on all the time."

"Sounds a painful process!"

4

"On Stage, please"

The ENSA auditions were the most extensive that have ever been held in the history of the Theatre anywhere. The work became so important that Harold Conway had to be transferred from Pope's office and made Auditions Secretary. The total number of applicants was approximately 50,000, of whom 14,000 people were given auditions; of this number 800 secured engagements. The majority of these came to ENSA as amateurs, and nine out of ten of them remained with the organization throughout the war.

Auditions were held three times weekly. There were numerous applicants at the preliminary morning sessions. These were weeded out by a small Auditions Committee, which included the Auditions Secretary and Mrs Percy Pitt, with William Armstrong to judge on the dramatic side. It soon became known through the grape-vine that to be asked to wait for another hearing at 4 P.M. meant that the artiste had a chance. The second session was attended by the heads of the producing sections. There was such a shortage of talent in the later years that, on the rare occasions when an applicant showed promise, producers would compete loudly with each other for his or her services, while the artiste waited patiently on the stage for a decision, and the Contracts' Manager stood by to issue the contract, only lacking a rostrum and hammer to be the complete auctioneer of this talent market.

During the air-raids it was customary to use the big stage until the roof-spotters gave a special warning by buzzer of the near approach of aircraft, when everybody had to retire to the basement. Consequently, many of the early applicants had the added task of putting their stuff over to the sound of gun-fire. When the volume of entertainment became so large that the stage was wanted for dress rehearsals every day and hour of the week, auditions were transferred to the Fortune Theatre across the way; driven from there by the demands of broadcasting, they were then held at the Duchess Theatre or the St Martin's, until finally the blitzed Kingsway Theatre was patched up and used continuously for the purpose.

All artistes were required to be in possession of a green identity card, and in cases where application for one was refused by Security we were not allowed to make the engagement. Cases were known of renewed application for an audition being made three months later under an entirely different set of names. Fortunately Harold Conway's secretary had a flair for faces, and a sort of tic-tac code was developed between them during interviews which warned Conway in time.

The Contracts' Manager was supposed to weed out the applications before sending the possibles on to Conway's office. Owing to pressure of work the system sometimes broke down, and then all manner of strange people, dangerous lunatics, faded aristocrats, and those boasting Rowton House addresses, would slip through the net and arrive on the big stage demanding an audition. Amongst the eccentrics was a white-haired old lady of about seventy who had made personal application at the stage-door, attired in the most impeccable Edwardian dress; she appeared on the stage a few mornings later in the full glory of a golden wig with ringlets and short skirts appropriate to a high-kicking tap dancer. After giving her notion of how to put over a highly censorable 'point' number, with dance thrown in, she asked if she might be allowed to go as she had not yet bought her meat ration. Then there was the sturdy gentleman who claimed to be an acrobat. He borrowed a chair from the side of the stage, jumped on it and went right through the seat; then he dashed off the stage and reappeared with a second chair, repeating the operation with the same result; he was about to operate upon a third chair from the orchestra pit when Bill Abingdon, who had been watching the proceedings with anxiety from a corner of the stage, forcibly took it from him. The amiable acrobat turned and bowed to the Auditions Committee in the stalls, and with an unconcerned "Well, cheerio, gentlemen," hurriedly left the theatre.

Our outstanding encounter with the world of eccentricity concerned two ladies who had corresponded with Harold Conway over a period of months regarding their most sensational variety act, with which they had toured the murkier pleasure resorts of South America. According to the correspondence they had also incurred various terms of imprisonment, not to mention forcible expulsion from certain of the smaller republics. Out of curiosity Conway granted them an audition. Word of this startling turn had gone the rounds. There was a full attendance in the stalls; typists and clerks were to be observed, viewing the scene from behind the dust-sheets covering the boxes. When their names were called two middle-aged ladies, looking rather like suburban housewives but wearing hula-hula costumes, walked primly on to the stage, one carrying an ordinary dinner-gong and the other an orchestral triangle. Standing side by side, they proceeded with deep concentration alternately to strike gong and triangle. After a few minutes sounds of merriment echoed from various corners of the darkened auditorium. When he had recovered sufficiently Conway invited these exponents of the latest honky-tonk to come to the end of their act. They silently exchanged instruments and, now squatting on the stage, resumed their exotic performance where it had been interrupted. By this time the theatre resounded with peals of laughter. Conway concludes his account of this strange event by saying, "I shall always remember the sweet smile the ladies bestowed on us as they walked sedately off the stage."

Sometimes there were incidents of an alarming character, as when a nervous R.A.F. man, waiting on the side of the stage to sing a song, felt his throat getting drier and drier. There was a small table near by, on which was a glass of water. Looking round to see if anyone were watching, he quickly drank it down. Unfortunately the water contained chemicals placed in it by a conjuror also waiting to do his turn. The singer had to be rushed to Charing Cross Hospital, while the baffled conjuror struggled on—without his star trick, as he had no more chemicals. . . .

There was a depressing side to all this: of the hundreds of girls of modest talent (earning £3 to £4 a week before the war and now with ENSA earning £7 or £8, acquiring thereby inflated ideas of their future prospects) less than fifty stayed in the profession after the war; the remainder suffered the inevitable disillusionment. In the end the auditions staff acquired a row of filing cabinets in which the case histories of all who gave auditions were fully recorded. Many tales of courage and heart-ache lay concealed within those close-packed files.

◇◇◇

Bright Obverse . . .

Among the crowd of applicants at one of the early auditions was Paula Beard, a young girl of sixteen from Hastings with a number of conjuring tricks up her sleeve. She proved to be very good indeed. Travelling the world under the ENSA banner, she later achieved front-page publicity as the first girl to be admitted to the Magic Circle, doing two tricks which baffled many of the older experts. At the end of her wanderings it was difficult to recognize in the smart woman of the world the shy young person who made that first schoolgirl's application at Drury Lane.

5

Room 6

"My dear chap, you can't possibly play that part."

"Why ever not?"

"What about your new leg?"

"I'll be able to walk on it soon."

Lefebure and I were standing at the door of Dressing-room Number 6, which was the office of the Drama Section; inside Henry Oscar was interviewing some of the tragical flotsam that necessity was forcing us to engage. The original Chairman of the Drama Section was Godfrey Tearle, and Oscar came in as his working assistant. When Godfrey left London I asked British Actors' Equity to nominate some one to take permanent charge of the Section, and 'Harry' Oscar was the unanimous choice.

Drama began as ENSA's Cinderella. There were two reasons for this: first of all, the lack of stage facilities to which I have already referred; secondly, the absence of any demand for plays in the camps. Although in the course of time we equipped several hundred garrison theatres with varying degrees of completeness, plays continued to be performed under primitive conditions in outlying places. If the men were still at supper when the company arrived, the hungry artistes had to wait until they had finished and then help them to fix up the stage, borrowing an odd blanket or two to hang up to make dressing-rooms and coping with the most primitive sanitary arrangements. (Neglect in this respect was a frequent cause of complaint among the girls, and when in one camp they were left to use the men's latrines I asked the War Office to circulate instructions to all units that they were responsible for making decent arrangements in advance.) Upon one occasion a performance of *Private Lives* took place on a billiards table, with table-tops laid precariously athwart it, supported by beer crates at the outer ends. Comparatively modest physical activity on the actor's part found him disappearing through the makeshift fire-place or sliding into the arms of the C.O. seated in a basket chair in the front row.

The Cinema was the nearest approach to Theatre that thousands of young troops had yet experienced. Thus conditioned to the aberrations of the loudspeaker, they were not trained to listen to the normal human voice, nor to keep reasonably quiet during a performance. They were full of impatience, indulging in running fires of comment which was great fun for them, but embarrassing for the actors. For example, if a servant drew back the curtains in a darkened room she would be greeted with uproarious shouts of "Mind the black-out"; and if in a café scene one of the characters ordered coffee there would be shouts from various parts of the house of "Three-ha'pence in the Y.M., tuppence in the NAAFI!" This reduced some of the actresses to a state bordering on hysteria. In some cases plays had to be compèred. An officer or one of the artistes would go before the curtain and tell the men what the first act was about. In the interval, to stop them from trooping out, he would have to go on again and tell them what the second act was about.

Drama's humble place in the programme was reflected in the poor accommodation allotted to Oscar's staff, which began, like the others, with a secretary and a typewriter but was rapidly increased. The over-crowding in Room 6 became unbearable. Added to which, for the first three years there was no window in the room, ventilation being provided by a fan operating with varying degrees of efficiency from the top of the door. This meant, of course, that everybody worked in artificial light. Oscar gives this as the reason why all his staff took to glasses before the end of the war and why most of them lost their hair, an amiable theatrical exaggeration that need not conceal the tremendous task accomplished by Harry and his lieutenants.

A modest start was made in 1939 with *Eight Bells* and *Heroes Don't Care*, in which James Mason played the leading parts; and two plays were sent to France: *Night Must Fall* and *While Parents Sleep*. After Dunkirk the Drama Section was closed down for five months. During that time a notable array of companies was engaged as complete units to tour the new garrison theatres, including the Sadlers Wells Ballet, the Sadlers Wells Opera, the Liverpool Playhouse Company, the Memorial Theatre Company from Stratford-on-Avon, the Intimate Theatre and repertory companies from Coventry, Bristol and Malvern. Early in 1941 a fresh start was made with companies playing two plays a week while rehearsing others.

Promoted to the dignity of a Division, the drama office was soon in the most desperate straits for actors. The demands of military service had to be satisfied first, the commercial theatre came next, and ENSA last. Because of our low salaries, agents did not recommend actors to ENSA; it did not pay them to do so. Therefore the Division had to rely upon written or personal applications from artistes and upon its own telephoned importunities. Whenever I made adverse comment on the standards of a company Oscar would burst into my room in a state of despair. "What can you expect?" he would exclaim. "The leading man has only got one arm, also he's going deaf." There is a well-authenticated story of how Oscar was struggling one morning to cast six plays at the same time, when the stage door-keeper telephoned to him.

"There's a man to see you, sir. Says he's an actor."

"Tell him, if he's white he's got the job!" was Oscar's reply.

Even when a play was cast we were not safe from the forays of one authority or another: either the recruiting sergeant, the intelligence officer, or the ubiquitous agent, discreetly offering commercial salaries in the world outside. Even the fire-service was known to raid our small store of talent.

Since choice of play eventually became dependent upon the number of actors available who were sound in wind and limb *Nine till Six*, with its all-woman cast, became extremely popular with Room 6. It was played so frequently and by so many companies that, whenever I visited a camp on inspection, the odds were more than nine to six on my having to sit through this play. I was moved to protest at the lack of variety in the programme. This so worried Oscar that thereafter he would telephone the secretariat to find out when and where I was going next. More than once he was heard to exclaim over the telephone, "For Heaven's sake, don't let him go there; it's *Nine till Six* again, and he's seen that company three times already!"

Oscar's two office assistants were Hamilton Price and Edmund Bailey. When sudden illness caused vacancies in the cast of a play and the camp was within motoring distance, they would hurry there after a hard day's work at Drury Lane and give two performances, making their way back to London long after midnight and usually through an air-raid. Soon there was quite a staff doing regular production work for us. In the list of those who lent a hand in the early days are to be found many whose names became well known to later playgoers, if they were not so already. Among the producers were Harold Clayton, Reginald Denham, John Fernald and Gabriel Toyne; among the players Eric Berry, Ann Casson, Charles Carson, James Donald, Rachel Gurney, Mary Hinton, Noel

Howlett, Phyllis Relph, Frank Royde, Olive Sloane, Mercia Swinburne and Amy Veness.

Despite the difficulties nearly 250 plays were produced under the banner of ENSA at one time or another. Among the early productions *Saloon Bar* was extremely popular: one company, in which Gordon Harker repeated his memorable performance for a time, gave a thousand performances in three years without repeating the locations. Another popular play was *Gaslight*. Irene Browne played *Private Lives* and *Hay Fever* for many months. Later in the war there were productions of Shakespeare, Shaw (*Arms and the Man*, *You Never Can Tell* and *Man and Superman*), Ibsen (*The Doll's House* held a popular place) and Strindberg—yes, Strindberg, who was represented by *The Father*. (Perhaps it was at one of these performances that a Scot in need of a programme was offered one, price one penny. He replied, "Oh, no, thanks. I can see everything.")

Robbed of the chance to go to France because of the evacuation, John Gielgud toured the camps in the summer of 1940, with a company that included Beatrice Lillie and Ivy St Helier: they played *Fumed Oak* and *Hands across the Sea* from Coward's *To-night at 8.30*, and Gielgud's own adaptation of Tchekov's one-act play, *Swan Song*. In doing so Gielgud led the way for other stars of the serious drama, as he was later to do overseas. There were many old Bensonians in the Shakespeare productions. Henry Baynton did *The Merchant of Venice*, *Othello* and *Julius Caesar*. . . .

At one time there were twenty-six companies at work, not counting those temporarily loaned by the commercial theatre in the later stages of the war. Yes, there is no doubt about it; the occupants of Room 6 at Drury Lane accomplished a gigantic pioneering task, in the course of which many thousands of young men and women found Theatre, and learned to love it.

Curtain Call . . .

An ENSA company was playing the famous old melodrama *Maria Marten; or, The Murder at the Red Barn*. When the curtain rose on the final gruesome tableau, with the villain on the gallows, the noose round his neck, the chaplain praying and the masked executioner with his hand on the lever of the drop, there was an audible gasp; and then in the silence a plaintive, quavering voice was heard to say, in the tone of Mrs Mopp, "Can I do yer now, sir?"

6

Top o' the Bill

The light musical stage was represented by the Musical Play Section under the charge of Frank Collins, released for this duty by C. B. Cochran. Among its productions were *Funny Face*, a revue called *Chins Up* (made up of specially chosen items by Herbert Farjeon and Ronald Jeans), *The Co-optimists*, *The Girl Friend* and *1066 and All That*. One of the companies was headed by Anna Neagle, and appearing in the cast lists were such names as Morris Harvey, Nellie Wallace, Richard Hearne and Billy Milton. This section also looked after the tours of the Sadlers Wells Ballet (with Margot Fonteyn and Richard Somes, and Constant Lambert as conductor and pianist) and the Sadlers Wells Opera (with Herbert Menges, Janet Hamilton Smith, Morgan Jones, Edmund Donlevy and many others). Later, a separate Revue Section was formed under Archie de Bear, whose intimate revues maintained a high standard and were always picturesque, although sometimes lacking in humour. Perhaps this deficiency lay at the root of his frequent and ebullient disputes with Seymour Hicks. Early volunteers to his section were Phyllis Monkman, Jasmine Dee, Cyril James, Tom Kinniburgh and Jerry Verno.

In the Variety Section the performers fought with the management and with the rival 'direction' of the V.A.F. representatives with the same gusto with which they delighted the ENSA audiences everywhere. Many 'old-timers' were to be found among the first volunteers in that section. Such famous variety names as Billy Bennett, Jack Barty, Joe Boganny, Carlton, Nat Mills and Bobby, Hal Jones, Randolph Sutton, Big Bill Campbell, Datas, Ella Retford, Keith Wilbur and Bransby Williams adorned its early contents bills. Skeets Martin deserves a separate mention for his persistence: two visits to France, where he broadcast with Gracie Fields, and where, on the second occasion, the G.O.C. 5th Corps gave leave to one of his soldier sons to stay with him in Béthune; eleven nights in the air-raid shelter at Drury Lane during the Blitz; taking part in the first factory concert from Woolwich; last mentioned in the records as about to leave for Burma, where he hoped to meet another soldier son!

<><><>

Wrong Number . . .

Irrelevancies buzzed daily in the ears of the overworked telephone operators, typical of the inability of some people to absorb matters of common knowledge. During the first winter dialogue like the following occurred many times a day:

"Can I book seats for the pantomime?"
"I'm sorry, madam, there's no pantomime here."
"But you always have a pantomime!"
"This is the headquarters of ENSA."
"Isn't *Cinderella* on there?"
"No, madam, no shows at all."
"Oh! Well, can you suggest a good pantomime I can take my small nieces to?"
"There's the Palladium—or the Coliseum."
"Er—which do you think the children would like best?"
"Sorry, madam, I can't help you."

One year later:

Officer's wife: "Is that the circus?"
Secretary (Aside—"I'll say it is!"): "No, madam, no circus here."
"Isn't the Chessington Circus working for ENSA?"
"Yes, but it's on tour."
"Can you get me some seats?"
"It's for troops only."
"Has it got an elephant in it?"
"I've no idea."
"Not very helpful, are you?"

"FRIEND!"

By permission of the proprietors of "Punch"

N

CHAPTER SIXTEEN

MORE ABOUT THE MERRY-GO-ROUND

1

"Seen, thank you"

THE initiation of our Treasury man was progressing rapidly as he stumped about Drury Lane, puffing at his pipe and meeting the most unexpected sights with a quizzical humour that concealed his astonishment: the troupes of young dancing girls scampering between air raid shelter and ballet room, clad only in sweaters and leotards ('bikinis in summer-time), or the dress parades at which every dissatisfied actress seemed deliberately to be wearing her dress back to front, or those final rehearsals which always appear to the chance visitor as unmitigated chaos.

He was interested in the routing room, the walls of which were close-covered with boards reaching to the ceiling in which were hundreds of little pegs, arranged horizontally in series and vertically in areas. There were coloured discs to hang on the pegs, with strange hieroglyphics on them, identifiable only by the manager of the Routing Branch (Eric Tissington) and his two confidential clerks. There was also a huge reference map for the whole system, kept under lock and key. It was possible to ring up the routing room and be told where any one of the hundreds of parties was on any particular day in the current week. With such a volume of entertainment, quick access to this information was necessary not only for the senior executives but also for the producing divisions. This was an example of how we taught ourselves to centralize information and decentralize responsibility, and thus to acquire the rudimentary principles of large-scale planning, previously quite outside the experience of any of us.

Then there was Theatre Control, where E. P. Clift presided over the work of hundreds of resident and travelling managers, the control of theatre box-offices, the issue of automatic ticket-machines and the innumerable details involved in the management of places of entertainment numbered by the hundred. As written, this appears to be a showman's exaggeration, whereas it is literal truth; but then everything was on that scale in this theatrical Gargantua. In Clift's office was another time-saving gadget, devised by Stanley Bell: on the slide-rule system and made like a roulette wheel. Thin slips of cardboard giving the names of the various companies playing the Category 'A' circuit, which was always routed from Drury Lane, were inserted into the machine each week. By revolving the discs Clift was able to remind himself in a few seconds of where a particular company was playing that week. I never quite knew why or how it worked; but it did. These and other devices of organization met with a cool, outward acceptance from Lefebure, but secretly won his warm approval.

2

Lamp for a Lady

"Basil, dear," said a gentle voice at my elbow, "may I have a word with you later on?"

"Of course. Any time."

"Who's that?" whispered Lefebure, as we left the auditorium.

"Lilian Braithwaite. I know what she wants. More money for hospital concerts."

"Well, she can't have it," snapped Lefebure. "They're costing too much already."

"You'd better tell her so. Come and meet her."

Lilian was well aware that Lefebure was riding in the Economy Stakes, but she had no intention of being forced on to the rails. As I introduced Lefebure to her she smiled with an air of calculated naïveté and said, "Oh, and what do you do? Add up the accounts?"

In September 1939 she and Sybil Thorndike had undertaken to look after the Hospital Concert Section. The work covered all three Services, and after Dunkirk became heavy and responsible. By this time Sybil had gone off with one of the Old Vic companies to play Greek tragedy to the miners in the north of England, although whenever she was in London her keen musical appreciation was invaluable in the selection of new talent for the hospital parties.

In her absence Lilian took sole charge of the Section. Every morning regularly at half-past nine, or thereabouts, she made her entrance, under the main portico, across the entrance hall and down into the stalls, threading her way with quiet dignity through the jostling crowds of singers, dancers, acrobats and what not who thronged all the passages leading to the great stage of Old Drury, until she finally reached her office in an upper-floor dressing-room at the back of the building, where she conducted the affairs of her Section with persistent calm and much acid good humour. She rarely troubled me in the front office, but whenever she did it was invariably on a point of importance, and just as invariably she would win that point.

Good male singers being always in short supply because of the call-up, Lilian secured two of the prettiest secretaries imaginable and installed them in her office, where they became generally known as 'Lilian's decoy ducks.' Across the landing the Music Division had the mortification of watching many of the best singers drift past the door en route for the Hospitals' Section; but any romantic hopes cherished by these visitants soon proved illusory in the face of Lilian's assistants, two stalwart characters, Naomi ('Mickie') Jacob and Jean Webster-Brough, whose keen sense of humour encouraged them to deny the same characteristic in others.

Personal attention to the nature and quality of hospital entertainment was part of Lilian's policy, and she was bitterly opposed to vulgarity and items that might upset the sensibilities of nervous patients. She took practical steps to safeguard that policy. Her discreet appearance on behalf of the Hospitals' Section at an audition was a sure sign that something good was likely to turn up, and she usually got away with the best of the spoils.

One morning after Lilian had put in two years of solid work at Drury Lane she came in to tell me she had been offered an important part in *Arsenic and Old Lace*. She had refused it once because she thought the humour too crude, but as the management (Firth Shepherd) was so insistent she felt that for financial reasons she should accept the offer. Would I mind very much if she did so? As she had not taken a penny piece for all her work with us, such devotion to duty took my breath away. Before I had time to reply Lilian hastily added:

"Of course, Basil dear, I shall come here every day when there is no matinée."

"But, Lilian, won't the work be too much for you?"

"Not at all," she said, and her face flushed with feeling. "Now you won't take the hospitals away from me if I play the part, will you?"

The indomitable woman kept her word.

After *Arsenic and Old Lace* had been running some eighteen months the arrival of the 'doodle-bugs' frightened the audiences away. The Strand Theatre had already been hit once during the 'Blitz.' So the management thought of sending the play on tour, where life was less dangerous. When the proposal was put to Miss Braithwaite she fastened a cold eye upon the manager:

"By all means," she said. "And we will open at Dover."

The original provision of ten hospital parties was inadequate to supply the 300 hospitals eventually receiving live entertainment. Some forty extra concerts were organized each month for special occasions; there were mobile cinemas, too, doing hospital duty, and a wide circulation of film programmes for those institutions that had their own projectors.

The supply of suitable artistes gave out, so the other producing Sections had to lend a hand. This led to some oddities. Five young actresses, all members of the same repertory company, performed three one-act plays in costume, one of which was an incident in the life of Queen Elizabeth I. Conditions were hard: no scenery, only one theatrical basket to contain all the costumes and wigs. . . . Thump! as a careless orderly tilts the basket into the road. Some one has forgotten to fasten the lid, and the queen's bejewelled wig and flounced petticoats tumble out into the road. Squelch, squelch! as the orderly retrieves 'sock and buskin' and bundles them back into the basket, streaked with mud. "Sorry, miss, but the audience won't know any difference here. This is a looney bin. . . ." It needed a sense of humour to do that sort of thing twice a day for weeks on end, especially as owing to shortage of transport the party was driven round in a hearse, not a very suitable vehicle in which to convey entertainment to a hospital.

V.I.P. . . .

The visit of an ENSA party made a break in the round of duty as help-ful to doctors and nurses as the actual concert was to the patients. On one occasion Richard Tauber and other distinguished artistes paid a visit to a large military hospital near Epsom; but owing to a misunderstanding there was no one to receive them on arrival. The concert was a huge success, and at the end the Senior Medical Officer hurried round to thank Tauber and to apologize profusely that the matron had not been there to receive him.

"Ach! Where is she then?" said the easy-going Tauber with a smile.

"Well, as a matter of fact she's gone to the pictures."

3
Bed and Breakfast

It will be seen that not all my Prætorians were men; among the dedi-cated women was Madame Vernon. Immediately after the evacuation from France she had begun to interest herself in the supervision of hostels for artistes working in the Aldershot and Salisbury Plain areas, where the frequent complaints had compelled NAAFI to accept the obligation of providing accommodation. But such restricted opportunity made her un-happy and restless. One day she tapped on the door of my office with unusual gentleness and entered, blushing like a young girl. I had a Hitlerian intuition that this boded no good for our continued co-operation. Sure enough, she told me she wished to apply for a special commission in the W.A.A.F. Hiding my dismay behind an air of callousness, I told her it was quite out of the question; we should have a really big job for her shortly. (I had not the faintest idea what it was and, fortunately, she did not ask me.) Persuading her to stay on was a lucky stroke on my part, for, with the coming of the Blitz, a really serious problem arose, one which threatened a complete breakdown in the service and which only a woman of her drive and capacity for sustained work could tackle.

Lack of accommodation was now being reported from all over the country; it was worst in the industrial centres, where artistes of modest salary found their national service of so little account that no one seemed to care whether they had anywhere to sleep or not. In normal times artistes are expected to look after themselves; but this was a different matter. The Area Organizers did their best; but landladies were grasping and not very co-operative. As one comedian sourly remarked: "We didn't expect a bed of roses. The trouble is there's no beds at all." There is the authentic story of a party manager's despairing search for billets in a Lancashire town, and of his knocking on the door of a house to which he had been recommended to ask the landlady if she had a bedroom to let. "Not for a day or two," replied the woman, adding, as an afterthought, "'e's not dead yet!"

In despair the artistes began to abandon the work. A constructive plan was needed, broad enough in scope to cover the whole country and based upon the Corporation's acceptance of responsibility for find-ing board and lodging for ENSA artistes everywhere. Within a fortnight of our interview I had written Madame Vernon a brief minute, proposing the formation of a Welfare Division with herself in charge.

We set out to solve the problem of accommodation in two ways. For the military parties there must be a country-wide extension of the hostel system: that much was clear. For the factory service the problem was more difficult. These parties could not be accommodated in the hostels as a general rule. The hours of work were different, which in turn affected the meal hours; also the military camps were usually some distance away from the factory areas, which made co-ordination of transport impossible. A system of subsidized billets was finally decided upon: that is to say, a weekly payment guaranteed to the landladies, provided they kept the accommodation permanently at our disposal. As the cost of living continued to rise, our nominal rates of pay became a hardship to those who were not well off. We met this by pegging the cost of board and lodging for all artistes at 35s. per week. Expenditure above that figure, whether at the NAAFI hostels or the guaranteed billets, was charged to the funds of the NAAFI Department of National Service Entertainment.

Welfare Assistants were appointed to each Area. Many of these women began as voluntary workers, after the manner of the W.V.S., but the volume of work became so great that paid whole-time employment was instituted. The Welfare staff worked closely with the Area Organizers, small cars enabling them to keep in touch with the hostels and to supervise the billeting.

For hostels the Corporation, through its Works' Branch, leased suitable premises, furnished them and provided the staff and rations. In some of the country houses that were taken over the furniture remained, which was a relief from the depressing NAAFI style of furnishing, with its rexine-covered fumed oak and its mass-produced lithographs. Actors and actresses have little liking for the communal life at any time. Under war conditions they were thrown into such close and intimate association both inside the theatre and through the long hours of daily travel that it was particularly hard to bear. It was one thing to have to endure the dressing-room comedian's raucous stories in the theatre, but quite another matter to find them ringing in one's ears across the breakfast-table!

Madame Vernon fought her way into the good graces of NAAFI's diet experts and succeeded in obtaining a greater variety of food and cooking than the Corporation was accustomed to provide elsewhere. Amongst other things she waged relentless war against 'NAAFI tea,' an esoteric brew of doubtful reputation with the troops and equally detested by the artistes, who soon discovered that no amount of wisecracking could improve its taste. Yet Madame Vernon eventually laid low the dragon. . . . I for one, gratefully recall many a delicious cup of tea drunk in hostels after a cold winter's journey.

Madame Vernon was as considerate towards the elderly actresses as she was fussy over the young girls touring for the first time. Her inquisitive energy sometimes carried her into dangerous waters. When the young people consulted her about their emotional problems, as they often did, the warmth of her response occasionally involved her in difficult situations. There were many stories—moving, painful and sometimes disagreeable—that she brought to my ears, in the hope that I would intercede on behalf of whomever she thought to be in the right, but which I most purposefully forgot.

The whole of this edifice of care and attention was based upon the support and guidance of an Advisory Welfare Council, meeting at regular intervals at Drury Lane under the Chairmanship of Lady Louis Mountbatten. Whenever, as the result of a Council decision, it was necessary to make an approach to NAAFI for a general ruling involving further concessions to the artistes, it was Lady Louis who did so. Her influence during those formative years, when the idea of welfare work for the theatrical profession was new, was of paramount importance in establishing precedents and securing a sympathetic approach to many problems.

By the end of 1942 the Welfare Division had covered the twenty-six military areas of Britain and the Command in Northern Ireland with a network of eighty hostels and over 7,000 registered billets. This achievement was due mainly to the energy and devotion of Madame Vernon. But the work could not have been carried out on such a vast scale without the co-operation of the extremely efficient Catering and Works Departments of NAAFI.

◇◇◇

Documentary . . .

Two half-open doors face one another across a narrow passage: within, vistas of desks with typewriters and telephones and bunches of fresh flowers; on the walls, rows of photographic enlargements of gracious country houses; the typewriters and telephones all in use together, mingling with excited female voices, a vehement orchestration of high-speed activity.

"What's all this about?" says Lefebure, as secretaries scuttle from doorway to doorway.

"Welfare Division, Madame Vernon," I reply.

"I've heard about her."

Then, riding the storm, comes Virginia's incisive voice, as she accepts a trunk call:

"Perth? Well, what is it? Why can't you? Nonsense. Take a night train! Well, make the Area Organizer give you his car."

Another telephone rings on her desk.

"Hello! Hello! What's the matter with this damned telephone? Switchboard!"

"Is it always like this?" mutters Lefebure.

"Most days."

"Yes, I can hear you, Truro. No, I haven't forgotten the dartboards. Yes. I'll see you get them. And the piano."

Lefebure turns to me with a grim look:

"She won't, you know!"

"She will, you know," I mutter. "Like to discuss it with her?"

"Not me!" And our Treasury watch-dog hastens away.

4

'Blue Nose'

"Out!" yells a stentorian voice.

"What?" replies a scared little comedian from the stage.

"Cut that out," the voice repeats.

"It went all right at the Gateshead pantomime last year."

"Maybe, but—out!"

We were standing at the back of the shrouded stalls, Lefebure and I, watching the rehearsal of a new revue before it went overseas.

Since medieval times English humour has always contained a strong element of vulgarity, not to say bawdiness. In that sense the modern red-nosed comic is heir to a tradition that even Shakespeare observed. After all, most of us prefer the straightforward vulgarity of the old-time music hall to the tedious innuendo that passes for a more sophisticated taste in such matters. The former is at least a safety valve, whilst the latter is mere indulgence. But there is a type of bludgeoning performer who wears a proboscis of another hue, best described as 'blue nose,' whose reliance upon lavatory jokes and indecent gesture is sickening when it is not frankly boring.

The thirst for entertainment was so great that indifferent performers of this type got more applause than they deserved, and this encouraged an inordinate belief in their abilities. They lacked the salutary experience of one comedian, sitting beside the driver of a coach on the way back to billets after the show.

"I used to be in your business," said the driver.

"Go on!"

"Fact. Earned many a half-guinea singing comic songs. Had to give it up, though. Couldn't make it pay."

"Oh?" said the comic, thinking of something else.

"Yes. But after seeing you I think I'll take it up again."

As the nuisance persisted a chain of supervision had to be introduced. An Inspection and Quality Committee was set up and given terms of reference which included the censoring of all script material beforehand and the right to withhold approval at the final dress rehearsal, which must be attended by a quorum of the committee. No party was to be given transport, either by road, rail, sea or air, until the Transport Divisions had received a certificate that the show was ready and fit for the road, signed by the Chairman of the Committee. Despite these precautions, vulgarity, blue jokes, suggestiveness and the like cropped up from time to time.

Such cases occurred when a comedian omitted from the dress rehearsal at Drury Lane any gags that he thought the Committee would object to, waiting until he got out on the road to reintroduce them. If they went well there he might go even farther; and so one vulgarity would lead to another until finally a complaint was received. The pest arose, too, when little parties, designed to give entertainment lasting an hour or so, were called upon to expand their programmes to last two hours. The artistes ran out of material, and began to pad out their turns with tap-room gags, often of the most abysmal vulgarity. (The majority of variety artistes work with a limited repertoire; their fund of invention seems limited.) To combat this I issued instructions that all artistes must in future carry with them typewritten copies of their material, signed by a member of the Inspection Committee, which they must produce on demand of either the Area Organizer or the entertainment officer. Further, the system of reports, first instituted in France and now brought up to date, was strictly enforced.

Continued breaches of the rules led to disciplinary action. This consisted of suspension from employment for varying periods of from three to six months. In persistent bad cases the suspension was made absolute. In such cases the Inspection Executive reported the matter to the Advisory Labour Council, so as to avoid trouble with the unions. Once the Council was satisfied as to the facts it was as insistent upon disciplinary measures as we were. Where dismissal was the penalty the *coup-de-grâce* was administered by the General Secretary with all the gravity that befitted the principal of the Royal Academy of Dramatic Art. It must have seemed rather like expulsion from school to some of these unfortunates, totally unused to discipline of any kind.

The content of the programmes had to be watched for other elements besides vulgarity. References to marital infidelity, getting girls into trouble and the like were not good for morale. Also, none of our audiences cared much for jokes about Hitler, Goebbels and Co. It was as though they instinctively recognized the menace of those war figures as too serious to be joked about. Therein lay a notable difference; the national approach to the Second World War was no less determined than in the First, but there were fewer illusions. Perhaps this explains, too, the dearth of popular war songs. At the outset it was the choruses of the First War to which the men had recourse in their canteens. Not until the Battle of Britain and the London Blitz did the indomitable humour of the people come to the surface.

At one time the criticism of undesirable elements in ENSA shows reached such a pitch of over-statement that it had to burst or be lanced before reasonableness could be restored. In this situation Macqueen-Pope acted with a calculated haste. Declaring that the remarks of a certain London newspaper upon the disclaimers he had issued reflected upon his "veracity and professional integrity," he issued a writ. At the same time all the Regional Chairmen signed a letter of protest, waited upon the newspaper proprietor concerned, and obtained a measure of retraction from the contributor. Only then did Pope withdraw his writ. It would be difficult to find another man in theatrical circles to act with such courage and independence in similar circumstances. Without his zest and energy neither ENSA nor I, personally, could have survived those early attacks.

Without Comment . . .

Mr Wilby Lunn took his 'Spotlight' concert party to a certain camp in the West of England. On his arrival the entertainment officer came to inquire if there were anything in the programme to which exception might be taken, as the commanding officer and his daughter were coming. He was told there was nothing. The officer returned a quarter of an hour later to tell Lunn the C.O. was not coming after all, only his daughter—adding, "so you can make it as dirty as you like."

5
"Good-bye for now"

One afternoon I invited Lefebure to watch the departure of one of our parties for overseas. . . . The whole business of dispatching artistes from Drury Lane had an air of mystery about it. The parties never knew exactly where they were going, not even the port of embarkation. It must be either north or south—yes, certainly, they knew that from the type of clothing they were asked to take with them—all else was unknown, a great void which one filled with high adventure or danger and anxiety, according to one's liking.

One manager was so impressed with the need for secrecy that he took all the luggage with its secret identification marks down to Euston in a lorry to hand over personally to the foreman porter, rather than allow it out of his sight.

"Where are you for, sir?"

"I have no idea. P8/5, wherever that may be."

"Bill!" shouts the foreman to another porter across the yard.

"'Ullo!" says Bill.

"More stuff for Greenock." . . .

In the half-light at the back of the stage the artistes are checking and labelling their luggage or making sure with a member of the Passports and Permits Section that their papers, medical certificates, identity cards and so forth are in order. They move about behind the scenery on tip-toe, talking in whispers, for another company has begun to rehearse a musical comedy.

"Where is the manager?"

"Being briefed by M.I.5," I am told in awestruck tones (All Security routine was M.I.5 to the actors.) Lefebure and I wander elsewhere. . . .

It is two hours later and night has fallen. Typewriter and telephone concatenate no more. Now there are only intermittent reminders of late work as I slowly cross the back of the stage to go home. The artistes are leaving at last, the final briefing speech of the Security Officer still buzzing in their ears. Parents and friends have gone home; they may not see them off nor send telegrams to the boat to wish them luck. Tired out with the excitement and the waiting, the artistes clamber into the coach. Even the elderly comedian's interminable fountain of chaff with which he has been splashing the company is stilled. Last in is the manager, grasping his briefcase and hurriedly shaking hands with the boss of the Overseas Division.

"Thank God we're off at last," mutters some one, as the siren sounds for yet another air-raid. But no, not yet! The Security Officer steps into the coach to examine the papers of each one by the light of a torch. This is done to prevent the last-minute substitution of undesirables, though how this could be, knowing the sharp wits of the players, I cannot imagine. The young girls sit awed and silent, watching him with eyes narrow with curiosity, as he thumbs through their papers. Now he flashes his torch into the face of the youngest and prettiest. This is too much for the talkative comedian: "Hey! You want a surprise pink[1] in that, guv'nor." The officer smiles in a superior sort of way and finishes his task. The coach door is slammed, as I stand silent and watchful under the dark portico of the stage-door. "Good-byeee" sounds faintly through the glass from the

[1] The name of a coloured gelatine medium used to glamourize women's faces on the stage.

irrepressible one. There is a lump in my throat as I turn to speak to Lefebure; but, of course, he has gone home long ago.

I go back to watch the dress rehearsal of the musical comedy. The merry-go-round of Old Drury: as one set of players slips away into the dark another takes its place.

CHAPTER SEVENTEEN

STAGE-DOOR TO FREEDOM

1

A Murmuration . . .

EVER since the beginning of her history Britannia has been taking in lodgers. In the old time they came with the sword of conquest. Later, fleeing from that sword, they came bringing new crafts and skills of hand and brain. Now they were here, not as refugees but as volunteers to fight for peace: Dutch, French, Belgians, Norwegians and, of course, the Poles. No sooner were the new arrivals comfortably settled in than they began to ask the landlady what there was to do in the evenings, where was the nearest cinema and was there a radio in the house?

The foreign troops evacuated from Dunkirk along with the British troops were admitted to our shows as a matter of routine, but soon came a direct request for entertainment specifically for Dutch troops quartered in South Wales. We were eager to comply, but in some perplexity how to go about it. We tried first to plan a sort of 'dumb crambo' entertainment, and I recall 'Tommy' Bates coming in to my room one morning very pleased with himself because he had found two turns that he thought would be just the thing: a clown and a juggler. "You see," he explained, "they neither of them speak a word." Then it occurred to me to consult Madame Vernon. I remembered her gift of tongues, her wide knowledge of the French theatre and her familiarity with the Continental approach to matters of entertainment generally, to which her long residence in Paris had been the passport.

An Advisory International Council was formed under the Chairmanship of the Earl of Cromer. Each of the Allied Governments was invited to appoint one or more official representatives to it: Bridges Adams and Miss Parkinson of the Resident Foreigners Department represented the British Council; staff officers from the War Office, accredited to the Foreign Missions in London, and our own Service Liaison Officers were *ex officio* members. Madame Vernon became Secretary to the Council and executive head of the International Section.

There was quite a turn-out at the Council's first meeting. All the foreign representatives attended in their respective naval, military and air-force uniforms, adorned with rows of clinking medals, which made many a junior typist forget her space-bar in contemplation of so much military distinction. Lord Cromer invited me to address them and to outline the terms of reference. I could not resist a thrill of pride as I looked round the crowded conference room and realized the opportunities which the British Theatre, through ENSA, was about to afford to the Theatre of the Continent. Thereafter Lord Cromer conducted the affairs of the Council with ineffable tact and diplomacy. What might have proved to be a whole kettleful of trouble in less distinguished hands never gave me an anxious moment.

The auditions for so many different nationalities were exciting occasions, particularly so the first. Word had gone round from the Allied Missions—and through the grapevine, whose tendrils are never stronger than in the world of the dispossessed. On the appointed day little knots of people began to gather in shadowy corners of the stage, standing silent for the most part, even though their dancing eyes betrayed their excitement at renewing acquaintance with the familiar back-stage life. About their clothes and bearing there was that special look of the refugee, now a common sight in once insular Britain. Presently there were muffled exclamations and emotional outcries as friends met after long intervals or recounted tragic separations. Madame Vernon buzzed excitedly from group to group, greeting them effusively, although not all could have been so well known to her as the warmth of the welcome suggested. Never mind; it flattered the nations and put the artistes at their ease. In the stalls waiting to begin the audition sat Lilian Braithwaite, William Armstrong, Bridges Adams and members of the Allied Missions. Grim reality lay beneath the romantic scene. As Virginia turned in conversation she saw a little golden-haired Dutch girl in black tights, lying unconscious in a dark corner of the stage. She had just been told that her fiancé, a Dutch airman, had been killed the day before. Nevertheless, she insisted on giving her audition, dancing enchantingly; she was engaged there and then.

Not all our distinguished foreign artistes reached Drury Lane in time for that first audition. The remainder came at intervals, hurrying through fire and tempest, hunger and fear, like questing birds seeking the opportunity to live as artistes and to add their individual notes to the defiant chorus. For France there was Paul Bonifas, the youngest actor at the Comédie Française when war broke out. After fighting through Belgium and Flanders with the French artillery, being wounded at Dunkirk and brought to England, he joined the Free French, represented his country on our Advisory Council and, with his Théâtre Molière, presented many French classics.

On the lighter side, Georges Rex, Belgian born, but a popular star of the Paris boulevards, organized and starred in our French Cabaret. Leaving Brussels in May 1940, he caught the last train from Brussels to the French frontier, where, after a journey lasting forty-eight hours, he started to walk in the direction of Paris. At Abbeville he found himself in the middle of a battle. After various hardships, extending over two months, he reached Liverpool disguised as a Czech soldier. Then, there was Vladimir Jahnssen, a magnificent Norwegian singer who escaped from Norway in an open boat, and within a few days of his arrival came to Drury Lane and was immediately engaged. Later he became the star turn at all Norwegian locations under our auspices.

Germaine Sablon arrived in England via the Spanish Pyrenees and Ireland. Twenty-four hours after her release from Wandsworth Patriotic School, whither she had been sent, she came seeking ENSA's Stage-door to Freedom. She had no stage clothes and no music. On a scrap of paper she sketched the sort of dress she wanted to wear, from which our wardrobe department made her a replica of the costume in which she had become famous in Paris. The music was more difficult. She sat at the piano with Elsie April and Hubert Greenslade, who subsequently became her pianist; she sang her songs over and over to them; she also hummed the accompaniments. They wrote the music down for her. Two weeks after she had walked into Drury Lane Madame Sablon was singing to the Free French Forces. Subsequently she went to North Africa and sang to General Leclerc's army in the desert.

Polish artistes were everywhere, going about their lives and work with an air of desperate brilliance that dazzled every one, not least of all the cautious Scots. Talented, exasperating, the Polish Cabaret and the Polish Ballet were magnificent contributions to ENSA International's achievement. Later on the Polish Choir also toured under our auspices. Among these Poles were artistes and singers from the National Theatre of Warsaw, elegant young men with unpronounceable names, infectious laughs and faded but well-decorated uniforms of the Polish squadrons of the R.A.F.

When the submarine war was at its height the need of entertainment for Allied seamen during their brief visits to English ports became urgent. There was no allowance in our budget for it, but Bridges Adams arranged for the British Council to meet the cost. Parties, composed of artistes of the nationalities concerned, were sent to ports designated by the Allied Naval Authorities, usually at short notice. It was at one of these concerts that pretty Suzi Marquis, Belgian-born Parisian *diseuse*, won

BEATRICE
LILLIE
SIGNS ON

NERVO AND KNOX AT MONTE CASSINO, ITALY

PERFORMANCE
IN A CARRIER
LYING OFF
GIBRALTAR

GERALDO ON TOUR IN THE WESTERN DESERT

BROWN STUDIES

a private reward for her devotion. She had landed in England without so much as a toothbrush, and could not speak a word of English. Suzi got in touch with L'Institut Français, learned to sing in English and found fulfilment of her cherished purpose when she too came to ENSA's first audition. But anxiety remained. Her brother, an officer in a Belgian shipping line, could not be found. She wrote letters to ports all over the world at which he might be likely to call, but no word came. One day Suzi went with an ENSA party to a distant port. During the rehearsal of her songs she noticed some men watching her from the end of the hall. As she hurried to get food before the show, one of them playfully put his foot out to trip her up. She turned round angrily and a voice said: "Aren't you going to speak to me, Suzi?" It was her brother, brought ashore for the concert.

Greeting . . .

At an operational air-force station, occupied by the Czechs, the first performance of a Czech artiste, Madame Herlingerova (recently escaped from Czechoslovakia), was announced. The majority of the waiting airmen packed in the hangar were in flying kit, as 'take off' was to be immediately after the concert. As Herlingerova walked on to the platform several hundred Czech airmen rose and stood in silent greeting for their famous opera singer, and remained so until she began to sing. Then they sat down, most of them in tears.

2

. . . in Divers Tongues

International ENSA came to be widely known and loved by the Allied troops. The news of what it was doing for them reached the ears of their compatriots in the occupied countries by means of the series of broadcasts which it gave in association with the B.B.C. and our own Broadcasting Division under the name of 'Freedom Cabaret.'

By a curious trick of memory I had forgotten all about the first broadcast until reminded of it by a friend the other day. It was a most distinguished affair, taking place in the presence of the Queen of Holland, the King of Norway, the Grand Duchess of Luxembourg and leading representatives of all the nations then at war with Germany. The joint hosts were Lord Cromer, representing ENSA, and Sir Stephen Tallents, representing the B.B.C. It was the first time that famous artistes from all these countries had come together in one programme to broadcast to their homelands; so it has its place in the story of war-time broadcasting. The performance closed with *Land of Hope and Glory* sung as a duet by Richard Tauber and Eva Turner, the rest of the company (which included some famous foreign singers) joining in as chorus. There was a reception afterwards in the Conference Room, which brings me to one detail that I do now recall. On the morning of the broadcast the General Manager of NAAFI telephoned to ask who was paying for the refreshments, because, of course, the Corporation could not do so. Happily, the difficulty was overcome through the generosity of the B.B.C.

Towards the end of 1943 I sent a minute to Lord Cromer in which I invited his Advisory Council to consider the possibility of making a contribution towards our Second Front plans. I had in mind that leading artistes of each Allied Nation should go into the liberated countries with our columns, ready to raise the national flag of entertainment as the Allied Armies entered each capital city. The idea was approved in principle, but it was impossible to get anybody to concentrate on the plan so far ahead.

Our service of entertainment to foreign troops helped to maintain morale during their long stay in this country; also it enabled many distinguished artistes of other countries to take part, equally with our own, in the joyful task of applying their life's work and accomplishment to the refreshment of friends and the overthrow of enemies.

Magic Circle . . .

Although most of the records of the International Division are now lost, burnt presumably in the holocaust of fired paper that preceded our evacuation of Drury Lane in 1946, some of Madame Vernon's reports remain to justify her claim that this was the most colourful side of all the ENSA work in Britain. Here is one extract, giving an account of her discovery of a Czech conjuror:

> Late one evening during an air-raid I was working in my office at Drury Lane when the stage-doorman telephoned to say that a gentleman who spoke very little English and looked "most peculiar" was asking for me. A man in an ill-fitting, dusty R.A.F. uniform, with face and hands none too clean, was shown in. He gave his name as Verdini and said he was a conjuror. He had been given permission by his Commanding Officer to come to Drury Lane, but had no travel voucher nor any cash for his expenses. He produced from the pockets of his trousers and tunic strange gadgets, packs of cards, string, etc. We went out

on to the vast stage, where I turned on a T-piece and sat down at one side to watch his turn. Within a few minutes I realized that here was a master-conjuror. . . . He never ceased to perform for ENSA until the end of the war. Romance conjured him into marriage, however, when he was with a party in Northern Ireland. He fell in love with his landlady's daughter. Not without some misgivings her mother agreed to the marriage, and Verdini taught his Irish bride to be his partner. I saw him right at the very end of the war in Calcutta on his way to entertain the troops in South East Asia.

CHAPTER EIGHTEEN

MUSIC IN THE AIR

1

Prelude

ONE aspect of our work that aroused more argument than any other was the general standard of the performances. The Government Report had stated, "The entertainments supplied by ENSA are of a type well suited to the audiences for whom they are intended." Although this was true enough at the time it was written, the matter could not be disposed of as easily as that. For how long should we continue to disregard all but the lowest common denominator of taste? It was a problem not unlike that of the B.B.C.; but in our case there were important differences. Whereas the civilian goes shopping for his amusement, picking and choosing the theatre, music-hall, or cinema he wishes to take his girl to, the ENSA audiences, consisting of a variety of ages and tastes, were all jumbled together to share the same entertainment; and whereas the radio listener has a choice of programme and, in the last resort, can always switch off his set, our audience, whether in camp or factory, had no such alternative.

Differences in the level of intelligence between the Services tended to confuse the issue. At first, owing to its technical training, the R.A.F. stood higher in this respect than the Army, where our audiences were largely gatherings of youngsters, with little taste save for distraction, plus a sprinkling of old soldiers. Appreciation varied also from camp to camp. According to the reports some training battalions of the Guards had the lowest standards, while second in this inverted honours list came the railway troops. Beef and brawn had evidently replaced intelligence for the time being. But the picture began to change as men of the higher age groups were called up, and more and more women joined the Services: the desire for better things grew steadily.

The change was a reflection of what was happening to the nation as a whole, which had ceased to be divided into separate classes and was being forged into one sentient mass by the emotions of war. Without any highfalutin, one might say that the people had rediscovered their Elizabethan magnificence. Mind and heart were clearer for the strenuous exercise of supreme danger.

Slowly I began to realize—all too slowly, my critics will say—that the simplest entertainments were failing to meet the spiritual challenge of the hour. Changes would have to be made, even though they might cause a rumpus inside the organization. Many of the staff had backward-leaning views as to what was wanted. And Ernie Bevin's "'ighbrow" was still a sanction not to be disregarded. But the modest alleviation of vulgarity, which was the most they aspired to, was inadequate to meet the changing situation. Soon those who declared that only low-brow entertainment, spiced with a little healthy vulgarity, was wanted were more out of step with the general trend than those who had maintained that our primary function was to educate the men. The latter exhortation was nugatory; time and the hour were doing that.

It is strange that those to whom Music is an unknown world, which they cannot or will not explore, should so often feel an active resentment towards it. They imagine they are being got at in some way. I was reminded of this when, at one of the many conferences at which the problem of standards was being discussed, I proposed that Music should be given a more prominent place.

"Music?" said some one. "But we're giving 'em plenty of it. What about the Bands Division?"

I spoke tentatively of classical music and symphony orchestras.

"Oh!" he said contemptuously. "You mean 'good music.'"

At this somebody laughed; but I thought, despite the euphemism— "That is a better title for ordinary wear than Classical Music."

I was uncertain how to set about the palace revolution I had in mind. It is one thing to care deeply for music, and quite another to speak with knowledge and authority to its votaries. I was still pondering the problem when Providence blew a stormy petrel into my office, with a cigarette drooping from its mouth and waving a walking-stick, a creature of un-certain temper with a supreme indifference to the feelings of those who sought to hinder its unerring flight towards that rarefied upper air where only the finest music can be heard. This was Walter Legge, the recording manager of the Gramophone Company (H.M.V.). He had applied to Seymour Hicks for a part-time job in September 1939 and been sum-moned to the fold in 1940 to take charge of Contracts 'A,' an office on the NAAFI side of the organization that dealt exclusively with artistes' con-tracts. But Legge soon made his presence felt in other ways. Ultimately it was mainly to him that ENSA's outstanding achievements in taking the finest music to millions of men and women in the Forces and the factories were due.

2

Overture

A start was made with the new policy when an experimental concert with a programme devoted entirely to serious music was given at the Garrison Theatre, Aldershot, one Sunday evening in October 1940. The artistes included Maggie Teyte, Eileen Joyce, Nancy Evans and Alfred Cave. Because of the response the visit was extended to the rest of the week. Two divisions of Canadian soldiers were quartered in Aldershot at the time, and Maggie Teyte's singing of French songs was known to many of the French Canadians among them. On the fourth day she received a letter, signed by twenty soldiers, asking her to sing a group of Debussy....

After that first week I suggested that there might be a series of 'good music' parties to tour the camps. Before very long seven of these companies were distributed through the Commands, and many distinguished artistes appeared with them.

It was at Aldershot, too, that chamber music received its first welcome when a concert given by the Czech trio—Walter Susskind, Maria Lidka and Karel Moritz—aroused the greatest enthusiasm. As Griffiths stood by the box-office, watching the tough Canadian types file past the window, he was in grave doubt how the latest experiment would be received and wondered whether the Canadians would express their disapproval by wrecking the premises. As a hefty backwoodsman fumblingly produced his shilling, Griffiths was impelled to utter a warning: "You know this isn't a variety show? It's highbrow music."

"That's all right, brother," replied the Canadian, "so long as they swing it in between."

In the Southern Command another pioneer had been at work, independently of ENSA. Herbert Lodge, his duties as conductor of the Margate Orchestra terminated by the war, was spending his time hurrying about Salisbury Plain, organizing soldier-musicians into rehearsal groups with the ultimate object of forming a Southern Command Symphony Orchestra. A vista of new opportunity was opening before our eyes, and I was determined it should not be missed.

About this time Harold Nicolson, who had become Parliamentary Secretary to the Ministry of Information, asked me to see Sir Victor Schuster, Bart., who was attached to his Ministry, to discuss "the development of good music for the Forces." As a result of our talks a small Music Committee was formed, with Sir Victor as Chairman and Walter Legge as secretary. By 1941 the work had become so important and so extensive that Legge was transferred from the Contracts Branch to take charge of the newly formed Music Division. An Advisory Music Council[1] was set up at the same time. Schuster and Legge were indefatigable in persuading many eminent composers, professors of music and critics to join, so that it became the most representative body of musical opinion that has ever been formed in Britain. It was this fact, quite as much as the call to national service, that ensured for us the practical support of all the leading conductors and soloists in the country, without which this part of our story would not have been the tale of unbroken triumph that it became.

Legge was inclined at first to take the approval of the Council for granted, and to prepare his plans solely in consultation with the Chairman, leaving the Council to rubber-stamp its approval; but in due course this exuberance disappeared; regular monthly meetings were held and minutes kept. Thereafter the Council continued to guide the development of our music policy with formidable success and to lend its combined authority to the plans which Legge laid before it from time to time until VJ Day and beyond.

The Council's first task, after accepting my draft of its terms of reference, was to interview and select the whole-time music advisers and their assistants for whom I had asked. These advisers were attached to our Regional Headquarters. For various reasons the entertainment officers demurred at first to their appointment: some thought we were wasting the soldiers' money on something they did not want; others thought the advisers should be commissioned officers, presumably because the notion of receiving advice from civilians was repugnant to them. There were one or two to whom a love of classical music appeared as decidedly effeminate. However, it is proper to record that the Directorate of Army Welfare backed up the ENSA 'good music' policy wholeheartedly and circulated, unaltered, a memorandum to all Commands drawn up by the Chairman of the Music Council.

3

Allegro

Herbert Lodge, who now became ENSA Musical Adviser to Southern Command, was first away with a Command Symphony Orchestra. The opening performance was conducted by Sir Henry Wood, with Moisei-

[1] See Appendix Four.

witsch as the soloist. It was given at the Garrison Theatre, Bulford, and attended by the G.O.C.-in-C. and senior officers from Salisbury. I sat with Legge and well recall the excitement of that first success. Here was an example of the will towards better things, an immense potentiality for the future. . . . My reverie was interrupted: "Aren't you coming to see the old man?" demanded Legge. The concert was over, and the audience was trooping down the muddied concrete roads, talking excitedly and making respectful lanes for the staff cars conveying the Commander-in-Chief and his officers back to Salisbury. I pressed forward to shake the beaming Sir Henry by the hand, but was taken aback by his brusque manner. The manager of the Concert Division had just handed him a cheque for two guineas, and he asked me what it meant. With my tail between my legs I replied clumsily that it was the standard ENSA fee for one night's work.

The other music advisers were quick to follow Lodge's example, notably Richard Austen in Northern Command; in Western Command Harold Gray was responsible eventually for two more. In Scotland there was none, as distances were too great and the troops too dispersed to permit this being done. Alas! these orchestras had no permanence. Military duties made regular rehearsals difficult; also postings and promotions removed essential players. They were no more than brilliant improvisations, made for the immediate pleasure of musicians who found themselves together in a particular district, and for audiences whose sojourn was equally transitory.

Perhaps the most rewarding side of this music-making within the Forces lay in the formation of chamber music groups. At one period during the years of training for the grand assault there were as many as thirty pianoforte trios, string quartets and quintets rehearsing in Southern Command alone, the music being provided from the ENSA music lending library. Recitals by eminent soloists helped these developments along by encouraging the young audiences to sympathetic listening. In this regard special place must be given to Solomon, who, throughout the war and beyond, consistently and repeatedly responded to the call of national service. During the war he must have given several hundred recitals for us and played to every kind of audience and in every land where our mandate ran. Always imperturbable, never out-at-elbows with circumstance, his modesty led him into strange situations from which his good humour always extricated him, sometimes with a wry chuckle. Upon one occasion he was asked to take the place of Dennis Noble, who had undergone a slight operation. When he arrived at the camp Dennis was there, recovered, and expecting to sing. Without hesitation Solomon seated himself at the down-at-heels institute piano and played Dennis' accompaniments.

Another time Walter Legge went with him to the big R.A.F. station at Londonderry, where, as it happened, Solomon's pretty niece was stationed. She met them, and, as Solomon had a headache and craved tea and aspirin, they went to a restaurant. There huge steaks were displayed on a counter at one end. Legge went over and ordered two steaks and chips and two pints of beer. Meanwhile the virtuoso sat, waiting. The steaks were half consumed before he said mildly, "I hope you haven't forgotten, Walter, that we originally came here for tea and aspirin?"

4

Marche des Fêtes

Despite the efforts of individual musicians already in uniform, such as Vivian Ellis, to whom the naval personnel in the Plymouth Area owed much, this desire for music-making could not continue to feed upon itself for long. It needed to acquire force and direction from the example of the professional orchestras. So Legge conceived the idea of collaboration with the Music Department of the B.B.C. In retrospect this seems an obvious move; but it was entirely due to his initiative that the enthusiastic support of Adrian Boult, Arthur Bliss and Julian Livingston-Herbage was secured for the new project. Each year the B.B.C. Symphony Orchestra, with the co-operation of many of the great soloists, gave a week's festival of music to each of the Services in turn. As many of the performances as possible were broadcast either on the Home Service or in the Forces programme from "Somewhere in England." The orchestra was placed at ENSA's sole disposal for the festivals, and the NAAFI Department of National Service Entertainment made itself responsible for the movement and billeting of the players. Elaborate staff plans and time-tables had to be worked out to secure the smooth running of what would have been a considerable undertaking even in peace-time; under the conditions then prevailing it was much more difficult.

The first festival was given to the Army from May 23 to 28, 1943, at the Garrison Theatre, Aldershot. The second, a week later, in the Royal Naval Barracks at Portsmouth.

Sir Adrian Boult, writing gleefully of the week at Aldershot, reminds me that the record for the Saturday night takings, previously held by Gracie Fields, was beaten by 1s. 9d. Of the Navy's music week he writes: "The gymnasium had been fitted out in the most lovely way with acres of bunting and a magnificently solid platform which would have supported a team of elephants." Legge adds to this account by pointing out that the two side bays of the huge building had to be opened in order to get the audience in.

The principal Music Festivals for the R.A.F. were given on the huge aerodrome at St Athan, near Cardiff. During the first of them John Barbirolli, whose return from America to revitalize the Hallé was a piece of good fortune for us, too, shared the conducting with Adrian Boult. After his first concert two Welshmen spoke to him just as he was leaving. They stood goggling for a moment, and then one of them gasped out, "There was fire there, man, fire!" This intense interest was not just a passing phase, for in succeeding years, when the composition of the audiences had entirely changed, the same reactions were observed. The following year Albert Coates, whom we had brought back from America to join in the work, was the guest conductor. This gave Boult an opportunity of mixing with the audience and sensing things for himself. He sat at the back of the hall,

> peering through a thick pall of smoke, waiting for the concert to begin. After the music had started not one of the boys and girls moved a muscle, and if by chance one of them kept a cigarette alight for even a short while the slight movement gave one quite a shock. By the beginning of the interval the air was perfectly clear. Exactly the same thing happened in Part Two.

When the members of the B.B.C. Symphony Orchestra were given the first set of programmes they were sceptical, wondering how a troop audience would 'take' such high-level classical music. Their doubts were soon dispelled; and they eventually looked forward eagerly to their weeks with the troops.

The high standard of the programmes was not confined to the B.B.C. festivals. Elsewhere, in a long list, I notice a performance of the Bach concerto for three pianos played by Dennis Matthews, Harriet Cohen and Cyril Smith, with Wing-Commander O'Donnell conducting the R.A.F. Central Band. . . .

In a formal report to me on the first year's festivals the Chairman of the Music Council wrote that the nightly and weekly attendances broke all records, and on some evenings a thousand people were turned away.

<><><>

. . . ., ... *and Song* . . .

During the festival for the Royal Navy the old salt in charge of the gymnasium at Portsmouth never missed a note either of the rehearsals or the performances, standing in the same corner with scarred face and gnarled hands and riveted attention: a statue by Epstein! He had never heard a symphony orchestra before, and now he could not keep away. On the last night, during the deafening applause, he gripped Legge's hands in a vice, and gasped out, "God! It's worse'n drink or women, the way it gets you."

5

Allegro Vivace

The standard of the factory entertainments needed to be raised even more than that for the Forces, especially now the fervour and excitement of the threatened invasion had begun to evaporate. But the conditions under which the shows were given made the task more difficult. It was not only the bad acoustics in the canteens and recreation halls, the incessant clatter of plates and dishes, knives and forks alternating with tramping feet and the sharp ping of the accurate check-takers—all the accompanying cacophony of crowds of people being fed in a hurry. There was the more subtle handicap of the psychology of the audiences. Encompassed by the relentless energy of the machine, their minds were conditioned to the return to work and subsequent release, and not to the relaxation of listening to music.

Although the Music Division sent out a number of parties on the factory circuit, similar in character and standard to those which CEMA was providing, neither Legge nor I regarded these as a satisfactory answer to the problem. They ruffled the surface of attention, but they did not stir the depths. Then, too, we ran into a strange difficulty, caused by jealousy within the CEMA organization at what was regarded as our unwarranted intrusion upon its policy. The CEMA rates of pay were higher than ours —eighteen guineas a week as compared with ENSA's ten, and a higher scale of hotel and travelling expenses—an encouragement to artistes, financially pressed, to by-pass our offers. I called the attention of the Treasury to this matter several times, pointing out that it was obviously undesirable that two organizations receiving support from public funds should have divergent rates of pay for performing similar service. When it came to our knowledge that artistes were being told that if they gave factory performances for ENSA they would not be re-engaged by CEMA, the time had come to register a stronger protest.

Sir Kenneth Barnes was a member of the Council of CEMA. I passed the matter over to him, and he handled it with force and dignity. He set out the facts in a minute to Maynard Keynes, the Chairman of the CEMA

Council, and subsequently attended a meeting of that body, at which he roundly castigated certain CEMA officials for their attitude. Receiving no support from the Chair, he referred the matter to the Minister of Education (R. A. Butler) but received only a waffling reply; whereupon he resigned from CEMA, a courageous and loyal action which we all appreciated, knowing that Kenneth set considerable store by his membership of its Council. This deplorable affair showed that Keynes, the individualist, was not prepared to co-operate in the affairs of the professional entertainment world, except in the way that suited him.

Wondering whether the success of the music festivals could not be matched in the factory service, Walter Legge proposed that we should give two trial symphony concerts for factory workers at Southampton during the Navy's festival week at Portsmouth. Their success was so pronounced that the Ministry of Labour agreed to a series of such concerts being given during the coming winter season, to which I gave the general title of ENSA Symphony Concerts for War-workers.

Certain principles had to be agreed on with the Ministry of Labour, such as the classes of war-workers to be admitted, the prices of the seats, and how their sale was to be controlled. The eligibility of factories was gradually extended by the Ministry as time went on. As to the prices, we were told to charge 1s. and 6d.; but when it was discovered that nobody wanted the cheaper seats the standard charge of 1s. was agreed upon. Controlling the sale of the tickets was not so easy. Each concert was shared by a group of designated factories, and the demand was so much greater than the accommodation that some means had to be devised to ensure that every worker stood a fair chance of getting a ticket. (In certain areas, such as Birmingham, the demands were so great that concerts had to be duplicated—i.e., given on two successive nights.) Direct sale at the box-office would not do; a special system had to be developed in the light of experience. Eventually I decided upon numbered and dated coupons exchangeable for the actual tickets at the hall on the night of the concert, each factory to receive an allotment of coupons proportionate to its size. Distribution was carried out by the Music Advisers, working in conjunction with the Area Organizers and the Ministry of Labour. The workers in each factory balloted for the coupons. But an illicit traffic sprang up when they discovered that coupons could be sold to the general public at a considerable profit. This abuse became so widespread, especially in Lancashire, that an additional check upon identity in the shape of a work-card or tally had to be shown at the box-office before a ticket could be purchased. Thereafter the system worked fairly well.

The Ministry chose the towns where there were the greatest concentra-

tions of war industry. As the scope of the scheme was increased halls of
sufficient size were not everywhere available. In such cases permission was
sought to use the cathedrals and larger churches. By the war's end a
number of cathedrals had been included in the schedule of engagements,
bringing those noble places into the minds and hearts of the people as
never before.

The opening concert was given at Wigan on October 11, 1943, by the
Hallé Orchestra, conducted by Barbirolli. The programme included
Debussy's *Prélude à l'Après Midi d'un Faune*. After the concert Barbirolli
invited half a dozen people from the audience to come and tell him what
they thought of the programme, and which piece they liked best. The
majority chose the Debussy, which he thought was because its delicacy
and sensitiveness was in sharp contrast to lives spent among the whirr of
machinery. The first London concert was given in the People's Palace,
Stepney, on October 22, by the London Symphony Orchestra, with Basil
Cameron conducting. Eileen Joyce was the soloist. I managed to inveigle
Ernie Bevin away from his official duties to go to it. He received a great
reception from the workers, but the reception for the concert was even
greater.

Everywhere the appreciation of these factory audiences was quite overwhelming. It is trite to say one could have heard the proverbial pin drop
in the pianissimo passages of a symphony. I prefer the opinion once
expressed to me by Barbirolli that every performance was for him "a
spiritual experience," a view which the players shared to such an extent
that they eagerly anticipated these bookings, despite the discomfort and
the unusual halls in which they were called upon to play, such as the
one above an underground ordnance factory, where both the Birmingham and Liverpool orchestras performed whilst high explosives were
being manufactured beneath their feet.

Much of the success of a programme depended on the choice of the first
work, because many of these new concert-goers had never seen a symphony orchestra in action before; and it was important to give them the
earliest opportunity of hearing the maximum splendour and brilliance of
orchestral sound. Among the pieces selected at first for this purpose were
Carnaval Romain, the *Hungarian March* from *The Damnation of Faust*, the
Meistersinger overture and the overture to *Prince Igor*. As the Music Council
desired the concerts to begin with British works, several composers were
commissioned to write overtures specially for us; and of these *Work in
Progress* (Arnold Bax), *Overture to a Masque* (E. J. Moeran) and *Street
Corner* (Alan Rawsthorne) were subsequently published, and now occupy
a place in the repertoire of British music. (The last-named was first given

in the 'Holidays at Home' week organized by us for the Royal Borough of Leamington Spa.) In the main programmes all the Beethoven symphonies were done, except the Ninth; the Fifth Symphony of Bruckner, the Walton Symphony, Sibelius' Symphony No. 5, Mozart's 'Jupiter' symphony and many more. It was at an ENSA concert given by the Liverpool Philharmonic Orchestra that the first performance was given in London of William Walton's *Sinfonia Concertante* in its revised form, with Phyllis Sellick as soloist.

All the leading orchestras of Britain were called to the ENSA colours during this time: the B.B.C. Symphony, the London Philharmonic, the London Symphony, the Hallé, the Liverpool Philharmonic, the City of Birmingham, and the Scottish Orchestra. When in the second season (1944–45) the Ministry of Labour asked us to take in some smaller towns, where neither cathedrals nor halls large enough for full symphony orchestras were available, co-operation with the B.B.C. was further extended by using their other orchestras: the Northern, the Midland Light, the Scottish, and the Theatre Orchestra. During one season Sir Adrian Boult took the Northern Orchestra to Newcastle for a week, where it played under our auspices in various factories as well as in the Newcastle Town Hall. Another light orchestra calls for special mention, the Boyd Neel which gave 300 ENSA concerts in one year.

By reason of the opportunities thus placed in their way many young conductors achieved greater recognition. Among these may be mentioned Walter Susskind (previously comparatively unknown as a conductor), George Weldon (now Associate Conductor of the Hallé) and Vilem Tausky, who came to ENSA in the uniform of a Czech soldier and later conducted at Covent Garden.

6

Rondo

One of Legge's early schemes had been the formation of record libraries in each region, boxed into programmes of various types, such as symphony concerts, chamber music, piano recitals and so forth. There were also libraries of individual composers' works, catalogued under their names, for use at lecture-recitals, also scores for the use of those who wished to follow the music while the records were being played. Each box was provided with programme notes specially written by Edwin Evans, the distinguished music critic (and brother of Dame Edith Evans). In these an effort was made to interest the prospective audiences in the lives of the composers and the meaning of their work. They were admirably done, quite simple and completely free from music jargon.

Distribution was controlled by the music advisers—usually their assistants acted as librarians—and more than once did I encounter a music adviser on the road with boxes of records stacked in the back of his car, like some itinerant village salesman. In due course distribution became so extensive that we had to institute a system of self-help, the various military units and factories exchanging the programmes among themselves by motor-cycle, or other means, and a time-limit had to be placed on the retention of each set—just like a lending-library. When the scheme was in full operation each regional library contained many thousands of records, and was continually being extended. In the London District alone the number exceeded ten thousand, because it was from this pool that the regional libraries were kept supplied. Recitals for civilians were often given under unusual conditions: during the London Blitz *The Magic Flute* (in German), with Beecham conducting, was played in an air-raid shelter from recordings made by Walter Legge in Berlin in 1938—so successfully that it was repeated the following night.

Next in this orderly development of interest in recorded music came the music centres, circles or clubs, as they were variously called, springing up everywhere along the trails blazed by our musicians, in military depôts and garrison towns (where the permanent cadres held out hopes of a continuing policy[1]) and in the main industrial centres where our symphony concerts for war-workers were given. Inevitably, musical activity gravitated towards those groups, so that in the end it was mainly to them that the records were circulated. One of the most successful was the Salisbury Study Centre, organized by the Army Education Committee, where, in addition to our record service, we provided weekly concerts, ranging from chamber music played by famous quartets and soloists to lecture recitals at which Walter Legge, Ralph Hill and others told the stories of famous operas in between playings of some of the better-known scenes. At some of these recitals records were replaced by living artistes. Matters were so arranged that, roughly speaking, each music circle in the course of a season received a conspectus in miniature of the best music of all periods. Sometimes the lecture-recital would be integrated with the programme of a forthcoming symphony concert, so that the workers would know something about the music they were to hear, after the style of a film trailer.

Musical competitions were organized: instrumentalists, singers, choirs,

[1] By D-day there were three thousand of these music clubs spread among all the three Services, the majority of which held weekly meetings.

ensembles, all taking part; and sometimes the team of judges reached rather surprising decisions, as when at Swindon they gave the principal award to a man who played a musical saw with genuine artistry. This seemed to me an intelligent decision and not just a whimsy. The music circles, some of them with as many as a thousand members, had taken such a firm hold on the workers' imagination that, when ENSA came to an end, they were handed over to CEMA, and afterwards greatly expanded by the Arts Council under Sir Steuart Wilson's direction.

7

Scherzo

An interesting scheme, little publicized but a source of much encouragement to instrumentalists, was the establishment of an orchestral rehearsal centre in London to help those anxious to maintain their techniques and unable to find orchestras with which to practise. It was given the gay title of 'Drop in and Play,' and was open to all professional, semi-professional and advanced amateur players in uniform. Music and, in certain cases, instruments were provided by ENSA. Rehearsals were held on Monday evenings in a room off the Marylebone Road. The resident conductor was Norman del Mar, but others lent a hand, among them Adrian Boult, John Barbirolli and George Weldon. Members were asked to attend for a specified number of consecutive weeks, so as to ensure a reasonable deployment of instruments, but there were occasions when it was little more than a freak orchestra. One evening del Mar was confronted with ten French horns, eight drums, eight violas, fourteen cellos and about six fiddles. He had to divide the horns into sections to give each player a chance; and the six fiddles were told that they must sound like eighteen! Despite such eccentricities the 'Drop in and Play' scheme was more than a recreation, and at various times many first-class players made use of its opportunities.

There seemed no end to the menu of good things offered to those who had the palate for them. There was the wonderful occasion when Casals played the Elgar Concerto with the Liverpool Philharmonic, conducted by Walter Susskind, in Chester Cathedral, crowded to the doors with troops and factory workers. For this performance the great man received our statutory fee, by now increased from two to three guineas! Then there was that lovely midsummer day in 1943 when, by good fortune, I found myself at Salisbury. The Hallé Orchestra, conducted by Albert Coates, was giving a serenade concert in the gardens of the

ALICE DELYSIA LEADS SOME COMMUNITY SINGING IN TRIPOLI

EIGHTH ARMY PROTECTION

ᴛHONY EDEN BREAKS ᴏ AN ENSA CON- ᴛ IN ALEXANDRIA TO ᴏUNCE THE COMING ᴛHE WAR TO THE MIDDLE EAST

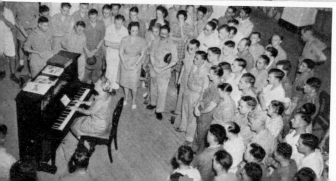

GRACIE 'HAS A BASH' AT AN INSTITUTE PIANO IN CEYLON

". . . MY LILI OF THE LAMPLIGHT, MY OWN LILI MARLENE"

MODERN SONG AND DANCE IN THE ANCIENT ROMAN AMPHITHEATRE
AT SABARTHA, TRIPOLITANIA

Bishop's Palace, with the Cathedral and Chapter House in the background. Over four thousand British and Allied troops were present. Before the concert was done the sky had begun to pale and the sunlight to slip from the ancient walls of the cathedral; then the evening star appeared. The troops stood or sat about on the grass, enwrapped. The whole effect was unbelievably lovely.

Although it was no part of the work of the Music Division—and, strictly speaking, has no place in this chapter—I must not forbear to mention the Brains Trusts for the Forces which Legge organized in conjunction with the Public Relations Council. It was just another side to his ubiquitous efforts to inject more originality and quality into the overall programme, in which I openly encouraged him, strongly supported by Alec Rea, William Armstrong and, whenever she was available— descending like lightning from the clouds—Virginia Vernon. Amongst the names that frequently appeared on those contents bills were Professor Andrade, James Agate, Edwin Evans, Desmond McCarthy, David Webster, P. P. Eckersley, Graham Howe, Professor Bernal, A. G. Street and William Barrett.

On one occasion six of the team had been doing a tour of Scotland— one-night stands—and had struck a noticeably dull audience in Arbroath. This depressed them greatly, as they thought they had been particularly brilliant. In the bus on the way back to the hotel Eckersley, Andrade and Legge fell to criticizing the dullness of the audience. During a pause in their tirade Desmond McCarthy remarked, "Well, gentlemen, I wouldn't go as far as you do, but let us say that when an express train passes, a cow usually raises its head."

8

Étude Fantasque

The struggle to raise our standards, of which the music policy was the major expression, was not carried on without some amusing mishaps. A staff accustomed to managing variety entertainment could hardly be expected to know how to handle the distinguished musicians now appearing for ENSA. Never before, I suppose, had such eminent artistes found themselves working side by side with patter comedians, crooners and dancers. Yet everybody worked with a will; and there was an overall acceptance of this unusual partnership because all were engaged upon the same national crusade. Nevertheless, the incongruity sometimes rose to the surface for all to see.

Upon one occasion the printing branch failed to correct a junior typist's

P

phonetics, and printed a poster announcing, among other items, "Orpheus and His Loot." Another poster announcing a lecture recital on the work of Hugo Wolf at the Aldershot Music Club caused much concern to the Passport and Permit Office. They could find no record of the name of Hugo Wolf on their Security files, and rang up the Music Division in a frenzy on the morning of the recital to know if "Hugo Wolf had his green identity card?"

A tour was organized through the camps for the Sadlers Wells Ballet, the music being played on two pianos, with Constant Lambert conducting and playing one of them. The official responsible for setting out the printing evidently had doubts about this 'attraction,' so he decided to improve matters. When the ballet arrived at the first camp on the tour, they read the following advertisement on the posters:

MISS CONSTANCE LAMBERT AND MISS MARGOT FONTEYN,
supported by a ballet of 40 lovely girls

9
Presto Furioso

The Music Division now occupied offices in the very front of Drury Lane Theatre, which was as it should be. The plaster-board partitions in the front lobby were used by the administrative staff, while in the box-office, where the walls were close-covered with contents bills of the concerts—as noble an array of announcements in the world of music as could possibly be imagined—sat Walter Legge, dispensing, not theatre seats, but exhortations and arguments in favour of classical music as the solvent of all ENSA ills. Musicians and singers alike had a healthy respect for the touch of genius which he displayed in the recording theatre. And behind the closed doors of the conference room, where a regular royal row on quality seemed to be in permanent session, his sweeping judgments and acid wit soon induced a similar regard for his opinions. I could not help admiring his contempt for those who would mix the classical and the popular, or, as he preferred to put it, the good with the bad, in the same programme. True, he would have stirred up less opposition to his plans by gentler methods. Yet his ruthlessness was a powerful ally; I was alternately exhilarated and annoyed by a tongue and temper that could cut through the broadcloth of complacency so swiftly.

Legge's secret contempt for the routine of organization amounted almost to an active principle of conduct; it seemed as though other people's hours must always conform to his. It was nothing for him to keep me waiting two hours or even two days for a conference for which, possibly, he had himself asked. "Where on earth have you been, Walter?" I would demand angrily. "Yesterday you said you would be up to see me in half an hour, since when you've not been near the place." "Sorry," he would smoothly reply, offering me a cigarette at the same time, "been to see So-and-So." Before I could protest further he would trot out a world-famous name as his latest acquisition giving the information with an air of studied indifference that carried with it the implication of yet more exciting news to follow. "That's all very well," I would splutter, "but you've forgotten to give the printing department the names for next week's R.A.F. festival, and I've had the station commander on the 'phone."

Eventually these vagaries were brought under a measure of control. But such reckless individualism can never be entirely suppressed, and the affairs of the Music Division were not conducted without a good deal of friction. Nevertheless, it was a shock to receive a memorandum towards the end of May 1944, signed by seven of the music advisers, which virtually demanded the removal of Legge from his position as controller of the Division. A copy of the memorandum was sent to each member of the Advisory Music Council at the same time that it was sent to me, which was perhaps a tactical error, seeing that at least one-half of it dealt with administrative matters. The point was an academic one, so far as I was concerned. But I was not prepared to have a pistol put either at my head or at the head of the Music Council, although I was prepared to become something of a 'devil's advocate' in respect of Legge's minor discourtesies. The story of the squabble, in which I found myself uncomfortably saddled with the task of sorting out fact from prejudice, is soon told. There were two main counts in the indictment: faulty organization at headquarters on the one hand, and lack of consideration for the point of view of the music advisers on the other. It was also suggested that there was favouritism in dispensing opportunities of conducting the symphony orchestras when their regular conductors were not available.

The criticisms of his administration were justified and were met by a rearrangement of duties. I also gave instructions that in future all music advisers would furnish monthly reports to be read by Legge at the meetings of the Council. Also, advisers would attend meetings if called upon, so that they could keep in touch with the distinguished musicians controlling the policy. The implication that standards were too high and that concessions should be made to more popular taste, which the second half of the memorandum contained, were in effect a reflection upon the Council, since that body endorsed where it did not initiate policy. In this respect Legge's position was impregnable, and it was a mistake to attack it.

The Council took a serious view of the charges of unsuitable standards and of favouritism, and had two exhaustive interviews with the 'Tolpuddle Martyrs.' It found itself unable to accept the criticisms and called for a withdrawal of the charge. The most eminent of the recusants, Dr Whittaker (Scotland), died before the decision was reached. Another withdrew his support of the memorandum, but the remainder preferred to resign. The only member of the Advisory Music Council who did not agree with its findings, Dr Vaughan Williams, also resigned.

There was the usual reaction of criticism in the Press and on the floor of the House of Commons, most of which fell upon my shoulders. In the case of the latter the Member's attack was made a trifle ridiculous because he had been briefed to complain that the Music Council had overburdened programmes "with renderings characteristic of Oriental and African races."

10

Trumpet Coda

To say that musicians up and down the country welcomed the new opportunities is an understatement. It was a fascinating crusade with certain victory in sight before the first battle was joined. The majority of the audiences had never before listened to music of such quality and serious intention. They had neither inhibitions nor traditions to overcome. Thus for the most part the seeds of musical appreciation were scattered upon virgin soil; some, too, upon stony ground, no doubt. But the cavalcade of strained and exhausted men and women who streamed in and out of the concert halls of Britain during those years was a triumphant vindication of the policy that Legge adumbrated with such aggressive confidence, and which the Council supported with the slogan, "only the best is good enough."

Good music became our 'Third Programme,' filling the air in the most unexpected places with its harmonies. Some will dismiss the phenomenon as merely the expression of war-time neurosis or as a need for relaxation from current anxieties; but the tremendous influence which the B.B.C. had had through the years must not be forgotten. It is an interesting speculation, although somewhat beside the point, as to whether radio drama has not similarly influenced the revival of poetic drama in the British theatre by training people to listen instead of to look, as in the cinema. If that be true then one is forced to the reflection that the influence is about to be reversed by television.

However the demand for good music may be explained by the social historian in the future, it was fortunate that ENSA was on hand with the will and the means to satisfy it on a scale that no other existing organization could possibly have achieved, CEMA not excepted, the amount of whose work was as a few spoonfuls to a full bucket. In justification of which it is sufficient to point out that, in the three concert seasons beginning in October 1943 and terminating in May 1946, 368 full-scale Symphony Concerts for War-workers were given. And the music festivals, the thousands of special concerts and recitals, the music circles and record libraries completed a vast programme of effort under one organization such as was never before seen, nor will be ever again. The fact that no concessions whatever were made to what is termed 'popular taste' makes the picture all the more impressive.

Happy Requiem . . .

On VE Day the Liverpool Philharmonic Orchestra found itself in Blackburn to give a performance of Verdi's Requiem with the local choral society. The choice of programme hardly seemed appropriate, and at the afternoon rehearsal Walter Susskind, the conductor, after surveying the growing hilarity of his players, expressed grave doubts whether either audience or orchestra would turn up in sufficient numbers for the evening, and whether the orchestra would be in a fit state to play if they did. Arrangements were made with each member of the choral society to take one or more members of the orchestra home for tea after the rehearsal, and to guarantee their return in time for the performance. In the evening the hall was packed to suffocation, and an exceptionally moving performance was given, joy and thankfulness adding spiritual fire to such physical warmth as may have been imbibed during the day's excitements.

CHAPTER NINETEEN

WIGS INTO UNIFORM

1

Off the Strength

BY the close of 1941 the increasing shortage of artistes had become a
major problem. The root of the trouble lay in the absence of any
overall plan for mobilizing the resources of the Entertainment Industry. Now it is clear what should have been done. As a first step, Music
and the Theatre should have been included in the schedule of reserved
occupations. The number of men and women engaged in these professions is relatively small. By a system of simple regulation all could have
been summoned to serve the needs of the armed forces and of the civil
population in turn, omitting only those whose youth and physical fitness
demanded their presence in the firing line. Thus, many of the glaring
incongruities and much of the heartbreak of the scramble for talent that
ensued could have been avoided.

The first arrangements for the deferment of actors and musicians were
haphazard in the extreme. For the commercial theatre a small committee
of managers was formed, representing both London and provincial
interests, to sift the applications and to advise the Ministry of Labour upon
them. This created invidious situations for those who were called upon to
oversee the applications of their brother managers. The call-up for military service had drained away the best of the younger talent, and when the
theatres and music-halls were permitted to reopen the needs of the civil
population had to be met. So it was in the nature of things that this committee of theatrical interests should seek to obtain deferment for as many
artistes as possible. And it viewed with alarm the inroads ENSA was
making upon the available talent and the possibility that its applications
for deferment might receive special favour, a needless alarm since the
Ministry of Labour declined to regard our applications as different in any
way and refused many of them. The fact that theatres and music-halls
were now crowded to overflowing, besides adding point to the argument
that public morale had to be maintained, increased the reluctance of

managers, anxious like everybody else to carry on, to part with any more actors to ENSA; it was also a visible enticement to men of low medical category whose inner call to duty was weak and made still weaker by our inability to hold out any promise of continuing immunity.

I was anxious that ENSA should not be regarded as a giant fox-hole, either by the profession or the general public, for that would have discredited our mission and might have brought the whole edifice toppling about our ears. For that reason I had insisted that all deferment cases must be carefully scrutinized at Drury Lane before being sent forward. Nevertheless, the attitude of the authorities raised the issue of our position vis-à-vis the rest of the industry in an acute form. We were at a further disadvantage when our conditions of employment were compared with the more lucrative commercial engagements. Patriotism at the expense of the actor's slender pocket was pitted against high salaries and all the comforts of home.

The Government Report had expressly stated that special consideration should be given to the deferment of artistes engaged in ENSA work, but our hopes in this regard were not realized. A separate committee was set up under the chairmanship of Lord May to recommend the deferment of artistes for both CEMA and ENSA; but whereas the managerial body was active in its recommendations, Lord May was pernickety to the point of exasperation. His reluctance, and that of the Ministry of Labour, was due to their anxiety to avoid public criticism. Seeing that the Ministry was gaining much benefit from our factory service and accepting the sacrifices the artistes were making to carry it out, it did seem to me that in this matter it was allowing discretion to outrun common sense.

2

Fall in!

We searched in every direction for means to make up the losses due to call-up. Amateur entertainment had dwindled to a mere trickle, as we had foreseen, because of the demands of civil defence and other essential duties. Short measure could not be made up from that source. The desire of the Treasury to use the lack of artistes as an argument for the reduction of our financial estimates added urgency to the search. But our efforts were circumscribed by the rapid expansion of the plans of the three Welfare Directorates for running their own entertainment schemes. Actors and producers were not slow to seize the opportunity of wearing the King's uniform and of keeping in touch with the profession at the same time, although the majority found themselves called upon to perform administrative duties in connexion with entertainment, for which previous experience had not fitted them. There were exceptions, of course, the most notable within my knowledge being Major W. J. ('Bill') O'Bryen, whose military accomplishments and wide theatrical experience appeared to me both to be wasted.

The number of artistes of low medical category, already working for ENSA, who found renewal of their deferments unexpectedly refused, began to increase. Refusal was usually followed by a call-up for service in a non-combatant unit, whence, after perfunctory training in such important military duties as standing to attention and knowing when and whom to salute, varied possibly by a spell of potato-peeling, the unfortunate artiste drifted sooner or later into a military concert party. The process was a waste of time and money in so far as the conversion of artistes into efficient soldiers was concerned, and a dispiriting opening to the career of an Army entertainer. One musician who had given two years hard and continuous service to ENSA in France and at home, only to find himself flung into a labour battalion at the end of it, wrote to his Section at Drury Lane complaining bitterly that after six weeks' idleness he was still without a pair of Army boots! No doubt an extreme case, but it will serve as an example of what was going on. Again, there were many talented artistes of foreign extraction possessing British passports who had been refused permission to work for us. Yet they had to register for military service and, eventually, were called up. They too found their way into military concert parties.

The inroads upon our manpower were not compensated for by the number of professional actors discharged from the Army. So many of them gave as the reason for their discharge that they were suffering from duodenal ulcer that I began to wonder whether the medical officers had hit upon this classification of unfitness as a means of getting rid of men unlikely to make good soldiers. The idea became so fixed in my mind that when one day a well-known actor in uniform came to see me and started to explain in a rather high-pitched voice that he was awaiting discharge, I said automatically, "What for, duodenal?" He stared at me, rather surprised and cross. "Certainly not. Hammer toes." The reply was so unexpected that I burst out laughing.

3

Toy Soldiers

The talent thus recruited by the Services was unevenly distributed, because the artistes tended to drift into units where they happened to have friends or where those responsible for gathering them in had contacts with the entertainment industry. And so pockets of talent were formed.

In an effort to overcome this the Director of Army Welfare decided to form a Central Pool of Artistes, and one of George Black's sons was put in charge of it. Very soon the theatrical Trades Union reported to our Advisory Labour Council that they had been asked to submit names of entertainers now serving with the Forces, or about to be called up, with a view to their transfer to the proposed Pool. Thus, a professional organization rivalling our own came into existence within the Army. Both the Pool and, later, the Army Bureau of Current Affairs (A.B.C.A.) absorbed a number of actors of quality, whom ENSA could have put to wider service. This activity made for impressive results on paper, but it did not alter the sum total of entertainment produced: it simply meant that it was given under different auspices.

Many of the war-time regimental bands were booked to appear with concert and variety artistes at provincial theatres and music-halls. The engagements were made on a commercial basis, either by payment of a royalty or a set fee. Highly skilled jazz musicians from the better-known civilian bands, who had been encouraged to join Army or R.A.F. units stationed within reach of the West End of London, were given passes to play in night clubs. All these soldier actors and musicians were being clothed, fed and, in some cases, transported at the public expense. It is difficult to see how such capers could be justified on any plea at all. At a time when the nation was meeting with nothing but frustration on sea and land it set a bad example to the millions of men, waiting, fully trained in Britain, for a chance to get at the enemy.

Our Public Relations Council raised the matter in the House of Commons and in the Press, campaigning for the abolition of "toy soldiers," a sobriquet which, if not complimentary, at least served to call public attention to the matter. There was everything to be said for the mobilization of all professional talent, and for its allocation to the commercial theatre and to national-service entertainment in accordance with requirements, but there was nothing at all to recommend a surreptitious "playing at theatres," when a fully accredited organization largely paid for out of public funds was already at work. Eventually a military inquiry was held and stricter regulations issued, governing the professional appearances of artistes while serving with the Forces.

4

"By any and every Means"

The early ENSA publicity had made glib reference to "a voluntary mobilization of all branches of the entertainment industry for national service," without realizing the disturbance of vested interests which the phrase implied, or the necessity for following it up with a compulsory scheme, if the voluntary one were to fail. But as early as February 1940 I began to write memoranda on the mobilization and co-ordination of entertainment resources and to make representations to those persons in authority who might be prepared to listen. I started by asking for a simple system whereby artistes not in medical category 'A' might be enlisted into employment companies and sent to France under our direction, pointing out that their talents would thus be employed for the benefit of all the fighting Services in turn and not for any particular unit. I also suggested that conscientious objectors might be recruited for similar purposes at home. I followed this up in July 1941 by asking for entertainment to be placed on the list of reserved occupations (much too late in the day), so that the direct recruiting of artistes and musicians of the higher age groups into H.M. Forces should cease. Finally I suggested to the War Office that recently recruited professional artistes should be transferred for short periods to ENSA, either as individuals or in employment companies. I hoped that by these means the Entertainment Industry would be safeguarded against further loss of personnel.

Nobody took any notice of my representations. Bevin shied at their controversial nature. Finance was not directly involved, therefore the matter did not particularly interest Lord May; and it definitely cut across the plans of the Welfare Directorates. I came to the conclusion that if we were to render effective service to the vast armies shortly to proceed overseas, the Minister of Labour must be persuaded to offer some inducement to those managements whose artistes were hanging back. From that point it was a simple progression to the idea that all artistes of either sex who were liable to national service should receive deferment only if they gave so many weeks' work each year to ENSA. This was as near to compulsion as I dare suggest; and it was very uncertain whether Whitehall would back me up. In any case the proposal would inevitably bring down much abuse upon my head.

I mentioned the idea to Bevin in our steam-clouded conference room one day, but his mind was full of more important issues. Finally I put the suggestion formally to Godfrey Ince. His reply was that the Minister would only consider the suggestion if it came to him with the unanimous approval of the entire industry. My spirits fell when I heard that. To obtain unanimity upon any subject within a profession where individual expression is the measure of success is a difficult proposition at any time; upon a matter closely touching the careers and pockets of all concerned it seemed hopeless.

5

Roll-call

On October 28, 1941, I addressed a special meeting of the London Theatre Council arranged for me by the President, Lord Esher. It seemed best to make the first approach to this body, which comprised representatives of British Actors' Equity and of the Society of West End Theatre Managers in equal numbers. I took the members fully into my confidence, gave them facts and figures and as much inside information as I felt entitled to do, and said that the time had come for the profession as a whole to give a certain amount of time each year to ENSA. The work was now recognized as essential to the war effort; and it was only by concerted action such as this that we could hope to set limits to the progressive denuding of the profession which, unchecked, might bring all show business to a virtual standstill. On the other hand if we could persuade the Government to a declaration of policy and to institute regulations to give effect to that policy, there was hope that commercial and national-service entertainment could be maintained in satisfactory proportion to one another.

A not particularly sympathetic discussion followed. The manager-representatives expressed doubts whether it would be possible to make what amounted to a bargain with the Government. However, it was arranged that two members of the Society of West End Managers and two from Equity should be appointed to act as a committee to discuss the matter with ENSA. So far so good. The plan had not been turned down out of hand.

To help things along I set down four paragraphs upon which I thought a memorandum could be drawn up and presented to the Minister by a deputation representing all sides of the industry.

I sent copies of my' four points' to Bronson Albery (representing the Society of West End Managers), to Percy Selby (now drawn into the discussions on behalf of the Theatrical Managers' Association, an influential body representing the provincial managers) and to each of the unions represented on our Advisory Labour Council. At the same time I drew up a further memorandum for members of the War Cabinet, urging the necessity for a "general strategic plan" to secure the distribution of entertainment in accordance with war-time priorities, and for tactical plans to implement that strategy on foreign fields and in the camps and factories at home. I had no means of knowing whether I was merely fanning the air with my lucubrations, but at least I extracted a promise from Bevin that he would study them.

Now began a wearisome search for the 'Holy Grail' of unanimity. There were thirteen organizations to be consulted, and a way had to be found of persuading them to accept my idea in principle and then to agree on a joint memorandum to the Minister. The Agents' Association was the bitterest opponent of the scheme at first, regarding it as an attempt on my part to come between them and the artistes they represented. A meeting was held at which I was exorcized by bell, book and contract. But in due course I gained the confidence of the Chairman, Harry Foster, sufficiently to secure the nominal support of the Association. Eventually, at a joint meeting held at the Savoy Hotel on January 14, 1942, with Bronson Albery in the chair, all but one of the thirteen organizations gave their consent in principle.

The business of drafting the memorandum might never have been concluded but for the patience and skill of Percy Selby, who, in company with Llewellyn Rees, then General Secretary of British Actors' Equity, did most of the work. Selby would have made an efficient civil servant. Possessed of a gift for negotiation and a love of balanced phrases, he had great influence with the tougher members of his Association, who were flattered to be addressed in such a dignified manner. In the background Bronson Albery gave hesitant support by trying to overcome the objections of the inner circle of West End managers who ultimately control London managerial policy. And Alec Rea worked hard as my deputy throughout this critical time, pouring ridicule upon fantastic rumours of my intended dictatorship of the theatre.

During the course of negotiations Selby warned me that a clique of managers and agents, despite formal approval of the plan by their associations, had begun to campaign against it, proposing as an alternative that any additional entertainment should be provided independently of ENSA. (Jealousy blinded them to the obvious financial and administrative difficulties of such a proposal.)

This was confirmed a few weeks later when I learned to my astonishment that the name of ENSA had been omitted from the final draft of the Memorandum. After consultation at Drury Lane I wrote to Albery and pointed out that if the document were to go forward as revised we should be bound to call the Minister's attention to the omission. I also gently reminded him that we had been charged by the Government with certain duties, and that it was in support of them that the scheme had been formulated. This last-minute hurdle being surmounted, a second joint meeting of all thirteen associations, which comfortably filled the ballroom of the Savoy Hotel, was held on February 23. As the arch-villain in this disturbance of the theatrical peace I was subjected to a good deal of heckling and felt like a speaker at an election meeting, propounding unpopular views to those of an opposing political faith. However, the Memorandum was finally approved.

6

Faith, Hope and Charity

March 2, 1942. The conference room at the Ministry of Labour was crowded with managers, actors and agents, all come to hear the Minister's answer. As Alec Rea, Kenneth Barnes and I made our way between the closely packed chairs to our allotted place we passed George Black, seated with a number of his associates. "Here they come, Faith, Hope and Charity," murmured George. "Which is which, George?" I asked brightly, but quaking inwardly. "Oh, I expect you'll play all three parts yourself," said George contemptuously, while his satellites laughed in chorus. We felt strangely cut off from former friends as we sat there waiting.

There was a hush, and then through the double doors facing us the Minister appeared, with Godfrey Ince at his elbow, followed by Lord Terrington (in war-time charge of deferment matters at the Ministry) and several more civil servants.

A nervous shuffling of chairs and arrangement of papers as the meeting gets down to business. The Minister welcomes the delegates with an expansive smile. Appreciating the difficulties of the industry at the present time and thanking them on behalf of the Government for the good work already done, particularly in the factories, he invites the chairman of the delegation formally to submit the Memorandum. One by one other delegates rise in support of it. Then Bevin calls upon me to state ENSA's case. The tone of hostility in his voice is something new in our relationship; he seems anxious to convince the meeting of his intention to keep ENSA firmly in its place. (Poker-face, I say to myself.) Following my brief, I produce facts and figures to show the present position and suggest that all artistes granted deferment from national service should give twelve weeks' work a year to ENSA.

Now the Minister makes his reply. The maintenance of entertainment for the civil population is an important part of Government policy. Nevertheless, in view of the national emergency sacrifices must be made. (Ah! Now we're coming to it!) Although he appreciates the industry's offer of national service he can give no general undertaking with regard to deferment. (The delegates look anxiously at one another.) However, he has decided that artistes who offer to give six weeks' work each year to national-service entertainment shall have that taken into consideration when their applications for deferment are considered. A moment's pause for breath, and then, as relief flows round the room in tiny wavelets, the Minister adds perfunctorily that offers of service must not be given in terms of personal convenience. Anxious looks give place to faint smiles and covert winks. The chairman of the delegation asks if the offers of service are to be made to the Ministry? "Certainly not," replies Bevin shortly. "To ENSA." Then, an unfortunate afterthought: "It might be advisable for the commercial theatre to form its own 'Bureau of Information' " (so he put it) "and let ENSA know from time to time what artistes are available and when." Deferment would continue to be recommended through the existing committees; that for the commercial theatre, now under the chairmanship of Lord Lytton, would be given enlarged terms of reference, while Lord May's committee would continue to deal with the applications from artistes working solely for CEMA and ENSA.

With bows and formal courtesies the Minister and his party retire. The delegates hurry to the doors at the opposite end of the room, sending the chairs slithering out of their neat rows in their anxiety to spread the news outside, while we three stand, dismayed.

"Six weeks! Just half what you asked for!" murmurs Kenneth wryly.

"I wish they hadn't invited Bevin to so many first-nights recently," I growled. And, remembering George Black's jibe, I thought, So Faith is destroyed, Hope vanishes, and we continue to live on Charity.

We made our way past the tumbled chairs out into St James's Square. "Not bad, eh?" grinned a loitering delegate. "I like old Bevin, even if he is Labour!"

I smiled. Whatever the ill-disposed might say and do, the entire Entertainment Industry was about to make a marriage of convenience with ENSA. The banns had been read, the terms of the marriage contract settled, and the day named by the Minister. All that remained for us was to gather the fruits of the union and to place them in the laps of the men and women fighting the war.

7

Deferment

Bevin's surrender to the glamour of the stage—there is no other explanation of his excessive leniency—had placed everybody in a difficult position, not least of all his own staff. It was not to be the actual service with ENSA but an offer of it that would secure the special consideration which, behind the guarded official phraseology, was tantamount to a grant of deferment. This flabby arrangement would remove any vestige of compulsion from the scheme and leave it as full of holes as a kitchen colander.

Those affected fell roughly into two groups, the managers and agents forming one and the artistes the other; but their actions and reactions were so interdependent that it is impossible now to dissect them, or to say where they criss-crossed or cancelled each other out. The continued existence of two committees, each recommending deferment for the same service but under different conditions, was the major embarrassment. Artistes naturally sought deferment through the Lytton Committee, where the obligation was limited, rather than submit their credentials to the precise examination of Lord May. We were at a further disadvantage in that the managers continued to have direct representation on the Lytton Committee, whereas we had none on its counterpart. This dual system could only have been worked successfully if requests for ENSA deferment had been given priority over those for the commercial theatre. In the end it was decided that artistes could not transfer their allegiance from one committee to the other; but our urgent request that the two committees should be merged in one was disregarded.

With regard to the offers of service, upon which deferment depended, it was impracticable for ENSA to accept these from individual artistes for such a short period as six weeks; the costs of rehearsal and production would have been prohibitive. Consequently, what were termed 'shows in being' took their place. And since offers of service were good currency in the deferment market the producers of shows were not slow in making them. All the new productions, presented either in the West End or in the provinces before coming to London, were offered to ENSA; but, since no dates were attached to the offers, these were of no immediate value. Many productions lasted for a year or more, as runs were consistently longer in war-time, and touring more profitable; so when the time came to redeem some of the long-dated promises we found Christ-mas pantomimes made available to us in the summer and summer shows in the winter. Yet the artistes had enjoyed deferment throughout the periods of each offer. Oftentimes the stars, without whom a production lost more than half its value, had mysteriously disappeared: they were filming; they were acting elsewhere—any excuse to avoid the despised ENSA. Admittedly, many of them were not liable for national service. Yet, if the manager had not obtained deferment for others in the cast, the stars could not have worked.

Gradually the larger loopholes were closed. To put a stop to managers and artistes slipping through the net of their own offers, lists of those who had been deferred by the Lytton Committee were sent to me; in return, we furnished the Ministry with the names of the shows accepted. Managers were later required to furnish cast lists and dates upon which the engage-ments would begin; but it was not until the autumn of 1943, at the in-stance of John Gielgud, that it was agreed to issue national-service con-tracts to each artiste at the time that the manager offered his production. . . . The Ministry of Labour officials were never quite sure how far the Minister was prepared to go in our support. In the circumstances it was remarkable that they succeeded in making the slovenly scheme work at all.

8

'Lease-Lend'

The Minister's suggestion that a bureau of information should be formed to collate the offers of service was not enough to overcome the general dislike of being directed to ENSA. In place of it an organization was set up by the original signatories to the Memorandum. This was called the Theatres' War Service Council (T.W.S.C.), a grandiloquent title that did not match its subsequent achievement and was too vague in its implication to catch the public attention. I preferred my own nickname of 'lease-lend' (an inversion of President Roosevelt's phrase) as a better description of the commercial entertainment about to be loaned to us. This name caught on, and was used within our own organization and throughout the profession generally.

It was not going to be an easy matter to absorb varying amounts of this 'lease-lend' into our far-flung and complex organization. However, we had invited the problem and must solve it. A lease-lend sub-committee was formed at Drury Lane under the chairmanship of Alec Rea, and given the most precise terms of reference, covering periods of service, size and cost of companies, security, health and billeting, and the other routine regulations which experience had shown to be necessary. Most of this was old stuff to our staff, but all had to be explained anew and, in some cases, fought over with the new T.W.S.C. office, which was now opened.

We had expected confusion to begin with; but there were times when we despaired of producing any sort of order out of the chaos. Nothing seemed to fit into our scheme of things: companies were too numerous and scenery too large, and the time allowed us for planning far too short. Productions that had ceased to attract were offered to us at one or two weeks' notice, whereas the average time we required to pass estimates, complete formalities and route the production was six weeks. Many touring companies wanted to appear for odd weeks and at remote places to suit the convenience of their other bookings; while variety turns favoured 'a trip with ENSA' as a means of filling in vacant weeks in their date books and doing their national service at the same time. All this made nonsense of our co-ordinated system, besides adding enormously to the transport bills, since we were under the obligation of taking companies and individuals from the place of their commercial engagement to the designated point on the ENSA circuit and thence to the town where the commercial tours recommenced or, alternatively, to London. I found myself reminding all concerned, in ever-sharpening accents, of the Minister's words that service was not to be given in terms of personal convenience.

In order to lessen the difficulties we were compelled to reduce the period of consecutive service, first of all to four weeks and, later, to two (in special cases). And to ease the complexities of booking, the grand tour of our twenty-six administrative areas was divided into three sub-circuits, centred on Glasgow, Manchester and London respectively, companies being routed from whatever centre was most convenient for them.

There were arguments over salaries. Artistes could not get used to the sudden drop in salary at the end of a commercial engagement; they seemed to think that a lease-lend artiste was a superior being to a mere 'rank-and-filer.' Being of contrary mind, I had no intention of altering the ENSA rates of pay for the newcomers, nor any other of our regulations for that matter. Our regular artistes were accustomed by now to the semi-military routine, to living in official billets or hostels, to medical examination and the usual Security measures; to travelling only in official transport and so forth and so on. The 'lease-lend' artistes had to learn by experience that they only brought discomfort on themselves if they tried to do differently. To toss one's head in disdain of the despised NAAFI

Q

catering often meant going without. Such independents soon grew tired of fending for themselves.

Following the formation of the T.W.S.C., Bronson Albery told me he wished to resign from the chairmanship of our Advisory Production Council, as he thought that body would no longer have a useful function to perform. The Council was the only professional link between the organization at Drury Lane and the vast audiences now gathering in all parts of the globe. At its monthly meetings it studied the reports collated by the Inspection Branch, and from them made its suggestions for the future. Moreover, several of its members, notably Edith Evans, John Clements and Richard Bird, were doing useful work in persuading authors and leading players to agree to simplified adaptations of plays with long casts and elaborate scenery. Many good things were reaching the camps by these means. If the Council were abolished, the staff would be compelled to rely upon information sent through official channels, not always helpful where truly frank opinion was the desideratum. However, the Society of West End Theatre Managers insisted upon Albery's withdrawal and that of two other members, Tom Arnold and S. E. ('Bill') Linnit.

The anxiety of the West End Managers to dissociate themselves from ENSA was difficult to understand, since it was only by close collaboration with us that the lease-lend organization could function at all. Standing out in contrast against the background of confusion and self-interest was Hugh Beaumont, managing director of the firm of H. M. Tennent, Ltd. Although the London stage was not then the field of monopoly it has since become, this weaver of contractual charms had already foreseen that, in an age of ration cards and queues, personality (the more colourful the better) was a sure element of success; perhaps an instinctive rather than a meditated judgment, but it was none the less correct. He had set out deliberately to draw as many box-office names within his orbit as possible; and in his war-time galaxy it was the female stars that twinkled the brightest.

He was the only manager present at my meeting with the London Theatre Council who had insisted that a clause *could* be added to the artiste's contract, binding him to work for ENSA at the end of his commercial engagement. Whenever he telephoned, telling me in his smooth, confident voice that he had something of interest to propose, I prepared my mind for good news; and as that cherubic face beamed at me across the table I felt elated, because here was certain to be a promise that would not be followed by disappointment. ENSA owed much to 'Binkie' Beaumont and the many stars whom he persuaded to work for it.

Bill Linnit, of the firm of Linnit and Dunfee, followed Beaumont's lead, and gave us valuable help. He organized special companies for Italy and the Middle East, above the limited requirements of lease-lend, and made personal journeys to supervise them. A handful of influential people behind the scenes in the variety world, such as Harry Foster, Horace Reeves and Val Parnell (who stepped into George Black's shoes at Moss Empires after the death of the latter), adding their personal influence to the inadequate regulations, were mainly responsible for better results from the variety stage.

Reports for the month of April 1943, roughly twelve months after the start of 'lease-lend,' disclose the following figures:

Of 42 Category A shows, 4 only were provided under 'lease-lend';

of Category B, 5 per cent.; and

of Category D, slightly more than 2 per cent.

Not surprising therefore that the gentle-tempered Alec Rea, with that sudden access of bile to which he was prone when deeply provoked, should declare to the Ministry of Labour one day that the T.W.S.C. was "a blasted bottleneck." Our stick and rag mountain had indeed laboured mightily, but only to produce such a tiny mouse that even the theatre cat disdained to kill it.

Request Item . . .

At a late stage in the war a famous comedian, who had been noticeably backward in coming forward, was asked to go overseas. His age and the number of his previous deferments seemed to indicate that this would be an appropriate action on his part. The head of the ENSA lease-lend office went to see him. The comedian said he would be delighted to go, but, unfortunately, he was waiting to make a film. Finding out that the preparations for it were far from complete, we returned to the charge. In the end the star reluctantly agreed to go for six weeks. Pressed to extend the time, he replied that he preferred "to stick to six weeks on paper," but if we were to publish a cable from Montgomery asking for him to stay on because of his success, he would make it another four weeks!

CHAPTER TWENTY

IN THE BLUE CORNER

1

Star Chamber

TO complete the picture of the mælstrom of conflicting interests in which we were struggling it is necessary to go back to what had been happening on our political front. The refusal of General Willans to become a member of the Entertainments Board proved to be the beginning of a determined effort to side-track the Government Report, to take over our functions and to run entertainment as a part of Army Welfare. What follows will supply ample justification for this sweeping statement.

The Army was ENSA's biggest customer. Since its appropriate senior representative would not be present at the board table there was little point in holding meetings of the Board. Consequently, none was held. Two results followed from this breach in the co-ordination network: it deprived us of any overall guidance on policy, and it enabled Lord May to keep all the financial strings in the hands of the Finance and Organization Committee. That Committee, apart from myself, represented only the NAAFI and Treasury interests; Lord May, the Chairman, was also Treasury adviser on the NAAFI Board.

Under the terms of the Report the total amount of entertainment required by the various Departments from time to time had first to be approved by the Board. But our estimates for the current entertainment year (1941-42), including the figures of expenditure incurred in its first months, had already been submitted direct to the Treasury. Sir Alan Barlow now suggested that the Service Departments should prepare revised estimates of their own—which, of course, they were quite incapable of doing, seeing that all the information enabling them to do so was in the possession of the staff at Drury Lane; and they displayed an obstinate reluctance to apply there for it. A good deal of haggling went on, the War Office refusing to accept our estimates in default of its own, while the Air Ministry pointed out acidly that the R.A.F. was in the front line and expected its requirements to be fully met. The delay was getting serious.

Already the summer was nearly over. Unless a decision were reached soon about the winter figures the machine would gradually slow down and finally stop for want of financial lubrication. We muddled through that autumn and winter, the Treasury grudgingly accepting our figures. The situation being what it was, they could hardly do otherwise. The brushing aside of the Board had removed the central authority whose primary function it was to determine these matters.

The Army Welfare people disliked my co-ordination plan; it took so much out of their hands which they had hoped to control that they did nothing to further its administration. Some of their entertainment officers, under the pretext of Security, refused to give our Area Organizers the locations. The more enterprising of our men went out and discovered them for themselves; the remainder gave up and left the work to the entertainment officers, who thereupon stated they could do the routing much better themselves. Eventually G.H.Q. Home Forces had to put its military foot down and issue instructions that the necessary information must be given to our staff.

Since little or no attempt was being made to follow the procedure laid down in the Report, I could not conceal my disappointment and spoke bitterly about it to Sir John Shute, the Chairman of our Western Regional Committee. He had been one of my sharpest critics in the early days of the Liverpool Repertory Theatre until the production of Hauptmann's *Hannele*, which he so much admired that he became my staunch supporter. We had kept in touch with one another throughout the quarter of a century that followed, and I was overjoyed when he consented to join us, only regretting that his many other public activities prevented him from taking a more important position in the ENSA hierarchy. The variety of his experience—first, as a leading member of the Cotton Exchange (who, in the First World War, had led the Liverpool Scottish with such distinction), and now as a Conservative Member for one of the City's Parliamentary Divisions and as Chairman of the Liverpool Playhouse—enabled him to grasp at once the various implications, military, poiltical, economic and professional, of our situation.

The Select Committee on National Expenditure was just then beginning a series of sittings in connexion with the Service Departments. Shute lost no time in discussing the matter with Sir John Wardlaw-Milne, the Chairman, who decided that the matter might properly be inquired into by the Sub-committee dealing with the Army. Determined not to lose the opportunity of making known all the facts about ENSA, I drove my unfortunate secretariat almost to the point of breakdown in preparing the dossier of our case.

On the first appointed day I hurried along Whitehall, almost empty of traffic save for buses, an occasional camouflaged Daimler transporting a senior official enthroned in mysterious anxiety, and the Fords and smaller 'pick-ups' crowded with back-room boys, many of them with brief-cases or rolls of plans under their arms, all hurrying to meetings and conferences or to the departure platforms of the railways. I too had formidable documentation under my arm, and I too knew my brief. Yet I was intensely nervous. This is worse than a first night, I thought. The palms of my hands are quite wet: must remember not to shake hands. I tried to laugh myself out of my foolishness. After all the Select Committee isn't the Star Chamber. This is a self-appointed task, and I'm doing it as well as I can! As I mounted the front steps of the War Office I longed for a dash of Seymour Hicks' breezy technique; so much better than relying on the bare integrity of a case.

Shute had warned me to support my statements with figures wherever possible, and as I sat down in front of the Committee and produced sheaves of documents and tabulated statistics from various folders, my examiners were taken aback at my preparations to storm the citadel of their good opinion. This did not look like a friendly little chat about entertainment!

When the examination began there was a certain vague hostility in the manner of the Chairman (Sir Ralph Glyn[1]). I assumed this was because General Willans' evidence had preceded mine. As the morning wore on, the Committee became so mentally waterlogged with the flood of facts and figures I poured over them that humour occasionally flew out of the window, as when one member said he had been told complaints were mainly about insufficient quantity rather than poor quality.

"How would you remedy that?" he asked.

"By providing more," I replied, and nobody laughed.

At the conclusion of the second sitting I made an urgent appeal to the Committee to persuade Army Welfare to implement the Government Report. On the way back to Drury Lane doubts began to jump up in front of me like so many sprites. Why be so positive that you're right? Why not let the War Office have its way? You're being Lady Louis' tank again, making heavy going for every one.

A week later Shute came breezing into my office:

"Well! You've certainly spilled the beans this time, my lad! Wardlaw-Milne says the Sub-committee's draft report condemns the War House so severely that he thinks it ought to be modified to avoid a public row. Also

[1] Now Lord Glyn.

he wants to know whether, if he delays publication, there's any chance of agreement between you?"

"Let's try," I said, with conscience heavy upon me. "Will you ask Sir John to hold up the Report?"

2

Mainly Cloudy

Round about the turn of the year I was asked to go to the Treasury to see Lord May and Sir Alan Barlow. The reluctance of the War Office to accept our figures was then explained. Army Welfare wished to provide their own Category 'D' entertainment and to take some of ENSA's financial allocation to pay for it. It was not proposed to employ civilians, but to rely entirely upon talent available within the Army. I was also told that any difficulties that had arisen were largely personal (as between General Willans and myself), and that these could be got over if Lord May presided over a weekly meeting between us. In reply I said the proposal would destroy co-ordination and therefore was contrary to the Government Report; as to the second point, it was not a question of personalities, but of principles. Surely the regular meeting of the Entertainments Board was the proper way in which to proceed? Lord May said this might be the ideal way, but the Army would not agree. However, perhaps I would submit proposals as a basis for comparison.

The ENSA Regional Chairmen were consulted, and a memorandum was prepared and signed by all of them. It was presented to the Treasury on January 17, 1942. On February 10 I went to the Treasury again, where I was told that our proposals were unacceptable. Sir Alan Barlow then handed me a short minute in which the views of the War Office were reiterated, the sum of £50,000 per annum being mentioned as the amount to be provided out of our funds for the Army's Category 'D.' I refused to accept the proposals, knowing they would destroy ENSA in the end, and said I must consult the various Councils and Regional Chairmen; feeling was high, and they might seek means to place the matter before the Cabinet. Sir Alan stared quizzically at me and Lord May polished his monocle. I left.

At a further meeting of our Regional Chairmen on February 16 strong views were expressed by all present, Lord Esher remarking that "the War Office was playing the German game with ENSA—taking Czechoslovakia to-day, and to-morrow it would be something else." A second memorandum was forwarded to the Treasury, pointing out that the shortage of entertainment was so great that the efforts of the Army should be devoted to supplementing the ENSA supply instead of to its replacement, and that any diversion of our funds to Army Welfare would adversely affect other parts of a co-ordinated service.

About this time Stanley Bell gave warning of a barometric change in the region of Adastral House, where a new Director of Air Force Welfare had taken the place of the friendly Halahan. Peake was an alert and youthful businessman who did not seem in the least intimidated by his sudden emergence in the exalted rank of air commodore. He was intelligent and inquisitive, and could double back round the corner of an argument quicker than most. He readily absorbed the information I poured into his ears. Then one day he thought it would be a good idea if the projection equipment we were installing at R.A.F. stations at the public expense, with a view to running an Air Force circuit, should be handed over to the individual stations to run for their own benefit. He went further than that—after all Willans was 'mixing it' for ENSA; why should he not do the same? When Ben Henry came storming into my office to tell me that Peake had been to a Ministry of Supply meeting to demand cinema projectors for the R.A.F. in competition with our own indents for the same purpose, it seemed as though the limits of topsy-turvydom had been reached.

3

Person to Person

Deeply as I resented the attempt to treat matters of policy as personal issues, I had no intention of putting myself in the wrong by refusing to fall in with Lord May's suggestion of having weekly meetings with General Willans. No doubt these little chats, more like tea-parties than serious conferences, were useful to the General in keeping himself informed of what was going on at Drury Lane. Lord May was always exceptionally anxious to be punctual at the weekly rendezvous, held alternately in the General's room at the 'War House' and mine at Drury Lane, as though he feared the antagonists would spring at each other's throats before the arrival of the referee. Upon one occasion, soon after the sessions started, his fears were almost justified. It was while the wrangling over the next year's estimates was still going on. Willans announced pontifically that the quality of our entertainment the previous winter had been beneath contempt.

"Are you referring to vulgarity, General?" I asked.

"Partly," replied Willans, superciliously.

"Then why don't you clean up your own Army shows?"

"Now, now, now," spluttered Lord May, polishing his eyeglass, and proceeded to tell one of his most dubious stories, while the General looked down his nose.

At another meeting a few weeks later the General announced that, as we could not afford to keep all the garrison theatres open with the expensive Category 'A' entertainments, he proposed to hire these from NAAFI for his own military concert parties and to charge admission prices so as to raise funds for more military entertainments. He blandly disregarded the fact that closure had been brought about solely by his own refusal either to support our requests for increased grants or to submit estimates of his own.

Lord Esher's words to our Regional Chairmen came into my mind. Evidently Army Welfare did not intend to await victory over its 'Czechoslovakia' before starting on its 'Poland.'

4

A Loose "Yes"

The time had now arrived for the next year's (1942–43) estimates to be prepared. . . .

But first, a backward glance at the figures to show how expenditure had mounted month by month and year by year since the days when NAAFI made a provision of £5000 for the first four weeks. By 1940–41 it was running at the rate of £1,300,000 per annum, of which £300,000 represented the cost of the factory concerts borne on the Ministry of Labour vote, and £200,000 was recouped from the admission charges, leaving a nett cost to NAAFI funds of £800,000. For the following year (1941–42) a further £200,000 was allocated, bringing the gross annual expenditure up to £1,500,000.

Anxious to avoid a repetition of the previous year's delays, I had the most elaborate statistics prepared for 1942–43, showing the exact amount of entertainment the troops in each area had received during the previous winter, and of what category. Out of a total of 10,764 military units, 4808 had received no entertainment at all, and many of the others had only received it at infrequent intervals varying from four to six weeks. The statistical survey included comparative tables, showing what the cost would be if all units were to receive shows at two, three and four week intervals respectively. If the frequency were to be once a fortnight for every one the cost would be about £2,500,000. The preparation of such accurate figures was made possible by the mass of data accumulated at

Drury Lane from our N.S.E. Committees and the system of separate reports for each performance. Nevertheless, the work kept our statistical branch busy for a fortnight or more. After making liberal deductions for the amateur and Service entertainments and for a reduced rate in the summer period, we decided to recommend expenditure for the Services at the rate of £1,750,000 per annum. Formidable as this amount appeared at the time, it was modest compared with the eventual annual figure, which exceeded £5,000,000 gross.

Meanwhile, our Regional Chairmen were getting very restive under a shower of criticism. Despite the fact that by January 1942 some 2500 separate entertainments (live and film) were being given each week in the Home Commands alone, thousands of men were getting no shows at all. The crop of complaints was heavy. Questions were asked in the House of Commons as to why the Entertainments Board did not meet; they received the usual stonewalling answers. But the Select Committee's strictures in their Report (now issued) could not be ignored. The Board was summoned to meet for the second time, eleven months after it came into existence, on March 18—ostensibly to settle the next year's allocation.

At the meeting Lord May still played for time, pointing out that the figures had been prepared by the Department of National Service Entertainment, i.e., ENSA, but were they in accord with the wishes of the Services? "What did the Army say? Were they not—er—proposing to— h'm—do more for themselves in future?" And he gazed with deceptive candour at the Army Welfare representative. Then, turning to the R.A.F.: "Would they not like more time to consider the matter, seeing that their Director of Welfare had only just been appointed?" Air-Commodore Peake rose to the fly greedily, and said he certainly would like more time.

"But," I protested, "the War Office has had the figures for the last fortnight and I know the R.A.F. want more."

"Now, now, now," replied Lord May, and out came the eyeglass for polishing. "You're always in too great a hurry."

"But the new period has already begun, sir."

"As to that, I'm sure the Treasury will agree to expenditure at the same rate as last summer."

"But that's hopeless," I spluttered, and then, observing a steely glint in the Chairman's eye, I said no more.

Meanwhile, across the street, Sir Alan, boggling at our totals, was in correspondence with the Permanent Secretaries of the Service Departments to persuade them to agree to a reduced figure. These officials, now brought into the picture for the first time, were concerned that such large sums of money should be expended on mere entertainment, and referred the matter back to the respective Directors of Welfare once more.

5

Tedious and Brief

There was no more hope of persuading Army Welfare to accept our estimates this year than last; they were obviously marking time, waiting for a high policy decision upon the continued existence of ENSA. Again I took Shute's advice and went down to the House of Commons and told my story to Wardlaw-Milne. He explained that the Select Committee could not interfere in matters of policy; but on the question of the estimates he acted promptly, telephoning then and there to the Treasury and requesting Sir Alan Barlow to come and see him at once—with some acerbity, I thought, but there! the Chairman of the Select Committee was entitled to cross-examine civil servants on matters which the Committee had under present review.

We had formed an Advisory Council on Public Relations as soon as it became apparent that there would be no Minister to speak for us in Parliament. Its members were well-known publicists and M.P.'s of various shades of opinion. They had already been most helpful in inviting backbenchers to visit Drury Lane and generally keeping us in touch with Parliamentary opinion. The Chairman was Sir Herbert Dunnico, an ex-Deputy Speaker of the House of Commons, who had been brought into the organization by Macqueen-Pope. I had kept closely in touch with Sir Herbert during the course of these events. When I told him of my talk with Wardlaw-Milne he offered to settle the Category 'D' matter for us. Much surprised, I nevertheless accepted his help. He wrote a personal letter, which he refused to let me see, to Arthur Henderson, the new Under-Secretary of State for War. This was towards the end of April 1942. On May 18, at our weekly meeting, General Willans demanded an explanation. I said I did not know what the letter contained. Lord May then sent to inquire if Sir Herbert Dunnico were in the building, and would he produce a copy of the letter? Here the two old gentlemen were equally matched, for Sir Herbert flatly refused to do so, whereupon the frustrated General remarked that in the circumstances he must seek further instructions. Shortly after this the Treasury informed me that Army Welfare was graciously pleased to abandon the Category 'D' project and its proposed raid upon our funds; but not before Sir James Grigg, then Secretary of State for War, had insisted upon the withdrawal of the

Dunnico letter. Of its contents I remain in ignorance to this day. The Air Ministry offensive died down at the same time. . . . This must read like some Iron Curtain fiction, but I am setting down events exactly as they took place.

The result of all this pressure was that a meeting was held at the Treasury on July 30. Those present were Lord May, Sir Alan Barlow and various officials representing the Treasury, the Directors of Welfare of all three Services, Sir Frank Benson (representing NAAFI), and myself. After various face-saving remarks as to stricter supervision of vulgarity in future, the allocation of expenditure for the winter period 1942–43 was formally ratified at the figure I had submitted in March.

6

Right you are, if you know you are

Although the campaign had been defeated our friends inside the House were far from satisfied. Clearly there would be no peace until General Willans took his seat on the Entertainments Board and that body met regularly, as it had been instructed to do. Therefore our friends, notably Sir Harold Webbe, an active newcomer to the Public Relations Council, renewed their pressure both on the floor of the House of Commons and in Minsterial circles. At the same time I did what I could to help by keeping in close touch with Ernest Bevin. He came with me on a one-day tour of the camps in the Aldershot Command, where he made brief 'whistle-stop' speeches to the troops in a style that mixed simple patriotism with the usual clichés of a Labour leader. He obviously enjoyed the authority which his position as a Cabinet Minister gave to these passionate exhortations; equally so the good supper which the hostess of the Anchor Hotel at Liphook laid before us before we began our return drive through the black-out. On the way home Ernie told stories of his early Trade Union days, interspersed with lively grumbles at the savage forays which Max (Lord Beaverbrook) at the Ministry of Aircraft Production was then making on his carefully husbanded man-power resources: "That b . . . r thinks he can do as he likes." He also expressed his admiration for that old b . . . r Churchill—the epithet popped up in his talk every few minutes— and his distrust of the War Office. He ended by telling me not to worry: "He'd see everything would be all right." An amiable sentiment, probably forgotten as soon as uttered.

After a tedious round of agitation and lobbying, in which Lord Tyrrell, all the Regional Chairmen and many private M.P.'s took part, an ENSA deputation interviewed Sir John Anderson, then Lord President of the Council. Major Milner, the Deputy Speaker, headed it, and John Shute and Harold Webbe were both present. They asked for full implementation of the Government Report. Further, in view of the public responsibilities that had now been placed upon me, they suggested I should be present at all meetings of the Entertainments Board. Both Lord May and Sir Frank Benson had previously desired my exclusion, regarding me as a servant of NAAFI and not as a person holding any outside responsibility. This was arrant nonsense, and I had not hesitated to say so. A minute was issued by the Lord President on October 22, 1942, appointing Major-General Willans as a member of the Entertainments Board and myself as its Technical Adviser.

The tragic death of General Willans in an air crash in the Middle East in the following year drew a warm tribute to his services from Sir James Grigg in the House of Commons. "De mortuis," etc., is a motto bearing a moral lesson that I have tried not to ignore. In reciting the facts I do not forget that I was always treated with personal courtesy and that I was dealing with a man as Hell-bent for his job as I was for mine. Yet there have been moments since when I have wanted to penetrate the shadows and to inquire of the General the reasons for his persistent opposition to ENSA. Confirmation that this was not a persecution complex on my part came quite unexpectedly in 1951, when the Countess de la Marr, one-time lessee of the Winter Garden Theatre, in the course of conversation told me she had offered her services to Army Welfare during the war. General Willans, refusing her offer, had said, "Dean's your man," adding as an afterthought, "We're out to fight ENSA, you know." . . . Perhaps after all there was no mystery, and the General was merely carrying out orders from his superiors?

Another battle was over; I hoped it would be the last. The principles for which we had fought so hard had been won in the face of determined opposition, first from NAAFI, which sought to keep ENSA as the star item in its catalogue of amenities, next from Army Welfare, that wanted to become entertainment impresario to the Forces, and, finally, from Lord May, whose whole skill and training lay in private and secret negotiation rather than in general conference.

From now on relations were largely a matter of skirmish and manœuvre, or better described, perhaps, as a boxing contest, in which the opponents were: In the Red Cor-nerr! . . . the Army, represented from time to time by officers of varying weight, according to their rank; and in the Blue

Cor-nerr! . . . ENSA, represented by myself, usually fighting as a fly-weight. I must be excused if metaphor now becomes somewhat mixed, but so was the fighting; it was never a properly conducted contest, and there were times when it became a free-for-all, when everybody joined in; when the struggle was more like one of those early Rugby matches in which one half of the school played the other half, and hacking was regarded as not only within the rules but as a manly trait in the player. When the R.A.F. felt that the loss of a bout might affect them they would volunteer to act as my second. The Ministry of Labour and National Service played the part of a spectator in the back row. Although it had put up part of the purse, it seldom interfered, unless it saw signs that one or other of the Service Departments was about to run away with the prize-money. Then intervention was effectively made, but with the ut-most discretion, through the judges at the ringside, namely, My Lords of the Treasury. Sometimes NAAFI itself would enter the ring when a round promised to be of particular interest. Alas! it was only as a sparring partner. The appearance of a War Office champion of superior weight invariably caused it to retire. Seeing that it had insisted upon having its name on the contents bills, we resented its failure to take part in the show. In retrospect, I realize that was impossible, since the Corporation belongs to the three Services, and must do as it is bid.

Although this analogy may appear flippant, the disagreements that are here set down were regarded with the utmost seriousness on both sides at the time. The Army was determined to claim the credit for everything that was done for the soldier during his military life, a laudable principle whose intrinsic weakness is that it sometimes excludes new ideas, as Florence Nightingale found out in a more important sphere. ENSA was equally determined not only to mind its own professional business but to prevent others from a form of interference that could only lead to waste of men and money. In this I claim we largely succeeded.

CHAPTER TWENTY-ONE

AMERICAN JOURNEY

1

The Prospect before us

THE entry of America into the war threatened to give ENSA an additional headache at a time when it had enough migraine of its own to contend with. The U.S. technicians and advance contingents of troops who made their appearance in Northern Ireland had been allowed to visit our shows, but before very long Major-General Hartle, on behalf of the U.S. Eighth Air Force, and the U.S. Navy Headquarters in Londonderry, both made formal applications for separate allocations of ENSA entertainment, which were arranged locally on a 'cost plus' basis. But when the main American Expeditionary force began marching down the gangways into Britain the question of what was to be done for its entertainment called for an overall decision at the highest level. To short-circuit discussion over finance I suggested that all entertainment for the Americans should be treated as reverse lend-lease or, to use the Whitehall phrase, as reciprocal aid. While the Treasury was thinking this over we were told that entertainment might be allocated to U.S. troops only if it were specifically asked for. Furthermore, a record was to be kept of such allocations. But it was impossible to keep any check on the attendances at the garrison theatres. By the autumn of 1942 large theatres like the one at Bulford were filled almost entirely by American troops.

Where should we find enough talent of a type likely to appeal to the Americans, without curtailing other parts of the ENSA programme? The obvious course was to invite collaboration from across the water. A plan had been on our drawing-board for some time for inviting American stars to undertake national-service tours in Britain, rather on the lines of those made by Gracie Fields. Approved by the Foreign Office, the Ministry of Information, the Treasury and the Service Departments, it had been held up at the last minute because of transport difficulties. Why not revive this plan and put it into action in conjunction with the Americans? With their greater transport facilities it should be possible to arrange for a steady flow of stage, radio and screen personalities to perform to the troops of both countries. We would reciprocate by supplying accompanists and additional turns to complete the programmes, and by providing bulk entertainment for U.S. troops in the remoter places which the stars would not have time to visit.

2

Round Trip

Meanwhile, in the United States various philanthropic bodies were in full activity. The largest, U.S.O. (United Services Organization), was made responsible for raising the funds with which the work of various constituent bodies, such as the Y.M.C.A. and the Knights of Columbus, could be carried on. This was to avoid the competition of separate financial appeals to the public. A subsidiary organization, known as U.S.O. Camp Shows Inc., which received its funds from the parent body, but otherwise was independent of it, was providing theatrical entertainment for the American Army Camps.

Copies of the reports of the Central Committee of ENSA, together with full details about the official side of our administration, had been sent to this new body through the New York ENSA Committee, formed eighteen months before under the nominal chairmanship of Gertrude Lawrence, with her husband Richard Aldrich as its first treasurer; and we had already received an acknowledgment of the great help which this information had been to our American counterpart.

The American reports which were sent to us in exchange exposed the same teething troubles that we had experienced. There were the same arguments about admission charges, the same rows over billeting and the late arrival of shows, and the same complaints about the condition of institute pianos. The men did not want "dirt or double entendre"; "girl shows" were preferred to straight plays; artistes were requested not to refer to the troops as "the boys," but as men. (Some difference there, for the British troops had no such inferiority complex!) There was the same demand for compères to explain the plots of straight plays to audiences who had never been inside a theatre before. Later, as in Britain, a developing taste for good music precisely followed our own pattern of events.

Although the organization resembled ours in certain respects, it was not financed from Government funds and remained outside the orbit of official responsibility. Consequently, it did not achieve either the scale or the importance of its British counterpart, despite the larger numbers it was called upon to entertain.

While I was cogitating over the possibility of full collaboration with the American organization, I received a summons to attend a meeting of the Bolero Combined Committee, formed at the behest of the War Cabinet to deal, *inter alia*, with welfare matters for American troops in Britain. The chairman was Sir Findlater Stewart, a distinguished Indian Civil Servant. Most of the American officers present at the meeting had only recently arrived in London. They were grateful to be put so promptly in the picture, and agreed that the arrangements begun in Northern Ireland should be extended to cover Britain. The difficulty over charges for admission, which were contrary to American policy, was resolved when the Treasury representative put forward my proposal of reciprocal aid. The meeting agreed this, subject to the approval of the Harriman Mission.

Next, co-operation between U.S.O. and ENSA was welcomed with so many compliments that the chairman was quite taken aback. He was unaccustomed to the American way in negotiation, which rightly assumes that facile courtesies waste no dollars and may conceivably soften the hard bargaining that must precede final agreement. That English words and phrases can have entirely different meanings on opposite sides of the conference table is a truth that every businessman should assimilate before he engages in Transatlantic negotiation. . . . The meeting closed in an atmosphere of great cordiality and with apparent agreement on all the points discussed.

Shortly afterwards we were painfully surprised by the arrival of a party of stars from New York, headed by Al Jolson. No prior notice had been given to us, and no dates left vacant for a visit to British troops. Consequently, with the exception of two performances in a factory, the party played only to American units. This caused adverse comment among our troops; to us it seemed a poor return for our efforts. About the same time Edward G. Robinson turned up, sent by the Office of War Information (O.W.I.) without prior notice either to U.S. Special Services in London or to any theatrical organization, but only to the Ministry of Information, which sustained its current reputation by informing nobody.

I made urgent requests to Lord May and to Sir Findlater Stewart to be allowed to go to the United States to establish personal contact with American organizations and officials before matters got any worse. After consultation between the Foreign Office and the Treasury authority was given, but I was to offer help only if the Americans desired it. I kept to myself the thought that we needed their help quite as much as they needed ours.

R

3
Boat Drill

I arrived in Greenock on Saturday, November 7, to take passage in the
Queen Elizabeth, then engaged in a series of coursing matches across the
Atlantic with German submarines—so far the hare had managed to win
every course—and boarded the ship by tender at first light the following
morning. When I went to the purser's office, armed with my secret movement order, there was a queue of senior officers—generals and brigadiers—
waiting to advance their claims to accommodation, while Air Ministry
clerks strove valiantly against the intimidations of superior rank. I
wondered whether my piece of paper carried the correct number of
cabalistic signs and signatures, if not I should find myself most ignominiously put ashore. In due course I was given a bunk in a large stateroom
with seven or eight senior officers and civil servants.

The passenger list numbered something over 8000. There were officers
of every rank and degree (mainly British and American), Canadian troops
going home on leave, Wrens, A.T.S., a sprinkling of nurses and a few
civilians like myself. This was trooping in the grand manner. Meals were
served in a series of sittings, the scurry and clatter reminding one of the
déjeuner served on the Boulogne–Paris boat express in the old days, when
those caught at table when the train rattled through Amiens usually found
a sprinkling of railway soup down their waistcoats.

Twice a day we had boat-drill, each passenger taking his allotted place
on the deck nearest the boat that he was to use in the event of emergency.
Highly necessary precaution no doubt, but if we had been torpedoed very
few of that mass of humanity would have escaped with their lives. However, we stood glumly in rows and did as we were bid without any of the
reassurance that the regulations were intended to give us.

As we steamed through the Western Approaches, infested at that time
with submarines, tension filled the air like a vaguely apprehended mist
blown hither and thither by every chance rumour; but after two days at
sea it was blown clean away and its place taken by a storm of excitement
as over the ship's radio came the first announcements of the North
African landings. The wireless operator's microphone technique was poor
and many people complained that they could not hear what he said. I
volunteered to become the ship's news-reader for the rest of the voyage,
an offer which the Captain gratefully accepted. Each evening the war news
was brought to me on slips of paper, and, as I made my way through the

crowded main lounge to the microphone placed on the platform at the end, passengers bombarded me with advance questions or tried to snatch the communiqué out of my hands. I quite enjoyed my one and only experience as an official announcer.

One passenger keeping apart from the heterogeneous company that thronged the upper decks was Alexander Korda. Day after day he was to be seen in a special corner of the smoke-room, imperturbably playing gin rummy with his friends, often into the small hours, and always with a bland disregard for the daily bustle of the voyage. It was like watching the performance of one of those small parts in a melodrama, which by exceptional composure contrives to secure all the notices from the critics the next morning. Alex's apparent indifference either to good or ill fortune, and his ability to bully money into obedience to his will instead of treating it like a bad-tempered master, as so many of us do, were traits that constantly won my admiration. On this voyage I could well have imagined him refusing to leave the table and go to the boats until the last 'gin' was called.

New York has an immense power to intimidate visitors. The canyons of tall buildings leaping from their granite cradles in the cold, hard light make no concessions to weakness; its relentless traffic screeches death to hesitation; the quick, brittle talk of its inhabitants acknowledges no doubt. Self-confidence is essential if one is to keep sane in this cosmopolis of the modern world, but I felt mine oozing slowly from me as the taxi-driver crashed into the rear bumpers of the car in front of us, damning "those German sonsovbitches" for making him drive in the dark. When I told him New York's 'dim-out' looked more like Piccadilly Circus on a holiday night his only reply was: "Say, stop kiddin', will yer?" Would he have remained as good-humoured as the London taximen in a real black-out, I wondered? . . . One must not expect to find the camaraderie over here to which we had grown accustomed at home. As the taxi jolted to a standstill outside the hotel I felt apprehensive for the first time about the success of my mission.

4

All the Answers

When I went to the office of U.S.O. Camp Shows the next morning I was told its chief executive, Abe Lastfogel, had just left by air for London. This was disconcerting in view of the cables sent from London announcing my visit. The times were not propitious for a game of Box and Cox across the Atlantic. At the office of Fanny Holtzmann I learned that Gertrude Lawrence was on tour in *Lady in the Dark*, a musical play in which she had scored one of the outstanding successes of her career, and that Richard Aldrich had joined the U.S. Navy.

Continuing my pursuit of ENSA committee members, I sought out John Golden, and found him seated in a barber's chair in the dressing-room adjoining his office, conducting rapid-fire conversations over a telephone perched on his knee, dictating letters and instructions to his secretary, and being shaved, while in the outer office a queue of people waited to be interviewed. John told me that Dwight Wiman, another member, was away in Washington, but that Gilbert Miller was expected in New York on the morrow. The affairs of our little ENSA committee were evidently in abeyance.

Gilbert Miller, an impresario operating in both New York and London, has succeeded in getting the best out of both worlds and for a longer period even than the great Charles Frohman. My talk with him filled in many gaps in the picture. I gathered that a political fight was developing in Washington between U.S.O. and the powerful American Red Cross for the right to entertain U.S. troops abroad. It behoved me to keep away from the ringside seats, or I might collect a chance blow or two myself.

Wandering down Fifth Avenue and across to Sixth, staring at the delicatessen stores with whole hams and cheeses stacked in the windows, I pondered over what Gilbert had told me, and felt rather disconsolate. The struggle over American national-service entertainment was so exactly like the storms we had been through. Apart from minor contests, which were endemic, we had at least produced a measure of order among the contending parties. Would the Americans achieve more or as much? By the time I had reached the hotel, having successfully resisted the temptation to eat steaks at every restaurant passed, and ice-cream from every drugstore, I felt a little better.

A visit to the Stage Door Canteen in the evening, where Alfred Lunt, with an apron tied round his middle, was helping in the washing up, took my mind away from politics. Similar canteens were being run in all the large American cities by the American Theatre Wing, an organization that included all the best elements in the American legitimate theatre. Actors and actresses resident in or passing through the cities gave voluntary service as dancing partners, or took part in more or less continuous cabaret, or helped to serve light meals to the troops of all the United Nations. This was probably the most original contribution of the American show world to the war.

The leaders of the Theatre Wing were keenly aware of the battle for ultimate authority going on in Washington. This made them vague about their own future intentions. I decided to waste no more time in New York, where uncertainty would sooner or later intimidate me to a standstill, but to go at once to Washington and seek enlightenment in official quarters there.

5
Carousel

Washington was crowded to suffocation with every type of expert and inexpert opinion, in uniform and out of it; the many citizens of the warring nations who thronged its hotel lobbies, piled into its taxi-cabs, and drank its cocktails, all wore the same air of portentous energy, as though conscious of the fact that they were living in the cauldron of world events. My taxi-driver volunteered the information that the hotel to which he was taking me had been refusing accommodation to his passengers for the last six months or more, including one three-star general, so what chance had a mere 'Britisher' without a uniform? As he had predicted, the receptionist smiled in a kindly sort of way when I told him I had wired from New York, and, pointing to a pile of telegrams containing similar requests that lay on the desk, turned without further word to attend to another client. Intimidation had begun to close in on me again. Fortunately I had held the taxi. When I ordered the man to drive to the British Embassy he thought better of my prospects and drove faster in consequence.

That august establishment was bursting at the seams with wooden huts, built in the gardens to house a small army of civil servants, officers on special list, cipher clerks, stenographers and other supernumeraries in the local cast of World Conflict, all reflecting in varying degree, according to temperament, the atmosphere of nervous hustle which the Americans thought proper to the circumstances.

The Ambassador gave up an hour of his severely rationed time to listen to my trivial story. At the end he warned me against expecting too much. Experience was a commodity the Americans preferred to buy in the open market. Anxious as I might be for immediate co-operation, any attempt to force the pace would have undesirable repercussions.

I suppose I must have looked a little crestfallen at this wise advice, so opposed to my own temperament, for the Ambassador hastened to reassure me of his personal interest. He sent for a member of the Military Attaché's staff and told him to arrange an appointment for me with

General Osborn, the titular head of U.S. Special Services, if possible the next day. I was to lunch at the Embassy afterwards to tell him how I had got on. The changed attitude of the hotel clerk when I presented my Embassy reservation was a modest salve to my shrunken ego.

The following morning I made my way to the vast, unfinished Pentagon Building where the multitudinous staff appeared to be in a permanent state of frenzy. Fighting my way through a throng of people at the main entrance, I eventually persuaded a minor official that the letter I held in my hand really was from the British Embassy and that there was no need for him to send for the F.B.I. to verify it. In due course my name, nationality and business were written on a large ticket that was tied into the lapel of my coat. Then I was conveyed like a parcel along endless corridors and from one messenger to another, each of whom appeared to have a clearly defined territory beyond which he must not trespass. I kept thinking of Seymour's story about 'General Sprike' and wondering what sort of yarn he would have made out of this adventure; something highly ornate, no doubt, but nothing that could exceed the extravagance of the reality.

General Osborn, a tall, urbane man, obviously not a professional soldier, listened carefully to what I had to say and then explained that he could give no direct instructions to Special Service officers abroad, where they came under the orders of the commanding generals concerned. "Sure, collaboration was desirable, and he hoped I could fix it, and anything he could do, etc., etc." Leaving the concentration camp that is called Pentagon, I made my way to my next appointment, with Elmer Davis, head of the Office of War Information (O.W.I.). More courtesies, similar enthusiastic endorsement of the proposals and, when it came to the discussion of practical steps, an obvious uncertainty about the whole position. "Anything we can do to help you, Mr . . . [a glance at the slip of paper to get my name right]—er—Mr Dean, we sure will."

Over lunch Lord Halifax expressed concern regarding the British artistes remaining in America. In the beginning their work for war charities had been useful; since the entry of America into the conflict their presence was causing unfavourable comment. He was in favour of their going home, but many could not afford to do so, neither could they obtain passages. Always on the look-out for useful pickings in the way of talent, I listened carefully to what the Ambassador was saying. Laurence Olivier and Vivien Leigh had returned home long since, but there were a number of lesser-known artistes still in Hollywood whose services would be invaluable to us.

The Government had recently announced a scheme for the repatriation of British subjects whose technical skills or professional training were urgently needed at home. They were to be transported at the public expense and given priority over other passengers. Actors and musicians had not been included in the schedule of occupations; but there was now sufficient reason for doing so. Those sent back under the scheme should sign a declaration before leaving the United States, undertaking to work for ENSA for the duration of the war. I put the suggestion to the Ambassador. He agreed to cable it at once to the Foreign Office.

The Ambassador told me I should find Mr Norman Davis and Mr Richard Green, of the American Red Cross, helpful and decidedly pro-British. It proved to be so. From them I heard the inside story of the political battle that was raging. The Red Cross had already begun to give shows to U.S. troops abroad, particularly in Australia. They now sought a general mandate, which the new organization was opposing strenuously. The struggle was so fierce that it might have to be taken right up to the President's desk for decision. The Ambassador did not much care for my proximity to such high-level American politics, even as an onlooker. He again advised caution and was relieved when I told him of my decision to return to New York to make another attempt to establish good relations with U.S.O.

<><><>

Conditional Negative . . .

Various stories were being circulated in Washington to illustrate the difficulty of obtaining decisions even upon quite simple matters, including the apocryphal one about a member of one of the foreign missions who, after a sojourn of several weeks, had failed to obtain definite answers to any of his inquiries. One evening he found himself dated with an extremely attractive redhead. He took the young lady out to a dinner-dance, during the course of which he made what he supposed were the expected advances, to which she responded by slapping his face. "Well," he said with shocked surprise, "that's the first definite answer I've had since I've been here."

6
'Fe—fi—fo—fum'—— period!

The first task on my return to New York was to resuscitate our moribund Committee and to strengthen its membership before inviting it to control the repatriation scheme from the American end. There was also an important job of production waiting for it. Concert parties for the R.A.F. Flying Schools in Canada were requested. These parties could be organized in New York without difficulty, but would require experienced business management. Now that the Committee would be vested with official responsibility vis-à-vis the British Government the adherence to it of some influential New York managers was imperative. From the hints that Gilbert had let drop it was evident that they would be reluctant to join if the chairman were a Broadway star and likely to be away on tour for most of the time. It seemed best that Gilbert should take Gertrude Lawrence's place as chairman; but this was not a matter that could be adjusted by correspondence or a telephone call; it must be explained to her personally. I set out for Cleveland, Ohio, where *Lady in the Dark* was running.

Not having seen her act for several years, I was amazed at the additional stature Gertrude Lawrence had acquired. The whole scale and significance of her acting seemed to have taken a leap forward. In the theatre interval I found myself thinking of those far-off days at the Liverpool Repertory Theatre, when she had played in my first Christmas production: a plain little sprite in pigtails, spending most of her time jumping in and out of the star-traps intended for the Demon King and not at all suitable for a woodland fairy. No one would have thought that she could cut and polish the rough diamond of her talent until it shone with such effulgence that when it passed away all the lights on Broadway and in Shaftesbury Avenue would be dimmed as though in despair of emulation.

After the play we had supper together. Our talk was not only of the business in hand, but of old friends, old jokes, and times past. Gertie wanted to be known as the Honorary President, and suggested Gilbert should be the Executive Chairman. Honorific titles would not affect the position at all, so I readily agreed, while Gertie renewed her promise to join us overseas at the first opportunity.

While I was waiting to see which way the political cat was going to jump I visited many of the theatres, but I can recall only the first night of Thornton Wilder's *The Skin of our Teeth*, in which Tallulah Bankhead created the part of Sabina. The memory of it stays with me, not so much because of the play (which I found pretentious) as for the impact of Tallulah's performance, brilliant in the first act, slightly less so in the remainder.

Tallulah's acting can offend all the canons of theatrical art and yet remain successful, even though, before the last act is over, the rest of the cast, and possibly the play itself, lie prostrate before her, like so many skittles in an alley. She is an aristocrat, and, like all aristocrats, remains an amateur at heart. Not for her the instinctive self-discipline of the professional artist. Her whole life has been a triumphant rebellion against the conventional and the commonplace.

Gracie Fields was in New York, too: star cabaret turn at the Waldorf Astoria. She was anxious to do another big ENSA tour in 1943. In the course of discussing the plan with Monty Banks I went to see her performance, and marvelled at the skill with which she held the attention of the smart café society of New York. As I sat there I could not help contrasting the careers of these three outstandingly gifted women, each of whom had appeared under my direction in the past. . . .

Gilbert Miller had now completed the plans for the reconstituted committee. The new members consisted of John Royal (of N.B.C.), Vinton Freedley, John Golden and John C. Wilson, with Gilbert in the Chair. Dwight Wiman had resigned because of his appointment as Director of Entertainments for the American Red Cross overseas, which eventually brought him to Drury Lane in search of artistes and other help. Meanwhile he generously placed his New York offices at the disposal of the committee, free of rent, and agreed that Forrest Haring, his general manager, should act as its executive secretary. Forrest undertook to accept a nominal salary, and to make a start on the companies for Canada right away.[1]

My urgent desire to establish good relations with U.S.O. Camp Shows remained. Lastfogel being still absent in Europe, I decided to seek out the President of U.S.O. itself. This was Mr Walter Hoving, head of a big department store on Fifth Avenue: a clean-cut, decisive American, who obviously belonged to the highest rank of stores executive. As he knew nothing whatever about the theatrical world, his approach to my plan of collaboration was conditioned by his business experience. Here was an attempt on the part of a British Government agent to sell him something he did not want, a situation that must be dealt with in summary fashion, yet with a certain diplomacy.

"It's dandy for the British troops, I see that. They'll get all the movie and radio stars. Sure! Why not? That's O.K. But what about the American boys? What do they get out of it? U.S.O. Camp Shows can provide all the entertainment they need." As to my offer to reciprocate by giving the U.S. troops a share of ENSA entertainment: "what did that amount to anyway? Americans wouldn't understand British Shows. As for theatrical equipment, that could be imported." . . . Then a perfunctory coda to this chorus of mistrust: "the matter was outside his province; it was up to the

[1] Forrest Haring carried out his assignment so ably that at the end of the war the National Service Entertainments Board sent special letters of thanks to him and to the committee.

Camp Shows people; he was concerned solely with bond drives, national campaigns to raise money. I would have to wait for the return of Abe Lastfogel from Europe."

I was seeing a good deal of Gilbert Miller at this time. One evening after a particularly tiring day he invited me to dine at the house of his father-in-law, Jules Bache, whose wonderful collection of pictures and *objets d'art* was evidence of great wealth wisely spent. Throughout the meal I was fascinated by the conversation, in which vast sums of money seemed to perform the most surprising feats of levitation, leaping across the table in a golden shower from one diner to the other, but always inconsiderately passing me by.

7

Stand and Deliver

The days went by. Still Norman Davis kept silent and still Abe Lastfogel remained in London. I grew restive and forgetful of the Ambassador's advice. All the organizations had given lip-service to Anglo-American unity, so why not take them at their word? My eagerness affected Gilbert, who must have suspended his cooler judgment out of kindness of heart. Together we planned a big public luncheon in New York. Prominent people would be invited, not only from the theatre, but from all walks of life, and the British Ambassador would outline our proposed scheme of collaboration. This was in keeping with the American way of doing things and would put an end to all hesitancies.

The date was agreed on with the Ambassador, and I promised to let his secretary have an outline of the speech for his consideration. A small committee was formed, in whose name invitations were sent out by telegram. As often happens when things are done at short notice, there was every promise of a highly successful function. Then one morning the telephone rang. It was Walter Hoving, who had not yet answered the invitation that had been sent him. He sounded so irate that it seemed best to go and see him.

The interview was a painful one. He began by asking why I did not wait for Lastfogel. I said I had waited several weeks, and could lose no more time. He declared that U.S.O. was opposed to the function because it would interfere with its forthcoming Bond Drive. This was a poor excuse. We were not appealing for funds. I asked what were the real grounds of objection, since every one had agreed in principle? He refused all discussion. If I did not call off the arrangements he would communicate with the State Department and request them to notify the Ambassador that his speech would be unwelcome at this time. This drastic threat made me realize that my exigence had created just that situation against which the Ambassador had warned me. There was nothing else for it but to beat a retreat with as much dignity as I could command, which, in the circumstances, was very little.

Gilbert was all for brushing the opposition to one side, saying that the State Department would not approve of Hoving's unwarranted action; it would certainly cause a scandal if it ever got about. This was all very well: Gilbert was speaking as an influential American manager, but there was the official British point of view to be considered. I telephoned to the Ambassador's private secretary, explained the situation to him, and asked him to cancel the arrangements. The attempt to borrow some American hustle had ended in failure, and my self-confidence was badly shaken.

While I was waiting for the movement order that would entitle me to squeeze myself into the bomb rack of one of the Liberators, the American-made bombers being flown nightly across the Atlantic for service with the R.A.F., I was invited to a dinner party by the Walter Hovings. Determined not to fall behind the Americans in tact, I accepted. The company consisted of influential businessmen and their wives. Our host and hostess could not have been more courteous, and insisted upon telling their guests all about the wonderful work that ENSA was doing. It was embarrassing to be so unexpectedly lionized; also, it was insufficient compensation for the sabotage of my luncheon plans.

Among the guests was ex-President Hoover. After the ladies had retired Havana cigars and a most excellent brandy were produced, and the progress of the war solemnly discussed. Mr Hoover took me on one side and plied me with questions about the position of the Labour Party in Britain, remarking that such people ought to be put down with a firm hand, by force if necessary. In the mirror behind him I caught sight of my own reflection, mouth gaping wide with astonishment, which made me laugh out loud. When the ex-President asked me what I was laughing at I had no answer.

Two days before I was due to leave there came word over the telephone from Norman Davis. The argument was over, settled by General Marshall, the American Chief of Staff. Firstly, entertainment for U.S. troops overseas would be controlled by U.S.O. Camp Shows. Secondly, the American Red Cross would continue to give entertainments in their own clubs and hostels. Finally, wherever the British were organizing entertainments U.S. Special Services were to act in collaboration with them. So now we all knew where we were! In the last of the three findings there lay some reassurance that my mission had not been a complete failure.

For the Record . . .

On April 5, 1943, the Americans acted upon their instructions to collaborate, but not quite in the way I expected. They informed the Minister of Labour that U.S.O. Camp Shows was now recognized by the U.S. Government as the sole organization to provide entertainment for their troops in Britain, and asked for such British artistes as they required to be provided through the agency of the T.W.S.C. and not ENSA. This request presupposed the superiority of 'lease-lend' to the ENSA companies. If the assumption were correct, the request could only have the effect of depriving British troops and factory workers of the better entertainment. It was not possible to allow our guests to order their own feast in this way.

ENSA kept its promise of reciprocal aid by continuing to send entertainment to remote areas where the American stars did not visit, notably in Devon and Cornwall (where Commander 'Dick' Aldrich was now administrative officer for amphibian elements of the U.S. Navy), and by providing large quantities of theatrical equipment. For example: in 1943 Drury Lane workshops made and supplied the U.S. Forces with 75 portable stages and 45 switchboards. In the following year the numbers of these items were 135 and 65 respectively.

CHAPTER TWENTY-TWO

RADIO ENSA

1

Tuning in

IN the days of restricted newspaper space radio was the obvious medium for keeping the British public informed of the development of ENSA's plans. That it was also a means of providing additional entertainment for the troops did not immediately occur to us. At the outset we wanted to convince the listeners of our ability to carry out the promises we had made and to convey to them something of the urgency that was propelling us forward, a spirit to be found neither in a plethora of gramophone records nor in the neutral voices of the B.B.C. announcers, Olympian spectators of our poor human world in flames. With such ideas in mind it was scarcely surprising that our early contacts with the B.B.C. were not encouraging.

Certainly we had our ears closer to the ground than those who lived in the rarefied atmosphere of Broadcasting House, where the declaration of war had found the organization singularly ill-prepared from the psychological point of view. The public, restless and dissatisfied, were beginning to listen-in to the malevolent slanders of Lord Haw-Haw, treating them as jokes, while hunting instinctively for sharper accents on which to whet their antagonism. The fretful customer in his 'local,' heard to remark after a couple of pints, "You'd think this war was an effing tea-party," had many sympathizers. Public anxiety was not lessened by the forced gaiety of variety artistes, whose personal jokes and excessive use of each other's Christian names—syndicated familiarity—savoured of self-advertisement and was out of key with the national mood. Also, the psychological effect of the juxtaposition of such items to the war news was imperfectly studied. In 1942, when the public mind was stretched to the very edge of suspense by the lengthening catalogue of disaster, it was embarrassing to listen to cross-talk between two variety artistes while waiting for the Prime Minister's speech on the fall of Singapore. At such times it was a relief to hear the prosaic voice of Mr Middleton, gently reminding us of the importance of giving all growing things "a good mulch now and then," practical advice the importance of which quite escaped me until I learned to tend my own garden.

It was not until a flood of protests overran the Corporation's listening posts, and seeped under the doors of the House of Commons, that a more virile attitude to the national danger was adopted. The early puerilities were erased from the record by subsequent achievement; by the European and other foreign news services, and not least by the ebullient humours of Tommy Handley and his fellow-comedians, and the script-writers who, inspired by his genius, gave expression to the national spirit in a series of brilliant comedy broadcasts of a standard quite unknown before the war. . . .To the sum total of that achievement ENSA made one or two minor contributions whose origin is now forgotten, like the name of the engineer who first thought of painting a white line down the middle of the road.

2
"We're on the Air"

Our first talks about a radio programme were tentative. A few enthusiasts used to meet in my room after the work of the day to exchange ideas and to discuss problems: Richard Llewellyn and Macqueen-Pope and Stanley Bell and one or two others; sometimes Rex Newman would look in and cheer us up with his gimlet eye for the ridiculous. At these meetings Richard would produce an astonishing crop of suggestions, but when he was invited to develop them he became lost in the Celtic twilight of a proliferate imagination. I remember one occasion:

"Let's begin with a fanfare of trumpets," said Richard, "*Aïda* trumpets. I know where there's a set in Wales. Then an announcement: Drury Lane Theatre calling all theatres of war! Then voices representing the great actors who've trod the boards here, to recall the past and summon the actors of to-day."

"How do you do that?" said a dubious voice.

"We'll use famous quotations . . ."

"Such as?" I interrupted.

"Well, I've thought of a quotation from Thucydides. . . ."

A momentary gasp of astonishment, and then Rex Newman said gravely:

"We shall have to refer that to General Ĭrŏn-sidees."

It was Pope who finally brought the talk down to earth by reminding us that the B.B.C. was an essential partner in the matter and likely to prefer ideas more clear-cut and definite than Richard's fancies. I was reluctant to see Richard entirely cast down. There was something in what he was groping for; but in the circumstances it was important to get on the air as soon as possible, and so Pope's greater experience of the medium and his personal contacts with the B.B.C. staff held present sway.

Our first appearance at the microphone came with some quarter-hour excerpts from forthcoming shows. These were sent out in the mornings from the stage of the theatre, and included one from Ralph Reader's *Gang Show*, which the Air Ministry arranged should tour the camps and visit France under ENSA auspices.

A start had been made, but that was all. I was in some perplexity as to the next step when that Very light of war-time entertainment, Gracie Fields, burst over the entrenched position of the B.B.C. Further broadcasts by her and other stars visiting France then followed.[1]

When the B.B.C. Forces programme was inaugurated on January 7, 1940, copies of our monthly schedules of entertainment were sent to the Controller of Programmes (B. E. Nicolls)[2] so that the programme planners could select those they wished to take, while Archie Campbell was sent overseas as B.B.C. producer to work in liaison with our staff there.

Although an ENSA Concert from France made more and more frequent appearances in the *Radio Times*, we were not satisfied with our progress. Our broadcasts were no different from any other items of light entertainment, except for the circumstances under which they were given. To express the wider scope of our responsibilities we should have to find a formula that would give our programmes individuality, and make radical changes from time to time in order to keep it vital.

All the producing divisions and sections were encouraged to submit ideas and to propose artistes; but we soon discovered that preoccupation with the day-to-day work tended to push broadcasting into the background of their thoughts, so that for the first few months Macqueen-Pope virtually carried the entire responsibility on his shoulders, with little help from the rest of us.

Early in 1940 Stephen Williams,[3] who had been producing sponsored programmes for Radio Luxembourg, now closed down, offered us his services. He appeared to live in a world wherein electrical impulses took

---

[1] Those I particularly remember were Will Fyffe's, given before an audience of Scottish troops on New Year's Eve; Harold Holt's party of distinguished artistes from the concert hall; Jack Buchanan's musical show; Leslie Henson and, later, George Formby.

[2] Now Sir Basil Nicolls.

[3] Not to be confused with the distinguished music and drama critic of the same name.

the place of human motives in the struggle for existence, a world peopled with song-pluggers and radio sponsors, and bounded by microphones and stop-watches. However, his practical knowledge was just what was required to render down our enthusiasm into common sense. I engaged him there and then. He quickly made his presence felt and remained with us until March 1944, working hard and unselfishly during those four years in presenting ENSA entertainment over the air.

Music was obviously going to play an important part in the work, and some one had to undertake general responsibility for it. Jack Hylton, still nominal head of the Bands Division, was unable to do so because of private commitments, and Geraldo, who had recently been deputizing for him in the Division, was appointed in his stead. 'Gerry', for that is his nickname, was well known before the war as the conductor of one of the Savoy Hotel dance orchestras. Like many other Londoners, I had danced to his music often enough. I had also met him in business, when he acquired a lease of the St Martin's Theatre after Alec Rea gave it up, and I had given a series of independent productions there. By hard work and strict attention to business he had acquired a considerable position, and was now about to set the seal upon his reputation, if not his fortune, by six years of ungrudging work as general musical director of our broadcasting, conducting his own orchestra in many of the principal programmes and scheduling the various civilian bands to the remainder. But for his cool competence this side of ENSA's work might well have broken down under the ceaseless pressure.

The job brought him much publicity, but I had no patience with the jealous sneers of those who said he only did it for that reason. Similar remarks were passed about George Formby and other prominent artistes. Publicity! After all, why not? It is the breath of life to those uncomfortable pole-sitters, the stars of the entertainment world.

'Gerry,' singularly devoid of snobbery or pretence at any time, took full advantage of contact with the distinguished musicians of the concert world which the work brought him, and acquired additional poise thereby. On one occasion he was rehearsing a specially augmented orchestra, consisting of his own people and a number of players from one of the big symphony orchestras, for one of our big events at the Albert Hall. Dissatisfied with a certain passage, he tapped the desk and stopped the music, remarking with admirable dignity, "We will now return to the andante," then silencing the mutterings among his own dance-band section by saying with an acid smile, "Foxtrot tempo to you."

The provision of adequate studio facilities was quite a problem. Broadcasting from the big stage, except late at night, became an embarrassment,

OND FRONT

NA WYNYARD,
MARGARET
THERFORD AND
R NOVELLO IN
L.S.T. WAITING
TO LAND

LOADING THE FIRST
INVASION COLUMN
AT HINDHEAD

GEORGE FORMBY,
VIRGINIA VERNON
AND WELFARE
SUPERVISORS ON
THE BEACHHEAD

A LAST-MINUTE
CHAT WITH
FLANAGAN AND
ALLEN

272

(1) Church Parade in our Camp at Bayeux: Cherry Lind, Margaret Rutherford, Florence Desmond, Kay Cavendish, Lyle Evans, Ivor Novello, &c. (2) After the Service: George and Beryl Formby, Forsythe, Seamon and Farrell, Richard Hearne

273 (Note the dog-fight above.)

Diana Wynyard and Ivor Novello play "Love from a Stranger"

Gertrude Lawrence arrives at t Beachhead

disorganizing the workshops and the surrounding offices and delaying important rehearsals. It was abandoned in favour of the stalls bar, which was underneath the pit and below ground level. The counters were removed and the place skilfully converted into a studio, the walls tastefully decorated with murals painted by Denis Wreford on hessian canvas, which also provided the necessary sound-damping.

Very soon this studio proved inadequate. I began to cast sheep's eyes at the Fortune Theatre across the way, which was already in our frequent use. In 1939 I had asked NAAFI if we might take it over and run daily café concerts there for troops at a loose end in London. The idea was rejected because it went beyond the Corporation's mandate. Now with the effluxion of time the Fortune Theatre came into ENSA occupation. There the Broadcasting Division established its offices; accommodation was also provided for the B.B.C.'s liaison officer, once more Archie Campbell. Two special land-lines, one from the Fortune, and the other from the stalls bar at Drury Lane, were run to Broadcasting House by the G.P.O., and a permanent monitoring panel was installed in one of the boxes.

Transmissions and recordings went on from both studios night and day for the rest of the war, many of the sessions at the Fortune Theatre taking place before audiences of invited guests. There were only two occasions when broadcasting had to be given from a B.B.C. studio because of enemy action, although on a third occasion it was a narrow shave. That was when a bomb fell in Bow Street which put the land-line to the Drury Lane studio out of action just as the musicians were waiting to begin. Gathering up their instruments, they scuttled across the road to the Fortune, dispossessed a recording rehearsal and were ready to go on the air just as the red light came on.

In the summer of 1941 Roger Ould, an old friend and associate of mine from the days of ReandeaN and, later, at Ealing Studios, joined ENSA to become Manager of the Broadcasting Division. At the same time an Advisory Council was formed under the chairmanship of Sir Herbert Dunnico, a development which the B.B.C. appeared to resent very much. To complete the now familiar pattern of organization a Broadcasting Executive was set up, of which I invited Dunnico to take the chair. At the same time Macqueen-Pope became Director of Programmes and Stephen Williams took his place as Broadcasting Officer.

There is no doubt at all that Dunnico's chairmanship of the Broadcasting Council was a success. He encouraged the prominent personalities who were members of it to submit ideas and to take part in carrying them out, and did himself widen the scope of the programmes with suggestions that

S

brought ENSA into contact with people who might otherwise have remained strangers to its work.

On the Broadcasting Executive things were not so happy. 'Popie' was just then entering a period of ill-health, when the tendency to resent criticism became more marked, and he found it impossible to ride the waves of controversy with his usual buoyancy. His complaints of interference, particularly against Dunnico, became frequent and bitter. I discounted them at the time, putting them down to physical causes, which subsequent events revealed as a serious error of judgment on my part. In my endeavours to keep the peace I too became involved in a series of petty differences that were the outcome of the frayed nerves set jangling between us. So we agreed to part company. But he was to return to Drury Lane towards the end of the war, when his vigorous efforts on my behalf were further evidence of a warm and generous spirit.

Pope's departure was a serious loss, for the programmes which he had written and produced himself had been outstandingly successful, and conducted with a complete absence of friction at Broadcasting House. After he left I placed responsibility for the programme planning in the hands of the Broadcasting Executive as a whole. The results were unfortunate. In the matter of broadcasting, as in every other branch of entertainment, harmonious relations are essential to good results. In an atmosphere cloudy with disputation the planning of our programmes began to break down, as each member of the Executive tended to leave decisions to his neighbour, which, in the end, meant Sir Herbert Dunnico. In July 1943 I abolished the system, and arranged for various individuals to take over the planning in turn. In October Charles Penley, general manager of the Paramount Theatres in this country, came in for a short spell, but he resigned after a few months; he found the buzz of politics too deafening.

Some part of the blame was mine, for I constantly prodded Dunnico about the programmes whenever the founts of invention appeared to be running low. In order to provide a reflection of the ENSA world—itself constantly changing and developing—as we had sworn to do, it was necessary to create fresh permutations and combinations, even though the numbers with which we could juggle were strictly limited. I began to understand the B.B.C.'s major difficulty in maintaining the standards of any given programme over a long period.

The Division was saved from complete internal collapse by the energies of Margaret Harper-Nelson, an extremely able young woman who had applied to Pope for a job in 1941, and been posted to Broadcasting as senior secretary, where she speedily made herself indispensable. She became Roger Ould's deputy, and towards the end of the war carried the administrative burden of the entire Division on her young shoulders, besides producing a large number of the later programmes. After the war she joined Army Welfare for a short while, left that organization in a state of mild shock and bewilderment and later was to be found conducting casting operations for Michael Balcon at Ealing Studios.

It was thanks largely to her and to Geraldo (whose flexible mind was better able to deal with palace revolutions than Roger's), to Walter Legge (who stood no nonsense and could exchange buffets as effectively as the next man) and, in some part, to Sir Herbert himself that the Division carried its burden of responsibility with reasonable success until the autumn of 1946. The sincerity of the conflicting purposes enabled a façade of solidarity to be maintained and the cracks in the parti-walls to remain successfully concealed from the outside world until the end.

3
"We beg to differ"

The B.B.C., through its Controller of Programmes, had reluctantly accepted my plea that ENSA should be allowed to present entertainment with a difference, but there was little sympathy with the idea. So long as we conformed to the B.B.C.'s restricted viewpoint of what this meant relations were cordial, but, at the first sign of deviation from the 'party line,' warning signals would go up and the tussle be resumed once more.

Some of the objections were childish and had to be overruled. At the time of Dunkirk our special relationship to the troops seemed to call for a more virile attitude to the emergency than that reflected in the general run of entertainment being broadcast. So I sent forth word that there was to be more energy and sparkle in our programmes. In the first of the new scripts Godfrey Tearle was to speak quotations from Shakespeare at the beginning and at the end. This departure from 'normality' aroused strong opposition. The correspondence that ensued was brittle, not to say acid, in tone: we were "falling between two stools, i.e., being sententious at one moment and light-hearted at the next"; again, "ENSA appears to be trying to put itself forward at a critical time to speak for the country as a whole, which it is not entitled to do."

I replied that contrast was an indispensable quality in all entertainment; to quote Shakespeare was no more sententious than to play the national anthems of the Allies before and after the transmission of a musical comedy. While the representative character of our organization did perhaps entitle us to speak for the entertainment profession as a whole, we were not seeking to do so, but only to reflect the popular feeling, as is the way in the theatre. Eventually the quotations were spoken in the middle of the programme, where sententiousness was presumed to be absent.

In January 1942 trouble arose when we proposed two Kipling programmes, which it was claimed were not representative of ENSA activities and more suitable for the B.B.C.'s own Drama Department, a view to which we did not subscribe. Our people had gone to immense trouble to secure permission for the use of the material, previous requests by the B.B.C. and others having been refused. The objection was overcome only after Roger Ould had approached Lady Violet Bonham Carter, one of the Governors of the B.B.C. at the time. Nicolls protested at such unorthodox procedure, but it achieved its object. The broadcasts were given and were a great success, Henry Ainley taking part in the first.[1]

As the pattern of our relations continued to weave itself into and out of agreement, I had informal talks with Robert Foot, one of the new joint Directors-General, in the course of which I drew his attention to the B.B.C.'s distressing habit of turning down our ideas only to adopt them at a later date for themselves—an experience that I implied was not peculiar to us. Following these talks, Nicolls and I drew up a set of 'working rules,' the first of which declared that ENSA's object was to reflect, as far as was possible by broadcasting, its various activities in the way that it wanted them to be reflected. Rule Two established the responsibility of the B.B.C. for seeing that the broadcasts were carried out in accordance with its requirements and standards. There were other rules, dealing with the engagement of artistes, finance and so forth, that are of little interest now, but they reflected the various sources of contention then existing.

Looking back on it all, one can only marvel that worse did not befall us, as the B.B.C. watched the emergence of a semi-Government organization that not only demanded the opportunities but proved capable of making appreciable weekly contributions of broadcasting hours, from a completely independent point of view. Such a situation was (and outside TV remains) unique in its experience.

At one time or another there appeared in our programmes Cabinet Ministers and leading politicians, officers of the highest rank in the Armed Forces, authors and composers, many of the leading conductors and concert soloists, singers by the score, leaders in the world of sport, radio personalities such as Freddy Grisewood and Tommy Handley, as well as the majority of the stars of stage and variety. There can be no

[1] Among the eminent actors who performed similar service for us upon subsequent occasions were Martin Harvey, Felix Aylmer and Henry Oscar.

doubt at all that this competition proved salutary as far as the B.B.C.'s own programmes were concerned. We, on our side, sometimes forgot that enthusiasm did not entirely make up for our lack of experience, and that we could not expect the official body to abrogate its ultimate responsibility. Yet, when all is said, the story of our war-time association with the B.B.C. remains as much a tribute to the forbearance of that body as to ENSA's pursuit of self-justification.

4

The ENSA Half-hour

This programme began our regular contribution to war-time broadcasting on March 18, 1940, with a fanfare from *Aïda* trumpets, all that remained of Richard Llewellyn's original conception. Then Henry Oscar announced: "ENSA calling all Theatres of War." And so it was to be, at regular intervals, from now on. Among the artistes who took part in that first programme were Horace Kenney, Minnie Rayner, Dennis Noble, Leslie Henson and the members of the *Piccadilly Revels*, a concert party that was on the point of leaving for France. The script was written by Ronald Jeans and Reginald Arkell.

Shortly after this Geraldo invited me to select the ENSA signature tune from a number of alternatives. I chose *Let the people sing*, a comparatively new song by Noël Gay, because of its gaiety and brightness. It remained our signature tune for the next six years, during which time it must have been played, recorded and rediffused many thousands of times, with profit to its composer and gratifying publicity for ENSA.

The second broadcast in the series (March 29) was the first occasion on which personal messages from soldiers overseas were broadcast to their families at home. The credit for this simple idea, which made an instant appeal to the listening millions, belongs to Stephen Williams. The messages were handed in at our entertainment posts in France, and teleprinted to London with the names and regimental numbers of the senders. Seymour Hicks read the first of them. In the excitement of the moment he lost his place in the script and gave one man's number as Gerrard 1234, for which he was duly admonished by the B.B.C. for flippancy. On the next occasion Williams proposed that the wife for whom the message was intended should be present when it was read, and should reply over the microphone, while her husband listened in overseas. Official approval for this was not received until about 8 P.M. on the day before the broadcast. The wife lived in the country and could not be located by telephone.

However, thanks to the intervention of the local exchange, a near-by grocer offered to contact her. When he reached the house she was in her bath, so he was forced to talk to her through the door. Hastily turning off the tap, she demanded sharply if it were good news or bad. Reassured on that point, she declared that it was impossible to give an answer while she was having a bath. . . . And so Mrs Elliott of East Grinstead inaugurated the system of messages from home to men serving in H.M. Forces abroad. Variations of Williams' simple, human plan were subsequently developed by the B.B.C. and the various Army Broadcasting stations overseas into a two-way traffic of great volume. Echoes of it are to be heard in the programmes of music broadcast at the request of serving members of the Forces to their families and friends and to the sick.

After Dunkirk the programme was given weekly, and so continued through various vicissitudes, internal and external, and in spite of the interruptions of the Blitz and the V1 and V2 bombs, until 1944. Over such an extended period the Broadcasting Division was inevitably hard put to it to meet my nagging requests for quality, sparkle and variety. The staff grumbled, and did their best: I grumbled, and secretly admired their achievements.

At one time or another various well-known writers helped with the scripts, including J. B. Priestley, Ronald Jeans, Wyndham Lewis, Macqueen-Pope, Jonah Barrington, Leslie Julian Jones and Michael Howard; Gillie Potter wrote his own scripts for a Hogsnorton series, in which Lilian Braithwaite played Lady Marshmallow with distinctive humour. Tactless censorship by the B.B.C. terminated Gillie's variations on our theme of "entertainment with a difference," to which we sometimes gave the sub-title of "The stuff we give the troops."

When the Music Division was fully in its stride I asked it to provide one broadcast programme of classical music each month, a notion that was as strenuously objected to by the B.B.C. as by our own Broadcasting Executive. The first took place on November 11, 1942, and, later, many notable broadcasts were given. Legge usually employed the London Symphony Orchestra for the purpose—until towards the end, when he used his own Philharmonia Orchestra. There were 'alarums and excursions' when the B.B.C. hierarchy decided that, between the hours of 6 P.M. and 9 P.M., broadcasting on the Forces Programme was to be limited to 'background listening,' a contradiction in terms that I found inexplicable, but which obviously excluded classical music. After a struggle, tense but mercifully short, we saved this particular variation on our theme by shifting the time of transmission to 5.30. The praise which it received left the pundits unrepentant.

The search for variations went on relentlessly. There was a series called 'Moods in Music,' with James Agate arguing the case for classical music against Spike Hughes on the side of jazz, illustrated by excerpts played by Geraldo's orchestra, augmented by instrumentalists from one of the big symphony orchestras. During a rehearsal of one of the classical items a musician put his hand up. When Geraldo stopped the orchestra he was told it was customary to be cued in at that particular passage, whereupon he replied, "So you want me to cue you in, do you? What a lot o' big bibies!"

In 'ENSA At Home,' members of the Broadcasting Council played host to theatrical friends whom they thought would please the troops, a pleasing idea put forward by Stephen Williams. Among those 'at home' were Irene Vanbrugh, Hugh Walpole and Clemence Dane.

Two good ideas came from Sir Herbert Dunnico. The first was a series of four programmes contributed by artiste-members of the Savage Club, including Moiseiwitsch, George Baker, Robert Easton, Gerald Moore, the Western Bros., Malcolm McEachern, Flanagan and Allen, and the 'Savage Club Choir'; the second, a series of short interviews on sport, in which the troops heard the views of Pelham Warner and 'Patsy' Hendren on cricket, Jimmy Wilde on boxing, and Joe Davis on billiards.

Several Scottish Half-hours were contributed by many well-known comedians from the North, among them Harry Gordon, Jack Ratcliffe, and Gordon Finlay. They were recorded in Glasgow and slotted in as Scotland's contribution. After the arrival of American troops in Europe U.S.O. Camp Shows contributed some characteristic broadcasts before combined audiences of American and British troops. Upon one occasion Sidney Carroll interviewed the beautiful creature for whose success he had been mainly responsible when he presented her in *The Mask of Virtue*: Vivien Leigh. This was shortly after her great success in *Gone with the Wind*. Then there was Charles Coborn, who insisted upon taking part. He sang his *The Man who broke the Bank at Monte Carlo* with immense gusto; he was then ninety-one. The list could be extended indefinitely, but it is time to speak of other parts of the work.

5

'Break for Music'

After Dunkirk there was quite a rush of broadcast entertainment into the factories. The B.B.C. was first off the mark with a programme called 'Music while you work' which began on June 23, 1940, and continued for many years. Then, shortly after the announcement of our Ministry of Labour Service, Stephen Williams suggested that we should include regular factory broadcasts in the scheme. The B.B.C. officials were loath at first to entrust the idea solely to ENSA, but after Ernie Bevin's 'plonk plonk' speech at the end of our first concert from Woolwich Arsenal they could no longer refuse us. According to the log-book, we broadcast two more concerts from munition factories before adopting Seymour Hicks' title of 'Break for Music,' and beginning the regular series. So much for the origins of the most effective of all the Radio ENSA programmes, and the one that achieved the longest run without ever swerving from its modest utilitarian purpose.

To begin with, it was given once a week in the Home Service from the Drury Lane studio; by 1941 transmissions were taking place bi-weekly in both the Home and Forces Programmes, once from the studio and once from the canteen of a London factory. Monday was usually the day for the studio transmission, and each Friday a number of artistes, musicians and technical people would set out at 8 A.M. from Drury Lane for a factory: a motor-coach for the orchestra, one or two cars for artistes and conductor, a lorry for the Bechstein grand piano (in charge of our own tuner), and a smaller one for the music-stands, portable rostrums and public-address equipment in charge of a staff electrician, besides the Post Office personnel to fix the land-lines: quite a cavalcade! Those weekly expeditions were organized with the care and precision of a military operation. The other day I came across minutes exchanged between the appropriate departments at Drury Lane regarding the dispatch by 9 A.M. of "one small door slam for Mr Peter Cavanagh." Telephones, tap mats, sleigh and bicycle bells and all manner of strange 'props' frequently appear on the requisitions.

As 'Break for Music' grew in reputation the cavalcade journeyed farther afield, eventually reaching cities as distant as Birmingham, Liverpool, Manchester and Bradford. On Bank Holidays, when the factories were closed, the programme was transmitted from military camps or R.A.F. stations, and most of the wonderful NAAFI clubs that made their appearance up and down the country in the later years celebrated their formal openings with 'Break for Music,' thereby receiving a great deal of publicity.

In 1944 'doodle-bugs' added to the anxieties. Whenever the purple light went up, which meant that missiles were approaching the neighbourhood, the show was taken off the air. As the works' canteens were not soundproof, the authorities took this precaution so that the listeners should not hear any catastrophe that might occur. Not so in the case of the supersonic rockets. Various V2 explosions came over the air during 'Break for Music,' adding ironic comment to each occasion, notably so one day when a baritone was singing *Bless this house* as the force of a near-by explosion blew in doors and windows and part of the roof of the canteen.

During the winter of 1942–43 broadcasts were organized for the night shifts. In spite of careful instructions from the Routing Branch our caval-cade often lost its way in the black-out, especially when snow cover-ing the ground made familiar outlines seem strange; but somehow or other the show went on. Often the artistes continued to entertain the tired workers after the broadcast was over. Upon one occasion, when work was temporarily halted because of breakdown, they gave a full two-hours' show, finishing at 2 A.M. The report read as follows: "Jack Simpson played every conceivable popular number on the xylophone and the audience sang tirelessly, and Jack Train—although in very bad health at the time—kept the party going with one brilliant impersonation after the other."

The reports are full of such matters: of a canteen plunged into darkness as the broadcast was about to begin, with Ruth Naylor singing *Vilia* from start to finish without a fumble from the accompanist, or a giggle from the audience; of Tessie O'Shea, released from a nursing home to journey by rail to a factory in Aylesbury, finding the line impassable from an over-night air-raid, and driving by car through dense fog and past endless Army convoys, only to arrive after the broadcast had started, of how she rested to recover her strength, while Stephen Williams (between announce-ments) and Margaret Harper-Nelson gave out her band-parts and scribbled instructions to Carroll Gibbons and to each member of the band on her complicated routine, and of how she went on the air entirely unrehearsed, but without a hitch.

Sometimes special programmes would be arranged, as when Gertrude Lawrence came from America in 1944 to join our Second Front line-up, and, within twenty-four hours of arrival, found herself leading a broadcast from Cossars Factory at Highbury. Then there was Josephine Baker (cap-ping her work for the Allied troops in the Middle East by entertaining British factory workers), George Formby and Arthur Askey, Alice Delysia and Anona Winn, and, oh! a host of others; in fact, all the famous dance-bands and all the top-line artistes appeared in 'Break for Music' at one time or another, many of them preceding or following their ENSA tours.

The compères included Bob Danvers Walker of Pathé News, Stephen Williams during the middle years, and, towards the end, Brian Michie, a highly-strung person who, apparently, stood in considerable awe of myself: inexplicable seeing that our relations had always been cordial.

One day he received a message "to go and see the Director, please." Probably just a routine matter, but conscience must have made him uneasy, for he took Margaret Harper-Nelson to one side and began to rehearse what he should say to me, ending up with the dramatic line: "Mr Dean, if you shout at me I shall simply burst into tears and run out of the room."

The list of happenings, grave and gay, appertaining to this programme —of obstacles overcome or bypassed, of talent encouraged and objections overruled—is as long as for any other. But repetition is tedious and there is a limit to all things, even ENSA's broadcasting. After VE Day the transmissions were reduced to once a week in the Home Service. In November 1945 I served notice on the B.B.C. that the programme was to close down. Its *raison d'être* no longer existed; as far as we were concerned the job was over. The 514th and last broadcast took place on the 30th of that month. On the programme were Vera Lynn, Rob Wilton, Carole Carr and, of course, the faithful Geraldo with his fiddles, drums and trumpets. Each of the compères who had served the programme so well through the years took turns to announce the items, and I said some words of farewell. After that last broadcast Kenneth Barnes opened a fresh 'Eulogy file'; it was soon bursting at the seams with appreciations, mixed with protests from the factory committees at the inevitable cessation.

Café Académique . . .

On State occasions, when official notables were visiting the factories opening new extensions and so forth, Geraldo would take his full orchestra, instead of sending one of the smaller dance-bands. The factory managements did their best to return the compliment by inviting the entire company to lunch in the directors' dining-room. On such a day Geraldo found himself seated beside the wife of the managing director. As she awaited the arrival of the soup she turned to make conversation with the popular band-leader. "Tell me, Mr Geraldo," she said, smiling graciously, "where were you trained?" "Well, Lyons' Corner House for one thing," replied the imperturbable Gerry.

6

Et Cetera

In addition to our two main programmes, there were regular broadcasts on the Overseas wave-length and a variety of contributions on special occasions. 'London Carries On,' written and produced by Macqueen-Pope, was transmitted overseas once a week from 1940 to 1942. The artistes taking part remained together for so long that they virtually became a stock company. The principal members were Joan Young, Harry Hudson, Bernard Clifton, Maidie Andrews, Gloria Kane and Jack Leon's band. This programme was compèred during the first year by Henry Oscar, and afterwards by Georgie Henschel, and became so popular that 'Popie' was inundated with fan mail, and men on leave would call at the stage-door, requesting permission to watch the transmission. The opening announcement always ran: "From that most famous playhouse, the Theatre Royal, Drury Lane, we, the show folk of Britain, send you half an hour of London," thus giving expression to its producer's abiding love for the historic building.

After Pope retired from our scene this programme gave place to 'By Way of Music,' and consisted mainly of revivals of old tunes and melodies popular between the two World Wars. This was devised by Stephen Williams and compèred by a young ENSA actress, Pamela Sholto. It continued until 1944, when its place was taken by 'Over to You,' transmitted for the last year of the war in the Light Programme as well as over the British Forces network. The names of those who took part are witness to the energy and enthusiasm of its producer, Margaret Harper-Nelson. The list included Frances Day, Florence Desmond, Reginald Purdell, Joan Cross, Dora Labette, Walter Midgley, Harriet Cohen, Irene Kohler and Vera Lynn.

Then there were the 'Naval Occasions': "ENSA calling all officers and men of the Royal Navy on shore and at sea." Evelyn Laye made these her special care and presided as hostess. The log-book records the artistes taking part in the first of these: Flanagan and Allen, Count John MacCormack, Teddie Brown, Cyril Ritchard and Geraldo's orchestra; on the second 'Occasion' (August 9, 1940, to be precise) Richard Tauber gave his first broadcast as a British subject after his naturalization. On the day of Pearl Harbour, Evelyn found herself hostess to Jack Buchanan, Dennis Noble, Eileen Joyce and Bunny Doyle. Trafalgar Day was always a 'Naval Occasion,' coming perhaps from Plymouth with the help of the

Polish Naval Choir and the Marines Orchestra and compèred by Lieutenant Vivian Ellis, R.N.V.R. (entertainments officer for the Plymouth Command), or from Scotland with Will Fyffe. On one 'Occasion' Evelyn Laye played hostess from the big stage in London, while Beatrice Lillie and others gave the concert from the Naval Base at Rosyth. They were supposed to talk to each other by the aid of earphones, but communication was difficult, and the sailors were edified by the following conversation carried on in rising tones, as they strove to make themselves heard:

"Hello, Bee, this is Boo. Bee, this is Boo!"

"Hullo, Boo, this is Bee. Boo, this is Bee!"

There were balancing programmes for the other Services, with the compensatory titles of 'To Meet the Army' and 'To Meet the Air Force.' Their respective hostesses during 1942 were Frances Day and Victoria Hopper.

There were the trans-Atlantic exchange programmes: one half coming from America, organized by Gertrude Lawrence on behalf of the New York ENSA Committee, and the other half contributed by us in London. These were beamed to America and Canada on short-wave and transmitted by the B.B.C. in the Home Service. Those who took part on the first occasion are unlikely to forget the experience. It was late at night. The great theatre was eerily quiet after the turmoil of the day, the auditorium shrouded in dust-covers and darkness. A little knot of people stood round the gaggle of microphones, waiting to hear the voices of their friends from across the Atlantic. Even in peace-time most people experience a certain nervous tension while waiting to speak on the transatlantic telephone, but in 1941, when the people of Britain felt cut off from all physical contact with the outside world, the tension had a special quality.

The programme had been given the general title of 'Broadway Calling,' but the first American items came from Boston, where Gertrude Lawrence was then playing. Harry Richman was with her as compère, while Evelyn Laye and Leslie Henson waited to do the same for the British half. Gertie was going to begin by introducing Governor Saltonstall of Massachusetts, who was to make a brief speech of welcome to the programme, to which I was to make brief reply. I waited with tensed nerves for the sound of Gertie's voice, listening to the strange roarings and buzzings of the gremlins before the engineers closed the circuit. Then somebody whispered, "Stand by." The red light flickered and then went out. Another pause, and then it glowed steadily.

The opening speeches would sound pompous to-day; perhaps they did so then, but the emotional atmosphere in which we were living was the excuse. When the time came for ENSA's contribution Leslie Henson relieved the tension with an unexpected gag that raised angry "Ssh-es" from the producer:

"This is a host to host cook-up, Gertie," he said.

The broadcast was over at last, and we could relax. As I turned round Evelyn Laye flopped on to a ginger-beer box at the side of the stage and started to laugh for no reason at all. . . . In later exchanges those taking part from London included Robert Montgomery, Grahame White, C. B. Cochran, Will Fyffe and Nelson Keys. Noël Coward acted as compère on one occasion.

Each Christmas Day in the afternoon it was my special joy to go with my wife to a military hospital, there to take part in an ENSA broadcast to the troops as well as to provide a full-length show for the patients. Sometimes Anna Neagle came with us, and parties of children singing carols; these were a special delight. It was fun helping to produce the show and acting as compère. I used to take the opportunity of including in the script a brief message renewing ENSA promises to the fighting troops. On one occasion 'Popie' wrote a complete radio pantomime in which I took the part of the 'Demon King.' I do not recall the performance, but Margaret Harper-Nelson assures me that I gave satisfaction.

Item . . .

The total number of broadcasts given by ENSA from March 18, 1940, to May 7, 1945, was 940. This figure refers to 'live' programmes only, and excludes the huge total of broadcasts from overseas stations.

7

His ENSA Voice

In the spring of 1940, while G.H.Q., Middle East, was noting with increasing impatience the inadequacy of our entertainment plans, and we at home were without an accurate picture[1] of what was really going on in Cairo, there arrived in Egypt one Major Peter Haddon, to take up a

[1] A state in which we were destined to be kept for a year or more, so that when in 1941 Major Randolph Churchill burst into my room with a catalogue of our failures in the Middle East and an account of what he had done for broadcasting there, ending up with a request for stars, I could only stifle my inner fury, plead ignorance and murmur, "Give us the transport and we'll send the stars."

staff appointment with Intelligence and so to renew his previous experience of a military life in Egypt. Peter, an actor of great charm in obtuse parts, is not the type of man whose arrival anywhere is likely to remain for long either inaudible or unnoticed. General Wavell sent for him and asked him how he thought his experience in civil life could best be employed. As a result of that interview the Middle East Forces Programme came haphazardly into existence, transmitted each day over the Egyptian State Broadcasting (E.S.B.) network and relayed by the Palestine Broadcasting Service. The programme was administered by a staff detailed from G.H.Q. and financed partly out of NAAFI funds. In view of the Corporation's financial responsibility it was clear that ENSA would soon be involved in the search for radio talent overseas. It was obvious that 'semi-professionals' and military bands could not sustain those daily broadcasts indefinitely. I began to worry increasingly about what should be done.

One day Stephen Williams reminded me that Radio Luxembourg and other commercial stations frequently transmitted their programmes on records. This seemed to be the answer to the problem: all ENSA broadcasts that were suitable should be recorded and flown to the Middle East to help to build up the new Forces Programme. This—and this alone—was the origin of the vast service of recorded entertainment that was later built up in the light of much disconcerting experience.

A recording section of the Broadcasting Division was set up, with Miss Elsie Cohen, lately managing director of the Academy Cinema in Oxford Street, as its secretary. The first recordings were made on acetate. This is a comparatively cheap process, but has the disadvantage of an extremely short life. Moreover, the inferior quality of the results obtained from the ramshackle equipment at Drury Lane led to complaints. We persuaded the Treasury Finance Officer to let us purchase better equipment, with which we continued to record minor items, musical links and so forth on acetate; but the method was too unreliable to carry the main burden of the service, and superior arrangements had to be made.

As there was a land-line direct from the H.M.V. studios to Broadcasting House, we invited the Gramophone Company to record our broadcasts. Later, we employed them to make direct recordings of all the programmes given at the Fortune Theatre. Very soon the supplies of vinyl, the material used to make the actual records, ran short. However, through the goodwill of the Ministry of Supply, essential supplies were made available to the Gramophone Company, provided each application was backed by myself.

In addition to trouble over the acetate recording, insufficient care was exercised in editing the programmes. References to occasions long past, such as Bank Holidays, Christmas time, Easter and so forth, gave the programmes a nostalgic force that was most undesirable from the morale point of view. Unexpected and highly censorable entertainment was sometimes provided when the voices of recording engineers, speaking in the strongest vernacular, were rebroadcast in Syria, Irak, and other out-of-the-way places, to the high amusement of the soldier-listener. All these minor faults were soon adjusted; but the need for close censorship of the material was constant.

Our first recordings were augmented by a number of programmes which Gertrude Lawrence made for us in New York under the general title of 'Broadway Calling,' with the subtitle of 'The New York ENSA Half-hour.' Her co-producer was Richard Haydn. These programmes were first broadcast by the B.B.C. in the Home and Forces programmes, for which we received considerable fees. Out of the proceeds we purchased a recording truck, known as the Gertrude Lawrence Recording Unit. The equipment did admirable service for the remainder of the war. It was borrowed upon several occasions by the B.B.C. itself—*e.g.*, to record an on-the-spot commentary of the bombing of the House of Commons.

For a later series Gertrude Lawrence secured American permission to record all the principal songs and singers of the New York production of *Oklahoma*. This was in October 1943. As we had no advance knowledge of the contents of the records we were considerably astonished at this proof of Gertrude's energy and enthusiasm, but not at all surprised when the owners of the British copyright refused consent to their use.

In February 1942 we received permission to take recordings of the B.B.C.'s own programmes without fee, except what might be demanded by the artistes making the broadcasts. But, since they were already receiving their usual B.B.C. fees, I felt justified in asking them to waive their claims.

A curious case of obtuseness provided us with a welcome addition to the schedule for 1943. Sir Harry Lauder was anxious to broadcast to the troops but, owing to his age, wished to record the programmes in Glasgow. The B.B.C. decided that he must come to London for the purpose, which he refused to do; whereupon, through our Scottish Regional Committee (of which, by the way, he was still President), he offered to make recordings of all his famous songs. These were duly flown out to the Middle East, where they were a sensational success.

8

O.R.B.S.

This recording scheme was obviously fair game for officers with entertainment experience serving at home, and there was little surprise in ENSA circles when the hounds of Whitehall began snuffing the air. Army Welfare minuted that the scheme should be run as a separate enterprise from our broadcasting—"Of course, with ENSA's help," being added as an afterthought. My briskly worded memorandum to Lord May's Finance and Organization Committee, calling attention once more to the overlapping and waste of money that always ensued from rival schemes, quashed the proposal for the time being. A Service sub-committee was then appointed to make selections from the B.B.C. programmes and to supplement them by recording programmes contributed by professional artistes serving with the Forces.

At first the sub-committee was attached to our own Broadcasting Division, but, as its members began to feel their feet, the association became irksome to them. By 1942 a new Inter-Departmental Committee, known as the Services Committee for the Welfare of the Forces (S.C.W.F.), had come into existence. This body now began to press for complete release of the recording scheme from the trammels of ENSA. Lord May did not care for this very much, for it meant bypassing the Entertainments Board. He put his foot down gently but firmly, saying that he could see no reason why the existing structure should not be used: extended, perhaps, but certainly not abandoned.

On his instructions I drew up a plan for the formation of an ENSA Advisory Recording Council, on which recognized experts in their various fields should be invited to sit, such as Major Christopher Stone, Compton Mackenzie, Tom Arnold and C. B. Cochran, together with J. H. Watkins (of the Gramophone Company) and Walter Legge, to act as technical advisers. Underneath the Council would be a Recording Executive, thus repeating our usual pattern of organization. The Service Departments would appoint representatives to both these bodies.

The plan did not appeal to the young officers responsible for the Services' share of the work. They were quite willing to use our facilities and to allow us to bear the cost. Outside these routine matters they desired complete independence, which was not possible because of our financial responsibility. After some brisk exchanges, conducted with increasing acerbity between the Entertainments Board and the S.C.W.F.—a soften-

GEORGE TAKES HIS UKE ACROSS THE ORNE TO A FORWARD POSITION HELD BY MEN OF THE SIXTH AIRBORNE DIVISION
(My snapshot.)

THE DIVISION'S COMMANDER, MAJOR-GENERAL ("WINDY") GALE, NOW GENERAL SIR RICHARD GALE, COMMANDER-IN-CHIEF, BRITISH ARMY OF THE RHINE
(I took this one, too.)

A REDIFFUSION VAN MOVES UP
(And this.)

OPENING NIGHT AT THE ENSA
(MARIGNY) THEATRE

CAEN:
ANOTH
OPENIN

World Pre
of the
Priestley f

ing-up process to which I was becoming hardened—it was decided that
the Services should have their own recording committee, to which Miss
Elsie Cohen would be transferred to act as its secretary. She was required
to remain a member of our Broadcasting Executive, and to attend its
meetings in order to report progress. Our Finance Control officer was
also appointed to the Committee to keep it straight on financial matters.
The total output was divided into three parts—one-third being provided
by ENSA, one-third from a selection of B.B.C. programmes and one-
third by original recordings provided by the Service Committee. Finally,
the whole scheme was given the general title of the Overseas Recorded
Broadcasting Service (O.R.B.S.), with distinctive sub-titles for each of the
three sources of supply—the name we chose was 'ENSA Calling'—and
the actual records labelled accordingly.

On the Committee that now took over responsibility for producing
the Service contributions the Army was represented by Lieutenant-
Colonel Eric Maschwitz, supported by Major Basil Brown (who later
joined Butlin's Holiday Camps), the Navy by Lieutenant-Commander
Kim Peacock, R.N.V.R., and the R.A.F. by Squadron-Leader Lamping.
In their planning deliberations they were greatly assisted by Harry Alan
Towers, an AC2 in the Air Force. Possessed of remarkable energy and
business acumen and a genuine flair for radio ideas, this brilliant and
thrustful young man speedily became the mainstay of the Committee. His
appearances before it in the early days were a subject for comedy. Arriving
in a taxicab with two secretaries, a dictaphone and a youthful bubble of
ideas, he would be kept waiting in the anteroom until the high-level
discussions were over, or until they had got into such a tangle that expert
help was needed to unravel them. He would then be summoned into the
presence, where he would tactfully explain to the Committee what was
required, salute smartly and disappear into another taxi. He was later
commissioned and given the somewhat cumbrous title of Deputy Services
Programme Director. He was the outstanding discovery on the administrative side of the scheme, and well deserves his subsequent success in
commercial radio.

A strong team of producers and announcers was at the disposal of the
Services Committee, including Philip Slessor and Douglas Moodie for
the Army, Ronnie Waldman, Roy Rich and Sidney Torch for the Air
Force and Kim Peacock for the Navy. Owing to the presence of so many
fine artistes in the Forces, their contributions often excelled in quality those
which ENSA provided. At one time the output of Service recordings was
double that of the B.B.C. and ENSA combined; but, like ourselves, the
Committee had to learn the lesson that quantity cannot replace quality.

T

The support of the three Directorates of Welfare was a great advantage to them, for artistes could be detailed by their units to report at the Fortune Theatre in London at "ack-ack hours for entertainment recording duty." These genial press-gang methods resulted in some unusual combinations, as when Rex Harrison was summoned from Fighter Command to perform a double act with Wee Georgie Wood. And Macqueen-Pope's radio pantomimes were flattered by later imitations, in the first of which two members of the Recording Committee (Eric Maschwitz and Kim Peacock) played the Ugly Sisters.

The keen rivalry between the military and civilian sections for the services of artistes not yet called up who were the mutual friends of both cut across the ENSA arrangements at times, so that the casting files became a sort of Tom Tiddler's ground. But I preferred to leave it so, rather than encourage the growth of what an official memorandum once suggested should be "a Service-designed and Service-produced entertainment conformable to Service policy," which had a formidable ring to me. Faced as we were by a vast round of daily routine, we should undoubtedly have fallen into complacency but for the zestful rivalry of the lodgers occupying our 'first-floor-front' at the Fortune Theatre across the road. Nevertheless, it was necessary to give one's sense of humour a shot in the arm sometimes after reading the minutes of their meetings.

By the end of the war forty-three radio stations abroad were relaying recorded programmes to the troops, sometimes for as long as ten and twelve hours each week. Eventually the majority of H.M.V.'s technical staff were employed on ENSA work, cutting the matrices and preparing the hundreds of records that were dispatched overseas each week, penetrating to the loneliest stations in the Persian Gulf and as far east as India, Ceylon, Burma, Singapore and Hongkong.

9

Rediffusion

Ian Macphail, a young Scottish fighter pilot, was responsible for what must have been the first music circle to be formed within the R.A.F. itself. In the first days of the war he used to give informal gramophone recitals for any officers and men on his station who cared to listen, using his own record library for the purpose. In due course he was shot down over Normandy, crash-landed his aircraft in Wiltshire and spent the next eighteen months in hospital. Soon he was at his old enthusiasm once more, and achieved quite a degree of musical appreciation among units of the

Army and R.A.F. in and around Aberdeen during his convalescence. This success inspired him with the ambition to take classical music to the men in the fighting line, although he had not the faintest idea how this might be accomplished technically. He got into touch with Walter Legge, who brought him to see me. I liked his enthusiasm. In due course he was appointed as assistant to Boyd Neel, musical adviser for the London District.

Although his time was fully occupied in the Music Division he began to pester our broadcasting engineers with his dream of taking music to the men in the fox-holes. Giving way to his persuasion, the engineers eventually worked out designs for a rediffusion van, and the first proto-type was built. This was a heavy-duty vehicle, equipped with its own power supply, a double turn-table for gramophone records, a microphone for the operator's announcements and two loudspeakers fitted to the roof of the truck, together with additional speakers on long leads, so that they could be hung on the walls of buildings or in the trees when large audiences were assembled. Specially designed racks provided space for a library of 500 records. The amplifiers were designed to withstand rough usage and tropical conditions.

The prototype was given exhaustive trials. Its success aroused great enthusiasm among our people. Soon there was a positive clamour from overseas for these rediffusion vans, which, after the gremlins had been chased out of the first set of equipment, were supplied in considerable num-bers not only to the Second Front but to Italy, the Middle East, Burma and Singapore. The record libraries which each truck carried included classical and light music and variety programmes, and were later reinforced by a selection of recordings from the O.R.B.S. service, for the use of which the various Trades Unions and copyright societies that exist to protect the interests of those concerned gave special consent.

10

Discovery Corner

Drawing the seine net of national service through the twin pools of amateur and professional talent brought rare finds to the surface at one time or another. Some of the discovered may now wish to ignore their origin; others of more generous mind will be glad to acknowledge the experience that working for ENSA brought them.

The process of discovery began of course with the auditions. To attend one of these came Brenda Bruce from the Birmingham Repertory

Theatre, the first of a small band of young people to win spontaneous applause from the Auditions Committee. She was engaged for one of Archie de Bear's revue companies, from which first success she never looked back. Cliff Gordon was another discovery; he was given an audition through the good offices of Collie Knox, subsequently went to the Windmill Theatre, was taken up by the B.B.C. and is now a variety star.

The Broadcasting Division evolved an extremely effective method of testing newcomers. They were recorded at auditions, the recordings afterwards being played back to the Selection Committee without divulging the name. In this way several notable discoveries were made. As the B.B.C. had the right to boss our prospective engagements we used to call attention to the talent we unearthed, but we received small thanks for our pains. Peter Brough was a case in point. He did a trial sketch with his Archie Andrews, which was so good that Stephen Williams arranged for him to make his first broadcast in 'Break for Music.' The B.B.C. reaction to the proposal was expressed in impolite vernacular: "You must be nuts." Lind Joyce also made her first broadcast in 'Break for Music.' Then there was the case of Val Merrall. He was employed on a war job at the G.E.C. factory at Hammersmith and volunteered to sing with Carroll Gibbons' band during an ENSA concert there. After a further audition at the Fortune Theatre he was given some overseas recording to do. Later, after several appearances in 'Break for Music,' Margaret Harper-Nelson persuaded Roger Ould to write to Michael Standing about his obvious promise. The answer: "although he might broadcast for ENSA he would have to go on a waiting list for the B.B.C." Sylvia Robin, returning from a long ENSA tour, was also given some overseas recording, while waiting in the queue. Ted Ray received great encouragement from ENSA which may have hastened his arrival at the top. Celia Lipton, whose band-leader father, Sidney Lipton, became an ENSA entertainment officer on the Italian Front, was another young artiste who profited by this war-time experience.

Then there was Norman Hackforth (long the mystery voice in 'Twenty Questions'), who did great service for us as a pianist in the Middle East, Marilyn Williams and Hugh French, also from the Middle East, Avril Angers ('Variety Bandbox') and Roma Milne, and many others whose names would be included if more information were available.

A number of artistes who were successful with the early ENSA companies went on to further achievement in our Broadcasting Division or with O.R.B.S. after they were called up. Terry-Thomas was one of these. He went to one of the general auditions in the days when Seymour Hicks was still with us. Seymour took a fancy to his work and placed him in the musical-comedy section under Frank Collins. He remained with ENSA until he was called up for the Army. Although his early attempts to persuade Stephen Williams to put him on the air were unsuccessful, he stuck to his guns, declaring his intention "to have a bash" sooner or later. He became a genuine Star in Battledress when he took part in the O.R.B.S. programmes.

Charlie Chester, a member of one of the first parties to go to France, took part in an early ENSA broadcast from the E.M.I. factory at Hayes, whereat he won his spurs by beating the competition of the rampaging hot-water pipes—apart from the orchestra, the only artiste to succeed in doing so. Other outstanding talent developed within the Services included Peter Cavanagh and Donald Peers from the Army, and Jon Pertwee and Eric Barker from the Navy.

Practically every stage, music-hall and radio artiste of note gave his or her services to one side or the other. Those that wore uniform took part in the Service programmes, while the civilians appeared in both, Harry Alan Towers rather naïvely remarking in a little book that he published after the war that 'the lack of a uniform made no difference to their talents.'

CHAPTER TWENTY-THREE

NOTES ON OCCASIONS

1

'Cathedral Steps'

THE end of the London Blitz saw the beginning of a boom in the Theatre which, except for a brief halt during the assault of the V1 and V2 weapons, continued until the end of the war and for many months thereafter. People crowded into places of amusement everywhere. As I sat in my little office at Drury Lane the crackle of notes and the jingle of coins in the surrounding box-offices made me restless. It was not that I wanted to hold out my hat to catch some of the golden shower, although that certainly would have been welcome; it was the loss of contact with life and work behind the scenes and, above all, with theatre audiences that I found so irksome. To spend the rest of the war tending a bureaucratic machine would be too frustrating. Some opportunities for self-expression must be found.

Neither the Treasury nor NAAFI placed any obstacle in my way, an attitude that immediately invoked restraint on my part. But, in the event, dabbling in the commercial theatre brought little satisfaction. I became obsessed with the desire to use music and drama in some kind of positive assertion of the nation's belief in itself. Then an idea came to me: a performance, nobly fashioned and given in a public place, perhaps before a cathedral, as in the days of the medieval mysteries, where people could forgather and draw comfort in more personal fashion than by listening to the radio.

"An Anthology in praise of Britain: extracts from our poetry and literature, accompanied by songs and music: a combination of English morality play with the Greek formula that used the Chorus by way of comment: an offering of British music and drama to stir the hearts of the people by making them conscious of their glorious heritage": these were some of the phrases I inserted into the brief paper I wrote for Dunnico's Public Relations Council. In the cold light of afterwards they seem flamboyant, but they were in the key of public feeling at the time.

The question at once arose as to how the project was to be financed. I felt sure the actors and singers would give their services, but a certain amount of expenditure for such items as costumes, transport, etc. was inevitable. Sydney Walton, an active member of the Council, secured a large contribution to the required guarantee fund from a friend who desired to remain anonymous. This benefaction and the promise of a good fee from the B.B.C. for broadcasting the first performance seemed to justify our proceeding with what had been, until then, little more than an idea. The obvious place for the first performance was in front of the West Door of St Paul's. While Sir Herbert Dunnico contacted the Cathedral authorities I looked round for a leading author to prepare the script.

My first choice was Eric Linklater. I found him buried in an obscure unit of the Army at a camp outside Ripon. After I had sketched out the lines which I thought the anthology should take he asked me what I was going to call it. At that moment I had no idea. "Where is it going to be performed?" he asked. "On the steps of St Paul's Cathedral, I hope." "There's your title, then," said Linklater. " 'Cathedral Steps.' " So, although he felt unable to undertake the task, our talk had not been wasted.

My next thought was of Clemence Dane, who at that time was acting with the Old Vic Company in the north of England. As I watched her on the stage I realized that in gaining a dramatist the English stage had lost a first-class dramatic actress. After the play we had a preliminary talk, at which she embraced the idea with her usual enthusiasm. The next day we spent driving over the moors, exchanging ideas. Her knowledge of English literature and her grasp of its historical significance soon convinced me that I had made an ideal choice. In a short while she sent me the script, which needed very little alteration, save to restrain a certain predilection for Queen Boadicea that might have involved Sybil Thorndike in a chariot race round St Paul's Churchyard.

Meanwhile the Dean and Chapter had approved the project; also the patronage of the Lord Mayor and Sheriffs of the City of London had been secured. The co-operation of our best classical actors was needed to bring weight and dignity to the performance. I appealed to Hugh Beaumont for permission to approach the stars under contract to him, which he gave ungrudgingly. Never has there been a more brilliant cluster of them in a single designed performance; the constellations to be seen at charity matinées usually lack form and direction. The War Office provided the massed bands of the Brigade of Guards and the trumpets and drums of the Household Cavalry, while Sir Henry Wood agreed to act as conductor. The massed singers included members of the Alexandra Choir, the Goldsmiths' Choral Union, a contingent of the Royal Choral Society and the London Fire Service Pulteney Choir.

The practical difficulties of production were enormous. As the Anthology was to be broadcast to America as well as to listeners at home, the amplification of the voices to safeguard the broadcast while ensuring that the words would be heard by the crowds filling St Paul's Churchyard and Ludgate Hill beyond was a major problem in itself. I hit upon the idea of having lecterns placed left, right and centre at the foot of the great flight of steps, and a faldstool immediately in front of the great West Door. In each of these positions the B.B.C. engineers concealed microphones which, in addition to feeding the broadcasting channel, were used for local amplification to the listening crowd through loudspeakers hanging on the lamp-posts up and down Ludgate Hill. The result was a triumph for the engineers. Years later, after that star of radio irascibility, Gilbert Harding, had failed to identify my voice in 'What's my line?'—the best he could do was to associate it with trumpets and drums—he told me he had been one of the commentators to America.

The Common Council of the City of London was by this time enthusiastic about the project and ordered the City Police to divert the traffic from Ludgate Hill and the precincts of the Cathedral half an hour before the performance was due to begin. This would give time for the crowd to assemble and for final microphone adjustments.

Between the base of the steps and Queen Anne's statue, in the wide semicircle formed by the granite posts, chairs for distinguished visitors were set down, for, with a wise sense of occasion, Dunnico had arranged that the Mayors and Aldermen of all the London Boroughs should witness the performance in company with the Lord Mayor and Sheriffs of the City.

The drums and silver trumpets of the Household Cavalry were posted in the upper cupolas of the West Front. When I airily proposed this position I did not realize what it involved; but Walter Legge told me it took the men the whole of the previous afternoon to get their drums into position, manœuvring them up the narrow, winding stone staircases that lead to these eminences.

With regard to the spoken part it was necessary not only to time the whole performance but also the entrances and exits from the Cathedral and the grouping of the Chorus. At least one 'run through' on the steps was essential. Preliminary rehearsals for the principals were held in the Albert Hall and at the Open-Air Theatre in Regent's Park, whither we repaired in the cold early mornings—it was now late September—before the regular day's work at Drury Lane began. Many of the stars who took part were engaged in films and stage productions, and this added to the difficulties. The programme of music was arranged by Walter Legge, under the authority of the Music Council, and this was rehearsed separately.

It was decided to have the final rehearsal at 7 A.M. on the morning of the performance, September 25. The traffic through war-scarred London at that time was infrequent, and it was just possible for us to do what we had to do before the attenuated rush-hour began. It was bitterly cold, yet all concerned displayed the greatest enthusiasm. Even Sir Henry Wood, whose health was already causing concern to Lady Wood, had insisted on turning out. The stars stood and shivered about the portico of the Cathedral or tried on their costumes in the cold vestry, while I stood with Sir Henry on the rostrum that we had erected in front of the statue of Queen Anne, shouting directions through a large microphone, and competing ineffectually with the raucous amplifications of B.B.C. engineers in argument. Press photographers hurried hither and thither in search of advance pictures of the event.

Madame Vernon had thoughtfully arranged with the W.V.S. to provide a coffee-stall for us, otherwise I think we should have broken off the rehearsal in despair. Soon the supplies of coffee and sandwiches gave out, and another canteen at a near-by taxi-rank was raided. Edith Evans had motored through the black-out after her evening performance in Coventry and was very tired. Yet both she and Sybil Thorndike set a splendid example. The Guardsmen stamped their feet, blew on their fingers and longed for breakfast; the Choir missed their cues or could not see Henry Wood's baton. Early City workers began to arrive and the buses became more frequent. One by one and in twos and threes the Choir began to slip away as enthusiasm froze and office hours drew near.

By nine o'clock the rehearsal had died away into a scramble to get through the last pages of the script. Lady Wood removed the conductor almost forcibly from the rostrum, the Guardsmen marched back to barracks, the engineers buried their faces in mugs of hot coffee, and I resigned myself to my usual mood of pessimism before a big production, from which all the efforts of Madame Vernon failed to rouse me.

For obvious reasons we had not been allowed to advertise in the newspapers, but we had erected two large boards on either side of the steps one week beforehand, giving details of the cast and of the performance, hoping they would help to draw the crowd. We need have had no anxiety. Punctually as the great clock of St Paul's struck twelve the noise of the traffic died away. From the rostrum I could see dense crowds of people filing up Ludgate Hill. Soon they were pouring into the circular space before the Cathedral from all the narrow roads and alleys that are a characteristic feature of that part of the City. They were prevented from

over-running the open space in front of our amphitheatre by the Drury
Lane Home Guard, turned out in full force to aid the City police.

I held a last-minute conference with my staff of stage directors, while the
B.B.C. engineers ran hurriedly here and there, adjusting the loudspeakers
and testing the levels of the microphones; then into the Cathedral again,
where Macqueen-Pope was marshalling the Press. They had been given a
preliminary briefing in the Chapter House by Sir Herbert Dunnico, but,
for some reason or other, too much stress was laid upon the fact that the
traffic was to be diverted. This was regarded as a news item, and given
prominence in some of the popular newspapers over and above the intention that lay behind our efforts. . . .

Nearly all the actors are assembled, but Henry Ainley is late, and there
is anxiety about Leslie Howard, who is filming *The Gentle Sex* at Denham.
How will he get through the crowds that are growing denser every
minute? A police car is sent to look for him. I hurry into our tiring house,
which is the vestry of the Cathedral, where Elizabeth Haffenden, the
designer, is superintending the costumes. Their bold patterns in purple
and red and gold look magnificent. There is the usual scramble for
properties, spears and crowns and wreaths, and the usual arguments as to
which belongs to whom. Sir Henry Wood arrives, calm, but with the light
of battle in his eyes. The procession of civic dignitaries has already begun
to form up. At last! The ringing sound of a police gong on the north side
of the building, and a few moments later Leslie Howard comes strolling
in. Thank God for that!

It is nearly time. Sir Henry stalks majestically down the centre of the
tiered steps to the conductor's rostrum. There is generous clapping for the
grand old man. I follow, glancing nervously to left and right. The precincts are packed with people. They are even standing on the coping-stones
of the bombed-out buildings. From every office window faces peer out
excitedly; and down Ludgate Hill there is a whole sea of them. My
nerves tighten, as I make the necessary effort of control that is essential
before this service in praise of Britain—for that is what it really is—can
proceed in orderly fashion to its appointed climax.

Now, just as the clock booms the half-hour, the two halves of the great
West Door are slowly opened and the procession of Mayors and Sheriffs
with their beadles and mace-bearers comes slowly into view, headed by
the Lord Mayor in his robes and the Lord Chancellor in morning coat and
silk hat, exercising his special privilege of precedence in matters affecting
public celebration at the Cathedral. There must be a hundred or more in
the procession. In their fur-trimmed robes and hats the civic dignitaries
lend a wonderful medieval air to the proceedings. Even as they walk the

pale September sun breaks through the clouds and lights up the scene, glinting on their chains of office and on the upturned faces of the crowd. The silver trumpets and drums in the cupolas sound a fanfare that echoes and re-echoes round the Churchyard. Clouds of frightened pigeons rise from the cornices, wheel once and disappear down Ludgate Hill. It is perfect timing. I could not have dreamed of anything more effective.

Sir Henry raises his baton, and the choir sings *Fairest Isle, All Isles Excelling*, to the Cathedral organ relayed from within. In single file the Fighting Men in red tabards, led by Valour (Eric Portman) in scarlet, and the Men and Women of Peace in blue and white, led by Patience (Sybil Thorndike) in light blue, and wearing a chaplet of laurel and oak-leaves, make solemn entry through the great doors. 'Any-Man' (Frank Cellier) and 'Any-Woman'—his wife—(Mary Clare) come quietly out of the crowd and sit on a bench at the bottom of the steps: just an ordinary working-class couple, resting at the foot of the Cathedral during the noon hour. She has a large basket of flowers; he takes off his hat, lights his pipe and opens his newspaper.

The singing dies away, and Valour speaks the first words of the Anthology, taken from Scott's *Lay of the Last Minstrel*:

"Breathes there the man, with soul so dead,
Who never to himself hath said,
This is my own, my native land!"

The Chorus invoke blessings upon the people of England, Scotland and Wales, and then Patience, in Sybil's most ringing tones, so that the very loudspeakers seem to echo upon each other, proclaims:

"We have a story to tell you. It took two thousand years to write, but we will tell it to you in a lunch hour."

And now, in the words of Scott, Shakespeare, Shelley, Spenser, Milton, Kipling, Tennyson, Hardy and others, and to the music of Arne, Purcell, Elgar, Stanford, Sullivan, Parry and Walton, great moments in British history are recalled.

As the tale is told the figures of King and Queen come and go: Henry Ainley, wearing his crown like a genuine coronation piece, albeit slightly crooked, and looking like the English counterpart of Le Roi Soleil, magnificent in decay; Edith Evans, with tossing mane and that astonishing ability to expand her personality to heroic size. Alternately, and antiphonally with Chorus and Choir, they tell the story, using Chesterton's *Ballad of the White Horse* for the English victory over King Guthram and his Danes; Kipling's *The Reeds of Runnymede* for Magna Carta; then John Barbour's *Freedom*, nobly spoken by Lewis Casson, and the song of *Agincourt* with Marius Goring as King Henry. Next, the fight for religious freedom: Cranmer, Latimer and Master Ridley (Robert Speaight):

"We shall this day light such a candle by God's grace in England as I trust shall never be put out."

Patience speaks words from Spenser's *The Faerie Queene*, and then the Choir sings *Now is the Month of Maying* to usher in the Golden Age:
"The Age of Youth," declares Patience;
"The Age of Wisdom," shouts Valour.
"Who calls Elizabeth of England?" cries Edith Evans in ringing tones from the great West Door. It is thrilling to hear those words, spoken by Queen Elizabeth at Tilbury before the defeat of the Spanish Armada.

After the English Revolution and Cromwell we hear Henry Ainley once more. The crowd falls quiet, listening to that noble voice speaking, from behind a pillar, words from Sir Thomas Browne's *Urn Burial*—a grave moment after the heroics. (Although I have taken the precaution of posting a stage-manager behind a pillar to prompt him, Harry does not falter.) Children play about the Cathedral steps in the times of Good Queen Anne while the Poet (Robert Speaight) recites verses from Gray's *Elegy*. The Queen puts her arm about them and goes with them into the Cathedral.

Arcady in the English countryside gives place to the Napoleonic wars, ushered in with drums and trumpets and more drums; a reference to the birth of the United States of America: "England beaten by her own sons," declares Patience. . . . Here and there comes naïve interruption from 'Any-Man' or 'Any-Woman,' acted by two supreme artistes in the characterization of ordinary folk. 'Any-Man' jumps to his feet, protesting angrily, "That was the Government." Valour chides him for not choosing a better one, and for shaking in his shoes when Napoleon threatened invasion. "I wasn't afraid, I had my Navy," declares 'Any-Man.' Valour, good-naturedly mocking, asks him to name some Admirals' names; but 'Any-Man' has to be reminded of a little man, blind in one eye and with one arm lost. He tells his wife how his grandfather served under Nelson—"he used to say he was just Drake come again."

The great doors are opened once more, and Leslie Howard, a small, frail figure, comes slowly out. It is the wraith of Nelson, risen from his tomb in the Cathedral, all in grey, even to the patch over his eye, the hilt of the sword and the colour of his face. He kneels at the faldstool and quietly, as the muffled drums and trumpets play *Drake's Drum* whisper-thin (magnificent control!), he speaks his prayer before Trafalgar. As it ends the voices of the Chorus creep in:

> "Call him on the deep sea, call him up the Sound,
> Call him when ye sail to meet the foe."

The figure rises and speaks the words of the famous signal: "England expects every man will do his duty," then, wraith-like, passes into the Cathedral. There is a deep sigh from the crowd, and a stillness, as though the people are unconsciously saying 'farewell' to the living actor. Who was to know that in fact it was just so? Or that Harry Ainley too was making his last appearance before the public on that memorable afternoon?

Waterloo ("Stand up, Guards") follows, and then the Victorian Age. Magic words from Tennyson and Emily Brontë, and Shelley: the Seed-Time and Harvest. Now 'Any-Man' interrupts again, rushing in among the Chorus, and protesting: "When I was a countryman I did wet my finger and held it up to know which way the wind was blowing. It was blowing in 1914, I tell you. A dangerous wind."

The First World War is ushered in, and the Chorus summons our memories to recollection: Mons, Gallipoli, Vimy Ridge, Passchendaele. . . . 'Any-Woman' has risen. Taking from her basket a steel helmet, she gives it to 'Any-Man.' He slips off his raincoat and stands in the khaki uniform of the First World War. Embracing his wife, he goes slowly up the steps, while the massed bands with slackened drums and muffled brass play *It's a Long Way to Tipperary* in slow time. At the top of the steps he turns: "If I should die, think only this of me." . . . He passes into the Cathedral.

The drums and trumpets take up the challenge of the Second World War. Phrases from Clemence Dane's *Trafalgar Day 1940* shake up the tempo of the scene. 'Any-Woman' rushes to the centre of the steps, crying in anguish, "What comes next, another lost peace and then another war?" The Chorus strives to soothe her, reciting lines from Douglas Gibbon's *The Secret Dream*, Valour speaking the last words:

> "So in the heart's bright seed; the same
> Glad future world that is not lost
> So long as man still dreams and sees
> Beyond our little world, the power
> That springs from present agonies,
> Breaking into glorious flower,
> The secret dream of mankind curled
> In this dark winter of the world."

'Any-Man' reappears in modern battle-dress. "A dream?" he cries.

"The holy city of a dream," says Valour, "and you are destined to build it." "Where?" cries Patience, speaking for all women. "Here, in your own Britain," replies the Poet.

'Any-Man' begins to speak the lines of William Blake's *Milton*, but immediately the Choir takes up the words in Parry's setting. The massed bands play louder together; louder sings the Choir; now the fortissimo notes of the organ, and embroidering all, the silver trumpets of the Household Cavalry, ringing out from the cupolas. The crowd joins in, as the last two lines become a great shout of emotional relief:

> "Till we have built Jerusalem,
> In England's green and pleasant land."

The second performance, before Coventry Cathedral on the Sunday following, with Basil Cameron as conductor in place of Sir Henry Wood (who had another engagement), was given before as great a crowd. The background of ruins bathed in the soft sunshine of a September afternoon added its own significance to the Anthology. The Lord Mayor of Birmingham and the Mayors of many surrounding cities were present as guests of the Mayor and Aldermen of Coventry.

Further performances were proposed at Exeter and Guildford, and two in London's Guildhall in October. But difficulties arose over the guarantee fund, and, as no more private subscriptions were forthcoming, NAAFI put an end to the proceedings. I was compelled to announce the abandonment of the project two weeks later in a broadcast talk after the nine o'clock news.

<><><>

Moonshine . . .

After the Coventry performance a number of us, emotionally exhausted by the efforts of the last few days, spent the night at a hotel in Warwick. We had a merry supper party, none the less. This is the favourite hour with most actors. The emotional effort of performance has exhilarated them. Now is the time to relax and allow the tempo of mind and body to slow down before going to bed.

It was a glorious moonlight night, I remember. But when Edith Evans proposed that we should wander along the battlements of Warwick Castle and imagine ourselves back in Elizabethan days, I did not respond. Edith is always fun, although her ecstasies sometimes induce the most surprising remarks, as when one day before the war I encountered her in Trafalgar Square, returning from her farm, and she clutched my arm, and said, "My dear, I've just experienced something more wonderful than the greatest painting, the greatest picture, a moment of divine ecstasy: an egg warm from the nest."

2

Grace and Favour

A gentler occasion lingers in the memory. Soon after co-ordination began a request was received from the Entertainments Officer of Area 22 (whose headquarters were at Oxford) for special film programmes to be routed to a special location once a fortnight. The air of secrecy about the request aroused my curiosity. I made discreet inquiries and found that the request came from the Equerry to Queen Mary. Her Majesty had taken up residence at Badminton House for the duration of the war. The entertainment was required for a detachment of troops quartered in the park there. This was in the nature of a Royal Command, and was so successful that it led to entertainment being provided regularly once a fortnight.

The films were shown in the picture gallery at Badminton House, and the stage performances took place in the village hall, where there was more room for the large number of neighbours engaged on local war tasks whom Queen Mary liked to invite and for whom she insisted upon paying out of her private purse, as well as for the troops. There was something very English in this pre-eminently Royal figure sitting quietly among her neighbours and the soldiers and estate workers, watching a concert party in the village hall.

When it came to the selection of the programmes Her Majesty had no intention of being fobbed off with out-of-date pictures. She knew what she wanted, and had no hesitation in saying so. Sometimes suggestions were not approved of, and alternative lists were supplied. These often contained the names of films not yet released in London. Ben Henry remarked more than once upon the shrewdness of her judgment on what was good value and what was not.

Later in the war a message came through from Oxford asking for an especially good 'live' programme for Queen Mary's birthday. Further, I was requested to present myself at Badminton, as Her Majesty desired to thank me personally for the services we had rendered. For the occasion a special stage had been built in the picture gallery. I drove down by car, arriving rather late—often my habit in those overcrowded days. I was given a hasty lunch in the steward's room, and the Equerry told me that Queen Mary would see me at the end of the performance.

It was a good show and delighted every one. I was seated among the troops immediately behind the rows of birthday guests, among whom were the Duke and Duchess of Gloucester. After the National Anthem, as Queen Mary left the gallery, I was summoned by the Equerry. Passing through the file of guests, feeling extremely shy and nervous, I was formally presented to Her Majesty in the drawing-room. Queen Mary said how much she liked the performance and how grateful she was for what had been done for the troops in her vicinity.

"They tell me you are responsible for all these ENSA entertainments that are given to the troops everywhere. Is that so?"

"Yes, Madam, I am afraid I am," I replied, unthinkingly.

"And what are you afraid of, pray? It's a very good thing to do." A remark of such devastating common sense that it left me completely tongue-tied. Her Majesty chuckled at my confusion and made some shrewd comments on the films she had seen. Then the Duke of Gloucester took me in hand, putting me at my ease by asking questions about Little Easton Manor. He had acquired his own home, Barnwell Manor, from the purchaser of my home, who had told him so much about it that he wanted to visit it one day. . . . Come to think of it, this is not a very important story viewed against the background of major responsibilities, but it meant much to me at the time. Letters from Commanding Officers and factory managers, welcome as they were, could not remove the occasional feeling of working in a personal void.

3

Hammer and Sickle

Towards the middle of January 1943 the Government instructed the Campaigns' Division of the Ministry of Information to organize a mass celebration in the Royal Albert Hall on February 21 to commemorate the 25th Anniversary of the founding of the Red Army. The Ministry applied to ENSA for technical assistance. Two officials came to see me, bringing further details. Beyond a high-level decision that the proceedings should be filmed and prints sent to Russia to be shown in the cinemas there, little else had been done. A memorandum had been prepared for the Minister, containing vague generalities: some concert items, and a suggestion that Service detachments might be used, and that Louis MacNeice would compose an ode for the occasion; certainly not enough material for a film.

As the talk went on I realized that here was an opportunity for developing the new form with which I had experimented in 'Cathedral Steps.' But time was desperately short. The best actors, singers and musicians would be needed, as well as representatives of every side of Britain's war effort. Moreover, the programme must be built round a single idea and have a genuine emotional climax. Having lashed my visitors and myself into a state of enthusiasm and given them, as forcibly as I could, some grasp of the magnitude of the job they had undertaken, I offered to do it for them. Sorrowful glances were cast at the memorandum which lay on the desk between us, but that poor brain-child was still-born. To close the discussion I asked for an answer by the morrow.

After the officials had left I called my faithful henchmen together, and told them what I had done. At first they said the task was impossible in the time, but I pointed out that it was a Government project, and this was a unique opportunity for showing what we could do in the way of quick, large-scale planning. The following morning I received a telephone message that the job had been handed over to us.

The suggested ode by Louis MacNeice had immediately caught my attention. I planned to make it the theme of the programme and to build up to and beyond it. The poet was enthusiastic about the enlarged proposals; we began the exchange of ideas at once. This would not be an anthology but a tone-poem with dramatic and musical illustrations, an attempt upon mass emotion in a new form, martial in character, but without theatricality. In this respect it differed essentially from 'Cathedral Steps,' a fact noted by *The Times* in its subsequent appreciation: the only newspaper to show any regard for what I was attempting in these theatrico-military displays.

The performance would be continuous, lasting about two hours, so as not to interrupt the mounting climax. Two narrators would be needed to describe the achievements of the Red Army; their narrations would be punctuated with Russian songs and music. By way of counterpoint, there would be British tributes, illustrated by British songs and music. Mac-Neice went away to write. He proved such an enthusiastic collaborator that on February 3 I was able to submit our proposals to the Ministry of Information for approval.

The ENSA Music Council was hurriedly summoned and took over entire responsibility for the music, and Walter Legge, quick to grasp the scale of the plan, followed up its suggestions with superb energy. Special fanfares were written by William Walton and Arnold Bax (the Master or the King's Musick), while Alan Rawsthorne composed the music for MacNeice's Ode. In addition there were orchestrations by Norman Del Mar of various Russian songs.

The production was to be on the grand scale, larger than the Albert Hall had ever before known. It is a pity the building is not more frequently

U

used for arena performances, for which it is specially suited. I decided upon three large acting areas: the existing orchestral platform with its tiers of steps would be the first; the second would be the arena proper, open and free of all obstruction; and the third, contrived by removing seats from the opposite end of the auditorium, would be for the combined orchestras and the massed choirs. An enormous backcloth, over 120 ft. wide and 60 ft. high, presenting a formalized perspective of the city of Stalingrad and designed by Denis Wreford, provided a panoramic background to the whole conception. On either side of the first acting area a rostrum was built high above the central arena for the narrators. These were approached by formal steel staircases.

Each of the three acting areas would be used in turn—or, alternatively, any combination of them; a powerful lighting system was installed to enable this to be done. A complete system of internal telephones and light signals was installed in a box facing the one occupied by the B.B.C. monitoring staff. Here Stanley Bell and I sat throughout the performance, controlling the various incidents by signals to the stage-directors posted in various parts of the building to marshal and control the crowds, and pushing buttons to light up the acting areas according to the requirements of the action.

Apart from the principals, the orchestras and the bands, over two thousand people took part in the performance, including detachments of the Royal Navy, Royal Marines, the Guards and Regiments of the Line. In addition, there were detachments from Civil Defence, the Home Guard and the Nursing Services, coalminers with their safety lamps, transport drivers in their white coats, firemen, munition and railway workers.

Music was provided by the London Philharmonic Orchestra and sections of the B.B.C. Symphony Orchestra, together with military bands of the Brigade of Guards (including Scottish pipes and the trumpets and drums of the Household Cavalry), the R.A.F. band, and buglers of the Royal Marines. The civil detachments came from areas as far apart as Scotland, Wales and Northern Ireland. The transportation of this huge cast into war-time London, and to and from the Albert Hall, was a major problem in itself. To deal with the mass of detail involved in a production of this sort a co-ordinating committee of senior ENSA officials was set up at Drury Lane, which remained in virtually continuous session for three weeks preceding the date. Liaison officers from the Service Departments worked with it in passing on its daily requests either for help or information.

Admission to the performance was by Government invitation only. There were representatives of all the public departments, Lord Mayors and Mayors of provincial cities and London boroughs, and delegates from many public bodies.

A few days before the performance I called the Ministry's attention to the complete lack of publicity. After all, this was a form of recompense to which the stars were entitled. I was told that publicity was undesirable for Security reasons. Certainly, a thousand-pound bomb dropped on the Albert Hall during the performance would have destroyed a number of distinguished persons; but it so happened that we had several radio enthusiasts on the ENSA staff, and one of them had told me that the programme had already been announced over short wave by Moscow Radio a week ago, giving the name of the Albert Hall and of the Foreign Minister, who was to speak!

The Salute began with a stirring speech by Lieutenant Laurence Olivier, R.N.V.R., taken from *Alexander Nevsky*. This was followed by the Royal Choral Society, singing the *Volga Boat Song* at the opposite end of the hall. Then, standing closely grouped in the middle of the empty arena, a Welsh factory choir sang *All through the Night*. . . .

Powerful arc lights from the roof criss-cross each other, picking out here the conductor, there a singer, now the Spokesman (Lieutenant-Commander Ralph Richardson, R.N.V.R.), now the Spokeswoman (Dame Sybil Thorndike) in their gold costumes and high-peaked helmets—their faces are golden, too—as the programme gathers in power and momentum.

So far the tale has been only of peace. Now the sinister figure of a Nazi SS man (Marius Goring), dressed all in black save for his arm badge, can be seen crouched by the microphone: "Germany calling! Germany calling!"

There is menace in MacNeice's rhythmic repetitions, spoken with power by Dame Sybil and Ralph, who is in magnificent voice for the occasion. Dennis Noble and the choir sing Red Army songs. War comes. It flows over the Russian border, and reaches its climax at Stalingrad, as the orchestra and chorus render the Soviet song, *Salute to Life*.

The orchestra plays the *Spitfire Prelude and Fugue* by Walton, as from every side factory workers and Civil Defence Services pour into the arena. As the different groups of workers are called, they cross the arena from one end to the other and mount the tiered stage beneath the huge Stalingrad decoration, shouting, "Here! Here!" in unison. The last to enter are the Metropolitan and City Police. There is rising excitement in the audience as they cheer and applaud the successive entrances.

Mary Clare calls upon the women at war in Britain to salute the women at war in Russia. They enter, group by group, named in clamant voice by the Spokeswoman. Some are in factory clothes, some in uniform:

nurses, wardens, Red Cross and ambulance staffs, representatives of all the women working in field and factory. They stream across the arena, while the orchestra plays the last movement of Elgar's Symphony No. 2. Mounting the steps, they take their places in front of the men, chanting softly and in unison one word: "Russia!" It is like a sea of sound, washing the shores of the platform and filling the audience with emotion.

Without pause or gradation, Joan Hammond and the chorus, dressed all in white, accompanied by the combined orchestras, sing Elgar's *To Women* from the *Spirit of England*. The Spokesman invokes the men of the Royal Merchant Marine:

> "Come up here, you seamen of Britain—
> You who have kept the route open to Russia,
> You who deliver the goods—
> You know who it is to whom you deliver the goods,
> Come up here and salute them."

A single line of merchant seamen comes down between the orchestra and the chorus and stretches out in a thin blue line across the arena; as they advance, files of naval ratings in Arctic equipment, headed each by a petty officer, come from left and right to meet them. The Spokesman hails them from above:

"Ahoy there, Jack!"

"Ahoy!" replies John Laurie, in a great shout.

"Everything under control on the Arctic Convoy?"

"Everything under control, sir."

"Right. Steer to close."

"Aye, aye, sir."

The action passes again to the orchestra: Vaughan Williams' magnificent *Sea Symphony* (first movement), sung by Dennis Noble and the chorus.

John Gielgud comes next as the voice of Moscow Radio, summoning the eyes and ears of the world to the heroic defence of Stalingrad. The crouching Nazi boasts that the city is all but captured. The radio voices describe the fluctuating struggle and rise to a climax with the surrender of Von Paulus' 6th German Army. The Nazi figure is blotted out and the voice of Moscow Radio cries in triumph:

> "Moscow calling!
> This is the hour of attack.
> Over to you, Red Army, over to you!
> And death to our enemies!"

The Spokesman and Spokeswoman chant in measured tones the slow retreat of the Germans to the opening bars of Shostakovitch's 'Leningrad' Symphony. Their voices rise and the music grows louder and louder, as the City of Stalingrad is seen in full light for the first time.

The Spokesman: "I now call upon the fighting services of Britain to greet and salute the Red Army."

With pomp and circumstance, the massed bands of the Brigade of Guards play the regimental marches of the various military detachments as they enter. The Scottish Pipers precede the formal entry of the British, Dominion and Colonial flags. Troops and civilians march and counter-march, until all the Service detachments with their colours are massed high on the tiered platform: an armed party from the Navy on the right, from the Army and the R.A.F. on the left; behind them the Service detachments, male and female; in the arena the regimental bands, with the pipers in the centre; behind them again the civil defence workers, and then the factory workers, male and female, line by line, stretching back until they merge with the symphony orchestra at the other end of the hall; it is a magnificent sight.

Louis MacNeice's Ode is now sung to Alan Rawsthorne's music, ending in a giant crescendo. The audience waits for the entrance of the Foreign Minister, some of them standing up and craning their necks, forgetting those behind them, in their excitement. Mr Eden stands in front of the flags. From the high gallery Bax's *A Solemn Fanfare* is sounded by the trumpeters of the Household Cavalry. Before the echoes have died away the Minister is speaking:

"I ask you all to stand and pay a silent tribute to the glorious dead of the Red Army."

The armed parties present arms, the Last Post is sounded on a single bugle of the Royal Marines, followed by sixteen bars of the *Dead March*. The detachments order arms, and the audience is seated.

The Minister's quiet, hesitant tones sound flat and uninteresting, but fortunately his speech is too short to dissipate entirely the emotion of the audience. Soon that emotion rises again as the *Internationale* is played and sung by many workers who seem to prefer this dreary, drab tune to their own national songs, and an enormous Red Army flag is broken high up in the roof over the stage, while a Russian actor, dressed in the uniform of a Red Army soldier, with fixed bayonet, is raised slowly upon a pedestal some twenty feet above the top platform: a living statue indeed. And then, capping all, loud and triumphant, the National Anthem, played by the massed bands and symphony orchestras and sung by all the company. . . . The whole audience rises. Portly mayors and dignified civil servants clap and cheer and wave their programmes. The effect is overwhelming. Too bad that the general public had not been allowed to see it. . . .

Anticlimax . . .

I sit beside Stanley Bell in our control box, exhausted. "Thank God, my scheme for lifting that Red Army chap without cutting the floor worked all right," he says. Then with his loyal theatrical sense he asks me if I am not going to take a call.

"Don't be ridiculous, Stanley. This is a solemn occasion."

"Well, I'm going to hear the comments." He bounces out of his chair and I am left alone.

A moment later Malcolm Sargent comes into the box, still in evening dress and with his red carnation:

"Well, it's a triumph all right."

"Is it?" I reply, flatly.

"Yes, I've been to see the Russian Ambassador in his box and various other people. They all congratulated me."

"Indeed!" I murmur. "I'm glad." . . . As I drove away from the Albert Hall with my small daughter, the cheers of the audience still ringing in my ears, I felt like a child that had lost a precious toy.

4

Our Gracie

During the war years Gracie Fields became a phenomenon, a symbol of the national refusal to be low-spirited, a portent of future triumph over present adversity. All theatre folk are inclined to develop personalities akin to those they project before the public. Gracie was no exception. By this time she was more the 'Our Gracie' of popular sentiment than ever Nature intended. Nevertheless, the integrity of her character remained. Under the emotional stimulus of the war and from the abundance of a full heart she poured out her exuberant vitality in an untiring effort which extended her performances beyond their theatrical significance, so that they became expressions of a mass emotion bordering upon hysteria. Such adulation imposes sanctions upon the private life of the recipient, which Gracie did shortly discover.

After her return from France in 1940 she told me she contemplated going to America with Monty Banks, the Italian-born film director to whom I had introduced her at Ealing Studios. I was gravely troubled about the public reaction to this step and put my doubts to her in a personal letter. However, her mind was made up. No sooner had the couple left than the storm broke, both in the Press and in the House of Commons. Gracie was accused of exporting vast sums in jewellery and other misdemeanours, while meanly disposed persons added to the chorus by declaring she would not be seen in England again during the war, and predicted her failure with American audiences. In contrast to this hysteria, the *Yorkshire Post*, on August 8, 1940, published an editorial on the turmoil, one sentence of which exactly expressed my own feeling in the matter: "If Gracie Fields were to prove anything but a loyal Lancashire lass, we should begin to doubt our very selves." There is no doubt she was bewildered by the sudden change in public feeling towards her. Her private letters to me at this time were filled with bitter hurt; but she stoutly maintained that since she had decided to marry an Italian it was her business and nobody else's. They were duly married in Hollywood in March.

From time to time Gracie wrote me excited accounts of the wonderful receptions she was having at her concerts for war charities and of the large sums of money that were being raised.[1] At the beginning of 1941 she wrote to say she proposed to keep her promise to return home to work for ENSA. Determined to keep her out of further trouble, I stipulated that the projected tour must be for national service only, no commercial engagements whatever being undertaken. When the announcement was made we received a number of abusive letters and postcards, most of them anonymous, threatening both Gracie and myself with dire penalties if she ventured to set foot in the country again. Even the most experienced members of the staff at Drury Lane were doubtful about the reception she would receive, but I brushed their objections on one side.

Gracie arrived in this country on July 8, 1941, prefaced by weeks of argument with the authorities over her air-passage, and followed in the first days by a sheaf of cables from Monty Banks requesting her early return. The tour began at Rochale, her home town, where a civic reception awaited her. We drove up by car, arriving at the municipal boundary at about noon, where we were met by the Chief Constable and the Town Clerk, and driven in slow procession to the Town Hall. Along the outlying parts of the route people stood at the gates of their little houses to see her go by—young mothers lifting up their infants-in-arms as so many sacrifices to the goddess of Popular Fame, and pointing her out excitedly

---

[1] Her first tour under the auspices of the Navy League of Canada netted £170,000 for British War Charities, and a subsequent one nearly £300,000.

to the older children so that in after years they could claim they had actually seen Gracie Fields, while more ancient faces peered at her from upper windows. As she stepped out on to the balcony of the Town Hall there was a roar of welcome, and factory whistles, both near and far, added to the din—warning of an approaching gaiety-raid upon the town's grim existence! All doubt and criticism as to the wisdom of the visit were drowned in that first roar. Wisely, she made no excuses for her absence, and the troops and munition workers forgot the unkind things they had said about her: she could marry whom she pleased, Italian or negro, so long as they could feel she had not deserted them entirely.

From Rochdale she covered the industrial areas of the North-west, thence to Greenock and Rosyth, to Orkney, back to Inverness, down through the East Midlands to Ipswich, Harwich, Chatham, Folkestone and back to London for the final concert at the Albert Hall on Sunday, August 17, in aid of the Red Cross and St John's War Organization, where she was supported by the Massed Bands of the Brigade of Guards and many stars. She came to Drury Lane Headquarters on the Friday before this final concert, exhilarating us all by her high spirits and warm appreciation, expressed in a message of personal thanks to me, published in the newspapers: "You have given us show-folk our biggest break, for you who made ENSA made us part of the war machine. Thank you for that."

The tour had lasted thirty-nine days, concerts being given on thirty-four of them, sometimes two and three in a day: eighty-six concerts in all, to a grand total of audiences computed to exceed 410,000. This was more in the nature of a triumphal progress than a theatrical tour. She left the Albert Hall with cheers ringing in her ears and her face wet with tears, driving through the night to Hurn Airport to catch the early-morning plane to Lisbon.

The success of her second progress in 1943 was even more remarkable, despite the unpleasant storm with which it closed. There was delay in her arrival because Monty Banks could see no reason why he should again be excluded from the *fiesta*, but the Air Priorities Board were as resolute in their refusal to grant him an air passage as the immigration authorities were to welcome him at all. As before, no commercial engagements were to be permitted, and, as before, the tour was to end with a grand concert at the Royal Albert Hall in aid of a Service charity.

Immediately the visit was announced the correspondence columns of the provincial Press and the General Secretary's office at Drury Lane were both pestered with demands: hospitals, bazaars, church parades, prize-givings, the new wing of a dog's home—all solidly convinced that a visit

535 Fifth Avenue @ 311 South Amalfi Drive
Santa Monica
CAL.

August 30th 1961

My Dearest Basil

Thank you so very much for all the lovely & kind words you have said about me, also for looking after me so splendidly. St. ... has been a tremendous experience for me to ... I am so sorry to have so many grandfolks in so short a time, I have met such an ... In ... me she chatted it wrong, (am ... I school ... missed) My journey to his ... was perfect. Late the rest to U.S.A. will be as good.

2

I haven't spoken to a soul since I left you & it feel a bit sorry for myself & hate being alone. (I am tired) I feel I want to say so much & I can't tell how to word it. Many happy hours I need ... on Broad east—was a huge success, due to ... — about it, am sure you ... me, why I ... love to you, & Vicki, & Teria, & so very very many thanks to you for making the most lovely exciting five weeks I've ever had in my life.

Always your friend
& Pal.
Grace.

GRACIE AS A LETTER-WRITER

from 'Our Gracie' would make just that difference to their future salvation—cables from the Lord Mayor of Sydney to the Lord Mayor of
London regarding an Australasian tour, an invitation to lunch with the
Navy League (preparatory to another Canadian tour) and, finally, a
fervent appeal to display her patriotism by kicking off at a Wembley
football match and perhaps singing a song or two first!

A committee of the three Services, together with Ministry of Labour
officials, sat for days, sorting out the requests, each determined that his
particular Service should get its full share of the star's time. This meant
that the tour had to be worked out with the exactitude of a military operation; any deviation from the rigid time-table was forbidden. Planning was
further distracted by unexpected obstacles. The star was tired and must
have two days in seven for rest; so cabled her director-husband. (But
Gracie refused to rest; in the end we settled for one day a week.) There
were complicated arrangements for hook-ups with the Mutual Broadcasting Company of America, who were to beam extracts from her
concerts in various parts of the country to America on short wave. The
NAAFI Transport Branch chose this moment for an excess of virtue,
deciding that it would be an "extravagance to provide Miss Fields with a
car. She should go to various centres by rail and then pick up local transport." It took a week to quash that piece of nonsense.

The success of my two experiments in mass drama had made me ambitious for further productions of similar sort. For some time before Gracie's
arrival I had been planning anthologies in praise of the achievements of
our fighting services, to which I gave the respective titles of 'Seascape,'
'Landscape' and 'Air Canopy'; 'Seascape' for the Royal Navy to come
first. I was about to begin the search for guarantors of the preliminary
expenses—public funds could not be used—when it occurred to me that
if I were to make the naval anthology the occasion for Gracie's last
appearance in the forthcoming tour, King George's Fund for Sailors
might be asked to undertake this quite nominal risk. The Committee of
the Fund readily agreed.

The key to the success of 'Seascape' would lie in the choice of a central
theme, historical or otherwise, illustrated by verse and drama, selected by
one mind (the reverse of that devastating procedure of the film studio
known as 'the story conference') so as to achieve a mounting climax. I
secured the co-operation of Arthur Bryant, the historian, spent a day with
him in the country discussing the theme, based on what the sea has meant
to Britain and the British way of life, leaving him to choose and link
together the various items. The music was once again in the hands of
Walter Legge and our Advisory Music Council, assisted by Julian Herbage,

who unearthed for us the Order of Service for Nelson's State Funeral at St Paul's Cathedral on January 9, 1806.

The composers represented were Sibelius, Elgar, Byrd, Stanford, Handel, Vaughan Williams and Parry; and there was an item of added musical interest in that three movements from Constant Lambert's *Merchant Seamen Suite* were performed for the first time in London, conducted by the composer. The same constellation of stars backed me up as so often before, and on this occasion Robert Helpmann was added to their number to design the choreography with which the Vic-Wells Ballet illustrated the sea-shanties.

Our vast backcloth was repainted to represent ships of the Royal Navy in review order, steaming across the horizon, watched by vessels from the time of the Armada. The platform in front of the organ was built up to represent the bridge and quarter-deck of a battleship, with look-out posts left and right for the Spokesman and Spokeswoman.

As in the case of the Russian show the most elaborate staff work was necessary, since two performances were planned, one at 2.30 P.M. and the other at 5.45 P.M. Both performances were completely sold out, and as the first did not finish until 5.15 it was an operation of some skill to clear the Albert Hall of one audience before the second took its place.

The Anthology closed with the first performances of Malcolm Sargent's arrangement of *Rule, Britannia*, with massed orchestra and the full chorus led by Nancy Evans, Gracie Fields, Heddle Nash and Dennis Noble.

The alternation of dramatic history, pathos and humour achieved by Bryant's arrangement, the solemn moments of Nelson's Funeral Service and the riotous gaiety of Gracie's concert on board our make-believe battleship combined to produce an effect greater far than I had dared to hope for: as refreshing as a brisk walk along the front at Brighton. The First Lord of the Admiralty (A. V. Alexander[1]) delighted us all with the warmth of his praise, shaking hands with me more than once with tears in his eyes. King George's Fund was usefully replenished, and Gracie Fields flew away in the darkness to face the clamorous impatience of the Eighth Army.

On the morning of the performance a cable had arrived from Monty Banks, requesting her return to begin an important new radio series. "Let 'em wait," said Gracie, as she climbed into an Army Dakota. The telegrams from her husband grew longer and more peremptory. Finally, he cabled holding me personally responsible for any action taken by the American radio sponsors against Gracie for breach of contract. This was a manifest absurdity, but I rewired it to Gracie, who was in the midst of a

[1] Now Lord Alexander of Hillsborough.

rapturous welcome from the Eighth Army. Evidently she now grew afraid, for a few days later the Press carried a story that she was terminating her visit and returning to America immediately. This brought a torrent of abuse from the troops, and an urgent telegram from General Montgomery asking me to extend the visit. It was too late; Gracie had already left. Shortly afterwards *The Crusader*, the Eighth Army newspaper, published an open letter from its editor, bitterly condemning her action. Poor Gracie no longer wore the radiant look of success, but at least it was a relief to know that the American radio sponsors had forgiven her truancy, even though her programme went on the air one week late. In the end the attacks overreached themselves and produced a reaction in her favour. Tributes to her work were paid in the House of Commons. Finally, to quell the tiresome disturbance, the Prime Minister gave instructions that Army newspapers must be subject in future to a certain amount of censorship.

My last recollection of her in those war years is as she strode singing at sunset along the hilly road to her villa on Capri with the darkness falling purple in the valleys; singing to herself for joy that the war was over, and yet well aware of the pleasure she was giving to all who listened: the cabmen halting their tired horses, soldiers and girls up from the beaches hushing their raucous laughter, Italian *bambini* staring goggle-eyed. The tumultuous sights of other days: her singing from the balcony of the Council House in the Civic Centre at Nottingham to the crowded square below, to an audience of 6000 in John Brown's shipyard on the Clyde during the lunch-hour, to groups of lorry-drivers, London-bound, gathered round the disabled ENSA transport; her emergence from stormbound Capri on Armistice Night, 1945, to sing to the thronging, impatient troops, first at the San Carlo Opera House and then at ENSA's Bellini Theatre in Naples, brought there, tousled and exhausted, in a crash-boat of the Royal Navy, not yet recovered from her final tours through Australia, India and the Far East—last and brightest flicker of that Protean lightning across the ENSA scene: all these memories were faded, like dreams long past. And when the B.B.C. attempted to convert her first post-war broadcast into a festival of nostalgic recollection the national psychology did not respond. Gracie was no longer a national symbol; her work in that regard was done: she had resumed her place as a great star of the music-hall, perhaps the greatest of her time.

TALLY TWO

The number of shows given to H.M. Forces and in the war factories during the twelve months ending March 1944:

Home

	Live	Cinema
H.M. Forces	94,204	64,065

Ministries of Labour,
 Fuel and Power,
 Agriculture,
 Shipping, etc.
(including Northern Ireland)   65,223   10,382

Total number   ..   233,874

Overseas

(including Malta, British North Africa, East Africa, Gibraltar, Iceland, the Faroes, the Middle East, West Africa, the Falkland Islands and the Central Mediterranean Force).

LIVE		CINEMAS	
No. of Shows	*Attendances*	*No. of Shows*	*Attendances*
12,185	5,556,071	29,252	13,509,915

Fifty-six garrison theatres and 185 garrison cinemas now opened in the Home Commands.

ESTIMATED TOTAL OF ATTENDANCES TO DATE: 100 MILLION.

THE THIRD PHASE

Climax and Anticlimax

SIGNPOST

Now we enter the last phase of the story. As the movement of troops overseas swells from stream into flood, and the pendulum of the war swings slowly past uneasy equilibrium into the confident initiative, so, too, ENSA's major responsibility shifts from Britain into foreign fields. Soon the climax of our work is reached in serving the fighting troops everywhere, even while entertainment in the factories and for the home troops continues to increase.

Then, after victory, the swift recession, when 'I couldn't care less' became the idiom of an expended interest. Artistes and staff made their several ways homewards, caught up in the general anxiety to find places on the band-wagons of civil life, leaving a few reluctant attendants to clear up the fair grounds and wait for the arrival of their successors. The story of ENSA was over.

CHAPTER TWENTY-FOUR

HOME AND AWAY

1

Operation Neglect

ENSA in the Middle East was born in travail in 1940, cradled in ignorance, and reared in the seductive whisperings of war-time Cairo—city of shrouded doorways and neon lights, hymns ancient and modern, animated rags and opthalmic eyes blinking at the rich meats and mountainous cakes stuffed with cream and almond-paste, city of spies and lust and tousled romance, a place where sooner or later one found oneself invariably doing the right thing for the wrong reasons or vice versa, so that in the end all activity was slightly suspect, most of all one's own. Thanks to the devoted work of a few individuals who fought down the early mistakes, ENSA did finally grow to honourable estate and accomplish its full purpose in the Middle East; else we might have been forced to stage a theatrical Dunkirk, reputation buried within a catacomb like some forgotten Pharoah, only in our case made of sand and unlikely to stir anyone's interest.

To understand the reasons for our poor start out there it is necessary to explain the situation that existed before we came upon the scene. The British troops in Egypt (usually referred to by the identification initials of B.T.E.) had long-standing arrangements for their entertainment in peace-time. They relied mainly upon cinemas run by an organization called United Film Services, which was virtually a one-man business owned by Thomas Shafto. In Palestine a similar circuit of camp cinemas was operated by a man called Monis, who was Shafto's partner. Some of the cinemas were permanent buildings, but many were temporary structures, made of breeze-blocks, whitewashed, or, in certain cases, faced with cement; some had corrugated iron roofs, some were little more than open-air places of assembly, provided with a screen, a projection box and rows of camp chairs or forms, surrounded by a high wall or barrier to keep out the impecunious. A form of contract entered into by the military authorities gave to Shafto the right to operate these 'encroachments' over a period of years. In some locations, but not all, rebates were paid by the concessionaire. For live entertainment there were some well-organized military concert parties and the regimental bands. Also, NAAFI, which had considerable installations throughout the Middle East, occasionally engaged for its larger institutes the professional concert parties to be found touring the Mediterranean areas. Finally, troops on local leave had access to the many fine cinemas in Cairo itself and, of course, to the 'night spots' there and at Alexandria; these had a sinister reputation.

When war came, and the British and Dominion troops began flooding into the Middle East, Shafto and his partner made plans to reap the certain harvest. Very soon, wherever the encampments of the modern crusaders were set up, new cinemas began to appear. So hot upon the scent were these showmen that often times temporary structures were ready for the soldiery, bored and restless amid the desert sands, almost before the last guy rope was in position. As for live entertainment, well, the 'night spots' increased their profits, despite the active disapproval of the British authorities, the military entertainers returned to more serious duties and a NAAFI concert party of doubtful value found itself marooned in Malta for lack of transport.

That, roughly, was the picture when ENSA came upon the scene. Mind you, there was nothing intrinsically wrong in a civilian contractor profiting by the emergency; but the existence of Shafto's enterprise ran directly counter to the national purposes for which ENSA (and FENSA)

ad been formed. Moreover, there were complaints about the quality of
he films and the prices charged, which some of the Dominion troops
egarded as unfair exploitation; they began to say bitter things about
Shafto's Shufties,' as they called them. Doubtless, the contractor had
is war-time troubles. I am merely stating the facts as they came to light
—not immediately, though; information drifted through slowly, so that
ve were only able to fit together the pieces of the jigsaw puzzle after a
ong interval of time. Indeed, I sometimes wonder whether we ever got at
he truth of what went on out there in the first two years of the war.
Men's motives and actions, stark and clear for a day, maybe, were then
ost in the swirling sands.

The situation from ENSA's point of view deteriorated rapidly as more
nd more cinemas went up; Shafto's profits increased, and so did the com-
laints. Round about the turn of the year live entertainment had also
ome into the picture when Bridges Adams, in charge of the Drama
Department at the British Council, received a request from the British
Chamber of Commerce in Cairo for a professional concert party. He
assed this to Sir Kenneth Barnes, who passed it to me. I, in turn, passed
t to NAAFI ('Passed to you, please') with an urgent request that ENSA
e allowed to start work in the Middle East.

The first essential was to get at the facts. The Corporation asked me to
ppoint an experienced civilian manager to go out immediately and submit an interim report on the situation. Associated with him there was to
e a military staff officer, who would make all the official contacts and
ee that the necessary regulations were carried out. This was our first
mistake, for we did not realize that soldier and civilian were like oil and
vater in the intrigue-laden atmosphere of war-time Cairo, neither mixing
vith nor helping the other.

Our civilian manager urged the immediate take-over of Shafto's
cinemas. But the Corporation's policy at this period of the war, whenever
new demands were made upon it, was invariably to say "No" first and
'Yes" later on, by which time there was usually a burden of accumulated
mistakes to be borne. This policy now involved us, since troop entertainment and ENSA were synonymous in the public mind. The proposal to
ake over the cinemas was rejected; we were directed to operate only in
places where Shafto was not doing so—as a sound businessman, the con-
ractor naturally made a bee-line for the most profitable locations—or
where the military authorities demanded additional facilities. The lack of
co-operation between our representatives directly contributed to the
worsening situation, for while they were agreeing to disagree commercial
competition was exploiting their neglect. And the attitude of the mili-

tary authorities towards entertainment generally reached a 'slow boil,' as cook would say.

On the question of film supply, the majority of the American companies controlled their Middle East distribution from Paris, where patriotic influences were not so deeply felt. However, the American members of the FENSA Committee applied direct to their New York offices for permission to release their latest films to us for the use of British troops in the Middle East, just as they had done in France, on the ground that such screenings were outside the jurisdiction of local exhibitors and, consequently, violated no contractual obligations. There was, however, an important difference which was glossed over; the up-to-the-minute releases now requested were full-size and not sub-standard films, as in the case of France. Consent was given. Precedent thus established, from now on, the troops everywhere overseas received a continuous service of the very latest and best American and British film programmes.

Gracie Fields volunteered to inaugurate the live-entertainment service; as my personal intervention at our headquarters was urgent, I applied for two air priorities, which were refused. Whereupon, acting on the advice of Group-Captain Halahan at the Air Ministry, I wrote to his opposite number at G.H.Q. Middle East to ask his help, for which direct action I received the customary reprimand from NAAFI, and a general directive that, if I wished to communicate with G.H.Q. Middle East or anywhere else abroad, copies of all letters must be sent to Ruxley Towers, so that the NAAFI staffs overseas could be notified. (The speedy break-down of this arrangement was inherent in its absurdity.) Before a reply to my request was received the fall of France brought about the closing of the Mediterranean Sea, Gracie Fields went off to Canada, and our plans fell into abeyance.

2

Icicles and the Rock

We always intended to make our work overseas the major preoccupation, but, since the disintegration of France, it had dwindled to a few threads in the giant carpet of home entertainment that had been woven by the national emergency. Gradually, as the war proceeded, those threads were brought together until they became the dominant pattern, and the service at home merely the background.

First, as to the threads: within only a matter of weeks after the evacuation from France—in August 1940, to be precise—we began again to send entertainment overseas. George Thomas took a party, called 'Eight of Us,' to the picturesquely named Alabaster Force, stationed in Iceland. A garrison theatre-cum-cinema had been built with the attractive title of 'Polar Bear Theatre,' and there we ran a mixed programme of cinema and live entertainment for the occupying British and (later) American troops. ENSA carried on in Iceland until June 1942 with little of interest to report, save for the tall stories, brought home by our officer-in-charge, of scenery arriving coated with ice and of icicles pendent from his own moustache, as he trod the deck of the little steamer that took him there. When the British troops left Iceland the theatre was handed over to the Americans, an early example of Whitehall's 'reciprocal aid.'

In the same year George Thomas took a concert party, the 'Swingtime Follies,' to Gibraltar at Christmas time. They played in the theatre as well as in H.M.S. *Ark Royal*, where they made a spectacular first entrance, after the fashion of the Folies Bergère, up one of the aeroplane lifts into view of the audience clustered thickly about the flight deck. The concert had to be kept secret so as not to embarrass the Germans, who had already announced that the ship was sunk. Another company was sent to Gibraltar in April 1941, and then the shortening horizon of the war brought an hiatus of twelve months, during which nothing could be done, and the troops were left to endure their boredom as best they might.

3

The Pipeline

Earlier in the same year the question arose of serving the troops in West Africa, that forbidding territory once known as "the white man's grave." It nearly became ENSA's grave, too, so far as reputation was concerned. We were given very little information about the situation to begin with; in the process of finding out we took some hard knocks. The men were training hard for a battle that might never take place; that much we knew from the newspapers. What we were not told was that the G.O.C.-in-C. (Lieutenant-General Giffard) had written to the War Office after the fall of France, demanding ENSA entertainment for his Command, and that the request had been pigeon-holed in the face of greater urgencies. Consequently, our response after a sudden telephone call from the authorities must have appeared dilatory in the extreme.

The West African Command comprised the four territories of Gambia, Sierra Leone, Gold Coast and Nigeria. Each was a military area, separated from the other by hundreds of miles of foreign territory. Communication between them was by infrequent aeroplane. Since officers and Government officials were constantly moving from one colony to the other, it sometimes took weeks to negotiate a passage for those who were without top priority. The number of white troops stationed in the Command was small but being rapidly increased in face of the threat of Franco-German action from Dakar.

The 16-mm. projectors needed for a cinema service were now in desperately short supply. The output of those made by Gaumont-British was small, and those made by Bell and Howell in America were hard to come by. The few we owned had been sent to outlying stations abroad, where such outposts of empire as St Helena, the Falklands and the Faroe Islands were now embarrassingly aware of our existence. The situation regarding motor generators needed to supply current in the remote areas where the machines were to operate was even worse. Agents in the United States and Canada were sent scurrying hither and thither in an effort to locate this equipment. And when it was finally acquired it was liable to be flung off the aircraft at the last moment or dumped at an airfield half-way to its destination, at the whim of a harassed supply officer. We undertook to provide standard (35-mm.) projectors for R.A.F. cinemas, one at Gambia, the other at Takoradi (African jumping-off place for the airlift to the Middle East). This equipment was too bulky to be flown out under existing stringencies: it had to go by sea. The first consignment was promptly sunk.

The troops were not silent about our failure to deliver the goods. Our impetuous Cinema Officer could scarcely wait to read the latest complaints from West Africa before he would come to my office, his cigar out, shouting that "every possible avenue had been explored!" Then some new channel would hold out possibilities, and off he would go on his quest once more. My mind shuns recollection of the dreary round of requests, refusals, renewed requests, telegrams, telephone messages and personal solicitation with which we reinforced the faith that is said to move mountains. Manna from Heaven! One day Ben Henry picked up a rumour that eight 16-mm. projectors might be available to us in South Africa if we acted quickly. By what devious means he managed to snatch them out of the jaws of the Y.M.C.A. I do not know, but when he came smiling into my office two days later with his cigar well alight I knew all was well. Nevertheless, a better method than this hand-to-mouth foraging was urgently required.

A short while before this I had met Sir Andrew Duncan, who had taken over the Ministry of Supply from Morrison, at a small dinner party given by Lord Ashfield in his private suite at the Ritz. Sir William Jowitt[1] was

_____
[1] Now Earl Jowitt.

another guest, I remember. Ashfield was interested in ENSA because of the weekly concerts we were giving to the staff of the London Passenger Transport Board; Andrew Duncan knew all about us by reason of our service to the Royal Ordnance Factories. The party developed into an animated discussion on the value of entertainment in war-time, punctuated by air-raid sirens and bursts of gun-fire. It was interesting to contrast those three distinguished men, the shrewd lawyer feeling his way carefully round a subject that he was not too sure about, the tired, good-humoured American transport visionary whose visions had been realized, and the hard-headed successful industrialist.

Remembering that meeting, I got into touch with Sir Andrew and by him was sent to one of his senior officers, whom I persuaded to set up a Cinema Equipment Allocation Committee, to which all three Services, the Ministry of Supply and the Ministry of Labour (in fact, all public or semi-public bodies using this material) should appoint representatives. There was also a Technical Supply Officer to represent ENSA.

At the first meeting I was dismayed to find that the Admiralty had already placed priority orders with the manufacturers for 200 35-mm. twin projectors and that our orders, submitted months and months before, had been shelved. The Army and the R.A.F. were also preparing exorbitant demands. To my plea that our indents were for the needs of the fighting troops I was given the stock answer that training must come first. The wrangle went on for two hours. When I began to hint at the necessity for taking the matter up direct with the First Lord, the Chairman of the meeting sat up and reminded the officers that "excessive demand at the centre led to deficiency on the perimeter." . . . The Committee met regularly throughout the war, and eventually the acquisitiveness of the supply officers was curbed and their requisitions sharply whittled down to enable the men fighting overseas to have their much-needed entertainment.

4

Ants and Artistes

While we were waiting for permission to send concert parties to West Africa we determined that at least their equipment should arrive in good time. The story of what happened to our first consignment of six mini-pianos is typical of the frustration of that period of the war. Lost sight of for weeks, they were eventually discovered buried among the mountains of Army stores that were dumped at the dockside after the arrival of each convoy. When they were unpacked they were mere skeletons; only the ivory keyboards and the metal parts remained. White ants had accounted for the rest.

In the circumstances it is not surprising that ENSA became something of a byword in the Command. We suffered the ultimate humiliation when a member of the NAAFI Board of Management, visiting West Africa in March 1942, discovered that ENSA live entertainment was non-existent and that the film service had broken down completely. There was a tremendous 'flap' in consequence; ways and means were found of granting facilities overnight that had been consistently refused during the previous six months. Our Senior Overseas Officer, Major Haygarth, was hurriedly withdrawn from the Orkney Scheme, and sent to West Africa to pull things together. He was accompanied by another experienced officer from France, and several N.C.O.'s. They left England by air in March 1942, happy in the knowledge that concert parties had at last been authorized. At the same time the Chairman of NAAFI arranged the transfer of cinema projectionists from the Army to take the place of the cadre from France which we had previously been ordered to disband.

The first live entertainment consisted of an all-male party, known as 'The Four Musketeers.' They set out that same month in the cruiser *Shropshire*, sufficient excuse for not sending any girls even if we had not felt reluctant to ask women to face the terrors of 'the white man's grave' without fuller information. But Major Haygarth and his staff were not long in setting matters right. Requests for mixed parties followed. The earliest of these were 'The Music Box' (a company of first-class concert singers, including Gladys Ripley), 'The Globe Trotters' and 'Stardust.' After that matters settled down to a regular routine. Artistes spent from three to six months in West Africa before going on to the Middle East, where they arrived as thoroughly 'seasoned troops.'

5

Travelogue

Lacking a true picture of the conditions under which those first companies worked in West Africa (official reports conceal the human side), I tackled Avril Angers about it one day, as I knew she had spent at least two years with 'The Globe Trotters.'

"Tell me, Avril, what was it like out there?"

"Well, first of all, nobody told us at Drury Lane that we couldn't land without yellow-fever certificates."

"I expect you weren't listening."

"Anyway, I hadn't got a certificate and I didn't get yellow fever. What I did get was an injection which went septic, so that I couldn't stand or have a bath or go swimming: it took me three months to get better."

"Well, go on."

"Nobody told us anything about the mosquitoes either. When we landed we hadn't a pair of boots between us; we knew nothing about leggings or woolly socks or trousers; we just put on evening dress and did the show. That's when the men of the party got malaria. In fact they got everything there was to get and just disappeared into hospital one by one. I suppose they were too old, or C3, or something. So the first three mixed parties finished up as a one all-girl show.

"Of course, we *were* told to use ENSA transport. But then ENSA didn't have any transport! Eventually an ambulance to hold twenty people turned up. So whenever the Governor or Colonial Secretary, or whoever he was, invited us to lunch and sent his own car to fetch us, we were not allowed to go in it. We all piled into the ambulance, and the car tagged along behind, empty! After we'd been kicking round in Freetown for about five weeks we got a plane to Takoradi. Nobody told us it got cold at 11,000 feet up. In fact, nobody told us anything. That was the trouble. So off we went in our light frocks in a transport Dakota: terrifyingly uncomfortable, no seats, just little aluminium trays running along each side; reminded me of bed-pans. We were absolutely blue with cold when we landed.

"At Accra a colonel implored us to go up into the bush and give a show to his troops; they hadn't seen any white girls for over two years. He said he would provide the transport. Hanged if it didn't turn out to be another ambulance! The journey took about ten hours, bumping over the laterite roads inches deep in that beastly red dust. We started by leaving the back door open for air, but the dust came in in clouds. Then we closed the door and hung blankets over it, but nothing could keep it out. We groaned to think of those officers awaiting the arrival of the ENSA glamour, six bedraggled girls more red than alive!"

"Where to after that?"

"After that to Lagos. While we were there we went to Abeokuta, the native capital of Nigeria, and the King invited us to tea."

"King? What king?"

"King Adimola the Second. He's the Alake of Abeokuta, you know," said Avril primly.

"I didn't know, but never mind."

"He lived in a wonderful old Victorian house. You know, fruit under glass, knicknacks, china ornaments, and thousands of women and children

all over the place! We had tea and cakes, and the King spoke beautiful
English and talked a lot about 'my friend Mr Churchill' and 'my friend
the Duke of Windsor' and how he sent the princesses two little thrones
exactly like his own. He told us his subjects had collected £5000 for his
Spitfire Fund, and that he'd got a letter of thanks from Mr Churchill."

"Anyway, I expect you're not sorry you went, in spite of the transport!"

"Rather not! By the way, that ENSA transport did arrive—just as we
were leaving for the Middle East. And what do you think it was?"

"No idea—not another ambulance?"

"A wog-waggon!"

"What on earth's that?"

"A sort of open truck like the natives use. Quite useless."

"But why?"

"My dear! Ladies couldn't drive about in that sort of thing. Frightful
loss of prestige."

6

Follow my Leader

One evening towards the end of July 1941 Rex Newman, who had now
taken charge of the Overseas Section, rang up Wilby Lunn[1] to tell him
entertainment was required immediately for the Middle East, and could
the Director have the names of artistes willing to go by the morning,
please? After waiting for sea passages for weeks we had suddenly been told
room could be found for a certain number of artistes in the next convoy.
As a result of that 'hurry' call, Wilby Lunn took out two concert parties
('Spotlights' and 'Hello, Happiness'), taking seven weeks to reach Cairo
via the Cape and the Suez Canal. The combined companies gave the first
ENSA performances on October 1, 1940, in the Cairo Opera House, in
the presence of the Commanders-in-Chief of the British, Australian and
New Zealand Forces. Later the two companies split up, 'Spotlights'
remaining in Egypt, 'Hello, Happiness' going to Palestine.

Seymour Hicks had always planned to be the first star to visit the
Middle East, even as he had been the first in France. It was now too late
for that. However, on his way to lecture in South Africa for the British
Council, he proposed to break his journey in Cairo and give some performances of *Sleeping Partners* there. I had high hopes that his presence

---

[1] Wilby Lunn was one of a small band of concert-party proprietors to whose work
I have previously referred. Among other proprietors who gave continuous service
were John Berryman, Ronald Brandon, Reg Lever, Gordon Marsh, George Thomas
and Cecil Johnson.

would stimulate our organization, which was still dragging its feet. Alice Delysia agreed to partner him. After thirteen weeks of uncomfortable sea travel in accommodation no better than that allotted to the humblest member of the cast, she arrived to find Seymour waiting for her. However, *Sleeping Partners* was never performed. After compèring some concerts and speaking over the radio Hicks departed for South Africa, but Delysia remained to become our first star in the Middle East.

Her devotion to the task was so outstanding that she must be mentioned above all others. When she first arrived she was appalled not only by the lack of morale among the players, but by the complete lack of consideration with which they were treated. Left largely to her own devices, she plunged into the work with energy, starring in revues and concert parties, singing over the radio and acting in sparkling style in many comedies, including an enchanting performance in *French for Love*, which I saw in Alexandria in 1943. She remained for three years in the Middle East, touring Tripolitania, Cyrenaica, Palestine and Syria, only returning to England in time to join ENSA on the Second Front.

After El Alamein several concert parties followed close upon the heels of the Eighth Army, not so close as in later campaigns when we were better equipped and had learnt the way of things, but, nevertheless, sufficiently close to give the artistes uncomfortable moments. During one performance a German Stuka came in out of the setting sun, shooting up our portable stage before the ack-ack could drive it away. A stray machine-gun bullet went through the comedian's baggy trousers, and a clarinet player fell off the platform in astonishment, breaking the instrument in the process. The troops thought this was the funniest part of the show. Another desert party was amazed at the end of its performance to see the whole audience waiting in a queue outside for the show to be repeated. The performance was given again in its entirety. But men still waited outside. To the manager's protest that they could not possibly face a third time the reply was: "We know that, chum, but perhaps your people would just come and talk to us." . . . It was the small companies such as these that secured the commendation of General Montgomery, that formidable critic of all laggards.

◇◇◇

Special Delivery . . .

During the period of the great 'blitzes' the troops were greatly worried about their homes and womenfolk. Their general feeling of neglect was intensified by heavy delay in the mails, some Service letters taking three months to arrive and others not arriving at all. Disturbed by the lack of news, the men began to lose heart. Knowing this, Anthony Eden broke into an ENSA show at the Fleet Club, Alexandria, to address the men. He began by saying, "I am bringing you a message from home," at which he was interrupted by a gruff voice shouting, "Blimey! Didn't bring us any letters, did yer?" Growls of approval at this sally came from all round the hall, but when the Minister added, "My message is that the war is coming to the Middle East," the men jumped to their feet, giving a great cheer that seemed to lift the roof.

7

'Laissez-passer'

Rumours of friction between soldier and civilian in our Cairo office continued to reach me throughout 1941. That the military authorities were openly dissatisfied with the meagre supply of entertainment was not surprising, for the Middle East was teeming with troops, and our progress had been slow and hesitant. Why were we not building or taking over more cinemas? Where was the garrison theatre in Cairo? Why no more parties in the desert?

In September, brushing on one side the crowding responsibilities at home, I made renewed application for air priority. In October the Air Staff gave grudging consent, adding a cryptic note on the file: "Mr Dean would be hard put to it to choose a more awkward time to go to the Middle East." By the beginning of November it seemed that I really would get away, but at the last moment the Director-General of Army Welfare sprang his mine of interference under my feet, and opportunity was lost for that year.

In the spring and summer of 1942 there was the crisis over manpower. To go abroad with that problem unsolved would have been like planning a major advance with insufficient troops and no hope of reinforcement. Then came my visit to the United States and the North African landings. An unfriendly poltergeist sat on my shoulder, nagging furiously all the time I was in America. British troops were streaming overseas. The southern shores of the Mediterranean were peopled with them. A demand for entertainment in North Africa was inevitable. Whatever the home anxieties I must go East as soon as possible.

The landings were prepared with such secrecy that no hint had reached us beforehand from any quarter, even NAAFI successfully withholding all information. In consequence, not an artiste, not a can of film, not a truck had been made ready. As for the officers and men we should require, they had not even been thought of. And after the campaign had opened the true state of affairs was submerged in a wash of rumour that followed in the wake of the amphibians. Other organizations besides our own were embarrassed by this secrecy, the Adjutant-General frankly admitting to me a few months later that his own Welfare Directorate had been equally unready.

The first urgency in North Africa was for an experienced officer of appropriate rank to set up the necessary contacts, but none was available. Haygarth had been passing from one pressing job to the next ever since Dunkirk. Hard upon his recent labours in putting the West African service on its feet, he was now engaged in clearing up the administrative mess in Cairo. Well might he be excused for harbouring thoughts of indispensability! Instructions were sent to a junior officer, who had been a member of the original cadre in France and was now doing well in West Africa, to make his way as soon as possible to Algiers to wait for me: the beginning of the exasperating process of robbing Peter to pay Paul that was to last for some months.

During Haygarth's last home leave I had persuaded Rex Newman to resume his commission of the First World War, and to go with him to set up a Middle East production centre, despite the rising scale of production at Drury Lane, which would make his absence increasingly felt. The short-sightedness of the War Office in insisting upon the disbandment of our military personnel after Dunkirk now became apparent. The staffing of the West African scheme and the preliminary requirements in Egypt had exhausted our 'cache' of trained men. Appeals to the War Office to allow others with the requisite experience to transfer to us had been mainly disregarded. Indeed, the fact that an officer or N.C.O. had had previous theatrical experience seemed a certain passport to refusal. This meant that new men had to be taken from civil life, given a month's military training at the R.A.S.C./E.F.I. depôt and then put through a course of instruction at Drury Lane.

However the overseas executive at Drury Lane worked out plans for a regular service of both live and film shows, while I made preparations for my own landfall, the intention being to see ENSA established in North Africa and then to make my way to the Middle East. As a civilian travelling in recently captured foreign territory amid a kaleidoscope of uniforms, each symbolizing the assertion of authority in one form or another, I should need to arm myself with a document of paramount importance, if my movements were not to be summarily terminated by one of the numerous Security agencies that would examine my credentials. Formal application for such a paper would have to go through both American and British channels, and might take weeks, so I decided to provide my own *laissez-passer*. A document was drawn up, addressed "to all whom it may concern," requesting facilities for my journey; it was signed by various Secretaries of State and by Lord May. But when a member of our Public Relations Council accosted the Secretary of State for War[1] behind the Speaker's Chair in the House of Commons, he would not oblige, demanding querulously, "What on earth does Dean want to go out there for?" However, the War Office later handed me a separate letter to General Alexander.

Armed with my paper, and with air priority to Gibraltar, provided by Lord Sherwood, Under-Secretary of State for Air, I thought the way clear at last for the oft-postponed journey eastwards. But no! Before inoculations were completed I was ordered into hospital for an immediate operation. I asked the sister how long this would take. Six weeks at least before I could travel long distances, she replied, adding with irritating cheerfulness that the operation I was about to undergo was on the painful list. Half-way to recovery, I was visited by Lord May and Sir Frank Benson, who came to suggest that some one else should go in my stead. I sat bolt upright in the bed, I remember, unpleasantly reminding myself of the nursing sister's warning. This was too much! I must go myself; nobody else.

Four weeks to the day since I entered hospital I set out for an airfield near Bristol, clutching my poltergeist firmly by the throat this time, and resolved to override all further obstacles, whatever they might be. Thoughtfully, Madame Vernon had provided me with an air-cushion which, most unthoughtfully, developed a leak within an hour of its first use.

[1] The Right Hon. Sir James Grigg.

CHAPTER TWENTY-FIVE

OVER THE HILLS AND FAR AWAY

1

Ridin' High

APRIL 30, 1943, Whitchurch Airfield, Bristol, at first light. A little knot of officers and senior officials is passing quickly through the Security barrier. The aircraft that is to take them to Lisbon is ticking over just outside. The officers are in mufti, for this is a civilian service and British uniforms may not be worn when passing through Lisbon, that Tom Tiddler's ground of neutrality. Each man quietly produces his 'documentation,' staring suspiciously at his neighbour after the fashion of British travellers everywhere, mildly resentful that others should use the same route as themselves. There is no one to see them off. It is all rather hush-hush. . . .

The passengers climb into the aircraft, putting on their parachute harness as they listen to the droning instructions of the second pilot on the inflation of their 'Mae Wests,' some with a smile of pretended indifference, others with scrupulous attention, according as they react to the vague anxiety lest on this particular day the enemy should fail to maintain the tacit agreement not to interfere with the American Clipper service. On the way down from London the previous afternoon we had seen clouds of parachute troops descending from the skies over the Wiltshire downs. It had looked easy enough, and graceful, too! But would one remember to count up to the prescribed number before pulling the cord?

Lisbon, city of bright lights, of shops crowded with food and trinkets, of espionage and currency rackets! We are lodged for the night at a comfortable hotel in Estoril—the Germans have other stamping grounds—and early the following morning I leave in a smaller aircraft for Gibraltar. The first sight of The Rock, poking up out of the early-morning mist, reminds one of a Japanese print. We circle and swoop down upon the tiny airfield jutting out into the sea; it is crowded with fighter aircraft, drawn up in rows. A car with an official pennant flying from the bonnet is ticking over beside the runway.

As I step out, feeling rather like a small boy facing his first term at a public school, an R.A.F. officer walks up to me and salutes smartly.

"Mr Dean?"

"Yes," I reply nervously, wondering whether I am to be sent home again.

"H.E. is expecting you."

"H.E.?" I stammer, my thoughts elsewhere.

"The Governor," he replies, a flicker of surprise in his eyes at my failure to recognize the abbreviation. "He would like you to stay at Government House."

Thank Heaven! I have not to go wandering about Gibraltar in search of the NAAFI office. An orderly takes my luggage, and I am in the car almost before I have time to ask the name of my escort. He is John Perry, later the close associate of Hugh Beaumont in the Tennent enterprises and part-author of successful Irish farces. Within a few minutes we are whisked away to Government House, sentries springing to attention and whitewashed barrier poles leaping into the air with admirable promptitude, a practical reminder of the value of high-level contacts in the war zone.

The Governor, Major-General Sir H. Mason Macfarlane, an intelligent soldier who did not allow the dignity of his position to cloud his quizzical interest in such peaceful matters as Music and the Drama, had surrounded himself with a youthful staff whose minds and tastes were congenial to him. There was Major Anthony Quayle, wearing the duties of his office with the same easy charm that was later to carry him to success as co-director of the Shakespeare Memorial Theatre, Stratford-upon-Avon; the Naval A.D.C., who obviously preferred the monosyllabic habit of 'the Silent Service' to the bright chatter going on around him, and the civil secretary with a monocle and a deceptively sheepish air that suggested one of those synthetic heroes of the popular fiction of espionage.

Government House procedure being new to me, I took the precaution of arriving in the anteroom in good time before the entrance of the Governor for dinner, the formal meal of the day, there to be discreetly instructed by 'Tony' Quayle as to my allotted place at table. On the night of his arrival the newcomer is seated next to the Governor, where he is expected to make the most of his opportunity and to pump His Excellency full of information on the purpose of his visit and to make informal requests for help and guidance on specific matters. On subsequent evenings the guest finds himself seated farther and farther away from the throne, as other guests come crowding in with their exigencies. He is expected to give early notice to the A.D.C. of his intended departure and, should he omit to do so, may have discreet inquiries addressed to him on the point, a fate which befell me and which I resolved should never be repeated.

Although I was intent upon getting to North Africa as soon as possible, the Governor had insisted that I await the arrival of the Adjutant-General from India. This meant staying in Gibraltar for four days instead of two, possibly longer, since H.E. in amiable mood had also promised to take me across to Oran in his own plane immediately thereafter. At dinner on the third night there was a positive gaggle of generals on their way home from North Africa, telling of their encounters with the enemy. By now my place was at the bottom of the class, where the necessity to keep the shuttlecock of conversation in the air was not so presumptive. I was able to relax and look about me. I counted the bag: two lieutenant-generals, three major-generals, including Lord Rennell of Rodd, at that time doing political administration in Abyssinia, and several brigadiers. I had not met Rennell since we were fellow-guests in Stephen Courtauld's motor yacht, *Virginia*, on a tour of the Greek Isles. After dinner he hastened to assure me that he was really a civilian in spite of his uniform, a remark that sounded like a boast in that company of Bellona's neophytes. Perhaps he had begun to appraise the value of the high-speed comings and goings in Government Houses during the war years: the higher the rank the greater the velocity—not exactly swanning, but lacking perhaps the searching quality of an eagle's soar.

At the moment ENSA was high in favour. The girls we had sent out to join the military concert parties were giving every satisfaction, their behaviour off-stage being apparently all that could be desired of well-favoured young ladies of the theatre. At a conference with the Fortress Headquarters Committee, summoned at the Governor's behest, I was asked to submit a complete scheme for future entertainment on The Rock. The talk with the Adjutant-General on the morning after his arrival was frank and cordial, despite his baffling habit of repeating the final words of each of my remarks before making reply. He spoke of the appalling dearth of entertainment in India, where the contumacious argument between Delhi and Whitehall as to who was to pay for an ENSA service was still going on. In the warm sunshine of the Governor's garden, with its flowering trees and shrubs—gardenia I remember, chiefly, and magnolia —its fountain and clean, sanded ways, official asperities melted away. The A.G. confessed that the War Office had been too prone to regard ENSA as a part of Army Welfare. Atonement was foreshadowed by the promised transfer of experienced officers and N.C.O.'s from unessential jobs to our military staff. In return I promised to go on to India, although our mandate was still unclear, and my solitary presence could effect little.

Y

However, observation at first hand would justify the visit. . . . I decided not to wait for a state ride in the Governor's aircraft; I would be off the very next morning, taking with me, as became a traveller in the East, frankincense and myrrh for those in authority. So I hied me to the NAAFI wine store, purchased two cases of the finest sherry in stock, and went back to Government House to pack my bag.

2

DUK[W]S and Drakes

May 5, very early in the morning: the sun has not yet dispelled the mist, as we skim a hundred feet above the Mediterranean on our way to Oran, first stop for the American courier plane taking me to Maison Blanche, airport for Algiers. American Air Transport Command was providing the only means of speedy communication behind the sprawling front of the Allied Armies: luxurious air-taxis that proved not so luxurious after all, as the passengers, seated in the little aluminium trays running down the sides of the aircraft, bumped their violent way up and down above the hot desert sands. At Oran came my first experience of an American Army breakfast: waffles and honey, eggs and bacon, eaten off the one plate and washed down with delicious American coffee, served by a loquacious mess waiter, whose attention to my wants sensibly slackened when he discovered my lack of interest in the writings of Mark Twain. At Oran, too, my first sight of the D.U.K.W's, those strange amphibians, boats that could both float in the sea and be driven on land, and of the new army jeeps: long lines of them being driven at frightening speed along the dusty roads and tracks, a too sudden turn upsetting them as easily as a child's hoop; many an American negro bit the dust in painful discovery.

The huge field at Maison Blanche, Algiers, was crammed with American transport Dakotas, lined up in rows, nose to tail; others were twisting and turning in the air like swarming insects; many of them had fantastic nicknames, and even more fantastic bikini-clad ladies painted on their sides; all were camouflaged and manned by casual, gum-chewing American boys, dressed in the distinctive golden-coloured drill of the U.S. Army that looks pleasanter than our British khaki. Behind that lounging indifference and quick informality there was the pulse of an intense vitality, so different from the comatose belligerence of the first days in France, or the routine life of the Gibraltar garrison, perched, crowded and vigilant, on The Rock, like a colony of sea-birds, with all the strength and pettiness that go with the close, communal life.

The officer I had ordered on from West Africa came to meet me, and hurriedly told me the position. Yes, he had brought three N.C.O.'s, three 16-mm. projectors and some films with him; also, two Category 'D' concert parties had arrived. For the rest, the picture was one of confusion and urgency. Transport was non-existent, and accommodation nearly so. The E.F.I. staff, overwhelmed with a dozen canteen problems, had managed to find us one small room at their headquarters while their Works' officer searched for offices to be requisitioned for our use. This was very complicated. Applications to requisition had first to go to the American Command, thence to the French authorities and then back to the Americans before British approval of the requisition could be granted. For office staff we had a junior French typist, speaking indifferent English and struggling with a second-hand typewriter that had arrived from London with the letter 'a' missing. Finally, the campaign was nearing its end—Tunis was expected to fall at any moment—and thousands of troops had begun to demand entertainment.

As we joined the long line of vehicles bowling along the road into Algiers I realized how badly we had been caught off balance. However, we must fight for a foothold somewhere. Madame Vernon was on her way out—I had left her in London fighting with the Air Ministry for a movement order—and she would be a tower of strength.

"We must organize, organize," I muttered aloud.

"Hell! What with?" exclaimed the young officer. "It's hopeless." He seemed to be in danger of losing his nerve.

"I shall go straight to the top. Take me to General Alexander's H.Q."

"He isn't here. He's in the field."

"His chief of staff, then."

"He's with him. They're fighting a battle, you know. Algiers is Eisenhower's headquarters. He's a sort of co-ordinator-in-chief."

"Well, take me there, then. I must find some one."

Two exhibition-size U.S. marines sprang to attention outside the Hotel St George as an American general preceded me into the new G.H.Q. I had decided to look up Arthur Tedder, now C.-in-C. of the Mediterranean Air Command, hoping that he had not forgotten our talk before the war broke out.

Tedder greeted me with his usual smile. No need to flourish my 'documentation' in his face. A pipe-in-mouth and feet-upon-the-desk attitude, doubtless borrowed from the Americans, but losing him neither dignity nor authority, accentuated the aura of lightly borne responsibility that surrounded him. He listened with a cheerful grin to my anxious tale.

"Arthur, I must get to General Alexander at once. Will you help?"

"Better find out first if he's at his camp or not." He pressed a button, and gave some directions to his P.A.

"Got any good shows for us?"

"Plenty, if we could only get 'em out here. Q Movements, War Office, won't do a thing. The Air Ministry's no good, either."

"Well, you'd better hurry up, or the campaign will be over."

"I've a splendid company waiting in Gibraltar, but no transport!" (The idea had only just occurred to me: the company was in truth waiting —to return to London at the end of their Gibraltar engagement.) "Can't you send a plane for them?"

"We'll see. I'll speak to Ike. Come back in an hour or so."

In the late afternoon I called again. The matter of air-lift for the artistes had been arranged, and I was to be sent on my way to General Alexander the next day. With the prospect of a cheery party in Tedder's mess that evening, to which a case of my sherry would serve as an amiable introduction, we went jauntily down the stairs into the main lobby of the hotel.

A flurry of activity outside: harsh words of command, sentries springing to attention, Security officers bobbing up mysteriously from nowhere; and then the swing-doors into the hotel revolved at speed to admit the striding figure of a three-star American general, armed *cap-à-pie*, two ivory-handled six-shooters dangling from his belt, boots and spurs, a riding-crop in his hand. He passed rapidly up the stairs, talking forcefully to an American colonel who maintained a respectful pace in the rear. Truly, an effective stage entrance: Donald Wolfit could have contrived nothing better.

"Who on earth's that?" I said in a too audible whisper. "Tom Mix?"

"Careful," whispered Tedder, his eyes twinkling as he nudged me in the ribs, "or you'll find yourself arrested for *lèse majesté*." Just one more sensation in a day of shock and surprises; it was General George Patton.

3

The Tumult and the Shouting

May 7: High noon at the top of the mountain road into Tunisia. I was seated on the stone parapet at the side of the road, eating a box lunch, with Air Vice-Marshal Robb[1], who was driving me in his little staff car to Constantine, where he had business with the U.S. General Spaatz, commanding the Tactical Air Force, and listening to his quiet voice as

[1] Later Air Chief Marshal Sir James Robb, Chief of Fighter Command.

he spoke of gardens and pictures and other matters not usually associated with a man of war. The plain lay shimmering beneath us; the red-brown rocks and the intense blue of the sky, turning white towards the sun, filling the senses with warmth and colour. The last military convoy of the morning had passed on its way and for the moment the air was unbelievably still. In this cerulean peace it was hard to believe that beneath us on the distant plain men were fighting, being wounded, and dying—some singly, some in groups.

Resuming the journey, we could not have gone more than a hundred yards when a horrible, clanking noise warned us of engine trouble. A dozen yards more, and the transmission gave out. Not a vehicle, not an Arab was in sight. If we were to pass the night there we were likely to be very cold indeed. We were just below the crest of the pass, so we got out, pushed the car over the top, and started a long coast down the other side. On we went, checking speed in the steeper parts and coaxing the lifeless vehicle over the occasional flat stretches. It was sublimely peaceful, gliding swiftly through that hot, bright air. As we drew near the plain the flat stretches grew longer and longer, and our coaxing more strenuous. Finally, the car crept slowly, ever more slowly, to a standstill, at the end of topographical advantage. Full stop. "Look!" pointed Robb. Not a hundred yards ahead of us was a R.E.M.E. recovery post.

The officer in charge provided us with over-sweetened, chlorinated tea and sent a breakdown vehicle for the car. This was my first experience of those lonely posts that lay behind the lines of march of the Allied Armies; supply or recovery, they were the same everywhere. The men who manned them had a forlorn look; no longer fighting men, mere spectators, as the convoys came and went amid the prevailing tea and sand (mud in Europe!); they were driftwood on the tide of military advance.

After tea we were taken on to Setif, temporary home of a night-fighter group under the command of one of the fabulous Atcherley twins. A small ENSA party had arrived, and a dance was being given for them in the officers' mess after the show. They were enormously enjoying the society of the young airmen who swarmed round them, only to leave shortly afterwards on one of their nightly forays, and then come roaring home an hour or so later for more dancing—all except Group-Captain Atcherley, who did not return till 8 A.M., having pushed his lone reconnaissance far out over Cape Bon peninsula and the sea. . . . These were men of the Desert Air Force; impossible not to catch something of their gaiety and bravura attitude to life. I was approaching the real war at last.

At Constantine we stayed with General Spaatz. Here was something different again. When we arrived the General was playing poker with some of his officers in a corner of the anteroom; in another corner cocktails were being shaken, while in a third the radio was blaring out indifferent American dance music. Robb treated all this rowdiness and informality as a great joke, which of course increased his popularity. At dinner the General sat in his shirt-sleeves, throwing wisecracks round the table and jeering at the failure of his subordinates to win at poker. But, after mess, when the reconnaissance reports and photographs were brought in, the atmosphere changed. Now it was a keen, aggressive mind at work, one that did not need the surroundings of an orderly room for the exercise of discipline: efficiency by different methods from those to which we British are accustomed; but the Germans found it no less effective.

.   .   .   .

"Yes, but where is General Alexander's Headquarters?" I demanded irritably.

"This is it," replied the army driver sourly.

Apart from some field telephone lines strung loosely over the thorn bushes there was nothing to be seen. Wait! What was that away there in the distance? Two bivouacs almost completely hidden by stunted trees, guard tents presumably, and, beyond, hardly seen in the undulating waste of silvery grey sand, some military caravans. After a bumpy ninety minutes' flight from Setif in a Mitchell light bomber, provided by General Spaatz, I had been dropped at the military air-strip at Il Kef, a lonely place far out in the Tunisian plain, whence an Army staff car had bundled me, my valise and my case of sherry to this desolate spot. My chase after the British C.-in-C. was at an end.

Hiding the sherry under a thorn bush lest an inquisitive sentry should decide to take it under his protection, I stumbled along the rough track to where, in a shallow depression among the dunes, the General's camp lay skilfully camouflaged. Field telephone lines, festooning the thorn bushes like the weaving of some giant spider, connected the signal caravan with the half-dozen or so other caravans, disposed at various crazy angles about the hollow. Apart from the buzzing of a lorried transmitter, the tapping of a typewriter and a single buzzard hovering in the sky on the watch for refuse flung out by the cooks, there was no other sound or sight of life. This ordered quiet was somehow more impressive than the clattering sentry-go outside the Hotel St George in Algiers.

Observing an Air Force roundel painted on a board beside one of the caravans, and remembering Tedder's promise to signal my arrival to Air

Vice-Marshal Coningham,[1] commanding the Western Desert Air Force,
I decided to 'make my number' there. General Alexander was away
receiving the surrender of Tunis, but the A.O.A. (Air Officer i/c Administration—Air Commodore Elmhirst[2]) was expecting me. He had quartered
me in a small tent next to his caravan, my first experience under canvas
since the First World War.

In the afternoon General Alexander returned to camp. I was immediately sent for and presented my credentials. The General struck me as
having the most lucid mind of any commander I had yet come across. This
and his modesty and fundamental simplicity of character, often the mark
of a great soldier, explained his prestige with all the Allied Commanders:
"You know where you are with him," is a passport to esteem in any
sphere. As he talked to me there were no frills, no adumbrations; just a
quiet discussion of my purpose, which, once accepted, received his whole-
hearted co-operation. I was in the camp of the three C's—Confidence,
Clarity and Calmness—all three qualities emanating directly from our
Commander-in-Chief.

The General decided to send a directive to A.F.H.Q., urging that all
entertainment provided for the British and for the Americans should be
co-ordinated through ENSA. Meanwhile, he asked me if something might
be done immediately for the troops about to enter Tunis. I undertook to
go into the city on the following day and to take over the most suitable
building.

'Maori' Coningham (pronounced 'Mary' by the troops), nicknamed
so because of his New Zealand origin, was of a more flamboyant type,
with something of the Elizabethan adventurer in his composition and a
panache for the good things of life that sometimes caused his brilliance to
be discounted. When, a few days after our first meeting, I put to him a
routine question as to where his next headquarters would be, he turned
to a large-scale map hanging on the wall behind him with a great show of
care.

"There," he said. "No, there!"

"Why?"

"My spies tell me they've got a good refrigerator." A flippant remark,
dismissed as soon as heard, only to be recalled when later one found the
Air Marshal quietly enjoying the aforesaid amenity.

Waiting for me outside the mess tent before dinner were three orderlies,
two waiters and a cook, who shyly handed me messages for their three
wives, written out on a single piece of paper, one underneath the other,

[1] Later Air Marshal Sir Arthur Coningham.
[2] Later Air Marshal Sir Thomas Elmhirst, and Lieutenant-Governor of Guernsey.

which they begged me to deliver when I returned home. I was glad to assist in the circulation of this cheerful round-robin of domesticity, but the only way I could do so was to send the paper to the wife first on the list and ask her to forward it to the next in turn. Since the messages varied little in the wording and not at all in the sentiment, there was no breach of confidence.

Inside the tent General 'Alex,' 'Mary' Coningham and the other senior officers drank toasts to the Allied Victory in my sherry, and made bets on the total bag of prisoners now flooding into the cages, bets that were no sooner laid than lost, as 'Signals' sent in little pink slips during dinner, announcing the leaping totals.

The following afternoon the General sent me in a staff car with his own driver into Tunis. The journey took four hours, because of the long columns of prisoners streaming away from the fallen city. Mingled with them were convoys of captured German trucks, lorries and horse-drawn vehicles of every description, packed with German soldiers hastening out of Hitler's war. Even the little Tunisian buggies that plied for tourist hire in peace-time had been pressed into service, driven mostly by the Germans themselves. Extra horses had been hitched to some of them to pull the crazy loads. In one vehicle no less than ten officers rode jauntily by, with one of their number as cabman, puffing at a big cigar. The fantastic procession reminded me of the trek home from Epsom on Derby Day which, as small boys, we used to watch from the school gates in the days before horse transport had been driven from the roads.

Few British troops were in evidence until we drew near the city. There, drawn up in the sand, clear of the road, were several squadrons of the 6th Armoured Division, the crews sitting on top of their tanks like a flock of sparrows, in black berets and shorts—no other clothing—their bodies burnt brown by the desert sun, grimly relishing their victory. Now and then one of their number made a remark to raise a laugh from his pals.

At the entrance to the town groups of civilians were fraternizing with the Germans, throwing them cigarettes and roses to put behind their ears as they clambered into their lorries to join the long procession into captivity—and freedom. The scene had the air of an Italian *fiesta*. Smoking and laughing and jostling one another, these men did not behave like a defeated army. Surely one of the happiest surrenders in history?

Tunis was drinking the wine of release: heady stuff, that! Once uncorked, it suffers no check until levitation has run its course. The confusion was almost beyond description: no electric light, no water—the streets crowded with Tunisians of every hue from European white to Arab brown. Cafés and wine cellars were already welcoming the new customers, many of whom, judging by their recumbent attitudes in the doorways, had yet to learn the superior potency of Algerian wine over British beer. The ferment of a city in the first hours of its release was an experience I was to undergo several times before the war was done.

With the help of the Town Major I ferreted out the Contrôleur-Civile of the town, and, in my flustered French, explained that by order of the British Commander-in-Chief le Théâtre Municipale was to be made ready for our use. A nominal rent would be paid, and he would hear more in due course from the Area Commander. In his enthusiasm he refused any suggestion of rent. I left—with profuse thanks for the rescue of his beloved Tunis ringing in my ears.

By this time it was dark. I was feeling hungry and wondering what we should do for a meal. But the General's driver was an old campaigner. He had foreseen the situation and stocked the back of the car with a complete dinner in tins. He drove the car into a palm grove outside a handsome Moorish residence, formerly the property of the Bey of Tunis and now taken over as a headquarters Mess. Lighting a portable petrol stove, he opened his tins and cooked a first-rate dinner—a meat stew, as I remember, with a fruit salad to follow—which was welcome, for by this time the temperature had fallen considerably. I refused the inevitable tea, because the water he had brought with him was so strongly chlorinated; but we scrounged several bottles of beer from the back door of the mess. As the officers were all out on duty there was no need to ask permission.

The return drive through the moonlit desert, in which the thorn bushes and sand dunes assumed strange shapes, some looking like sentries at the alert and others like pill-boxes, took us another four hours. Cautiously uttering the password to the outer ring of sentries, I stumbled my way back to my tent, falling over the guy-ropes and waking up Elmhirst, who demanded where on earth I had been. "General Alexander was getting quite anxious." "Not the least need," I replied grandly, "I've got the theatre anyway."

At his conference the following morning General Alexander approved the terms of the directive to be telegraphed to A.F.H.Q. It was more sweeping and categorical than I had expected. In the afternoon I paid calls to various units of 242 Fighter Group, each with its landing strip named after a British railway terminus, such as Paddington, Euston and so forth. One of them had to be renamed because the Free French pilots objected to landing at Waterloo, which was understandable enough.

Flying back to Algiers in an American courier plane, I arrived simultaneously with Madame Vernon from London. She had nearly blown Adastral House into the air with importunity in her determined efforts to join me, and in the first excited minutes brought news of the early dispatch of artistes and staff, and of frenzied efforts by Ben Henry to hijack 16-mm. cinema projectors from every source known to him, at which I flung up my arms with joy, and withdrew the imprecations that I had hourly flung at Drury Lane during the past week.

Lost, Stolen or Strayed . . .

One of the first parties to go to North Africa was headed by Morlais Morgan, veteran Welsh baritone. Twenty-four hours after the party had left, the Concert Division received a cipher message which read: 'Morlais Morgan left ship U.K.'

Morgan was the artiste-manager of the party, and his disappearance caused the greatest anxiety. Movement Control, War Office, assured us that he had embarked, so Scotland Yard was called in. Exhaustive inquiries, extending even to the Liverpool Morgue, where a newly arrived corpse, long and thin, did not answer to his description, yielded no result. The suggestion of an hysterical secretary that the River Mersey should be dragged was not well received by the authorities.

Reluctantly, Drury Lane came to the conclusion that Morgan had jumped overboard. It was decided to send a Welfare Assistant down to break the sad news to his wife. The door was opened by a small daughter who, in response to the usual question, replied, "Daddy has gone to North Africa." (So much for Security!) As his wife was not in, the Welfare Assistant thought it best to come away.

Thorpe Bates, who was something of a crossword fan, passed nights of anxiety until it suddenly flashed through his mind that the operative word might be 'skip,' the professional name for a theatrical basket, and not 'ship.' Eventually a signal clerk at the War Office admitted he had altered the word to 'ship,' as he had never heard of a skip.

4
'Ring up the Curtain!'

"Virginia, can you be ready to fly to Tunis with Air-Marshal Coningham in an hour's time?"

My question broke off Virginia's interview with a French official, whose voluble objections to the take-over of certain offices as the ENSA headquarters were being rapidly reduced to a mere expostulatory stammer.

But there was no time to stop and admire her *Sturm und Drang* methods, nor the decisive Parisian charm with which she extracted the assent of the Frenchman and bundled him out of the room.

I had just returned from Tedder's headquarters. There was to be a Victory Parade in Tunis five days hence, with General Eisenhower and the other military leaders present. Determined to open the theatre on the same day, I had asked for immediate air passages for Madame Vernon and an E.F.I. Works Officer to go to Tunis to complete arrangements for the take-over and to obtain hostel accommodation. Air Marshal Coningham, who was in the office at the time, offered to take them in his own plane, leaving in an hour's time.

Hardly waiting to take in my brief instructions, Virginia hurried to the hotel to pack her valise and caught the Air Marshal's plane just as it was ticking over at Maison Blanche, a good half-hour's drive away. She must have turned that flight with Coningham to good account, for ever after both she and I were assured of his help and interest wherever his writ ran. In my case this took the practical form of a standing order to the staff of 2nd T.A.F. to give me an air-lift whenever I needed it.

The immediate problem of the theatre disposed of (I had not an instant's doubt of Madame Vernon's ability to unravel the tangle[1] at Tunis), there remained the question of a programme for the opening week. A signal was sent to John Berryman's 'Laughter for To-night' Company to close their visit to Gib. and stand by for instructions to proceed to Algiers. Formal application through Army channels for the necessary air transport having been turned down as "not an operational necessity," Tedder arranged with American Transport Command to send a special plane over for them.

That evening, at the suggestion of Colonel McCormack (chief P.R.O. and a well-known journalist), I announced the Tunis opening to all the war correspondents, British and American, as the beginning of ENSA's service in North Africa. I felt like a schoolmaster, standing up there on the master's daïs with all the good little boys sitting in front of me at their wooden desks, each equipped with a portable typewriter. These were the pick of the world's reporters and their place of meeting a school building.

I spent the next days looking into the broadcasting position. Almost the whole of the available air time of the local stations was given over to the Americans, who were also using a number of field transmitters. British representation over the air was decidedly inadequate. The Chief Adminis-

[1] Within hours of her arrival she had settled up the theatre and borrowed a jeep and was touring the town demanding billets for the artistes, only to be told to wait until the Germans had left them.

trative Officer (C.A.O.) to General Alexander, General Humfrey Gale, invited me to lunch to meet his opposite number on the U.S. Army Staff, General Sawbridge, an amiable and co-operative man who readily agreed that we should share equally with the Americans, and undertook to instruct U.S. Special Services accordingly.

Our recorded programmes for North Africa had been consigned to Gibraltar before the Front opened. Apparently they were still piling up there. Something had gone wrong with our distribution scheme, another matter to be inquired into when I reached Cairo. Meanwhile, I induced the official in charge of local rediffusion in Gibraltar to fly over to Algiers, bringing with him some of the accumulated supply of programmes. In the process of finding out what had happened I came into contact with Henry Caldwell, then a young warrant officer in a cipher section of Army Signals, who was doing his best to remedy the deficiency by broadcasting gramophone records and such bits and pieces of entertainment as he could scavenge. I was much taken with his energetic personality, and suggested he should transfer to ENSA, where he would be free to develop his broadcasting ambitions. This was eventually arranged through the good offices of General Gale.

Two days before the Tunis opening 'Laughter for To-night' flew in from Gibraltar in two aircraft. The company was accommodated for one night at the G.H.Q. mess in the Hotel Aletti, normally reserved for V.I.P.'s and General Staff, and the next morning packed into a coach and sent to Bougie, where they gave one performance that night and two more on the following day. Their unheralded appearance was like rain in the desert to our men.

The next day they were taken by coach to Setif, where they arrived several hours late, but complete with their theatrical baskets and scenery. The pilot who was to fly them on to Tunis watched all this baggage being piled into his aircraft (as crazy an example of overload as ever could be) with apparent unconcern, judging by the 'dead-pan' expression on his face, but when an attractive blonde got in and took possession of the seat nearest his he spat out the usual chewing-gum and, with a laconic "Let's go," climbed into the plane and began furiously to rev up the engines.

To land at El Ouina, the airfield for Tunis, called for the utmost skill. Wrecked Junkers and Messerschmitts littered the ground, looking from the air like squashed aluminium flies on a dirty tablecloth. There seemed to be no space to land at all. But the pilot brought the overladen aircraft down with superb skill and a pretence of sang-froid that would have done credit to a great actor.

"Weren't you worried about the overload?" I asked over a cup of coffee.

"I sure would ha' been but for that dizzy blonde. She kinda took my mind off."

May 20: A day of celebration for the Allied troops and a testing time for ENSA. Very early in the morning, while the scavengers were still preparing the streets for the Victory Parade, I hastened to the Théâtre Municipal, gay with flags and large wooden shields, displaying the ENSA badge. "Trust Virginia for that," I chuckled, as I hurried into the place.

There, with a borrowed apron over her skirt and the largest pair of officer's marching boots imaginable, was our Senior Welfare Officer, furiously cleaning out the stage boxes, while an aged Arab with a native broom drove dust into further corners and an emaciated French Tunisian sat at the Contrôle with a scared look on his face, as though personal arrest were imminent. Between flourishes of her broom Virginia told me the arrangements that had been agreed on for the marshalling of the audiences for the two performances which were to follow the Victory Parade, the first at 1600 hours and the second at 1830 hours. I went on to the stage to escape the dust clouds. There a gendarme handed me an official invitation to attend the luncheon to be given to Eisenhower and the other military commanders by the French Resident General.

"Virginia, what does this mean?" I called out.

"I rang them up," she said briskly, "told them who you were and that they ought to send you an invitation at once."

"Really!" I exclaimed. "I can't possibly accept such an invitation."

"Nonsense," she replied, "you're the head of ENSA, aren't you? Go and see the Victory March first. I've picked out quite a good place for you. Just opposite the saluting-base. Take some photographs if you can, and then go straight on to the Residence." I started to protest. "Now, then, off with you! You're doing no good here. See you when the theatre opens at four o'clock."

Meekly accepting her orders, I went to the spot indicated. The processional way was gay with flags, and there was a good turnout of local inhabitants, kept at a respectful distance by troops lining the route.

Martial music! Ah! Here they come, the victors, headed by detachments of the Eighth Army, free at last of the sand, marching as if down Whitehall. But there are not many British troops. Following them come detachments of French Algerians, company after company, far too many to my thinking. These are not the troops that won victory over the Afrika Korps. Doubtless, they have been paraded for political reasons. Indeed,

some look as if they had just left their shops and hotels and put on uniform to take part in a show in honour of *la belle France*. Not so the
Moroccan detachments that follow them, ghoums in burnouses with
long-barrelled desert rifles and murderous knives in their belts. Splatter,
splatter, splatter sound their sandals on the tarmac as they go quickly by with
their loping strides, bloodthirsty-looking ruffians. Now the thin line of
spectators has stopped cheering and fallen into an absorbed silence. "Thank
God for the ghoums and the Guards," murmurs a British officer standing
beside me. There is a fly-past of numerous aircraft, dipping their wings as
they go by the saluting-base where General Eisenhower stands, shy and
unassuming, supported by his field commanders, American, French and
our own.

Now to the Residence for the official luncheon. There must be over a
hundred officers and civil functionaries seated either side of the long table.
I find myself between two generals, French and American, with whom
conversation is difficult, except to praise the feast, chosen with such
Lucullan care and cooked as only the French know how—everything
genuine, nothing ersatz: a delicious fish with fresh mayonnaise made with
cream, Tunisian baby lamb that melted in the mouth, a sweet and French
cheese—brie, possibly. The wines include a vintage champagne.

"How is it possible," I ask of General Juin on my left, "to serve such
wines after the Occupation?"

"Ah!" he replies with a wink, "they have some very deep cellars in
Tunis, you know."

Upstairs, in the reception room, French brandy, coffee supplied by the
Americans, and Havana cigars. The air is thick with important conversation. General Eisenhower sits on a settee, with Tedder supporting him.
He has a charming air of detachment, like a prefect listening to professional talk in the masters' common-room. I tell him about the opening
of the theatre that afternoon, but he tactfully declines to carry out the
opening ceremony, saying that it is the prerogative of the British First
Army Commander. He is pleasant and amiable, asking me when all his
troops will have entertainment. I reply confidently enough until suddenly
I have a vision of Madame Vernon in her coarse apron, sweeping the
grime of months out of the theatre, and of a young officer left behind in
Algiers with an indifferent French typist and a machine with the letter 'a'
missing, anxiously awaiting the arrival of reinforcements from Drury
Lane.

The Théâtre Municipal is well placed, fronting one side of the principal square, which is generously shaded with trees. It was packed from
corner to corner with troops when I arrived a few minutes ahead of the

official party. Virginia, still in her working-clothes, her face streaming with perspiration, was standing by the main entrance, watching the long lines of men, under their N.C.O.'s, clump their way into the little theatre. The building was already over-packed, yet there was no diminution of the waiting crowd outside. If anything, it became denser, as the First Army Commander drove up with Tedder.

When General Anderson walked on to the stage and announced that the first ENSA garrison theatre in North Africa was open, cheer after cheer went up from the Eighth Army men—brown as berries, hardened by the struggle in the desert: nobbly, humorous faces from Lancashire, cheeky Cockneys with their caps at odd angles, Scots in their kilts—row upon row of them, laughing with tears in their eyes at the sight of the girls, their lips unconsciously repeating the words of the songs and the jokes of the comedians.

General Anderson and the other commanders had difficulty in leaving after the performance, the soldiers pressing so hard one upon another that it seemed as though they would push the very walls of the theatre down. It was long past the time when the second performance should have begun, and the men cheered with impatience as we struggled to extricate one audience and admit the next. . . .   The following morning General Alexander sent me a letter of congratulation, which was carefully preserved in the 'eulogy file' at Drury Lane for a long time, but now is most unaccountably lost. No matter. I am not likely to forget my exhilaration at seeing the ENSA flag unfurled under foreign skies and flown at the summit of effectiveness.

Repairs Promptly Executed . . .

Solomon made many tours overseas. The pianos from which he was expected to extract superlative music covered the whole gamut from excellent to the virtually unplayable. The instrument for his first concert in Algiers was more than usually decrepit, with broken pedals, notes that stuck and sundry other imperfections. A number of British and American soldiers were lounging in the concert hall, used as a canteen in the daytime, when Solomon went to try it. One of them noticed the virtuoso's look of despair and offered to put the piano in order for him.

"I'm afraid it's quite hopeless," said Solomon, much amused.

"Give me a couple of hours," said the G.I. "I'll fix it."

Solomon came back later to find him quietly putting back the case. The piano was in reasonable order.

"You seem to know quite a lot about it," said Solomon, surprised and delighted. "What's your name?"

"Steinway," replied the American.

This story gained such currency in ENSA circles that many eminent musicians were credited with the experience in places as far apart as Singapore, Eindhoven in Holland, Foggia in Italy, Sierra Leone and Rangoon. Perhaps there was more than one scion of the house of Steinway serving with the Allied Forces?

5

Early and Late

Leaving Virginia in her officer's shoes to go clumping her indomitable way in and out of the orderly rooms of Tunisia and patiently instructing scrofulous hostel staffs in the elements of hygiene, I hurried back to Algiers in time to welcome Haygarth from Cairo. As artistes, military personnel, stores and equipment were now coming in from England it was necessary to change the direction of our routing. The days of the long hauls round the Cape or across tropical Africa were over. We began organizing Algiers as our supply base for the Mediterranean.

Many of the artistes now arriving were veterans of our time in France. The glitter in their eyes spoke their eagerness to resume contact with the fighting troops. The terrace of the Hotel Aletti became a place of pleasant congregation and unexpected encounters. There one day Benn Levy was to be seen, wearing his R.N.V.R. beard with a difference, and James Hilton, the novelist, whose fascinating talks to the troops over the local broadcasting station had brought him fresh renown. The second or third day after my return my youngest son arrived with his sergeant in a desert truck from the Eighth Army. Apparently he had persuaded his colonel that the speediest way to secure a show for the troops was to send him to Algiers to buy wine for the officers' mess. After a brief visit to a little seashore restaurant just outside the town, where, under the pine trees, we drank potent wine, swatted flies and indulged in family gossip, I sent him on his way with promises that for the sake of his future standing in the mess I hoped ENSA would be able to fulfil.

One morning Caldwell asked me with a great air of secrecy to attend a special broadcast that evening to be given by Josephine Baker. She had been living in retirement for two years, and Military Intelligence was in some doubt about her because of the competing claims of Vichy and the Free French to her loyalty. The broadcast was such a success that I invited

BUD FLANAGAN, WILL HAY AND "CHES" ALLEN IN BRUSSELS

ANGLO-AMERICAN CO-OPERATION: THE FIRST ENSA PERFORMANCE ON GERMAN SOIL, SUPPORTED BY A U.S.A. 'SHOW' BAND

BURMA

Snapshot of the
Fourteenth Army
Commander
(General Sir William Slim)
taken in his Camp

Myself reporting Home

her there and then to join ENSA, to visit the Middle East and later to come to England. She agreed to do so, provided she might give a certain number of concerts to French troops; she also undertook not to accept any commercial engagements while she was in England. To make things easier I went to see Harold Macmillan, then Resident Minister in North Africa, who cleared the way for her with the French civil authorities. Her unexpected appearance raised the temperature of our work overnight.

June 1: Maison Blanche, looking more like a Clapham Junction of the air than ever. In vain I wave my special paper with all its formidable signatures in the U.S. transport major's face. Glaring resentfully at my 'civvies' as though I were trying to 'put one over on him,' he shouts, "I see no pips, bud!" Then a second claimant for the remaining seat in the Tripoli plane appears in the person of a thin, soft-spoken young man, newly arrived from Whitehall. "Oh, hell!" says the major. "Youse guys better toss for it." So we solemnly toss, and I lose.

It is dark when at last I arrive in Tunis. I begin a weary trudge along the road, lumping my kit; then I thumb a passing jeep and climb on to somebody's knee. It is very late indeed when Virginia, who does not of course expect me, secures a movement order for Tripoli and insists upon showing me over the ENSA hostel, lining up her heterogeneous staff—obviously dragged out of bed for the purpose—and berating the manager for the untidy toilets.

A few hours later, in a cold dawn, she took me to La Marsa in a dilapidated taxi, explaining that it was her only means of transport for the present. The Bisley mail plane had guns in its nose and tail, mailbags piled high to the roof of the fuselage. My passage appeared to be in jeopardy, for there was an Army Chaplain waiting, too. However, as there was no co-pilot that meant one seat for sure. The pilot revved up the aircraft, and the officer in charge of the air-strip invited us to climb in. I was introduced to a bishop from New Zealand: very young for such high dignity. "Will you sit by the pilot?" said he, courteously. "Oh, won't you?" I countered with calculated hesitancy. "No, please," said the Bishop, "I shall be quite happy on the mailbags." "Very well," I replied promptly, and clambered up, not before Virginia had time to whisper in my ear, "Basil, you are shameless."

Tripoli, monument to the energy of Mussolini's colonizers, presented an extraordinary sight, the slimy yellow-grey water of its harbour dotted with the funnels of sunken ships: a devil's wedding-cake, with a large Italian troopship with engines blown out for centre piece, known to our troops as "Angostura Bitters."

z

The O. i/c ENSA, Captain Harrington, first manager of the Transport Division in London, had contrived (with the co-operation of Army Welfare) to open one garrison theatre and two garrison cinemas, a remarkable achievement seeing that he had no clerical staff, except what he could borrow. Performances were going on all day, long queues of men forming up outside all three places from nine o'clock in the morning. Thus were the 'desert rats' slaking their thirst for entertainment at the ENSA water-hole, before attacking that soft under-belly of which the Prime Minister had spoken. . . .

Troops crowding into the town everywhere, jostling unit to unit, and spilling over into the surrounding desert. Eager inquiries after the folk at home: "Are they in good heart? Tell them we shall be home soon." The spirit of these men is infectious. I try to see too many of them and my driver loses his way. It is long after dark before I arrive at the headquarters of Lieutenant-General Horrocks, commanding 10th Corps and the Tripoli Base. The distinguished soldier looks tired and ill, but not too tired to give thanks for ENSA. No need to linger here: all is well in Tripoli. And now Malta!

Identity Disc . . .

The reception clerk at the Hotel Aletti was a British sergeant, unaccustomed to the smooth requirements of the position. He was not at the reception desk when Pouishnoff was escorted to the hotel. The following day it became necessary to change the virtuoso's room. The ENSA office told the sergeant over the telephone to notify Pouishnoff when he returned to the hotel.

A distinguished white-haired civilian approached the desk shortly afterwards.

"Pushin-off?" asked the sergeant abruptly.

"Certainly not," said an irate civil servant. "I shall not be pushin' off, as you so politely term it, until the morning."

6

'Knights of Malta'

Once more skimming the blue Mediterranean, in a Hudson this time. I am in the nose of the machine, with nothing between me and the sea but a few metal struts and a round dome of Perspex. There is a brown smudge on the horizon. We are approaching the island. The pilot gains height in order to prepare for landing. Beneath us lies Malta, a chromatic study in browns and yellows, ringed blue and white by the sea. We come down so rapidly that I expect to be flung like a sack of potatoes out of the machine's nose at any moment. So this is Malta, island of medieval fortitude!

The Governor and Commander-in-Chief, Field-Marshal Lord Gort, seems little older than when I had first met him in France, more worn perhaps, but as courteous and humourless as ever.

As we drive round the island in the midday shimmer, looking for sites for a garrison theatre—to take over locally owned buildings would arouse too much hostility, says Lord Gort; he would prefer not—the bomb damage does not look severe. In the Manoel Theatre the civilian owner charges the troops 2s. 6d. for out-of-date film programmes, brought in by submarine or by aircraft. Something wrong here. Now that things are easier ENSA should be able to do better. Ah! Here is an open-air skating-rink which the R.E.'s undertake to convert into a theatre with a temporary stage at one end.

The Navy has stowed itself away in homely fashion, as sailors are wont to do—only underground. Tomatoes and lettuce and marrows growing lush and defiant in ammunition boxes; and pigsties, too, housed in the ruins of an underground canteen. There is more joy in Valetta Harbour over one first prize gained for a sow in litter than over a whole squadron of night bombers chased away in the darkness. Meanwhile Vice-Admiral Power, commanding the Naval Base, strides restlessly up and down his office, equipped like an Admiral's cabin, chafing to get back to his Second Cruiser Squadron.

Among the Spitfire squadrons and on the gun sites there is no vociferous welcome for the promises I make. These men are stripped bare for the fight: "If it happens, it happens; that's all." Things are taken in their stride.

At lunch with the A.O.C., Air Vice-Marshal Keith Park, known to his staff as "old Battle of Britain," an arrow of a man with a gift for the terse phrase, news comes in that a Spitfire returning from patrol has crashed in one of the little fields enclosed by stone walls that remind one of Derbyshire. "Umm!" says "Battle of Britain," "no future in forced landings in this place. Pass the mustard, will you?"

At the afternoon conference with the new Garrison Entertainment Committee, under the chairmanship of Brigadier de la Bere, every one is quietly helpful and co-operative. More cinema projectors, a regular supply of better films and seven more hours a week of recorded programmes (they are already transmitting fourteen hours) are promised. Then a last meeting with the Governor, lonely and depressed, chafing at inaction, before a drive round the Island as the sun goes down. The pale primrose light suffuses even the commonplace with indescribable beauty. We leave Malta, grimly earning its George Cross, and are over the Mediterranean once more, travelling by R.A.F. Transport Command to Cairo. In very little time a smudge of brown mist appears on the horizon. We cross the coastline of Africa once more, and come down at El Adem in the heart of the Western Desert. Sand, sand, blowing in one's eyes and ears and down one's throat: the heat is intense. I stumble against a half-buried steel helmet. It is German. I look round, startled. We are making our way through a little patch of wooden crosses, some erect, some lying flat: German graves—men hastily buried, maybe at the height of Montgomery's battle with Rommel. I want to turn aside, but my companions straggle on, their eyes fixed upon a large marquee with a piece of canvas with the familiar NAAFI lettering flapping in front of it. No one despises the excessively sweet chlorinated tea. The desert is a great leveller of taste where drink is concerned.

Refuelled, and heading east for Cairo.

The afternoon advances, the temperature begins to drop; the aeroplane goes rocketing up and down, over and through the air pockets. One learns to share things in the air in war-time, including one's neighbour's lap. As the great ball of sun sinks in the smoky red distance the pilot turns and nods to starboard. The Pyramids! The first glance is disappointing, but then nothing looks much from the air. So this is Egypt! The poltergeist slips from my grasp, and I have butterflies in my stomach as the aircraft slowly circles and drops on to the tarmac.

What shall I find here? The long neglect will bear a harvest of trouble; that is only to be expected. Besides, we have been given frequent warnings. For instance, that farewell lunch with Lord May before I left England, when he had put his finger down the side of his nose, winked and said, "Better keep close to the R.A.F.; they'll see you through." Just that—no more—then shut up like a clam.

Anyway, we've woven a strong fabric of co-ordination in spite of the War House. Newman's efforts won't have begun to tell yet. Hope Haygarth is getting the military side in order. He hampers himself by his strange longing for a military hierarchy with theatrical acolytes. Impossible combination in the circumstances. Anyway, we've made him a lieutenant-colonel (what a struggle with NAAFI there was over that!) and given him the title of Overseas Senior Entertainments Officer (O.S.E.O.). What more does he want? . . . Ah! There he is!

The car had stopped with a jolt outside the ENSA office in the busy Sharia Kasr-el-Nil, and for the first time during the long drive into the city I took notice of the new sights and sounds and, above all, the smells of the Middle East. It was evening. Neon lights in red and blue and emerald green—advertising shops, cinemas and dance halls—were beginning to define the darkness. All the scented staleness of the daytime city, burning camel dung and petrol fumes, was rising into the violet sky; wisps of sharp, desert air were taking its place, as though the Angel of Mercy had flung open the windows of the *bordel* to gaze at the stars.

There was no time for more than the briefest survey of the political arena that I was to enter on the morrow. I was expected at Air House. Air Marshal Sir William Sholto Douglas[1] (A.O.C.-in-C., Middle East) had invited me to stay with him. Remembering Lord May's advice, I had accepted with alacrity. Sholto's cheerful welcome and strong good humour minimized the anxieties. Here was a place of friendly understanding where the professional 'empire-builders' did not seem to fit in. Of all the official residences at which I was privileged to stay during the war I think I was happiest there.

[1] Now Lord Douglas of Kirtleside.

By permission of the proprietors of "Punch"

CHAPTER TWENTY-SIX

DUSTY ARENA

1

Written in Sand

UNDER the jacaranda-trees in full bloom that border the roads near Air House, crossing the iron bridge that spans Old Nile—the fashionable Gezira Club round the river's bend to the right—gazing at the heterogeneous life of the streets, dust, smells, flies, honking motor-cars, shabby tramcars grinding and wheezing under the human freight that clings to them like greenfly to the stem—a daily swarming of the beehive before the sun is fully up—breathing the same tired air that whispers in the reeds of Upper Nile, blows round the pillars of ancient temples and wafts scented dust and filth over the palm trees in the Ezbekiah Gardens: my morning walk was no preparation for all the thrusting anxieties in the ENSA office, flowered by the hot sun and blown to seedless triviality by the whirring electric fans. Against such a background it was difficult to preserve a sense of urgency about our place in the war effort, for theatrical production is normally a thing of lamplight, darkened streets and evening's ease.

When Rex Newman arrived in Cairo at the beginning of 1943 the back-log of lost opportunity in the Middle East was still formidable. A meagre staff, trained to passive acceptance of shortage as the first working rule of a quiet life, were no match for artistes to whom the attractions of Cairo appeared superior to the call of the desert. Cut off from home and compelled to stay far beyond the term of their original engagements, those so inclined were soon sucked into the vortex of café idleness: ices and cream buns at Groppi's, entrance cards for the Gezira Club, cocktail bars and other allurements. Strange rheums and fevers would attack these people when they were booked for a tour of Ismailia and Suez (known as the Punishment Zone), but never so fiercely as to prevent their attendance at the office on Saturday mornings to draw their pay. To mitigate the recurrent staleness, artistes were later given shorter contracts, but for the hard core of confirmed idlers the application of a kind of 'Pride's Purge' remained the only cure. Another black spot was Baghdad, where later Newman's broom, sweeping clean, was to drive out of hidden corners performers who had been there for as long as two years.

Previous to Newman's arrival artistes had received little encouragement or understanding from the military personnel sent out to look after them. His influence quickly restored their morale. His method was to pick out the adventurous members of a party and tease them with blandishments.

"Very nice company going to East Africa, my dear. Lovely climate. Brand new." ("Brand new" meant that it was new to ENSA.)

"I want to go home."

"Opening up in India. Brand new there, too," persists Rex.

"Don't think I'd better go to India."

"Well, come to Italy. It's July now. The troops will love you there."

"I dried up in my second number last night. I'm tired out."

"Go to Cyprus, then. Absolute rest-cure."

The Thespian dove, surrendering to the wiles of the managerial serpent, packs her bag for Cyprus, where the troops are so hungry for entertainment that she is forced to give them three hearty meals a day.

Rex appeared quite unaffected by his surroundings, quite unashamedly British in his single-minded purpose to do the job and then go home. As he told me his story on that first morning, brightening the recital with his sharp wit, I could not help wondering what would have happened in 1939 if we had adopted the Seymour Hicks suggestion of making Paris our headquarters.

Each succeeding day of my visit brought me to a clearer realization of how the pendulum of our efforts must inevitably swing farther and farther away from entertainment at home. I cordially approved of Newman's plans for dealing with the changing situation. As a first step, he proposed to fly home to use his personal influence with the stars and their managers to persuade them to come out. For garrison theatre we were renting the Ritz cinema, which at that time had a rather unsavoury reputation; but this was only a temporary measure. A night-club, known as the Printania, had been purchased, and was now being gutted and rebuilt as the ENSA Garrison Theatre. Here Newman proposed to stage a series of plays of all kinds (musical and dramatic) and to give regular Sunday concerts, a move that was in accord with the general trend, for the demand for good music, which had reached a shout at home, was now being reiterated overseas. A Middle East Advisory Music Council had been formed, and Lance Dossor sent out as music adviser. A Cairo Symphony Orchestra was on the way, made up largely of R.A.F. personnel, under the baton of Squadron-Leader Hugo Rignold, a development owing much to the encouragement of Group-Captain Stubbs, Director of R.A.F. Welfare.

Contemplating these plans and the invaluable experience they would provide for the Second Front, our major task of the future, I felt profoundly relieved that Newman was installed in such a key position. It was well, too, that I was able to announce some of his plans at my first Press conference held at Shepheard's Hotel, for the atmosphere was decidedly hostile. Asked why I had not come out sooner, I had to take evasive action, and replied that it was a long story. This did not sound very convincing.

◇◇◇

Marching Orders . . .

Rex had a sharp wit for the bone-idle. One comedian so got on his nerves with the number and variety of his ailments that Rex sent for him one day and told him he and his party would be sent to Khartoum on the morrow.

"But you can't send me there, Rex," the comedian protested. "It's a hell of a place. Why, they tell me it's 120 in the shade!"

"Don't worry, old boy," said Newman shortly, "there's no shade there at all."

2

Stars in their Courses

Apart from Delysia and a small group (including among others Edith Evans, Jeanne de Casalis, John Gielgud and Michael Wilding) who had managed to get as far as Gibraltar—a visit which made no impact on the fighting troops—stars had been conspicuously absent, owing mainly to the restrictions upon all forms of civilian travel. The expeditious way of reaching the troops was of course by air, but even requests from commanders-in-chief for visits from famous personalities had been set aside up to now by officials in Whitehall who either could not or would not see any justification for air travel. The alternative route by sea round the Cape had been known to take as long as thirteen weeks. The time which the stars could give to ENSA was limited, and they naturally objected to spending the greater part of it at sea. As for those working under the 'lease-lend' system, their period of service was so short that they must either be flown out or stay at home.

Thus, the lack of air transport became the chief excuse for the reluctance of the stars to join ENSA in the Middle East. There were other excuses, too. A well-known actress was unable to go because her "nanny had given notice," an absurdity that was surpassed when an established West End star refused to go out because he "had no one to look after his dog."

However, a visit had just begun that was to raise the temperature of our entertainment service throughout the Mediterranean Basin. This was the group of stars assembled by 'Binkie' Beaumont under the title of 'Spring Party,' including Beatrice Lillie, Vivien Leigh, Dorothy Dickson, Leslie Henson, Cyril Baker and Richard Haydn: a positive galaxy. By the time I reached Cairo they had already played Gibraltar with enormous success, and were now in North Africa.

The routing of the party was immensely difficult, for they were wanted everywhere at once. It was not so much the intrinsic merit of the performances. (Vivien Leigh, anxious though she was to visit the troops, had modestly protested that she was no good as a concert turn: she could only recite; this 'Binkie' countered by declaring that it did not matter, as the men would appreciate her beauty in any case. Both were right.) It was the fact that they were the first British stars to visit the troops after their victory. Yet they had been so long a-coming that when Leslie Henson opened the show in Tripoli with the time-honoured remark of all clowns: "Well, here we are," a disgruntled voice at the back shouted, "Bit late, aren't yer?"

While they were playing in Tunis, King George VI arrived unexpectedly to inspect the troops. He stayed at the famous villa at Hammamet, whence a command was issued for 'Spring Party' to come on after the performance at the Garrison Theatre (Madame Vernon still in charge) to entertain the distinguished company that had been dining with His Majesty.

This was ENSA's first and only Royal Command performance overseas. I would have preferred one of the small companies that had borne the burden of work since El Alamein to receive the honour, but at least Leslie Henson was a member of the party, and already his cheerful croak had been heard up and down Britain from Scapa to Plymouth, and was to reverberate along the shores of the Mediterranean and as far east as Singapore. Madame Vernon, dressed in a peculiar coat and skirt, made of French officer's khaki, and still wearing her officer's boots, went with the party, eating her dinner on the way, an enormous bully-beef sandwich, wrapped in a copy of the Army newspaper, *Union Jack*.

The King sat in the centre of a circle of officers on the upper terrace, and blue-clad R.A.F. filled in the background; before them the white marble courtyard for a stage, lighted by spotlights hidden among the ornamental shrubs; overhead the stars, a new moon, and a lone fighter circling the sky on the look-out for sneak enemy aircraft.

After the performance the artistes were presented to His Majesty by Leslie Henson, Madame Vernon self-consciously keeping out of the way. But when the King heard of her devoted energies he asked for her to be presented. Afterwards she wrote:

> I put out my cigarette and clumped down the length of the verandah. "Why did you put out your cigarette?" said the King, smiling. "Have another?" His Majesty then asked me to tell him about ENSA in Tunisia. I forgot the absurdity of my costume and the size of my shoes in telling him how, since the 15th May to this June night, ENSA had entertained 400,000 men from Bizerta to Sfax.

The stars went everywhere by air (thanks to the co-operation of Air Chief Marshal Tedder), ranging from Gibraltar, along the North African coast to Cairo, Ismailia and Suez, and back again to Gibraltar on the way home.

The rough flights over the desert tried the nerves of some of the party. It was due mainly to 'Binkie's' tact, to Leslie's humorous grumbles (which took the sting out of every catastrophe) and, above all, to Beatrice Lillie's witticisms that the displays of temperament were not more frequent. Bee's wit is as light and inconsequent as a feather duster. What matter if a feather here and there has a razor's edge to it?

En route for Tripoli, the port engine of the Dakota began to splutter and finally gave out altogether. One of the girls became hysterical:

"This is frightful. What will happen if we crash?" she cried.

"Two minutes' silence in the Ivy, dear," remarked Bee with admirable calm.

Upon another occasion one of the girls was criticizing another member of the company:

"You can't tell X anything," she declared, "she's just a broadcasting station."

"A whole blue network, dear," responded Bee.

After Tripoli the company was due in Malta; but at the last minute the Governor cancelled the visit for Security reasons. The time saved proved a godsend to the commandos already embarked in ships at Alexandria, aptly described by the Area Commander as "waiting in the dentist's chair." However, the stars were only extricated from Tripoli with difficulty. General Montgomery, wanting to commandeer the extra time, sent me a politely worded request which I, backed up by General Maitland Wilson, as politely refused.

The arrival of the galaxy in Cairo was a wonderful opportunity for advertising the fact that ENSA meant business at last, and I did not intend to let it go by. We organized a buffet supper-party in the roof restaurant of the Mahommed Ali Club (the resort of Egyptians of the highest rank and famous for its cuisine), attended by the British Ambassador, Lord Killearn, the Minister of State, Lord Moyne, the Commanders-in-Chief of the three Services and members of the Egyptian Government. The official reception at the British Embassy had to be cancelled at the last minute because a child was born to Lady Killearn the day the company was due.

The party was timed for nine o'clock, three hours after the special Dakota carrying the artistes was due to touch down. When nine o'clock came I was told the aircraft might be half an hour late! Ten o'clock came, ten-thirty, eleven o'clock—still no sign of them. Was ENSA about to fail once again, and in front of so much distinction? I felt sick at the thought. The effort to sustain conversation among the great ones was exhausting. By this time many cocktails had been consumed and most of the hors d'œuvres; the hungry glances at the laden buffets, which, so far, none had dared to touch, grew longer and longer. It was nearly half-past eleven before the company arrived, tired, but happy in the memory of the al fresco concert they had given at El Adem on the way—the cause of their late arrival!

'Spring Party' opened the ball in stately measure. After Newman's return home others were to follow, until the floor was close-packed with performers to every tune and tempo. Before that, jolly old Will Fyffe had arrived in Tripoli in his kilt and tam o'shanter, singing *I belong to Glasgie* to the boys of the 51st Division on the night before they embarked for Sicily. Then, *en route* for Cairo, his aircraft crashed, and he was compelled to pass the night in the desert under the shelter of its undamaged wing. He arrived exhausted, but eager to tell his story to every kilted Tommy he met on the street. A very gallant old man.

Later came George Formby with an assortment of ukeleles, encouraged and restrained alternately by the redoubtable Beryl. . . . Companies of stars, dramatic and musical, followed in the wake of individuals, and, finally, popular band-leaders with full panoply of brass and string. . . . Before I left Cairo it was satisfactory to observe the first trickles of this eventual stream coming through the pipeline we had begun to lay down even before the reopening of the Mediterranean.

3

A Concourse of Harps

The evenings at Air House were delightful. The cheerfulness of our host, the absence of ceremony, and the interesting personalities who came and went—men like the Earl of Bandon, Alec Coryton, Harry Broadhurst, the Atcherley twins, and many more—created an atmosphere of verve and high spirits that was in sparkling contrast to the carping critics at G.H.Q., sitting ensconced in a great block of flats behind a barricade of barbed wire.

Soon after my arrival I was privileged to be a guest at a dinner given to Lord Trenchard on his way through to India. It was fascinating to watch the faces of the distinguished airmen as they sat respectfully silent round the dining-table, listening to the words of the gospel according to the R.A.F., expounded in that deep, booming voice that none would dare to contradict.

Another guest was Lord Moyne, newly arrived to take over as Minister of State from Mr R. G. Casey. He appeared greatly concerned at the inadequate presentation of British views over the air. Although I was careful to explain that we were responsible solely for our own recorded programme service, he insisted that my presence in Cairo was an excellent opportunity for a general get-together of all concerned with broadcasting. Gradually I found myself drawn into a major process of reorganization.

Examination revealed a chaotic state of affairs. The original agreement between Egyptian State Broadcasting and the Military Authorities provided for an hour's programme each day—unfortunately, at a time when the majority of the troops were busy with military duties. This was later supplemented by broadcasting an additional five or six hours daily on an alternative wavelength, one which the men could not pick up on their sets. The actual transmissions were supervised by officers of the Middle East Broadcasting Unit (M.E.B.U.), some of whom had had previous theatrical experience and rather fancied themselves as radio producers. They preferred to organize their own programmes, using local talent, rather than to make use of visiting ENSA artistes or the recorded programme service. Thus, plenty of harps were being played, but their vigorous twanging was inaudible to the majority of the soldier-listeners, and the tunes were often conflicting; no one had bothered to set the key in which the whole symphony was to be played. Dissatisfaction was general and loudly expressed.

Arising out of my talks with Lord Moyne, the G.S.O. I in charge of Public Relations (Lieutenant-Colonel Chisholm) invited ENSA to take general charge of the Forces Programme; but news and propaganda were integral parts of the service, and these were not our concern. So between us we evolved a plan which in essence was this: at the head, a Middle East Broadcasting Co-ordination Board, three members of which would be the programme planners, representing the three Departments responsible, namely, the Ministry of Information for news, Army Public Relations for Propaganda and ENSA for Entertainment; M.E.B.U. to be responsible for the actual transmissions; the hours of transmission to be altered to suit the listening-time of the troops, an obvious reform that I secured after talks with Ferguson of E.S.B. and with the Postmaster-General, Palestine.

The whole scheme was accepted with considerable relief by the authorities. With regard to ENSA's share in it, I gave instructions for a Broadcasting Executive to be formed on the London model, to which the ENSA officer i/c each Area would furnish monthly reports on the number of broadcasting hours contributed each week, the contents of the programmes (whether live or recorded) and the general listener reaction. At the same time I took the distribution of O.R.B.S. records out of the hands of Army Welfare and made it the responsibility of our own staff, who were directed to see that the correct number of recorded programmes was delivered to M.E.B.U. at each station.

After my return home Nicolls of the B.B.C. found me a good radio research man who was commissioned and sent out to report and advise. The verbatim reports of this officer's talks with the troops were illuminating:

"What stations do you listen in to?"

"London, of course, unless there's something wrong with the set."

Another remark: "If London doesn't come through all right, or the programme is dull, we fiddle with the set until something cheerful turns up, usually Germany. Their stations are much more powerful than the B.B.C." (It was thus that *Lili Marlene* achieved its popularity with the Eighth Army.)

Listening under good conditions, *i.e.*, in a canteen or barrack-room, meant that the will of the majority prevailed, and so classical music was usually switched off, despite individual protests. Facetious references to marital infidelity and sudden increases in the birth-rate unhappily linked in the men's minds with the swarms of American, Canadian and other forces on leave in Britain were sombrely resented. The retransmission of the more popular B.B.C. programmes was of little use in the main concentration areas, because the troops had heard the originals; besides, it fostered the idea that ours was a second-best service.

Stephen Williams' idea of exchanging messages between the men and their families over the air formed the basis of a special feature which Peter Haddon built up under the title of 'Cairo Calling.' The programme became so successful that Peter preferred to remain with it until the end of the war instead of taking general charge of ENSA broadcasting in the Middle East.

'Cairo Calling' was broadcast by the B.B.C. from August 1940 until August 1945. During that time Haddon recorded and introduced over 250 programmes, sending home the best part of 12,000 messages. These were recorded on aluminium discs, which were flown to Cairo and thence to London. Bumping his way in and out of the Western Desert, climbing the companionways of Naval ships, greeting lonely aircraftmen, always with a recording machine tucked under his arm, so to speak, and a Cyrano-like panache for compassionate stories, Peter did a great service in providing personal interest for the troops at a time when correspondence with the folks at home was subject to prolonged interruption. It was not his fault if the men were disgruntled when they failed to hear the return messages intended for them.

The absence of variety in the messages worried Haddon a good deal. On one occasion during the Alamein offensive, scenting the possibility of fresh interest, he took his recording machine to an advanced dressing-station where three wounded men lay side by side, waiting to be sent back to base hospital. Alas! Their messages were almost identical. "Dear mum and dad, I hope this finds you in the pink as it leaves me at present. Give my love to everyone at 42 and 53 and The Nest. Your loving son." In Baghdad he did, however, secure one amusing variation: "Dear mum, I have not seen the Magic Carpet yet, but I have seen every one of the forty thieves."

During the Blitz he was approached by a soldier in Palestine, wanting to send an urgent message.

"Any special reason?" demanded Haddon.

"Well, sir, I want to find out what's 'appening. My wife says in her letter it was ever such a lovely funeral, but I'm blessed if I know oo's dead."

Bedtime Story . . .

Entertainment for the troops in Irak and Iran ('Paiforce') was cancelled after the first 'hot weather' season on the instructions of the G.O.C., because of the large number of heat casualties among the artistes. But when the stars began to arrive in the Middle East the 'Paiforce' men complained bitterly of neglect. Hearing of this, Joyce Grenfell very gallantly offered to fly out there and give a series of concerts to the sick and wounded. The opening performance of her tour was given in the main ward of the largest military hospital in the Command. It was thronged with stretcher cases. She was introduced by the A.D.M.S., who concluded his references to the work she had already done at home by saying, "And now this wonderful lady has come all the way to Baghdad just to entertain you men in bed."

4

"More Matter for a May Morning"

When I arrived in Cairo two formidable documents were demanding attention in the military branch of our headquarters, just across the corridor from Newman's office. Both papers blandly disregarded the taproot of ENSA authority, namely, the Entertainments Board; both indicated that, although Army Welfare had abandoned its attempts to interfere with ENSA at home, considerable 'empires' were in the making overseas.

The Army was now running its own mobile cinemas at home under a new organization known as the Army Kinema Service (A.K.S.). A report recently submitted by a young officer who had been sent overseas to take a peep at our set-up contained two alternative proposals: one, to create an Army film service abroad side by side with our own; the other to take over the entire ENSA film organization. But Q.M.G./War Office had decided that no action should be taken until G.H.Q., Middle East, had ascertained my views: this was Document Number One.

Document Number Two was a draft order, virtually handing over the administration of *all* entertainment in the Middle East to Army Welfare, our organization to become a sort of delivery service. The Government Report made no specific reference to overseas, but its general implication by which the actions of all concerned had hitherto been guided was that it was to be a case of "*status quo ante* Dunkirk." The proposals contained in these two documents implied otherwise.

Pondering the cinema situation as I watched three or four hundred men, far out in the Western Desert, enjoying a Technicolour film called *Cover Girl*, featuring Rita Hayworth, then having its pre-release run in the West End of London, I came to the conclusion that the War Office might duplicate our progress; it could not hope to exceed it. Projection equipment was coming in steadily through the Ministry of Supply Committee. Talks with Shafto had been opened, as Lord May had instructed me, although, now that our former civilian general manager had 'crossed the floor of the House,' negotiation had become difficult. Eventually I sent a cable to the Treasury, outlining satisfactory terms, to which Lord May replied that negotiations must be suspended for the time being. This was reasonable enough, for, if the War Office were going to take over the job, there was no point in NAAFI buying the cinemas for us; it might just as well keep its money in its pocket. . . . Within a fortnight of my arrival I had submitted a memorandum to G.H.Q., Middle East, which was accepted out of hand.

As for Document Number Two, I anticipated little difficulty in settling that matter with my old ally of the B.E.F. days, Lieutenant-General Lindsell, now i/c Administration, M.E.F. But at my first interview with him the old confidence between us, often expressed in the past by a tone of cheerful raillery, was gone. ENSA was now a recalcitrant organization.

"Well, you've got here at last," said Lindsell, as we shook hands. That's a quick one, I thought, remembering that he had sent me a cable via the War Office on February 3, saying that my presence was not required, and followed it by another on February 20 to the effect that he had changed his mind: "I hope you're going to co-operate," Lindsell went on.

"Of course, General," I replied cheerfully, not yet appreciating the significance of the changed atmosphere. "I'm always out to help, you know that."

"Splendid!" said Lindsell, indicating a copy of Document Two lying on his desk. "Then I propose to publish this order right away. Any objections?"

"I should like an opportunity of commenting on it first."

"Oh, certainly," said the General, with an air of pained surprise. "I held it up because I heard you were coming, but I hope you won't take long."

5

Travelogue

The daily trivialities at Shepheard's left me bored and restless: the endless gossip before lunch and at cocktail time round the bar or on the terrace overlooking the street; the somnolence of the early afternoon, broken by the creaking wood floors of the passage-ways and the surreptitious opening and closing of bedroom doors; and then the purple night made hideous by the screaming mechanization of American voices from the open-air cinema in the Ezbekiah Gardens. In the phantasmagoria of my dreams I

POTATO-PEELING TO MUSIC—
IN BURMA

THE
FORMBY
FAMILY
IN THE
ARAKAN

GENERAL PRACTITIONER: CEYLON
(My camera could not resist this one.)

368

ON THE
ROAD TO
MANDA-
LAY: AN
IMPROMPTU
AT A
FORWARD
AIR-STRIP

THE SACK OF BERLIN

(These pictures were
taken by myself.)

HARVESTING THE
DEAD OUTSIDE
HITLER'S BUNKER

INSIDE THE
CHANCELLERY

BLACK MARKET
IN THE
UNTER DEN
LINDEN

planned a new sort of musical comedy, with an opening chorus of staff
officers waving fly-whisks and drinking pink gins.

The time had come to inspect the outer marches of our responsibility. I
left Cairo on July 1 in the flying-boat *Corsair* for Jerusalem, taking with
me Major Eric Dunstan, who belonged to one of those mysterious war-
time branches of Military Intelligence wherein social contacts were the
cards of membership and leave to pursue private lines of inquiry appeared
to be unlimited. Eric had written to us in London, caustically inquiring
whether the rumour that I was about to visit Cairo were really true, and
inviting me to the villa at Maada which he shared with Geoffrey Amherst,[1]
then holding a staff appointment at R.A.F. Headquarters. Through the
various stages of Eric's career, as he became in turn private secretary to
Gordon Selfridge, B.B.C. announcer and film critic for the *Star*, I had
always admired his ability to combine an easy efficiency with a disarming
dilettantism. So during that first lunch I invited him to take charge of our
affairs in India. The present journey was to enable him to see something
of ENSA at work before taking up his new appointment.

The flying-boat came down on the Dead Sea with an almighty splash.
Major Fairfax was waiting for us with a full schedule of engagements,
which he insisted must begin with an initiatory baptism in that warm
brine, which makes bathing a joke and a medicinal exercise in one. It was
impossible not to feel exhilarated by the hot, dry wind that had burnt the
waving grasses bordering the shore to palest gold and yet could not quite
conceal its threat of bitter cold. The harshness and cruelty of so many of
the Jewish stories seemed justified in the first impact of that stony land.

The brevity of the notes in my diary bears witness to the strenuous day
we passed, as conference succeeded conference, complaint piled upon
complaint, and praise, that occasional flower, was plucked from some
half-forgotten military unit, astonished to find it had not been overlooked.
And the characters in those crowded scenes go jiggling past the memory,
like the figures in a child's 'wheel of life,' Victorian exponent of the first
principle of cinematography. Eric seemed always to be at my elbow,
waiting patiently for military distractions to cease so that he might show
me the Grand Mosque in Jerusalem, the *suks* of Aleppo, or what other
sights might be to hand.

First a visit to the A.O.C.-in-C. at the airport, where, in exchange for
promises of more shows for the R.A.F., we secured air-lifts for the rest
of our short tour; then to Government House, Jerusalem, where Sir
Harold MacMichael showed me the wonderful rock gardens planted by
the first High Commissioner and brought to present beauty under his

[1] Earl Amherst.

2A

regardful eye; next visits to the small but efficient production centre where Fairfax was reproducing and re-equipping Service parties before returning them to their units, and to the main rest camp at Nathaniya accommodating 5000 troops. This camp had been wired for rediffusion by one of our staff sergeants; our recorded programmes were played daily, and all camp orders and news broadcast by the same means, a service greatly appreciated by the authorities at H.Q. Palestine Base.

Next, to Haifa, looking like some vast ill-kept petrol station: Lieutenant-General Holmes, C.-in-C. Ninth Army, set to guard the western approaches to Irak and Iran against the possibility of German invasion, was not interested in entertainment; he was satisfied to leave such matters to his Welfare staff. Already one could sniff the air of disgruntlement that follows the decline of a fighting force into an army of occupation.

On to Syria. It was nearly dark when we reached the hotel in Beirut where we were to stay. A group of officers was waiting to see me. We sat down in a corner of the lounge and ordered coffee. Eric and I were tired and hungry, and he began to fidget, as I ran rapidly over the inquiries I wished to make. On the subject of broadcasting G.H.Q. had authorized me to call attention to the undesirability of employing women to read the war news. Before I had time to elaborate the point an officer's effeminate voice interrupted me from the shadows: "Oh, my dear, you needn't worry about that here. I do it all myself."

Early the following morning Eric took me for a swim at the French Officers' Club on the shore, one of the best natural pools I have ever seen. Next to Naval Headquarters, Captain Rutt-Kean, R.N., being in charge. I had first met him in 1940 in Londonderry, marching up and down his office, swinging a bunch of fresh pineapples like an Indian club, a present, so he explained, from one of his destroyer captains, while I sat, uncomfortably reminded of the rarity of such greengrocers' items in beleaguered Britain.

He insisted upon taking over as my guide, welcoming the opportunity of a break from routine and leaving Eric free for the afternoon. He drove me at breakneck speed to see the Highlands, thoughtfully distracting my attention round the hair-pin bends with a selection of the latest quarter-deck stories. We reached the snowline in what seemed less than the hour: fantastic change from the Riviera atmosphere of the town below. I longed for more time to explore this beautiful hinterland and the ruined strongholds of the Assassin country. Half-way down we stopped at a charming café on the corner of a village square where we drank Syrian wine and smoked Turkish cigarettes. Then to the best wine-shop in Beirut to purchase a case of the wine for the Air Marshal's mess in Cairo.

Pleasant to meet Mary Borden[1] again, at dinner, during which both she and her husband pressed for some entertainment for the French troops in the area. The loyalty of these men, as between Vichy and de Gaulle, had been somewhat divided recently, to say the least. However, I agreed to help, having in mind the promise I had made to Josephine Baker. (In due course she gave a series of special performances to the French troops there in company with one of the ENSA parties.)

Next to Aleppo, farthest outpost of our troops, flying too high over the Lebanon to see much of that monument to Christian valour facing an infidel world, le Krak des Chevaliers. The authorities were grateful for what we had already sent and pleased at the promise of more for men described as "definitely browned off." We stayed the night in the NAAFI Officers' Club, a good building in which a delightful meal was served. After dinner, off in the dusty dark to see a small ENSA party, called 'Between Ourselves,' at a place called Ryak: a company of talented people, Roma Milne, Hugh French, Marilyn Williams (now Marion Harris) and Norman Hackforth (fresh from a tour as accompanist for Noël Coward). There is a black mark in my diary against that performance: "one filthy joke-Out!!" Although I can no longer remember it, evidently it was one that the artistes had better have kept 'between themselves.' The next morning to the castle of Aleppo and the suks, the most picturesque of any that I had seen, renewing my longing for Samarkand, apex of romantic travel for me since Flecker's Hassan.

High in the clear air, returning via Lydda airport, where a cluster of officials of the Palestine Broadcasting Service reminded me of a promise to broadcast. I spent ten minutes of fluster while the microphones were set up in the ladies' cloakroom—rather unusual, but, as one of the officials airily explained, "it is the only quiet spot on the airfield; if any women want to use it they will just have to wait."

That was soon over. Now we are flying through the brief, smoky dusk to Cairo. No sign of a car anywhere on the airfield. In a few minutes it will be dark. Some urgent telephoning to the ENSA office, where an excited officer on duty protests that two cars have been sent.

"Why two?" I ask mildly.

"Well, sir," he explains, "that's in case one breaks down." Eric, unused to our transport vagaries, is inclined to be irritable. I let him take the first car that arrives, as he has arranged an urgent dinner party at his villa and cannot possibly keep Geoffrey Amherst waiting. A quarter of an hour later I follow him into the city, and hand over my case of Syrian wine to the

[1] Lady Spears, wife of Sir Edward Spears, First British Minister in Syria and Lebanon.

mess waiter at Air House. The Air Marshal gives me a cheery greeting, adding, as his P.A. hands me a cocktail, "By the way, a letter has just come for you from G.H.Q., marked urgent." I open it. It is a peremptory summons to appear before General Lindsell in his office on the following afternoon at 1800 hours. Evidently the climax to our recent discussion is about to be reached.

In an effort to placate the Army without nullifying our mandate I had twice drawn up revised drafts of Lindsell's entertainment orders, the second incorporating a suggestion made by the Commander-in-Chief (General Sir Maitland Wilson) after discussion with Sholto Douglas. As I had been given to understand that the second draft was acceptable I gave myself up to the pleasures of a cheery evening. Twenty-four hours later I was confronted by an extremely angry general who declared that I had let him down, an accusation that I was quite unable to understand, unless he meant by it to express his resentment at the support of the Navy and the R.A.F. for my views and the embarrassed neutrality of his own C.-in-C.

General Lindsell either could not or would not accept my view of our mandate. Equally, I could see no reason to recede from the position I had taken up. Principles were fully established, and I was impatient of further intrigue. There was much to be said for the control of entertainment amenities by the Services themselves in peace-time—and matters have now been so arranged—but there was nothing at all to be said for a complete disruption of the existing arrangements in the middle of the war to satisfy the desire of certain persons to make imposing jobs for themselves.

As we talked I realized it would be folly to undertake enormously increased responsibilities in the Far East until I knew where we stood. I told the General I should not go on to India but return to London, where the matter must be fought out by the Entertainments Board. "Do as you think best," he replied; "I shall send the papers to the War Office. . . ." A silly, painful story.

<>< ><>

Reprimand . . .

In the autumn Noël Coward, recently returned from his tour abroad, asked me to lunch, as he wanted to have a chat about ENSA. Gladys Calthrop was the only other person present. I spent a surprising hour, for while I dissected the meat of an admirable cutlet from its surrounding tegument, Noël, with superior adroitness, dissected my various mistakes in the Middle East from the wrappings in which unfriendly rumour had swathed them. Warming to his subject, he accused me of ballooning about the countryside with too much energy and too little regard for the wishes of the Army Staff. Gladys observed my apparent docility with some surprise, not knowing that my mind was reconstructing the scene in terms of a nautical comedy in the Ian Hay manner: a wardroom youngster, lectured by a splenetic rear-admiral (George Grossmith type) for some roguery of the heart with his daughter, decides upon silence in the face of superior authority; yes, that would do.

"'OW MUCH FURTHER TO 'ELLFIRE CORNER?"
By permission of the proprietors of "Punch"

CHAPTER TWENTY-SEVEN

IN PREPARATION

1

General Call

MY first task on returning home was to orientate ENSA to its original purpose of following the fighting troops. Home entertainment was now upon such an enormous scale[1] that the Divisions at Drury Lane, struggling to meet their mounting totals of obligation, had come to regard the demands from overseas as little more than an additional irritation. But the years of military preparation were over. The climax of world conflict was looming over the horizon of history. Nothing less than a complete reversal of our order of thinking would meet the case.

We had to double and treble the number of artistes to go overseas at a time when the ranks of the profession had been ultimately depleted by the demands of military service and when those that remained were in constand demand for commercial entertainment. And we had somehow to do this without increasing too much our administrative staff, already overflowing into every nook and corner of Drury Lane and the various theatres and office blocks that we had taken over in the vicinity. . . . Our staff must be roused to further efforts.

So it was that on the morning of July 29 I found myself on the stage of Drury Lane, addressing the strangest audience ever assembled within its walls. Every nook in the auditorium was crowded, except such as were so bomb-damaged as to be unsafe for perching. Gazing at the sea of faces, it was impossible not to feel proud of the machine we had created. I told my eager audience stories of what I had seen and heard while I was away. But when I spoke of the time, not so far distant, when ENSA would be called upon to run up the flag of entertainment in the liberated capitals of Europe—in Rome, in Paris, Brussels, Vienna and Berlin, and all along the extended lines of march—there were incredulous smiles on

[1] By the autumn of 1943 the number of ENSA performances of all kinds given *each week* in Great Britain and Northern Ireland had risen to 3750.

many faces. There was an incredulous feeling in my own heart, too, for even while I was speaking uncertainty lurked in the background as to whether ENSA would be allowed to carry out its plans. The explosive element in the two documents I had tried to answer in Cairo might blow us clean out of the water. At the end of the meeting, as the younger members of the staff crowded round me with excited questioning, the senior officials who would bear the brunt of the new responsibility walked back to their offices, murmuring among themselves. Staff enthusiasm was all very well, but where were the artistes to come from? Against the background of national endurance and suffering how base appeared that excuse we all knew so well: "Well, of course I'd like to help, but I don't like ENSA." The measure of our success could be no greater than the sum total of enthusiasm which the profession as a whole put into the work.

August 1943. Pause for a moment in your reading while we half-mast the big ENSA flag high above the great, flat roof of Drury Lane, in happy recollection of Owen Nares, the sweet-natured, gently cynical *jeune premier*, last of the matinée idols.

Owen was on an ENSA tour, staying in Brecon and visiting the remote garrison theatres of Central Wales. On the Saturday afternoon before the Bank Holiday he went with Constance Cummings and other members of the company to the house where Mrs Siddons was born, now a local museum. As he listened to the guide's story of the connexion of the great tragédienne with the little market-town he was overcome by the heat, collapsed and died on the premises. He was fifty-four. When the news came through my mind went back to that first meeting at Leslie Henson's house in 1938, hearing again Owen's diffident promise of help at a time when many actors were only prepared to scoff. The promise had been fulfilled.

By this time I had instituted annual staff conferences, attended by all the regional supervisors and provincial staffs, as well as by the heads of Divisions, Sections and Branches from Drury Lane, and, at the opening sessions, by Regional Chairmen and members of the various Advisory Councils. The main purpose of these conferences was to smooth away any roughnesses that had developed in the running of the machine during the previous year and to explain future policies. They were notable arrays, filling the ballroom of the Waldorf Hotel to capacity.

The second was held in October 1943. In my opening address I foreshadowed the home reductions that would have to be made to meet overseas expansion. Half-hour 'Ensatainments' were no longer adequate to the changed psychological atmosphere; the number must be drastically reduced, and their places taken by the Symphony Concerts for War-workers scheme, already a huge success and to be extended in the coming winter. We must be on guard against the danger of becoming bogged down in a morass of local obligation. The fact that the Lord Mayor of London, wearing his robes and chain of office and attended by a posse of sheriffs, had visited Drury Lane, and that both the Lord Mayors of Birmingham and of Nottingham had sought our help in planning their 'Holidays at Home' schemes, must not blind us to where our first duty lay.

The conference atmosphere was confident and assured; but when super-visors stood up in their places to proclaim their achievements I retorted brusquely that our objective now was overseas; work and more work was the order of the day for all. No doubt this sounded exacting, but we were living in exacting times. Fortunately my acerbity was softened by the arrival of Alfred Lunt and Lynn Fontanne, come to bring the conference fraternal greetings (I believe that is the usual phrase) from the artistes of America, and to give details of a series of special Sunday evening invita-tion performances for both British and American troops which they were proposing to give during their forthcoming tour of the provinces.

Boat Stations . . .

The first fruits of our recruiting drive were embarked in a Dutch ship, the s.s. *Marnix Van St Aldegonde*, sailing in the first convoy to pass through the Strait of Gibraltar during daylight since the reopening of the Medi-terranean. She was carrying troops and a contingent of South African nurses, in addition to 123 ENSA artistes. This formidable reinforcement of talent included several concert parties and variety acts, a well-known dance-band and numerous actors and actresses *en route* for the production centre in Cairo. They had with them all the musical instruments, band parts, costumes and theatrical equipment necessary for a prolonged stay in the Middle East.

November 6, 1943: time, 6.30 P.M. The artistes were assembled in the lounge for dinner, one comedian boasting: "We'll show those ruddy Germans and 'Eye-ties' who's boss in the Mediterranean." Crash! Then a crunching sound, deep in the bowels of the ship, followed by an explo-sion. The lights went out and the alarm bells rang for 'boat stations.' The ship was listing heavily to starboard. Fortunately all the lifeboats were not destroyed. The women were taken off and put on board an escorting destroyer. The troops and the actors remained. The professional comedians began to abandon their jokes; the amateurs among the troops took over. By 11 P.M. the torpedoed ship had begun to settle by the stern. So the artistes spent the night tossing about in the remaining ship's boats; there were submarines in the area and all rescue craft had been ordered away. In the early dawn the destroyer reappeared, threw ropes to the tossing boats and drew them alongside. "Wait for the top of the swell, and then jump," yelled the petty officer. Not too easy for Leslie Julian Jones, the author-composer, suffering from lameness, who scattered sheaves of manuscript music prepared for the new musical shows as he did so. Maybe the crayfish and the red mullet would enjoy the opening choruses.

Twelve hours later, in a French Army camp outside Philippeville, temporarily occupied by British troops, the quartermaster's stores were raided for blankets to put on the stone floors; and there was a frantic search for soap and razor blades. In the morning the sight of so many English girls wandering about the camp in beaded evening frocks under the noonday glare must have astounded the Arabs.

Meanwhile, at home, the news editor of the Press Association had telephoned a report on the sinking to Jonah Barrington. At first we were told there were "few survivors," then that "some" had been saved. It was three days before we were told that all were safe, to the relief of those responsible for engaging them.

Back in Tunis, whither our castaways had been sent, American Transport Command pilots, nonchalant and obliging as ever, found compelling reasons for additional flights into Egypt, preferring cargoes of pretty girls to mail-bags and military stores. But it was several weeks before all the shipwrecked players reached Cairo, sans clothes, sans music, sans instruments, sans everything but their professional high spirits, until Madame Vernon presently arrived to make hay of an extravagant crop of compensation claims.

2

Disputation and Great Argument

The expansion of our foreign service would involve a drastic upward revision of the Treasury estimates, but I was in grave doubt how Lord May would react in the light of his cable to me about the Shafto cinemas and his evident intention to adopt the businessman's caution of waiting to see which way the cat was going to jump before committing himself.

But the time for sitting on the fence had passed. If he stayed too long in that position he was liable to find himself carried away in the bustle of preparation. And that is exactly what happened to him.

Ways of implementing the two documents that had confronted me in Cairo were now under examination at the War Office by one of the so-called 'working parties' that were soon to spread like a rash across the face of Reconstruction. There was plenty to show the way the wind was blowing in the increasing difficulty which our officers were meeting with in carrying out their instructions. Determined not to repeat the unreadiness of North Africa and remembering the success of our mobile columns in the chaotic last days in France, I had told Haygarth to get ready two of them to go into Sicily, with two more to follow when the invasion of Italy took place.

"Hadn't we better get the approval of G.H.Q.?"

"Get your columns ready first, and ask for approval afterwards," was my over-confident reply. I had learnt by this time that it was useless to keep schemes shivering on the brink of adoption while the temperature of the water was precisely ascertained. The only thing to do was to push them in, and hope they would swim.

We waited anxiously for news of the departure from Algiers of No. 1 column. Instead there came a spate of telegrams, telling us first that permission to land was being withheld,[1] then that living entertainment was not to be sent, next that the mobile cinemas and their staffs were to be handed over to the newly appointed A.K.S. staff, and, finally, a despairing telegram from Haygarth asking whether he himself was to be superseded. I replied that he was to hand over nothing, either of material or responsibility, until he received direct orders from London, and that there was no intention of superseding him; I concluded with the admonition to "adopt a policy of patience with firmness." This "patience with firmness" telegram was often referred to in ENSA circles afterwards with a certain sardonic humour.

Although the Chairman of NAAFI succeeded in obtaining permission for our columns to land in Sicily, matters could not be allowed to rest there. Our Public Relations Council had long since realized that lack of Government status was the root cause of the recurring interference. Earlier representations to the Lord President of the Council that all concerned should adhere to the terms of the Government Report having brought no result, they now began to press in the House of Commons for revision of the whole set-up. They wanted ENSA to be responsible to a fully constituted and active Entertainments Board, in its turn responsible to a Cabinet

[1] By direct wire from the War Office, we learned later.

Minister. These views, which I did nothing to discourage, came into public light in sudden fashion.

At the close of our second annual conference Sir John Shute gave a luncheon in the Pinafore Room of the Savoy Hotel to all the Regional Chairmen and senior officials at Drury Lane, at which he took everybody by surprise, including myself, by bluntly announcing that he intended to propose to Parliament the complete separation of ENSA from NAAFI. This announcement lighted a bonfire that raged throughout the remainder of the year, but unfortunately Shute had irons in several other political fires and was unable to give this one sufficient attention.

Meanwhile, Lancelot Royle, the Chairman of NAAFI, forced to take notice of the growing storm, was pondering various ways of calling ENSA to order. In his view the constant squabbling with the War Office was nullifying his efforts to improve the relations between his Corporation and the Service Departments, not hitherto noted for their cordiality. Yet he was resolutely opposed to the separation envisaged by Shute in his lunch-time indiscretion. The Chairman of the Entertainments Board should control the situation; if he were unable or reluctant to do so, then another must be appointed in his place.

At the beginning of 1944 Royle presented himself at Drury Lane, accompanied by the General Manager, and announced with a mixture of nervousness and determination that the Corporation found the situation intolerable and had resolved to end it. After consulting the Treasury and the Service Departments it had been decided that Lord May should give up the Chairmanship of the National Service Entertainments Board but remain Chairman of its Finance and Organization Committee. His place on the Board would be taken by Marshal of the R.A.F. Sir Edward Ellington, a distinguished officer who had at one time been Chief of the Air Staff. This officer would also become the NAAFI Director of Entertainments. The Corporation proposed to retain my services by appointing me as its technical adviser. Beyond remarking that I already held that appointment under a minute from the Lord President of the Council, and that theatrical management would be an abstruse subject for a Marshal of the R.A.F., I remained silent. The brief interview was conducted, as it were, upon ice, the words slipping away from their true meaning as though they wore skates. I was left to ponder the situation.

Some of my staunchest supporters, Sir Louis Sterling among them, urged me to resign. But, however tempting it might be to go back into the theatrical market-place where there were golden prizes to be won, the climax of our work, the return to Europe, lay immediately ahead. After much cogitation I decided to place myself unreservedly in the hands of the

Central Committee of ENSA. A series of meetings with representatives of the NAAFI Board followed at which my deputy, Alec Rea, fought the battle more strenuously, and certainly more indignantly, than ever I could have done. The following conditions were set to my acceptance of the ultimatum: Sir Edward Ellington was to be known as the Chairman of the N.S.E.B. only, my own position and responsibilities were to remain unaltered; ENSA was to be legally embodied (with a Provisional Council taking the place of the Central Committee), one of its members[1] being appointed by the Lord President to represent ENSA on the N.S.E.B. Sir Edward Ellington took up his appointment in April 1944, and in the following August ENSA was legally incorporated, its Articles of Association having been approved by the Treasury.

The Chairman of the Provisional Council was Sir Walter Monckton. Under the new dispensation, while Lord Tyrrell remained our titular president, we had Monckton to represent our views at the Treasury, where, hitherto, Maynard Keynes, representing CEMA, had had things all his own way. Grateful as I had been for the early support of Lord Tyrrell, that aged diplomat had proved quite unable to withstand the political pressures of the war at its height. He would sit, frail, thin and gentle at the head of the long table in the Conference Room, huddled in his overcoat and, whenever contentious items appeared on the agenda, would hurriedly excuse himself in order to view a film. His position as titular head of the British Board of Film Censors made the excuse plausible, although I doubted whether his intervention in the day-to-day affairs of the censors was really necessary. However, it did give us the opportunity of voting Lady Louis Mountbatten into the Chair, where she would conclude the day's business with charming dispatch.

Royle had 'saved' ENSA for NAAFI, and could now look forward with relief to the disciplining of myself by superior authority, but he failed to appreciate how the facts of the situation would impress themselves upon Ellington's logical mind. Throughout the whole period of our association my relations with the Air Marshal remained cordial. I cannot recall a single difference of opinion upon any matter of importance. One might say without offence that his behaviour was that of "an officer and a gentleman," a commonplace phrase of Victorian melodrama that raised a laugh when it turned up unexpectedly in one of the later plays of Galsworthy, and yet one which exactly expresses the regard I felt for my new Chairman.

His brusque tone to me at Board Meetings was a reflection of his desire to show that he had no intention of being unduly influenced by Drury

[1] This was the Right Hon. Lord Elton.

Lane. Yet where matters of principle or common sense were concerned he could be resolute. When a draft of that document dealing with the control of entertainment in the Middle East was submitted to him he curtly reminded the War Office that Welfare was a 'Service' just as much as ENSA was, and that it was contrary to military regulations for one Service to give orders to another.

Finally, the cinema argument was disposed of, although it was not until December 1944 that G.H.Q. Middle East was instructed to make a deal with Shafto and to hand the cinemas over to us, by which time of course a vested interest of high capital value had been created out of the soldiers' war-time needs, and the majority of the fighting troops had gone elsewhere.

In the face of the overseas developments the shortage of artistes once again became an issue. As early as May 1942 Lord Terrington had written warning us that young women between the ages of twenty-one and twenty-four were to be called up for national service, and suggesting that actresses and chorus girls coming within those age-groups should not be referred to either of the two Deferment Committees. To this I made caustic reply that the official responsible for the proposal must be remarkably ignorant of the nature of our work: youth in its female performers was a specific requirement.

By the end of that summer the position had become desperate, and the Entertainments Board, meeting for the third time in its career, passed a resolution calling the attention of the Minister of Labour to the shortage of artistes. In October I sent Bevin a memorandum at his request, showing that the current deficiency in personnel amounted to 1100 artistes, which would increase to 1500 during the coming winter. One year later the Minister asked Sir John Forster, Chairman of the National Arbitration Tribunal, to hold an inquiry into our manpower position. But it was not until the needs of the Second Front had begun to grip the popular imagination that we won our last and greatest agitation to secure "the tools for the job." The labour exchanges were then instructed that girls on the stage summoned to register for national service might be allowed to opt for ENSA instead of being ordered into other forms of war work. The Ministry of Labour allowed us fourteen days in which to make a decision in each case. The newcomers were given contracts for six months' work overseas and sent to fill the gaps caused by calling home some of the artistes who had been longest in the service of ENSA— veterans of our '39-'40 days in France, shortly to return there displaying the Africa Star which they had won in the Libyan Desert.

3

Three Meals a Day

Quite early in the North African campaign it became clear that the scale of welfare to which artistes had grown accustomed at home was inadequate overseas. Certain health measures had now to be included. In France we had begun by assuming that artistes volunteering to work abroad were strong enough to do so; but during that harsh winter the sickness rate became abnormal. In one of Leslie Henson's pantomime companies 75 per cent. of the artistes went sick within the first ten days, including the hind legs of the horse, so that all that remained was a number of variety turns performing to small groups in the lobbies of hotels and other odd places.

A Red Cross section had been formed at Drury Lane during the Blitz to deal with minor casualties. When work was resumed overseas inoculations were given against typhoid, yellow fever, tetanus and malaria. Sutherland Felce, one of the first artistes to visit the Middle East, lost his life through partial evasion of these precautions. His death gave impetus to the demand for complete medical supervision. Two doctors were added to the staff, who took duty in turns, so that one of them was always in attendance. A complete system of medical inspection was set up, including X-ray examination, so that what was virtually an ENSA health service came into being, involving a routine of co-operation between our Welfare Division and the medical authorities at home and abroad.

On the administrative side it became the business of the Welfare Division to shepherd the artistes, often excitable and resentful of procedure, through the maze of formalities. There were so many regulations, such as green identity cards, security checks, military permits, insurances and home allowances, with, at the apex of preparation, a Geneva Convention card, entitling the artiste to be treated as a "junior officer" in the event of capture by the enemy, that, in the end, each person passing through the turnstile was given a card listing the regulations in the order in which they should be complied with. Not until every space on the card had been stamped by the appropriate branch was the artiste judged ready for embarkation.

Throughout the period of expansion Madame Vernon, now known as Chief Ensa Welfare Officer (C.E.W.O.), rose purposefully to each successive urgency, flying back to London to interview new welfare supervisors and their assistants, and disappearing as quickly as she had come. To carry on the administrative work in her absence a deputy was appointed, Mrs Newall, an able woman whose charm and distinction secured compliance from refractory artistes by methods radically different from those of her chief.

The fitting out was mostly done at Drury House, a large office building opposite the stage-door. Here on the various floors and back in the theatre itself thronged performers of every sort and calibre, collecting or returning uniforms and equipment, queueing for passports, and generally 'shopping' for their official requirements, while members of the staff hurried from room to room and from building to building, co-ordinating the routine work of preparation. No wonder that Noël Coward once described Drury Lane as a cross between a recruiting office and No. 1 platform at Crewe Station on a Sunday morning.

4

Dress Parade

So far ENSA had not acquired the distinction of wearing uniform, although other non-combatants, such as the war correspondents and the Y.M.C.A., had long since done so. This was not because the privilege had been refused: there had been no occasion to ask for it. But the spread of the war in the Mediterranean increased the distances to be covered. And days spent in bumping over the desert roads were no help to the nightly display of glamour; the women's clothes wilted under the process. Then, too, travelling as civilians, our people were subjected to exasperating delays over passports and permits, especially when crossing minor frontiers and zones of influence. But when entertainment units of the South African Field Force appeared in the Middle East wearing uniform, and when American artistes, similarly attired, began to drift into North Africa, enjoying many of the privileges of the soldiery, including the right to buy at their shops and stores and unrestricted use of their aircraft, our people began to make comparisons. The fat was flung sizzling into the fire when civilians were ordered to remain indoors during the military parade for the King in Tripoli. It was hard upon the ENSA girls who had been entertaining the Eighth Army for weeks past to peer through the lattice and watch American actresses wandering about in smart uniforms with their cameras and chewing-gum. Perhaps there was something in this uniform business after all?

Constance Carpenter arrived in Cairo about this time. There was no diffidence about this amusing and vital personality. She dealt with the situation in a practical way by demanding outright of Sholto Douglas why artistes were not allowed to occupy vacant places in R.A.F. transport planes, when this would mean more entertainment time for the troops? The Air Marshal replied, half jokingly, that it might be arranged, but of course the actresses would have to wear uniform. A week later Miss Carpenter appeared before him, attired in her version of what that uniform should be. When I arrived she 'modelled' it for me, announced herself as its designer, and begged me to give permission for its adoption. This I had no power to do, but, after discussion at high level, G.H.Q. gave permission for its local use. Thus I suppose it was true to say that we had helped ourselves to a uniform.

On my return home I was rather startled to read a war correspondent's sarcastic account of the uniform I had invented for my entertainment army, which he amusingly nicknamed "Basil dress." This sent the official balloon swirling into the sky: quick pens were ready in the Press to set down this clear evidence of my bent for dictatorship; a private Member put down a question on the order paper in the Commons, and the War Office inquired brusquely, "What all this was about?"

The sample uniform I had brought back with me was duly inspected and pronounced too attractive and insufficiently identifiable as a military uniform, but, after modification, it was officially approved for overseas use. Thereafter, all civilian members of the organization were required to wear it in the war zones. To ease the susceptibilities of those who viewed this approach to militarization with suspicion I gave orders for it to be known as ENSA Standard Dress, a pacific gesture that was nullified by the later issue of British battle-dress (complete with greatcoat and choice of skirts or slacks for the women) as second dress for all artistes overseas. Shoulder flashes with the initials E N S A worked in white on a black ground were provided for both outfits, and badges in gunmetal, or red, white and blue enamel, for cap or beret.

Many of the stars were reluctant to wear the standard dress at first. Not so George and Beryl Formby, about to pay their first visit to North Africa and the Middle East. Without waiting for confirmation of the forthcoming "dress-up" they hurried round to Moss Bros. and selected uniforms of a highly decorative character, complete with 'guardee's' buttons and ENSA badges in gold on the coat lapels. Two days later I was escorting a number of M.P.'s across the stage when, rounding a corner by some scenery, we came upon George and Beryl in full regalia, posing for a Press photographer!

In the excitement of finding themselves in uniform some of the younger people assumed a truculence which they thought becoming to their military status. For example, six C3 chorus men, released from the dress rehearsal of a musical comedy, rushed into the Cavour Bar one evening, newly arrayed in their standard dress. Pushing their way obstreperously through the throng, one of them shouted an order to the over-worked barmaid: "Six lights, Elsie, and sharp about it!" This drew the unscripted reply: "You wait your turn, Mr Basil Dean's bleeding light infantry!"

Unidentified . . .

When 'Mickie' Jacob came to see me before taking up her new job in North Africa as welfare supervisor, she was wearing a khaki tunic of slightly antique cut, with claret-coloured facings and brightly polished captain's pips on the shoulder-straps. Striding about the room, telling me what was wrong with ENSA—so far as I can recall, its major defect sprang from my own appalling lack of humour—and emphasizing her points by tapping the furniture authoritatively with her cane as though to command its attention, she filled my mind with recollections of Vesta Tilley at the Palace and those smoking-room cartoons by Spy. Apparently it was the uniform of a woman's organization of the First World War, but it was an error of tact on my part to ask whether she had permission to wear it.

Shortly after her arrival in Algiers a succession of signals in cipher arrived at the War Office, angrily demanding who was the woman parading about Algiers in unauthorized uniform and purporting to belong to ENSA? Finally, there came one from our senior officer: the military authorities were threatening her immediate arrest if she were not recalled. In all fairness I must add that Naomi Jacob won her point and continued to wear the uniform of the defunct organization for the remainder of the war, the only instance known to me of a 'one-man band' among all the millions of men and women in uniform on either side.

Identified . . .

The unassuming manner in which Solomon went about his work was a trap for the careless and the ignorant. When they fell into it—and they often did—it seemed to enrich rather than to lessen his store of good humour. About to leave for his first overseas tour, he called at the standard dress department for his clothes. The over-worked clerk, new to her

2B

duties, asked abruptly what division he belonged to. Solomon replied vaguely:

"I am a pianist."

"So you've just said. But what party is it?"

"I belong to no party," replied Solomon.

"Oh," said the clerk, "a pool pianist."

5

Mr Puff

The public relations side of our expansion needed to be carefully watched overseas, where Service newspapers had made their appearance in various theatres of war. After Macqueen-Pope's resignation our publicity struggled on for a month or so under the impetus of his energy and enthusiasm, like a decapitated chicken. We were constantly in the news, but too frequently in the wrong way. Ever since the fracas in France reporters had always gone a bit 'gay' in writing about our doings. Above and beyond the too frequent appearance of ENSA's name in Hansard and in the tattle-tale columns of the provincial newspapers, there was ridicule, that most potent form of disparagement—it was on too many lips, and misapprehension was widespread.

A fully fledged public relations division with a top-ranking journalist at its head was needed. Collie Knox was approached, and eventually persuaded to become its director, with Jonah Barrington as his deputy. The new division was quickly set up with separate sections to deal with editorial, pictorial, advertising and printing matters. Later, a photographic section was added, housed in separate premises in Covent Garden, where a staff of photographers and laboratory assistants was fully employed in the tedious business of taking, developing and printing thousands of passport photographs, in addition to the usual newspaper coverages. Press officers were appointed for each theatre of war.

Collie was insistent upon the need for frequent Press conferences. He knew that I disliked these affairs (which made me nervous, and which I would have avoided if I could), but as the time drew near for one of them he would become ubiquitous, hovering in the background of other preoccupations with a look of smiling expectancy more minatory than the loudest protest. Under his tactful direction my technique began to improve.

Ever since the beginning of the war we had published an ENSA Bulletin each month. Unlike that issued by CEMA, ours was a humble, roneoed affair, involving little or no expense beyond the small amount of paper used. When the 'save paper' campaign was started I gave orders to stop it. But the establishment of a public relations division seemed to justify its reappearance. A special Section within the Division was formed to deal with the resuscitated publication, which I named *The ENSA Record*. Patrick Hamilton, the dramatist, joined us to become its editor. Statistics were interspersed with readable articles and amusing stories from camp and factory; there were photographs and on the back a map showing "Spheres of ENSA entertainment," stretching from Iceland to Madagascar. Publication ceased after two issues because of the objections of the Paper Controller. If our original bulletin had not been stopped through my excessive zeal *The ENSA Record* would have escaped his regulations.

In spite of this rebuff, Collie was determined upon the regular circulation of our news, not only in Fleet Street and throughout the provinces, but to the Service newspapers and to the Commonwealth. This was achieved by means of two broadsheets, one called *ENSA Show News* and the other *ENSA Picture News*. The photographs in the picture-sheet were numbered to correspond with written paragraphs in the news-sheet. By application to Drury Lane the Service newspapers could obtain prints of any photographs they desired to reproduce. Thus, information was kept in constant flow.

About the time when I was trying to persuade the Russians, through the Foreign Office, to send leading artistes to sing in our factories, I learned that the *ENSA Show News* was being sent regularly to Moscow, there translated into Russian and later distributed in Red Army circles. We occasionally received their reports in exchange, from which we learned that their artistes were being formed into units, called *brigadas*, to tour the front lines. The photographs were interesting too. I remember one showing the lighting of the stage by torches carried by Cossacks, which had its counterpart in the picture of Gracie Fields in Burma, calling on all present to strike a match when she said "three."

Jealousy continued to smoulder beneath the surface of our relations with NAAFI. Its origin lay in the superior amount of public notice which the ENSA work attracted. It would burst into little bright flames of resentment whenever we received outstanding publicity. Proposals to cut down on our Public Relations Division, after the manner of Parliament when it desires to express lack of confidence in a Minister, then followed. By the winter of 1943 we had several times won the Oscar of publicity, a cartoon in *Punch*, and I was beginning to hope that the Corporation had ceased to trouble itself about such trifles. Suddenly there was flung into our political hot-pot, now simmering nicely, additional 'herb o' grace' to sweeten the dish of trouble. Peremptory circulars were issued by the

Corporation's Secretary that in future all shows were to be advertised as NAAFI/ENSA entertainments: foolish instructions since the public had long ago made up its own mind on the subject, and no amount of caterwauling would change it. The Corporation's connexion with the work remained in the public mind precisely what it was, a financial one for which great credit was due; beyond that the bouquets and the brickbats belonged, very properly, to ENSA.

It was a complex situation, and Collie handled it brilliantly. Thanks to his tactful intelligence and to shrewd assistance from Jonah Barrington, now deeply engaged in producing programmes for the Broadcasting Division—two jobs at once—he succeeded in a short while in creating a machine of remarkable efficiency. His charm and good humour compensated for the difficulty he had in speaking his thoughts. Maybe the pauses in conversation which this imposed gave time for heads to cool and thoughts to be more diplomatically expressed.

One morning he came smilingly into my room. Standing in front of the desk, he stared at me in silence for so long that I wondered what bad news he had to impart. Then with sibilant difficulty he uttered one word only:

"M—mm—misapprehension!"

"Well, what about it?" I asked rather savagely.

"It's gone!" The words popped out of his mouth with a little shout. "N—nn—no ridicule either. Do you mind if I have a week's leave?"

6

On Wheels

When the political discussions referred to at the beginning of this chapter were at their most violent I received a hint from the Deputy General Manager of NAAFI that the Corporation was well advanced with its own preparations for the Second Front and that it would be as well if we put ourselves in the same position. I was grateful to him for this advance notice. The scheme I had in mind required months of planning.

Transport would be the main difficulty. At home we were always in trouble over this. Although the Corporation's Transport Branch did its best to keep us on the road, it was hard put to it to maintain its own fleets. In the end we were forced to hire motor-coaches for the orchestras and larger parties, every bus company in Britain being called upon at one time or another to meet our requisitions, many of them being contracts on a long-term basis.[1] Even so the bulk of the home entertainment, both military and civil, continued to travel on its own wheels. Our various garages were crowded to bursting. Finally, Aldridge's famous auction mart in Upper St Martin's Lane was taken over, where guards kept day and night watch over our precious headquarters transport, ready to answer calls for break-down assistance from all parts of the home counties.

Overseas, transport lay at the root of most of our administrative troubles. The pattern of early mishap in France had been repeated in North Africa and the Middle East. And now the mobile columns sent to Sicily, and thence into Italy, began to show the same weakness. It was like a recurring decimal to which there is no end. NAAFI in its anxiety to help made unsuitable purchases. Most of the adapted vehicles were draughty and extremely uncomfortable; all were second-hand and broke down at the smallest provocation. When this occurred the artistes had to beg, borrow or steal a lift, which induced carbuncles of grievance, liable to burst at any moment. Even the cheeriest comedians lost their dressing-room humours under the clouds of desert sand that rattled against their dentures like hail on the window-pane. Equally trying to the nerves were the chill winds that froze the mud of Flanders, turning the roads into switchbacks and making coughs and colds a prevailing condition.

Sometimes officers in remote areas, left to their own devices, resorted to unorthodox measures in order to keep us moving. In Greece the problem was solved by the arrival of a South African party of twenty-two, all teetotallers and under no impulse to draw their whisky rations, supplied to them at the duty-free price of 8s. 6d. a bottle. The brigadier of a certain R.E.M.E. headquarters liked to keep a good mess. For a case of Scotch (at the proper price, of course) he allotted stranded ENSA one 3-ton lorry and a battered jeep, once captured by the Germans and subsequently recovered. Patched up by one of the R.E.M.E. staff, it enabled the ENSA officer to go triumphantly about his business.

For the Second Front I intended to rely upon R.E.M.E. for major repairs, not realizing what a broken reed this would prove to be: we were only camp-followers, and there were higher priorities. It was not until the liberation of Europe was in full swing, and we were threatened with complete and final breakdown, that it was decided to commission transport officers and to build up our own M.T. sections. But we came late to the

---

[1] In the Home Commands during the year ended April 30, 1943, over 175,000 miles were covered by motor-coach and hired car alone. This was in addition to the mileage of our own transport fleet and the distances travelled by rail. Later records are incomplete because the statistical section of our transport division was overwhelmed with a mass of detailed returns, and the compilation of general statistics fell into arrear.

scheme, when the barrel had been drained of technical competence. So the sections never became 100 per cent. efficient. However, this flaw in our planning lay in the future. For the present we all gave ourselves up to the eagerness of preparation.

7

Kettle on the Hob

A Second Front Committee was formed of senior officials at Headquarters, to whom I gave a rough outline of what was required. The complete scheme, as finally worked out by the committee, consisted of twelve columns, divided into two groups of six, each group subdivided into two sections of three columns each; the groups were commanded by majors and the sections by captains; each column had a subaltern in charge, and the whole 'expeditionary force' was under the command of Colonel Haygarth, with the usual adjutant and headquarters staff. The only civilian members of it were the women secretaries, who wore ENSA standard dress.

There were two ENSA parties in each column in addition to the mechanical entertainment, the average number of artistes in each party being six, including the stars: 144 artistes in all. The military personnel included electrical engineers, projectionists, drivers and stage technicians, as well as the administration: for the latter there were twenty officers and 180 warrant officers and N.C.O.'s Each column was equipped with sleeping- and day-coaches for the artistes, two mobile cinemas, a fully equipped mobile workshop, one rediffusion van (later increased to two) and two motor-cycles; finally, diesel-engined power trucks were added, capable of generating enough electric current to light a full-sized cinema—a last-minute stipulation of my own, because of the blitzed cinemas we might have to operate, an impossible task without our own electric power: 130 vehicles in all. The equipment included portable stages, lighting-sets, numerous pianos, microphones by the dozen, thousands of feet of film and hundreds of records; typewriters, draperies, scenery and properties; also the usual domestic articles, such as blankets and electric kettles and irons, Red Cross supplies, and innumerable smaller items of theatrical impedimenta. All these 'bodies,' vehicles and material had to be assembled in places and at times specified by the embarkation authorities, ready to be conveyed at short notice to the landing beaches.

The work of assembling and training the military personnel—training them, that is, in the running of our administrative system and in the handling of artistes; training them as cinema projectionists and as stage-manager/electricians, able to build the portable stages, run the motor generators and deal resourcefully and good-humouredly with every emergency—was carried out at one of the larger hostels at Hindhead, which was converted into a training centre. Here, by degrees of coercion and persuasion, the vehicles were collected from builders already harassed by the competing priorities of the rapidly approaching D-Day; here drivers were taught to manœuvre their coaches in military convoy; here projectionists gave trial film shows on their new equipment, and here the stage technicians erected and dismantled their stages and practised the rudiments of stage lighting.

As the weeks of preparation slipped by I began to feel the weight of responsibility. If anything were to go wrong with our entertainment army I should be held as fully responsible as is any commander in the field for his troops. Therefore, in the spring of 1944 I took over the chairmanship of the special committee, and at our daily meetings did my best to ensure that no detail, either of material or personnel, had been overlooked.

When the military side of our preparation was complete Air Chief Marshal Tedder, deputy to the Supreme Allied Commander, drove down to Hindhead to make a general inspection. The spacious grounds of the hostel could not contain so many vehicles, and more than half of the transport had been spilled on to the grass verge lining the main road. The array of numbered columns, manned by their appointed officers and technicians, each vehicle bearing the ENSA signet and the white star of identification as part of the Allied Invasion, made a brave show. Many of them emulating, too, the whimsical habit of the American transport pilots in painting slogans on their aircraft, displayed the titles of famous plays as a further mark of identity.

8

Ready to serve

Second Front preparation had reached its final stage when suddenly, on May 18, Gertrude Lawrence arrived. Her dearest wish had been granted. She had arrived in time to join the 'Second Fronters,' full of zeal, attired in American Red Cross uniform with ENSA flashes adorning the shoulders, and a U.S.O. badge on the left breast. A steel helmet covered with a camouflage net for use when visiting military camps completed the martial effect. Some of our people were inclined to chortle a little at this 'get-up,' but they forgot that behind that theatricality and nose for publicity was a woman of grit and character. In America her proposal that one thousand citizens should donate their blood for the exclusive use of British soldiers had been received with enthusiasm. Returning home, she sought to organize a similar gift for U.S. troops. It was her theatrical way of expressing the blood-brotherhood of our two nations, but she forgot that the realities of total war made such gestures unwelcome to her countrymen.

There was no lack of volunteers among the stars. They were so caught up with the fancy of landing on the beaches that we were compelled to allocate them weeks in advance, so many stars to each sailing. The authorities proposed to land one section (*i.e.*, three columns) at a time, calling them forward whenever the complicated logistics permitted. The irrepressible George Formby and his wife were to be in the first sailing, in company with the commanding officer and his headquarters staff and Madame Vernon. Close behind the Formbys would be Alice Delysia, Richard Hearne and Forsythe, Seamon and Farrell with Lyle Evans; then, in quick succession, Ivor Novello, Diana Wynyard and Margaret Rutherford to play *Love from a Stranger*, Gertrude Lawrence with her own party, Sandy Powell and Billy Scott Coomber, Jessie Matthews and, at the tail-end of the team, two of its top laughter-scorers, Flanagan and Allen. These lively sparks, freed from George Black's restraints, filled in the waiting-time by performing at their craziest wherever we asked them to go. Upon one occasion, taking 'Monsewer' Eddie Gray with them—a natural comic as funny in private life as he is on the stage—they turned up at a secret camp just outside Watford, and soon had the Mayor of Watford sitting in the centre of the stage taking his shoes off to prove there were no holes in his socks. . . . All these entertainment 'commandos' were ready, and waiting to land on the beaches by the dates specified. It was a swarming of the entertainment hive.

9
Opening shortly

The troops were swarming, too. In the southlands—in the narrow lanes of Kent and Sussex, in the New Forest, in the deep valleys of Devon and Cornwall the assault forces were gathering. They were lodged in secret invasion camps behind barbed wire. Our Area Organizers were hot upon the scent of this new opportunity; but when we asked permission to take entertainment into the cages we were met with blank stares, as though such places were figments of our imagination. When, for reasons that are now a matter of history, the invasion was postponed, the full-blooded highly trained young troops began to resent being treated like animals in a zoo. There were break-outs, and discipline began to deteriorate. Panic seized Whitehall. One afternoon there came a peremptory call from the War Office, requesting entertainment immediately for the secret locations. Our Army liaison officer (Graham John) had been convinced that sooner or later there would come this sudden demand, so we were not entirely taken by surprise. Within twenty-four hours we met the call.

I set out for an extended tour of the invasion areas, working my way gradually from the South-east down into the West Country. Everywhere the quiet byways were filled with long columns of men and vehicles wending towards the coast, past ancient churches where medieval knights lie beneath their stone effigies, kissing the earth while they gaze upward at the stars—and their faithful liegemen, long mouldered to equal dust in the yew-lined churchyards. Once more the young men of Britain were setting forth to fight overseas for the freedom of the island home. How often before had those green lanes and quiet towns been the background for similar scenes! Men-at-arms following their lords to what personal quarrel they knew not, save only that it was with a foreign enemy; pipe-clayed toughs on their way to the Peninsular War (tough—my God, how tough!), drinking, wenching, blaspheming their way to victory and perdition; men in Lincoln green and greasy leather, in scarlet coats, in khaki jackets and puttees: no need to lengthen the list or to labour the point.

But there were some notable differences in the latest crusade. Now it was mostly machines that bore the armour: columns of tanks lurching down the narrow roads, or, nose to tail, lying up on the grass verges beneath the trees, waiting for darkness; young officers standing up in the turrets, having a last look at scenes so familiar they had scarce noticed them before. These young men were different, too, from long ago—more fine-drawn, perhaps—yet they had the ancestral look in their eyes.

This was a crusade with a wider significance than those that went before, for here were American troops treading the remote byways: tall men with open faces like their own prairies, in loose-fitting blouses and trousers fitting tight over self-conscious posteriors, chewing gum with ostentatious indifference. And the columns of their transport, houses on wheels seemingly, vast structures that heaved and tossed the earth like snowballs, all painted dark green and bearing the white star of the West, driven by negroes from the deep South: they too were moving down to the sea, bound for foreign parts.

In the heart of the New Forest, in a camp so secret that guards were posted every few hundred yards to check identity, a concert had been arranged in a large marquee by a party from one of our mobile columns. It had just begun. The troops were craning forward with special eagerness to catch every sound, every gesture. "Good up to a point," I said to myself. Then the comedian began his turn. So few laughs that he was obviously disappointed; but then he was not very funny. To improve matters, he changed his routine, and went hunting for laughs in the compost heap of his mind. Presently out popped a filthy joke that made me go hot all over, received by the young soldiers with a few incredulous titters. "The fool! Can't he see that's the last thing these dedicated men want?" Immediately the performance was over I went to the artistes' tent. The wretched little man started to defend himself. In a white heat I told him he was sacked, and instructed the column officer (new to his job, obviously) to send him back to London in the morning. I was so stirred by all that I had seen that I drove back to London with bitter anger sitting at my elbow.

There were some special concentrations in Outer London, which gave the Bands Division their finest opportunity. Geraldo and his orchestra were playing at the London Palladium, where the performance was over by 8.30 P.M.—broad daylight in those days of double summer time. Each night coaches and cars waited at the stage-door to take the artistes and musicians to the extra special task. Then on one particular night, June 5 to be precise, 'Gerry' begged me to come to the West Ham Football Ground. We had received a request from the highest quarters to send him to these commando troops.

A fine night, as I remember, but rather chilly. When I arrived the grandstand was packed with troops, listening enwrapped to the singers and the orchestra grouped below them: one of those rare occasions when audience and artistes are in full communion, sensibilities sharpened by an unspoken awareness of coming events. The shadows lengthened round the feet of the soldiers; soon only their faces could be seen through the gloom. I was trembling with an emotion I could not express. Suddenly arc lamps sizzled away the darkness. Would the cries for the songs and favourite tunes to be repeated over and over again never stop? At last the senior officer present declared an end. Scarcely had the last strains of the National Anthem died away before Geraldo and his company were surrounded by young soldiers, begging them to autograph the five-, ten- and twenty-five-franc notes issued to them as invasion money. So much once again for Security!

The departure of the troops was obviously imminent, and equally obvious their destination. I moved quickly among the musicians, reminding them that they had been sworn to secrecy. Nothing was to be said, even at home; it would be a breach of trust. All understood and agreed: they had only one thought, one hope that night. While I lingered talking to Geraldo's wife a young soldier hurried up to her with a new pair of nylon stockings, asking her to send them to his wife as a parting gift. A bugle was sounded, the floodlights were switched off, and the men drifted away in the dark. The visitors moved to the waiting cars in silence, feeling as empty of life as the grandstand above them. . . .

Now we too are ready, down to the last knife, fork and spoon, the last stick of grease paint and the last roll of film. Our players are rehearsed and equipped; our French, Dutch and Belgian liaison officers stand poised like divers, ready to make the plunge. How long shall we have to wait?

THE FAR SHORE

1

Gangplank

JUNE 6, 1944: outwardly no different from any other day. And yet from the moment when I was roused in the blue light of the early summer morning by the threshing of hundreds of steel wings in the sky and peered up at the aircraft flying under and over and through the high white cumulus, I was conscious of an inner difference. It was as though the nation had suddenly been made aware in full sobriety of a moment in high history, as though each one of us, openly or covertly, according to his wont, were saying to his neighbour in the current slang, "This is it!"

For ENSA the great crusade would be the supreme test and ultimate justification. Hurrying to Drury Lane, reading the news flashes over and over again, I could already see in my mind's eye our little entertainment army on the march. In my impatience I made small allowance for the enormous complication of the transport and security arrangements, and forgot that camp followers must come late on the list. A thousand and one practical details, on which it had been impossible to obtain decisions beforehand, came popping back into my mind. Before our columns landed a reception area would have to be chosen and approved by the invasion authorities; it must be laid out like a military camp with field kitchens, messing tents, transport lines, latrines and so forth: this was a job for the sappers. Camp guards would be needed: a matter for the provost-marshal. As for messing, it had been settled that army rations were to be drawn in the usual way, supplemented by supplies from NAAFI. Crossing Covent Garden, I could already hear Madame Vernon demanding the inclusion of fresh vegetables in the diet sheets. The thought made me laugh out loud. A constable on duty at Bow Street stared hard and suspiciously at me.

I had long ago determined to be the first of our people to visit 'the far shore'; by the time I reached my office I was already half-way there. I could see no reason why the ban on the movement of civilians overseas should apply to myself, so I sat down and wrote out my application to the

War Office for permission to land. After waiting a week I renewed my application, only to be told that nothing could be done until my status under the Geneva Convention in the event of enemy capture had been determined. On pressing the matter I was met with the bland suggestion that it might be best for ENSA to wait until Army Welfare was moved to France. It was likely to be months before all those administrative hangers-on to Montgomery's 21 Army Group got under way. Meanwhile the fighting troops might be half-way across France. Already, on D +6, the arrival of a party of "Stars in Battledress" at the beachhead had been announced.

Both the Chairman of the Entertainments Board and the Chairman of NAAFI sustained my eagerness. So, one bright morning, the invasion already two weeks old, we drove down, all three, to interview the Major-General i/c Administration, Miles Graham, in his caravan among the laurel bushes beside the Wentworth Golf Course. There was tremendous activity in this hideout, the tapping of typewriters replacing the click of golf balls, sentries lurking behind every tree-trunk and junior officers popping out of their camouflaged caravans with frowns at our intrusion: the lower the rank the deeper the frown. It seemed a century of time since my first visit to those other British Headquarters in France. Now the officers were younger and more alert; also, there was no farmyard and no chickens.

Miles Graham, recalled to the Army from his City directorships, added business training to a natural charm of manner, but over my business he was disposed to be evasive. I explained my sense of personal responsibility towards the artistes.

"But surely it is the Army's business?" queried the general.

"From the safety angle, yes, sir. But in the first instance it is mine."

I wanted a permit that would give me the right to come and go across the Channel as freely as I had done in the first year of the war. Faced with Sir Edward Ellington's superior rank and Lancelot Royle's tactful phrases, the general gave way. The privilege was conceded and a directive issued to leave me to my own devices.

'Q' Movements shook its important head when I asked them to implement the permit: "Request out of order; must be 'phased-in' in the proper manner." This was just common or garden obstruction, so I grabbed my kit and my papers, jumped into a car and departed for BUCO (Build Up Command Operations), the holy of administrative holies so far as embarkation for the Second Front was concerned. It was now the fourth Saturday after the invasion. No cunning on my part, just a happy accident that the particular office to which I addressed myself had been left in charge of a young duty-officer over lunch-time. He discounted the bill of urgency I presented by signing my movement order, remarking that there was an American L.C.T. just about to leave if I cared to "have a go" for that? Without pausing to reply, I dashed out of the office and told my driver to drive like Hell to the jetty. The little ship was casting off as I arrived. I waved my permit at the American commander on the bridge just as the last gangplank was about to be withdrawn. A longshoreman obligingly held out his hand. Not looking where I was going, I stepped ankle-deep into the water. Recovering myself, I managed to scramble on board, helped by a grinning negro sailor. My American hold-all was flung after me. The ship gathered way quickly, leaving my faithful Channel Islander standing by the staff car, his mouth wide open with astonishment. . . . Thus it was that I left 'Pompey' (code word for the embarkation port) and voyaged once more to France. No galleys with dressed oars to see me off; no Cleopatra to wave a mocking farewell: just a pair of extremely wet feet.

2

Moving in

Plumes of smoke ahead and numerous buoys on either quarter told where countless Allied ships were discharging at Mulberry Harbour, now firmly established as the Piccadilly Circus of the British Zone of invasion. We joined the queue and drew near the shore line. The place was like a beehive: everywhere men, ships and the machines of war; dock companies in khaki battledress and naval caps shifting piles of stores; ships coming, ships going, ships beached after the recent storm, others sunk by enemy action; away to starboard a huge battleship steaming slowly, camouflaged almost to invisibility, on the other quarter a line of destroyers moving fast.

Presently our ship drew alongside, opened its bowels and excreted a line of tanks and loaded lorries. Shouldering my kit, I made my way through the crowd, passing a long line of bewildered German prisoners, staring at the bustling port risen by magic from the deserted beaches they formerly knew. Great swathes had been cut in the sand dunes, and steel mats laid down, over which endless lines of vehicles made their way inland, their straining engines drowning the roar of aircraft overhead and the booming of the distant guns. I made the usual pillar-to-post inquiries, and eventually discovered a NAAFI officer unloading stores, who found me a seat in a lorry about to make its way to NAAFI Headquarters. The lorries bumped and crashed their way, head to tail, along the road, or threaded their way over the verges through gaps torn in the hedges and back on to the road again, avoiding groups of pioneers filling up pot-holes with road metal and squirting tar almost under the wheels of the interminable crocodile, their faces so caked with dust as to make them indistinguishable from their uniforms.

The chairman of NAAFI, his grey flannel suit incongruous amidst the khaki, was waiting at Headquarters to greet me. After a night passed in listening to the occasional patter of spent shells on the roof, reminding me of that first Sunday morning in Arras, I went with the NAAFI works officer to select our camping-ground. We chose a field just off the main road into Bayeux, and about five kilometres from it. It was well suited to the purpose, with good turf and trees at one side that would serve to screen our transport park. While the major went off to make arrangements for the pioneering of the site, I called on Major-General Naylor, in charge of the base area. The moment he saw me he asked why there was no ENSA, and when I told him of the difficulties we were having he popped off a signal to the War Office, asking for the immediate phasing-in of the columns. Next day to Courcelles to Naval Headquarters to spread the news of our impending arrival, which brought me a pleasant lunch with the Admiral; in the afternoon to the R.A.F., where the privilege of using 2nd T.A.F. transport whenever I needed it was renewed. There was an extraordinary exhilaration in being among this multitude of men working with such energy to one purpose. The office wallahs with their tea-chests laden with documents and red-tape had not yet arrived. One could get a direct answer to any question, yea or nay, without shillyshally or argument.

Back and forth along that dusty, bumpy road into Bayeux I went during the next days, hurrying the preparation of our camp, contacting the French civil authorities regarding the take-over of the little Théâtre Municipal—where legend declares that the French Revolution was planned—watching day by day that fantastic oil pipe-line creeping along the grass verge up to the little pumping-stations and on again. Bull-dozers, steam-rollers, tons and tons of road metal, fountains of tar overlaying the dust, savage rents in the tall hedgerows to make way for the ring road flung round the outskirts of Bayeux: the weals of war were spreading relentlessly across the rich Normandy farmlands, sweeping aside the giant poplars and luscious boscage that stood in the way. At evening I drove up to the little Hôtel Lion d'Or at the top of the main street to meet and talk with the war correspondents, Alan Moorehead, Chester Wilmot and the others, driving in from the battle-front in their battered jeeps, hammering at their portable typewriters between sips of coffee. The local population seemed to have disappeared, flushed out by the flood of young British soldiery parading the narrow streets, tough and purposeful, encountering new sights with bold, confident eyes. Everywhere eager inquiries for the first show: "Where's George Formby?" "Tell Bud and Ches to hurry up!" Everywhere a sense of elation, an assurance of victory. Life behind the front was altogether different from the Arras days, queerly satisfying and concealing no element of uncertainty within it.

Back in London, the change in tempo from the eager battle-front to home affairs came as a shock. Our artistes had been waiting in their columns for days, roused to a kind of patient fury by the repeated delays. I obtained a promise of the immediate call-forward of No. 1 contingent and returned to BUCO, waving my permit once more—it was Saturday, July 15—and secured passage in an M.L. on the Sunday morning. A good idea, this week-end technique, I thought. Our camp was ready, and a guard of military police already mounted. There was a large messing tent with anteroom for the artistes, a separate Mess for officers and one for the N.C.O.'s. It was agreed to admit the stars to honorary membership of the officers' Mess, a decision that called for an adjustment of military etiquette and a blind eye to pomposity. At Royle's request I returned home to represent ENSA at the ceremonial opening of a new NAAFI Club in Manchester by Lord Sefton in the presence of Lord Derby, for which we were providing a star programme. Thus I missed the great thrill for which I had longed. While the speechifying was going on in Manchester our spearhead on the Second Front landed in Normandy.

The landing was not without mishap. Negotiating the steel ramps from the L.S.T.'s threw too great a strain upon the chassis of the heavily laden sleeping-coaches; the back axles of two of them gave way. They had to be towed ignominiously into the camp by giant American lorries, preceded by their passengers, chorus girls for the most part, riding on top of a Sherman tank—much to the surprise of German prisoners trailing wearily down to the shore. Not quite how we had planned our arrival: never mind, we were in!

◇◇◇

Wash and Brush-up . . .

Campaigning conditions were the same for our people as for the troops. Those who took the embarrassing moments in their stride usually came off best. Our columns were kept waiting on the outskirts of the embarkation areas for long hours, sometimes for a whole day, wedged as like as not between long lines of tanks. In the case of one contingent brought to a standstill in a suburb of Southampton, the officer in charge allowed the artistes to roam, telling them they would be warned by the hooting of motor horns when the column was about to move off again. When the signal was given all the artistes reassembled, except one pretty little chorus girl. She had taken advantage of the long halt to solicit a bath at a near-by villa. With complete disregard of her circumstances, she leaned far out of the bathroom window and shouted, "Hi! Wait for me!"

3
The Build-up

The August Bank Holiday week-end saw me on my way again, this time in a 2nd T.A.F. transport plane. The duty-officer at Northolt (an operational type, complete with D.F.C.), looking up, bored, from his Sunday newspaper, gave me the seat intended for a senior staff officer who arrived just as the plane began to warm up. The young man returned his senior's look of fury with a cool stare, puffing out his cheeks and sucking at his moustache in an effort to hide his glee.

Recent storms had converted our "fair field of France" into a quag-mire. Duckboards, adornment of every military camp sooner or later, had already made their appearance. Virginia had now established a hostel for overflow in a farmhouse near by, called "La Colline." The competition to enter it was less in fine weather than in wet. Here, and later in a house in Bayeux itself, where Madame Louise cooked and Mademoiselle Louise swept, where 'père' Louise and 'mari' Louise cleaned the vegetables, smoked and got in the way, while the remainder of this French refugee family of eleven stole food and cigarettes and chocolate from us, and shouted garrulous delight at the return of "Les Anglais'—here and at other temporary homes along the line of advance our artistes came into touch with the personal realities of invasion, a kaleidoscope of minor inci-dent, of courage and humour, the seamy side of character turned upper-most, in a way that I could not hope for, swinging pendulum-wise be-tween the hours of an overcrowded schedule.

George Formby and the parties in the first section had been stirring things up, playing here, there and everywhere, never less than two shows a day and sometimes three. Mobile cinemas and rediffusion vans were now in operation, and the Théâtre Municipal at Bayeux was crowded nightly. French civilians and bomb-wounded children were admitted to many of the shows. The cruisers and transports lying off-shore were not forgotten, the artistes going out to them in D.U.K.W.'s and suffering badly from seasickness on rough days. Shell-fire provided an interruptive comment not only upon the performances but in moments of relaxation, as when one of the parties, having its dip in the sea at Luc s/Mer under the protective eye of a sergeant-major, was rudely interrupted by the arrival of two heavy shells in quick succession, sent over by the German gunners at Le Havre. In the excitement the sergeant-major lost his set of false teeth, which a fatigue party lined up for the search failed to recover.

The ENSA build-up was now in spate, and our camp teeming with personality and temperament. Part of the second contingent, led by Forsythe, Seamon and Farrell, was already in, with Richard Hearne as the star of another party. Three days later the remainder came in, headed by the indomitable Delysia, disgruntled because she had hoped to be the first star to re-enter France. But for the moment personal grievance was drowned in a mood of patriotic fervour, expressed with admirable theatricality. As she stepped ashore she seized a handful of French soil and swore she would not rest until she had placed it on the tomb of the Unknown Soldier underneath the Arc de Triomphe.

On August 16 the Adjutant-General, still Sir Ronald Adam, made his long-promised inspection of the camp. A posse of famous comedians in uniform standing rigidly to attention beside the Mess tent made an imposing display; but the parade-ground atmosphere that our senior officer had intended was ruined by my presence, busily photographing the scene with a Leica. The A.G. seemed more at his ease talking to the old soldiers among our military staff than to the artistes. These people in their ENSA standard dress, were they to be treated as officers, N.C.O.'s or just 'other ranks'? However, he carried out his inspection assiduously, climbing in and out of the sleeping-trucks and mobile cinemas and listening to a demonstration of one of the rediffusion vans. Delighted with all he had seen, he complimented the O.C. in appropriate official terms upon the ingenious technical equipment and excellent turnout. Then he turned to ask me how long I was staying in France.

By this time I had made the acquaintance of the colonel in charge of Second Army Welfare, an energetic, ubiquitous person: the type of man —one meets them in all walks of life—that knows instinctively where is to be found the best of everything and the right price to pay—or not to pay—for it. From him I learned that the 6th Airborne Division under Major-General Gale[1] were out in the blue on the other side of the River Orne, clinging to advanced positions after successful glider landings. It had not yet been possible to replace them with more heavily armed troops, and they were without any amenities whatever. George Formby clamoured to be allowed to go. Before I would agree I had to see things for myself.

---

[1] Later General Sir Richard Gale, C.-in-C. British Army of the Rhine.

My colonel friend offered to come with me. We set off early the follow-ing morning, taking the coast road through Saint-Aubin and Lion s/Mer, skirting Ouistreham and crossing the Caen Canal at Benouville. The destruction wrought in the little pleasure resorts, with their casinos and seashore restaurants smashed to matchwood and the gaily painted villas with great holes torn in their sides, seemed more cruel and heartless than in the case of great cities. Perhaps it was because these little places speak more directly to the eye of peace and happiness.

On the grassy flats beyond the canal lay the abandoned gliders of the Division in orderly rows, looking like a covey of great sitting birds. We hid the rediffusion van we had brought with us in a fringe of trees, and made our way forward. We came to high ground, thickly wooded. Here the paratroopers were doing duty as infantrymen, manning fox-holes and sandbag entrenchments, enduring heavy losses from attacks by elements of the 21st Panzer Division, and longing to return to their more familiar mobile rôle. The general's dug-out was in a sand-cliff beside a sunken road; a sentry with tommy-gun at the ready conducted us to his presence. My offer to leave the rediffusion van with the Division and to bring George Formby over the next day was welcomed. In battle areas there is no beating about the bush; co-operation is offered and accepted out of hand because it is assumed that you have weighed the chances and know what you are about.

After lunch with the staff, sitting under a hedge with a plank for a table (army rations of course: bully beef and biscuits and cheese washed down with some excellent beer, with a musical accompaniment provided by the rediffusion van not so very far away—if the music reached German ears, they doubtless regarded it as a propaganda stunt), the general took me to a seashore villa at Lion s/Mer, organized as a rest-centre where exhausted men from the line could be given twenty-four hours' rest. He led the way in a jeep, with men holding tommy-guns at the ready, preceded by two dispatch-riders on motor-cycles. A garage at the side of the villa provided ideal stabling for the rediffusion van. Our sound engineer began at once his preparations for a concert that evening, setting up loudspeakers in the various rooms. Alas! An enemy plane bombed the rest-centre during the night but was itself shot down in flames over the adjacent villa. Our sergeant managed to rescue his precious van, but the rest-centre suffered heartbreaking casualties.

Early the next morning I found George Formby, impatient to carry his uke across the Orne, waiting by my car, and his wife with him. I tried to dissuade Beryl, but she would not be denied, and so became the first woman of the invasion forces to cross that river. We joined one of the interminable convoys, often waiting at traffic intersections in the choking dust for ten minutes or more. The little Normandy towns and villages through which we passed had been mostly blown to pieces, their tiny streets buried under piles of rubble, and fresh ways carved by the bull-dozers, oftentimes where formerly there had been homes and little shops. Everywhere the stink of long-neglected dirt, blown from the rafters of ancient buildings, and the still fouler sweetness of death.

Between 12 noon and 3 P.M. on that day George gave six shows to the men of the Airborne Division, none of them more than 300 yards from the German lines and, in one case, a mere eighty yards. Standing with his back to a tree or a wall of sandbags, with the men squatting on the ground in front of him, he sang song after song, screwing up his face into comical expressions of fright whenever shells exploded in the near distance, and making little cracks when the firing drowned the point lines in his songs. On the long drive back to our camp, wherever sufficient numbers of men were gathered to warrant a performance, in stables and in courtyards, out would come the uke.

On August 19 Ivor Novello landed with Diana Wynyard and Margaret Rutherford. The following day they set up their portable stage in a Normandy orchard and gave a performance at the Headquarters of 2nd T.A.F. to the distant boom of artillery fire and the nearer rattle of the Bofors guns. The audience squatted on the grass or lolled against the apple trees, with Air Marshal Coningham seated in their midst in a canvas chair, just like a film director 'shooting' a crowd scene, while the sun slowly gave up its task of illumination in favour of our spotlights, glinting pink and amber through the green leaves.

It required moral courage of a high order to go out and face the troops so soon after his release from prison, but Ivor wisely had accepted Macqueen-Pope's advice; in doing so he gained the regard of the invasion troops as well as of the public at home. Ivor lived all his life in terms of melody, gay or sad, as the case might be, with just a dash of cynicism, not too deeply felt, to flavour the tunes: an attitude of mind not far removed from the wisest philosophies. The hit number of his forthcoming success (*When the Lilacs Bloom again* in *Perchance to Dream*) was composed while he was in Normandy, and sung in public for the first time after the play at the Garrison Theatre, Bayeux, the composer going down into the orchestra pit and playing it on the little piano there.

Gertrude Lawrence, her keenness undimmed by an exhausting two months' tour from Land's End to John o' Groats, and beyond, over the stormy Pentlands to Orkney and the Shetlands, arrived with her party on the same day as Ivor. Finally, on August 25, the last contingent, consisting of parties headed by Flanagan and Allen, Sandy Powell, Florence Desmond and Kay Cavendish respectively, came in, after exasperating delays which included disembarkation and re-embarkation, and four days fog-bound in the Channel.

While our people went steadily about their business, building up a systematic routine, the affairs of the "Stars in Battledress" parties were not progressing so well. The system of attaching them to operational units for rationing and billeting had broken down under campaign conditions. Some of these soldier-artists turned up in our camp looking like members of the lost tribes. Our commanding officer took charge of them for the time being. Later all military parties in overseas theatres of war were routed by the ENSA officers, a commonsense arrangement that should have been made from the start. With this addition to our strength our build-up might be said to be complete.

4

Pressing on

By now the British troops had passed beyond the narrow confines of the beachhead, squeezing the Germans out of Caen and successfully drawing counter-assault from Panzer Group West to make possible a rapid turning movement by Patton's U.S. troops on the other side of the Peninsula. Little of the great events portending was known to us at work behind the lines, absorbed in contemplation of the next objective, which for us was Caen, where we must, as speedily as may be, pitch our tents. I tackled my friend at Second Army Welfare. If anyone could get me into Caen before the other Auxiliary Services it would be he.

We drove there on a blazing hot afternoon from Bayeux, taking Haygarth with us; the poplar trees bordering the road gasping beneath a coating of chalk dust, away to the right the great plain of Caen brooding in a kind of heavy stillness, broken occasionally by muffled explosions, like the blasting operations that punctuate the summer silence in the Derbyshire hills: a smitten, sultry landscape, conscious of the evil it concealed. We were stopped by Canadian sentries a few hundred yards short of the town, but the Second Army Headquarters pass which my escort carried silenced the objections to our further progress. Nevertheless, we were required to leave the car and walk in the middle of the road, no vehicles of any sort being allowed in.

Caen was deserted: not a person to be seen. Much of it, particularly the older parts, is built of the beautiful local stone. Great masses of the stuff lay about the main thoroughfares; the narrower ways were quite impassable. In many places tape or wire had been strung across, with an assortment of notices swinging in the gentle breeze: "Closed—Snipers." "Booby Traps." Here and there German warnings had been left: a skull-and-crossbones, painted white on black, with the single word *Minen*. Presently the car overtook us; the driver, a fly young Cockney, only winked when I asked him how he had managed to pass the sentries.

Second Army Welfare went about his particular mission of acquisition, while Haygarth and I wandered in search of the town major, hoping he could help us in ours. We found him eventually, seated amid the debris of what must have been an important business office, with a sergeant and a number of orderlies trying to put the place into some sort of order. Evidently he regarded my request for information about theatres and cinemas as evidence of the higher lunacy: "Theatres? Not that I know of. Good Heavens, man, this place was in the front line a couple of days ago!" Following the reverberations of the big guns, plaster fell in fine showers from the ceiling as we talked. Reluctantly he consented to go with us in search of what was wanted. His tin hat lay upturned on the trestle table beside him. Nonchalantly tipping the plaster-dust out of it, he led the way to the street. Why did I suddenly think of *Journey's End*? Of course! It was the last time I had seen that piece of 'business' done; but that was in a theatre, and this was real life.

Our driver had prudently withdrawn the car behind the ruins of a tall house tumbled pell-mell into the street, a fountain of rubble, from which concealment he peered inquisitively at us as we came out. "Got a car?" asked the major. There are moments in a campaign when disregard of regulations is taken for granted. Without a word I waved our driver forward, and we all got in. The major directed us towards the eastern outskirts, where the evidence of recent combat was everywhere: all the side-roads criss-crossed with tape, an occasional rifle shot corroborating the warning notices hanging from them; odd bricks, a shattered doorway and small articles of clothing lying in the middle of the fairway; in the gutter, a German cap and parts of a rifle. We came to an open space where several roads radiated towards the open country. The small modern cinema on the far side of it seemed to have possibilities; we decided to examine it. The major made objection: the roof was unsafe; if we went inside it was at our own risk; there had been quite a battle in that corner of the town two days ago. With a final warning about booby traps he left us to it and went back to his office, taking our car. German contents bills were still in the display frames. A great hole had been blown in one wall, exposing the roof trusses. There was a stage, small but large enough to accommodate our mobile play companies: I decided this should be our garrison theatre.

Leaving Haygarth to rescue the car from the town major's clutches, I continued the search for a garrison cinema. The town was eerily quiet, in spite of the distant diapason of gunfire. Between two high walls I came upon a flight of steps piled high with rubble and great blocks of Caen stone. At the foot stood a watchful French gendarme, armed. A moment of frightened hesitation lest he should decide to shoot first and ask afterwards, and then I spoke in my halting, nervous French; but he would volunteer no information until I offered him a packet of Player's cigarettes, when he kissed me violently upon both cheeks, pointed to the top of the steps and disappeared round the corner.

The deserted *place*, with young trees round all its sides protected by iron railings, looked exactly like a film set after shooting is over for the day and artistes and technicians are gone home. At the far side was a cinema, a large modern building with a brasserie beside it. While I was staring at the empty scene Haygarth rounded the opposite corner with the car. We walked into the brasserie through a large plate-glass swing-door. An enormous black cat, miaowing passionately, sprang at us; it was not hunger that caused its distress, but thirst, for when we offered it pieces of ham sandwich it refused to eat and cried louder than ever. The brasserie was full of marble tables and chromium chairs, with a long bar at one side and glass shelves behind it stacked with unused glasses; but of drink, not a sign! The cinema was a fine building with a manager's flat above the entrance hall that had been hurriedly deserted, because there were child's toys scattered on the floor and the remains of a meal on the table—but no milk for the cat! The Germans had most unkindly smashed the electrical gear and removed the projectors, but the place was precisely what we were looking for. Our engineers must get in here and light up as quickly as possible with one of our power-lorries.[1] As we turned our backs upon the square, the cat, divining our intention, followed us, raising the most extravagant echoes with its yowlings.

Appetites for reconnaissance whetted by this expedition, we gladly accepted an invitation from our Welfare acquaintance to go with him to Granville, where he assured me he had business to transact, adding, with an air of studied detachment, that he knew of a small restaurant in the

---

[1] The Majestic Cinema, Caen, was opened as an ENSA Garrison Cinema on September 1 with the world première of J. B. Priestley's *They Came to a City*. The Trianon Cinema became the Garrison Theatre on September 4, when *Love from a Stranger* was presented. A hostel, later discovered to have been a Gestapo interrogation centre, complete with coshes and thumb-screws, was opened on the same day.

town, famous for its cuisine, particularly the *langouste*—an afterthought that was not to be lightly set aside.

Beyond Saint-Lo and Coutances, in the wake of the American advance, the ravaged quiet of the countryside had an air of emotional emptiness, the passion of warfare spent. In the *bocage* country wrecked 'Tiger' tanks poked their noses at us from tall hedgerows, while the open roads along which German reinforcement had failed to arrive gave evidence of the savage punishment meted out by the Allied bombing. At one crossroads where there had been a great killing we got out to look at the fantastic litter: a whole convoy tiptilted into the deep ditch beyond the grass verge, a mess of personal belongings, caps, belts, small-arms, newspapers, photographs, mess-tins, water-bottles; and there, beside a burntout tank, glistening in the sun, the shin bone of a Nazi, neatly severed at the ankle, no clothing upon it, looking like a joint of fresh meat dropped from the butcher's cart: not a pleasant preliminary to the culinary anticipations of Granville.

The departure of the Germans and the arrival of the Americans had been so swift that the inhabitants of that little seaport were still dazed, moving circumspectly about the streets, doubting the evidence of their own eyes. The *patron* of the restaurant received us with dubious smiles, reflecting the pervading sense of impermanence. From his secret store he produced excellent white wine to take with the *langouste* (*spécialité de la maison*), a delicious omelette, fresh vegetables, cheese and butter and some real coffee, obviously acquired from the American PX, although brewed in the French style. The bottle of Calvados produced to top up the feast was so potent that my mind became a complete blank. When I came to I found myself seated with the rest of our party in a primitive *salon*, inspecting a collection of silk lingerie in an uproar of laughter and incomprehensible polyglot badinage. These strong Normandy women with their rosy cheeks, deep breasts and thick, sprawling limbs would make superb models for any artist, I thought, but not for the scanty garments in pastel pink and blue, trimmed with lace, which they were displaying with such outlandish gestures. They told us they had supported themselves during the German occupation by making these articles for German officers' wives and girl friends. The *Frauen* must have been flattered to receive such filigree underwear. Watching this vernal collection of femininity was so depressing that I broke up the party, much to the annoyance of the 'modistes,' and made for the car, leaving the others to straggle after me.

It was dark when we reached camp. As I stumbled to my tent I was met by Florence Desmond, demanding battledress and gum-boots. She and Kay Cavendish had withstood every sort of persuasion at Drury Lane to put on the ENSA standard dress. Now they were complaining that living under canvas had ruined their clothes, although they had only been ashore for twenty-four hours. It was my opportunity for a pert rejoinder. Instead, I could only giggle at the contrast in my mind's eye of 'Dessie' in a battle-dress and gum-boots and those Normandy peasants in their lingerie.

<>—<>—<>

Under the Influence . . .

An eccentric captain of the Royal Navy came out of retirement to take charge of one of the captured ports in the bridgehead. He was deeply affected by the films he saw at our mobile cinema shows and modelled his conduct upon them. Thus, his staff had an uncomfortable time when one week the good captain saw Charles Laughton in *Mutiny on the Bounty*. Fortunately, the next week's film was *Good-bye, Mr Chips*, so all was genial affection again.

5

Liberation Express

And now the cauldron of invasion boiled over as the Americans completed Montgomery's plan by overrunning Brittany and opening the way to Paris. In the surge forward that followed our column officers were overwhelmed with conflicting orders: "Go forward!" "Move back!" "Wait for instructions!" "Clear your people out of here, it's wanted for a hospital!" The confusion was made worse by the universal chorus of "get cracking! get cracking!" sung in varying accents of urgency according to seniority.

Gertrude Lawrence was out on the left flank; of all the stars she had most caught the urgency of my plea to keep close up to the advancing troops. A share of credit is also due to the commander of the group to which her column belonged, Major Stokes Roberts ('Stokey'),[1] whom I had encountered as entertainment officer during my first visit to Malta, where his ability to establish the friendliest atmosphere among those with whom he worked was humorously exemplified by the meetings he arranged between Solomon and Wee Georgie Wood during the coincidence of their visits at which, after mutual exchange of compliment, these North and South Poles of entertainment solemnly sat down to play poker. Noting his efficiency, I had marked him down for our impressment, secured his transfer and brought him home for the Second Front.

[1] Now the Director of the *Daily Mail* "Ideal Home" Exhibitions.

Gertrude was giving two and three performances each night in the little bombed-out casinos along the Normandy coast, and spending her days in soothing the nerves of the returning inhabitants, moving in each other's tracks with cat-like circumspection for fear of booby-traps, and growing increasingly dubious of the benefits of British invasion as they observed the wreckage of their homes. She did not in the least mind performing by candlelight or, she wrote rather ruefully, using cowsheds as lavatories, although it was embarrassing to have to share them with the troops. The determination that had lifted Gertie out of the side-streets of Lambeth and placed her among the twinkling stars of Broadway and Shaftesbury Avenue drove her on: in and out of Deauville—running no light risk of drowning in her zest to get across the Seine—through Bolbec and into Fécamp; Saint-Valery next, close to the heels now of the 51st Division (straining to wipe out the memory of its earlier surrender), then Dieppe, and beyond to reopen the Casino Theatre in Ostend, where huge portraits of the King of the Belgians and King George VI stared at each other from opposite boxes. Let us leave her along that line of march and turn to pick up the tracks of another indomitable trouper, pausing perhaps at Louvain to watch Nervo and Knox giving a matinée performance of their famous balloon dance, the accompanist in a too sunken orchestra pit unable to see even their legs, the troops roaring with laughter at the agonized expressions that chased themselves across the comedians' faces, with each jerk of the head. How were they to know that this was the morning after the night before?

One evening a young officer came spluttering into camp on a don-r's motor-cycle, spreading alarm and despondency. Alice Delysia had disappeared!

"Disappeared?" I cried. "Nonsense! Where to?"

"Don't know, sir. One of the company saw her waving from the back of a French truck. She was in a convoy; shouted something about Paris."

I grinned in the young man's face. The liberation of Paris was an event in History not to be missed. What better excuse for the journey could I have than to go in search of my lost star? Besides, I had certain plans in mind, which made it necessary to be early in the city before the Americans monopolized attention.

By this time the urge to advance was universal. All that was needed was a vehicle that could move, never mind whether it was yours or your neighbour's. This form of larceny, known as 'winning,' became so widespread that dozens of vehicles were known to change hands in a day. One of our brand-new sleeping-coaches disappeared in this 'general post.' Towed in by a R.E.M.E. recovery unit for a new axle after landing on the beach, it was later seen to be in use as the field headquarters of a senior commander of that efficient, if too acquisitive, arm. However, by making sure that my car was never out of sight either of myself or the driver, I stood a reasonable chance of early arrival in Paris. So I joined the endless crocodile of vehicles nose to tail, kilometre after kilometre, pouring through the Falaise Gap, still heavy with the scent of the dead. Thence to bomb-shattered Lisieux, where the pious spirit of Sainte Thérèse seemed to linger among the brutal ruinations; from there onwards to the Seine crossings, where it looked as though we might remain in the queue all night. Leaving the main road, we drove to where we had been told a local ferry had resumed working. There, quite close to the river, we came upon a sparse plantation of poplars, the space between the swaying trees tight-packed with abandoned horse transport of various kinds (carts, hay-wains, even ancient carriages) that had evidently been requisitioned from the French countryside; many of the vehicles had dead horses still harnessed to them. The ground too was carpeted with articles of clothing and accoutrements dropped by the enemy in flight. The scene would have made a perfect subject for some Royal Academician of Victorian days: title, *Rout!*

Virginia was at Dieppe, trying to conjure water out of the taps of her latest hostel. She agreed to come to Paris, where her assistance in contacting the French authorities was essential. As we drew near the capital we were borne forward upon a relentless flood of vehicles of every sort and description: giant American trucks, tank transporters, mobile guns and staff cars in descending sizes down to Virginia's PU. Stop, change down, start and stop again; gears grinding, engines revving; clouds of dust, knots of excitement at the roadside whenever we stopped; laughter and kisses given as a matter of right. It was the day after General Leclerc's French 2nd Armoured Division had rumbled down the Champs-Élysées, and excitement was still sizzling hot. Crowds of enthusiastic bicyclists, with British and American flags tied to the handle-bars or worn as scarves, surrounded the Étoile and Avenue des Champs-Élysées. Every few minutes these festive groups, coming together of no set purpose save to laugh and sing, would give way before lorries packed with American troops standing up and cheering, equally without reason. I felt greedy, wanting to suck in all the pure emotion to which the city had surrendered itself: the mad encounters, the joyful reunions, the ache of discovered loss —I wanted to lose none of it, so that in years to come its distillations might enrich and humble my memory.

Parking the car in the Place de la Concorde and bidding Virginia go and see if anything were left of her former home with Frank Vernon, I retraced my steps, but had not gone a dozen yards before I found myself the centre of flattering attention from excited Parisiennes who flung their arms round my neck and kissed me. My French was neither quick nor fluent enough to explain the difference between combatant and non-combatant, and, as they would not have believed me anyway, I accepted the vicarious battle honours without the slightest twinge of conscience. As I walked on, distant cheers came floating up the side-streets in sudden waves of sound, like the chattering of many starlings; shots and the clatter of fire-engines told where the last snipers were being flushed out by members of the Resistance. And then, for violent contrast, I came upon the stamp collectors' booths in some garden just off the Champs-Élysées, and watched the studied concentration of the buyers as with meticulous care they turned over the rarer specimens with long, slender forceps, some-times holding them up to the light in their little cellophane jackets. I caught myself smiling at their ridiculous absorption in the midst of world events.

All the bars and restaurants were filled with excited, singing customers. At Fouquet's the crowd and the noise seemed greatest. An impulse of curiosity drove me inside the place. There, standing on a marble-topped table surrounded by a wildly excited mob of cheering and singing Parisians, was Alice Delysia, wearing the uniform of the French Red Cross, adorned with ENSA flashes and various ribbons she had acquired during her long service in the Middle East. She was not in the least put out at the sight of me. Anyway, the noise was too great for explanations. Besides, who cared? Paris was free! She flung her arms round my neck and promised to return to her troupe in due course. She did for a short while, but really her gallant pilgrimage was over: France was free.

6

Nach BERLIN

In the early confusion of liberation nobody quite knew whether Paris was to be in the American or the British Zone, which made it difficult to find out whom to approach about entertainment. In the event, the city became mistress in its own house again, permitting American and British Military Staffs to remain only as house-guests to take charge of leave-centre arrangements. Through British Army staff I obtained an interview with the U.S. Commanding General. After convincing him that I was not just another Britisher trying to sell him something he did not want I offered him the usual dish of co-ordination: Americans and British each to provide a share of the entertainment; ENSA to run one theatre and one cinema and allocate a certain number of seats to Allied troops other than British, provided U.S. Services would reciprocate; a joint committee to deal with the allocation of seats; a central booking-office, run by U.S. Special Services, to control ticket distribution, and so on. I proposed a general title for the scheme of "Allied Entertainments, Paris," adding a rider to the effect that we should follow the American practice of admitting troops free to all shows, and permit a limited number of French civilians to purchase tickets in the ordinary way.

The general was disposed to acquiesce in the plan, which seemed to offer U.S. troops an opportunity of more live entertainment than they were likely to receive from U.S.O., whose major commitment was in the Pacific. On our side nothing more could be done without Treasury approval. Back in London our Finance Officer, with unwonted celerity, obtained Treasury approval for a scheme that was evidently in line with current official policy, the expenditure to be treated as part of reciprocal aid. At the next meeting of the Entertainments Board the *fait accompli* was greeted with a few disapproving looks, and some shoulders were shrugged: "Oh, well, if the Treasury has agreed . . ." and the meeting passed to other business.

In Paris Virginia found the theatre position complicated by a decision of the re-established civil authority not to grant licences to those managers who had collaborated with the enemy. Any request to requisition a theatre for the use of Allied troops would have to be made with the utmost circumspection. And with charming courtesy the managers, realizing that 'compensation rental' would in fact be no compensation for the richer harvest now in prospect, strove to evade that possibility. It was fortunate that Madame Vernon with her intimate and specialized knowledge of the French theatre scene was able to steer me clear of grosser error. Fortunate, too, that the new British Ambassador was so accessible and sympathetic. In the intervals of helping Lady Diana to marshal the packing-cases—the beautiful Embassy building was being reopened— Duff Cooper found time to talk things over and to introduce me to the resuscitated Ministry of Fine Arts. This had no practical outcome, but it did give my quest an official status when Virginia secured me an interview with Édouard Bourdet, the distinguished dramatist and Administrator of the Comèdie Française, to whom had been given the job of deciding which of the French theatres were to be reopened and by whom. He used his influence with M. Volterra, the French manager, who later won much success on the English turf, to let us have the Théâtre Marigny in the Champs-Élysées. Similarly, a large cinema, also on the Champs-Élysées,

was requisitioned for us through the French association of cinema proprietors.

The Marigny was opened as the ENSA Garrison Theatre, Paris, on
November 15, 1944, in the presence of members of the French Provisional
Government, the British Ambassador, and senior officers of the American
and British Forces, with the Brigadier of the British Army Staff, Paris,
acting as host. The Ambassadorial party was twenty minutes late. I cast
many anxious glances at the Presidential box, where the French party sat,
glum but expectant, but as Duff Cooper was attending officially it was
impossible to proceed without him. It was no satisfaction to be told that
the party at the Embassy had been a gay one nor to overhear the sharp
admonitions which the Ambassador's lady addressed to her lord—a
curtain lecture in more senses than one!

The performance was memorable more for the names of those giving
the entertainment than for its coherence: Noël Coward, Frances Day,
Will Hay, Bobby Howes, Nervo and Knox and Geraldo with his concert
orchestra. Noël enlivened a rather dull star programme by introducing
two songs that were new to the audience, one of them the now famous
satire about the South American lady, and Frances Day threw underclothes
into the stalls during one of her numbers.

The following week the galaxy appeared for us in Brussels, being joined
on the first night by Josephine Baker, who presented herself at the stage-
door, thus disproving the rumours of her death. She insisted upon taking
part, much to Noël's delight. On the last night of the visit Frances Day
again threw those underclothes into the stalls, this time at General Montgomery—with equivocal success. The Brussels visit terminated Noël
Coward's uneasy association with ENSA. Our organization was now
so vast that it had not been possible to give that individual attention
to the wishes of each star to which he had grown accustomed. Consequently, deficiencies in our organization loomed over-size in his mind.

Many companies of our British best performed at the ENSA Theatre
in Paris, including the Old Vic Company and the Sadlers Wells Ballet. At
least one West End production was tried out there before opening in
London: *The Lady from Edinburgh*, a play by Aimée and Philip Stuart,
displaying to the critical stare of the fashion-starved Parisiennes the latest
models of London's coupon-controlled *haute couture*. Most of the better-
known stage bands appeared here as part of their 'lease-lend' obligation,
among them the ever-popular Henry Hall, who donned ENSA uniform
and took his orchestra and singers through the liberated areas in 1945.

As more theatres became available to us in the principal cities of Europe
a special circuit was arranged for those attractions which, by their very

nature, were too big or too difficult to be distributed as mobile entertainment, to which I gave the office title of ENSACAP. Horrid fabrication! The tour was the means of displaying the first achievements of the post-war British Theatre in such cities as Paris, Brussels, Antwerp, Amsterdam, Rome, Naples, Hamburg, Berlin and Vienna.

7

Über Brüssel u. Antwerpen

Our principal headquarters in Western Europe (henceforth known to Army Signals as ENSA MAIN) were established in Brussels from September 1944, shortly after our first mobile columns arrived, until hostilities ceased in the following May. We soon had a fine super-cinema running, and an up-to-date newsreel theatre next door. Accommodation for live entertainment was more difficult. My attempt to secure regular use of the lovely Théâtre du Parc on certain days of the week broke down because the Belgians objected strenuously to having their premises requisitioned, pointing out that they were Allies. However, some of the most notable companies, including the Old Vic, did appear there. Ultimately a large variety house was secured, a modern building with white plasterwork and red plush which made a cheerful setting for the musical shows. This became known as the ENSA Music Hall, and was always packed. It was also used frequently for Army lectures and other official gatherings, and, once, as a casualty clearing-station when collaborators and non-collaborators fell out with one another and rioted through the streets.

When I arrived in Brussels Gertrude Lawrence was already there. She was the first star to enter the city. Billeted first at the Excelsior Hotel, she quickly moved out, saying she detested its empty façade of luxury, and joined the rest of her party at a smaller hotel where the conditions were sordid and unhappy. Calling to investigate, I was angry that our officers had allowed an inexperienced welfare assistant to make such a mistake while they had billeted themselves comfortably in a large, well-furnished private house. However, Madame Vernon arrived a day or two afterwards and soon put things to rights.

Headquarters for the Lines of Communication (ENSA REAR on official messages) were established in Antwerp. Here Lance Fairfax, from Palestine, now a lieutenant-colonel, took charge. The Scala was taken over as the garrison theatre and the near-by Eldorado as the garrison cinema, where also Fairfax had his administration. But the enemy's harassing fire from across the Scheldt, to say nothing of the bombing, gave our people many awkward moments. And, on December 16, a V2 fell on the Rex cinema, adjoining the theatre, during the matinée performance, demolishing the roof. Our people were badly shaken. Performances were continued with the help of new scenery and properties sent from Brussels. But shortly afterwards the garrison cinema was bombed and the offices completely wrecked. Whereupon, the Army authorities ordered our transfer to Ghent. It was here that I saw the production which Lewis Casson made for us of *St Joan*, with daughter Ann in the name part—a most excellent performance in a fine theatre, and well attended. Incidents continued to occur in Antwerp, until one morning we received sudden orders to cancel all entertainments forthwith. Nan Kenway and Douglas Young had just arrived; they were told to get some breakfast and leave immediately: "a case of spam and scram" wrote the comedian in his diary.

The advance of the liberating armies across Western Europe uncovered towns possessing first-class theatres. The Municipal Theatre at Lille calls for special mention because of the number and similarity of its war-time vicissitudes. In the First War it was taken over by the Germans as an entertainment centre when they overran Northern France. Both the Kaiser and Field-Marshal von Hindenburg attended the official opening. When the Germans were driven out it became the home of Leslie Henson's 'Gaieties,' the comedian arriving at the stage-door to take over immediately after the German director had left. This was Franz Arnold, who visited England after the 1914–18 war to arrange the adaptation of several of his farces for Leslie's use. In the Second War ENSA took up the story, giving performances in the Municipal Theatre regularly until the Blitzkrieg, after which the Germans once again resumed occupancy—on May 10, 1941, to be precise—when the theatre was opened by Propaganda Minister Goebbels as the headquarters of Das Deutsche . . . Theater am Westen. The photographs reproduced here are from a captured enemy brochure, and show how closely the organization followed ours, not omitting the use of uniformed personnel to run the administration and the assistance sometimes called for by the stouter members of a company in boarding military lorries!

As soon as Brussels was liberated we appointed music advisers to N.W. Europe. This was opposed at first by the B.L.A.[1] Entertainment Committee, who thought that if good music were required, it should be provided either by Army Welfare or by Army Education, and not by ENSA. However, the Music Council, egged on by Walter Legge, had begun this particular march overseas, loading the ENSA knapsack with the

[1] British Liberation Army.

THE END OF THE AFFAIR

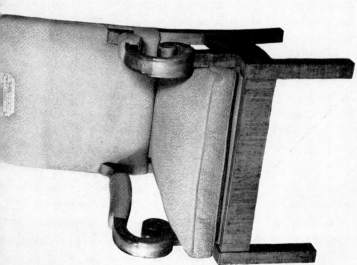

THE SO-CALLED "HITLER" CHAIR

From the Reich Chancellory
Berlin
Renovated and presented to Drury Lane Theatre
by BASIL DEAN
as a memento of the occupancy of the Theatre
as the ENSA Headquarters
During the Second World War
1939 — 1946

"THE MERRY WIDOW" (MADGE ELLIOT AND CYRIL RITCHARD) WALTZED HER
WAY TO EVERY FRONT

Here the company is in Brussels after touring the Middle East and Italy.

FRANCES DAY MAKES HER BOW AT THE MARIGNY THEATRE, PARIS

best music and the batons of well-known conductors, and with water-bottles well filled with enthusiasm, setting out to conduct local orchestras, resuscitated after the holocaust of double invasion. A triumphant start had been made with the visits to Italy, first of all, of John Barbirolli and, later, of Constant Lambert. Now further objectives had come into view. To hand over the work to another authority was out of the question.

Our plan to raise the national flags of entertainment in the various countries as they were liberated came unstuck for the simple reason that in the general joy and excitement it was impossible to secure the co-ordinated effort which they required. Artistes and managers were scattered far and wide; many had been deported, others, from the Resistance, were rejoining their national colours. Moreover, some of the Allied liaison officers[1] who had accompanied our columns to the beachhead had gone off to fling their arms round their families. Who shall blame them? When we heard at Drury Lane of their defection we thought it rather funny, and laughed as though we had ourselves been present at their joyful reunions. However, we did help in the rehabilitation of individuals; Belgian and Dutch artistes were employed, either in mixed parties in association with our own people or in companies of their own. Many of them, particularly the concert artistes and circus turns, were immensely popular with the troops. They were a bunch of assorted characters, and if not all of those who claimed to have escaped from German prison camps or the torture chambers of the Gestapo had in fact done so, they were talented people none the less. And allowance must be made for the romantic temperament.

All the companies passed back and forth through Brussels, so that at times our headquarters there was like a miniature Drury Lane. In the end the Hôtel Georges Scheers was taken over, with additional accommodation later at the Hôtel Trappiste, both in the Boulevard Adolphe Max. On certain days in the week the foyer of the Georges Scheers reminded one of a hotel lounge at Southampton immediately after the arrival of one of the big liners; crowded with actors and actresses, musicians, singers, variety artistes, some mounting guard over their hand-luggage, others sitting in corners reading, all waiting for convoys home or to take them up the line. Here and there a welfare assistant moved among them checking on journey details. All wore the ENSA uniform or khaki battledress, the stars easily distinguishable from the chorus even at a distance by the air of embarrassment with which they bore their submersion beneath this flood

---

[1] These were the officers selected by Lord Cromer's International Council on the recommendations of the various Governments-in-Exile.

2D

of uniformity. A babble of voices filled the place like an over-amplified sound track. Yes, positively an entertainment army!

My personal recollections of the next few months are of endless car journeys, slithering through mud and darkness, to which a cold fog was usually added, when the main preoccupations were to keep one's car or truck out of the ditch and in the track of the vehicle in front of one. The only signposts were the military ones: Maple Leaf Up, Club Route Down, Diamond Up, 250 Up and Down. What scenes to recall along those military traffic routes! How well one learned to know them, especially the tricky places where, owing to some strange conformity of light and shadow, one continually went wrong: all too easy in that darkened countryside, where topographical features displayed a mocking similarity.

All but our heaviest transport had been handed over to Mrs Peake's Motor Transport Corps (M.T.C.). Seizing an opportunity to serve overseas, previously denied them since the first months of the war in Egypt, the more venturesome, among them Lady Stuart-Wortley, now Duchess of Newcastle, added ENSA flashes to their uniforms and trooped over to Brussels to drive ENSA trucks and cars through the Flanders winter: some in the spirit of the chase, some with an additive charm that did not fade for lack of notice. It was well they were expert drivers, for road incidents were encountered daily, almost hourly, amid the surging traffic. . . .

"Don't those men look funny; just like Germans," giggles a little Cockney chorus girl, as a dashing sergeant drives his coachload of talent slap into a German forward position near Apeldoorn. Whereupon he goes on through the village, turns round and drives back again before any of the party have time to realize their position.

Evening Dress Operational . . .

It was a constant source of wonder to me how the most delicately nurtured musicians stood up to the hardships and the danger. Pouishnoff is particularly remembered in this regard. Wherever he went the flying-bombs pursued him. Yet nothing daunted him nor tarnished his immaculate appearance on the platform. At Eindhoven while he was changing for his concert one of these missiles hit the power-station, putting out all the lights. After a hurried search some candles were produced. As they were being lighted Pouishnoff stalked from his dressing-room in full evening dress, quite a sartorial achievement for an elderly man in pitch darkness. The effect of such coolness upon the morale of other artistes was magical.

8

Its Finest Hour

Great preparations were made to give the B.L.A. a rich spread of entertainment at Christmas time. As a principal item in the menu, Barbirolli proposed to take over the full Hallé Orchestra. He had returned to England from his visit to the troops in Italy, full of enthusiasm for the new soldier-audiences, but irked by the amount of time lost in rehearsing the foreign orchestras. It would be the first time in its history that the Hallé had left England; and it would not be a small undertaking, for eighty-seven musicians, half of them women, would take up quite a lot of room both in transport and billets. 21 Army Group Welfare seized upon this fact to negative the idea at first. In view of what transpired the troops have cause to be grateful to our Treasury Finance Officer for the support he gave me in the argument.

The orchestra sailed from Southampton in the charge of Ernest Bean, now the manager of the Royal Festival Hall in London. After being delayed in the Channel for three days by fog, that biting kind in which north-western Europe appears to specialize, during which they gave an impromptu concert on board, they reached Brussels in time to give two concerts on December 22 and 23. Meanwhile, Ian MacPhail—of the re-diffusion scheme, you remember—had been sent on ahead to assist the music advisers and to ensure that the necessary transport was procured. Only one coach was available, the rest being troop-carrying vehicles, but he managed to borrow a Mercédès car, formerly the property of the German Assistant-Chief of Police in Brussels, for Barbirolli, his wife (Evelyn Rothwell) and the leader, Laurence Turner. The eminent conductor refused to ride in it: the car and the coach must be for the ladies and older men; he would travel in one of the troop-carriers. And, like Gertrude Lawrence before him, he refused to stay at the Excelsior Hotel: "he must be where his orchestra is."

On Christmas Eve they played in Ghent, returning to Brussels for two more concerts on Christmas Day, at which Solomon played piano concerti. Long queues of officers and men surrounded the Salles des Beaux Arts for hours, waiting to get in. It had been suggested to Barbirolli that if he were to include some Jewish music in the programmes this would convince the local population that Freedom really had been restored to them, more so perhaps than any material gesture, since performances of Jewish music had been forbidden during the Occupation. The only piece they had with them was the Mendelssohn violin concerto, and as the soloist had been unable to leave England because of the bad weather, the leader of the Hallé, Laurence Turner, played it. This was the first Jewish music to be played on liberated soil.

After a visit to Lille the orchestra was to go to Eindhoven on New Year's Eve to play to forward troops. It was lucky that Madame Vernon was in Brussels. On the day in question she knocked on MacPhail's door at 3 A.M. and insisted upon his getting up to go with her in the car to Eindhoven, adding by way of explanation that she had a hunch all was not right with the billets. Her intuition saved a serious situation. She and MacPhail arrived at 8 A.M. to find that the large house requisitioned for the orchestra was filthy: no other word for it. After a hasty cup of tea they set to work to scrub the place out, summoning drivers, clerks and even our junior officers to fetch and carry pails of hot water from the nearest Army cooking unit.

The convoy of vehicles, including a lorry laden with extra blankets and bedding, arrived in time for dinner. It was snowing, bitterly cold, and the icy fog had come down once more. After their six-hour drive the musicians were certainly ready for the bully-beef stew ("appetizing only because it steamed") eaten in a ground-floor store room that did duty for a dining-hall, its bomb-blasted windows and walls supported by heavy baulks of timber. There was one stove, round which they crowded, four or five at a time, to thaw their fingers, for that of course was their greatest anxiety, before making their way down the road to Dutch billets that were as cold as the icy roads. Barbirolli had retired to look at a score, but at 11 P.M. he and MacPhail were out on the road again, touring the billets in the Mercédès, followed by the lorry, from which the conductor personally supervised the distribution of extra blankets to each member.

Now began an adventure which Barbirolli has himself described as the Hallé's finest hour. No sooner had the orchestra arrived than Von Runstedt's thrust for the Channel ports began. The result is an item of military history, but one of its immediate consequences was that 'the Hallé' found itself marooned on the fringe of a major battle. The musicians decided to give two full orchestral concerts each day throughout the emergency, playing in the beautiful Phillips Theatre. The enemy provided frequent reminders of the dangers outside, machine-gunning the players from the air on one occasion as they were getting into the coach; upon another, just after the *Fledermaus* overture had been broadcast in the Forces Programme, shooting down seven or eight soldiers waiting in the queue outside: poor return for an admirable performance of some of their own music.

The concert on New Year's Eve will never be forgotten by those who took part in it nor, indeed, by those who heard it over the air. Frank Gillard, the B.B.C. commentator, described the scene to listeners at home. The final item was a selection of Scottish songs, ending with *Auld Lang Syne*, prepared by Barbirolli's brother-in-law. The orchestra, shrouded in Balaclava helmets—no one who has not experienced it can imagine the penetrating cold of those frost pockets in Holland—the brass section with just their lips showing, the double-bass players in thick woollen gloves—playing without music for the most part, Barbirolli orchestrating as he went along, calling out to the various instruments the parts they were to play (one included a marvellous descant by the horns), the impromptu singing by the weary troops sitting in the stalls in their battle-gear with rifles and Sten guns on their laps and machine-guns piled in the aisles, their breath ascending in clouds in the unheated building. The atmosphere was as emotional as a Welsh revivalist meeting. The programme over, a secondary concert began at once, the men calling out their requests, including items from Debussy and Ravel, while 'Tommy' Cheetham, the librarian, rummaged through his music, almost flinging the parts at the various musicians. At the end there was a wild rush for the platform, because every member of the audience wanted to shake Barbirolli by the hand. Those young men had undergone an experience that might never be repeated. Undefined, unspoken was a prophetic sense of the brevity of life, brought into focus under the spiritual illumination of the music.

Thus, the two days at Eindhoven lengthened into a week. Our British troops returned to the battle fortified by music played by an orchestra founded and made famous by a German, while the musicians found ultimate justification of their national service amid the blood and cold of the most critical battlefield of the war.

CHAPTER TWENTY-NINE

THE OTHER SIDE OF THE HILL

1

Dawn Chorus

THE Entertainments Board gave permission for work to begin in India some time in 1943, while the departmental discussions were still proceeding, but on an extremely modest scale because of the uncertainty as to our mandate and the ultimate financial authority. The first office was opened in our Cairo headquarters in the Kasr-el-Nil, in what was little more than a cubby-hole opening on to the first landing. It possessed neither window nor telephone, but the outside of the flimsy door bore the brave title, 'ENSA—INDIA.' In charge of this office was a certain sergeant-major, whose reply to every remark made by Dunstan was, "Yes, mijor," to which Dunstan would invariably reply, "You should never forget—there is no 'I' in major."

The first officer to join Dunstan was Captain Donald Neville-Willing, transferring from the staff employed on rehabilitation work by Mr Casey, then Minister of State. Of mixed English and Dutch extraction, his keen sense of humour and acid wit invariably gave him the victory in any battle of words to which personal idiosyncracy may have given rise. He had attended his first ENSA show at the Ezbekiah Theatre as the guest of Colin Keith-Johnson, a well-known British actor in America who had been brought back by us under the Government's repatriation scheme and given a commission. As he entered the box he was surprised to see Colin turn his chair with its back to the stage. He asked why, and Colin replied, "Dear boy, because I'm here on duty, that doesn't mean I have to look at the show," which gave Neville-Willing a misleading impression of his forthcoming duties.

Dunstan flew to India alone, leaving him to bring on the advance party, consisting of two junior officers and several N.C.O.'s. Just before they were due to sail Haygarth, whose sense of duty appeared always to be in competition with his sense of humour, paraded the party at the Cairo office and solemnly warned them against the wickedness of

India, adding certain precepts on the proper conduct of officers and men towards "the natives," complacently unaware of the sharp eyes and ears that were taking in his remarks.

The staff waited seven weeks in a transit camp at Suez for a ship, watching with mordant interest the gradual filling up of a still larger camp near by for Service women, known to the waiting soldiery as "The Aviary." In addition to the military personnel, Neville-Willing had with him various dogs belonging to Dunstan (including a litter of five puppies) and his pet pigeons, trained to sit at table when meals were served. The officer in charge of the camp, with a lively sense of what was to be expected of ENSA, took one look at the little menagerie and immediately asked Neville-Willing for a performance.

"But I don't do anything," protested that officer.

"Not by yourself, but with the pigeons and dogs. Let's have the whole lot."

On board the troopship *Derbyshire* was an ENSA party also bound for Bombay, bearing the optimistic title of 'You're Welcome' and looking very smart in their standard dress, the first artistes to be so equipped. They had been sent from Cairo to open the new service. The parties who later followed them from England were equipped with white topees— to the huge delight of the troops. The mistake was soon corrected, but not before the comedians had discovered the laughter-making properties of this form of headgear.

'You're Welcome' had arrived in Cairo at the top of the crisis preceding El Alamein, after journeying from Britain in the *Aquitania* via Sierra Leone, Cape Town and Madagascar, only to find themselves confined to their hotel until they could be moved to a less vulnerable area. They were sent to Palestine, Syria, Irak (where, from Mosul onwards, they lived in their own railway coach) and to Iran, where photographs show them displaying their 'poshteens'—the sheepskin coats worn as protection against the bitter night winds; then back they went to follow the Eighth Army as far as El Agheila. Finally they were flown back to Cairo to make ready for this new duty. The company was managed by Stafford Byrne and included Alec Halls, an admirable Scottish comedian.

In India their first performance was given in an open-air theatre on a hill above Bombay—the headlights of vehicles, jeeps, staff cars and 3-tonners, climbing the hill from every direction, setting the countryside alight with fiery anticipation. The six rows of gold braid and red tabs, come from near and far to vet the first ENSA show, included the Governor of Bombay (Sir John Colville[1]) and Lady Colville. At the Govern-

[1] Later Lord Clydesmuir.

ment House reception which followed the Governor made graceful reference to the appropriate name of the company and concluded the evening by playing the bagpipes up and down the entrance hall with Alec Halls. The official report upon the tour[1] ended with the sentence: "the whole of British India is astonished to find the artistes behaving like ladies and gentlemen."

The first stars to arrive by air were Elsie and Doris Waters, briskly military with khaki berets and ENSA shoulder flashes. Notice of their coming had been short, so the officer sent to meet them at Karachi expressed amiable anxiety as to the accommodation they would find in Bombay.

"Oh, it doesn't matter," remarked one of the sisters with easy nonchalance. "We can go back to England, if they're full up, and come some other time."

Warm hearts and a rich endowment of humour made for quick adjustment to new surroundings. Spending their mornings drinking tea with the troops in their canteens and on spare evenings giving turns in the hospital wards, the sisters made friends wherever they went, up and down the sub-continent and over the Manipur Road as far as Imphal.

Their frontal assaults upon the traditional snobbery of the British Raj further extended their popularity among the troops. Invited to a smart social gathering at the exclusive Poona Club, they found they were expected to give a turn to the assembled guests.

"If we give you a turn will you do us one?" one of them asked forthrightly.

"What is that?"

"Allow the O.R.'s in here?"

There followed some whispering in corners, but the hostess was firmly told it was the only condition upon which the Waters sisters would consent to entertain her guests. It was finally agreed that each lady present

[1] Neither officers nor men forgot the companies that had pleased them at home. When 'You're Welcome' arrived at Trincomalee (Trinco for short) the fleet had just returned from a raid on Sebang. Vice-Admiral Power, remembering the company's visit to Scapa in 1941, sent his flag-lieutenant to ask for an immediate visit to the Fleet. All other bookings were cancelled, and the company gave two shows a day in *Queen Elizabeth*, *Valiant* and *Renown*, also in the French battleship *Richelieu*. The loyalties of this ship's company at that time were divided between General de Gaulle and Vichy, so that the artistes faced a sticky atmosphere in more senses than one. But *les matelots* soon showed their appreciation by throwing their hats on to the stage for the girls they favoured to kiss the red pompoms on the crowns. At the end of the performance the stage was littered with hats. The captain presented each of the players with a medal with the *Richelieu* crest in thanks for the lift that had been given to the morale of his ship's company, telling the manager that *La Marseillaise* had been sung in the ship for the first time in two years.

should invite two O.R.'s to take tea with her in the Club once a week. Remarked one of the hostesses after her first experience of this enforced hospitality:

"My dear, you've no idea; they behaved better than the officers!"

Meanwhile, the 'You're Welcome' Company had been entertaining the Chindits in their training quarters, living in huts and tents under jungle conditions: one bed-roll and one suitcase per person the limit of luggage. Among the British troops was a unit of the Black Watch whom they had first entertained at Thurso in 1941.[1] The Indians were mostly Gurkhas, who always greeted the opening chorus with loud hisses.

"Don't they like us?" asked one of the chorines on the first occasion.

"They think you're wonderful," replied a British officer with truth and tact.

In due course the Chindits were flown into Burma while the players remained behind for another week for Security reasons, contemplating with satisfaction a unique experience.

With the Waters sisters came 'Stainless' Stephen, who mysteriously disappeared shortly after his arrival in Calcutta. He was located eventually among the front-line troops at Imphal, giving hourly turns to the men, almost in their foxholes. The exploit remained in the memory of all who fought in Burma, for they continued to show him their gratitude in riotous welcome at the Fourteenth Army rallies in the Albert Hall.

Next to arrive was Vera Lynn, in travel-stained shorts and shirt, carrying a small holdall like a football bag.

"Where's your luggage?" asked the ENSA officer.

"That's all I've got."

"What about your dresses?"

"Rolled up in there," she said, indicating the holdall.

Within an hour they were taken out, laundered, and beautifully pressed —a service only possible in the land where dhobies swarm. Even as she viewed her strange surroundings with child-like interest and met every mishap with disconcerting simplicity, so her nightly transformation from a travelling Cinderella into the 'Forces Sweetheart' remained a triumph of single-hearted integrity.

While she was going to lunch one day with Eric Dunstan the car stopped first at Government House to drop Elsie and Doris Waters.

"Who lives here?" demanded Vera Lynn.

"The Governor," replied Neville-Willing, in a tone of awe.

"Whose Guv-nor?" said Vera, quite unabashed.

[1] The company had the unique experience of playing to men of the 5th Division in seven different countries, and they were indeed 'welcome' in each of them.

At a casualty clearing station within a few miles of the fighting line in
Burma she was told that the Japs played her records over loudspeakers "to
lower the morale of British troops"; at her first concert in Dinapur the
front of the minipiano fell out and had to be held in place by an officer
for the rest of the evening; in Calcutta, when Imphal was surrounded,
'Dicky' Sharp of the B.B.C. proposed that she and he should be dropped
inside 'the box,' so that he could record her singing to the troops within
sound of the guns. "Fine," said Vera, "but how do I get out again?"
"Never mind how you get out. All that matters is to get in."

From the beginning Dunstan was determined to leave no doubt in the
official mind as to the importance of his position as Colonel Commanding
ENSA (INDIA)—with the NAAFI connexion kept discreetly in the
background. In view of the tenuous nature of our early mandate this was
undoubtedly wise. Among the influential friends he had encountered
in Cairo was the Princess Aly Khan.[1] Before he left for Bombay she
suggested he should occupy the Aga Khan's beautiful villa on Malabar Hill;
at least that would save it from being requisitioned.

From this social fortress he surveyed the position with an eye persuasive
and benign, giving frequent parties, not only to the visiting stars but to
senior British officers and officials, establishing thereby the ENSA position and his own at the same time. By means of his generous hospitality
V.I.P.'s from England were drawn into a personal interest in ENSA and
its doings. It was fortunate for his plans that the first companies we sent
out justified the large confidence which he displayed on our behalf.

Cecil Beaton came out for the British Information Service. Dunstan,
with a lively sense of photographs to come, arranged his accommodation
at the Taj Mahal Hotel. The morning after his arrival Beaton went to the
native quarter and came back with a gharry full of flowers, which three
servants bore into his room. As the 'Taj' did not possess any flower vases
he placed his purchases in a row of chamber pots round the veranda,
much to the annoyance of the hotel management, who were already short
of that particular receptacle.

The social round brought valuable reinforcement to the ENSA net.
Invited to join the Governor's entourage at a special performance given
by the 'Cross Keys' Divisional concert party at the Town Hall, Bombay,
Dunstan took with him Neville-Willing, who, his keen eyes lighting upon
an attractive Spanish señorita, complete with billowing skirts and fan,
decided that impersonator Jack Hawkins would be an asset. Dunstan's
'pull' at G.H.Q. made the transfer of this accomplished actor an easy
matter. This was good fortune for Jack in a more personal way, too, for

[1] *Née* the Hon. Joan Yarde-Buller.

during the course of his duties he met and married Doreen Lawrence, then touring India in the ENSA production of *Private Lives*. Jack ended the war a full colonel and occupying a dominating position in our hierarchy in India.

Despite his obsession with the social side of the organization, Dunstan possessed great moral courage. An important show with stars was about to begin at the R.A.F. H.Q. in Bombay when he noticed that the first four rows of armchairs were empty. He was told they were being kept for the officers.

"Hi! You fellows," called Eric to the crowded benches at the back, "fill up these front seats."

Twenty minutes later the Air Marshal sauntered in, smoking a cigar, followed by his staff and their ladies.

"What's all this?" he demanded.

"I gave orders for the seats to be occupied, sir," replied Eric. The Air Marshal began to splutter. "Sorry, sir, but I am in charge of ENSA in India. And I cannot allow the artistes to play to empty seats."

Garbled accounts of this incident, for which Dunstan ran the risk of disciplinary action, passed rapidly through the military grape-vine with salutary effect upon subsequent punctuality.

The welcome that greeted our arrival in India had a very practical outcome in offers of accommodation for the artistes, oftentimes at personal inconvenience, but this could not be expected to continue indefinitely, especially since want of consideration on the part of individuals invariably led to the withdrawal of privilege from those who followed them.[1] Dunstan had been given no specific instructions regarding welfare procedure, but unless the matter were given expert attention there would be painful incidents. Accordingly, within a few weeks of his arrival he received a cable from me which read:

"Virginia Vernon Chief ENSA Welfare Officer arriving shortly." Evidently he had other ideas, for he cabled back that he had made his own welfare arrangements. The reply to this *démarche* was equally unexpected: a brief cable from C.E.W.O., *en route*, which said:

"Arriving this afternoon, Virginia Vernon."

Her impact upon this glamourized set-up can be imagined. Asked whether she should be accommodated at the Taj Mahal, Eric had replied

---

[1] Hermione Baddeley and Leslie Henson once let off steam at a gay party in the officers' transit hotel in Tunis: quite harmless, really, if a little noisy. Some high-ranking staff officers, who were due to be called at 4 A.M. for an onward flight, lost their sleep thereby. It was months before we could regain the privilege of using the hotel. Meanwhile the complaint had travelled along the wires until it came to a halt in a War Office file.

that a good second-class hotel would do. Virginia took one look at the pension—"filthy place" was her terse comment—and demanded the whereabouts of Dunstan; he was just then busy with one of his exclusive cocktail parties. When she telephoned to him he replied off-handedly, "I'll see you to-morrow morning at the office at 10," to which she replied, "You will see me now." Virginia—in her travel-stained khaki, carrying her overfilled dispatch case, perspiring freely, but, as always when over-tired, at her most trenchant—did not impress his friends.

Nevertheless, Dunstan was profoundly right in seeing to it that our entry into the official life of British India was upon a proper social status. By such means he met half-way any resistance that might arise in Delhi and elsewhere to the new organization that depended for its success upon facilities never before granted. And he did not hesitate to use his personal fortune to further this objective. Indeed, upon reflection, although matters subsequently went awry when the size of the organization proved too great for Dunstan's personal approach to its problems, we could not have made a better choice for O.C. ENSA (INDIA).

◇◆◇

The Ladies of the Raj . . .

Some of our officers, observing the social round from its circumference had mischievous stories to tell. In one remote area the senior Army officer was named King. Chatting to impress our young men at tiffin, his wife remarked, "We're very popular here, you know, particularly me. Last year we had a durbar, and the natives put a streamer across the street and on it 'God Save the King and Mrs King.' Wasn't it sweet of them?"

Another officer, attending an important social function, was introduced to a general's wife whose face seemed familiar. Then he realized he had known her as a barmaid at a favourite haunt in the West End of London. The evening grew late. When he was about to leave she stopped him, pointing out that her husband was in command of the District and no one could leave until she did. "Fun, isn't it?" she added.

2

Cairo revisited

Shortly after midnight on December 17, 1944, I found myself airborne once more in an R.A.F. Dakota, bound for India via Gibraltar and the

Middle East. Following a general report on the welfare of British troops in India from Lord Munster, in which ENSA was criticized for inadequacy, there had been a debate in the House of Commons. Whereupon the argument between the Treasury, the India Office and Delhi was swiftly concluded, galvanized into finality by the direct intervention of the Prime Minister. Then some telephone inquiries from the Cabinet secretariat, and, presto! within a week or two I was on my way, shivering with cold under a couple of Army blankets, listening to the incomprehensible jokes of the Polish pilot and his navigator, both wearing the D.F.C. and both highly contemptuous of the transport duties to which they had been relegated.

The flight had been specially arranged. There were only two passengers, myself and Captain Kershaw, a young man who was to act as my p.a. on the tour before taking up his duties as adjutant of our headquarters in Bombay—the only way in which I could overcome the resistance of the NAAFI chairman to the idea that such help was necessary to me. While the Polish crew smoked interminable cigarettes in the cockpit, filling me with apprehension in the process, my mind went rummaging over the past to compare it with present circumstances. Copies of the letters that had been exchanged between Delhi and London, setting out the terms of agreement, had been given to me, together with full authority to settle any outstanding details with the Finance Member of the Government of India. The Secretary of State[1] had personally assured me of his backing if I ran into any bureaucratic difficulty, and the Entertainments Board had given full steam ahead. Finally, my mission was to come under the remote watchfulness of the Prime Minister himself. The days of carpet-bagging for ENSA were over. I felt responsible and important.

A vicious bumping over the Bay in the bitter cold of the small hours caused much merriment in the cockpit, and, for further measure, just as the dawn began to hint at its presence we were jerked wide awake by a violent lurch to starboard which flung us out of our bucket seats on to the floor. More merriment from the Poles. Through the white morning mist the dark shadow of The Rock loomed up on the port side. Soon we were threading our way round and among the masts of fishing vessels a few hundred feet above calm water. To attempt to land on the crowded airstrip in such weather seemed a speculative venture. Judging by the animated discussion in the cockpit, the pilot thought the same.

"Gibraltar?" I asked.

"Gibraltaire, yes."

"All right to land?"

[1] The Right Hon. L. S. Amery, P.C., C.H., M.P.

"Perhaps, yes, perhaps, not." He gave me the thumbs down sign. "Radio—kaput—no signals."

A red Very light coming up at us out of the mist warned the pilot against any such recklessness. Another sharp swerve, more laughter, and we gain height and speed away. No Gibraltar yet!

After radio repairs at Oran, flight calls at Gibraltar and Tripoli and a further breakdown at El Adem, all to the accompaniment of Polish enjoyment of every mishap, we reached Cairo at 6.45 P.M. on the night of December 19: not bad after the inauspicious start.

In the eighteen months since my last visit immense changes had been wrought, the bad reputation of our early days completely wiped out and lost confidence regained. Forward planning was ambitious and assured. While the Garrison Theatre was being made ready, and to set the pace for the ambitious plans to follow, the Cairo Opera House had been loaned to us on nominal terms for a production of *The Merry Widow*, with Madge Elliott and Cyril Ritchard, Mark Daly and Diana Gould (now Mrs Yehudi Menuhin) in the cast, for which Jack Hylton lent his London scenery and costumes. Our own theatre, very spick and span, was opened with Rex Newman's production of *No, No, Nanette*, with Dave Hutcheson, Lois Green and Enid Lowe to head the cast. The play ran for eight weeks to capacity audiences. It was followed by the Middle East production of Priestley's *How Are They at Home?*, and, later, Benn Levy's comedy, *Springtime for Henry*, the four parts in which were played by Kathleen O'Regan, Victoria Hopper, Lieutenant Nigel Patrick and Flight-Lieutenant Richard Littledale, R.A.F.—the two officers being given special leave from their respective units for the purpose. Even Harry Welchman arrived in due course to cast his 'Red Shadow' in *The Desert Song*.

The Cairo Symphony Orchestra was going strong, and its Sunday night concerts under the baton of Squadron-Leader Hugo Rignold were always sold out.[1] Gerald Gover had joined Lance Dossor as a second music adviser. Together they gave piano recitals that were immensely popular, except perhaps with the British N.C.O.'s responsible for the transport of their grand pianos, whose general complaint it was that the pair would never stop playing. The first of Walter Legge's 'Good Music' parties (Miriam Licette, Nancy Evans, Dennis Noble, Walter Widdop, Alfred Cave and Ivor Newton) had come and gone on to India, after rapturous welcome everywhere.

---

[1] 'Music for All,' a scheme started and brilliantly conducted by Lady Russell, wife of Russell Pasha, that had kept alive a taste for good music in the barren years, was by now relying more and more upon the help of our artistes, until finally circumstances compelled us to take it over.

The Music Division, continuing its policy of encouragement of young musical talent, asked Hubert Greenslade, accompanist to another good music party, to keep his eyes open, which he did to good effect. It was thus that Manoug Parikian was discovered and sent back to England, where he studied for a year before joining the Philharmonia Orchestra. Within six months he became its distinguished leader.

Popular band-leaders were bringing out their bands, *e.g.*, Maurice Winnick, whose band, together with the 'Dorchester Follies' stage show, had recently arrived after a strenuous three months' tour of Italy. Geraldo's appearance later in the year was eagerly anticipated. Young Henry Caldwell's latent confidence and ability, enormously developed since his transfer to ENSA, had carried him from control of the entertainment side of all British Forces Broadcasting from Algiers, Tunis and Sicily to the production of theatre shows in Cairo under Rex Newman's supervision. Sent to investigate the arrival at Haifa of an illegal shipload of European refugees, he reported the presence of a number of Hungarian artistes of undoubted ability. From their number he created two complete variety entertainments under Rex's guidance, one of them being given the title of 'Café Continentale.' This was the origin of the B.B.C. television feature.

The production centre was bustling with activity. Members of companies that had disintegrated through illness or termination of contracts were no longer kicking their heels, awaiting sailing-dates for home; they were put into new shows produced at the centre by well-known artistes encouraged to try their hand at production. Among these was Noel Howlett, who, after joining ENSA as an actor, later became a conducting warrant officer for us, during which 'pilgrim's progress' he found himself understudying the part in *George and Margaret* which he had originally created in London! Later he was given a commission and produced a large number of straight plays for Newman. Eric Berry was another good actor who did useful work in this way. The chief designer and scene painter was Captain Anson,[1] whom Newman had discovered as a sergeant-typist in Algiers, with Sergeant 'Tommy' Hudson to run the scene and property workshops. Under these expert technicians a staff of Egyptian craftsmen was eagerly absorbing the 'know-how' of stage production.

My stay of twenty-four hours gave time for no more than a solid meal of satisfaction with all this progress, not forgetting warm congratulations to the principal chef, Rex Newman, before I was winging my way to Baghdad, where similar improvement on a smaller scale brought com-

[1] Much of the scenery in current West End productions bears the hallmark of his craftsmanship, for he is now chief scenic artist to the Alick Johnstone studios.

mendation from the G.O.C. Thence to Basra, smelling like an untended oil lamp, where our stage shows were evidently appreciated, one of them receiving the following encomium in the Basra *Times*: "The four dancing girls, Muriel, Josephine, Carol and Ruth, were like vestal virgins, figures of vital vitamins." Garrison cinemas for the R.A.F. at Shaiba and Abadan were also doing a good job.

I had promised to be in India before Christmas, and it was now December 22; and so on over the muddy waters of the Persian Gulf through deepening blue skies to Karachi, picking up news on the way of the fantastic success of Walter Legge's 'Good Music' party[1] as it flew over the desert wastes with its mini-piano, fiddle and glorious talent.

The damson bloom of Indian darkness was spreading over the airport buildings as my aircraft touched down. My visit had been announced in the House of Commons and given considerable publicity in the Press, which put an extra edge on my determination to achieve its purpose.

We were driven through the scented dust to the transit mess at Somerset House, where a telegram was handed to me from Eric Dunstan. He proposed to spend Christmas in Ceylon, as he felt run down, and suggested that I should fly on to Delhi and report there. I felt like the unwelcome guest arriving unexpectedly at the feast. Gulping down the anticlimax with a stiff whisky and soda, I sent a terse telegram to Dunstan, instructing him to await my arrival in Bombay, and went to bed.

<><><>

Classic Praise . . .

Sailing in convoy to the Middle East, the 'Good Music' party had been warned that in the event of six short blasts being given on the ship's hooter (indicating the possibility of submarine or air attack) all passengers must immediately make their way to boat stations. One calm morning in the Mediterranean the warning was given. Dennis Noble, acting as manager of the party, saw Miriam Licette and Nancy Evans out of their cabin and then went along to that shared by Alfred Cave and Walter Widdop. Walter Widdop was dressed and ready to go; Cave was putting

---

[1] At Sharjah, a lonely R.A.F. station on the Persian Gulf, reached after considerable delays caused by persistent sandstorms, the party decided upon a plebiscite concert—all requests to be sent in writing to the orderly room by 1 P.M. The only concession to popular taste was the *Warsaw Concerto*, the remaining items, selected by majority vote, being as follows: the duet from the first scene of *Madam Butterfly* (Miriam Licette and Nancy Evans); Mendelssohn's Violin Concerto (Alfred Cave); excerpts from *Carmen*; two Beethoven sonatas (Ivor Newton); various operatic arias (Dennis Noble and Walter Widdop); Gounod's *Ave Maria*, and *One Fine Day* from *Madam Butterfly* (Miriam Licette).

"THE SCHOOL FOR SCANDAL," CAIRO DRAMA FESTIVAL, 1946
Ursula Jeans as Lady Teazle   Malcolm Keen as Sir Peter
Charles Carson as Sir Oliver
Roger Livesey as Joseph Surface   Norman Claridge as Charles Surface

MY FAREWELL PRODUCTIONS

"THE APPLE CART" FOR THE TROOPS IN GERMANY
Barry Jones as King Magnus, George Howe as Proteus, Julien Mitchell as Boanerges

432

PARADE OF UNIFORMED PERSONNEL ON HITLER'S BIRTHDAY

GERMANY'S ENSA

(Reproductions from a captured enemy booklet.)

GALA PERFORMANCE AT THE
MUNICIPAL THEATRE, LILLE

HOISTING THE PRIMA DONNA

on his lifebelt when he looked up and said in a quiet voice, "Walter, have you got such a thing as a clothes brush?" to which the Yorkshireman replied with open-mouthed astonishment, "Well, if tha's not th' best bloody fiddler since Nero!"

3

Protocol

None of the detail of our early work in India was known to me when I landed, only a general outline of what had so far been accomplished. As for the sub-continent itself, it was wrapped in a mystery as remote as the British officials who still nervously controlled its destinies. There was only one thing to be done: climb to the highest platform and jump in with a good splash, a technique that had paid good dividends on previous occasions. As a first step I asked Dunstan to inform Delhi that I wished to report in person to the Viceroy, whereat he was taken aback; still more so when he learned that he was to accompany me there. There was a further titillation of surprise when he received a prompt reply, inviting us to stay at Viceroy's House.

Meanwhile we spent a delightful Christmas Day at Juhu Beach in the company of Mr Turner of the *Times of India* staff and his enchanting young family, swimming and sun-bathing, eating roast turkey, plum pudding and all the usual trimmings, making no concessions whatever to climate. No hospital broadcasting to do this year, but a speech to be made on Boxing Night after a performance in the Town Hall, Bombay, by Forsythe, Seamon and Farrell, Lyle Evans, Cherry Lind and other excellent artistes, just arrived by air from home to spend Christmas with the troops. My announcement of further good things to come was received with rapturous cheering which wafted me all the way to New Delhi and my interview with the Viceroy.

Friends had warned me that conversation with Lord Wavell would prove difficult. But, seated at his right hand at luncheon, taken on the terrace beneath the shade of a graceful little *pavillon*, I found him less intimidating than the Sikh servants hovering behind the chairs in their scarlet uniforms with the Royal coat-of-arms emblazoned in gold on their chests. After a feeble remark or two about the weather—the Englishman's traditional opening wicket which scores few runs abroad—I began to stare at the imposing building in red sandstone standing out under the full glare of the Indian sun, defiantly asserting Lutyens's compromise between two widely different ways of life. Lord Wavell interpreted my look.

"Yes, it's fine," he growled. "But nowhere to sit down; too much

2E

marble. Witty fellow, Lutyens," he added after a pause. "He used to stay with me while he was building the place. That was when I was commander-in-chief here. I asked him one day why he was puttin' in so much marble. 'Well,' he said, 'I was told to raise an Imperial pile.' Good, eh?"

In the search for ground of common interest, the Viceroy made graceful reference to my stage work, particularly the production of Flecker's *Hassan* at His Majesty's Theatre. This soon put me at ease. I felt uplifted that he should remember the details so clearly, for it was long ago, but I was cast down again when he began to recite long passages from the play in tones of such deep feeling that those seated nearest to us fell silent, and I to regretting how many of the lovely lines I had forgotten.

Afterwards, in his study, with the Military Secretary present, listening to my oft-told story, he promised to smooth the way with the big-wigs who reigned in the Secretariat. There was to be a Governors' Conference in a few days, and he would tell them that the Prime Minister desired me to have every assistance in preparing my report. There would be difficulty in requisitioning any premises under Indian ownership, he warned. Air transport was vital—he could see that—but it was a matter for the R.A.F. However, he would "have a word." I was to stay with him while the arrangements for my tour were being made and to let him know if I ran into trouble. Yes, he would like to see a copy of my report, but it should be addressed in the first instance to the G.O.C.-in-C. India (General Auchinleck) and to the Supreme Allied Commander, South East Asia Command (Admiral Lord Louis Mountbatten)—"er—simultaneously," he added with just a suspicion of a smile.

Top-level contacts followed in close succession: lunch with the Commander-in-Chief the next day to meet the Adjutant-General, I., Lieutenant-General ('Tiny') Deedes, a shrewd terrier, that one, who would bark at any provocation, and who already, before the meal was concluded, began to express his doubts about each this and that; conferences with the Finance Member and his staff in the lovely Secretariat building, where the bearers—squatting outside the office doors, warming themselves over open charcoal braziers—struck an incongruous note; talks with Brigadier Portman of the Army Welfare Services and the Welfare staffs of the other arms, at which I explained the set-up at home, which I proposed should be paralleled. The Inter-Services Entertainment Committee at Delhi should correspond to the Entertainments Board at home. Since the Government of India was going to pay there should be a Finance Sub-Committee similar to the one at home. NAAFI had already appointed an accountant officer to represent them, which was reasonable enough seeing that expenditure in India was inextricably interwoven with the financial responsibilities at home. For the rest, co-ordination of supply and allocation, with ENSA officers everywhere to do the routing. The reader fully understands the system by now; there is no need to dwell on it.

The Viceroy was as good as his word, for when I called upon the A.O.C.-in-C. (Air Marshal Hollinghurst) and told him that I planned to visit all the Commands in India, Burma and Ceylon, he at once offered to place an aircraft at my disposal. In no other way could I have covered the ground in reasonable time. While it was being made available—a twin-engined Beechcraft with a sergeant-pilot and a sergeant-navigator for crew, and room enough for my p.a. to nurse a busy typewriter on his knee and for myself—I paid hurried visits to Agra to inspect the cinemas patronized by the R.A.F.—a note in my diary mentions the old films being shown and the exorbitant prices charged—and to Cawnpore to do the same thing. From Agra I was taken to see the Taj Mahal in lucky moonlight, filigree lace of unbelievable delicacy standing ghostly against the violet blue of the night sky; by day this monument to Indian Muslim art seemed hard and indifferent, a building with quite another personality. The night of my visit there were rows of brand-new jeeps parked outside, waiting for American officers to finish their tireless sightseeing.

New Year's Eve was spent with Brigadier Desmond Young,[1] and his wife, renewing a friendship begun when he was an Oxford undergraduate, and I visited there as a member of the Horniman Company. After adventures in and out of Tobruk, and a daring escape from North Italy, he was now Director of Public Relations to 'The Auk.' His useful advice included a cryptic reminder of Bismarck's saying that "a man's value was his ability minus his vanity." The following morning (New Year's Day) we were winging our way to Calcutta, first stage in a journey that was to continue up and down without pause for more than a month.

4

Whistle Stop

Calcutta was to be no more than a whistle stop on the way through to Burma, where General Slim's Fourteenth Army had already begun its return through the jungle, soon to become a triumphant scamper into Mandalay and Rangoon.

Here was another opportunity for our mobile columns. A dozen or so jeeps, some half-track vehicles for heavy stuff, scenery made to fold up

[1] Author of *Rommel* and other books.

and go in baskets as in the invasion days at home, half a dozen small parties of experienced artistes who know the ropes, and away we go! Too easy! Virginia must get her welfare show going, of course. After that wave of optimism I felt better. Then bump, bump, and a gentler bump! a three-point landing and a quiver through the fuselage as the aircraft turned down wind to taxi to the control tower. We were landing at Alipore, Calcutta.

Two majors—Bontemps, in charge of our Calcutta administration, and Jack Hawkins—were there to meet me with their plans and anxieties. The faces of both men fell when I said that mobile columns for Burma must be No. 1 priority. "I thought that was coming," said Jack with that strangulated laugh of his. "We've got no premises. We're making scenery on the side-walk, as it is."

Bontemps chimed in: "I've been trying to get a decent office for the last six months."

"Can't you requisition?"

"All requisitioning for ENSA has been refused."

"We'll soon put that right. Both the Viceroy and the Commander-in-Chief have promised me their support," I said, over-grandly.

"Huh!" said Jack, "the top boys are bound to tell you that. Wait till you get down to the Indian civil servants. They're worse than the British, and that's saying something." Again, the pleasant, surly laugh.

The complexity of commands was worse here than in Cairo: garrison headquarters for each of the three Services, headquarters for various training establishments, for Air Transport Commands, British and American, and, finally, an advanced headquarters for Lord Mountbatten's Command. This was known as ALFSEA, with Sir Oliver Leese, transferred from the Eighth Army, in charge. I was glad I was to stay with Mr and Mrs Casey at Government House. The Governor's influence would be needed to convince the various authorities that ENSA was now one of their official offspring, entitled to a share of their much divided attention. At dinner that evening the Governor began by remarking that the entertainment should be fully sustained during monsoon, to which I replied that it would be impossible without air transport: "We had fifty per cent. casualties last time." The senior R.A.F. officers present devoted themselves to the soup. At a conference at ALFSEA on the following day I asked for co-operation in getting the artistes forward into Burma quickly. "For example," I said, "there is the case of Kenway and Young.[1] We want them flown right forward. By rail it takes five days."

---

[1] These fine artistes were eventually flown in and about Burma by the Americans, although their upright Broadwood piano was something of a problem, being greeted with huge delight or bland indifference according to the mood of the pilot who was lifting them.

A brigadier waved a sheaf of pink signals at me:

"See these? Signals from Kandy all about Noël Coward, some of 'em from Supremo himself. Dates, cancellations, requests for this and that. We simply haven't time to bother about actors. There's a war on." He went pink in the face. I tried to soothe him with the most positive assurances that ENSA stars never travelled under their own steam; routing was our responsibility, and a greatly increased staff would take care of future developments.

"Oh, well, that's all right then," said the brigadier, and lost further interest in the proceedings.

I raised the question of premises.

"We can't requisition," snapped a staff colonel.

"How about transport?" I continued relentlessly. "Can't our coaches and luggage-vans be hooked on to the fast mail-trains?"

"You'll have to see Delhi about that."

"I intend to."

The background to my report was darkening.

5

'The Forgotten Army'

On the flight to Cox's Bazaar I began to have doubts: no good making promises to 'The Forgotten Army' if the means of carrying them out were denied us. In the round of inspections and conferences which followed I forgot these doubts. I was invited to spend my first evening in Air Commodore Lord Bandon's mess. He commanded the fighter pilots in the area. We had a riotous evening, and I won money off the A.O.C. without finding out what game we were playing. When I asked if I could get into Akyab the next day to find a building where we could give a show, he laughed and said, "Yes, provided you don't get shot down before you get there." I was breathing the atmosphere of a fighting front once more.

Driving to Maunghaama on the following day over the most atrocious roads made me wonder how troops could be moved at all during monsoon, let alone entertainers. Writing of movements puts me in mind of a queer little story I heard about the elephants that were an invaluable part of the British Army's transport system. On one of the main roads through the jungle cut by the R.E.'s the precipitous verge had been marked out with white-washed concrete posts in regular Aldershot style. But the elephants took the strongest exception to what they regarded as obstacles, and proceeded to remove them one by one, tossing them aside into the bush before proceeding on their way. At Maungdaw there was news of one of our little parties, 'The Sun Rays,' which had played there recently in an excellent *basha* theatre, a local type of construction in bamboo and straw that would make an L.C.C. fire inspector jump with fright. Pleasant to record in my notes the energy of the recently appointed ENSA officer, Captain Glyn.

Back at Maunghaama air-strip my crew agreed to try for a landing at Akyab. It was perfect flying weather. The scenery was magnificent, the mountain-ranges running down to the sea in straight lines like giant ribs, one behind the other, deepening gradually in colour to deepest purple. The forward horizon was lost in pale blue mist, and in the valley beneath us was a dense green carpet of forest. Presently the signs of cultivation began to increase, native huts giving place to small buildings, the beginnings of Akyab. Peering anxiously for the air-strip so meticulously pinpointed on my pilot's map the night before, we failed to notice a destroyer lying under the shadow of the farther shore. An Aldis lamp began winking violently. The pilot banked the aircraft sharply to starboard, nearly pitching me on to the floor of the fuselage while the navigator hurriedly threw Very lights out of the window.

"What are they saying?" I asked.

"Asking for our identification," said the navigator grimly.

"What now?" I asked, as the lamp went on winking more violently than ever, and the aircraft continued to turn away.

"Telling us to sheer off, or else——" muttered the pilot.

And that was as near as I got to Akyab.

Leaving the Arakan Peninsula, we flew to Chittagong, an inexcusably dirty and evil-smelling place, and then on to Comilla. The programme of inspections was falling into a pattern: questions answered or evaded according to the impression it was desired to create; always the proffered 'char,' and then a jolting ride to the next spot. Dinner with Major-General Symes and members of his staff was ended for me just as it began, when what appeared to be cannon-shells started to explode inside my head, announcing the arrival of a bout of dengue fever which took me back to the 21st British General Hospital in Calcutta and to a two-day convalescence at Government House, watching Casey's little boy tearing up and down its broad garden paths in his toy motor, and in contrast, driving to the office for a talk with the staff past a Hindu festival with fantastic images mounted in gharries, and sacred cows nosing among the fruit and vegetables, all the scrabbling fecundity of the city's streets. On the second evening Mr Casey took his dinner guests to the opening performance of Priestley's *How Are They at Home?*, given by the Reper-

tory Company recently arrived from England, in a Y.M.C.A. building
now doing duty as our Garrison Theatre. I tagged along as a matter
of duty. A good performance—good, that is, as far as the appalling echo
would permit one to judge, since each sentence demanded a second
hearing for itself.

Back to Comilla and the inspection dance: along the lines of communication, in the reinforcement camps and rest-centres, theatres of bamboo were going up. One of them, named the Mountbatten Hall, had a
single film projector provided by an enterprising Indian contractor who
charged high prices for his out-of-date films, changed them three times a
week and out of the takings paid 4 per cent. as rental for the building,
retaining 96 per cent. as reward for his trouble: a division that pointed a
finger at the business ability of both parties. At another place the theatre
was being built on the side of a hill so as to provide a sloping floor, recall-
ing the very first design that George Harris had sketched a quarter of a
century ago. This one was exceptional because it was to have a corrugated
iron roof. Will the performances be audible in monsoon? I wondered, but
said nothing.

Flying over the mountain ridges at 10,000 feet on my way at last to the
Headquarters of the Fourteenth Army at Indaingale; beneath us a solid
green carpet of jungle, mile after mile: I remember 'Battle-of-Britain'
Park's remark in Malta: there is certainly no future in a forced landing in
this country. All of us are relieved, crew included, when the flight is over.
The ENSA officer, Captain Crabtree, takes me immediately to General
Slim's camp along a road cut through elephant grass, the mud underfoot
beaten into a treacly paste by the incessant traffic.

General ('Bill') Slim—a thick-set, soldierly figure with a forthright
manner and an aura of complete confidence in himself, his staff and his
army—shakes off his cares for half an hour after Mess and chats of pleasant
things. He approves my desire to see conditions at first-hand and suggests
I should visit his two corps commanders and then go on to the divisions.
In that way I shall be following up the main line of advance, seeing everything that it might be useful to see, and more besides.

He is amused when I tell him I want to photograph some of the wild
life for which Burma is famous: "Although I'm disappointed I haven't
seen anything so far."

"And you're not likely to," laughs the General.

"Why not?"

"Well, what would you do if thousands of strange beings came crash-
ing into your haunts from all directions, firing guns and refusing to go
away?"

"Move on, I suppose."

"Exactly." The remark was conclusive.

The M.G.A. (Major-General Snelling) unrolls a big map: here I should go, and here. "Perhaps there, too," says Slim, pointing a stubby finger. "Mandalay will fall soon. There'll be a rest-camp in the hills at Maymyo. It will be large, accommodating five thousand men. ENSA should arrange continuous entertainment, especially in monsoon."

By nine o'clock the pleasant chat is over and the General has turned in. I linger for a while with the Welfare officer, polishing off his whisky ration. The camp is quiet except for some tented voices among the trees. One by one the shadowy lights go out, the General's first. I stumble to my tent, next to his, by the aid of a torch.

6
"ENSA, I presume?"

Pleasant to wake at dawn in the cool air under the trees; most surprising, without one mosquito-disturbance, thanks to DDT. I badger my host, while he is shaving, for a snapshot, and then set off as planned to visit Lieutenant-General Sir Montague Stopford, commanding 33rd Corps at Kalemyo.

In a marquee pitched among the scrub I sit at lunch with the General and his staff. Talk is brisk and encouraging, the simple meal well cooked and charmingly served. The undulating country stretches before us in a glorious canvas, shimmering green and purple and blue under the heat; it is more like a holiday picnic than war. The commander sees no reason why campaigning should be carried on in unnecessary discomfort.

In the afternoon to the 4th Corps for a brief talk with the Corps Commander (Lieutenant-General Messervy), after which I am passed on to a divisional headquarters, where amenities are in little regard. There is an air of neglect over the divisional Mess-tent; even the muslin cages over the butter are clogged with dead flies and dirt. One can only suppose this indifference to hygiene indicates a more rugged conduct of the battle. Next, to a place called Ye-Hu in search of General Nicholson's 2nd Division, which is moving rapidly in pursuit. The general is out on the Shwebo Road. We drive for miles beside a canal; not a soul in sight, only an occasional paddy bird standing poised and motionless in an empty green landscape under the soft blue sky.

Presently a military car with two officers in the back, and an orderly with a tommy-gun seated beside the driver, comes rapidly into view, trailing clouds of dust. One of them looks round as we pass and then stops the car. I get out of our jeep as a tall, thin figure strides towards me. His companion follows at a more leisurely pace. We meet in the middle of the road.

"ENSA?" he asks abruptly.

"General Nicholson?" I counter.

We talk, standing there in the middle of the road, while the chief-of-staff redirects my escort, and Kershaw stands respectfully silent under the trees. "Shows for his men? Nothing he would like more, but advance is too rapid for the moment. We are entering Shwebo now."

"Any chance of a theatre there, general?"

He grins at my naïve question. "We'll be gone before you can get there."

"But later?" I persist.

"Later, oh, yes! Later."

A look of abstraction comes into his eyes, the look I have seen before when talking to generals with important things on hand. He gets into his car, waves his hand and disappears behind a curtain of dust.

We drive on in search of the 19th Division and lose our way. While my escort goes to reconnoitre the outskirts of a village I stroll into a near by Buddhist temple that has the forlorn air of all ravaged buildings. There is a gaping hole in the roof and other signs of violence. The cells built round it for the monks are deserted. The interior is dominated by a stylized image of the Buddha, brooding upon a world in which the beatitude of abstract contemplation has no place. Clear stones sparkle on the fingers and toes: are they glass or diamonds? The jewelled eyes have been removed, as though to spare the saint the spectacle of desecration; or was the operation performed by a British bayonet? At his feet are overturned brass pots with decayed flowers in them; dead leaves and sheets of a Japanese army newspaper, which for no good reason I take away with me, litter the floor. An occasional sigh of the wind through the broken roof intensifies the aura of the place. A ghostly whispering of long-forgotten prayers?

Farther on, a patrol of the Royal Scots are squatting round a little fire of sticks, laughing and making tea in a billy-can, while three scrofulous vultures glower at them with impudent eyes from the grass verge opposite, looking like three Douglas Byngs in a row! Reading my shoulder flashes, the men let loose a flight of questions, each putting forward his special candidate for Fourteenth Army applause. Will Fyffe, Gracie Fields and George—"Oh, yes, mustn't forget George Formby," says one— are the most favoured. Refusing an offer to share their 'char'—I know all about that sort of tea by now—and to a chorus of good-byes in accents that range from the Clyde to the Thames, we drive on. The vultures have hopped disdainfully away; no 'char' for them, either!

We reached the Headquarters of the 19th Division to find Major-General Rees briefing Ian Colquhoun of the *Manchester Guardian*, and other correspondents whom I did not know, on the crossing of the Irrawaddy, which was to take place that night. This energetic Welshman was known to his staff as "the fire-eater" as he moved about among his Indian troops in their foxholes, with complete disregard for his own safety, his only means of identification a flaming red handkerchief which he wore knotted round his neck.

In the little Mess-tent, lighted by smelly oil lamps that either smoked or went out, everybody was waiting for the time to pass. The officers slipped away one by one, followed by the war correspondents. Then General Rees, ignoring my hint that I too would like to see something of the action, asked to be excused.

Kershaw woke me up at dawn. The General's A.D.C. was crouching outside the bivvy. "Yes, the river had been crossed during the night, and there were hardly any casualties." But he brought a message: "his General was anxious to have a conference with General Festing at 36th Division and would I give him a lift?" Of course I was glad to be of service, but would the general allow me to take a peep at the river-crossing in return? Permission was granted, provided the A.D.C. came with me as escort.

We set out in a jeep, with Gurkhas armed with tommy-guns seated in front and behind us. Another jeep led the way, and a third brought up the rear. As we glided past the foliage shining bright green against the yellow sand of the road, only the rhythmic throbbing of the jeeps' engines to disturb the quiet, I tried to imagine the sinister struggle going on in those jungle depths as General Rees had described it to me: sudden, fierce conflicts breaking out of the silence, then once more the stillness—a forest fire that burns subterraneously until it reaches flash-point in unexpected places.

Shortly after leaving Brigade H.Q., where the A.D.C. was 'given the form,' we came upon a group of British officers, squatting in a little hollow, drinking tea and eating rations, the headquarters staff of a battalion of the Rajputana Rifles. We talked for a while of this and that, drinking tea while they gobbled up the tidbits of news from home that I offered them. Again that special quality of quiet within the immediate battle area that I had felt with the 6th Airborne Division across the Orne.

Gurkhas to right of me and Gurkhas to left of me as we set off for the village on the river bank where the Indians had crossed, the A.D.C., still with his rifle, marching in front. My embarrassment at the precautions struggled with curiosity for what I might see.

In the centre of the village—most of the larger two-storey wooden houses had been fired by the Japanese—there was a large post on which the headman had been hanged (for alleged collaboration) before the enemy retreated. The A.D.C. motioned to me with his rifle to follow him. We crossed to the shelter of a large house by the river, and crept on hands and knees slowly towards the river bank, I unslinging my camera as I went. Behind a low bank the young man edged to one side and made signs to me to take my snapshot, and quickly. Obviously he was itching to be off, disliking this civilian responsibility. Gingerly, I raised my head to take a look at the opposite bank. Through field-glasses I could see two figures who I supposed wrongly to be enemy soldiers laying wire. On the near bank, to my left, men of the Rajputana Rifles were washing their clothes and throwing water at each other like elephants at play, taking the first opportunity after last night's engagement of cleansing themselves according to Muslim habit. A more peaceful anticlimax could not be imagined. . . . The General was waiting impatiently by the Beechcraft when we returned.

Word had been sent to General Festing by field radio of our coming, but the war was moving fast. When we reached Katha, both he and his troops had gone, leaving only the D.A.A.G. and a few details. We were directed to a place called Yanbo. This journey was impossible in the Beechcraft because the temporary landing-strips carved out of the jungle were too small. Lateral communication between the lengthening fingers of the British advance was being maintained by means of little spotting planes, known officially as L.5's but colloquially as 'flying fleas.' Forerunners in usefulness of the present-day helicopters, they were capable of landing within a hundred yards at a speed of little more than fifty miles per hour. They were flown by American transport pilots attached to the 36th Division. We changed over into these, General Rees flying on ahead in one, and I taking the next available. Strapped into a little cradle at the back of the pilot, with one's feet on the struts either side of him, deafened by the noise of the engine, the plane twisting this way and that like a falling leaf in autumn: it was not a comfortable mode of travel. The giant of a man behind whom I was ensconced wasted no words: he just sat there, chewing an enormous mouthful of gum. At Yanbo the two generals had disappeared into the blue together. I was advised to take a chance and go to a place called Koto; I might find them there.

This pursuit of a famous general from air-strip to air-strip seems ordinary enough in retrospect, but it was exciting at the time. Approaching Koto, the pilot beckoned me to look over the starboard wing, where I could just make out the tiny shape of another L.5 travelling in the same direction. Then it banked in readiness for the run-in to the tiny air-strip below us. My pilot made the thumbs-down gesture.

"What's the matter?" I shouted.

"Too fa-ast," he shouted back. We continued to stare below us as the tiny machine landed and began running along the grass towards a bank of earth which marked the end of the landing-ground. In an instant it overran the strip, hit the bank full tilt and crumpled up on its side, like a child's fallen kite.

"Good God," I shouted, "it's crashed!"

"Sure," said my American calmly. "I ses it was too fa-ast."

They were carrying the crashed pilot away as General Festing came bumping along the strip towards me in his jeep: a tall figure, carrying a long Highland crook, followed by a hulking sergeant from Lancashire, who decanted himself into the bushes bordering the field with his tommy-gun under his arm, while the General and I sat down on the running-board to have our talk. As I began my little recitation about mobile columns and air passages for the stars the familiar look of abstraction appeared in the General's eyes. "He was pleased I'd come all this way and sorry I'd had so much trouble to find him. Yes, he'd let the troops know that entertainment would be laid on once they were out of the jungle. One day he hoped to be sitting among his men enjoying an ENSA show. Good-bye!" And he was in his jeep and away!

The Beechcraft took us to Imphal, arriving just as night was falling over the purple-black mountains beyond the airfield. There was little to do there now that the Fourteenth Army was gone. The theatre they had used was derelict, and the young subaltern in charge of ENSA (Lieutenant Cooper) had the thankless task of carrying on entertainment before steadily diminishing audiences. That did not excuse the filthy condition of the hostel. My protest was cut short by the information that Dunstan had circularized all officers that Madame Vernon's requests for improvements to hostels must await his approval: a whiff of internal disagreement, and a depressing note on which to end the Burma tour.

7

Country House

January 16, 1945. Time was in the slip-stream rushing past the windows of the aircraft as we flew back into Assam. I was impatient to get to

S.E.A.C. Headquarters at Kandy, for the build-up in Burma had become urgent, and to be a week overdue for my appointment seemed a poor return for the cordial telegram Lord Louis had sent me in Delhi. Nevertheless, it was manifestly absurd to travel all the way down to Ceylon with the certainty of having to fly back again to complete the tour in this part of the world. Hence I found myself staring out of the windows of the Beechcraft at the indigo clouds that hung over the foothills, sorting out my impressions of the job in Burma. Had my journey really been necessary? Well, perhaps not. The troops were moving fast through difficult country; among the forward units our columns would be in the way. Yet the officers I had contacted would pass on the news of our preparations to the men. To that extent the visit will have done good.

We landed at Sylhet, thence through the gate and up that marvellous mountain road—one-way traffic for much of the way—to Shillong, the capital of the province, situated in the gorgeous scenery of the foothills. It was now being used extensively as a rehabilitation centre, particularly for flying crews of the R.A.F. There was an excellent theatre with good seating, dressing-rooms and a stage so tiny that our company, playing *Love in a Mist*, had been unable to use their scenery and lost several days contriving substitutes.

At dinner with the Governor and his Lady, Sir Andrew and Lady Clow, the talk soon swung away from entertainment to matters of more personal interest within the official circle. It seemed that these British enclaves borrowed little from the countries in which they lived, save perhaps the flowers in their gardens and their native servants. (Was that why Lady Wavell and her two daughters brought the atmosphere of an English deanery into Viceroy's House?) The feeling of uncertainty that ran like a fine thread through the conversation was so unmistakable that in the billiard-room afterwards I asked the Governor a direct question that had been rattling about in my mind all the evening. "Of course, we shall have to leave India after the war," came his reply. The shock I felt showed how ill-prepared at that time the average Englishman was for the eventual transfer of power.

The following day being Sunday, I was invited to attend early morning service at the English Church, from which I excused myself because I was tired out, whereupon the A.D.C., adopting a firmer tone, informed me that breakfast would be at 9.30 A.M. sharp, which indeed it was. As I entered the breakfast-room the slight look of disapproval on Lady Clow's face vanished in the sweetest of welcoming smiles. After grace had been said, a large silver tureen of porridge was placed before her, from which she carefully ladled out a portion for each person. I kept my wits sufficiently about me to accept the offering, which pleased my hostess, but alas! fell from favour by refusing salt and asking for sugar.

8

An Admiral's Signal in Clear

Ceylon—"Fairest isle, all isles excelling"; justifiable paraphrase for this peacock-flashing place where the scented air seems spiced with the further scent of happiness, a deeper fragrance than of flowers. The Supreme Commander knew all about us through Lady Louis' close association with our various Councils. It was because of this that he had sent for me shortly before his appointment to S.E.A.C. was made public, and while he was still head of Combined Operations, to find out what ENSA was prepared to do for the troops of his new Command, a talk which ended in a promise of ready access and full support for any reasonable request that I might make.

Dunstan and I arrived in Kandy in the late afternoon. We were bidden to dinner that evening and spent an hour or two having a look round. Here was a G.H.Q. with a difference: alertness the first quality to be noted, with just that touch of bravura to be expected of one lately in command of His Majesty's Ship *Kelly*. Even the staff of WRNS doing the office chores looked smarter and prettier than those to be seen elsewhere. The atmosphere of elegant informality that Lady Louis spread around her was a special quality of hospitality that had almost passed from memory in wartime London. Dinner over, we moved into a drawing-room, where I gave the Supreme Commander a general outline of the report I proposed to make, stressing our need of transport in all its forms. When I had done there were none of the expected hesitations, no partial reservations of this and that. I was to see the head of each branch of his Headquarters the following morning and tell them what was wanted; after which he would quickly decide what could and what could not be done. Finally, of his own accord, he raised a matter that was beginning to trouble Dunstan.

"One more thing. In future, artistes must not come out here under their own steam; they must be sent out by their own organization, which is ENSA. It's taking up too much of my officers' time and it's got to stop." He paused, adding by way of an afterthought, "And that goes for Noël, too." Was there just a glimmer of a twinkle in his eye as he said that?

My interviews the next day took place in an atmosphere of friendliness that blew anxieties away like smoke: "Certainly, representatives from S.E.A.C. would fly once a month to attend the monthly meetings in

Delhi of the Inter-Services Committee, to make sure they got their fair share of the allocations."

At R.A.F. Headquarters Air Marshal Garrod promised a directive that air-lifts should be arranged wherever practicable; he also undertook to expedite the transfer to ENSA of R.A.F. personnel with managerial or technical experience.

"Of course," said the Chief Engineer, Lieutenant-General Harrison, "the plan for new garrison theatres should conform to those at home."

A brief farewell to 'Supremo,' who promised to inspect our offices in Bombay in a week's time, and we were bowling down the road back to Colombo, my mind dancing with the exhilaration of all this showered encouragement, and my camera busy with unusual sights, including a doctor's notice of his ability to deal with a surprising conjunction of diseases.

At Trincomalee a young naval officer attached to ENSA showed me the plans for two theatres, each to seat some 500 men, one for the Navy and one for the Army. My suggestion that a 1000-seater, shared by all arms, would enable the companies to entertain larger numbers during their visits aroused such opposition that I decided to interview the Captain of the Fleet in the battleship *Queen Elizabeth*, then in harbour. As he was ashore, Admiral 'Hooky' Walker consented to see me. I was piped aboard in true Navy fashion, and managed to salute the quarterdeck—with embarrassment. The Admiral plied me with pink gin so rapidly and in such quantity that presently I found myself staring in fixed fascination at Captain Hook reaching for the Doodledoo! Having secured the high-level approval for the single-theatre policy that I sought, I went ashore in search of similar consent from the Army people. On the return flight to Colombo my zoological curiosity was at last rewarded, for I saw both elephant and buffalo, although so far distant that I needed the pilot's confirmation, else I might have ascribed the sight to the Admiral's gin.

Those few days in Ceylon stand out in halcyon memory. Swimming every morning in the warm sea at Mount Lavinia, talks and interviews with the various authorities to whom the word had gone forth to help and not hinder, lunch with the Governor, dinner with an old friend and theatre associate (Commander George Curzon, in charge of Fleet Public Relations), a night with the Fleet Air Arm at Katakuranda to see one of our companies, called 'Follow the Sun,' and a climax of relaxation on the Sunday morning when certain naval officers invited me to a curry lunch at their headquarters: a desperate adventure that began immediately after Church Parade and lasted until about three in the afternoon.

On the west coast of India building activity was greatest round Cochin and Coimbatore where vast training-camps were being set up in anticipation of amphibian operations in the Far East. At Cochin two large theatres were building within a short distance of one another, to the War Office plan which we had condemned in 1939 as being unsuitable for 'live' entertainment. (The same thing was going on at Vizagapatan—'Vizag' for short—on the east coast. I had then decided to say nothing until I had seen whether the folly was being repeated elsewhere.) The theatre for Naval personnel was approaching completion, and while I was at the camp I secured a promise to remove the 'slice of cake' walls on the stage. In the Army camp, where the offending obstructions were only three parts built, the garrison engineer refused, with a considerable show of temper, to stop the work.

"But," I protested, "you are putting up something that will be useless."

"What do I care?" he replied unhelpfully. "As a matter of fact," he added, "I've already been on to Delhi about those blasted walls. They say the partitions are to be completed according to contract. Later on instructions may be sent about taking them down." There followed a brisk exchange of telegrams with the Chief Engineer's Department in Delhi, in the course of which I sent them the file numbers of the revised drawings which had been circulated by the War Office early in the war.

At Coimbatore more activities, more cinema theatres, a spate of interviews and, finally, an hour's flight to Bangalore, there to be met by Captain Plunket-Greene, in charge of ENSA in Southern Army, and whisked off to a performance by Waldini's Band in a giant Nissen hut at the R.E.M.E. Advance Base Workshops. A conference with the M.G.A. and the A.O.C. 225 Group followed the next morning. By this time my note-book was crammed to its last page with the names of units and locations, of theatres and cinemas and converted institutes either projected, in course of construction or actually built, all of them clamouring for equipment of various kinds, from pianos to electric-light bulbs. As I flew back to Bombay I wondered grimly whether Drury Lane would be able to satisfy all the promises I had scattered during my long paper-chase.

The last day of January. While I sat with a secretary in the bungalow at work on my report Eric went off to attend the Supreme Commander's inspection of our headquarters.

By this time more stars had arrived. George Formby had just flown in with the unconquerable Beryl, and Pat Burke, come to join her mother, Marie, who had already visited Burma single-handed and been a great success.

In the evening George gave the opening performance of his tour on the

football ground, in the presence of the Supreme Commander and Lady
Mountbatten, Sir John and Lady Colville, and many military and civil
dignitaries. There were over 5000 troops present. The portable stage was
to be erected in front of the grandstand immediately after the Indians had
finished football, but the game was nearly two hours late; as the sports
crowd went out the troops came surging in. The stage, the wiring for the
electric light, the microphone and loudspeakers, all had to be rushed up in
a matter of minutes. It was like a display at a military tattoo. Shortly after
the show began some one or something severed the main cable, cutting
out the microphone and throwing the stage into darkness. With the aid
of motor-car lamps Formby carried on for thirty-five minutes. When the
microphone was finally restored he resang many of the songs he had sung
in darkness, without any sign of audience impatience: a genuine triumph
of personality. George, indefatigably strumming on his uke, did more to
sustain morale in the war years than many performers of less restricted
talent.

Writing the report took me the best part of a week, employing two
secretaries working in relays, one of whom delayed matters by a remarkable display of phonetic typing. It was done at last: a charter of entertainment for Allied troops in India and the Far East. Copies were dispatched
by quickest means to London, for the Treasury, the S. of S. for India,
the Service Departments and the Entertainments Board; to Delhi, for the
Commander-in-Chief, with copy to the Viceroy; and to Kandy, for the
Supreme Commander, South East Asia. The Report was not published
officially, but the copies which I sent to the *Times of India* and to *SEAC*,
the Service newspaper, received warm approval, and I felt a twinge of
pride when the Prime Minister in reply to a question in the Commons
read from the slip of paper that had been given him: "Mr Dean's report
is now being studied with great care by the Departments concerned." It
was something that one's name had passed the great man's lips.

9

"For Information and Action"

The array of generals assembled to pass judgment on the Report was
certainly impressive. The Adjutant-General took the chair. As I sat down
beside him, with Eric Dunstan just behind in a close support trench lined
with senior staff officers, the distant tapping of typewriters sounded
ominously like the click of knitting-needles.

The chairman began by introducing a lieutenant-general of the Royal

Engineers, sent out on special mission by the Prime Minister to report to him personally upon all welfare matters and to co-ordinate action where required. This seemed a political smoke-screen of less than average density, for in the general run of my experience R.E. officers were not notably eager to co-operate in matters outside their normal sphere.

My cross-examination was conducted with an Olympian impartiality that nevertheless required me to justify any unflattering statements which the report contained. Sentences such as that "the visit of an ENSA party should be regarded as an event, and not as an 'amenity ration' supplied at stated intervals," and that "the granting of air passages only after prolonged discussion, and as a kind of favour that cannot be repeated, is not in accord with realities" were, I thought, to the point. But the assembled rank and power took little interest in such generalities; it was when we came to the recommendations at the end that they went into concerted action.

Transport requirements had been listed under three heads; each was neatly decapitated in turn. First, air transport for the stars: this matter must be referred to the Air Priorities Board (India). (I decided to keep quiet about the hopes held out to me at S.E.A.C.) The request for the attachment of coaches to the mail-trains was a matter for the Indian State Railways. As for road transport, each item as it was read out induced progressive lowering of temperature until we came to the request for twelve jeeps for mobile columns in Burma. At this point the circle of faces surrounding me took on a look of frozen horror reminiscent of Bateman's cartoon of the Guardsman who dropped his rifle on parade. The rows of jeeps that I had seen parked outside the Taj Mahal in the moonlight prompted me to suggest that some might be borrowed from the Americans. After a shocked silence the meeting passed to other business.

I was in process of justifying the demand for the requisitioning of premises by pointing out that scenery and other equipment for Burma was being made on a public sidewalk in Calcutta, when the Prime Minister's emissary broke in.

"I can see no need for these special facilities—premises, transport, technical staff and what not. Why don't you get the Engineers to make the scenery for you? You'd like to have a go, eh, Mac?"

Brother Engineer played up joyfully: "We would certainly do our best." (A few quiet chuckles.)

With this encouragement the general raced on. "When I was out here years ago we often used to amuse ourselves makin' scenery in our spare time—for the amateur shows at Simla, you know." Reminiscent far-away looks appeared on some of the countenances confronting me. "Yes, and my wife used to come along and help us to paint it. Jolly good fun, really."

I could think of no way of repulsing these friendly hostilities, and accordingly abandoned my forward positions for the time being and fell back upon a demand for wardrobe facilities.

"Wardrobe facilities?" The general looked puzzled.

"Yes, premises for making and fitting the artistes' costumes."

"You can do that at an Army clothing depôt. Get on to Ordnance. Haven't you got a place in Calcutta, Bill?" Whereat a somnolent figure in a corner started awake. "Yes, I think so."

The general turned to me with his attractive smile: "There you are! General X will see you kitted up."

"But an Army clothing depôt is not a suitable place for trying on chorus girls' costumes."

"Why not?"

"Not very good for discipline."

"I should think the chaps would enjoy it." (General laughter.) "Besides you could use the W.A.A.C. (I's) as mannequins." (More laughter.)

As the proceedings drew to a close the general passed to the counter-attack: what was being done about the lack of pianos in rest camps and institutes? I explained that ENSA's pianos were ordered in London by NAAFI through the Ministry of Supply. The general pounced.

"Ah! Serious lack of co-ordination. All requisitions for Welfare equipment should be forwarded to War Office for co-ordination with the requirements of the other Services, application for shipping-space being made at the same time." (I kept quiet: waste of time to point out that a large number of our pianos had already arrived.)

We had come to the end. The chairman directed his gaze at each somnolent figure in turn, using the hieroglyphics that are the common terms of reference on such occasions:

"Any comments, D.X.Y.?"

"I don't think so, sir."

"How about you, M. and B.?"

An elderly brigadier with the puffy, sweetly complacent gaze of a budgerigar started awake.

"Well, actually—actually—I don't think we are affected."

"You'd better have a copy of the notes all the same, Tim," said the chairman cooingly.

"Very well," sighed the general.

The chairman closed his file of papers. "Notes will be distributed to all concerned." (To a clerk) "Usual distribution."

"Send your comments to A.G. (I) x y z, please; we will meet again in a fortnight's time to see how much of Mr Dean's report we can adopt. Thank you, gentlemen."

10

Turn out the Guard!

I did not fancy the prospect of waiting about in Delhi for the decision. The place was picturesque enough under the wintry sky in its prevailing tones of grey and brown, to which the women's saris and, here and there, magenta turbans worn by the men added spots of bright colour. But the dry winds were uncomfortable, blowing hot in the bright sunshine and cold in the shadows, like the delicacy known as 'pouding Alaska' that is some people's fancy but never mine. So I welcomed the C.-in-C.'s suggestion that I should go to the Central Command at Lahore and thence to the North-West Army at Rawalpindi and Peshawar. The Beechcraft being still available, I and my assistant set off once more.

The pattern of things was the same as elsewhere: established cantonments, preparing to face a long war in the Far East, were bursting their buttons; new rest-camps and leave-centres were springing up everywhere. The talk was all of the great need for entertainment, especially during monsoon; but when I found at Rawalpindi that ENSA parties were spending twenty-seven days out of the month in travel, and began to expostulate across the Commander-in-Chief's dinner-table at the shocking waste of time, the M.G.A. silenced me by remarking that, even if air transport could be provided, it would only save about five of those twenty-seven days because most of the locations were without air-strips.

In Peshawar brown leaves and white frost patterning the tree-bordered roads under a white sun suggested February in the English shires. While the young staff captain who drove me to see the Khyber Pass told legendary stories of 'The Road,' I stared with romantic interest at the wild tribesmen, mounted on mules and armed with long-barrelled rifles, occasionally to be seen on the narrow pathways leading to the little hill forts. The blood-feuds persisting between families were by common consent rarely pursued on the sole artery of communication in that wild country, for to do so would have been to challenge the Pax Britannica, to say nothing of stopping the flow of traffic upon which the life of the community depended. But when we reached Landikana my escort warned me on no account to cross the frontier line, for the Afghan guards lolling outside a hut there would not stop at smashing the camera.

On the way back to Delhi Brigadier Duncan, whose daughter Joanna had been a member of one of our drama companies and was now back in India serving as an ENSA welfare officer, invited me to visit him at Jodhpur, where he commanded the State troops. The picturesque native city, all pink and white like ice-cream, stood out in contrast with the bright yellow palace which the ruler had recently built for himself a few miles away, an enormous structure reputed to have cost a million sterling and furnished *en suite* by Maples of London. Within the palatial *massif* there was a complete bijou theatre of modern design and excellent proportions, but heavily decorated with plaster work in the style and quality of Frank Matcham, architect of Edwardian music-halls. The boxes were heavily latticed so that the Indian ladies might view the performances without themselves being seen. Here the R.A.F. personnel would occasionally give their own concerts and a welcome to ENSA companies.

The Old Fort, really a fortified palace, now used mainly to house State officials and the Prince's dependants, was more picturesque, with its huge, crumbling white walls and iron-latticed windows. When Brigadier Duncan invited me to inspect the State guards, turned out in my honour, I, being no Köpenick, made a poor showing, but the tall, bearded guards, their breasts glittering with medals, gave no sign. Atop the ancient crenellations pieces of ordnance of the time of the Indian Mutiny and of Clive were still used to signal the noon hour to the native population, and for other public notice. Within there was a small museum of Indian costumes and a considerable armoury of ancient weapons of priceless historical value.

In the cool of the afternoon, to a polo match between a team captained by the Maharajah and one by his neighbour, the Maharajah of Jaipur, played with tremendous dash and speed on gloriously sleek, well-groomed ponies. The ground was verdant, the pavilion gracious and comfortable, the drinks served on the little terrace in front of it beyond compare. After play was over and the teams had said good-bye to their host and driven away in their fast American cars, the two Princes invited me to sit and talk with them. But for certain differences of light and shade in the vista before us and some changes of emphasis in their speech and sentiment, one might have been a guest at one of the stately homes of England, sitting there listening to the sounds of the fading day. Night fell as the brigadier drove me back to the city. Countless twinkling lights appeared low on the horizon, lifting as we drew nearer to become the lights of shop and street —garish, unshaded, contrasting into blackness the many little alley-ways under the soft Indian night.

11

Seeing it through

The next day I was back in Delhi for the final verdict on my report. The Supreme Allied Commander, South East Asia, had already telegraphed his acceptance of my proposals. Agreement upon its financial implications had also been reached with the Auditor-General (Sir Cameron Badenoch) and the Finance Member, so that really all that was required was a formal acceptance that could be circulated in a defence Department Letter.[1]

Very few officers were present when Dunstan and I repaired again to the A.G.'s conference room, the passing interest of the curious and the not-directly-concerned having by now evaporated. In half an hour all was over, and Eric and I were kicking our heels in the fresh air. Time unexpectedly on our hands, we drove back to Old Delhi, where Eric was once more at his best, showing me those glories of Indian Muslim architecture, the Red Fort and the Pearl and Friday mosques.

The remaining days in India could be devoted to ENSA's personal affairs, untrammelled by official anxieties. To keep pace with the rapidly developing campaign against the Japanese, we decided to make Bombay our Rear Headquarters, ENSA Main to be in Calcutta; the organization for Burma and beyond would be echeloned from there. Before leaving Delhi I spent a fruitful morning with the Engineer's Department at G.H.Q., where the revised theatre plans had been found, tucked away in a drawing-office.

While I was at work one morning in the Bombay office there came a personal telephone call for me from Karachi.

"She's gone, sir," came the voice of the ENSA officer, crackling over the telephone.

"Who's gone, what's gone?" I asked irritably. The telephone crackled some more. "What is all this?" I asked of the secretary.

She took the receiver and listened awhile. "Something to do with Frances Day," and handed me back the receiver.

I spoke again to the agitated young man at the other end of the wire. "Frances Day? She's flying in from England. One of our welfare officers is accompanying her."

"I did my best, sir. When she landed I told her I'd booked her onward passage to Bombay, but she said she hadn't come out for ENSA. She was

[1] This was issued to all Commands in India on February 21, 1945.

flying down to Kandy to see the Supreme Commander. Then she walked away. Before I could think out what to do next she was gone." (Censorship cut, our ensuing conversation being unprintable.) When she later appeared in the Arakan to give her first concert, heralded but without a pianist, the happy fiction that Miss Day was travelling independently of us had to be abandoned in the face of inexorable circumstance.

Affairs having been sorted out in Bombay, I flew to Calcutta, using the little Beechcraft for the last time. There I said good-bye to my faithful crew of two who had flown with me up and down the sub-continent almost continuously for six weeks, always cheerful, always laconic, mildly amused at the para-military duties assigned to them. Now they are swallowed up in the maelstrom of memory, but thank you—just the same!

In Calcutta, thanks to the energetic action of Major-General Stewart, taken in conjunction with Mr Casey's persuasion of the civil authorities, we had been given commodious offices; workshops also were promised. Preparations for Burma were now well in hand. 'Stokey' Roberts, transferred from N.W. Europe, was to lead the expedition, while Jack Hawkins, now promoted to be lieutenant-colonel, was given command in Calcutta. We had an enthusiastic conference in the new offices, Jack's face wrinkling with doubt when I said we had undertaken to keep going during monsoon. Virginia, in the best of form, brushing aside all difficulties, announced that the hostels she proposed to open in each of the big towns would be known as ENSA House, after Viceroy's House in Delhi, presumably. She also proposed field hostels for the jungle country. . . . Altogether an encouraging time, staying with Sir Renwick Haddow the while, a Scottish nabob, possessed of a gentle humour and the largest collection of geraniums in pots I have ever seen.

There was a Press conference on my last night in Calcutta, followed by a broadcast from All India Radio, in which I deprecated "this business of favoured artistes coming out under special privilege, and when they get here, rushing about all over the place like scalded cats." This brought a heated rejoinder in *The Times*, signed by George Formby and Wee Georgie Wood, which surprised me, for there were no stars in the ENSA firmament to whom my remarks applied with less reason.

On the mail-plane to Karachi I tried to work out the order of priorities for our people at home. My mind was nauseated with excess of detail and refused to function that way. . . . Good to have seen something of India, even in the twilight of the British Raj. Understandable why British officials are scared to requisition for our needs. They are sitting on a political volcano. Moving rapidly about the country, one can sense the latent heat, without the discomfort of having to sit on top of it.

Sky and water were no longer blue over the Gulf. We were drawing near to the Middle East. On Bahrein the bright dresses of the East gave place to the browns and black of Arab habit. We had to spend the night there. But I was in luck. Captain Shillington, R.N., was the Naval officer in charge. I had helped him to equip a theatre on Scapa in the early days, so now we had a happy evening together, sampling the strangest assortment of liqueurs. What's more, I had a comfortable billet instead of sleeping in the transit hut where sand was the inner and outer cover to a catalogue of discomforts.

Approaching Cairo, my thoughts flew back to the uneasy country I had left. . . . Those Victorian stories of men and women at the outposts of Empire who solemnly dressed for dinner in order to drink the Royal Widow's health: their superb confidence kept control over situations that otherwise would surely have got out of hand. But now? Confidence was no longer sustained by events. A change was coming, and everybody knew it.

Cairo and trouble were apparently to remain synonymous. I heard on arrival that Edith Evans and the company she had got together to play *The Late Christopher Bean* in India had broken their journey there. By some carelessness our senior officer, appointed to take Haygarth's place when he left for the Second Front, had failed to call upon her. I went to the hotel. There in the lounge was Edith, ecstatic, alert, a trifle disconcerted by the lack of welcome, but full of duty. Sitting beside her was beautiful Dorothy Hyson, with that air of faint perplexity she wears so charmingly. This was the notable advance guard of the parade of stars of theatre, concert platform and music-hall that had been promised for India.

CHAPTER THIRTY

THE PARTY IS ON

1

Italy revisited

THE general was seated on a low stone wall, dangling his feet, a pile of neatly cut sandwiches in a mess-tin by his side; behind him a grove of olive trees in spring leaf and, in front, at a turn in the rutted lane, a small staff car, inconspicuously parked. The outline of the seated figure seemed familiar, so I stopped my car and began a diffident approach. But he spoke before I could state my name and business. It was General Alexander, Supreme Allied Commander, Central Mediterranean Force.

"Well, how are you getting on? Come to stir up the entertainment?"

"Yes, sir. Just been to G.H.Q., hoping to see you."

"Out to lunch," said the General, twinkling.

On my way back from India I was paying a belated first visit to the C.M.F., and had just left the Royal Palace at Caserta, built in the eighteenth century for the honour and dignity of the Kings of Naples and now battered and shop-worn after various utilitarian occupancies, culminating in its present use as the Allied G.H.Q. The matchboard division of the noble rooms into office cubicles, the mutely protesting statuary used as hatracks, the files of Army papers nailed to the wooden shutters in the deeply embrasured windows: these and other indignities contrasted the current violence with a more graceful past.

"I hope we are giving satisfaction, sir," I ventured in uncertain gambit.

"Music, more good music—that's the thing," the General murmured vaguely.

The sight of brigadiers and colonels waiting in the queues with private soldiers to gain admission to Barbirolli's concerts had evidently impressed the General deeply. But his momentary interest in the subject of entertainment was soon lost in contemplation of more important matters. As the familiar look of abstraction returned to his face I realized it was my cue to retire.

"Come and dine to-night, and I'll have the complaints ready for you," he called after me.

I drove away, marvelling at the power of a personality completely adjusted to itself to soothe and renew another's confidence so quickly. And then I began to fuss lest the complaints proved serious. . . .

Nothing further has been set down about the work in Italy since our mobile columns drove on to the Sicilian beachhead, George Formby, venturesomely, the first star to land there. This is not from any wish to minimize its importance. Rather the reverse, for those columns, ploughing their way through the bitter rain and mud in the wake of the Eighth Army in the winter of 1943, received special eulogy for their ability to keep close behind the advancing front, and it was their example which had finally decided me to use the same system in the Normandy landings. But we were flinging stones so fast and far into the pool of national effort, one ripple merging into the next, that, in retrospect, strict chronology becomes impossible.

In the Mediterranean Command the necessary administrative personnel had been ready to hand, and so the muddle of small beginnings and too swift expansion was avoided. On our team were several energetic and resourceful young actors, transferred after service with fighting units. Prominent among them was Nigel Patrick. After his initiatory term in the Middle East he had been given charge of the ENSA headquarters in Algiers, where, fired by Newman's example in Cairo, he had applied himself with zest to tightening up our affairs, especially production. A company whose stage equipment had been lost at sea was put to work, giving play-readings over the air to augment Henry Caldwell's broadcasting efforts. The plays, greatly appreciated in hospital wards and messes, were *Romeo and Juliet*, *The Importance of Being Earnest* and *Libel*. Circulation of the Inter-Services Committee's allocations through ENSA channels was resumed, so that when Frank Cellier and the London company playing *Quiet Week-end* arrived by air—passages arranged by Air Marshal Tedder—and announced their intention of playing to R.A.F. units only, Patrick was able to adjust matters to the Army's advantage: a useful preliminary exercise in the duties that lay ahead.

Brian Reece was another new broom. He came to us from the gunners. He was sent first to the sub-area of Bône in North Africa, where on his first morning he found a welfare officer usurping his office chair and our military personnel still abed at 9 A.M., their cars and lorries parked outside the billets in a filthy condition.

Some of the new men came straight from responsible managerial positions in civil life, such as Harold Mellor from The Tower, Blackpool,

Derek Salberg, whose conduct of the family business in the Alexandra Theatre,[1] Birmingham, since the war, remains an oustanding example of what theatre management should be, and Michael Brennan, assistant stage-director at Drury Lane before the war.

The first ENSA column had landed at Salerno: Norman Harrington in charge, with Michael Brennan as his 'Number One.' The second column went into Bari with Fraser-Green in charge. Harold Mellor, landing in January, began to co-ordinate the work of the now widely separated columns. Later, Reece took Harrington's place on the tail of the Eighth Army, maintaining through snow and mud a record for close contact first set up in the African desert. After the fall of Rome the Allied H.Q. moved from North Africa to Naples, and Patrick went with it, taking with him Leon ('Ding') Davey, a clever designer commissioned from the ranks and given charge of our Naples production centre, where his work achieved a high professional standard. But it is not possible to mention all these young officers by name nor their wanderings; they were here, there, and everywhere, working hard without the publicity and adulation to which their professional contemporaries were grown accustomed. Nor must it be supposed that they were moved higgledy-piggledy about the country at the whim of those immediately superior to them. Their postings and promotion were controlled by a Military Postings Committee, sitting at Drury Lane under the chairmanship of Stanley Bell, where qualities and defects were carefully conned before changes were authorized.

Garrison cinemas were opened and operated in the same thrusting spirit that animated the mobile columns, beginning with the Municipal Theatre at Tarano, reopened on June 8, 1944, with the film *Springtime in the Rockies* —exactly two days after the Germans had evacuated the place. A free performance for the civil population followed—the first English-speaking film ever to be shown in the town. By February we were in Ancona, our column bringing with them the Anglo-Polish Ballet, which stayed for a week, giving nine performances to a total of some 20,000 troops in a theatre with a seating capacity under 2000. And so the march went on.

Along the line of advance the theatres were roofless, or else gaping holes gave on to sky and rain and frost. Where electric installations had been

---

[1] A whimsical reminder of his days in Italy used to hang in the office there, a poster advertising the performances of an ENSA party in Perugia. A sergeant, left alone in the office, mistook an official billeting sheet for the usual advertising matter and dispatched it to the local printer, with the result that the following information was plastered on the ancient walls of the city:

EVE ON LEAVE

6 men, 4 women, 2 married couples.

destroyed the headlights of a jeep were shone through a hole in the wall; if this proved insufficient the audience would always oblige with their torches. It was a day to remember when the ENSA officer in charge of a theatre received a dozen or so lamps from Naples to go on with. In Foggia it was so cold that an open brazier was kept burning at the back of the stage. The place possessed only one backcloth, made of paper stretched on canvas, and the audience could see the flames of the brazier through it; they could also hear it crackle and splutter in vociferous competition with the singers on the stage.

In Rome conditions were better. There we ran the beautiful Argentine Theatre for nearly two years. Originally founded in 1731 by Duke Sforza Cesarini as a private theatre, and three times rebuilt, so that its original appearance is much changed, it still retains a certain eighteenth-century atmosphere. Opera and ballet were the main attractions for the first 150 years; it was here (on February 5, 1816) that Rossini's *The Barber of Seville* was first presented. Strict instructions were given to our staff to take great care of the fabric. On the first anniversary of ENSA's occupancy I was gratified to receive the letter of thanks which the Italian director sent to our sergeant-in-charge, recording the fact that, although approximately half a million Allied troops had attended the performances, the theatre had suffered no damage.

One fact stood out notably clear from the patchwork of difficulties: ENSA was at its best in the really dangerous areas. For example, there was that company 'Eve on Leave,' which arrived at Forli immediately after the town had been heavily bombed. The artistes took over two top-floors of a hotel that had been burnt, and set to work with buckets and mops, scrubbing the floors and rigging up two dormitories before giving a show that night in the city square, the smoke of conflict still playing about them.

Many well-known artistes have cause to remember the war-torn theatres of Foggia, Bari, Ancona and other places. Names that come to mind are Sandy Powell, Maurice Winnick, Waldini, Bebe Daniels (sent out on a special tour by her husband, Ben Lyon, a colonel in U.S.O. Special Services—later their show, 'Hi Gang,' was handed over to ENSA to route) and Cicely Courtneidge, who visited some of them briefly.

All our best clowns played here either before or after their visits to the Second Front, among them Nervo and Knox, seizing every opportunity for hard work; always playing tricks, never coming to harm, safeguarded by the simple rule that each looked after the other on gay nights. And if the jerky head-movements of that famous balloon dance were sometimes a baleful exercise, what did it matter since those excruciating grimaces were all the funnier?

There were famous American names, too: Jack Benny, who loved to take moments off to peep at the ENSA shows (which he much admired), Joe E. Brown, Humphrey Bogart, Katherine Cornell (who brought a full New York production of *The Barretts of Wimpole Street* to take part in a joint Drama Festival at Naples) and many more. These artistes came to Italy for U.S.O. At last there was complete co-operation and interchange between the two organizations, U.S.O. and ENSA, such as I had sought in New York. But I had nothing to do with it: it was brought about by the fact that the troops of our two countries were so intermingled—the Fifth American Army had a large number of British troops attached to it —that any other policy would have been foolish in the extreme. On the cinema side, too, there was a complete interchange of programmes, greatly to the benefit of our organization.

Towards the end of his time Nigel Patrick, wearing his promotion to the rank of lieutenant-colonel with the self-assurance of a *mousquetaire*, had nineteen officers under his command responsible to him for the running of thirty-four theatres and 120 cinemas. And from his headquarters in Naples he administered our entertainments throughout Italy, Austria, Corsica, Sardinia, Malta and Greece, as well as those remnants that still lingered on in North Africa. All the Directors of Welfare whom he encountered were senior to him in rank, but histrionic wits and an irrepressible good humour kept him on the surface of serious argument, whence no amount of official artillery could blow him into the crevasse of Army Routine.

2

Commedia dell' Artisti

All our headquarters overseas had begun to develop individual characteristics, reflecting the personalities of those in charge as much as the general atmosphere of the Commands to which they were attached. Here in Naples life with ENSA took on something of the quality of opera bouffe, Nigel Patrick's detachment and the acid humours of Neville-Willing (transferred to the C.M.F. from India) colouring every contretemps with a kind of Neapolitan variegation.

Our reputation in the Command, dating back to the opening of the Tunis Theatre, was too well founded for interference to amount to more than the usual pin-pricks, and for these ridicule was ample compensation. The opportunity for its exercise was not missed when a senior officer, presiding over an important meeting summoned to discuss Army amenities, opened the proceedings by remarking, "Gentlemen, I have serious news for you. We must carry on as best we can, but as a result of recent sinkings in the Mediterranean we have lost no less than four consignments of ping-pong balls." A certain Brigadier Newth (newly appointed Director of Welfare), highly critical of our inadequacy, was heard to remark jokingly one day in the bar of the senior officers' Mess that ENSA might be responsible for entertainment, but its officers were incapable of doing anything about it themselves. Patrick took up the challenge. In company with Brian Reece, he organized a show called 'Staff Party,' presented two Sundays later at the Bellini Theatre, Naples, in aid of the Prisoners of War Red Cross Fund. His performance of a lisping staff officer whose comment upon every situation was: "Well, no newth is good newth," was received with delight by the crowded audience.

Encouraged by success, the staff at Naples produced further shows. One, a Nativity play called *Behold the Man*, well produced by 'Ding' Davey, was a co-operative effort of all three Services, including A.T.S., W.R.N.S. and a combined Services choir. This ran for two weeks at the Bellini Theatre, now officially known as the ENSA Garrison Theatre. William Devlin was the narrator, and the faithful Mary Barrett—not permitted to accompany Gracie Fields to America and now wearing our uniform and the insignia of a Welfare Supervisor—played Joseph's mother. The young ladies of a disbanded Revue company provided the angelic chorus. To complete the cast, a languid sergeant-major, very tall and thin, attached to the our office, who had been a ballet-dancer, offered to perform in Herod's Palace. When he appeared in abbreviated trunks covered in sequins, and with larger sequins on each of his eyelids, the troops went mad with glee. Unfortunately he forgot to remove the sequins from his eyes when he attended at the office next morning, and was severely reprimanded.

Just before one of the evening performances Naomi Jacob stood at the corner of the street, watching the crowds, and talking to Neville-Willing. Both were in uniform and both wore slacks, Naomi Jacob with hair cut short and sporting the usual monocle. A young Cockney soldier approached, saluted smartly and said:

"Excuse me, sir or madam, is this the way to the ENSA theatre?"

As he walked away in the indicated direction Naomi Jacob murmured: "Charming boy."

"I thought the remark rather insolent," said Neville-Willing.

"Oh, but he wasn't addressing me," said 'Mickie'; "he was talking to you."

Billeting the companies provided by Army Welfare's Central Pool of Artistes caused friction. Whereas the ENSA artistes had been given officer status, the soldier-actors were mostly N.C.O.'s and consequently not permitted to lodge in our hostels. One of the companies included an array of well-known actors and actresses, including John Longdon, John Wyse, Geoffrey Keen, William Kendall, Robert Sansom and Faith Brook. Arriving in Naples after an exhausting four-hour journey in an army truck, they were disgusted at the billets allotted to them, and trooped off in a body to the ENSA H.Q., where the officers were dining. A message was sent in to Lieutenant-Colonel Patrick that some "Stars in Battledress" wanted to see him. Such brevity was not calculated to assist good understanding. "Tell 'em I'm at Mess and can't be disturbed," said Patrick grandly. Whereupon Corporal Faith Brook burst into the room and gave the commanding officer such a dressing-down that in the effort to save face and cover up his mistake he lost his head and shouted, "Put that woman on a charge."

It was Neville-Willing who finally succeeded in pacifying the disputants, reminding them that, after all, they were only actors and actresses in spite of the uniform. The row brought about the cancellation of an unpopular and deeply resented regulation that became impossible to maintain when numbers of 'non-belligerent' Italian artistes, whom we were permitted to employ, came to dwell in the tents of the victors. Thereafter the Army companies stayed in our hostels, properly claiming precedence over their late enemies.

One of Neville-Willing's duties was to meet the artistes on the incoming ships. This gave further scope for observation of the unusual and untoward, from which laughter at his own expense was not excluded. Sent to warn the Polish Ballet that their lurid behaviour elsewhere must not be repeated in Italy, he obtained the cabin number of the principal dancers, went below and tapped smartly on the door.

"Come in!" said a girlish voice.

He found three or four young men in various stages of undress, apparently in no hurry to land.

"Well, what is it, sweetie?" asked one of them impudently.

Drawing himself up to his not very considerable height, Captain Neville-Willing pointed to his shoulder badges:

"Look, boys, doesn't this mean anything to you?"

There was a chorus of laughter as one of them cried:

"Oh, my goodness, she's a captain!"

The same company was later involved in a shooting affray in Rome. At the usual party after the performance in a club for Indian troops one of the dancers with Polish exuberance let off a revolver. The shot went through the ceiling and pierced the posterior of an Indian N.C.O., as he lay in his bed in the room above. (Was it a foreshadowing of a later Goon: "You rot-ten swine, you!") When he was cross-examined the N.C.O. only grinned and said:

"Now I've been wounded I shan't have to go."

Captain Reece turned to the offending Pole:

"You know, what you really need is a bloody good hiding."

The young man replied, "My dear sir, I couldn't agree with you more."

The list of bizarre personalities decanted on the quayside at Naples, and embellished by Neville-Willing's impish tongue, included two variety artistes of indifferent talent but marked amiability. Their only comment upon the direst experience was: "Smashin', Captain, lovely country, lovely scenery, lovely people." In the end one of them had to be taken to hospital, suffering from internal hæmorrhage, brought on by overwork. After several blood transfusions he left hospital a positive skeleton, but it was still a case of "lovely hospital, lovely nurses." And when Reece went to see him off on his return to England he was greeted with: "Thanks, Captain, I have enjoyed it." The pair were never told that it was not the variety act that made them popular with the troops, but a touching performance of good heart.

Not all the opera bouffe was confined to our headquarters, nor to Naples. It spread among the actors of every shade and talent, including the chorus girl sightseeing in Rome who was told she should not miss the Colosseum. "Coliseum?" she chirruped. "Why, what's on there?" It was blown hither and thither by the spirit of the *improvisatori* whose special gifts, though sadly attenuated, still delight our children's children at pantomime time. It played round my own head for a moment when an officer of American Transport Command, never having heard of ENSA, viewed Patrick's application for a movement order for my visit to Rome with the deepest suspicion. He disapproved of 'sky-pilots' mixing with enemy nationals—"it just meant trouble." The order was signed only when he realized he had mixed me up with the Dean of St Paul's.

An early visitor to C.M.F. was Grant Anderson, who came with his sister to give readings in costume from Dickens and Shakespeare. The first show was in H.M.S. *Orion*. The two artistes had fourteen quick changes between them. Grant Anderson dressed behind a screen rigged up with flags at the side of the stage while his sister was accommodated in a torpedo room on deck. She was warned not to let the iron door close on her, as it only opened from outside. This injunction she forgot, but remembered when she found a cockroach in her shoe, and started to scream and bang on the door just as the torpedo 'chiefy,' who had been making merry in Naples, came aboard. He was mightily intrigued and, although her cue had now arrived, flatly refused the appeals of 'Sarah Gamp' (Grant Anderson) to release his 'Betsy Trotwood.'

"To hell with that," said the slightly fuddled C.P.O., "there's a tart in my torpedo room and there she stays."

In the Forward Areas Patricia Burke and Gabrielle Brune, each the toast of a division, joined together in riotous conflict, breaking into each other's songs and cross-gagging in an exhibition of professional fun that created a furore in the Eighth Army. Inspiring, too, to see them in the daylight hours doing the rounds of the hospitals (twelve fifteen-minute sing-songs in a day, perhaps) and most touching to watch as they sang softly outside the wards where the very sick lay.

Then there was Geraldo, after a triumphal tour of the Middle East, flying in with his parcel of glamour—the orchestra had been sent home in the cruiser *London*—and crash-landing in the mud five miles south of Palermo. The sight of Sicilian peasants giggling as the shoeless and muddied Dorothy Carless and Doreen Villiers ploughed their way to firmer ground was no more soothing to the temper than to overhear themselves described on the American air-strip as "just another ENSA party." Laughable enough in retrospect to hear of 'Gerry' tramping through the dark of an officers' transit camp at 5 A.M. armed with towel and sponge, in search of the commanding officer's promise of a bath; but not at all amusing to be in Bari the night two munition ships blew up in the harbour, depriving the hotel of doors and windows. Imperturbability won the day when he was removed to hospital, stripped and placed on a slab for sun-ray treatment for lumbago, and overheard a nursing sister in the next cubicle say, "Geraldo? I must take a look at him. I named my canary after him in Palestine." As she stared at the recumbent bandleader he surprised her by saying, "Well, how do I compare with your canary?"

There were moments in the opera bouffe when fun and absurdity gave place to scenes of emotion that lifted entertainment out of the normal rut of soldiers' amenity and gave it another and deeper significance. Of such were the concerts given by the Welsh Choir. This manifestation of native musical genius owed its existence to the exertions of a little-known organist and choirmaster from Swansea, Lionel Rowlands, who had been appointed ENSA Supervisor for the South Wales Area under the Factory Scheme. He had travelled the hills and valleys of his native land, sifting the best of the musical talent that abounds there. Rowlands welded his singers into such a close-packed expression of belief in the mission to which he had summoned them that their success became universal. In the end I yielded to his entreaties and gave orders to make the Choir ready for overseas.

After a memorable embarkation concert on the terrace of the House of Commons before Mr Speaker, many members of the Welsh Parliamentary Party, including Lady Megan and Major Lloyd George, and other political notables, they set out. From Naples, in March 1945, through rain and slush to Rome, and thence north to Perugia, Arezzo, Siena; across country to the Adriatic and up with the Eighth Army as far as Gradox; back over the Apennines to Florence and Milan: everywhere tumultuous welcome and closing scenes that had in them some of the special quality of religious revival—officers and men shaking hands with each other in silence; American G.I.'s with sentimental tears asking if the Choir could visit the folks in U.S.A.; New Zealanders and South Africans of the same mind. We had nothing to reproach ourselves with in regard to Good Music for the troops in Italy.

There was no need for me to linger where all was going so well. Patrick was keeping a careful check on the certified audience returns. By VE Day these reached the huge total of 54,000 performances to 27,000,000 men—approximately one show per man each eight days. No wonder that General 'Alex' had few complaints to make when I dined with him that first evening.

<>

In the Manner of the Word . . .

Leslie Henson, touring his 'Gaieties' round the Mediterranean, with a Yorkshire musical director to conduct the local orchestras, arrived at Bari. The orchestra went busily to work in the pit while he stood on the stage supervising the arrangement of the scenery. But the conductor ran into difficulty when he tried to explain what he wanted. One of their number, who claimed to know a few words of English, proved a broken reed. Others joined in the argument. Tapping his score angrily, the conductor lost his head and shouted above the din that he wanted so many bars played louder, and more abruptly. Leslie decided it was time to intervene:

"Why don't you say staccato, Bill?"

The Yorkshireman looked up with open-mouthed astonishment: "Eeh, but would they understand?"

3

Little Odyssey

Lurch and bump! Bump and lurch! Breath held and then a slower and heavier lurch, followed by a grinding noise and a crash! A tiny procession of vehicles comes to a halt in clouds of dust, the three-ton lorry, driven in first gear for the last hour, steaming like a cauldron. Men and women in battledress climb tiredly out of the vehicles and draw together in knots. The speed limit of eight to ten miles per hour imposed by the innumerable pot-holes, some partly filled with road metal, some with loose stones, some not at all, has been exceeded. Another back axle gone! . . . The concert party in Greece, for such they are, discuss anxiously the possibility of reaching their location in time to give a show that night. It is forty miles on, and already they are exhausted by their two-hours' journey. Even tough 'Mike' Brennan, in charge of the column, finds the going hard.

A few months later a high-level meeting of Welfare Officers in Athens is discussing the urgent need of amenities for their troops, encountering street revolution in this country of quondam liberation with the good-humoured grouse that is the soldier's privilege. The usual atmosphere of such meetings prevails: a mixture of discipline, frustrated enthusiasm and polite informality. A senior R.A.F. officer from Salonika is on his feet.

"I don't know about the Army but with us Welfare has been a complete wash-out. No sports gear, no footballs, no gramophone records and very few radio sets. As for ENSA, it simply does not exist."

A murmur of agreement from the disappointed: others who have no cause to grumble hold their peace; after all they can always 'do with more.' Although he has come unbidden to this feast of criticism, a young officer who, as actor, has a nose for Situation rises to protest. The presiding brigadier looks up, noting with surprise the junior rank confronting him.

"Name, please?"

"Captain Reece, sir."

"Unit?"

"In charge of ENSA, sir."

Interest stirs among the slightly bored officers; some look up curiously.

"Well, what have you to say?"

"It's true there have been few ENSA shows in Greece so far, sir. Very soon there will be none at all."

"How do you mean?"

"I've written to my headquarters in Naples, suggesting no more should be sent for the present."

"Perhaps you'd better explain yourself."

"Well, sir, I've had a party waiting for ten days for air-lift to Salonika. They could have entertained another thirty thousand men in that time."

"There's no priority for ENSA," snaps Air Movements.

"ENSA should move them by road," says the chairman.

"All our transport has been shaken to pieces. Besides, it's too much for the girls; they arrive exhausted."

"What practical suggestion has this officer to make?" asks the R.A.F. member.

"Only one, sir," says Reece. "If you want shows you must give us priority in the air."

"Out of the question!"

Four days later the artistes are still haunting the airfield, while their stage costumes and properties lie idle in baskets, and the troops hunger for shows. Then Reece's protest pays its dividend, and our parties, augmented by leading singers from the Athens Opera, paid for by a special financial grant from Drury Lane, are flown to various control points, and distributed thence in military vehicles.

Another month later. The buildings on the Acropolis, serenely beautiful, look down in classic disdain on the unkempt crowds, soldiers and civilians alike in their shabbiness. There is dust in clouds as British Army convoys go hurtling and banging down narrow streets, while shambling pedestrians dodge out of the way. A staff car draws up at a block of flats. Out steps a brigadier and—Lieutenant-Colonel Patrick. The latter, recently arrived to survey the situation, has decided that we must take over the National Theatre, since all efforts to obtain cinemas for our films and live shows have been blocked. He has managed to secure the largest car in Athens and a Greek interpreter, as well as the presence of the Director of Welfare, for this foray into officialdom. Much virtue in rank! The Minister of Education having referred them to the Prime Minister as the only person able to deal with the matter, what more natural than to drive up to the flat where a cabinet meeting is being held and demand to see the august one?

The British officers wait in the lobby. As the Ministers file out of the meeting the interpreter speaks to a secretary, who stares and shakes his head. But the Prime Minister's wife, busy cooking lunch, overhears the conversation. She tells Patrick that she was once an actress and would be glad to help. Patrick, with a gallant bow, seizes the occasion. He too is a well-known actor, although, alas! we have no National Theatre in Eng-

land. Of course he is only doing this work *pour la patrie*, etc., etc. The
Director of Welfare is nowhere at all in this professional fraternization,
but his presence lends it official sanction. The actress persuades her husband to agreement. And so the use of the National Theatre with all its
staff is granted to ENSA without charge, with only two provisos: no song
and dance shows, and one box to be reserved for the use of the Cabinet.
Patrick and his brigadier drive away in a cloud of dust and glory to lunch
at the senior officers' Mess. . . . So this was ENSA—in Greece!

Glamour Stations . . .

Over now to the Middle East. Date: February 1945. Place: ENSA
Headquarters at Alexandria. The telephone rings: Flag-Officer to Rear-
Admiral Levant calling.

"We have a flotilla of destroyers and M.T.B.'s patrolling off Rhodes
and Leros, keeping the enemy troops there inactive. The men have had no
leave and are pretty browned off. Can you send a show?"

"A mixed party, sir?"

"What do you mean, mixed?"

"Well, girls as well as the men?"

"Hardly."

"Won't do much good without the girls, sir. You know how it is."

"I'll call you back."

'All the Winners' was the company chosen, because of its experience
in more than one theatre of war, and perhaps because it included six
attractive girls. In high anticipation they were piped aboard H.M.S.
Ledbury, each player armed with a single suitcase. Off Cimi a heavy swell
tossed the Greek caiques about like corks as the artistes were rowed from
ship to ship. Three shows a day was hard going for the girls. And, as they
clambered up the heaving companion-ways, not even a liberal coating of
Max Factor could entirely conceal from the inquisitive *matelots*, peering
from every nook and cranny, the greenish pallor beneath.

En route from Cimi to Khios, *Ledbury* received a signal that a German
party had raided a small island and was burning the Allied installations.
Ledbury was joined by *Exmoor*, and the two ships were ordered to destroy the landing-craft. Our girls, ears stuffed with cotton-wool to
deaden the sound of the 4-inch guns, were shepherded into the wardroom,
intended for later use as a casualty ward. Throughout the night the
destroyers circled the island to prevent the landing of enemy reinforcements, and in the morning assault groups went in to mop up. The German

prisoners taken aboard *Ledbury* were astonished at the glamorous cargo she carried, an astonishment as complete no doubt as would have been that of My Lords of the Admiralty had they been present.

4

"Who goes Home?"

Back in London there was a change of atmosphere. The Allied Armies were across the Rhine, and victory in Europe was near. Problems of demobilization came into view as people began to think and talk of the return of their men and womenfolk. As early as December 1944 proposals for the reduction of ENSA entertainment by stages after the cease-fire had been put before the Entertainments Board; they were resisted at first by the Service members, but strongly supported by the Treasury. We tried to back up this policy by an orderly withdrawal of talent from the Forces. Our Advisory Drama Council, under the chairmanship of John Gielgud and, later, Aubrey Blackburn, prepared a scheme whereby professional artistes awaiting demobilization from H.M. Forces would be allowed to transfer to ENSA units, thus providing opportunities of further study for those who were little more than students when the war broke out, and useful refresher courses for the older artistes. In no circumstances was a person's demobilization to be postponed, except at his own wish. The plan was to be operated in co-operation with British Actors' Equity. The work of our Advisory Music Council reached the apex of its importance about this time, too, the Army Council requesting it to submit a memorandum on the rehabilitation of soldiers wishing to adopt a musical career in peacetime. Both Councils submitted their schemes to the War Office, where they were duly pigeon-holed in that graveyard of so many well-intentioned documents, the Central Registry.

The change of priorities at Drury Lane had brought no lessening of administrative tasks. While the need for artistes, particularly stars, to go to the Far East still had to come first, and home entertainment was drastically cut, the opening of NAAFI Clubs at home and abroad brought a last-minute widening of our responsibilities. These Clubs owed their existence largely to the enthusiasm and drive of the NAAFI Chairman. They showed the Corporation's work at its best, and were as far removed from the beer canteens of the First War as can be imagined. Providing a wide variety of amenities, they were an immediate success and popular with both sexes.

In the first flush of enthusiasm NAAFI wanted us to service them with regular entertainment. But at home this would have been contrary to our original undertaking not to operate in direct competition with commercial interests. Overseas, it would be impossible to avoid the appearance of artistes whom the troops had already seen in the normal course of our visits. Yet blank refusal would lay us open to the charge of non-co-operation. I pondered over the problem for some while.

Anxiety among the younger men and women in the Forces about their future careers was widespread. (This anxiety was to find political expression in the following year.) If we could arouse interest by an informative approach to some of the peacetime avenues that lay open, we might help to canalize that anxiety and provide a powerful magnet of support for the Clubs at the same time. I therefore proposed ENSA Leisure Centres, attached to the NAAFI Clubs wherever possible, where exhibitions, lectures, and recitals would be given on such subjects as (here I quote from my original minute):

> Architecture; Town Planning; Industrial Design; The Ideal Home; The Air Age; Television; Literature; Drama; Music; Painting;
> the whole scheme to be announced under the title or slogan of 'THE WORLD OF YOUR FUTURE.'

The proposal was accepted.

An Advisory Council on Club Amenities was formed under the chairmanship of Sir Herbert Dunnico, with a Club Amenities Executive to co-ordinate its activities with the rest of the organization. As in previous cases, this Council was an authoritative body, including among its members Lord Brabazon of Tara, Sir Henry Lamb representing the Royal Academy, Sir William Rothenstein the Tate, and Sir Hugh Allen the Royal College of Music, together with a representative of the NAAFI Board of Management. Other members were Professor Patrick Abercrombie and Professor Herbert Reilly, both then taking part in the resurgence of planning that trumpeted the post-war years.

The first Centre was opened in Paris in the Atelier attached to the Théâtre des Ambassadeurs in the Champs-Élysées. Here an exhibition of town-planning was set out by Denis Wreford from material supplied by members of the Council. Here, too, the Music Council later arranged recitals by distinguished musicians, and lectures illustrated by gramophone records. Later there was an exhibition of Contemporary French Painting. In Brussels the lovely Palais d'Egmont had been taken over by NAAFI and converted into the Montgomery Club, where similar exhibitions were held. Meanwhile at home the firm of De La Rue prepared a display setting forth the many opportunities in the Plastics Industry. So far so good.

This collaboration with our foster parents put an end to the cold war between us. But the scheme soon ran into difficulties. Coming so late upon the scene, it received little moral support from the rest of the ENSA family. The sense of mission that had driven the staff at Drury Lane forward through the dark days of the war was now largely dissipated. Our people were mentally, if not physically, exhausted. Abroad, our officers disliked the intrusion of civilian notions and civilian personnel; they sided with the Army Education people, who felt that the plan was an intrusion upon their province. Some of the distinguished men on the Advisory Council felt uneasy under Dunnico's chairmanship and left it after a while. The near prospect of the war's end made the launching of new ideas more and more laborious. In the end the plans to make our Leisure Centres places where young soldiers could acquire a practical interest in the new world they were about to face were submerged beneath the turbulence of demobilization.

The financial implications of that turbulence took me frequently to the NAAFI Headquarters at Esher. There I was present at an end-of-term prize-giving, only on this occasion the term was the Second World War and the prizes were rewards for duty carried out in circumstances of danger. One could have wished for a more picturesque quality in the gifts instead of the usual utilitarian dullness. But there was no lack of sparkle in the ensuing competition to choose the Ideal NAAFI Girl. The other judges were Lady Astor and Godfrey Winn. The former disapproved vehemently of the accent upon glamour, holding that it did not consort with efficiency. Godfrey Winn, on the other hand, would have the glamourizing process raised to the nth degree of perfection. In his view it was more helpful to the morale of the troops than any show of efficiency. The argument waxed hot between the judges.

"Such goings-on put ideas into young men's heads," declared Lady A.

"Why should drinking beer lead to temptation?" asked Godfrey, at a slight tangent.

"There is a war on. Young men are fighting and dying for Freedom." The Puritan hackles were up. "Girls should strive to be worthy of them, not fill their stupid heads with thoughts of romance; all that can wait."

"Romance never waits," shouted Godfrey, in glutinous accents and with a pink face.

The rows of NAAFI 'Ideals' sat, scrubbed and starched, listening with open mouths and excited giggles to the verbal crackers exploding underneath their chairs. I succeeded in bringing down the curtain to a hearty round of applause by putting the compromise that glamour and efficiency might yet walk hand in hand, even through that vale of temptation ever present in Lady Astor's mind, the beer canteen.

While all these expanding and contracting duties were milling about in my head, I could see little chance of getting back to the Second Front, where it seemed that the climax of our work must be reached at last. Hitherto that climax had always been a little farther on. It was like walking in undulating country: in the end you reach the summit and begin the descent without realizing it. Then a pin-point of crisis gave me the opportunity I wanted.

Shortly before leaving for India I had come across an old newspaper containing photographs of Laurence Olivier and Vivien Leigh looking at bomb damage in the City after their return from Hollywood. This had put me in mind to invite the Old Vic to visit the Second Front. Not wishing to offend any of the triumvirate then managing the Company, I had written to each one of them. On my return I was delighted to find that the suggestion had been accepted and preparations begun for the visit. But now there came word from Brussels that G.H.Q. did not wish it to take place. I flew to Brussels to discuss the matter with Major-General Chilton, who had taken Miles Graham's place as M.G.A.

The General began by saying that in the opinion of his staff the visit of such a large company would place too great a strain on ENSA's resources, to which I tartly made answer that that was our responsibility. When he referred to the shortage of transport I made the same answer. Neither of those bantams being willing to fight, and the General being in some uncertainty how to continue the conversation, he asked if I would call on the morrow. I said that if cancellation were insisted upon I should be obliged to inform the Press. Among those summoned to the kill the next day was Frank Medlicott, M.P.,[1] Director of Army Welfare, 21 Army Group—no longer in the uniform of a private, as when first encountered in the Welfare Office at Aldershot (even then sharply critical of ENSA), but bearing the rank of brigadier. I repeated my threat to tell the whole story to the Press. After some desultory, face-saving remarks about poor-quality shows (irrelevant in the circumstances), consent was given subject to agreement on the plays to be presented. This was a great relief to General Chilton.

As the final surrender of the Germans was imminent, I hurried back to London, wanting to be with my own people for that great day, and arrived a few night-hours before the event. When the news was released the following morning we all rushed out in front of Old Drury, like a flock of children released from school. Nothing premeditated or arranged: just an

---

[1] Now Sir Frank Medlicott, M.P.

involuntary surging into the street, filled with the joy of peace, such as I had witnessed in Tunis and Paris and more recently in Holland. Here was an end—for so we thought—to the abominable anxieties of extinction from on high and, passing from the supreme to the trivial, to the glee with which minor bureaucrats and all those in brief authority (waiters, bus-conductors, shopkeepers and other important persons) were wont to say, "No." Fortunately for our joy on that day, Disillusionment once again hid its face.

What's in a Name? . . .

At a conference held to approve the repertoire for the Old Vic's visit to the B.L.A. a stout colonel, who had been somnolent in a corner, looked up with alarm when *Peer Gynt* was mentioned:

"*Peer Gynt*? Isn't that a German play?"

"No, sir—Norwegian."

"Yes, but don't the Germans play it?"

"Yes, sir, but not to the same audiences."

By permission of the proprietors of "Punch"

On VE Day the following message from our President was posted at Drury Lane, and copies were dispatched to all our offices in Great Britain and to our Headquarters in every military area overseas:

SPECIAL VICTORY DAY MESSAGE

FROM THE LORD TYRRELL OF AVON, P.C., G.C.B., G.C.M.G., K.C.V.O.

To All ENSA Artistes and Technicians

I cannot let this great day of release from the anxieties of total war pass without sending greetings and congratulations to all ENSA artists and technicians who have worked so hard and so well to entertain the troops and factory workers everywhere. I feel that a special word of thanks is due to those who have been organizing the ENSA work, both at Drury Lane and elsewhere, right from the beginning. Many of you do not come before the public eye, but your work and unflagging loyalty have been essential to the success of the organization.

As President of ENSA and on behalf of the Provisional Council, I send to all advisory councils, regional committees and members of ENSA companies my warmest appreciation and thanks for the wonderful work that has been done in connection with the NAAFI service of entertainments to troops at home and overseas, and also to the millions of war-workers in various fields at home. Personally, and on behalf of ENSA, I wish you all continued good fortune both now and in the future.

TYRRELL OF AVON

CHAPTER THIRTY-ONE

˙ THE PARTY IS STILL ON

1

Germany revisited

EACH country has its own fragrance, an association of scents and smells that linger in the mind as an aid to recollection. The Germany of my first memory smelt of lime trees in flower and the thicker scent of cigars smoked over little marble-topped tables on summer evenings, of beer-halls and cellars where the chairs and tables gave out the aroma of gallons of lager beer swallowed in their company.

The memories begin with 1911, when, tired of watching Liverpool strikers hurl at the charging police the bricks assembled to rebuild the old Star Theatre into the present Playhouse, I had grabbed my small savings and hurried to sit at the feet of Max Reinhardt, then the wonder-boy of theatrical Europe. Nightly visits to the Deutsches Theater, or to the Kammerspiele next door, alternated with days among the new German lighting equipment that was a stage electrician's wildest dream come true. That plaster cyclorama travelling slowly towards me across the hundred feet or more of the vast Charlottenburg Opera stage in readiness for the evening performance of *The Flying Dutchman*!

My visits after the First War were less starry-eyed, with Reinhardt already in retreat under the searchlight of the new *Expressionismus*, and the scent of the lime trees replaced by the synthetic perfumes and sweaty powder of the crowded *kabarette* in Berlin's Kurfürstendamm. The new Germany had lost its appeal. Nevertheless, I felt honoured when Reinhardt staged the German production of Galsworthy's *Loyalties* under the title of *Gesellschaft* in the Theater in dem Josefstadt in Vienna, and asked for the loan of my prompt-book.

The *schwärmerei* faded as I stared through the window of the little French Rapide, crowded with R.A.F. relief pilots, in which I was being pitched and tossed across the Rhine. George Smith was with me. He was now chairman of our Transport Executive and also helping me with the reorganization overseas. The blades of the port propeller began to glitter in the fitful sun like a single yellow diamond, suspended. Next there were two diamonds, then a whole string; soon the eye could separate the blades and almost count the revolutions. The engine was slowly giving up its power. Yes, the port engine had stopped. We must be preparing to land. I swung round in time to see the pilot turning his thumbs down at us.

Calmly and without haste, the airmen began to fasten safety-belts and to put their feet up against the struts of the fuselage. The plane swerved this way and that in search of a landing. We began to lose height. Not a word was spoken. Some of the passengers made comic faces at the pilot in his difficulty. Presently he turned round, thumbs up this time. I looked through the window again. An emergency landing-ground was below us, just a strip of expanded metal, half-buried in the sand. We came down wind at tremendous speed. Claws of ice gripped my stomach muscles: impossible not to over-shoot. Admirable, the look of calm curiosity on George Smith's face. On and on we went, bumping and lurching to the end of the runway and into the soft sand beyond. The plane shuddered as its landing-wheels tore into the yielding stuff. A clump of tall fir trees loomed in front. We pulled up not a dozen yards from the tallest tree. Desultorily, we tramped through the trees until we came to a road, and stood about in twos and threes, waiting to hitch-hike. The young men began to pull the pilot's leg for dropping us where no *bistro* was in sight. As I listened to the usual flip-flap of R.A.F. conversation the heels of my shoes began to beat a tattoo on the hard macadam of the road. It had certainly been touch and go, this return to Germany, and quite in keeping with current violence.

George and I were on our way to Bad Salzuflen, known to the troops as 'Bath Salts,' whither our headquarters had been moved in company with other 'voluntary' organizations. For some time past I had been anxious for our headquarters staff to get out of Brussels, where they had become attached like limpets to 21 Army Group Rear, nourished in complacency by the flow of 'chittage' that is the plankton of such waters. As in Cairo, the close proximity of the administrative empire of G.H.Q. intimidated our small professional world, setting up a constant see-saw between obedience to instructions sent from London and subservience to the wishes of the Army staff.

In the rush forward into Germany our people had not kept up with the troops as well as they had done in Italy. Consequently, the State and Municipal theatres which had been requisitioned by the advancing Corps had to be prised from the grasp of Welfare officers and handed over to professional control, for which some of our best men, who had been running Ministry of Labour areas during the strenuous days at home, had been detailed. This substitution of civilians was opposed by our military hierarchy in Brussels. They also failed signally to display the same enthusiasm at the arrival of famous companies in the B.L.A. as we felt in announcing them. It was surprising that their interest remained alive at all, for the air they breathed was heavy with frustration, each new idea they conceived half strangled at birth in the effort to cut the umbilical cord of red tape which the military machine wrapped round it. Nevertheless, I had come to the conclusion that changes in our 'High Command' were overdue. The war was over, and different qualities from those required for the actual campaigning were needed. After discussion with Sir Edward Ellington these changes had been effected. Now I had come to see how the new commanding officer was shaping, to note the regrouping of our personnel into static areas and to inspect the fine theatres for which we had become temporarily responsible.

Bad Salzuflen, a pleasant little spa town, had not been touched by the war. Contact with the inhabitants left me strangely embarrassed, an embarrassment that our officers appeared to share. The sly, resentful looks of the German women waiting upon them suggested they had been recently admonished for stealing from the store cupboard, and the constrained abruptness of the officers when they gave their orders suggested that they somehow shared in the blame. The sullen glances of people in the countryside belied the obsequious silence. I might have felt better if they had been openly hostile. The place was a backwater, away from the comings and goings of the great towns and their environs, and most unsuitable for our headquarters. The new commanding officer was taken aback when I told him to get permission to move forward at once, to Hamburg for preference. "But I've only just got here!" he exclaimed.

We set out on our tour, George Smith with his dispatch case crammed with documents about missing ENSA vehicles which our officers thought had been written off long since, and I full of curiosity to revisit an old love. The Army vehicles, left to rust and decay in mile-long parks beside the *autobahnen*, were an offence to George's economical soul, and an exasperating reminder of his failure to obtain Treasury consent to the purchase of further transport to relieve our appalling shortage. Although there was little time for sightseeing as we rushed from place to place, helping our people in their new housekeeping, some sights stay in mind, vignetted through the windows of a military car. But no scent of lime trees now; that was smothered in the stench of those entombed cities, crying aloud of blood and suffering. Did no one bury the dead?

Cologne: the deserted Domplatz, a monstrous hill of rubbish in its middle and, near by, a burnt-out electric tramcar, halted there by a bomb presumably; the skeletonized roof of the great railway station; the windowless Cathedral and the other large buildings fronting the Square buttressed to inaccessibility by fallen masonry—these juxtapositions made a dramatic spectacle. We arrived on the day that the British took over the city from the Americans, and watched a rather feeble military ceremony, with fluttering flags and a slightly self-conscious guard-mounting, smacking of make-believe in the face of calamitous reality.

The spectacle was worse in the Ruhr: Düsseldorf, last visited in 1922, when grinning French black troops gesticulated at us with bayonets at every road block—George Harris and I were on our way to Mannheim to see the first performance in German of *Hassan*—and where now ENSA was in occupation of the Opera House, the Schauspielhaus having been destroyed; Duisburg, dreadful Essen, where grim tales were told of workers' sabotage; Dortmund, Bochum; mountains of rubble had converted their main streets into sunken roads, with here and there shoes or articles of clothing protruding from the mess, sometimes children's toys planted atop, veritable rock gardens of destruction. With relief we travelled north to the newly liberated towns and villages of Holland, the little houses as ugly as ever but newly swept and garnished, and still flying their flags; the burghers and their wives and sweethearts arm-in-arm in the streets, too excited to work; their dancing joy and gay laughter contrasting with the scraping of those hundreds of shovels slowly eating their way through the waste heaps of Germany.

ENSA in Holland deserves separate mention, not for any particular achievement but because of its successful liaison with the liberating forces during a time of the utmost confusion.

As the First Canadian Army slowly completed its mopping-up operations following the onward rush into Germany, crowds of soldiers on leave (Americans, Canadians, Poles, Dutch, every Allied nationality), making their way to Amsterdam in search of relaxation, found their impatient homing submerged in the fermentive joy of the Dutch towns and villages. Welcome was inevitably outstayed because the shortage of food and supplies of every sort was an embarrassment to the hospitable Dutch, who began to find liberation a heavy burden. For entertainment the crowding troops had to be satisfied with Canadian Army shows, most of which they had already seen; not surprising that they preferred to fraternize and generally get into mischief.

Fortunately officers with the right qualities were to hand. For some months prior to the Allied crossing of the Rhine this sector of the Front had been in charge of Major Jamieson, a Scot of proved experience who had been with us since the beginning, done good work in West and North

Africa and capped this reputation by getting on well with the Canadians. Now he was joined by Neville-Willing, who, during my visit to Naples, had importuned me to transfer him to the Second Front. As he spoke Dutch fluently and had a practical knowledge of the public-relations side of the American hotel industry, his claims to consideration could not be denied.

It was entirely due to him that we acquired an exemplary reputation in the matter of artistes' welfare in Holland. One hostel was at Soestdijk in the grounds of the Queen's Palace; it was known as the Hotel Soest. Another, not far away, was the Zyler Hotel, run by two spinsters. At the first interview with Neville-Willing they told him that after their experiences with the German storm-troopers they had had enough. But they relented when he promised them meat, flour, coal and light, and pointed out they would be asked to accommodate ladies and gentlemen only. One week later, calling at the hotel to make sure all was ready for the first arrivals, he was met in the entrance hall by the Misses Zyler, dressed in their black satin best, and wearing mittens. He had barely time to ask what they were doing and to receive the answer that they always received their guests so, when three truckloads of soldiers with kitbags on their shoulders clumped up the grand staircase, a Canadian Army party, known as the 'Tin Hats.'[1] The good ladies burst into tears, protesting that they had been promised ladies and gentlemen, not soldiers. But the Canadians behaved so well in their luxurious surroundings that the gentle ladies burst into tears again when they left.

As we approached Hamburg, George Smith and I, the countryside filled with silent, shambling men in twos and threes, or groups of fifty and more, sometimes in roughly improvised concentration camps with tired sentries staring with self-conscious dignity at what the cat had brought in: a defeated army on its way home. Not far from Luneberg at the gate of a huge German barracks, well-turned-out British Guardsmen stood at ease watching those companies of the lost trudging by on the opposite side of the road. Some had bundles, some had nothing at all.

The streets of Hamburg stretched endlessly through acres of desolation; in the ruined dock basin giant ships lay bottom-up in the fairway to bear witness to the power of the British blockbusters. The fine old Schauspielhaus had escaped, and it was here, two weeks after the surrender, that the Old Vic Company, headed by Sybil Thorndike, Laurence Olivier and Ralph Richardson, had given their first performances in Germany. The success of the visit exceeded our expectations. The troops came in from

---

[1] The leading 'lady' of this Canadian Army show was John Heawood, who subsequently scored a personal success in the London production of *Guys and Dolls* at the Coliseum.

places fifty miles away, driving in their jeeps and lorries through a country-side still encumbered with the surrendering enemy. The fine old theatre was so packed that, in the words of one exuberant reporter, the troops seemed to be hanging on to the chandeliers. Never has classical drama been performed to greater enthusiasm.

The Opera House had been unlucky: twice blasted during the raids, once by fire. The second attack destroyed the front of the building, including the auditorium, so a temporary one was built upon the original stage, the huge scene-dock in the rear being converted into the new stage. Here we saw a performance of *The Marriage of Figaro*, done with enforced simplicity, but great taste. Owing to underfeeding, neither singers nor orchestra could sustain the whole evening; by the time the last act was reached both music and voices became deplorably flat. The auditorium was packed: seemingly neither war nor hunger can quell the German passion for opera. Both the audience and those behind the scenes used the original lavatories intended for the artistes. It was strange to see performers in their costumes joining the queues waiting to relieve themselves, but the incongruity was accepted by every one. 'Figaro,' taking his place beside me, begged in broken English for a cigarette, explaining that it helped to stave off his hunger.

From time to time the opera company gave special performances in the Schauspielhaus for the troops. These were well attended on the whole, even though a large part of the audience had to be lorried long distances into the city. Some operas were more popular than others. A great favourite was Smetana's *The Bartered Bride*, which the men always called *The Battered Bride*, rolling up in their hundreds in anticipation of a lively evening in the style of Fred Melville.

The crowds of officials (with forests of initials) roaming the streets high-lighted the centre of military occupation which Hamburg had become. In the officers' club I met an acquaintance whose shoulders were adorned as follows:

CIVILIAN
MIL: GOV:
OFFICER

which seemed to be a contradiction in terms. Our own ENSA flashes were but one more note added to the general orchestration of alien activity. I was more than ever determined that our headquarters should move here as soon as possible; after the exchange of some breezy telegrams between Sir Edward Ellington and 21 Army Group I had my way.

◇◇◇

Candid Camera . . .

The British soldier, out with his girl friend, takes nothing for granted. 'Show me' is standard currency. A not-very-good revue was sent to Hamburg with Nellie Wallace as leading lady. Many of the youngsters in uniform (girls and boys, little more) had not seen her before, and did not realize that she was a star. Miss Wallace, dissatisfied with her nightly reception, would put on her uniform (without ENSA flashes), dash out of the theatre and mingle with the troops just like any other woman in battledress. "What'd you think of the show, luv?" she'd say. And the troops would invariably reply, "Bloody awful!"

2

Ankunft

At last to Berlin. As a schoolboy I had often wondered what the sack of Imperial Rome must have looked like; now I knew. All the pleasaunces and power of Modern Germany naked to the view in jagged flesh of tree and stone; the Unter den Linden bare and contorted like those dreadful skinned rabbits one used to see in the butchers' shops; the trees of the Tiergarten blasted by Russian gunfire or chopped down for firewood, the statues from the Sieges Allee uprooted or lewdly defaced: one marble lady in scanty classical drapery had her breasts hacked off and an iron spike driven between her thighs. The Brandenburger Tor matched the black ruins of the Reichstag building. A shored-up waiters' entrance gave admission to the Adlon Hotel, fitting Nemesis for its former display of arrogant wealth. Gangs of grey-haired women toiled with wheel-barrows and long-handled shovels among the mountains of rubble, while Siberian troops in fur caps swaggered everywhere. One of them lurched into me on the Unter den Linden, wearing two cheap American alarm clocks tied into the lapels of his overcoat with string, medallions of the grosser brutality.

The Deutsches Theater was still standing; its satellite the Kammerspiele, where I had once watched the lovely Konstantin rehearsing for Sumurün, was gone; so, too, the Charlottenburg Opera House. The forest of Russian slogans and the huge cut-outs of the Communist bosses were a fitting endorsement of the city's torment.

Cigarettes were as highly prized as Bank of England notes, with daily quotations of value impudently displayed in odd places. Elderly men and women carrying tattered attaché cases of imitation leather—who knows what cherished trinkets they contained?—journeyed daily to the black market, tauntingly permitted by the Russians in one corner of their sector —selling the wherewithal to buy food. But they were not given cigarettes; they had to be content with paper money of doubtful value. One morning I saw a Cossack officer bargaining with a little old lady in a ragged black silk dress over her worn fur coat. Twice he threw it back in her face before finally thrusting some notes into her hand and stuffing the coat into a bag. Sometimes the Russians would raid the place for a change. Then there would be shouts and scampering feet, and black figures running in all directions, as snub-nosed Mongolians with tommy-guns came sweeping round the corner in their jeeps and then out, running among the stunted trees. Arrests, searches, rape, screams in the night and—silence! No wonder the Berliners whispered to each other that National Socialism and Russian Communism were the same, except that it was colder in Siberia—a discovery good no doubt for their political souls.

The British troops quartered in Berlin must have their entertainment equally with those in less nerve-racking situations. That was going to be difficult for two reasons. The encircling Russian Zone would make the unfettered passage of artistes difficult to arrange at short notice, and the only suitable theatre that had existed in the British Zone—the Schiller— was gone. We had to content ourselves with a small building, not far from the main broadcasting station (which was still under Russian control although within the British Sector, and from which was poured out an endless stream of vituperative broadcasts, as abusive to war-time friends as to recent foes).

The proposed Garrison Theatre had been a cinema: it boasted an inadequate stage, but some room for extension. I was all for fitting the place out in first-class style, so as to do credit to us in the enemy's capital, in which I was strongly supported by Lancelot Royle, on behalf of NAAFI. And the technical know-how came knocking on the door.

One day when I was discussing things with our Works Officer a sergeant came to tell us that a German civilian was asking to see me.

"What's he want?" I said.

"Says he met you in a theatre, sir."

"What name?"

"Lindy something or other. Calls himself a professor. He's a 'professor' all right." He appeared to have a poor opinion of the visitor.

"That will do, sergeant. Show him in," I said.

A half-starved figure in a seedy black overcoat appeared in the doorway, drew his heels together and bowed. It was Professor Lindemann, famous throughout Europe during the last quarter of a century for his work in association with his brother in modern theatre-building. I was delighted to see him and to know that his brother was alive and living in Munich. There is a confraternity of artist-technicians in the theatre world whose mutual regard transcends the enmities of war. When I told Lindemann I had work for him the thin grey face lit up; before we had done talking his hand was busily sketching some preliminary ideas. In a matter of days he had produced a complete set of plans with revolving stage, lifts and much besides. The stage he planned was not built, because our anticipation of a large British Garrison, which alone would have justified it, was not realized. We did, however, make some modest alterations and improved the dressing-rooms, renaming the place the Jerboa Theatre, in memory of the 'Desert Rats.' It was not easy to maintain the programmes at the highest level because of the restrictions, but we did our best, and many good shows were played at the Jerboa.

Sometimes the artistes crossed the encircling Russian Zone by air in an official aircraft. At other times they drove by road along the *Autobahn* through Helmstedt, past grinning boys at the British control point who, immediately they saw the ENSA badge on the windscreen, made cheeky demands for a show. The good humour of the British soldier was the best possible advertisement of our country in all the lands where we fought; this has been said before, but it is worth repeating. The Russian Control was sharp in contrast. Armed to the teeth, the Red Army soldiers poked tommy-guns under the cushions and scowled at passes which they could not read. We, the ordinary people, who wondered what our Prime Minister had been at to allow such a situation, had to wait for the published records to realize the enormous American mistake which the great man could not gainsay.

ENSA artistes were among the very first British civilians to enter Berlin, staying in a suburban villa close to our headquarters. For a long time they were not allowed out of its compound except under escort. I paid several visits there during the next few months. During one of them I said I should like to visit Hitler's Chancellery. Our senior officer looked rather dubious, as it was in the Russian Zone. We decided to make a reconnaissance and drove there in his car. A Red Army soldier stood indifferently by the outer gate. We decided to try our luck. Perhaps it was the red flannel round my companion's cap, perhaps it was the cigarettes we left on a pile of masonry in the outer courtyard; at all events we were not stopped.

The destruction that had been wrought was bestial: marble columns split and blackened by fire and chipped with indecipherable Russian names, sconces wrenched from the walls, settees and chairs ripped open by bayonets. So might Nero's palace have been wrecked. We wandered through the building and out into the garden beyond. There in a far corner was the celebrated bunker, and, to the right of it, in a corner of what had once been a garden, groups of frail women in black were turning over the soil, harvesting the dead. We went down, down, into the bunker, where, a week or two before, Hitler had played out his last hours in company with the rest of his crew. This too had been savaged and wrecked; offices and bedrooms, the conference room, a small dining-room—all were full of broken chairs and tables. There were bloodstains here and there. What a contrast with Churchill's bunker beneath the Treasury building in Whitehall, orderly and businesslike, with the names of his Cabinet colleagues printed on neat cards, set on the table before each his allotted place: austerity in keeping with the historic struggle that was there directed to its just conclusion. I was glad to stumble up the steep steps again into the fresh air. Phew!

But the air was not fresh; it stank. Even as we came out into the pale afternoon sun searchers had uncovered a body and were placing it on a stretcher to one side under the watchful eyes of lounging Russian officers. On the way out I noticed several chairs protruding from a pile of half-burnt rubbish stacked in the inner courtyard of the Chancellery. Unthinkingly I turned to our senior officer and said:

"We ought to rescue some of those chairs."

"What ever for?" he demanded.

"Oh, I don't know," I said; "might be useful as props."

"Aren't they too big?" he demurred.

"Never mind about that," I cut him short; "send a lorry in the morning and pick up two of them if you can."

The lorry returned next day with three, two of them so badly burned that they could not be repaired. I told the staff to patch up the remaining one, use it if they could in the shows and, if not, to send it back with one of the companies to England in due course. This thoughtless action was to become an item in my indictment at a later date.

Looking back, the destruction of Hitler's Chancellery appears senseless from the historian's point of view. The halls of Infamy can illustrate History quite as effectively as the palaces of Fame; the monument of yet another dictator turned to dust can be an object-lesson to future generations. Might not Nero's fiddle sound a note of better ways, could it now be heard?

Party Line . . .

Late one evening our car broke down on the *autobahn* between Bad Salzuflen and Iserlohn. An Army lorry towed us to the nearest R.E.M.E. recovery post, a large Nissen hut in a muddy field. A smaller hut, shared with the military police, did duty as an office. Nudes in a variety of attitudes and flesh tints, torn from foreign magazines, were pinned round its walls in a frieze, which the habitués regarded with complete indifference. There was a radio to bring the men *Lili Marlene* and other tunes, but their main source of interest was the telephone. This was a party line, connecting orderly rooms, Messes and officers' quarters with the nearest military switchboard. Whenever the bell rang the R.E.M.E. sergeant in charge, a chirpy Cockney, picked up the receiver without waiting to find out from the number of rings whether the call was for his post, and listened with close attention or boredom, according to circumstances. In between long-drawn-out attempts to contact Major Webster i/c ENSA at Iserlohn, this 'cheeky chappie' regaled us with an account of the passionate affair going on between a British captain and a German Red Cross nurse. Progress was held up, he explained, by the caution of the lady in the case; but last night the captain offered to rent a house so that she might bring her "mother" with her; now it was "on" again.

The telephone rang again. I looked up expectantly. The sergeant shook his head at me as he grabbed the receiver.

"This'll be the captain. Always tucks her up last thing."

"He's got it bad," grinned the corporal of police, winking at me.

The sergeant was listening in, waggling his head to and fro as though arguing with the girl, and making lewdly shy grimaces. Then he gently replaced the receiver.

"He's got the house," he said.

"Strewth!" said the corporal. "He ain't 'alf goin' after it! Wonder what she's like in bed." And he stared inexpressively at one of the nudes.

"Ah!" said the sergeant. "'E hasn't got there yet, though."

He put on a mincing voice—something of an actor, this fellow. "She ses she can't possibly live with him now, 'cos she's 'ad a postcard from a P.O.W. camp. She thought 'er 'usband was dead, she ses, but 'e's not; 'e's still alive-o."

He clapped his hands on his knees and roared with laughter.

"The captain's in a hell of a stew. 'That's wimmen all over,' he ses, 'leadin' me on and then makin' excuses.'"

The headlights of a car appeared on the *autobahn*. Out of the darkness appeared Major Webster, bearing a bottle of champagne, a packet of sandwiches and a mouthful of apology.

3

Schinkenbrote

Our most northerly entertainment Post was in the lovely old town of Lübeck, where there was a fine, modern theatre with a revolving stage. It was like passing from nightmare into reality to go there from other parts of Germany. The attitude of the people was independent and sturdy, like the sea-traders they used to be. Here Rex Newman had established his production centre for N.W. Europe, bringing with him from Cairo his trained assistants, including Henry Caldwell, still in pursuit of foreign talent to sit at the tables of his Café Continentale, and Sergeant 'Tommy' Hudson, to do the construction work. Not that technicians were needed, for the theatre was fully staffed and well equipped in all respects, including an elaborate wardrobe of historical costumes and a collection of wigs of all periods, row upon row of them on wooden blocks, some behind glass cases and all most beautifully trimmed and curled. When the ENSA officer drove up in his jeep to take over he found the aged perruquier at his work-bench, cool and absorbed, like Rebecca West's gardener tending his cyclamens in Nuremberg. He was still bent to his task at my first inspection, and continued so throughout our tenancy, even though the wigs were never used. My heart went out to the old man.

It was like that with the German Theatre. Somehow or other aged men and women, left over from the war, had clung to their jobs, preserving the places from wanton damage during the tumultuous days of final surrender, and now only too thankful to save themselves and their families from starvation by working for us. I noticed little recognition of this devotion among younger members of our staff, who found it only bewildering. I wished for more humility from the officers placed in charge of those magnificent theatres when the ENSA flag was run up. And I wished, too, that they would not gesticulate so much with those ridiculous little leather sticks. After all they were not field-marshals' batons.

German artistes had a grim time for the first months after the collapse, floating just above the Plimsoll line of starvation. We were permitted to employ all those in possession of D.P. (displaced person) cards, and did so as much as possible. Some of them were former stars of the theatre or concert artistes of great distinction, and their co-operation was welcome. For his Sunday entertainments Newman used to send Caldwell out with a lorry to search out and bring in these forlorn people, many of them so hungry they were glad to give their services in return for a meal. Invariably they asked if they might come again. Although it was contrary to NAAFI regulations to feed them in this way, the instruction was ignored as much as possible. It had to be so, else the troops would have been deprived of much entertainment of outstanding merit, particularly concerts. . . .

It was Sunday night in Lübeck. I had been to an admirable show with some of our officers. Back in the Mess we were talking over the idea of farewell drama festivals in Germany and the Middle East, on which I wanted to put the seal of my own workmanship as a producer. The telephone rang: a London call, transferred from Kiel. It was Collie Knox, followed minutes later by Stanley Bell, both making impassioned appeals for my immediate return. There was a shocking row in the ENSA pantry; some of the domestic help, both hired and voluntary, had walked out, with the Reverend Sir Herbert Dunnico at their head. His exit had been accompanied by a fanfaronade of Technicolor statements to the Press. "It's frightfully serious. Please come back," urged Collie. I realize now that my friends were probably right; but in the mood of the moment I could only laugh. The climax of ENSA was at hand: let who will fall by the wayside.

The Bread Line . . .

One of our variety parties included a comedian dressed as a tramp. His act contained some business with thick slices of bread which he took from an old handkerchief. The first night at Lübeck, one piece fell into the orchestra pit. Whereupon the orchestra stopped playing and fought for the scraps. The business had subsequently to be cut out.

Lawlessness descending into violence went hand-in-hand with hunger. In that same orchestra was a double bass who was invaluable as an orchestrator and did great work for the production centre. One evening he failed to turn up—murdered by a Polish soldier that afternoon. The following evening the pianist of the same orchestra fell off his bicycle—dead from starvation—just as he was arriving at the stage-door.

4
All Stations beyond

In Burma, where we left the story with promises made but not fulfilled, Stokes-Roberts justified the confidence placed in him by tackling the twin problems of staff and equipment—upon which success depended—with resolution, leaping over obstacles that in other theatres of war had to be laboriously circumvented. In the matter of staff our requirements had never been officially recognized to the extent of approving a military establishment for each theatre of war. But the password of co-operation, given to me in Kandy by the Supreme Commander and repeated by Sir Oliver Leese at ALFSEA, had been passed down the line to Army Welfare, where Brigadier Darley Bridge backed our application for a war establishment and, when there was delay, flew to Delhi, taking Stokes-Roberts with him, to return with an allocation for India and SEAC of thirty-five officers and 140 other ranks: an instance of effective co-operation with Army Welfare that it is a pleasure to record.

The equipment problem was solved in similar fashion. By a fortunate circumstance there had recently arrived to take up the post of Senior ENSA Welfare Supervisor, SEAC, Mrs Ireland-Smith, whose husband, Colonel Ireland-Smith, was the Deputy Director of Ordnance Supplies (D.D.O.S.) in Delhi. (She had joined ENSA in 1942 as Welfare Assistant for Yorkshire, traipsing through the streets of Hull, Doncaster and York in fog, rain and sleet for two dreary winters in search of billets for the artistes.) By means of this contact 'Stokey' managed to secure a large number of light and heavy trucks and—corn in Egypt!—some jeeps: eighty-five vehicles in all. And so the promise I had made in some dubiety to General Slim was kept, for men and vehicles, artistes and staff were dispatched to the Burma front before the monsoon destroyed the bridges behind the Fourteenth Army. Little was known about this feat of organization at home, but the commanders in the field knew and were not slow to write their thanks at the war's end.

Jack Hawkins and Stokes-Roberts were among the passengers in the first seaplane to land in Rangoon Harbour, thanks once again to co-operation: the R.A.F. this time. The Jubilee Hall was at once opened as an entertainment centre; it also became the administrative headquarters for ENSA, BURMA.

Next, when ALFSEA Headquarters moved back to Ceylon to prepare for the recapture of Singapore, Stokes-Roberts took his small military staff with him, there to make ready for the onward march. This came sooner than was expected, but our people were well in time. Three hours after Admiral Mountbatten accepted the surrender of the Japanese at Singapore, an ENSA 'recce' party, including Mrs Ireland-Smith and Lieutenant Greenfield (recently commissioned after spending the early years of the war running ENSA cinemas in Devon and Ceylon), landed from the hospital-ship *Sussex*. Excitement was intense as the liberators streamed ashore, each heart filled with a joy too diffuse to focus upon individuals. The quayside was crowded with prisoners-of-war, who until that morning had been under Jap guard; so out came cigarettes, chocolate, spare tooth-brushes, razor-blades, in a general shower. And the inevitable question, "What's the news at home?" brought shouted answers, just as vague and unrelated: "Quite all right. Hurry on home." And then a triumphal procession through cheering crowds, every one feeling uplifted, blown up to heroic size like some huge photograph that included in one corner a very small ENSA 'recce' party seated on top of its luggage in a three-ton lorry.

Days of frenzied activity, searching for hostel and office premises and the laying-in of food supplies, alternated with lorry-hops to all the prison camps to find out which of them wanted ENSA shows. "The whole lot," cries one commandant. On the fourth day there was news of another ENSA landing. The 'recce' party hurried down to the docks to find a small unit, appropriately titled 'Keep Moving,' giving an impromptu performance in a shed to a crowd of P.O.W.'s waiting to embark for home. There must have been 500 packed in that little space—standing, sitting on each other's knees, astride the rafters some of them. This little company's first show at Changi coincided with the visit of 'Supremo' and Lady Mountbatten, both delighted of course to find our people so well up in front.

The Victoria Building, a theatre in one wing, a concert hall in the other, an interruptive clock-tower that the stars tried unsuccessfully to have silenced, surmounting a block of offices in between, was requisitioned for our use. No finer premises were at ENSA's disposal anywhere, in spite of an infestation of starlings flying back and forth through the unglazed windows of the theatre, hitherto their undisputed home. Every rafter and perching place was black with them. They took such noisy exception to the visits of the stars, Leslie Henson in particular, that in the ensuing campaign, fought on our side, I regret to say, with nets and tear gas, over 5000 of them died in defence of their 'squatter's' rights.

By this time Stokes-Roberts (now lieutenant-colonel), with Madame Vernon and the ENSA main body, had arrived. While 'Stokey' made his plans for the next forward rush, so closely resembling that other leap forward from the Normandy beach-head, except that here distances were much greater, climatic conditions unspeakable and facilities less, Virginia and her staff planned to make Singapore the base for ENSA welfare in the Far East. Soon no less than three hostels were in full use. One curious sidelight: in the process of settling in on this latest and liveliest Tom Tiddler's ground, we acquired so many refrigerators 'surplus to requirements' that several of these highly negotiable assets were bartered for jeeps, of which we were still in short supply. Report is silent as to the precise rate of exchange.

Within twenty-four hours of the arrival of our main body the Army Broadcasting Unit was relaying a batch of O.R.B.S. programmes to Malaya, Burma and the Bay of Bengal. A daily stream of local ENSA announcements followed: "Booking office at the Victoria Theatre open from Monday next. Service personnel may bring one civilian guest. Professional musicians interested in orchestral work, please contact ENSA Headquarters; also variety acts and turns suitable for cabaret." And then the signing off, that by repetition became a chant:

> Remember, everybody, you've got a date,
> Every night at eight; any night at eight;
> In the Victoria Theatre, Singapore.

A larger party, 'Laugh Awhile,' had now arrived to take over the burden, with Alec Halls at its head. This admirable comedian, making a habit of early arrival, had been among the first to visit Orkney in 1941; he led one of the first companies into the Western Desert; then there was that bag-pipe incident with the Governor on arrival in Bombay; now he was first into Rangoon: quite an established opening batsman! In the same ship came Mary Honri; after singing her way from the Normandy beach-head through France, Belgium, Holland and into Germany. She had been last seen in Berlin—still singing!

For its next attraction the Garrison Theatre had only a little four-handed party called 'Lucky Dip' to rely on, but the arrival of Douglas Byng at the last minute from Calcutta kept the flag of entertainment flying.

Dr Cecil Chisholm, ENSA music adviser for India and SEAC, arrived to organize the Singapore Symphony Orchestra to play in the Victoria Concert Hall, whipping sixty-eight players of nine different nationalities into shape for the arrival of the concert stars at Christmas. Possibly the librarian doubled the duties of interpreter?

Here I must turn aside to explain how we kept the pipe-line filled at our end. The days when individual attractions could be competed for were past. The N.S.E.B., at my request, had formed a small sub-committee to settle the priorities for each Overseas Command. (This kept me conveniently out of the argument.) But they could only deal with matters wholesale, so to speak: thus, in a given allocation period, say, 400 artistes for the Mediterranean Basin (which included Middle East, North Africa, 'Paiforce,' East and West Africa and C.M.F.), 300 for India and SEAC and 500 for Western Europe: the latter transferred from home entertainment. The allocations included artistes in transit as well as those actually in each theatre of war.

The end of the fighting had brought such demand for more amenities, especially from returned prisoners of war, that arguments arose between India and SEAC, each proclaiming the greater need and hence a right to the larger share. Finally, SEAC, dissatisfied with the decisions of the Delhi Committee, put in a direct demand to London for a hundred additional artistes for themselves only. This made a difficult situation for Jack Hawkins, wearing the red tabs of his colonelcy with becoming solidity. He had recently taken over the command after the breakdown in health of Dunstan's successor, and was now suffering the tribulation that went with the top administrative jobs in wartime. SEAC declared he was too much under the influence of Delhi, and blamed him for giving way to pressures he could in no wise withstand.

In October 1944 there were 244 artistes in India, twenty-five standing by and three stars; at the time of the Japanese surrender the huge total of forty companies had been allocated to India and SEAC; and by Christmas 1945 Stokes-Roberts was able to report thirty-four separate ENSA shows performing in SEAC. All things considered, there was little cause for complaint.

For the story of ENSA's part amid the final scramble of contending revolutions that as often as not bit their own tails, reports and cables from Virginia were the only reliable source of information, for by the time official reports arrived from India the news they contained was hopelessly out of date. Her terse comments, hectic with enthusiasm, caustic in criticism, give a clear picture of the Hell's broth of nationalism in revolt that the war had set bubbling throughout Indo-China and Java: fifth-columnism, black-market luxury and starvation, all the instruments of unrest. She gives a graphic description of how she, Stokes-Roberts, and the others rode forward on the successive waves of Allied reoccupation, first in to Bangkok and then Saigon.

In Bangkok there was no suitable theatre for large parties, but the troops would need entertainment for three months at least. In Saigon she successfully vamps Monsieur *le Maire* on the instructions of the Area Commander and secures "an adorable little ENSA garrison theatre, holding 350 approx., and the large Eden cinema is to be hired by the week for star events and by the day for music recitals (£8 *per diem*, including use of grand piano)."

Could there possibly be a more fantastic background to entertainment? While the local Annamites, arming themselves at the expense of the Japanese, occupy the air-strips and strive for the control of the whole of Cochin China, a mixture of French, Chinese and American Forces gather in alliance against them; some Japanese too! Our men, watching the political struggle with cynical indifference, await the arrival of the Free French to clean up the mess, longing to do the job for them, so that they can be on their way. No cafés are open, the shops for a few hours only. By four o'clock there is a strict curfew because of after-dark sniping in town and suburbs. Not to be wondered at that a great cry for entertainment goes up and is echoed in far-away Sumatra, where the 36th Division find themselves in equal case.

Next Virginia flew to Hongkong with 'Mike' Brennan, once again out in front on the toughest assignment: a perilous hop, made worse by unexpected monsoon weather, and, still more so, by Chinese Communist occupation of the airstrips.

The Star Theatre at Kowloon on the mainland had been allotted to ENSA as a garrison theatre, but our people found that first the Japanese, and then the Chinese, had stripped it bare of everything, except some dilapidated seating. Now it so happened that an R.A.F. force, dispatched from U.K. to help the Americans on Okinawa in the air battle of the Pacific, had been liberally supplied with theatrical equipment from Drury Lane (lights, curtains, costumes, etc.) since there was no possibility of landing our shows on the island. After the Japanese surrender the force was diverted to Hongkong to reoccupy the Colony. Our equipment was being used to equip a small R.A.F. headquarters theatre on Hongkong Island, instead of for the main body of troops at Kowloon. The officer responsible, summoned to appear before the Commandant of the force, found himself confronted by an outraged ENSA official, wearing travel-stained khaki drill, who, with nostrils dilating, treated him to a flow of female eloquence quite outside his previous experience. In the end he was told somewhat tartly to hand over.

The vast distances and the uncertainty of transport put a tremendous strain on our workshops in Calcutta, and so others were installed in Singapore to supply scenery and equipment for the most forward areas. In an effort to lessen the difficulties duplicate sets of scenery were made and forwarded in advance to the countries the drama companies would visit. Thus, for Gielgud's *Hamlet* three sets of scenery were prepared. Even so, it was the mobile parties that carried the main burden.

All Virginia's reports were peppered with urgent requests that I should visit the Far East, where she assured me repeatedly that ENSA activity was at its best. One of them, sent by quickest means, ended with the words, "only you can make ENSA in Far East what it should be": a piece of blatant flattery that merely high-lighted her own achievement. Whereas for the greater part of the war Virginia had been absorbed in her care for the artistes, so that it was no uncommon thing to hear chorus girls, waiting to appear before a factory audience, inquiring for the whereabouts of Madame Vernon—she was probably in Rome or Cairo—or some Cockney comedian in search of special privilege taking her name in vain in a hostel in the sweltering heat of the Persian Gulf, now in its closing stages she made the whole ENSA world her province. Therein her exigence brought her into conflict with those who held a more restricted view of her functions; but it was of inestimable benefit to me whenever an unbiased opinion of the causes of breakdown or failure was needed.

To hear her bright voice and confident laugh in the passage outside my door was like a draught of champagne in the desert of official frustration.

"Director in?" Virginia would inquire of the outer office.

"He's in conference," would come the stereotyped obstruction.

"Tell him I'm here, please," Virginia would snap out, abruptly. "He'll see me!"

In would stride Virginia, usually in faded battle-dress, proudly displaying her ribbons of service, travel-stained, after an all-night flight from Cairo perhaps, or Bombay, but buoyant as ever, greeting me without pause for formalities:

"What is this I hear about closing the hostel at X?" (mentioning some small town in, say, Northern Ireland). . . . "The troops at Bahrein want more music." . . . "Cairo has gone to pieces again. Found an Army officer in bed with a girl out of a revue company in one hostel."

"What did you do?" I manage to interject.

"Told him to get out at once and asked the girl what she was thinking of."

"Italy's all right though. We're keeping well up to the front line. Shocking hostel at Bari, lavatories choked, fleas, bugs and God knows what; Germans had occupied it: had to set to and clean it out myself."

Somehow, as one listened to her, spirits were lifted and determination renewed, even though one's over-tired nerves resented the spur of her persistent enthusiasm as much as the trail of messages that followed me through the various theatres of war.

Those messages! Arriving at all hours of the day or night, and in the most unusual places: telephone calls, 'teleprints,' bits of paper left in offices or with transport drivers, top priority cables; the phrase 'by any and every means' was thoroughly understood by Virginia. Somehow or other the messages always reached me; in the North African desert, in Cairo, on the mountain roads of Italy and in the forests of Burma, in Paris and Berlin, all couched in forthright terms that left no doubt at all as to her requirements or her views on the particular matter in hand. The name of Madame Vernon was one to conjure with in ENSA circles, an open-sesame in some cases, a door-slam in others. ENSA and all who care for its record of service owe her a debt of gratitude.

In all his Glory . . .

Hitherto Solomon had faced every mishap with imperturbability, but he ran into an entomological experience in Bangkok that nearly defeated him. Tired out after a difficult flight from Saigon, he omitted his usual practice of trying out the piano beforehand, and only went to the concert in time to play. The hall was a disused theatre that had been hurriedly cleaned out for the occasion. As the virtuoso made his entrance, all the lights in the building were extinguished, except a powerful spotlight over the piano. The weird sounds given out by that aged instrument were as nothing compared with the shock that was to come. Presently insects began to crawl out from inside the case and from in between the keys, attracted no doubt by the brilliant light overhead. In less than five minutes the keyboard was covered with them. Solomon was even squashing them as he played. They got up his sleeves, on to his face, inside his collar. Never more miserable in his life but not wanting to make a fuss, he endured the ordeal for half an hour, and then went off, tearing his collar from his neck, repeating hysterically to himself, "I can't stand it, I can't stand it!" The troops, in unwitting mockery, clamoured and shouted for more. Some one suggested switching off the light, in the hope that the insects would retire whence they came. This was done, and the second half of the concert was played in pitch darkness.

Solomon had another concert the next day, but he refused to face the ordeal a second time. The officer i/c ENSA, determined not to lose his second concert, drowned the piano in DDT and every other form of insect-killer that he could lay his hands on. The virtuoso strode on to the stage, once more under the bright light. Not an insect! This is wonderful, he thought. But after several minutes the heat of the spotlight once more attracted disaster, for the fumes of the DDT, having won the battle with the insects, rose to threaten Solomon with a similar fate. He became dizzier and dizzier, more and more uncertain of the notes he was playing, finishing a nightmare performance in a state of frenzy that might have been taken as the result of a generous evening in the officers' Mess.

The great pianist's work for ENSA was all but over. He had travelled by plane, ship, truck, lorry, train, and on foot, playing to every type of audience for whom we catered, always struggling with broken-down instruments—in a far-off staging camp in Iran he stopped the frantic efforts of a local tuner to charm sand out of the top notes while the troops waited impatiently: "Never mind those. I won't play them"; he even carved his name on a minipiano with a bayonet before paratroopers went on a secret mission to destroy radar establishments in Northern France.

I was insistent that, if the work of distinguished artistes were to be officially recognized, Solomon must be among the first. Yet when Sir Edward Ellington came into my office to tell me that the patronage office had rung up to say that Solomon's name was not to be found in the lists of variety artistes they had consulted, I was not entirely surprised; it was all of a piece with the strange adventures of this Triton among the minnows.

5

Grand Parade

We come now to the climax of the show: the Grand Parade, as they call it in the Christmas pantomimes, when the lines of chorus girls wait and watch for the welcome each leading player receives from the cheering audience. In our case, as the procession of talent debouches before our audience of recollection, some of the players merge into the scenes they graced, others stand apart, stars to shine in any firmament. One would like them all to have their separate bows, but upon such a crowded stage there is time only for a brief retrospective glance as the spotlights pick out a feature here and there, ere the curtain finally descends.

We reached the climax of our effort round about Christmas 1945, and held it for many months. Millions of men and women in uniform had departed for the great crusade; so, too, the players, even to the most laggard of them, had found their way to duty. In the last months of actual conflict and for twelve months thereafter there was mounted such a scale of entertainment as had never before been seen.

The ENSA badge was everywhere. Beginning as side decoration on hundreds of stages and platforms in camp and factory and over the doorways of requisitioned houses and offices, it had quickly spread to foreign lands. Affixed to the façades of theatres and cinemas, adorning the sides of lorries, coaches and trucks as they bumped and hurtled themselves over the desert roads of Libya or the *corniches* of Italy, or the jungle tracks of Burma, or proceeded more sedately along the boulevards of capital cities —everywhere the red, white and blue badge of ENSA entertainment was to be seen. Amidst the multiplicity of military signs there was always an occasional notice-board, crudely painted on a bit of wood or, maybe, on the side of a jerrican, and fastened to a tree or telegraph pole. Such notices as in France: ENSA H.Q. 30 Corps. 200 yds. ☞ guided the artistes to their destination, and reminded the advancing Armies of the Commonwealth of the fun and relaxation to be had under that sign.

Our hostels stretched like a line of posting-stations across two-thirds of the globe: from Lübeck across North-west Germany, through Holland, Belgium, France and Italy to Greece; beyond the Hellespont through Asia Minor, Egypt, India and the Far East. Few of them could be regarded as 'safe hotels' after the fashion of Nathaniel Gubbins; some were within rifle range of the enemy. At Maesget in Holland only 400 yards of the River Maas separated the artistes from enemy troops.

In the following rough assessment of ENSA's scope the probability of accidental omission must be borne in mind. Among the plays and players that had come and gone in North-western Europe were the following: Shakespeare's *Julius Cæsar* and *Twelfth Night* (apart from performances of his plays given by the Old Vic Company), Somerset Maugham's best play, *The Circle* (played by Leslie Banks and Yvonne Arnaud), and Shaw's *Saint Joan*, *Arms and the Man* with Richard Greene, *Pygmalion* and *The Apple Cart*. Special mention must be made of Robert Helpmann and the Sadler's Wells Ballet, Cedric Hardwicke in *Yellow Sands*, Emlyn Williams in *Blithe Spirit*, Madge Elliott and Cyril Ritchard in *The Merry Widow*, and Eliot Makeham in *Acacia Avenue*. And the evergreen successes: Priestley's *Dangerous Corner* and *When we are Married*; *French without Tears*, *Saloon Bar*, *Ten Little Niggers*, and so on. Many of these attractions appeared under 'lease-lend,' at last so fully vindicated that little-known managements began to advertise offers of a six-weeks' ENSA engagement. The implication of deferment which these contained compelled us to put a stop to the practice.

Farther afield, there was a double-barrelled Festival company playing to the troops in Italy and Austria—triple-barrelled, you might almost say, because of the production of *The Barretts of Wimpole Street* contributed by

USO. One half of that Festival Company was led by Godfrey Tearle, the repertoire consisting of *The Man who came to Dinner*, *The Light of Heart*, *The Amazing Dr Clitterhouse* and *Time and the Conways*, the productions being rehearsed and staged by Major Leon Davey from the production centre in Naples. The second half of the company, headed by Barry Jones, was sent out from England under the direction of Major James Parish. Godfrey's 'Man Who Came to Dinner' and Barry's 'King Magnus' were outstanding performances in the two most popular plays in the repertoire.

In India Edith Evans' success in *The Late Christopher Bean* had been followed by Roger Livesey and Ursula Jeans in the Cairo production of Bridie's play *It Depends What You Mean*, after their tour of Irak and Iran. In January 1946 *Canaries sometimes Sing* opened at the Garrison Theatre, Damascus; another first-class company played a contemporary success, *Pink String and Sealing-wax*, in Alexandria. Seven full-size repertory companies, including the Colchester 'Rep,' were working overseas at this time, more than half the number in India or the Far East. So much for Drama.

Achievements in vivid contrast appear momentarily under the spotlight, as when John Barbirolli conducted the Hamburg Philharmonic Orchestra for performances of the Sadler's Wells Ballet in Hamburg, and Donald Wolfit played Shakespeare in Paris.

John Gielgud played *Hamlet* in the Garrison Theatre in far-away Singapore, while Solomon contributed a piano concerto or two with the Singapore Orchestra in the Concert Hall next door.

The policies of the Music Council were being pursued vigorously everywhere. No Command either at home or overseas was without its music advisers, who organized music clubs and dispensed gramophone records by the thousand. The rediffusion vans were still hard at it. During the Cairo Festival I noted Thomas Matthews, touring with his string ensemble in Palestine and, later, the Middle East, playing Bach's 'Double Concerto' with Percy Coates, leader of the Middle East orchestra; included in that group was piano soloist Eileen Ralf.

'Music for All' sponsored the first performance, on February 18, 1946, of *Song of England*, a narrative ballad with chorus written by Flight-Lieutenant Albert Arlen, R.A.A.F.: unimportant musically, perhaps, but interesting as an example of how the Services were getting together to make their own entertainment.

Among the virtuosi Pouishnoff followed Solomon to India and beyond; in Europe Barbirolli, in the track of Constant Lambert, went from Hamburg to conduct the Sadler's Wells Ballet in Paris. In addition to those concert stars whose names already figure in these pages, others came from America to take part in our climax: Melchior, tired but undefeated, and Marjorie Lawrence, the Australian singer, crippled by polio, travelling everywhere in an invalid chair with her husband, Dr King. Valda Aveling, the brilliant young Australian pianist, joined the party. Arriving at Flensburg, they found themselves occupying quarters where in an adjacent room Himmler had committed suicide a few days before. Most notable of all the late arrivals, Elizabeth Schumann, now in ENSA uniform, carried out an extensive tour of one-night 'stands' in Germany—a magnificent effort; she was then nearly sixty years of age.

Among the popular name bands the imperturbable Geraldo, by his visit to the Middle East, had effectively removed any shortcomings to our reputation in that department, although his opinion that the first performance of the *Warsaw Concerto*, played in the University Hall, Cairo, by his own men combined with the Middle East Symphony Orchestra, represented the climax of ENSA's musical achievement in the Middle East is open to question.

Admiral Fraser's Pacific Fleet was not forgotten: Bernard Miles was to lead the first show. With finance granted, and NAAFI's agent instructed to provide office facilities, the Lord Mayor of Sydney assured me of a warm welcome as I prepared to fly out. But the surrender of Japan scotched that.

In the Middle East we stood high in regard, all the early mistakes forgotten. On the occasion of our final performance at the Garrison Theatre on August 17, 1946, General Sir Miles Dempsey, the new C.-in-C., published a cordial letter of thanks. On the following day, August 18, the last twinkle of an ENSA star in India came from Tommy Trinder.

In turning the spotlights upon these well-known faces in our Grand Parade let me never forget the thousands of little shows that were rank and file to that leadership. They were everywhere. One of the first, and actually the last of them, called 'Stop, Look and Listen,' proudly sent in a report sheet, endorsed and signed by General Slim himself. It is before me as I write. The same company went with the British Commonwealth Expeditionary Force to Japan in February 1946. They were the last ripples on the farthest shore since first we threw those stones at the war's beginning.

CHAPTER THIRTY-TWO

NOTES UPON TWO FURTHER OCCASIONS

1

High Festival in Cairo

THE Festival Idea had been blowing in and out of the offices at Drury Lane like pollen ever since the success of Walter Legge's music festivals. It was easy to carry out at home by inviting the co-operation of West End companies under the 'lease-lend' system, and selecting towns where the commercial theatre had ceased to function during the war, such as Folkestone and Eastbourne, or areas where troops were congregated, such as Salisbury Plain and Aldershot. They were not festivals, strictly speaking, but they raised the temperature of anticipation and brought together in one audience young men and women of better than average taste, with good effect upon the general morale.

Overseas nothing could be done until after VE Day, except in Cairo, where the pre-war collaboration between the Egyptian Government and the British Council in arranging the visits of dramatic companies was resumed under the ægis of ENSA early in 1944. A plan was put forward by Bridges Adams, when he represented the British Council on our Advisory International Council, and taken up and kept alive in Cairo by Soliman Bey Naguib, the Director of the Royal Opera House, whereby drama festivals would be held for the joint benefit of the Allied Forces and the civil population, a proportion of the seats being reserved for the latter at prices to be fixed by the Government, with cut rates for student matinées, and the remainder allotted at our usual prices to men and women in uniform.

During my first visit to Cairo Naguib took me to see the Minister of Education, an amiable person wreathed in cigarette smoke and quiet eloquence. (Can that rumoured ingredient of the Egyptian cigarette really produce such fragrance?) The principles of the tripartite collaboration were soon agreed on. The Egyptian Government would provide the

Opera House and the services of its staff without charge; it would also pay the NAAFI Department of National Service Entertainment a subvention. (This amount was increased upon each occasion; in the case of the third and last festival it amounted to a good round sum.) The British Council would give a financial guarantee against any losses that might be incurred over and above the cost of providing the same amount of entertainment solely for H.M. Forces. ENSA would provide the productions and the companies, their transport, salaries and living expenses.

The Opera House was built in the time and style of the Second Empire to celebrate the opening of the Suez Canal and to provide a stage for the first performance of Verdi's opera *Aïda*, commissioned for the same purpose. Its decorations in white and gold and crimson speak hauntingly of that momentary flamboyance in French history. Constructed mainly of wood and plaster, its creaking floors are a perpetual reminder of the obvious fire risk, so much so that the Egyptian authorities are compelled to exact an unwonted discipline in the matter of smoking both in the front and at the back of the house.

Soliman Naguib was a typical Cairene, bubbling with inconsequent gaiety. His topsy-turvy use of the English idiom endeared him to every one, and effectively concealed the workings of a mind determined to keep the interests of his beloved theatre uppermost. The fact that the Mediterranean was closed did not deter him from the enthusiastic contemplation of plans in which ENSA and the Cairo Opera House would soar together to the topmost heights of achievement, not only within the next few months or years but for ever and a day.

The first Drama Festival took place in March 1944. It was given by Emlyn Williams and a company including Adrianne Allen, Kathleen Harrison, Ivan Samson, Emrys Jones and Leslie Dwyer. They played *Blithe Spirit*, *Night Must Fall* and *Flare Path*. The artistes had been assembled by Bill Linnit, who flew out to Cairo before they arrived to make sure that everything was in readiness for them. Owing to some misunderstanding they had been engaged on terms very much higher than those normally paid to ENSA artistes, which meant that a large proportion of the seats would have had to be sold at civilian prices to meet the higher cost, thereby disadvantaging the troops. At the meeting called to explain the position to the artistes, Kathleen Harrison was first on her feet: "Put me down for five pounds, ten pounds, or nothing at all if you like. My son is in the Air Force." The Festival was such a success that the British Council guarantee was not called upon.

Donald Wolfit was the star of the second Festival, hurrying to Cairo after a brief 'Ensacap' visit to Paris and Brussels. He opened at the Opera

House on March 5, 1945, and played a season of four weeks with *Hamlet*, *Twelfth Night, Volpone* and *Much Ado about Nothing*. His gusto and downright way with Shakespeare were immensely popular, both in the camps at home and overseas, but the suggestion made in his autobiography that these tours were arranged in the face of ENSA's fear and trepidation must be regarded as a momentary surrender to the temptation to throw a pebble or two that we all experience at one time or another when confronted by a large and grimacing Aunt Sally.

A mighty effort and a strong element of luck—never far from a theatrical manager's thoughts—would be required to top the success of those two festivals and make the third a memorable swan-song of ENSA in the Middle East. Much depended upon the stars who were willing to go. The sudden ending of hostilities everywhere dangled the brightest prospects in front of artistes grown accustomed to over-crowded theatres and music-halls, which they imagined would remain for ever so. Therefore they needed to be convinced that the Festival was going to be a worthwhile occasion, and that they would not be lost in the crowd of ENSA companies that were still at work around three-quarters of the globe.

Now it so happened that John Gielgud was touring India and the Far East during that autumn and winter, playing *Hamlet* and *Blithe Spirit*—perhaps the least advertised and most memorable of his many undertakings for us. If the dates were adjusted to enable him to give some performances in Cairo on the way home, the prestige of the Festival could be established at a stroke. This was agreed on, and when Roger Livesey and Ursula Jeans accepted my offer to lead the London company the initial difficulties of recruitment were solved. With them went Malcolm Keen (who had scored so many successes with me in years gone by), Charles Carson and a number of other fine artistes.

The plays selected were *The Barretts of Wimpole Street*, James Bridie's *It Depends What You Mean*, and *The School for Scandal*: to be produced in that order, with performances of *Hamlet* spread through the season for as long as Gielgud had time to spare. This was a well-balanced programme of classical and modern drama, and gave great satisfaction in Cairo when it was announced.

I was determined to abandon not one particle of my own standards, but a certain simplicity of setting was inevitable. Draperies of hessian canvas, forty feet high, would provide the surrounds and background, with architectural features such as doors and windows set in front: a method that necessity had originally forced upon us and which our scene designers and painters had now brought to a state of near-perfection. While Hamilton Price, who was going out as my assistant, opened preliminary rehearsals of *The Barretts*, I went on ahead, taking our overseas engineer (Lorraine) and the chief designer (Denis Wreford) with me, so that all would be in order at the Cairo end.

A planned whistle stop at our new headquarters in Hamburg turned into a ten-day incarceration in hospital. I was two weeks overdue when I arrived in Cairo. There was no news of the departure from London of either the artistes, costumes or equipment. Also, our headquarters staff were wrestling with the problems of demobilization, senior officers being hurriedly replaced by those from other Commands, and the most experienced of them, Major Noel Blenkin, involved in a serious air crash on his way up from East Africa, which did not help matters. While Lorraine ransacked the *suks* for glass lustres with which to build up the three big chandeliers for lighting *The School for Scandal* after the manner of the first production in 1777, while Wreford initiated our smiling but only faintly comprehending Egyptian craftsmen into such mysteries of period furnishing as the rejection of an American alarm-clock for Joseph Surface's study and the acceptance of Nottingham lace curtains for *The Barretts of Wimpole Street* but not for *The School for Scandal*, I went off to Helwan, a nondescript little Delta town, possessing hot sulphur springs that held out the prospect of a cure for the sundry aches and pains left over from my Hamburg visitation.

The treatment certainly justified its local reputation in my case. By noon on the following Sunday I was waiting in the dusty main street for the car to take me back to Cairo, listening to a priest chanting the midday prayer from the tower of a mosque opposite, while from a loud-speaker in the little tourist hotel behind me a B.B.C. news bulletin came blazing forth in precise British accents. The Mahommedan was chanting his message to Heaven, the Englishman to the Earth. There was no one in sight to pay attention to either.

Local interest in the Festival was growing, running side-by-side with the mounting political tension. The British Ambassador remarked one day at lunch that the season was really most opportune; both he and the Minister of State (Lord Hankey) intended to give it every support. Members of the Egyptian Government were to be present on the first night, as well as the accredited representatives of the Allied Powers in Cairo, including the Russian Minister to Egypt and the Polish Chargé d'Affaires. Yet one week of our allotted rehearsal time in Cairo had already gone by, and there was still no news of the departure of the company from London.

As I turn over the sheaves of telegrams exchanged between London and Cairo I realize what a risk we ran of having to postpone the opening date.

One morning, in an excess of anxiety, I cabled to Jack Hawkins, suggesting the postponement of Gielgud's departure from India by one week, to which I received the reply that he had already Priority Two for the whole company to move on the agreed date, and it was impossible to "chop and change like this."

To prolong the fun the R.A.F. ran into a bout of the worst flying weather experienced in years. The plane carrying Roger and Ursula, Malcolm Keen and Ann Bennett, forced to detour over Spain, was grounded for two days at Rabat. Another plane was struck by lightning and forced-landed in Sardinia. The last members of the company straggled into Cairo three days before the opening. Fortunately they knew their lines, but it was cutting things a bit fine.

No sooner had the company arrived, fretful and nervous after all the delays, than Meadows White, cast for Crabtree and Moses in *The School for Scandal*, was taken to hospital. His absence from the Sheridan cast was a great worry until George Howe, playing Polonius with Gielgud, agreed to play his parts and to remain behind after the *Hamlet* company had left. Brian Reece, who had come from Italy to take charge of the production centre, looked so forlorn in his office job and cast such sheep's-eyes when he saw me interviewing the artistes from the Cairo pool for the minor rôles that I offered him the parts of Captain Surtees-Cook in *The Barretts* and, later, of Trip in *The School for Scandal*. He made a real success of both these modest opportunities and justified my prophecy that if he stayed in the theatre he would one day be a star light comedian. To his place at the production centre I posted Major James Parish from Naples, where he had just staged the festival production of *The Apple Cart*. 'Jimmy' Parish had transferred to us from the Intelligence Corps, "via the Savoy Grill," as he puts it. I had encountered him in that caravanserai in October, when he was awaiting demobilization.

At last we were all set to open the season with *The Barretts of Wimpole Street* on Friday, February 9. Gielgud had flown in the night before with his company, and was scheduled to give *Hamlet* on the 12th. But now the political anxiety threw its shadow over us: we might not be allowed to give the Festival after all! Neither the British Embassy nor the officials at the Abdin Palace would commit themselves, so our P.R.O. in the Middle East went off to interview the Student Committee of the Nationalists and extracted a promise that they would neither sabotage the Festival nor burn down the Opera House, which was a great relief, seeing that all our theatrical possessions were stored in that wooden box of enchantment.

The official junketings began with a reception in the foyer of the Opera House at 5 P.M. Speeches were made, healths drunk in various liquors (not provided by NAAFI) and a large number of flashlight bulbs expended in the effort to create a friendly atmosphere. Gielgud announced that the eight performances he would give during the first fortnight of the Festival would be his last appearances as Hamlet, because he felt it was essentially a young man's part. Sad to think that the most notable Hamlet of our generation would be seen no more, but it was a decision he has wisely refused to change; and, of course, it added exceptional interest to an already exciting programme.

My own remarks had an alcoholic fervour, induced by the over-sweet cocktails with which the Drama representative of the British Council kept me fortified. It was the proper occasion for a complete circus of thanks: the Egyptian Government, the British Council, the City of Cairo for its hospitality during the war years (we had not bothered to ask if we were welcome), the Director of the theatre and his staff, and so on; all of which was received by my own countrymen with dignified "Hear! Hear's!" but I could see no Egyptian faces reflected in the upraised cocktail glasses. The speech, repeated in the evening from the Opera stage and broadcast in the Middle East Forces Broadcasting, must have made a good impression on the Egyptians, for it was translated into Arabic and rebroadcast over E.S.B. No doubt I exaggerated the politico-cultural importance of the Festival, but surely it would help to alleviate the political situation? In fact, it did nothing of the sort. None of the Egyptian Ministers was present on the first night, except the Minister of Finance, come to see how his money was being spent, I suppose. Neither were any of the seats allotted to the Palace entourage taken up. This was ominous.

The opening performance went smoothly. The actors rose to 'an occasion,' as they always do, Ursula Jeans giving a moving performance as Elizabeth, Roger Livesey effective but somewhat too robust as Robert Browning, and Malcolm Keen demonstrating once more his emotional powers, of which he had given London that startling first taste in *A Bill of Divorcement* in the nineteen-twenties. The acoustics of the Opera House are not flattering to the speaking voice, and Ursula, lying prone on that couch in Wimpole Street, was sometimes inaudible. Discussing the repertoire one morning for a subsequent tour of India, she said:

"Let's drop *The Barretts*."

"No need to. You do it every night, my dear," was my thoughtless rejoinder.

The second great night of the Festival was, of course, the entry of Gielgud into the lists. The date originally chosen being King Farouk's birthday, a Palace official politely suggested that this should be changed. He evidently feared lest some members of the audience should find encouragement in the murder of the King of Denmark. The play was given very simply in black curtains and the few essential properties. It was enormously effective, proving once again that Shakespeare can be enjoyed by those who have ears to hear as fully on the bare stage for which he wrote as in the over-carpentered productions of the present day. John was very ably supported by Marian Spencer as the Queen, Ernest Hare as the King, Helen Cherry as Ophelia and George Howe as Polonius. The notices published in the English, French and Arabic newspapers were ecstatic. Sometimes the ecstasies spilled over into the most startling inaccuracies, as when one contributor to an English newspaper in the course of an article on Gielgud's career referred twice to his courage in dispensing with the traditional Delius music in his recent production of *A Midsummer Night's Dream*, while a French-language paper published a large photograph of a completely bald young man as the head of ENSA.

I strove to make *The School for Scandal* the high-spot of the Festival. Rehearsing a comedy of manners against a seething background of Egyptian nationalism called for exceptional concentration. Going to the theatre in the early morning before the heat of the day was some-thing of an adventure. The air was charged with tension. There was that particular day when I set out from Shepheard's Hotel to find the streets quieter than usual and the theatre locked and barred. Soliman Naguib, who had been in enthusiastic daily attendance at our rehearsals, had disappeared and, with him, his genial stage director, Shukri. The door-keeper too had vanished. Some of the actors went off to drink coffee in a neighbouring café, while I telephoned. Naguib arrived later with the keys, rather shamefaced. He was not communicative, beyond saying that there had been some rioting in the students' quarter and that it might spread into the main streets. I saw no reason why that should stop our rehearsals, but after an hour or so we thought we could hear a strange noise, nothing very definite, a faint ululation of the atmosphere. It was nearly lunch-time, so we decided to break off.

There is a flat roof to the foyer of the theatre, fronting the Opera Square, which gave us a grandstand view of all street incidents, whether it was the portly King, driving by at a scorching pace in his red motor-car, surrounded by hooting motor-cyclists in the best American manner or, as on this day, when the downpour of nationalism began. The vast square was deserted, save for the traffic policeman sweltering under the umbrella on his stand. All the shops had been closed, except here and there where a few laggards were hastily repairing the omission. The noise of shouting crept nearer and nearer. Presently the tinkling of falling glass mingled with it, and the banging of sticks against steel shutters. Groups of men appeared at the head of the main street leading to the square. They came forward, rioting, little knots of them selecting the shops with British signs for special attention. There was no leadership. They appeared to be working themselves up to the required pitch of desperation, gathering in little groups and haranguing each other, and then as suddenly breaking off to form other and more excited groups, suppurations that burst in all directions when carloads of police and soldiers appeared. Wisps of smoke began to curl up from some of the shop-fronts. Next on the scene came the fire-engines to put out the shopkeepers' fires. In the shimmering noon-day heat the figures had a marionettish look, giving to the whole performance an air of unreality, like an extreme long shot in a film.

Gielgud had joined us on our grandstand, and after a while he and I fell into keen discussion about the future of the publicly endowed Theatre at home, John declaring that all theatre schemes were the outcome of personal initiative and tended to pass with those who originated them. The incongruity of time and place for such discussion did not occur to us. But it was foolish, standing there like that in our ENSA uniforms. If the attention of the mob had been drawn to us, the promises of the Students' Committee would have been worthless. We had just decided that the moment the square was clear we would go to lunch, when I received an urgent message from G.H.Q., relayed by our own office: "To-night's performance will be cancelled. British troops are confined to barracks. All ENSA staff and artistes will return to billets immediately, and remain there until further orders; also, they will take off their uniforms and wear civilian clothes until further notice."

At Shepheard's, neat little Egyptian soldiers in tin hats mounted guard at the entrance. The terrace was crowded with officers, twirling their fly-whisks and ordering drinks. Most of them wore an aggrieved look, as though hurt by this violent exhibition of dislike. An A.P.M. saw me approaching the hotel and told me off severely for going about the streets "in what purports to be British uniform." In the afternoon Jimmy Parish and I went off to the Gezira Club to watch a hot and dusty game of rugger; I was in grey flannels and Jimmy had borrowed a civilian suit from the ENSA wardrobe. By the time the game was over all taxis had left the streets. On the walk back we came to a squalid street that was an obvious short cut to the centre of the city. Jimmy was in considerable doubt about going down it.

"Come on," I said, "it'll be all right, if we don't talk."

"You look like a Turk anyway," said Jimmy, grinning in my sunburnt face.

"Nonsense," I retorted, and strode forward.

There were scowling faces on either side as we entered the street. Half-way down the crowd became more threatening, but we persisted in our vow of silence. We passed a little Arab boy relieving himself in a doorway. He called out after us in a shrill, piping voice: "Left, right, left, right, left . . . left." We had been so busy with our vow of silence that we had forgotten we were marching in step.

The next night was a *Hamlet* night. Following the unwritten law of the theatre, I was in hopes the show would go on; but in the morning a friendly Sudanese waiter with bazaar information soon disabused my mind of that idea. "Mr Gogo, he not play 'Ămēelĕt' tonight." But rehearsals must go on, so I strode out in my grey flannels. Opera Square was more deserted than on the previous day; even traffic policemen had disappeared. Then I noticed more of the little tin-hatted Egyptian soldiers standing in doorways and in groups at the roadheads. The situation was getting worse. A frightened stage-doorkeeper let me into the theatre. From the grand-stand I watched a few groups of excited students being chased by the soldiers. But where were my actors? I telephoned to Roger Livesey at the Hotel Continentale.

"Yes, I know you're waiting. We could see you standing on the roof. But the manager refuses to let us leave," said Roger.

"Nonsense," I replied, "I'm coming across to fetch you."

By the time we had collected all the company the demonstration had begun again. However, we marched back across the square without any trouble, but Soliman Naguib, fearful for the safety of his Opera House, begged us in tears to go away. He must have got into touch with G.H.Q., for a quarter of an hour later a staff officer telephoned and ordered an immediate retirement.

The School for Scandal looked, as I intended it should, a lovely picture. The moulded eighteenth-century windows and doorways and big candle brackets framing the dark brown hangings were a perfect background for the lovely dresses in silk and brocade. In the warm candlelight the waving fans and courtly bows had an especial grace. Ursula's Lady Teazle and Roger's Joseph Surface were completely in the mode, while Malcolm Keen, wilting at first under the severity of my rehearsals, made Sir Peter the doting, perplexed husband he was meant to be, with no fanciful modern reading of the character, out-at-elbows with Sheridan's intention; Heather Thatcher's musical-comedy attack gave special zest to Lady Sneerwell's tantrums, and George Howe's Crabtree was like an over-ripe medlar, but there! I should mention the whole cast if space did not forbid.

The bickering between the two Governments had grown more bitter, so much so that rumour had it that Prime Minister Sidky Pasha no longer addressed his diplomatic Notes to Britain in English but in French. It was the greatest triumph for us that he attended the first night. I sat with him in the diplomatic box. At the end of it he was effusive in his congratulations, saying that he had not seen what he was pleased to call West End acting since his undergraduate days at Balliol.

We were still without open support from the Palace, although the Queen Mother and one of her daughters attended a students' matinée of *Hamlet*, incognito. A strange sight that was: the rows of nodding tarbushes following the play from printed texts held before them like prayer missals, accompanying the exciting moments with sibilant gusts of pleasure, much pleasanter than their fire-eating oratory in the streets.

Soliman Naguib made many excuses for the Palace neglect until one day he announced triumphantly that Hassanein Pasha, the Court Chamberlain and an acknowledged Anglophile, had been to see *The School for Scandal* and requested me to call on him, which I did the following evening. A man of great charm and refinement, he spoke so feelingly of his days in England and of his many friends there that I could well believe the hints that Naguib had dropped as to the delicacy of his present position. After giving me his thanks for the work we had done in Egypt, he said that a movement had been started to build a new and larger Opera House in Cairo. What did I think of the existing building? Should it be torn down and the new one erected in its place, or should a site be chosen in the Ezbekiah Gardens? So far as I can recall, I was all for a new building and for retaining the present one as well, a little gem of its kind. Hassanein listened without comment until I had done, when he said that, if anything came of the plan, I would be invited to return to Cairo as Government adviser on the project. Two days later he was killed in a motor accident while driving across the Kasr-el-Nil Bridge. Watching the impressive State funeral from our grandstand deepened my regret for the loss of that friend of an afternoon, for with his passing went the last hope of giving the ENSA Drama Festival any political significance.

The Festival lasted from February 9 to March 12, 1946, inclusive: thirty-nine performances were scheduled, of which three were cancelled because of the riots, including one *Hamlet*. Final performances of each of the three plays brought out from London were given on the last three consecutive nights. For none of them was a seat left vacant. I was satisfied that we had achieved the climax of our work for the troops in the Middle East, but a little sad that the proportion of seats occupied by Egyptians had steadily declined.

2

Passed by Censor

My farewell production for the troops in Germany was made in July 1946. The play chosen was *The Apple Cart*. My first choice had been *The Devil's Disciple*, but Shaw refused his permission, declaring that the recent General Election had shown that America was not popular. Later he tried to fob me off with *On the Rocks*, which he said had only failed in London because the theatre in which it was presented had not been properly heated.

To give the play an up-to-the-minute appeal to the troops in their new political consciousness, I made Magnus' Cabinet resemble as closely as possible the new Labour Cabinet in Britain. It added to the difficulty of casting, but we achieved it beyond my best hopes, George Howe as Proteus looking remarkably like Mr Attlee, and Julien Mitchell, complete with tortoise-shell glasses, the physical embodiment of Ernest Bevin; some of the other likenesses were also excellent. 'King Magnus' was dressed in the uniforms of each of the three British Services in turn: in the first act as a Field-Marshal, in the second as an Admiral of the Fleet and in the last act as a Marshal of the Royal Air Force. This removed any element of charade that might have clung to Barry Jones' appearance before a military audience in fancy uniform, but to satisfy propriety we decorated his chest with ribbons of strange and fearsome colour.

Using again the draped-stage technique, with solid features placed in front, Denis Wreford designed scenery, simple but nobly proportioned to the fine stages on which it would be set. They were the best designs he made for ENSA, a fitting climax to six years' brilliant service.

It was a glorious day towards the end of May when I flew to Germany ahead of the company. Rainclouds were chasing each other across the sky, the lime and larch trees in their newest green; I remembered again the characteristic scent of the country. My purpose was to get into direct touch with the American Headquarters Command at Frankfurt, because I had the fancy to make a farewell bow to the G.I.'s too, in return for the many performances given to British troops by U.S.O. I was given air passage to the American Zone, where reckless driving was still causing many casualties. A lurid warning of the consequences stared me in the face as I left the Airport: a huge skeleton, painted white on a black board, and underneath the words:

DEATH IS SO PERMANENT. DRIVE CAREFULLY

To top up the object-lesson a broken-down jeep with a dummy American soldier, heavily bandaged, flanked the notice-board with the further slogan:

WILL THIS BE YOU?

Everybody seemed to be out at cocktail parties when I reached U.S. Headquarters. The social round of an army of occupation had already replaced the campaigning spirit. I got along famously with the commanding general, once he was convinced that I was not trying to sell him anything, but had a genuine desire to give the G.I.'s a sight of my farewell production. (Strange, I thought, that so many Americans should be suspicious of salesmanship.) A decision was promised as soon as possible, the date and place to be notified to ENSA H.Q. in Hamburg. I stayed to an excellent dinner.

It was to this same American Headquarters that Walter Legge had offered a visit from Elizabeth Schumann, which was refused as being unlikely to please the G.I.'s, a Security evasion that was the more unaccountable since she had paid a visit to American troops in the previous year; but that was before the Rhine had been crossed. In due course we were invited to give two performances to U.S. troops in the beautiful Opera House at Wiesbaden on July 9 and 10.

In Berlin I ran across Ashley Dukes, assisting at the rebirth of the German Theatre. With his standing as a British author and his German scholarship, the Allied Control Commission could not have picked a better man for the job. Ours was a fortunate meeting because ENSA's continuing tenancy of the German theatres was obstructing the policy of the Commission. We ironed the matter out in a couple of meetings. In future ENSA would occupy the theatres only when it had full-scale attractions to present to Allied troops, and on due notice given. At other times the Germans would run their own opera and drama for the civilian population.

There was free admission to ENSA entertainment for all members of the Allied Forces in uniform, but no German civilians were admitted, either as guests of the troops or otherwise. This seemed to me unwise, and Ashley agreed, but so far he had been unable to overcome the prejudice of the military hierarchy against permitting any amenities for their late enemies. I intended to try again, and Ashley promised to back me up.

The following day I lunched with Major-General Nares (a cousin of Owen's), who was in charge of the British sector, and who was quickly persuaded to our point of view. He further proposed to make the first night a festival occasion. The ENSA Jerboa Theatre being too small for the purpose, we arranged to hire the Theater des Westens, now renamed the Städtische Oper. I returned to England and the final rehearsals, hugging to myself a secret delight that ENSA would be the first to break down the no-fraternization order in favour of a wiser policy.

All the representatives of the Occupying Powers accepted General Nares' invitation, except the Russians, who, mindful of the author's recent flirtation with the Dictators, evidently regarded the political talk in the last act with dark suspicion, for they asked that quite a slice should be cut out of the interview between King Magnus and Mr Vanhatten, the U.S. Ambassador, particularly mentioning the sentence: "I suppose you mean by Germany the chain of more or less Soviet Republics between the Ural Mountains and the North Sea."

I could well imagine the fun G.B.S. would have when he heard this news; it would be an amusing piece of publicity for us, too. So I wrote to him, proposing a visit. The usual Shavian postcard in reply was not cordial: "I'm not free until 4 o'clock and am short of petrol, tea and domestic service." Before I could fix the date a signal came in from Berlin, stating that our office had agreed to make the cut. I was annoyed to have lost the opportunity of a little mild fun at the expense of the Russians.

The play opened in Hamburg on July 1. Apart from the fun of recognizing famous Labour leaders under the actors' disguises, the political talk, received with riotous laughter as a typical example of Shavian extravagance when the play was first presented, seemed to have drawn nearer to reality with the years. The Americans went for the Orinthia scene in a big way; poor tragic little Shelagh Furley making an astonishingly good shot at the part. Barry Jones' report on the second Wiesbaden performance described its success as "almost heartbreaking, with a sort of Bank Holiday crowd backstage afterwards."

As a return gesture, the U.S. commanding general offered me a day at the Nuremberg Trials. It was a long, long drive through heavy rain and over some of the roughest roads. I had to get up at 5 A.M. in order to reach the Court House by 10 A.M., after which no one could be admitted. It was not a day of outstanding interest (by that I mean there was no cross-examination of the criminals), but every detail of the scene remains clear in memory. The court room was like a film set, with the array of judges seated on the long daïs beneath their national flags, Lord Lawrence, President of the Court, in the middle, the row of interpreters in their cage high up above the dock, the American military police, unutterably bored, over-fed and over-pipe-clayed, and the prisoners looking a very ordinary middle-class lot in their nondescript clothes, all except Goering. His deportment still suggested a leader, as he sat hunched in the right-hand corner of the dock facing the judges, contemptuous of his fellows and indifferent to the Court procedure.

My deepest impressions were reserved for two unexpected and unconnected matters, the astonishing speed of the interpreters, whose voices came over the ear-phones scarcely a second later than the original speakers', and the President's complete command of the proceedings. During the morning an American police sergeant handed me a note from Lord Lawrence inviting me to lunch. I told him how much the British public admired his effortless control over the Court. Further comment on what I had seen was inappropriate. Instead, the talk drifted away to the theatre. It was heart-warming to receive his praise of my productions in the theatre, and courtesy most welcome his hopes for my early return there.

After the Court had risen a small party of the day's visitors was permitted to visit the cells while the prisoners were at exercise in the yard. The Commandant of the prison was a Texan colonel of cavalry, whose racy speech and American idiom called for a note-book which decency forbade; now much is forgotten. Each of us was handed an elaborate booklet, which set out in detail all the arrangements for the custody and health of the criminals. The colonel certainly did his job of conducting officer very thoroughly, explaining the number of ounces of food of different kinds that went to make up each meal, lifting up baking-tins in the cookhouse to show how clean they were kept, flushing the toilets to show they worked.

His brochure set down the prison routine in full: the times of meals (only a spoon allowed), daily visits from the prison officer, the doctor, the barber (no talking allowed), a minister of religion of the appropriate denomination (if requested), eye-glasses removed at night and returned each morning. The portholes in each cell door were protected by heavy wire mesh and had lights suspended above them to assist day and night observation. Insecticide was in constant use "to prevent ingress of vermin and parasites from other parts of the prison." As the colonel marched us along the cat-walk past the cells, he drew attention to the names on each door, with revealing comments now and then on the occupant's general behaviour and other characteristics. I noticed that Ribbentrop had remained in his cell. After we had passed by I asked about him.

"He sure is a dirty bastard, that guy," replied the colonel. "Always making trouble. Doesn't keep his cell clean and won't take exercise."

In spite of all the elaborate arrangements the place smelt like a zoo. I

2K

half expected to read under the names, where appropriate, the words: "Habitat: Prussia."

I drove back to Wiesbaden, feeling rather sick.

On the first night of *The Apple Cart* in Berlin the Russians, with full panoply of medals, quite put into the shade the other Allied representatives. During the ten-day season the queue of British troops at the box-office gradually gave way to German civilians, each with a copy of the play in hand. By the last night this queue extended right round the building. There was a humorous side to this conclusion of my seven years' work for the troops, for whatever our men may have thought of my farewell production, at least the Germans enjoyed themselves.

Heil, Cæsar! . . .

Before my production the Drama Division had made up its mind to have its own farewell. *Julius Cæsar* was staged with an admirable cast, including Francis Lister, James Dale, Cecil Ramage, Henry Oscar, George Skillan and Vivienne Bennett. The company ran into mishap, almost immediately it arrived on the Continent. George Skillan, on the verge of a nervous breakdown, consulted an R.A.M.C. doctor, who advised mental relaxation, so Skillan went off to the local zoo. Presenting himself before the doctor next day, he said, "I've been to the zoo. I did as you told me. Now look at me! Still shaking. I must have had a shock." He was flown home.

After playing in Holland and Belgium the company moved to Düsseldorf and Dortmund, and thence to Berlin and Hamburg. A German symphony orchestra was provided in each town, sadly deficient in woodwind, (the players too hungry to blow their instruments), and an eager crowd of a hundred supers for the forum scene, which Henry Oscar rehearsed each Monday morning through interpreters. These crowds consistently failed to understand the difference between, "Hail, Cæsar" and "Heil, Cæsar." The latter was a cry to which they were more accustomed.

CHAPTER THIRTY-THREE

LIGHTS OUT

1

'I couldn't care less'

BY the time the Cairo Festival was ended, World Theatre, a title first used by ENSA and proclaimed everywhere in an arresting lithograph, was virtually over too. The 'house' was emptying, and I naturally wanted to 'go behind,' as we say, to bid 'good-bye' and 'thank you' to as many of the staff as I might encounter.

I went first to 'Paiforce,' where, in the G.O.C.'s Mess at Baghdad, a visiting brigadier from the War Office, no less, made public acknow-ledgment of the one outstanding fact about us that no amount of adverse criticism could gainsay: at least ENSA had been the first to realize the necessity of mobilizing entertainment as a positive weapon in the national armoury; he thought the Services should pass a public vote of thanks to the theatrical profession.

Doubling back through Cairo to pick up Madame Vernon, I visited our various offices throughout Italy, and then on into Austria and Ger-many. Nearly all the officers previously mentioned as being in the Com-mand were gone by now, but here and there were others (Captain Cheney i/c Milan Area was one) whom I had met as N.C.O.'s during our first days in France and, subsequently, in various parts of the world, and invariably found busy on the job. There were many that I did not know—but it did not matter, for Virginia, who knew most of them, enumerated their virtues and failings with the accuracy of an expert valuer of human character.

Vienna was grey and sad: the lovely Opera House in ruins, streets of half-melted snow, dirty little tramcars, the tawdriness of a once-popular night-club seen by day, tinkly tunes that suggested a former gaiety with the blood run out of it. But the C.M.F. Festival Company seemed happy with its success, Godfrey Tearle greeting me with the same dubious air he had worn at that Sunday morning meeting in Leslie Henson's house, as though he were still unsure of the propriety of our proceedings. Yet he made no complaint when he was lodged in a hostel without a front door; nor did he when he was sent to mess in an extremely unkempt restaurant with boarded windows, among a crowd of Austrian employees of E.F.I.

Our affairs were in the care of one of our civilian managers, Mr Caine, formerly of the R.A.F., who was originally sent up to take charge of one cinema, but found himself in possession of sole responsibility. The type of man who undertakes little and promises less, yet invariably delivers the goods, his feats of wizardry in keeping our crazed transport on the move were not the least of his achievements in a position that was crumbling daily; and I here record a belated recognition of his work.

From Vienna we went on to Graz and to Klagenfurt, headquarters of British Troops in Austria (BTA) and of the 13th Corps, which had its concentrations at Trieste, Udine and Treviso. Our neglect of those troops was due to the failure to get ENSA Main shifted out of Naples in good time. On Virginia's insistence, I sought out the Army Commander, Lieutenant-General Sir Richard McCreery, in his caravan, to admit our shortcomings and to promise that, although my own work was coming to an end, I would do my best to arrange for some special entertainment to be flown out via Vienna. I had in mind to include this in the Ensacap tour. But it was too late in the day: the scheme died of inanition, leaving those troops bereft.

In Germany my good-byes included a visit to 2nd T.A.F. Headquarters, where a farewell party was in progress for Air Chief Marshal Coningham. I recall the occasion well, because it was the only time that I heard him express his views freely about the war. I particularly remember his comparison between the war just over and any future conflict: "In this war," he said, "sixty-five per cent. of the people prepared weapons for the remaining thirty-five per cent.; in the next one ninety-five per cent. of the people will be preparing weapons for five per cent. to use. It might even be won by threats alone," he added. Recent events have brought his views to mind. At the time, however, it seemed to be an air marshal's fantasy, spoken jauntily against the deafening background of an R.A.F. jazz band.

The current state of affairs defeated me. Anticlimax was expressing itself in a hundred ways. One longed for the camaraderie and spirit of service of the war years. Entertainment of one kind or another had now become everybody's business. ENSA had lost a great part of its significance in the daily round of military events. As our importance declined, that of the Army's own entertainment officers increased. Many of them were young actors of modest experience whose competence to give advice was questionable. Yet they were often called into conference, whence it was but a short step to positive interference. In such circumstances self-discipline, never easy for us in the entertainment world, became an added trial to those who exercised it, and a bore to their acquaintances. One could not blame our officers; they were in the grip of a national 'hurrah!' most of them with their eyes fixed on the demobilization charts.

Transport was another infective spot in our body politic. In Germany, after the habit of the day, our officers reacted to our congenital shortage by 'winning' German cars, their special predilection being for those made by the firm of Mercédès. As these acquisitions were bound to come to roost one day, I asked the Transport Division to call for an immediate return of all enemy vehicles; but I need not have troubled. Before it was completed the Army stepped in and put an end to the requisitioning circus.

Among the artistes the decision to close down produced a sort of 'double take.' Good artistes were chafing to return, while the indifferent ones were up to every dodge to prolong their stay, lacking the comforting assurance of full employment at home. This was amusingly described by Brian Reece, reporting from Cairo: "When I first arrived the staircase to my office was lined every morning with artistes waiting to see about renewals of engagement, holidays and so forth. Now that entertainment is to be reduced by two-thirds the main concern of everybody seems to be to keep out of my way; if I go into Groppi's for an ice-cream, artistes I wish to interview jump up, pay their bills and hurry out."

In the various Messes and hotels I was regaled with numerous stories all extolling the current inversion of outlook, that regarded the successful 'winning' of other people's property as legitimate enterprise. That farewell shout of the *démobilisés*, "see you in gaol!" might easily become a possibility. Our artistes could not be expected to remain unaffected by what was going on around them; it was only surprising that there was so little to complain of. Some import and export traffic, yes, certainly; an occasional Persian rug and some Eastern jewellery, perhaps, but not 'winning' in the soldier's sense. I did hear of lighter flints imported into Italy in jam-jars by a band-leader at a time of great scarcity, but that doubtless was merely to assist the balance of trade. Conjurers and sleight-of-hand people had the best time of it. One illusionist, whose stage properties included trunks with false sides and bottoms, adopted the highly successful technique of distraction. When asked to open up his trunks for inspection he appeared to misunderstand, and began to perform various conjuring tricks which so delighted the Iraki Customs officers that they forgot to look inside.

Well, there it was. The party was breaking up; the show was over—choose which analogy you prefer—there was nothing to be gained by prolonging it. . . . In the aircraft I began idly to turn over the papers in my brief-case. I came across a minute from Madame Vernon about an Arts Festival in Rome. The paper was intended to arouse my anger because no public acknowledgment had been made to ENSA for securing Gracie Fields' appearance at the opening concert. As I put the file away I caught myself muttering the common phrase: 'couldn't care less.' I too had caught the infection.

<><><>

pro ENSA . . .

One figure stood out, unmoved amid all this coil: 'Mickie' Jacob, our public relations officer in Italy from January 1945. Her warm humanity endeared her to the troops, and her long residence in the country enabled her to undertake a variety of duties not only for them, but for the local inhabitants, who evinced a touching belief in the importance of the magic initials, ENSA, on her shoulder.

The following items are taken from her reports:

> Please help us, signora, to get our bells rehung in the church tower. The Fascisti took away two, but we've kept the others.

> We have no fuel in the town for next winter. Will you help the syndico to get some for us from AMGOT?

> Will you write to the Missus and tell her to do what's right towards me and the kid? [This from a corporal of her acquaintance.]

I like best the account of the evenings in her home in Sirmione: the men from near-by units crowding into her study, lined with books, ostensibly to ask for her photograph, but really to borrow those books, all of which were faithfully returned; and especially that last night when a party of her regular clientele came to say good-bye before going home; the windows open to the soft, night air, the only refreshment some bottles of cheap wine; the young soldiers talking eagerly about the new world they were about to enter; a debate, ranging from politics to religion, and then to home and children. Mickie, with all her resource, is unable to find satisfactory answers to all their questions:

"I'm an atheist, all right," says one, "and wot I ses is, why should humanity suffer like what it's doing? Answer me that, ma'am?"

A youngster with a more practical mind produces another poser.

"Religious talk's all right, but what's to 'appen to the likes o' me now the war's over? Are we going to be unemployed, like my dad was last time?"

She turns another aside with one of her own: "When did you write to your mother last, son?"

"I'm not much of a hand at writing letters."

"Then I'll do it for you," promptly replies Mickie. The threat is received with delight by the others.

She signed her reports PRO/ENSA, except for the last, which was signed pro-ENSA. Both meant the same to her; the troops, artistes and staff all came to respect an impeccable loyalty.

2

"miching mallecho"

Our climax was sustained in spite of the hubble-bubble of shifting political emphases and national readjustment that followed VE Day. But the serio-comic political storm that eventually burst over our heads—I got most of the shower—was vastly different from the chorus of "Bravo!" and "Well done!" that we had anticipated. The story, or such of it as they were told, has long since been forgotten by the general public, but it has to be retold here because it robbed ENSA of its share of public acclamation and led, ultimately, to its passing. Therefore it has its place in the microcosm of theatrical history.

The reader will recall my account of early difficulties in the Broadcasting Division. They had grown steadily worse as victory drew near. Roger Ould, Manager of the Division, may not always have responded as generously as he should have to the ideas of his Chairman, Sir Herbert Dunnico, many of which were highly successful, but he had every right to object to changes in the minutes which completely altered their intention and to the persistent engagement of artistes useful to Dunnico in his other activities, often against the advice of the Broadcasting Executive. To his formal notes, always sedulously polite, Dunnico responded with open missives, dictated in ever more abusive terms, but not always signed, and dispatched about the building by messenger. When I could no longer acquiesce in this persistent gunning for a senior member of the staff, Dunnico threatened resignation, withdrawn only after patient manœuvre on my part.

It was not persons alone but policies that incurred his increasing displeasure. When Walter Legge offered to provide recitals of classical music in the NAAFI Clubs to supplement our other amenities, Dunnico objected, saying that variety would attract more customers. Wary of the disputatious Walter, he brought his complaint to me. When I refused to accept his view, he again offered his resignation, and once again I staved it off.

The situation was now extremely worrying. It was all very well to make jokes about this modern Friar Tuck with his broad smile, his office drinking-parties and fund of salacious stories, set down in a little black book that in the course of time had acquired an exaggerated reputation among the junior typists; it was a simple matter, too, for senior officials to keep out of the old gentleman's way, rather than risk the explosion of a cannon-cracker when least expected; but such sapience could not be expected of younger members of the staff, who fell under the influence of his trailing joviality and began unwittingly to provide him with ammunition for the subsequent explosion. It had been a serious blunder to invite him to take over the Amenities Council when his goodwill was already exhausted by the constant bickering over broadcasting. An overriding factor which I should also have noted was Dunnico's health. He had already had one serious attack of thrombosis and the marks of strain were visible on him. My exigence blinded me, and I was much to blame.

Friends of ENSA who expressed surprise at his presence at Drury Lane had no knowledge of the valuable services which he had rendered in the early years. A skilful negotiator, with useful contacts in many walks of life foreign to the entertainment world, he did not hesitate to use his political skill to help me in the early struggles for recognition of ENSA's official status. For that I remained grateful; for that reason I strove over a period of more than twelve months to adjust differences and to disregard untoward incidents. And I declare most positively that it was no fault of mine that just before the final rupture we were hardly on speaking terms, my appeals for yet another friendly talk over differences being met with frigid messages conveyed by a secretary.

Then there was that fateful day when I passed him in one of the corridors with his arms full of ENSA standard dress. "Just off to Brussels," he remarked jauntily, in response to my stare of surprise. When I made inquiries of the Overseas Division I was told that he was proposing to go over in charge of a Sports Brains Trust. In recent months he had been taking a more and more active part in the broadcasting of the ceremonial openings of the new NAAFI Clubs, a proceeding which NAAFI regarded with disfavour. I supported that view, because to enter the professional arena was to step down from his high seat as a judge of what should take place. Now he was going a step farther.

Acting more by instinct than anything else, I decided there and then that the visit ought not to take place. The ENSA ship was tossing on the tumultuous waves of demobilization. In the prevailing restlessness the officers overseas would be quite unable to control him. Stated baldly like that, my decision may seem like the exercise of that dictatorship of which Dunnico subsequently complained, but after this lapse of time it is impossible to recapture for the reader the atmosphere in which it was made. At all events both the Chairman of the Entertainments Board and the Chairman of NAAFI jumped at the opportunity of putting an end to a troublesome situation. I wrote a letter, polished by Ellington and others to the smoothest edge of tact, stating that it was thought undesirable for him to go abroad on the score of his health. This was unfortunate, for it touched a sensitive spot, and led to the most violent repercussions.

Dunnico's final letter of resignation had been couched in such ambiguous terms that the news of his public attack telephoned to me that Sunday night in Lübeck found me quite unprepared. Hitherto I had regarded our differences as a domestic matter of no public importance. It was this which caused me to treat it so lightly over the telephone from Germany. I might have continued in the same mood of light-hearted denial when I met the knot of reporters waiting for me at the stage-door on my return home had not some of my closest associates warned me to read what had been published before making any statement. The reporters were told to come back at noon the next day.

When I read the pile of Press cuttings that lay on my desk, and realized the quasi-political twist which Dunnico had given to his statements, I saw things in a different light. His loud cries for a public inquiry before a Judge of the High Court, with evidence taken on oath, were calculated to arouse the gravest suspicions. The reader who has followed the story thus far will have no difficulty in understanding my reaction to such absurdities as that I was "the sole executive authority over an expenditure of £4,000,000 per annum," and "an absolute dictator, overriding the decisions of my executives." But to many people ENSA had represented a collection of concert parties, too numerous all to be of good quality, nothing more. Now the suggestion that millions of pounds of the taxpayers' money had been at the disposal of one man, and a theatrical manager at that, implied a public scandal of some magnitude, especially since it had been made by an ex-Deputy Speaker of the House of Commons.

Few stopped to ask themselves the question: "Why, if Sir Herbert Dunnico was so profoundly convinced that waste of public funds and mismanagement had been going on for years, had he remained within the organization?"

It is ten years since all this happened. Turning over the papers in the files and pondering events, I feel it might have been better if we had all had a course of treatment from a psychiatrist. Yet, mentally twisted as we all were by the strain of those war years, I doubt whether such ministrations would have been effective. If they had the fate of ENSA might have been otherwise.

3

"skimble-skamble stuff"

To inquire or not to inquire? The question was fully canvassed in the ensuing weeks. The Treasury was strongly opposed: it would imply criticism of their supervision. The War Office very properly passed the matter to the Entertainments Board. The Chairman of NAAFI said that, if ENSA insisted upon inquiry, the Corporation would raise no objection. For my part, I was not blind to the fact that our many mistakes and short-comings would certainly be exaggerated, else the newspaper reports of the inquiry proceedings would be without interest to the general reader. In that atmosphere public opinion too often becomes a court of summary jurisdiction. Our Public Relations Council (the appropriate body to advise me on the matter) had ceased to function, and I could hardly con-sult its individual members now; it would place them in an embarrassing position vis-à-vis their late Chairman. Fortunately E. P. Smith, Member for Ashford (Edward Percy, the dramatist, known to his friends as 'E.P.'), had not been on the Council, and to him I went in my perplexity. He was all for an inquiry, and said so in the lobby and on the floor of the House. But I was so completely confident of the outcome that, as the days went by and discussion waned, I began to resent more and more the appall-ing waste of time that would be involved in giving way to intolerable conspiracy. In the end I came down on the side of no inquiry.

Meanwhile, 'E.P.' took steps to clear up the matter in the House of Commons, rising on November 1 to ask the Lord President of the Council whether the National Service Entertainments Board had now con-sidered the request for an inquiry into the work of ENSA and whether he had any statement[1] to make.

MR MORRISON. The National Service Entertainments Board are of opinion that there is no need whatsoever for an independent public inquiry into Ensa's activities. I have also consulted the Service authorities concerned, who consider that the scope of the task undertaken by Ensa and the enormous difficulties which they have had to face in bringing entertainment to the forces all over the world have been insufficiently appreciated. It is natural that there should have been local failures and criticisms, but viewed as a whole the work of the organiza-

[1] *The Times* (Friday, November 2, 1945). Report of proceedings in the House of Commons the previous day.

The newspaper reprinted this statement for me in leaflet form. Copies were sent to our Councils and Committees and to the artistes and staff in all overseas territories.

tion has been highly commendable. The complaints may perhaps be seen in a better perspective if it is mentioned that between the outbreak of war and May 8, 1945, Ensa performances to the troops and factory workers numbered over 1,000,000, and the attendances exceed 318,000,000.

Dunnico did not remain idle, of course; he was constantly to be seen, bustling about the House or in the smoking-room, dispensing items for my discomfiture and sworn overthrow. On the day that the Lord President made the Government statement, Sir Waldron Smithers rose to inquire of the Home Secretary who had exempted me from personal fireguard duties at Drury Lane: such a farthing cracker that I was surprised anyone had bothered to explode it. The conspirators, piqued at the failure of their demand for an inquiry, went underground for the next week or two. But the calm was outward seeming only. They had gone home to collect ammunition for the grand detonation.

On November 29 Wing-Commander Millington, M.P. for Chelmsford, successful in the choice of speakers on the motion for adjournment, rose in his place to deliver the grand attack upon ENSA—and upon myself, the head and front of all offending. In accordance with custom, he had given the Vote Office a list of the accusations he proposed to make and of the evidence he would produce in support of them. A copy was passed to me. Much of the evidence was contained in a report from the young man who had been promoted from the secretariat and given, at his own request, the title of General Administrative Secretary (G.A.S.). Other items were supplied by officers and civilians whose engagements had been terminated.

Never having been involved in a political row before, I viewed the prospect with alarm. Although I had no wish to appear at the Bar of the House of Commons as a miniature Warren Hastings, I hoped to comport myself with dignity. There was some doubt as to the appropriate Minister to speak in my defence. The Lord President of the Council (Herbert Morrison) seemed to be indicated, but the day before the debate I was told that the Under-Secretary of State for Air (John Strachey) had been given the task. I sat up half the night, preparing yet another ENSA dossier, and had the supporting documents carefully collated. An appointment was made for Alec Rea and myself to see the Minister in the morning. Several glamorous secretaries stared at us, lambs for the slaughter, as we waited in an outer office before being shown into the Minister's sanctum.

"Well," said Strachey, staring at us in a rather abstracted way. "It seems I've got to reply to this debate, but I really know very little about it. Why it should be left to me . . ." His voice trailed away uncertainly. I placed my parcel of documents in front of him. He shied as though it contained a bomb.

"What's this?"

"The answer to the list of accusations they sent us," I said. "It's fully documented. If you care to study the papers . . ."

"Study?" he cried.

Unfortunate choice of a word! "I'm frightfully busy, you know," he protested, and put the papers to one side.

"It's a very difficult case," he resumed.

"I don't see why," said Alec, his hackles up.

"Well, the shows aren't very good, are they?" said the Minister in a lofty tone, looking over the top of Alec's head.

Alec began to splutter: "D'you realize the whole profession at one time or another . . ."

"Yes, yes, yes," interrupted Strachey.

"This attack is scurrilous," pursued Alec, while I kept silent, the accused listening to his advocate.

"Well, I'll do my best," again interrupted Strachey, "but I can't promise that you will like what I'm going to say." And with that parting beneficence he showed us out of the room.

The hon. and gallant Member for Chelmsford in the course of his windmill tirade[1] handed out so many charges of graft, corruption, inefficiency, favouritism, waste and dictatorship, that even with the perspective of time it is difficult to pick out the grosser absurdities. But here are a few, taken at random from Hansard: "High-ranking stars would not give their services, willing as they might be to entertain the troops, because they could not stand his [my] direction." (An unworthy slander on the patriotism of the stars, that.) Millington on waste: "Not many people realize that £14,000,000 of public money has been spent by ENSA during the period of its existence. Much of this money, troops' money, public and semi-public, has been literally and absolutely wasted." Many companies rehearsed, kitted up at the cost of thousands of pounds, which failed to pass the quality test at the final dress rehearsals were put back to be re-formed "at the whim of the Director." A scheme to develop German opera under ENSA auspices had been devised for my personal aggrandisement. (In truth, no such scheme existed.) The hon. and gallant Member could hardly be blamed for these and many other extravagances; he was speaking from a brief provided for him by a past master in the dubious craft of political over-emphasis.

Millington's polemic occupied seventeen minutes of the precious half-

[1] Hansard, Vol. 416, No. 50, Cols. 1777–85.

hour, instead of the customary ten. This left E. P. Smith one minute in which to deny flatly everything he had said, and no time at all for Benn Levy to rise in support.

The Minister began his reply at 1.41 A.M. Anxious to establish his impartiality in the argument, he produced the brisk statement: "I must admit that some of the worst hours of that [his] career have been spent in ENSA shows." This was well calculated to titillate the curiosity of somnolent members, but was scarcely an adequate answer to charges of fraud and corruption. No case for a public inquiry had been made out. Such irregularities as had occurred were probably inevitable; it would be an impossible matter to determine. In conclusion, he thought it would be more useful to examine the new situation which had arisen since the end of the war: "We must not allow the ENSA organization which is still providing entertainment on a vast scale all over the world to die."

This was all very well, as far as it went, which was precisely nowhere. The Government had not specifically refuted the charges; there had been no time. In fact, they had not taken the matter seriously at all.

I was left face to face with a situation new in my experience, having been publicly accused of fraud and corruption, with no hope of redress unless my detractor could be induced to repeat his charges outside the privilege of the House. Without much confidence but with the help of my solicitor I wrote a letter to *The Times*, challenging the hon. and gallant Member to repeat his charges in public when I could promise him immediate action. The Editor showed what he thought about the matter by giving it a prominent place in the next day's issue.

Members are rightly jealous of the dignity and privileges of Parliament, but when individuals are slandered by a Member during the course of its proceedings, there should be some means of calling him to account. There was editorial comment in this sense in several newspapers. Admittedly, the circumstances were unusual. Although I was engaged on public business I was not a civil servant; technically I was still an employee of NAAFI.

Surplus to Requirements . . .

Amongst the accumulated material which it had been suggested in Parliament was waiting to be 'picked-up' (*i.e.*, stolen) was an enormous music library, thousands of copies of sheet-music, band-parts of musical plays, symphonic pieces, songs and special orchestrations, estimated to be worth at least £5000. It was in charge of an old concert-party pianist,

Pennystone Miles, known as 'Penny,' whose experience with entertainment officers during the war had not endeared them to him. When the time came to hand over this library to the Services, a deputation of staff officers attended at Drury Lane to interview 'Penny' on the subject. They knew little about music but were aghast at the quantity. "How do you suggest we dispose of all this stuff?" asked one of them. Penny, anticipating this question, had prepared an answer in line with his own caustic humour. "Well," he said, rubbing his stubbly chin, "I suggest the R.A.F. has the wind, the Navy the strings and let the Army take the brass." "Good show!" said the officer. "Press on!"

4

"Read All about It! Pap—err!"

I came back from my farewell tour in Germany full of plans for ENSA's future. In consenting to the formation of the ENSA Council, NAAFI had tacitly accepted the principle of our separate existence after the war. Accordingly, in April 1945 I had submitted papers on Music and Drama to our Provisional Council that were in some part blueprints for the work subsequently undertaken by the Arts Council of Great Britain. Continuance in some form of the work for the Service Departments was also envisaged. I had had several conversations with Lancelot Royle on the basis that it might be financed by direct subsidy from NAAFI, both parties feeling at the time that the machinery that had been created at the cost of so much effort might well be retained in skeleton form.

Walter Monckton had apparently convinced the Treasury of the validity of our claim to share in post-war reconstruction in cultural matters. The British Council was about to appoint representatives to our Council, and was listening sympathetically to our proposal that ENSA should present some representative British plays at the Comédie Française during the peace talks in return for a visit of the French Company to London, both seasons to be under joint auspices. The political barometer was set fair after the recent storms. But I underestimated the persistence of our enemies.

Dunnico knew all about my plans. For reasons which I did not appreciate at the time, he had elected to remain a member of the Provisional Council, receiving all papers; and we had not bothered to ask him to resign. Another attack on my personal integrity was being planned.

On the very first day that Parliament reassembled after the Easter recess (April 30, 1946) the then Member for Darlington rose at 10 P.M. to speak on the motion for the adjournment. For twenty minutes he covered me and my associates with the coarsest abuse, although the ostensible purpose of the speech was to secure a reduction in ENSA expenditure. Rousing street-corner stuff, all to be found in Hansard.[1] Here are some choice samples. "The old gang" (by which presumably was meant those who had remained loyal to ENSA from the beginning) were described as "the Colonel Blimps of theatre-land," delaying their own demobilization, "hanging on to four-figure incomes with grim determination," while "the smaller fry" (by which was presumably meant the little concert parties) "had been completely liquidated." "The Director-General of ENSA went all the way to Egypt to stage-manage or present British drama for rich Egyptian civilians given at public expense, out of the soldier's pay-packet."

Poor Sir Edward Ellington even caught some of the mud. Dealing with the previous refusal of an official inquiry, the orator posed the following question: "When the Lord President says that the matter had been gone into thoroughly by the National Service Entertainments Board, does he not know that that only means Basil Dean? It is only one man, it does not mean a committee."

I did not mind particularly being called "the Lord Pooh Bah of the land of bluff and make-believe," for this was the usual stuff of the hustings, but the renewed suggestions of corruption were a different matter. "A nice little carve-up is taking place at ENSA, Hitler's chairs, for example. . . . Who has them at the moment I do not know, but some folk have a good idea." And more of a like nature. Replying for the Government, Mr Glenvil Hall, then Financial Secretary to the Treasury, was more emphatic in our defence than Strachey had been. He ended his speech with the warmest tribute to myself personally, which was gratifying but did not conceal from me that I was once more fighting from my 'blue corner,' and obstinately refusing to leave the ring at the behest of the barrackers.

Three reporters, scenting a good story in Hitler's chairs, presented themselves at my flat at midnight the following day and jostled their way into the hall: "Where are the chairs, Basil?" grinned one of them. "Come on, be a sport!"

For a moment I was tempted to let them search the flat, but my wife had already gone to bed. As an alternative I invited them to go to Drury Lane to inspect the exhibit when it came back from the upholsterers. My wife was wakened by the racket. "What have you been up to now?" she asked—a trifle unsympathetically, I thought, in the way that women have when faced with unwelcome publicity about those nearest to them: the

[1] Hansard, Vol. 422, No. 128, Cols. 150–158.

corollary to which is, of course, that in public they will defend these same persons to the death, even though evidence be black against them. For a day or two that chair certainly hit the headlines, which must have given the dictator's ghost a cackle or two. Now it rests, suitably inscribed, at the Theatre Royal, Drury Lane, symbol both of our war-time occupancy of the famous theatre and of the successful accomplishment of the national mission in which ENSA may claim to have had a tiny share.

5

Trumpets before Jericho

All who knew the work of ENSA were unanimous in their indignation at the continued smear campaign, and many who did not were equally so; some of the expressions of sympathy were delivered to me in person, others in writing. One of my earliest callers was Lord Cromer, who voiced his disgust at what had occurred. But anything in the nature of scandal was so distasteful to the gentle courtier, who had passed so much of his life in the atmosphere of St James's Palace, that no practical help was to be expected from him. Another sympathizer, Commander Locker-Lampson, M.P., a complete stranger to me, went so far as to send a long telegram, urging me to write to Mr Speaker and demand a complete withdrawal of the statements.

For some reason that I cannot now recall this course of action was changed in favour of a personal interview with the Lord Chancellor.[1] Owing to a lapse of memory on the part of a secretary who failed to order my car, I was a quarter of an hour late. When I reached the House of Lords an extremely annoyed Lord Chancellor was waiting for me in his robes, having left the Chamber on purpose to keep the appointment. In my confusion, instead of making up some dramatic excuse, I told him the truth. This *naïveté* annoyed him exceedingly. "Why, I left the Woolsack for you," he exclaimed inconsequently. Refusing to discuss my business, he gathered up his long robes, tucked them under his arm, and made an indignant exit, preceded by his attendants.

The renewed political fracas aroused fresh buzzing for and against an inquiry. I was inclined now to accept 'E.P.'s' original view, to abandon other preoccupations and to press for one immediately; but by this time the Authorities, in their quiet, methodical way, had satisfied themselves that it would be a waste of time and money. No case had been made out,

[1] Lord Jowitt.

and they would have none of it. As to whether they were right—well, the reader has all the facts and must draw his own conclusions.

As a last cast for good opinion, E. P. Smith suggested a visit of three M.P.'s to see our work in N.W. Europe and to report to the Prime Minister. The three Members, chosen because of no previous connexion with ENSA, were A. C. Bossom[1] (Conservative), John Paton (Labour) and W. J. Brown (Independent). I gave instructions that they were to be taken wherever they wished. Untrammelled by party politics—this was a non-party matter—their personalities expanded with the unwonted freedom: Bossom, good-humoured, shrewd and genial; Paton, rather cautious with a slightly portentous anxiety to get at the truth, and W. J. Brown, rather too easily declaring that everything was all right before he had seen it. Greatly impressed with all they saw, it was agreed that Paton, who strongly disapproved of the recent conduct of certain members of his party, should make a verbal report to the Prime Minister, while Bossom was to write to Walter Monckton. But it was too late. Really important matters were occupying public attention.

An unfavourable reaction to the sensational publicity was inevitable. The day came when Lancelot Royle told me that NAAFI had decided to give up directly interesting itself in entertainment after the war. The decision caused me no surprise, although I could not help regretting that the Corporation should have held on so determinedly to ENSA during the war, thus preventing it from coming to full estate. As we had never abandoned the view that ours was a voluntary service I decided that we should go before we were dismissed, and accordingly gave six months' notice that ENSA would end, so far as the troops were concerned, on June 30, 1946. The Adjutant-General, in whose eyes our semi-independence had always been an abhorred thing, replied by informing Sir Edward Ellington that it had been decided to bring ENSA to an end on August 31. . . . Now the Services are happy in the control of their own entertainments, which is just as it should be in peacetime. The arrangement would undoubtedly have to be revised in the event of another world conflagration.

On the civil side, the British Council called off the Paris plan—there were to be no peace talks in Paris anyway—and no representatives to sit on our Council were appointed. Finally, the Government announced the formation of the Arts Council of Great Britain. It was obvious that our plans had been brought to nought. All that remained to be done was to fold up our tents and steal away. The conspiracy had succeeded.

The ENSA Provisional Council was dissolved at a meeting held at

[1] Now Sir Alfred Bossom, Bart.

Drury Lane on July 18, 1946, with Sir Walter Monckton in the Chair. He read out Bossom's letter, which, after praising the organization, called attention to the fact that on two previous occasions he had served on Government committees whose duty it was, *inter alia*, to investigate the conduct of ENSA. In both instances it had been proved completely satisfactory. First the Chairman, next Sir John Shute, then all the members present made flattering speeches to me in turn. Not very long after this, senior officials of the Treasury and of NAAFI invited me to a private lunch in token of their appreciation of the work I had done; all of which was highly gratifying, but nothing could assuage my sense of failure in the larger purposes.

The system of Government support for the Arts that has grown up out of the CEMA infancy represents the most forward step in the advancement of British culture that a British Government has yet taken. In the creation of the Arts Council of Great Britain, the British gift for political compromise is seen at its best. And only the ungenerous would refuse to admit that, by its struggles before and immediately after the outbreak of war, and by the magnitude of its later operations, ENSA made a direct contribution to this achievement.

6

Humpty Dumpty

Preparations were now in hand for the Victory Parade. Theatre people have an instinctive, anticipatory delight in curtain calls; they never miss them if they can help it. And this was to be a parade of the nation's thanksgiving. So when it was announced that the civil organizations were being invited to take part I regarded our place as assured. I told our people in Germany to reconstitute one of the mobile columns exactly as it had been landed in Normandy: portable theatre, mobile cinema, sleeping- and day-coaches, a rediffusion van—the whole lot. The question of whether well-known artistes or some of the little concert parties should be invited to occupy the vehicles could be left for the moment. Sir Edward Ellington offered no objection to the preparations, although, I think, he was secretly amused by them.

As time went by and no invitation came to ENSA I grew alarmed. When I heard that the column was ready and waiting in Brussels, I rang up the War Office to ask what arrangements had been made to include us. "None," was the answer. "It is a matter for NAAFI." But the Corporation said the matter rested with the War Office. Back I went, to ask this time that a place should be made for us. "Too late; application should have been made much earlier," came the reply. To cover the omission we were offered some four or six places in NAAFI's marching detachment, which I indignantly refused. . . . Whether our exclusion was the direct result of the recent publicity or not makes no matter. The affront to the profession was the same.

I sat with a friend watching the parade from a stand at the back of Carlton House Terrace, facing the Mall. The places had been found for me at the last moment by the Treasury. The columns of marching men, the rumble of the tanks—now near, now far—filled every one with joy. We cheered madly with the rest as that undulating serpent of vehicles glided slowly by: but the plane trees, still in their first leaf, hid most of the spectacle. After a while my attention wandered; I began to hold a victory parade of my own.

Here they come: the little companies first, those that had endured Icelandic winters, the heat of the Bahrein Gulf, been torpedoed perhaps, some giving their lives equally with sailor, soldier and airman. The stars join them as the kaleidoscope of memory slowly revolves, changing the pattern of scene and sound. The audiences too are part of my secret parade, those wonderful audiences proclaiming the comradeship that was every one's glory: Queen Mary, sitting bolt upright among the soldiers of her guard in the picture gallery at Badminton; little women humping shells in the deafening roar of armament factories; the troops outside the theatre at Tunis; the first broadcast from France; the rush into the streets everywhere on news of final victory.

And the solemn occasions when people and players merged in one communion: 'Harry' Ainley speaking in front of the great West Door of St Paul's; Leslie Howard kneeling before that same door, murmuring Nelson's Prayer and, mingled with the simple, pious words, the voice of Dennis Noble, singing Drake's Drum. . . . Everywhere there are voices, single voices, voices in chorus, voices! They echo and re-echo above the cheering and the laughter. Sailors' voices drowning Leslie Henson's quips on Hoy; the R.A.F. men in their converted hangars; the factory girls drowning the clatter of plates and dishes with shrill gaiety; foreign voices, French and Dutch and Norwegian, calling freedom across the narrow seas. And the quiet, unprepared-for occasions, as when accidentally I came upon a group of little children being held up in turn before the microphone by their mothers to record shrill messages of Christmas greeting to fathers overseas, the flat, toneless voices unbearably moving. It had been one vast anthem of national hope and fear and courage. Impossible not to feel proud that we had a share in its composition.

My parade comes to an end and the cheering dies away; one backward glance remains. Shall we ever forget those deserted London squares, Belgrave especially, blue-grey in the autumn mornings, like faded gentle-women waiting patiently in the memory of a gallantry lost in the war? . . . Yes, it was good to have lived through THE TIME.

My companion nudges me awake. The real procession is nearly over; now come the boot-repairing outfits and the travelling sewing-machines. Resentment comes back with a rush. Surely the artistes and the organiza-tion which represented them deserved a place before these contraptions? As we joined the Government guests slowly making their way across Waterloo Place I blamed myself for failing to re-enter the ring for the last time. I had let down the side. Now it is no matter, but public acknow-ledgment given at the right time is doubly worth.[1]

Of private and individual thanks there were plenty. I paid little regard to them at the time. Now it is pleasant to turn over the files to find thanks from Mountbatten of Burma, Alexander of Tunis, and the other great figures, jumbled up with letters from factories (Rolls-Royce, Vickers, Reyrolle, Sanders-Roe, all the big names in industry) and from quite small units, tucked away in forgotten corners. Here is one from 'Battle of Britain' Park, praising to the skies the improvement in the Middle East; another from the French Ambassador (M. Massigli) on behalf of the Free French; others from the Polish C.-in-C., the U.S. Special Services General in Europe—I must flick over the pages faster and take a chance where my eye falls; another American General thanks us for Florence Desmond's visit to Corsica; that telegram from Montgomery, asking for the stars to stay longer; Ernest Bevin; L. S. Amery on behalf of the India Office; General de Lattre de Tassigny on behalf of his First French Army—two letters, one in gratitude, the second to ask us to accept a tour of *Veronique* in Britain in aid of his welfare funds. (That we could not do. Instead, we sent the company to the Marigny in Paris for a week.) . . . And then in a file apart from the others, as though it might dispel the grateful atmos-phere, is a copy of a letter from Ronald Adam, about to retire as Adjutant-General, sent to Sir Edward Ellington, thanking him for all that his Department had done for the Army. Very properly, this letter was sent down to me, with Sir Edward's comment that it should have been so addressed in the first case. . . . Recognition could scarcely go farther in reverse! Humpty Dumpty had certainly had a great fall.

[1] On the tenth anniversary of VE Day B.B.C. Television gave a commemorative broadcast of war-time entertainment. Presumably this was intended solely as an advertisement of what the Corporation had achieved in this direction, since no men-tion was made of ENSA, nor were the stars most prominently associated with our work invited to take part.

'One more endeavour remained with my opponents: to prevent any official gesture being extended to me, for that would confirm the Government's denial of their charges. . . . And then one morning I found myself standing in line with others who had "done the State some service," conscious of nothing but the end of the journey. . . .

I bowed as the King placed the ribbon round my neck and shook hands. Then a smile came into his eyes, and in a clear voice that those near to him could plainly hear, he said, "This is given you for your work with ENSA."

A queer sense of elation flooded my being. I fumbled a second bow and was about to turn away when the King's voice stopped me.

"And what are you going to do now?" he asked.

"I'm hoping to return to the theatre, Sir."

A momentary hesitation while I waited in case any more should be said —a flicker in the Lord Chamberlain's eye warning me that conversation must not exceed the prescribed few seconds.

"Oh, are you?" said the King. "When?"

"As soon as possible, Sir."

"I'm glad. You're needed. I wish you every success." And he shook hands again, giving me a smile of Royal sympathy. . . .

Then Humpty and his daughter went gaily off to lunch.

7

Time over again

Clemence Dane asked me gaily the other day whether I would be willing to undertake the job all over again and, if so, which mistakes I would try most to avoid. A light question, lightly asked, and quite impossible to answer, for conduct is conditioned by character and experience; if both remain unchanged, the same mistakes are inevitable. Looking back, it is clear that, if I had not fought against the 'empire-builders,' the road would have been easier and pleasanter; if I had surrendered our claim to independence in professional matters and allowed the War Office to do as it liked with us the suppression of ENSA, or an intolerable overlordship, would certainly have followed. In either event, without independence of operation much less entertainment would have been produced for the troops. Yet it is also true that if I had not spent so much time struggling to keep the decks free from official encumbrance more of the productions could have been personally supervised, and earlier and more frequent visits paid overseas. It would be false modesty to pretend that the shows would not have been better in the former event; in the latter much of the lack of initiative, of which people complained in the early years, might have been remedied.

Raking over old records and memories has been a dragging work, inducing retrospection—a bad habit, prisoning one's thoughts in past follies. This is especially true of theatre folk, who must ever live on the surface of life while they pretend to plumb its depths. Yet I am glad this book was not written earlier, for then it might have contained bitterness, a worthless element that clouds all issues.

But this is not answering Miss Dane's question. Taking the second half of it first, then, I should pray for greater insight into the situations I was called upon to face, so that I might proceed with less exigence and so avoid hurting people's feelings and raising unnecessary opposition. As to the main part, yes, assuredly I would go through it all again, for, after all, what is more exhilarating than to be one of an ardent company, working with single enthusiasm in the national cause? And what more decisive than a satisfactory conscience?

CHAPTER THIRTY-FOUR

TESTAMENT IN POSTSCRIPT

1

RETURN to the theatre, yes, that was all very well, but what should I find there? Seven years is a long time to be absent from that distorting mirror of the human scene that must ever be shifting and changing to catch the light of public approval. After the upheaval of world war, followed by a peaceful social revolution, things were bound to be different. ENSA itself had been a sign of change.

When I did finally step out into the market-place, the huckster's fair was in full swing: quick returns and no argument, quality not asked, success to the loudest mouth. Over at the Quality Booth Shakespeare decked out in strangest fancy, now a blaze of colour, now dark and sombre, *A Midsummer's Night Dream* in depth of winter—his poetry concealed beneath the accents of the lecture room. In the Cinema tent there was Shakespeare again, his glorious, trailing cloak cut to new size with a patch here and there, the rhythm of his verse abandoned in favour of the bastard rhythm of the movie camera. . . . Here's a bright wonder: a beauteous young lady snatched from a restaurant table to play one of the great classic rôles on the screen, positively for the very first and— very sensibly—the last time.

Everywhere television aerials, the modern periscope, are popping up over the housetops "the better to see you with, my dear." Shows for the million. Something of everything. Plays? Dig out the old ones; write new: the maw must be satisfied.

The players act their parts as well as ever, and better—but not on Sundays, for that would break the law, and there are elders and common informers watching. On Sundays they must do their tricks in the Modern Marvels tent. True, they may wear costumes and paint their faces just the same, but the iniquity of Sunday performance is not directly visible to the elders in the market-place, so they can pretend it is not there. The common informers are powerless because that tent is largely a Government show.

Come and see the very latest marvel: love and passion on ice! Singers trilling like larks even while they whirl at top speed, every note in its place! How is it done? Something went wrong there. She opened her mouth, flung wide her arms, and not a sound came out. Alas! They are only beautiful skaters after all.

Success, success, success! Walk up, walk up!

Up at the Castle, where the actor's art used to be encouraged, things are different too. The private patron is no more. His place is taken by an officer of national or local government, rather scared of stirring up that witches' brew called The Arts. . . . The Theatre has been put on the dole. And that is the very heart of change for its servants.

Leave now the realm of fantasy, and join me in examination of some Facts or Theory, however you look at it. If it should prove controversial, all to the good: away with the habit of never saying what one really believes, lest it offend. The fear of disturbing accepted beliefs is like effeminate play-acting: it doesn't trouble the heart, increases no glandular secretions.

First, as to my personal standpoint: I believe in the living Theatre, whole and indivisible between actor and audience, an instrument of the human spirit that has given freely of its knowledge and experience to the electric shadows that now entertain the majority, and received nothing in return. This is not to deny the shadows their virtues of speed in action and speech, but those secrets were known to Shakespeare too.

I also believe in the Theatre as an instrument of Revelation, if only of follies and meanness: the Divine inspiration of Man writing about Man, one against the gods. I believe in the living audience, present in communion with the players, for which mechanical perfection is no substitute. I believe in the discipline of technique, and the inspiration of the moment.

What must the Theatre do to be saved? It must stop saying to itself, "I am a camera," because it is not true. Although it seek new ways, proclaim new beliefs, these are but a reassertion of the old. (The modern cult of incomprehensibility that flatters the audience by assuming comprehension may conceal a pearl of price or it may not.) It must throw away the graven images, such as the microphone and the loudspeaker. It must cease to regard Realism (I prefer the word Naturalism) as the only salvation, for that is the temptation of the devil who suborns the artist with rich reward. I do not want to see the blood dripping from the eyes of Œdipus, nor living animals capering upon the stage. The blood of the lamb is for sacrifice, an offering to Dionysus. Finally, and in triumph, the theatre must return to Evocation, the genesis of its being and the justification for its survival.

2

The cornerstone of State aid for the Drama should be a National Theatre. By that is meant not just a monument in stone and steel to the importance of Drama in the national life, but—the more important part, soul to the body—a company of artists: dramatists, actors, musicians, designers (and their craftsmen), without which the theatre would be about as much use as a railway station without trains. This simple truth was plainly stated in the early teachings of Granville Barker and William Archer which inspired the group of distinguished amateurs to form themselves into a National Theatre Committee. Unfortunately the gift of a considerable sum of money by a public benefactor for the express purpose of building the theatre canalized the Committee's further approach to the subject. It has bedevilled its thinking ever since.

The sole function of a National Theatre should be to provide a rallying place for all that is best in the dramatic art of the country—*i.e.*, to enshrine tradition and to maintain and improve current standards. This means authorship as well as acting. It also means regard not only for Shakespeare and what are commonly called the classics, but programmes designed to exemplify the British (and foreign) dramatic genius of all periods, including the present day. Its artists must sustain criticism and draw strength from every kind of audience. The performances must ultimately be broad-based upon popular approval; otherwise the institution will become a coterie theatre, satisfying only to the few and likely to become fossilized. These principles are admitted by all theatre people, but they need restatement, because the extravagant claims put forward on behalf of the mechanized drama, and the influence of those claims upon standards of writing and performance, make the need for such an institution greater than ever.

The Committee's fumbling attempts to acquire a suitable site—even now the foundation stone has been Royally laid in a place where it is not to remain—led to a widespread belief that the scheme was really the hobby-horse of cranks and enthusiasts. The lack of professional know-how through the years was a serious handicap to the Committee. Bernard Shaw, its best-known member, never understood the theatre in the professional sense. He only understood that it had kept him waiting outside until past middle age, typically and most unfairly, because he had new things to say. Yet G.B.S. was profoundly right in one respect, for he used often to say the public would never want a National Theatre until they were given it.

In bitterest mood he could not have expected to see that principle successfully applied in the matter of a national opera house, yet not to the theatre of Shakespeare, Sheridan, Congreve, Garrick, Kean, Mrs Siddons, Irving and the rest.

The Committee's war-time marriage of convenience with the Old Vic foundation certainly gave it a visa to enter the realms of Government recognition, but in maintaining the union each is being false to its original purposes, and the sooner the National Theatre obtains separate citizenship the better.

In the resurgence of national pride following the exhilaration of victory, it seemed as though the National Theatre, in company with the brave plans for rebuilding the precincts of St Paul's Cathedral, would come to fruition. But the economic pressures that now assail the country make that unlikely in the immediate future. Therefore any compromise that holds out a prospect of positive action in place of the present doldrums should commend itself. Why should not the Government be called upon to do with the Theatre Royal, Drury Lane, as it has done with the Royal Opera House, and to set up a Trust to acquire the freehold of the theatre? An opportunity of doing so in lieu of death duties occurred quite recently. Alternatively it should be possible to work out some plan of co-operation with the existing leaseholders, whereby, at stated intervals, national companies such as the Old Vic and the Stratford Company would appear under the auspices of the Trust. One immediate effect of the scheme, which admittedly could only operate with the willing co-operation of all concerned, would be to break the stranglehold of American musical comedy over what is still regarded as the national shrine of our theatrical tradition.

Some of the present generation of actors have been known to declare that Drury Lane is too big for a National Theatre.

"Young man," said Sir George Alexander to me one day in 1917, "if you ever go to Drury Lane, you will find out it's a theatre that flatters the good actor and damns the bad one": a statement that I was subsequently able to verify.

In any case its amplitude is a point in its favour, for it would encourage the art of acting in the living theatre to draw farther away from the pseudo-naturalism of the screen and television, which it must do if it is not to be sucked into that vortex in which it must inevitably drown.

◇◇◇

Conversation Piece . . .

Towards the end of the war Austen Hall, one of the group of architects and planners forming Lutyens' Royal Academy Committee, then engaged upon the fascinating job of redrawing the face of London, told me that they had been discussing the Covent Garden area.

"What would you do with it?" he asked casually.

"Make it the greatest war memorial of all time, a cultural centre for the British Commonwealth and Empire," I replied.

"That seems a good idea. How would you set about it?"

"Centred on the Opera House and the Theatre Royal," I said, warming to the fun. "You'd need to clear the front of Drury Lane. It's on rising ground. Make a fine, sweeping approach from Waterloo Bridge. Fountains and statuary in the centre of the roundabout. Why, you could make a wonderful show! A concert hall, academies for drama and opera and ballet. Central booking-halls."

"Restaurants?"

"Certainly. You'd clear away the vegetables and fruit for that. Disclose the piazzas. The market is a costly anachronism anyway."

"Traffic?" queried Austen. "You'd want an enormous car-park."

"Underground," I said, adding, in the tones of an L.C.C. building inspector, "Of course, all those ramshackle, nondescript buildings would have to come away."

To my huge delight I heard later that Lutyens had incorporated the idea in his drawings.

A pipe dream? Well, why not? If one does not look upwards at the smoke sometimes one never knows where it is going.

3

I live within sight of the barracks of the King's Troop of the Royal Horse Artillery, where the bugles sound daily the obdurate summons to work. And when I hear the horses and the gun-carriages clattering by I see in my mind's eye the troops of another century in their bobbing shakos and jingling harness, and the mobcaps of the maids nodding with excitement from the upper windows of the Regency houses. The overall happiness of the common people was greater then in spite of squalor and political injustice; or so it seems, as I watch, for example, the anxious faces of municipal workmen re-laying the paths outside. For them the one glad note comes when Retreat is sounded, proclaiming an end to tea-drinking and back-straightening and gossipy work for that day.

Too many people have forgotten that the most satisfying moments of Anyman's life come with achievement. We cannot all be craftsmen, working in wood and iron and stone, but there are other satisfactions: a field well ploughed by a pair of trained Percherons, or swift and straight by the modern tractor, a scientific problem solved, new and quicker ways of obtaining better results—there's satisfaction to be had in varying degrees from all these things. The artist, feeling his satisfaction more deeply, ever sustains and renews himself in contemplation of work well done.

In the Theatre it is right that the wider opportunities that public subsidy has brought should be given to the younger men, for it is they who must carry the banners of the vanguard. We, the rest, can join the main body and, when too old to keep up, stand on the side-lines, grumble a little, criticize a lot, and, altering Matthew Arnold's famous declaration, shout, "The theatre is dead: long live the theatre." . . .

There goes that darned bugle again. But it is not sounding Retreat; it is sounding Reveille: Time to fall in again and join the onward march.

TALLY THREE

From September 1939 to March 2, 1946, the grand total of ENSA performances given to H.M. Forces and the various branches of Industry was   2,656,565
The attendances during that period exceeded   300,000,000

FIGURES OF THE CLIMAX

The output of entertainment reached its maximum during the winter of 1945. For the four weeks ended February 24 the figures of actual performances are given:

	United Kingdom (Services and Factory Workers)	North-west Europe (Troops only)	Other Overseas Commands (excluding India and SEAC)
LIVE	8,840	1,073	3,479
CINEMA	7,761	1,515	10,928
			Total 33,596 shows

Thus, 8399 separate shows were being given each week, spread over two-thirds of the globe. Of this total roughly 40 per cent. was live entertainment.

The annual gross cost of the maximum output was estimated at £5,489,900.

More than 80 per cent. of the entire Entertainment Industry gave service to ENSA at one time or another.

The Theatre in Emergency

"The Theatre is irresistible;
organize the Theatre!"

MATTHEW ARNOLD

We must dedicate the Theatre to the National Service without delay. The present careless view of both Government and the public that in time of great national emergency theatrical entertainment is a luxury, fit only to be taxed out of existence, must give place to a different attitude. The change can be wrought by the scope and magnitude of our efforts. In the first years of the last war the army generals secretly regarded entertainment as a serious interruption of the work of training and discipline. Later, they reached a better understanding of the psychology of the citizen soldier. Ultimately, the whole nation provided incontrovertible evidence of the theatre's important function in time of emergency. Apart from the official and semi-official efforts made by the fighting Services to provide entertainment for themselves by means of their garrison theatres and cinemas in this country, and their various army and navy concert parties abroad, the theatres of London and of the big provincial cities went through a period of hectic prosperity quite out of proportion to the intrinsic value of the entertainments they provided.

The hysterical assumption that in the next war all theatrical entertainment will close down for good may be dismissed at once. The civil population will turn to entertainment for relief from their anxieties even more avidly than did the fighting Services in the last war, for the strain upon the occupants of what may be termed the civil trenches will be greater than that imposed upon those who man the firing posts. Nevertheless, the theatre's task in upholding the morale of the nation cannot be performed in war-time at all without official support and sanction. But it has to be admitted that for Government the immediate problem is twofold, and most obstinate of solution in London itself. On the one hand there is the obvious undesirability of exposing considerable numbers of people to grave danger in what are extremely vulnerable buildings, and of the crowded use of public thoroughfares and internal transport such as tubes and buses at certain stated periods of the day. On the other hand there is this insatiable demand for entertainment in time of war which no modern government dare neglect for long. In the general state of unpreparedness it is not surprising that no solution of this twofold problem has yet been proposed, but there must be a solution. All purveyors of entertainment have a lively sense of their responsibility in keeping their houses open when the people have such need of comfort. On the other hand they do not disguise from themselves the harm it would do their businesses if heavy casualties were suffered in theatres, music-halls and cinemas during times of performances. The matter should be taken up by the competent authorities immediately. Not London alone but all the larger cities should be divided into zones radiating from the centre outwards. At the beginning of the war entertainment within all the zones might have to be closed down entirely, not for the panic reasons mentioned previously but in order not to obstruct the general national mobilization. But later on the various zones could be opened or closed on receipt of instructions from the competent authority. Control of public places of entertainment in this manner should be organized beforehand after the most careful deliberation by a Government Committee on which the various representative bodies of the whole entertainment industry were fully represented. Not only should the various zones of entertainment be worked out beforehand, but the whole question of the rationing of the entertainment that would be available after the institution of universal national service needs to be considered. It would be troublesome and laborious work with many heart-burnings, but an infinitely preferable position to the chaos that must ensue, following upon a general order to close all places of entertainment without previous knowledge as to which of them were to be permitted to reopen and in what order of time.

Then there is a secondary problem of almost equal magnitude to the one that concerns Government. This involves the provision of entertainment, not only for the fighting Services, but also for the civil population concentrated in the munitions areas and in evacuation centres. This problem is different from that of the zoned town areas because normal facilities for entertainment are unlikely to exist in what may be termed the emergency communities. Entertainment in the permitted town areas can safely be left to whatever will remain of normal professional enterprise after national mobilization has taken place. Human ingenuity is remarkably elastic in adversity. Although many of the accepted entertainment houses may not be allowed to reopen until after the war, the work will go on somehow. If the national life is to dive under ground, then entertainment will follow it there!

Radio will undoubtedly play its part, but its importance in war-time from the psychological point of view is not so great as that of the flesh and blood performance, nor of the talking picture whereat both eye and ear are engaged. It is the humanity of these war entertainments that constitutes their major appeal. The entertainments that we provide must be high spirited and courageous and give pride of place to the brightest jewel in our theatrical wardrobe, the spirit of British comedy.

The Theatre's great opportunity for National Service then lies in the organization of entertainment in the emergency communities. For the fighting Services the experience of the last war will be a useful guide; the garrison theatres and cinemas will undoubtedly repeat themselves although probably in a more mobile form. To service these, to provide for the evacuated populations of big cities and the occupants of munitions centres and the hospitals and base camps abroad, many groups of actors, singers and music-hall artistes of both sexes will have to be formed. The actors will, of course, be over military age or officially exempted from other service for undisputed health reasons. Some of these companies might travel their own theatres by road and be capable of giving performances in the open air as well as indoors, after the modern Italian plan. This war work will require some form of official support in order to secure room for it amongst the thousand and one pressing requisitions of the day.

Have we not here the beginnings of a true National Theatre, a living organism, fashioned to serve the entertainment needs of the whole nation? By our hard work under the most trying conditions and by unswerving loyalty to the ideals of National Service we shall stake an irrefutable claim to fuller recognition of the value of our profession than we have yet received. This will be our great reward.

1st April, 1939

APPENDIX TWO

Minute to Minister of Labour and National Service outlining my proposal to form a National Service Entertainments Board

1. The Board to meet once a month under the chairmanship of the Treasury Representative to allocate such funds as are made available by the Treasury for the purpose of providing entertainment for H.M. Forces and for Munition Workers.

2. The Board to receive reports from whatever source upon general questions of morale, and how it is being affected by the entertainment service.

3. In the light of these reports and according to the funds available, the Board to increase or decrease the allocation for the various Services, as it sees fit.

4. The Board not to undertake executive responsibility for the provision of entertainment, the latter to be controlled both financially and administratively by NAAFI through their Entertainment Branch Headquarters at Drury Lane Theatre.

5. The secretary to report monthly how the Board's allocations are working out.

6. ENSA to provide for NAAFI all the professional entertainment, as heretofore.

A Letter of Appreciation from the Air Council

AIR MINISTRY,
LONDON, W.C.2
23rd October, 1940

SIR,

I am commanded by the Air Council to inform you that they have recently had under their notice a report upon the provision of entertainments for the Royal Air Force for the first twelve months from the outbreak of war. It is evident therefrom that the work which has been carried out in this regard by the Entertainments National Service Association, both at home and overseas, under your guiding direction, has been of great value among the factors making for the contentment and good spirits of the personnel of the Royal Air Force.

The Air Council realize that the results achieved have been due not only to your energy and powers of organization since the outbreak of war but also in considerable measure to the thought which you had given to the subject and to the preparatory work carried out for several months before the war began.

The Air Council desire me to convey to you their warm appreciation of the services which you have rendered.

I am, Sir,

Your obedient Servant,

(Sgnd.) J. B. ABRAHAM

BASIL DEAN, ESQ.,
THEATRE ROYAL,
DRURY LANE.

Advisory Councils

MUSIC

Sir Victor Schuster, Bart., *Chairman*
Dr William Walton, *Vice-Chairman*
Walter Legge, A.M.C., *Liaison Officer*

Sir Hugh Allen, G.C.V.O., Mus.D.
Sir Kenneth Barnes
Sir Arnold Bax, Mus.D.
Professor E. J. Dent
Sir George Dyson, Mus.D.
Edwin Evans, M.B.E.
Captain R. Francis

Cecil Gray
Dr Patrick Hadley, Mus.D.
Constant Lambert
Wing-Commander R. P. O'Donnell
Lieutenant M. Roberts, D.R.A.M.,
  A.R.C.M.
Malcolm Sargent, Mus.D.

DRAMA

John Gielgud ⎱ *Joint*
Aubrey Blackburn ⎰ *Chairmen*

William Armstrong
Leslie Banks
Sir Kenneth Barnes
Richard Bird
W. Bleach
Dame Lilian Braithwaite
Miss Judy Campbell
T. D. Clarke
John Clements
Horace Collins
Roland Culver

Miss Edith Evans
Will Fyffe
Patrick Hamilton
Leslie Henson
Miss Irene Hentschel
E. J. Hinge
Miss Victoria Hopper
Miss Cathleen Nesbitt
Alec Rea
Emlyn Williams
Miss Diana Wynyard

LABOUR

Sir Kenneth Barnes (ENSA)
F. Dambman (Musicians' Union)
A. V. Drewe (Variety Artists' Federation)
Fred Morris (Concert Artists' Association)
T. O'Brien (National Association of Theatre and Kine Employees)

Alec Rea (ENSA)
Llewellyn Rees (British Actors' Equity Association)
Miss Rose Smith-Rose (Concert Artists' Association)
H. R. Wright (National Association of Theatre and Kine Employees)

WELFARE

The Lady Louis Mountbatten

Sir Kenneth Barnes
Mrs Nancy Bridgeman
Edward Hayden

Mrs Hunter
Alec Rea
Mrs Van der Byl

PUBLIC RELATIONS

Rev. Sir Herbert Dunnico, J.P., *Chairman*

Cyril E. Asquith, C.B.E.
F. Seymour Cocks, M.P.
Alec Critchley, M.P.
Collie Knox
Colonel A. M. Lyons, K.C., M.P.
G. L. Reakes, M.P.

Colonel Sir John Shute, C.M.G.,
    D.S.O., T.D., M.P., J.P., D.C.
Sir Louis Sterling
Evelyn Walkden, M.P., J.P.
Sydney Walton, C.B.E.
Sir Harold Webbe, C.B.E., M.P.

BROADCASTING AND RECORDING

Rev. Sir Herbert Dunnico, J.P., *Chairman*

Miss Adrienne Allen
Sir Kenneth Barnes
Aubrey Blackburn
Gerald Bright
C. B. Cochran
The Earl of Cromer, P.C., G.C.B.,
    G.C.I.E., G.C.V.O.
Miss Clemence Dane
Collie Knox

Walter Legge
L. V. Manning
Roger Ould
Herbert C. Ridout
Miss Athene Seyler
Sir Victor Schuster, Bart.
Sir Louis Sterling
Dame Irene Vanbrugh

INTERNATIONAL

The Earl of Cromer, P.C., G.C.B., G.C.I.E., G.C.V.O., *Chairman*

Captain O. Aardal (Norwegian Ministry of Defence)
Sir Kenneth Barnes, *General Secretary*
Thorpe Bates, *Executive Head, International Division*
T. Bayer (The Danish Council)
Lieutenant Paul Bonifas (Department of Information, Fighting French Head-
    quarters)
Dame Lilian Braithwaite, *Supervisor, Foreign Concert Parties*
W. Bridges-Adams (The British Council)
Squadron-Leader Bujalski
Lieutenant-Colonel Sir Thomas Cook, M.P., Liaison Officer, Allied Forces
Lieutenant Drzewiecki (Polish Army Education Bureau)
Squadron-Leader M. W. Kowalski

Major Kronacker (Military and Air Attaché, Ambassade de Belgique)

Colonel Harold Mitchell, J.P., M.P. (British Liaison Officer, Polish Forces)

Lieutenant-Colonel Morbitzer (Bureau of Polish Propaganda)

Lieutenant-Commander C. M. Morrell, R.N.V.R. (Office of Principal British Liaison Officer to Allies)

Miss N. B. Parkinson, O.B.E. (The British Council)

General Radovitch (Military, Naval and Air Attaché, Royal Yugoslav Legation)

Principal Raulin (Forces Navales Françaises Libres)

Major Schoonerberg (Office of Dutch Military Attaché)

Captain F. Snabl (Czechoslovak Republic Ministry of Foreign Affairs)

Mrs Virginia Vernon, Secretary, ENSA Advisory International Council

Lieutenant-Colonel Vleck, G.S.O. (Czech Department of Military Information)

Wing-Commander H. D. H. Wardrop (Air Ministry, D.A.F.W.)

Flying-Officer W. Zagorowski

Commander Denis Zepos (Naval Attaché to the Royal Hellenic Government)

CLUB AMENITIES

Rev. Sir Herbert Dunnico, J.P., *Chairman*

Professor Patrick Abercrombie, M.A.

Sir Hugh Allen, G.C.V.O., Mus.D.

J. Bateman, R.A.

The Right Hon. the Lord Brabazon of Tara

A. K. Lawrence, R.A.

Professor Sir Herbert Reilly, O.B.E., M.A.

John Rothenstein

Sir Victor Schuster, Bart.

L. C. Wynne-Tyson

REGIONAL COMMITTEES

SOUTHERN

Emile Littler, *Chairman*

Wilson Blake, *Organizing Secretary*

Birmingham Area:	The Lord Mayor of Birmingham
	The Venerable H. McGowan, Archdeacon of Aston
	Alderman Sir John Burman, J.P.
	Mrs Laurence Cadbury
	Derek Salberg
Bristol Area:	Mrs Egbert Cadbury
	C. M. Haines
Cheltenham Area:	Mrs Van der Byl
Coventry Area:	S. H. Newsome
Malvern Area:	Sir Barry Jackson
Oxford Area:	Stanley Dorrill
Stratford-on-Avon Area:	Sir Archibald Flower

SOUTH-WESTERN AREA SUB-COMMITTEE

Cyril Maude, *Chairman*

Cornwall Area: The Hon. Sir Montague Charles Eliot, K.C.V.O., O.B.E.

Exeter Area: The Very Reverend the Dean of Exeter (Dr S. C. Carpenter, D.D.)

Percy Dunsford

Plymouth Area Mrs Mary Hoyle

Torquay Area: E. W. Goss

EASTERN

Patron: His Grace the Duke of Grafton, J.P., D.L.
Chairman: The Viscount Esher, M.B.E.
Organizing Secretary: Captain W. E. Greenland
Committee:

W. E. Butlin
Rupert J. Costerton
A. E. V. Dennis
Charles H. C. Doré
Elton Halliley
Michael Hillman

Bernard Knowles
Nugent Monck
Barry O'Brien
Percy Rowland
R. W. Davies Taylor
J. Hastings Turner

Geoffrey Whitworth

NORTHERN

Patrons:

His Grace the Duke of Northumberland, J.P.
The Earl of Harewood, K.G., G.C.V.O., D.S.O., T.D.
Sir Arthur Hazelrigg
Sir Arthur William Lambert
The Lord Mayors of:

Bradford	Newcastle-on-Tyne
Hull	Nottingham
Leeds	Sheffield
Leicester	York

Committee:

E. J. Hinge, *Chairman*
A. E. S. Barker
John Beaumont
Councillor H. Bowerman
Richard Clegg
Herbert Elton
W. Lindsay Everard
Councillor F. S. Gent
W. S. Gibson

W. D. Stewart, *Organizing Secretary*
Councillor A. R. Jones
Lady Nutting
J. Prendergast
Sir H. V. Price
Professor Searls
Sir W. A. Forster Todd
John E. Wilshere
J. H. Wright

WESTERN

Patrons:

The Earl of Derby, K.G., P.C., G.C.B., G.C.V.O., J.P.
The Earl of Lonsdale, K.G., G.C.V.O., D.L.
The Earl of Shrewsbury, J.P., D.L.
Sir Robert J. Webber, J.P., D.L.
Alderman Sir Sydney Jones, J.P.
Alderman G. Harold White, J.P.
Alderman Henry Johns, J.P.
Lady Whitten-Brown
Lionel Lightfoot

Committee:

Colonel Sir John Shute, C.M.G., D.S.O., T.D., M.P., J.P., D.L., *Chairman*

T. D. Clarke, *Hon. Supervisor*
William Armstrong
John E. Blakeley
J. Bleakley
W. Harold Brett
Louis Cohen
F. E. Doran
C. Priestley Edwards
Alfred Francis
Jesse Hewitt

G. F. Clarke, *Hon. Organizing Secretary*
Dudley Joel
Hon. Ruth Lever
Prince Littler
Harold Mellor
A. H. Merrett
H. Moorhouse
H. Porter
G. O. Sharman
Malcolm E. Smith

David Webster

SCOTTISH

Honorary Patrons:

The Lord Provost of Aberdeen, Thomas Mitchell
The Lord Provost of Dumfries, John Lockerbie
The Lord Provost of Dundee, John Phin, J.P., D.L., Ll.D.
The Lord Provost of Edinburgh, Henry Steele
The Lord Provost of Glasgow, P. J. Dollan
The Lord Provost of Inverness, Hugh Mackenzie

Committee:

President: Sir Harry Lauder
Hon. Supervisor: Horace H. Collins
Hon. Organizing Secretary: J. Alfred Collins

A. Stewart Cruikshank
Harold B. Dickson
Will Fyffe
William R. Galt
Right Hon. Lord Inverclyde, D.L.
Alec B. King, J.P., O.B.E.
Jock Kirkpatrick, J.P.

Miss Greta Lauder
Stewart McBean
Dugie Macdonald
James Stevenson, C.A.
Lady Swan
A. J. Wark
Chalmers Wood

NATIONAL SERVICE ENTERTAINMENTS BOARD

CHAIRMAN: THE LORD MAYOR OF WEYBRIDGE.

FINANCE AND ORGANISATION COMMITTEE MEMBERS: THE CHAIRMAN OF N.S.E.: THE GENERAL MANAGER: THE CHIEF ACCOUNTANT OF N.A.A.F.I.
THE TREASURY FINANCE OFFICER: THE DIRECTOR OF NATIONAL SERVICE ENTERTAINMENT
(SECRETARY TO THE BOARD: MR. C.H.M. WILCOX, TREASURY CHAMBERS, GT. GEORGE ST. LONDON, W.1.)

DEPARTMENT OF NATIONAL SERVICE ENTERTAINMENT E.N.S.A.
HEADQUARTERS ORGANISATION CHART

E.N.S.A. REGIONAL COMMITTEES

SCOTTISH — CHAIRMAN: HORACE COLLINS, ESQ.

NORTHERN — CHAIRMAN: E.J. HINGE ESQ.

WESTERN — CHAIRMAN: COL. SIR JOHN SHUTE, M.P.

EASTERN — CHAIRMAN: REV. SIR M. DUNNICO, J.P.

SOUTH EASTERN — CHAIRMAN: THE VISCOUNT ESHER M.B.E.

SOUTHERN — CHAIRMAN: E. LITTLER, ESQ.

NORTHERN IRELAND — CHAIRMAN: ALEXANDER DALZELL J.P.

THE BRITISH BROADCASTING CORPORATION EXERCISES TECHNICAL SUPERVISION OVER ALL E.N.S.A. BROADCASTS IN GREAT BRITAIN THROUGH ITS SUPERVISOR ATTACHED TO DRURY LANE HEADQUARTERS.

The E.N.S.A. Advisory Councils meet once a month
AND
Sub-Committees of Councils twice a month (or as required)
H.Q. Executives meet once a week.

H.Q. NATIONAL SERVICE ENTERTAINMENT COMMITTEES ALLOCATE ENTERTAINMENT TO AREAS BY COMMITTEES AS FOLLOWS:

SCOTTISH AREAS 1 — 4
NORTHERN AREAS 5 — 9
WESTERN AREAS 10 — 14
EASTERN AREAS 15 — 17
SOUTH EASTERN AREAS 18 — 20
SOUTHERN AREAS 21 — 26

The F.E.N.S.A. COMMITTEE, ACTING ON BEHALF OF THE KINEMATOGRAPH RENTERS SOCIETY, ADVISES THE DEPARTMENT ON ALL MATTERS RELATING TO THE RENTING OF FILMS.

ADVISORY WELFARE COUNCIL — CHAIRMAN: THE LADY LOUIS MOUNTBATTEN

ADVISORY LABOUR COUNCIL — CHAIRMAN: SIR KENNETH BARNES M.A.

DEPARTMENTAL LIAISON OFFICERS

CO-ORDINATION EXECUTIVE — MR. ALEC REA — GENERAL SECRETARY SIR KENNETH BARNETTA

DIRECTOR OF NATIONAL SERVICE ENTERTAINMENT

PRODUCTION EXECUTIVE — MR. ALEC REA

INSPECTION EXECUTIVE — SIR A. BARNES M.A.

TRANSPORT EXECUTIVE — MR. GEORGE SMITH

CINEMA EXECUTIVE — MR. JAY SMITH

EQUIPMENT EXECUTIVE — MR. O. LLEWELLYN

BROADCASTING EXECUTIVE — SIR S. DUNNICO J.P.

MUSIC EXECUTIVE — SIR WALTER J. SCHNEEFLETT

STAFF RECORDS
WELFARE SECTION
SALARIES
ACCOUNTS BRANCH
FINANCE BRANCH
THEATRE CONTROL
OVERSEAS BRANCH
OVERSEAS ACCOUNTS
CENTRAL FILING
PUBLIC RELATIONS OFFICER
STAFF CONTROL
ADVERTISING
BILLING
INSPECTION BRANCH
CHIEF INSPECTING OFFICER (LIVING)
CINEMA INSPECTION
PERMIT SECTION
AUDITIONS SECRETARY
BOOKING BRANCH
TRANSPORTATION
MOTOR TRANSPORT OFFICER
ADMINISTRATION SECTION
BOOKING MANAGER
STORES
FILM REPAIRS
TECHNICAL SECTION (MANAGER)
CINEMA ENGINEER
CINEMA DIVISION
INTERNATIONAL CONCERT SUPERVISOR
ENTERTAINMENT SECTION
REVUE AND CABARET SECTION
VARIETY SECTION
PLAYS SECTION
MUSICAL PLAYS SECTION
LECTURES SECTION
CONCERT SECTION
CONCERT PARTY SECTION
HOSPITAL CONCERT PARTY SECTION
MUSIC DIVISION
CONCERT DIVISION
PROGRAMME DIRECTOR
RECORDING ENGINEER
MANAGER
WARDROBE AND STORES
DESIGN SECTION
E.D.I. THEATRE EQUIPMENT
E.D.I. GENERAL EQUIPMENT
BROADCASTING DIVISION
EQUIPMENT DIVISION
PUBLIC RELATIONS COMMITTEE

R.N. LIAISON
R.A.F. LIAISON
ARMY LIAISON
M OF L. LIAISON

ADVISORY INTERNATIONAL COUNCIL — CHAIRMAN: THE EARL OF CORNER GCB GCIE GCVO

ADVISORY PRODUCTION COUNCIL — CHAIRMAN: BRONSON ALBERT ESQ.
SUB-COMMITTEE OF ADVISORY PRODUCTION COUNCIL

ADVISORY LECTURE COUNCIL — CHAIRMAN: MAJ. LEMA ARTWELL O.B.E.

ADVISORY MUSIC COUNCIL — CHAIRMAN: SIR VICTOR SCHUSTER B.T.
SUB-COMMITTEE OF ADVISORY MUSIC COUNCIL

ADVISORY BROADCASTING COUNCIL — CHAIRMAN: SIR HERBERT DUNNICO J.P.

ENTERTAINMENTS NATIONAL SERVICE ASSOCIATION

CHAIRMAN OF CENTRAL COMMITTEE: THE LORD TYRRELL OF AVON, P.C.

NORTHERN IRELAND

President: The Right Hon. the Lord Mayor of Belfast,
Sir Crawford McCullagh, Bart., P.C., J.P., D.L.
Chairman: Alexander Dalzell, J.P.
Vice-Chairman: Captain C. J. Brennan, Mus.Bac., F.R.C.O., L.R.A.M.
Hon. Treasurer: W. M. Fullerton
Hon. Programme Director: S. M. Goldstein
Hon. Auditor: Cecil V. Smylie
Committee:

J. Crothers	James Lockhart
R. E. Forbes	J. R. Mageean
Councillor W. J. Gillespie	A. Frazer Mayne
District Inspector T. P. R. Kenny,	Captain T. D. Morrison, M.C., D.L.
D.C.M.	W. D. Morrow

APPENDIX FIVE

GRACIE AMONG MY "PRÆTORIANS"

Key to plate at page 96

1, Lancelot Royle (Chairman of NAAFI). 2, Basil Dean. 3, Gracie
Fields. 4, Alec Rea. 5, Sir Kenneth Barnes. 6, E. P. Clift. 7, Stanley
Bell. 8, Walter Legge. 9, Virginia Vernon. 10, Lilian Braithwaite.
11, William Armstrong. 12, W. Macqueen-Pope. 13, W. Abingdon.
14, E. Everett. 15, Greatorex ("Rex") Newman. 16, Thorpe Bates.
17, B. Lecardo. 18, Henry Oscar. 19, R. Layton. 20, C. Morris.
21, J. Waller (representing Geraldo).

INDEX

566 THE THEATRE AT WAR